KING JOSIAH
of Judah

KING JOSIAH
of Judah

The Lost Messiah of Israel

MARVIN A. SWEENEY

UNIVERSITY PRESS

2001

OXFORD
UNIVERSITY PRESS

Oxford   New York
Athens   Auckland   Bangkok   Bogotá   Buenos Aires   Calcutta
Cape Town   Chennai   Dar es Salaam   Delhi   Florence   Hong Kong   Istanbul
Karachi   Kuala Lumpur   Madrid   Melbourne   Mexico City   Mumbai
Nairobi   Paris   São Paulo   Shanghai   Singapore   Taipei   Tokyo   Toronto   Warsaw

and associated companies in
Berlin   Ibadan

Copyright © 2001 by Marvin A. Sweeney

Published by Oxford University Press, Inc.
198 Madison Avenue, New York, New York 10016

Oxford is a registered trademark of Oxford University Press, Inc.

Library of Congress Cataloging-in-Publication Data
Sweeney, Marvin A. (Marvin Alan), 1953–
King Josiah of Judah : the lost messiah of Israel /
Marvin A. Sweeney.
p.   cm.
Includes bibliographical references
ISBN 0-19-513324-2
1. Bible. O.T. Prophets (Nevi im)—Criticism, interpretation,
etc.   2. Deuteronomistic history (Biblical criticism)   3. Josiah,
King of Judah.   4. Jews—History—to 586 B.C.—Historiography.
5. Bible. O. T. Former Prophets—Historiography.   I. Title.
BS1286.S94   2000
222'.54092—dc21   99-37745

1 3 5 7 9 8 6 4 2

Printed in the United States of America
on acid-free paper

For my Sayangs,
Muna and Leah

ACKNOWLEDGMENTS

One of my greatest pleasures in writing is the ability to acknowledge those who provide support or otherwise enable a volume of this nature to be completed. Research for this study began during the term of my appointment as the 1993–1994 Dorot Research Professor at the W. F. Albright Institute for Archaeological Research, Jerusalem, Israel. I am indebted to the Dorot Research Foundation and to Seymour Gitin, professor of archaeology and director of the Albright, for making my appointment possible. The staff of the Albright went to great lengths to ensure that my stay was successful. I would especially like to acknowledge Munira Said, secretary of the Albright, and Edna Sachar, administrative assistant to the director. Albright fellows provided insights on various topics and otherwise made the year so much more enjoyable: thanks to Uzi Baram; Amy Fisher; Larry, Denise, and Garrick Herr; Lisa Kahn; Ann Killebrew; Bruce, Flora, and Elizabeth MacKay; Beatrice St. Laurent; Benjamin Saidel; William and Jean Schniedewind; Ranjit Singh; Bryan Jack Stone; James Strange; Andrew and Amy Vaughn; and Jan and Eileen Wilson.

I also am indebted to the University of Miami, Coral Gables, Florida, which granted me a leave of absence so that I might accept the Dorot appointment. My thanks go to Daniel Pals, formerly chairperson of the department of religious studies, and Ross Murfin, formerly dean of the College of Arts and Sciences, for their efforts on my behalf. In addition, I thank John T. Fitzgerald and David Graf for their friendship and insights. I am grateful to the Hebrew University of Jerusalem, which provided its incomparable library facilities for my research. I am especially grateful to Shalom Paul, Simha Kogut, and Emanuel Tov, for enabling me to present the results of my research on Jeremiah 30–31 to the Hebrew University Bible faculty. Wayne Horowitz, department of Assyriology, provided a great deal of insight on historical and Assyriological matters, and his family—Leylach, Lisa, Michael, and Liam—provided wonderful respite from research on a long dead king. Moshe Greenberg, the late Jonas Greenfield, Avi Hurvitz, Sara Japhet, Anson Rainey (Tel Aviv University), Alexander Rofé, Haim Tadmor, the late Binyamin Uffenheimer (Tel Aviv University), Yair Zakovitch, Israel Knohl, Joan Goodnick Westenholz (Bible Lands Museum), and librarian Zvi Schneider provided valuable insights and hospitality as well.

The Research Council of the Institute for Antiquity and Christianity of the Claremont Graduate University has graciously accepted my work on King Josiah as one of its ongoing projects and provided research funding. I am grateful to director James Robinson and associate director Jon Ma.Asgeirsson for their support. The Claremont School of Theology has provided travel funds, library resources, and a stimulating context in which to work. I am indebted to my colleagues in Hebrew Bible, Tammi Schneider and Kristin De Troyer, and to my students in both the Ph.D. and M.Div/M.A. programs for their insights and support. Antony Campbell, S.J., Jesuit Theological College, Parkville, Australia, lent a willing ear to many ideas concerning the Deuteronomistic history. Rev. Seung-il Whang, Ph.D. student in Hebrew Bible at Claremont Graduate University; Christopher Miller, M.A. student at Claremont School of Theology; Geri Newburge, B.A. student at the University of Miami, M.A. student at Claremont School of Theology, and now rabbinical student at Hebrew Union College; and Jami Flatt, M.A. student at Claremont School of Theology, provided valuable research assistance.

None of this would be possible without the love and understanding of my wife, Maimunah, and my daughter, Leah. It is therefore to them that I dedicate this book.

AUTHOR'S NOTE

Throughout this volume, I employ the designations G-d, L-rd, YHWH, JHWH, *yhwh*, and so on, for the Deity in the text, notes, and bibliography. Although this practice is not universally employed in Jewish circles, it is intended as a demonstration of respect for G-d.

CONTENTS

ABBREVIATIONS

AASOR   Annual of the American Schools of Oriental Research
AB   Anchor Bible
ABD   *Anchor Bible Dictionary*, ed. David Noel Freedman et al.6 vols. New York: Doubleday, 1992.
ABS   Archeology and Biblical Studies
ad loc.   at location
AJBI   *Annual of the Japanese Biblical Institute*
AnBib   Analecta Biblica
ANET   *Ancient Near Eastern Texts Relating to the Old Testament*, ed. James Pritchard. 3rd edition. Princeton: Princeton University Press, 1969.
AOAT   Alter Orient und Altes Testament
ARAB   *Ancient Records of Assyria and Babylonia*, by David D. Luckenbill. 2 vols. London: Histories and Mysteries of Man, 1989.
ASTI   *Annual of the Swedish Theological Institute*
ATD   Das Alte Testament Deutsch
AThANT   Abhandlungen zur Theologie des Alten und Neuen Testaments
ATSAT   Arbeiten zur Text und Sprache des Alten Testament
BA   *Biblical Archaeologist*
BASOR   *Bulletin of the American Schools of Oriental Research*
BBB   Bonner Biblische Beiträge
B.C.E.   Before Common Era
BETL   Biblioteca Ephemeridum Theologicarum Lovaniensium
BFCT   Beiträge zur Förderung christlicher Theologie
BHS   Biblia Hebraica Stuttgartensia, ed. K. Elliger and W. Rudolph. Stuttgart: Deutsche Biblegesellschaft, 1977.
BibB   Biblische Beiträge

BibInt   Biblical Interpretation Supplement Series
Bibl   *Biblica*
BibSem   Biblical Seminar
BKAT   Biblischer Kommentar, Altes Testament
BLS   Bible and Literature Series
BO   Biblioteca Orientalia
BTS   Biblisch-Theologische Studien
BWANT   Beiträge zur Wissenschaft vom Alten und Neuen Testament
BZ   *Biblische Zeitschrift*
BZAW   Beihefte zur Zeitschrift für die Alttestamentliche Wissenschaft
CBQ   *Catholic Biblical Quarterly*
CBQMS   Catholic Biblical Quarterly Monograph Series
cf.   compare
col(s).   column(s)
ConBibOT   Coniectanea Biblica, Old Testament
CR:BS   *Currents in Research: Biblical Studies*
CTM   Calwer Theologisch Monographien
DtrH   Deuteronomistic History
EB   Études Bibliques
ed.   editor, edition
EncJud   *Encyclopaedia Judaica*, ed. Cecil Roth. 16 vols. Jerusalem:
           Keter [1971]
ErFor   Erträge der Forschung
ET   English Translation
EvTh   *Evangelische Theologie*
f   following (one verse, page)
ff   following (multiple verses, pages)
FOTL   Forms of the Old Testament Literature
fp   feminine plural
FRLANT   Forschungen zur Religion und Literatur des Alten und Neuen
           Testaments
Fs.   Festschrift
fs   feminine singular
GBS   Guides to Biblical Scholarship
GCT   Gender, Culture, and Theory
HAR   *Hebrew Annual Review*
HAT   Handbuch zum Alten Testament
HSM   Harvard Semitic Monographs
HTR   *Harvard Theological Review*
HTIBS   Historic Texts and Interpreters in Biblical Scholarship
HUCA   *Hebrew Union College Annual*
ICC   International Critical Commentary
IDB   *Interpreter's Dictionary of the Bible*, ed. George Buttrick.4 vols.
           Nashville: Abingdon, 1962.
IDB[S]   *Interpreter's Dictionary of the Bible, Supplementary Volume*, ed.
           Keith Crim. Nashville: Abingdon, 1976.

idem	the same
i.e.	that is
IEJ	*Israel Exploration Journal*
Int	*Interpretation*
IOS	*Israel Oriental Studies*
JAOS	*Journal of the American Oriental Society*
JBL	*Journal of Biblical Literature*
JCS	*Journal of Cuneiform Studies*
JETS	*Journal of the Evangelical Theological Society*
JNES	*Journal of Near Eastern Studies*
JPS	Jewish Publication Society
JSOT	*Journal for the Study of the Old Testament*
JSOTSup	Journal for the Study of the Old Testament Supplement Series
JTS	*Journal of Theological Studies*
KAT	Kommentar zum Alten Testament
KS	*Kleine Schriften zur Geschichte des Volkes Israel*, by Albrecht Alt. 3 vols. Munich: C. H. Beck, 1953.
LXX	Septuagint
mp	masculine plural
ms	masculine singular
MT	Masoretic Text
NCeB	New Century Bible
NEAEHL	*New Encylcopedia of Archaeological Excavations in the Holy Land*, ed. Ephraim Stern. 4 vols. Jerusalem: Carta; Israel Exploration Society, 1993.
NRSV	New Revised Standard Version
NTT	*Nederlands Theologisch Tijdschrift*
OBO	Orbis Biblicus et Orientalis
ÖBS	Österreichische Biblische Studien
OBT	Overtures to Biblical Theology
OTG	Old Testament Guides
OTL	Old Testament Library
OTS	Oudtestamentische Studiën
PIOL	Publications de L'institut orientaliste de Louvain
r.	reigned
RevScRel	*Revue des Sciences Religieuses*
RB	*Revue Biblique*
RHPR	*Revue de l'histoire et de philosophie religieuses*
RSV	Revised Standard Version
SB	Sources Bibliques
SBB	Stuttgarter Biblische Beiträge
SBLDS	Society of Biblical Literature Dissertation Series
SBS	Stuttgarter Bibelstudien
SBT	Studies in Biblical Theology
SEÅ	*Svensk Exegetisk Årsbok*
SJOT	*Scandinavian Journal of the Old Testament*

TAPS	Transactions of the American Philosophical Society
TRu	*Theologisches Rundschau*
TLZ	*Theologische Literaturzeitung*
trans.	translated by
UUÅ	Uppsala Universitets Årsskrift
v.	verse
vol.	volume
vols.	volumes
VT	*Vetus Testamentum*
VTSup	Supplements to *Vetus Testamentum*
vv.	verses
WBC	Word Biblical Commentary
WMANT	Wissenschaftliche Monographien zum Alten und Neuen Testament
ZAW	*Zeitschrift für die Alttestamentliche Wissenschaft*
ZBK	Zürcher Bibel Kommentar

KING JOSIAH
of Judah

Introduction

King Josiah of Judah (r. 640–609 B.C.E.) is potentially one of the most significant, and enigmatic, figures in the Hebrew Bible.[1] The Deuteronomistic History's (hereafter, DtrH) account of his reign in 2 Kings 22:1–23:30 (cf. 2 Chronicles 34–35) relates that he came to the throne at the age of eight following the assassination of his father Amon in a coup by elements within the royal court that was put down by "the people of the land." The DtrH reports that during the eighteenth year of his reign, a Torah scroll, commonly identified by scholars as some form of the book of Deuteronomy, was discovered during the course of Temple renovation. As presented in the DtrH, this scroll became the basis for an ambitious reform program in which the king removed all pagan religious installations from Jerusalem; closed all worship sites throughout the lands of Judah and Israel including the altar at Beth-El; centralized all worship exclusively at the Jerusalem Temple; and reestablished the covenant between the people and YHWH, in which the people pledged to observe the commands of YHWH as written in the Torah scroll. In carrying out these reforms, the narrative maintains that Josiah corrected the cultic transgressions of his predecessors, including Solomon, Jeroboam, Ahab, Manasseh, and the other kings of Israel and Judah, and thereby he laid the basis for resolving the fundamental problems of the Israelite/Judean people as identified in the DtrH account.

The DtrH narrative consequently lauds Josiah as one of the most righteous monarchs of Israel and Judah, who "did what was right in the eyes of YHWH, and walked in all the way of David his father, and he did not turn to the right hand or to the left" (2 Kings 22:2) and before whom "there was no king like him, who turned YHWH with all his heart and with all his soul and with all his might,

---

1. For an overview of scholarship on Josiah, see Robert Althann, "Josiah," *ABD* I, 1015–1018.

according to all the Torah of Moses; nor did any like him arise after him" (2 Kings 23:25). Although several monarchs are compared to David, the notice that "he did not turn to the right hand or to the left" and the reference to his adherence to "the Torah of Moses" otherwise applies only to the ideal monarch in Deuteronomy 17:14–20 and to Joshua in Joshua 1:7. Likewise, the reference to Josiah's turning to YHWH "with all his heart and with all his soul and with all his might" takes up the language of the fundamental commandment to love YHWH in Deuteronomy 6:5. In short, the application of this language to Josiah indicates an interest in portraying Josiah as a monarch who surpasses even David in his righteousness. After all, David is criticized in the DtrH for his affair with Bath Sheba and the murder of Uriah. Instead, Josiah is to be regarded as the ideal monarch of the Deuteronomistic History, who alone among the kings of Israel and Judah fully observes YHWH's commands as expressed in "the Torah of Moses."

This idyllic picture of Josiah's reign is qualified in the DtrH by his early death at Megiddo. According to 2 Kings 23:29–30, Josiah went to Megiddo to meet Pharaoh Necho of Egypt, who was moving north toward the Euphrates River to support the Assyrian army in a last desperate attempt to hold back the advancing Babylonians and their allies. According to the DtrH narrative, Necho killed Josiah upon seeing him and thereby put an end to Josiah's reform program. Josiah's death is foretold in 2 Kings 22:14–20 by the prophetess Huldah, who informs him that he would die in peace and thereby not see the evil that YHWH was bringing upon "this place," that is, Jerusalem and Judah, due to the words of the Torah scroll that Josiah had read. This of course must be read in relation to the statements in 2 Kings 21:10–15, 23:26–27, and 24:3–4 that YHWH had decided to destroy Jerusalem and Judah on account of the sins of Josiah's grandfather Manasseh, who is said to have shed much innocent blood in Jerusalem and to have caused Judah to sin as well. The remaining material in 2 Kings 23:31–25:30 relates the rapid collapse of Judah under Josiah's successors, culminating in the destruction of Jerusalem and the Temple and the exile of the people to Babylonia as a result of Manasseh's sins.

The DtrH leaves the reader to wonder why this righteous monarch had to die. The DtrH provides no clear answer to this question. Indeed, the narrative portrays Josiah's attempts at reform as entirely futile, because YHWH had already decided to destroy Jerusalem because of Manasseh's sins. This prompted Stanley Brice Frost some years ago to observe that "a conspiracy of silence" surrounds the death of King Josiah in that the authors of the DtrH and various others of the biblical writers were unable to come to terms with the demise of this righteous monarch which contradicts the most fundamental moral teachings of the Hebrew Bible, viz., the reward of the righteous and punishment of the wicked.[2] The chronicler later attempted to blame Josiah for his own death by portraying him in opposition to YHWH. When Josiah approaches Pharaoh Necho for battle in 2 Chronicles 35:20–25, Necho tells him, "Cease opposing G-d, who is with me, lest he destroy you." Josiah is thereby portrayed as disobedient and therefore deserving of punishment,

---

2. "The Death of Josiah: A Conspiracy of Silence," *JBL* 87 (1968) 369–382.

but earlier generations were unable to account theologically for Josiah's death and simply passed over the matter without comment.

Although Frost correctly notes the relative lack of comment on Josiah's death in the ancient sources, this has certainly not been the case in modern biblical scholarship. The remarkable narrative about Josiah in the DtrH has proved to be a pivotal text in scholarly discussion and has shaped the entire discipline of Hebrew Bible studies.[3] It provides the fundamental linchpin by which modern critical scholarship reconstructs the development of Israelite/Judean religion and the compositional history of much of biblical literature. Based on the correlation of the features of Josiah's reform as presented in this narrative and the laws of Deuteronomy, especially the command for cultic centralization, scholars identify the Torah scroll as an early form of Deuteronomy and argue that Deuteronomy's concerns with monotheism, cultic centralization, social justice, and the codification of Torah as the basis for the covenant relationship between the people and YHWH represent the apex of Israelite religious development in the late monarchic period. Deuteronomy (or the D source of the Pentateuch, as it came to be known) thereby becomes the focal point that determines the dating of the other Pentateuchal sources. J and E are determined to be earlier in part because they accept diverse conceptions of the nature and identity of YHWH, other divine beings, and Israelite worship, and because Deuteronomy appears to repeat and to reformulate some of the basic content of J and E. P is reckoned to be later because it emphasizes a priestly and legal conception of YHWH and the covenant with the people that supersedes that of Deuteronomy, and because it appears to provide the final framework of the entire Pentateuch. Based on its relationship to the account of Josiah's reform in 2 Kings 22–23 and its characteristic vocabulary and theological perspective, Deuteronomy also provides the basis for dating the so-called Deuteronomistic History (DtrH); many of the prophetic books such as Jeremiah, Hosea, Amos, Isaiah, and others; and the books of Chronicles and Ezra-Nehemiah.

Clearly, the DtrH account of Josiah's reign constitutes part of the foundation on which modern biblical scholarship rests, in large measure because scholars accept the historical reality of Josiah's reign and reform program as presented in the DtrH. Nevertheless, the narrative presents many problems, particularly to scholars concerned with assessing the historical reality of Josiah's reign and reform. Based on the view that the DtrH narrative provides a relatively secure basis for reconstructing a historical portrayal of Josiah, many posit that Josiah successfully carried out his reform program and extended his power over the former northern kingdom of Israel, thereby reestablishing the old Davidic-Solomonic empire.[4] This

3. For discussion of the development of modern critical biblical scholarship, see John H. Hayes, *An Introduction to Old Testament Study* (Nashville: Abingdon, 1979); Douglas A. Knight and Gene M. Tucker, eds., *The Hebrew Bible and Its Modern Interpreters* (Chico, Calif.: Scholars Press, 1985); Hans-Joachim Kraus, *Geschichte der historisch-kritischen Erforschung des Alten Testaments*, 2nd ed. (Neukirchen-Vluyn: Neukirchener, 1969).

4. For discussion of this viewpoint and bibliography, see Bustenay Oded, "Judah and the Exile," in *Israelite and Judaean History*, ed. John H. Hayes and J. Maxwell Miller (Philadelphia: Westminster, 1977) 435–488, esp. 458–469.

view is buttressed by such features of the DtrH as the notice of Josiah's death at Megiddo and his destruction of the Beth-El altar that indicate the extent of his hold over the north, and by archeological factors, such as the Yavneh Yam inscription and the *lammelek* jar handles that many interpret as evidence of Josiah's hold over the Mediterranean coastal region and the entire land of Israel. Josiah's powerful empire came to an end, however, in its confrontation with the Egyptians and later with the Babylonians, both of whom proved to be too large and powerful for the nascent neo-Davidic state.

More recent advances in the literary study of the DtrH and the archeological study of the land of Israel during the seventh century B.C.E. call this conclusion into question.[5] Numerous studies of the DtrH, from the foundational study by Noth to the present, point to the theological or ideological character and the historiographical viewpoints of the DtrH—including its postexilic, exilic, Josianic, and perhaps earlier editions—that posit YHWH's control of history based on a scenario of reward or punishment for the people's adherence to Deuteronomic Torah. When combined with the study of ancient near-eastern records and archeological sources, these considerations raise doubts about the historical reliability of the DtrH narrative. After all, the DtrH narrative posits the downfall of the Assyrian empire during the reign of King Hezekiah; this is in contrast to extrabiblical evidence that points to the reign of Hezekiah's successor Manasseh as the period when Assyria, under King Esarhaddon, reached the apex of its power, conquered Egypt, and kept Judah and the rest of the Syro-Israelite region firmly under control. Excavations at Tel Miqne, identified as the ancient Philistine city of Ekron, demonstrate that the Assyrians were in full control of the Philistine coastal plain and the Shephelah; in that they were able to establish Ekron as an industrial center for the production of olive oil to serve the needs of the entire empire.[6] Furthermore, the Assyrians em-

5. For current overviews of the study of the Deuteronomistic History, see Steven L. McKenzie, "Deuteronomistic History," *ABD* II, 160–168; H.-D. Preuss, "Zum deuteronomistischen Geschichtswerk," *Theologisches Rundschau* 58 (1993) 229–264, 341–395; Steven L. McKenzie and M. Patrick Graham, eds., *The History of Israel's Traditions: The Heritage of Martin Noth*, JSOTSup 182 (Sheffield: JSOT Press, 1994); Thomas Römer and Albert de Pury, "L'historiographie deutéronomiste (HD): Histoire de la recherche et enjeux du débat," in *Israël construit son histoire: L'historiographie deutéronomiste à la lumière des recherches récentes*, ed. A. de Pury, T. Römer, and J.-D. Macchi (Geneva: Labor et Fides, 1996) 9–120. For discussion of the archeological aspects of the land of Israel in the seventh century B.C.E. and its application to the study of Josiah's reign, see Nadav Na'aman, "The Kingdom of Judah under Josiah," *Tel Aviv* 18 (1991) 3–71; Israel Finkelstein, "The Archaeology of the Days of Manasseh," in *Scripture and Other Artifacts: Essays on Bible and Archaeology in Honor of Philip J. King*, ed. Michael D. Coogan, J. Cheryl Exum, and Lawrence E. Stager (Louisville, KY: Westminster John Knox, 1994) 169–187; Andrew G. Vaughn, "The Chronicler's Account of Hezekiah: The Relation of Historical Data to a Theological Interpretation of 2 Chronicles 29–32," Ph.D. dissertation (Princeton Theological Seminary, 1996) 38–112. For general reassessments of the reign of Josiah in addition to that of Na'aman, see J. Maxwell Miller and John H. Hayes, *A History of Ancient Israel and Judah* (Philadelphia: Westminster, 1986) 377–401; Gösta W. Ahlström, *The History of Ancient Palestine* (Minneapolis: Fortress, 1993) 763–781.

6. Trude Dothan and Seymour Gitin, "Miqne, Tel (Ekron)," *NEAEHL* 1051–1059; Seymour Gitin, "Tel Miqne-Ekron: A Type-Site for the Inner Coastal Plain in the Iron Age II Period," *Recent Excavations in Israel: Studies in Iron Age Archaeology*, ed. S. Gitin and W. G. Dever, AASOR 49 (Winona Lake, Ind.: Eisenbrauns, 1989) 23–58.

ployed a great deal of Israelite labor to carry out this production, thereby limiting the influence of Judah in the region. The settlement at Yavneh Yam, frequently cited as evidence of Josiah's influence due to the presence of a Hebrew ostracon at the site, proves to be a Greek trading colony that lay outside of Josiah's control.[7] The famed *lammelek* jar handles, frequently cited as material evidence of the extent of Josiah's power, are now conclusively dated to the reign of Hezekiah and point to his preparations for revolt against the Assyrians in the late eighth century B.C.E.[8] A string of Judean fortresses in the Negev indicate the vulnerability of Judah to Edomite encroachment during the late seventh century; perhaps they were built by the Assyrians to protect Negev communications and trade from Egypt or the Edomites.[9] In any case, they point to Josiah's weakness, not to his strength. The discovery of a Judean altar with a *maṣṣēbâ* at Arad, apparently never destroyed by Josiah, raises doubts about the extent of Josiah's reforms in that Arad was one of Josiah's key Negev administrative and trade centers.[10] Finally, a study of Judean demographics during the late seventh century indicates that the Judean population contracted during this period, and shifted eastward away from the fertile Shephelah dominated by Assyria to the central Judean hill country surrounding Jerusalem.[11] All of these factors indicate that Josiah's influence must have been very limited. Some have even suggested that Josiah never presided over an independent Judean state; rather, he was an Assyrian and later an Egyptian vassal, who was killed by Necho as a means for Egypt to strengthen its hold on its weak Judean subject.[12] If any reform program took place at all, it must have been very limited in scope and in success.

Obviously, archeological and historical study of the land of Israel during the late seventh century B.C.E. places certain limits on scholarly reconstructions of the reign of King Josiah and his reform program, but the fact that Josiah may not have succeeded in establishing the full neo-Davidic empire that earlier scholarship envisioned does not justify the dismissal of Josiah's historical significance or the claim that the account of his reign and reform program is fictitious. The DtrH account makes it very clear, after all, that Josiah's program was a failure and that, in the aftermath of the king's death, the nation was forced to succumb first to Egypt and then to Babylon during the last twenty-two years of its existence. Several key works in biblical literature, including the DtrH, the book of Deuteronomy, and a number of the prophetic books, have played particularly important roles in scholarly discussion of the reign of King Josiah in that they provide evidence that con-

---

7. Na'aman, "The Kingdom of Judah under Josiah," 44–51.

8. Nadav Na'aman, "Sennacherib's Campaign to Judah and the Date of the *lmlk* Stamps," *VT* 29 (1979) 61–86; Na'aman, "Hezekiah's Fortified Cities and the LMLK Stamps," *BASOR* 261 (1986) 5–21; Vaughn, "The Chronicler's Account of Hezekiah," 38–112.

9. See Itzhak Beit-Arieh and Bruce C. Cresson, "Horvat 'Uza, a Fortified Outpost on the Eastern Negev Border," *BA* 54 (1991) 126–135; Lynn Tatum, "King Manasseh and the Royal Fortress at Horvat 'Uza," *BA* 54 (1991) 136–145; Finkelstein, "The Archaeology of the Days of Manasseh."

10. See David Ussishkin, "The Date of the Judaean Shrine at Arad," *IEJ* 38 (1988) 142–157; contra. Miriam Aharoni, "Arad," *NEAEHL* 82–87.

11. Finkelstein, "The Archaeology of the Days of Manasseh."

12. Miller and Hayes, *A History of Ancient Israel and Judah* 381–401.

tinues to point to Josiah's reign and reform program as key factors in the development of ancient Judah's political, socioeconomic, and religious history. Each of these compositions presents its own set of interpretative problems that must be addressed in order to establish their applicability to the historical study of King Josiah's reign and his role in the development and expression of Israelite/Judean religious thought. Nevertheless, scholars must come to grips with the evidence presented by this literature, and the problems that it poses, in order to have any clear understanding of Josiah's reign and reform program. Indeed, the study of King Josiah and his reform cannot be limited to the historical reconstruction of the events of his reign. It is most fundamentally a matter of proper assessment of the literature relevant to Josiah's program in order to identify its religiopolitical and socioeconomic ideology, presuppositions, and goals. What was Josiah's reform designed to accomplish, how was it designed to do so, and why would it have been expected to succeed?

The DtrH obviously provides the primary motivation for the study of King Josiah's reform not only because it presents the basic account of Josiah's reign and reform program but because a significant group of scholars has arrived at a consensus that an earlier edition of the DtrH, written in the late seventh century to support the reform program of King Josiah, stands behind the present form of the DtrH text. In his initial establishment of the existence of the DtrH, Noth argued that it was written to chronicle the ultimate demise of the people of Israel from the time of their entry under Joshua into the promised land until the time of their exile to Babylonia.[13] Although Noth recognizes a great deal of literary tension within the work and argues that the DtrH employed earlier compositions and traditions in assembling this great history, he essentially views the DtrH as a single edition that is derived entirely from the period of the exile. Other scholars observe elements of hope in the work that suggest that the DtrH was not limited simply to the retrospective agenda of chronicling the decline and failure of the people of Israel. Von Rad, for example, points to the emphasis on the Davidic promise in the work and the release of King Jehoiachin from prison,[14] and Wolff notes the theme of repentance,[15] both of which suggest a programmatic concern by which the DtrH was designed to address the needs of the future—that is, how might the lessons of Israel's past experience be used to build a community for the future that would not repeat the same mistakes? Various other studies hold to Noth's model of an exilic edition but modify it to account for such programmatic concerns, as well as for the literary tensions evident within the work. Smend, Dietrich,

---

13. Martin Noth, *Überlieferungsgeschichtliche Studien I*, 2nd ed. (Tübingen: Max Niemeyer, 1957) 1–110; Noth, ET: *The Deuteronomistic History*, JSOTSup 15 (Sheffield: JSOT Press, 1981).

14. Gerhard von Rad, *Studies in Deuteronomy*, SBT 9, translated by D. M. G. Stalker (London: SCM, 1953) 74–91.

15. Hans Walter Wolff, "The Kerygma of the Deuteronomic Historical Work," in *The Vitality of the Old Testament Traditions*, ed. W. Brueggemann and H. W. Wolff (Atlanta: John Knox, 1975) 83–100; contra Norbert Lohfink, "Kerygmata des Deuteronomistischen Geschichtswerks," in *Die Botschaft und die Boten*, Fs. H. W. Wolff, ed. J. Jeremias and L. Perlitt (Neukirchen-Vluyn: Neukirchener, 1981) 87–100.

and Veijola posit three distinct exilic editions for the DtrH that address basic programmatic concerns within the history: the foundational layer (*Grundschicht*) (or
DtrG) presents the basic historical work that looks forward to an eventual return
to YHWH; the prophetic redaction (or DtrP) that reworks DtrG to emphasize a
retrospective view that Israel was warned of potential catastrophe by the prophets,
but failed to heed the warning; and the nomistic redaction (or DtrN) that reworked
DtrG/P to posit the eventual restoration of the community based on its observance
of Deuteronomic law.[16] Hoffmann, by contrast, returns to Noth's model of a single
exilic composition but argues that the DtrH presents a model of reform as the basis
for the restoration of the Jewish community in the land of Israel.[17]

An alternative treatment of the issue appears in the work of a number of
scholars, beginning with Cross,[18] who point to the role that King Josiah plays in
the composition of the DtrH and in the expression of its perspectives for Israel's
and Judah's future. Cross and his followers take a more nuanced view of the composition and outlook of the DtrH that points to the existence of earlier preexilic
editions of the work. Cross notes the presence of two primary themes throughout
the DtrH: YHWH's promise of eternal rule in Jerusalem to the house of David
and the condemnation of the northern kingdom of Israel based on the typological
sin of Jeroboam. Given this dichotomy of promise to David and the southern kingdom of Judah and condemnation of the northern kingdom of Israel, Cross argues
that the DtrH originally culminated in the reign of King Josiah, insofar as his reforms were designed to reunite Israel and Judah under Davidic/Josianic rule and
thereby to correct the sins of Jeroboam by reestablishing the Jerusalem Temple as
the sole legitimate center for worship by the entire people of Israel.With the unexpected death of Josiah and the subsequent Babylonian exile, the DtrH was modified
and updated in the exilic period to account for these events, thereby removing Josiah's
reform as the capstone of the entire DtrH. Cross is followed by a cadre of scholars
who have refined his basic hypothesis in various ways.[19] Furthermore, a highly

16. Rudolph Smend, "Die Gesetz und Völker: Ein Beitrag zur deuteronomistischen Redak-
tionsgeschichte," in *Probleme biblischer Theologie*, Fs. G. von Rad, ed. H. W. Wolff (Munich: Chr.
Kaiser, 1971) 494–509; Walter Dietrich, *Prophetie und Geschichte: Eine redaktionsgeschichtliche
Untersuchung zum deuteronomistischen Geschichtswerk*, FRLANT 108 (Göttingen: Vandenhoeck
& Ruprecht, 1972); Timo Veijola, *Die Ewige Dynastie: David und die Entstehung seiner Dynastie
nach der deuteronomistischen Darstellung* (Helsinki: Suomalainen Tiedeakatemia, 1975); Veijola,
*Das Königtum in der Beurteilung der deuteronomistischen Historiographie: Eine redaktions-
geschichtliche Untersuchung* (Helsinki: Suomalainen Tiedeakatemia, 1977).

17. Hans-Detleff Hoffmann, *Reform und Reformen: Untersuchungen zu einem Grundthema
der deuteronomistischen Geschichtsschreibung*, AThANT 66 (Zürich: Theologischer Verlag, 1980).

18. Frank M. Cross, Jr., "The Themes of the Books of Kings and the Structure of the
Deuteronomistic History," in *Canaanite Myth and Hebrew Epic* (Cambridge, Mass.: Harvard University, 1973) 274–289.

19. Richard Nelson, *The Double Redaction of the Deuteronomistic History*, JSOTSup 18
(Sheffield: JSOT Press, 1981); Nelson, "Josiah in the Book of Joshua," *JBL* 100 (1981) 531–540;
Richard E. Friedman, *The Exile and Biblical Narrative: The Formation of the Deuteronomistic and
Priestly Works*, HSM 22 (Chico, Calif.: Scholars Press, 1981); Iain W. Provan, *Hezekiah and the
Books of Kings*, BZAW 172 (Berlin and New York: Walter de Gruyter, 1988); Steven L. McKenzie,
The Trouble With Kings: The Composition of the Books of Kings in the Deuteronomistic History,

influential study by Weippert of the regnal evaluation formulae in the DtrH demonstrates that the DtrH presentation of the death of Josiah and the reigns of the kings who followed him constitutes a later expansion of the DtrH.[20] Her work further points to the possibility of an earlier edition of the work from the time of King Hezekiah. Halpern and Vanderhooft build on Weippert's study to argue for such an edition.[21] Campbell and O'Brien argue for an earlier prophetic record.[22]

These studies point to a great deal of evidence for the existence of a Josianic edition of the DtrH that was designed to present King Josiah's reign and reform as the culmination of Israel's history in the reunification of the people of Israel around the Jerusalem Temple as YHWH's central sanctuary and the house of David as YHWH's designated dynasty. Key elements in this scenario include Nelson's argument that the image of Joshua as ideal leader of the united tribes of Israel is based on the image of Josiah, Cross's argument that the portrayal of Josiah in 1 Kings 13 as the one who will eventually destroy Jeroboam's idolatrous altar at Beth-El points to Josiah's actions as the culmination of the DtrH, Weippert's argument that the regnal formulae indicate the presence of later exilic expansion in 2 Kings 23:31–25:30, and Knoppers's argument that the figure of Solomon provides the basis by which to validate the independent kingdoms of Israel and Judah prior to the failure of the north and the need for reform and reunification under Josiah. Furthermore, the presentation in 2 Kings 23:25–26 of YHWH's decision to destroy Jerusalem and Judah completely negates not only Josiah's actions to reconstitute the covenant but also the entire DtrH program to identify the people's adherence to Deuteronomic law as the basis for their continued existence in the land.[23] According to 2 Kings 23:25–26, none of this matters; it is only Manasseh's actions that determine the fate of Jerusalem and Judah. Clearly, this undermines the narrative concerning Josiah's reforms, as well as that of the entire DtrH, and indicates the likelihood of an earlier edition of the text.

VTSup 42 (Leiden: E. J. Brill, 1991); Gary N. Knoppers, *Two Nations Under G-d: The Deuteronomistic History of Solomon and the Dual Monarchies*, 2 vols., HSM 52–53 (Atlanta: Scholars Press, 1993–1994).

20. Helga Weippert, "Die 'deuteronomistischen' Beurteilungen der Könige von Israel und Juda und das Problem der Redaktion der Königsbücher," *Bibl* 53 (1972) 301–339.

21. Baruch Halpern and David Vanderhooft, "The Editions of Kings in the 7th–6th Centuries," *HUCA* 62 (1991) 179–244; cf. Erik Eynikel, *The Reform of King Josiah and the Composition of the Deuteronomistic History*, OTS 33 (Leiden: E. J. Brill, 1996).

22. Antony F. Campbell, *Of Prophets and Kings: A Late Ninth-Century Document*, CBQMS 17 (Washington, D.C.: Catholic Biblical Association, 1986); Mark A. O'Brien, *The Deuteronomistic History Hypothesis: A Reassessment*, OBO 92 (Freiburg; Universitätsverlag; Göttingen: Vandenhoeck & Ruprecht, 1989).

23. See Stanley Brice Frost, "The Death of Josiah: A Conspiracy of Silence," *JBL* 87 (1968) 369–382, who points to the relative silence concerning Josiah's death in the Hebrew Bible as an indication that the biblical writers were unable to deal adequately with Josiah's early demise. Frost correctly notes that the early death of the righteous monarch and the failure to realize his program challenged the general biblical scheme of reward for righteousness and punishment for wickedness. Rather than attempt to explain this issue, Frost argues that the biblical writers chose to ignore the theological problems posed by Josiah's death and simply reported the facts of Judah's subsequent demise.

Nevertheless, the hypothesis of a Josianic edition of the DtrH is not fully accepted by scholars for two key reasons. First, Cross and his followers are unable to provide a convincing redaction critical analysis of the DtrH accounts of the reigns of King Manasseh in 2 Kings 21 or of King Josiah in 2 Kings 22–23. The account of Manasseh's reign is crucial because it presents the rationale in vv. 10–15 for YHWH's decision to destroy Jerusalem and Judah on account of Manasseh's sins, but scholars do not succeed in demonstrating a means to remove these verses and to reconstruct the hypothesized original account without destroying the narrative altogether.[24] A similar situation applies to the account of Josiah, which likewise relates YHWH's decision to destroy Jerusalem and Judah because of Manasseh in 2 Kings 23:25–26. The key issue here, however, is the narrative concerning Huldah's prophecy in 2 Kings 22:11–20, which predicts Josiah's early death together with YHWH's decision to destroy Jerusalem and Judah. Again, scholars are unable to eliminate or to reconstruct Huldah's oracle in a manner that demonstrates support for Josiah's reign and reform.[25] Second, apart from Nelson's study of the correlation of the image of Joshua with that of Josiah, scholars do not successfully demonstrate how the DtrH as a whole builds up to Josiah's reign. Indeed, O'Brien points to the need to assess the overall outlook and conception of the Josianic DtrH.[26] Most of the attention focuses on the books of Kings and, to a much lesser extent as a result of Nelson's study, Joshua, but various questions remain unanswered. The role played by the books of Judges and Samuel within such a Josianic composition is not defined, especially since neither book gives any explicit hint of concern with Josiah. This problem is especially acute in that both books seem to posit David, and not Josiah or any other Davidic monarch, as the ideal king of Israel. The role of the Succession Narrative or Court History is not adequately explained, especially since it presents David in a relatively unfavorable light as a result of his affair with Bath Sheba and murder of Uriah. Many therefore argue that it must be a relatively late anti-Davidic addition

24. See the discussion by Provan, *Hezekiah* 145–147, who outlines the difficulties in attempting to demonstrate a preexilic text underlying the present form of the narrative. See also Ehud Ben Zvi, "The Account of the Reign of Manasseh in II Reg 21, 1–18 and the Redactional History of the Book of Kings," *ZAW* 103 (1991) 355–374, who applies the Smend–Dietrich model of three exilic redactions to this text, and Klaas A. D. Smelik, "The Portrayal of King Manasseh: A Literary Analysis of II Kings xxi and II Chronicles xxiii," in *Converting the Past: Studies in Ancient Israelite and Moabite Historiography*, OTS 28 (Leiden: E. J. Brill, 1992) 129–189, who examines the literary character of the account.

25. See the discussion by Provan, *Hezekiah* 147–151, who points to the difficulties in reconstructing a preexilic edition of the account of Josiah's reign, especially with relation to Huldah's oracle in 2 Kings 22:11–20. See also Norbert Lohfink, "The Cult Reform of Josiah of Judah: 2 Kings 22–23 as a Source for the History of Israelite Religion," in *Ancient Israelite Religion*, Fs. F. M. Cross, ed. P. D. Miller, Jr., P. D. Hanson, and S. D. McBride (Philadelphia: Fortress, 1987) 459–475, who attempts such a reconstruction, and W. Dietrich, "Josia und das Gesetzbuch (2 Reg. XXII)," *VT* 27 (1977) 13–35, who applies his model of three exilic editions to this text.

26. O'Brien, *The Deuteronomistic History Hypothesis* 12. His own attempt provides possibilities, but his inability to define an independent redaction critical base for his overall structure hinders his ability to explain some components of the DtrH text, as indicated by his exclusion of the Succession Narrative from consideration.

to the DtrH in the exilic or postexilic period,[27] but this would leave Solomon's accession to the throne unexplained in earlier editions of the work. Likewise, the roles played by the narrative in Kings concerning Elijah and Elisha require definition in the context of a Josianic DtrH, and those played by the narratives concerning Solomon and Hezekiah require clarification as well.

A second major issue in the study of King Josiah and his reign pertains to the book of Deuteronomy. Obviously, this is related to the issues posed by DtrH in that Deuteronomy provides the historiographic foundation for the DtrH evaluation of the history of Israel and Judah. Scholars are virtually unanimous in arguing that the narrative concerning the discovery of a Torah scroll in the Temple during the reign of King Josiah must be identified with the book of Deuteronomy, or at least with an early version of the book, due to the correspondence between Josiah's reforms and the commands of Deuteronomy.[28] The focus on cultic centralization constitutes the primary correspondence between Josiah's reform and the book of Deuteronomy insofar as the reform identifies the Jerusalem Temple as the exclusive site authorized by YHWH in Deuteronomy 12 for worship. Other correspondences include polemics against pagan or Canaanite worship, the command to celebrate Passover, and the role of YHWH's Torah in establishing a covenant relationship between YHWH and the people.

The basic problems in establishing the relationship of the book of Deuteronomy to Josiah's reform revolve around the provenance of the book and its portrayal of the role of the monarch. Deuteronomy presents a model of leadership in which the Levitical priests and the prophets are given special consideration; the king appears to be placed under the supervision of the Levitical priests (Deut 17:14–20). The primary authority figure in the book, after all, is Moses, a Levite and prophet who exercises power much like that of a king insofar as he promulgates the basic laws by which Israelite society and religion are to be governed. Given the relative strength and stability of the Davidic monarchy in southern Judah, and the relative weakness and instability of the various dynasties that ruled the northern kingdom of Israel during the course of its history, this has suggested to many scholars that Deuteronomy derives from a northern provenance. This view is reinforced by the role that Moses and the Exodus play in northern Israel as the basic tradition concerning the foundation of Israel as a distinctive people and in its concept of a conditional covenant based on adherence to YHWH's Torah, in contrast to southern Judah, in which the Davidic tradition of an unconditional promise to David of eternal rule and divine protection in Zion stands as the foundation for

---

27. For example, John Van Seters, *In Search of History: Historiography in the Ancient World and the Origins of Biblical History* (New Haven and London: Yale University, 1983) 277–291; cf. O'Brien, *The Deuteronomistic History Hypothesis* 139–142.

28. See Horst Dietrich Preuss, *Deuteronomium*, ErFor 164 (Darmstadt: Wissenschaftliche Buchgesellschaft, 1982) 1–74, esp. 1–12; R. E. Clements, *Deuteronomy*, OTG (Sheffield: JSOT Press, 1989) 69–83; Moshe Weinfeld, "Deuteronomy, Book of," *ABD* II, 168–183. See also M. J. Paul, "Hilkiah and the Law (2 Kings 22) in the 17th and 18th Centuries: Some Influences on W. M. L. de Wette," in *Das Deuteronomium: Entstehung, Gestalt und Botschaft*, ed. N. Lohfink, BETL 68 (Leuven: Peeters, 1985) 9–12.

Judean self-identity and the relationship to YHWH. As a result, many scholars argue that Deuteronomy was brought south, probably in the aftermath of the Assyrian destruction of northern Israel, and that it was incorporated into Judean tradition by Josiah who made it a foundation of the southern covenant tradition in place of the old Davidic tradition.[29] Hence, Deuteronomy severely restricts the authority of the king by requiring him to observe YHWH's Torah under the supervision of the Levitical priests.

Nevertheless, the commonly accepted view of a northern provenance for the book of Deuteronomy raises questions about its relationship to Josiah's reform and points to the need to consider the interrelationship between religious considerations on the one hand and socioeconomic and political considerations on the other in the overall conceptualization of the laws of Deuteronomy and the Josianic reform. No one adequately answers the question as to why a Judean monarch should adapt the covenant ideology of the northern kingdom of Israel when Israel had been so roundly defeated and destroyed by the Assyrians. The argument that Josiah feared a similar destruction of Judah for sin against YHWH is hardly compelling, especially during the period of the collapse of the Assyrian empire. If anything, the experience of the Assyrian invasions and hegemony in Israel and Judah during the late eighth through the seventh centuries B.C.E. would validate Davidic ideology and undermine the northern Mosaic covenant tradition. Judah survived the Assyrian onslaught, and Israel did not. In the DtrH conception of reward and punishment, this would suggest that Judah was righteous but Israel was not.

Indeed, scholars point to the role of Judean or Davidic ideology in Deuteronomy and the means by which the laws of Deuteronomy enhance the power of the Davidic monarch and the Judean cultic establishment.[30] Many of the features of Deuteronomy's program appear to be quite Judean. As Clements demonstrates, the language of election for the people of Israel in the book of Deuteronomy reflects that of YHWH's election of the house of David. The requirement of a centralized site for cultic worship conflicts with the tradition of the north, which maintained sanctuaries at Dan and Beth-El and perhaps in other locations as well, whereas Judah tended to focus on Jerusalem. Furthermore, the centralization of the cult has substantial socioeconomic and political implications that enhance the power of the Judean state and its ability to control the economic resources of the land. Fundamentally, the centralization of the cult entails the centralization of the collection of economic resources or taxes from the people in the form of tithes, offerings, and so on, and places them in the hands of the state.[31] Although

29. For discussion, see Clements, *Deuteronomy* 79–83. Prominent examples of this position include Albrecht Alt, "Die Heimat des Deuteronomiums," *KS II* (1953) 250–275; E. W. Nicholson, *Deuteronomy and Tradition: Literary and Historical Traditions in the Book of Deuteronomy* (Philadelphia: Fortress, 1967); Gerhard von Rad, *Deuteronomy: A Commentary*, OTL, translated by D. Barton (London: SCM, 1966).

30. For example, R. E. Clements, "Deuteronomy and the Jerusalem Cult Tradition," *VT* 15 (1965) 300–312; Moshe Weinfeld, *Deuteronomy and the Deuteronomic School* (Oxford: Oxford University Press, 1972).

31. W. Eugene Claburn, "The Fiscal Basis of Josiah's Reforms," *JBL* 92 (1973) 11–22; Naomi Steinberg, "The Deuteronomic Law Code and the Politics of State Centralization," in *The Bible*

Deuteronomy emphasizes care for the Levites by the people, it actually reduces the income due to them by closing down the noncentral altars and by allowing the people to eat a portion of the tithes that were designed to support the Levites. This essentially undermines the role of Levites outside of Jerusalem and enhances the role of the Jerusalem priests. Finally, the image of the monarch who is subsumed under the authority of the Torah actually gives the monarch wide-ranging powers. The narrative in 2 Kings 22–23 demonstrates that Josiah was able to exercise considerable authority over the life of the people of Judah and Israel by appealing to the Torah found in the Temple as his warrant for doing so. Although Deuteronomy employs the imagery of the northern Mosaic traditions, it seems to allow for a very centralized concept of king and cult in keeping with Judean tradition that undermines the covenant concept of the north. The indications of both northern Israelite and southern Judean concerns within the book require closer study in order to clarify the nature of Deuteronomy and its relationship to Josiah's reform. Because Deuteronomy is identified with Josiah's reform, this points to a very clear religious and sociopolitical agenda to employ northern ideology as a means to extend Davidic authority over the north and thereby to consolidate Davidic rule over a reunited kingdom of Israel.

The third major area involved in the study of King Josiah and his reign pertains to the prophetical literature, much of which appears to be associated with it, including Jeremiah, Nahum, Zephaniah, and Habakkuk. This suggests that a great deal of information concerning Josiah's reign and reform might be available, but such has not been the case as problems emerge in the study of each of these books and have raised questions.

Jeremiah is the most prominent case in point. Although the superscription to the book in Jeremiah 1:1–3 states that Jeremiah's prophetic career began in the thirteenth year of Josiah's reign (627 B.C.E.), there is relatively little indication in the book that Jeremiah's prophecies date to the period of King Josiah, or that Jeremiah played any major role in relation to Josiah or his reform.[32] Jeremiah 25:1–38 portrays Jeremiah's frustration at speaking to the people since the thirteenth year of Josiah's reign because the people did not follow his instructions to return to YHWH. As a result, Jeremiah states that YHWH will bring about the Babylonian exile for a period of seventy years. This might suggest that Jeremiah was a supporter of Josiah's reforms, insofar as he called for adherence to YHWH, but there is no clear indication that adherence to YHWH entails adherence to the teachings

---

and the Politics of Exegesis, Fs. N. Gottwald, ed. D. Jobling, P. L. Day, G. T. Sheppard (Cleveland: Pilgrim, 1991) 161–170, 336–339.

32. For discussion of the problems in establishing the relationship between Jeremiah and Josiah, see Leo Perdue, "Jeremiah in Modern Research: Approaches and Issues," in *A Prophet to the Nations: Essays in Jeremiah Studies*, ed. L. G. Perdue (Winona Lake, Ind.: Eisenbrauns, 1984) 1– 32, esp. 4–6; Siegfried Herrmann, *Jeremia: Der Prophet und das Buch*, ErFor 271 (Darmstadt: Wissenschaftliche Buchgesellschaft, 1990) 1–37; Klaus Seybold, *Der Prophet Jeremia: Leben und Werk*, Urban Taschenbücher 416 (Stuttgart: W. Kohlhammer, 1993) 68–91; Josef Schreiner, "Jeremia und die joschianische Reform: Probleme—Fragen—Antworten," in *Jeremia und die "deuteronomische Bewegung,"* BBB 98, ed. W. Gross (Weinheim: Beltz Athenäum, 1995) 11–31.

of Josiah's reforms in this text. Jeremiah chides Jehoiakim in Jeremiah 22:1–30 for building a sumptuous palace for himself while ignoring the needs of his people. In carrying out this critique, Jeremiah refers to Jehoiakim's father, Josiah, as an example of a righteous monarch who ate, drank, and did justice and righteousness for his people. Nevertheless, this is a retrospective view of Josiah that provides no indication of the prophet's views or actions during the lifetime of Josiah. Likewise, Jeremiah 3:6–10 refers retrospectively to the word of YHWH concerning Israel in the days of Josiah in order to criticize Judah for acting in a manner like that of Israel. This might suggest that Jeremiah's message was directed against Israel in the days of Josiah. Indeed, many scholars have noted that Jeremiah 2–4 and 30–31 contain material that condemns Israel and calls for its return to YHWH, but in the present literary context of Jeremiah 2–6 and 30–33, this material relates to the punishment of Judah in the Babylonian period. A number of scholars have attempted redaction critical analyses of these passages to establish an earlier text of Jeremiah's prophecies that would relate to the period of Josiah's reform, but none has proved to be convincing.[33] This is due in large measure to the uncertainty as to whether "Israel" refers solely to northern Israel or to Judah as representative of Israel as a whole. The northern kingdom after all had been destroyed about a century prior to the reign of Josiah, which would suggest that "Israel" in these texts could not refer to the northern kingdom. Nevertheless, the statements concerning the return of Israel to Zion (Jer 3:14; 31:6, 10–14), the reunification of the house of Judah and the house of Israel (Jer 3:15–18), and the restoration of a new covenant with Israel and Judah (Jer 31:27–34), suggest the possibility that Jeremiah did in fact support Josiah's actions to reunify the people of Israel and Judah. Many argue that these statements represent postexilic eschatological sentiments, but the political dimensions of these statements must not be overlooked because they point clearly to the political aims of the Josianic reform. Both Jeremiah 2–6 and 30–33 require further redaction-critical study to determine whether or not this is the case.

The book of Nahum would seem to be a prime candidate for a prophetic text deriving from the period of King Josiah insofar as it celebrates the downfall of the Assyrian empire, particularly the capital city of Nineveh, which took place in 612 B.C.E.[34] Nevertheless, questions have been raised concerning the applicability of the book to the period of Josiah's reform. Many have been perplexed by the apparently incoherent literary form of the book with its references to Belial in Nahum 1:11 and 2:1. Since Belial is frequently identified as a Satan figure in late–Second Temple period texts, many have argued that Nahum is the product of extensive postexilic redaction that represents an eschatological scenario of judgment against evil symbolized by the Assyrian empire. Consequently, Nahum would have little to do with Josiah's reform.Others have argued that the reference to the sack of Thebes in Nahum 3:8–10, which took place in 663 B.C.E., indicates that

---

33. See Seybold, *Der Prophet Jeremia* 68–91, for discussion.
34. For an overview of current research on Nahum, see R. Mason, *Micah, Nahum, Obadiah,* OTG (Sheffield: JSOT Press, 1991) 57–84.

the book should be dated to a much earlier period and that the projections of Assyria's downfall only express the hopes of the writer, but not the reality of Nineveh's fall. Nahum, too, requires renewed redaction-critical analysis.

Much the same applies to the book of Zephaniah.[35] The superscription of the book in Zephaniah 1:1 places the prophet's oracles in the days of Josiah, but many argue that the book is the product of extensive postexilic redaction that posits an eschatological scenario of judgment against Israel and the nations prior to the establishment of YHWH's worldwide blessing in Zion. This is due in large measure to the problems caused by the references to YHWH's destruction of all creation in Zephaniah 1:2–3 and the oracles against the nations in Zephaniah 2:4–15, which many take to indicate a worldwide eschatological scenario. The nations mentioned, however, do not represent the entire earth, but only those that were of relevance to Josiah—that is, the Philistine cities where many Israelites had been relocated by the Assyrians to support their olive oil industry; Moab and Ammon, which had taken control of former Israelite territory east of the Jordon; Ethiopia, which had once controlled Egypt and failed to come to Israel's aid during the Assyrian invasions; and Assyria, which had dominated Judah for over a century. Again, the exhortational elements of Zephaniah, the condemnation of pagan religious practice, and the call for the restoration of Zion all point to elements of Josiah's reform.

Habakkuk also must be considered, not because it dates to the period of Josiah, but to its aftermath.[36] Again, there are tremendous problems in discerning the literary structure and character of the book and in identifying the "righteous" and the "wicked" that figure so prominently in the prophet's statements. Many have argued that the "wicked" must refer to elements within Judah, and that the Babylonians are brought by YHWH to punish them (Hab 1:2–4, 5–11). Unfortunately, the identification of the "wicked" with the Babylonians in Habakkuk 1:12–17 introduces an element of confusion, prompting many to argue that Habakkuk is a postexilic redactional pastiche like Nahum and Zephaniah that presents the "wicked" as part of an eschatological scenario of punishment in Habakkuk 2:1–20 and 3:1–19. The issue is of great concern for understanding Josiah, however, because the identification of Babylon as the wicked party that is accused of treachery and violence is particularly pertinent. Josiah died supporting Babylonian interests, apparently following a long tradition of alliance with Babylon begun by his great grandfather Hezekiah and supported by the prophet Jeremiah. The book of Habakkuk apparently conveys a great deal of disillusionment in Judah concerning Josiah's former ally for whom Josiah and Judah had paid so dearly.

Finally, prophetic books that present the period prior to the late seventh century also must be considered because of their potential relevance to Josiah's reform. There has been considerable discussion of a Josianic redaction of the book

---

35. For discussion of current research on Zephaniah, see R. Mason, *Zephaniah, Habakkuk Joel*, OTG (Sheffield: JSOT Press, 1994) 16–58; Marvin A. Sweeney, "Zephaniah: A Paradigm for the Study of the Prophetic Books," *CR:BS* 7 (1999) 119–145.

36. For discussion of current research on Habakkuk, see Marvin A. Sweeney, "Habakkuk, Book of," *ABD* II, 1–6; R. Mason, *Zephaniah, Habakkuk, Joel* 60–96.

of Isaiah, in which the prophet's oracles were read in support of Josiah's reform.[37] The downfall of Assyria predicted in the book and the predictions of a righteous Davidic monarch who will preside over a period in which a restored Israel and Judah will be reunited clearly lend themselves to Josiah's reforms. Likewise, there has been considerable discussion of Deuteronomistic redaction of the books of Amos and Hosea.[38] Amos culminates in oracles calling for the destruction of the Beth-El altar and the restoration of "the fallen booth of David" over Israel, and Hosea culminates in a call for Israel's return. Whatever the original referents of these statements might have been, the present forms of both books lend themselves to support the aims of Josiah's reforms. Likewise, the book of Micah, which applies the model of Israel's punishment to that of Judah, must be considered. Its calls for the return of Israel to Zion and the restoration of Davidic rule over Judah and Israel in the aftermath of Assyria's defeat also must be considered in relation to Josiah's reform. Each of these books appears to have been known in some form or another by Jeremiah or the writers of the book of Jeremiah, insofar as the book cites them and employs many of their expressions and ideas.[39] Altogether, there are substantial indications that the earlier prophetic books were read or reworked to support King Josiah's interests in reuniting northern Israel and southern Judah around the Jerusalem Temple under the rule of the house of David.

It is the purpose of this study, therefore, to examine each of these literary works, the DtrH, the book of Deuteronomy, and the relevant prophetic books—in relation to the reign and reform program of King Josiah of Judah. In carrying out this agenda, I employ several methodological perspectives or guidelines. First, I take seriously the results of archeological study of the land of Israel during the late seventh century and the study of extrabiblical sources that point to the limits of Josiah's influence in the land. Whatever the intentions of Josiah's reforms might have been, archeological and extrabiblical literary evidence indicate that Josiah ultimately did not succeed in establishing Davidic control over a substantial territory beyond the Judean hill country.

Second, I employ advances in redaction-critical methodology that take seriously the final form of the biblical text as the unequivocal starting point for the

37. See esp. Hermann Barth, *Die Jesajaworte in der Josiazeit*, WMANT 48 (Neukirchen-Vluyn: Neukirchener, 1977). For a full discussion of research on this issue, see Marvin A. Sweeney, "Reevaluating Isaiah 1–39 in Recent Critical Research," *CR:BS* 4 (1996) 79–113, esp. 84–92.

38. See W. H. Schmidt, "Die deuteronomistische Redaktion des Amosbuches: Zu den Theologien Unterscheiden zwischen dem Prophetenwort und seinem Sammler," *ZAW* 77 (1965) 168–193; H. W. Wolff, *Joel and Amos* (Hermeneia; Philadelphia: Fortress, 1977); Wolff, "Hoseas geistige Heimat," *TLZ* 81 (1956) 83–94; Wolff, *Hosea* (Hermeneia; Philadelphia: Fortress, 1974).

39. For studies of the interrelationships between Jeremiah and these prophetic books, see Ute Wendel, *Jesaja und Jeremia: Worte, Motive und Einsichten Jesajas in der Verkündigung Jeremias*, BTS 25 (Neukirchen-Vluyn: Neukirchener, 1995); Walter Beyerlin, *Reflexe der Amosvisionen im Jeremiabuch*, OBO 93 (Freiburg: Universitätsverlag; Göttingen: Vandenhoeck & Ruprecht, 1989); Martin Schulz-Rauch, *Hosea und Jeremia: Zur wirkungsgeschichte des Hoseabuches*, CTM 16 (Stuttgart: Calwer, 1996); Jun-Hee Cha, *Micha und Jeremia*, BBB 107 (Weinheim: Beltz Athenäum, 1996).

reconstruction of earlier text forms.[40] In contrast to earlier redaction-critical studies that attempt to identify redactional material at the level of the individual phrase,
verse, or pericope, this study recognizes that the final form of the text as a whole
(including the entirety of the DtrH, the book of Deuteronomy, or any of the prophetic books under consideration) is potentially the product of its redactors. They
were the ones who selected, read, interpreted, and reworked earlier traditions in
keeping with their own theological, ideological, or historiographical perspectives
and agendas. Redactors are not only editors but also authors with theological,
historiographical, and ideological agendas of their own that must be considered.
It is only after the structure, genre, perspective, and setting of the final form of
the text is analyzed and understood that earlier text forms can be posited insofar
as this is possible. Barton's warning concerning the disappearing redactor—that
is, the redactor who does his/her/their work so well that literary tensions are no
longer evident—must be firmly kept in mind.[41] Evidence for literary historical
reconstruction may not always be present, or it may be limited, so that such work
may be severely restricted or even impossible. Nevertheless, when such literary
historical work is possible, the structure, genre, perspective, and settings of reconstructed texts also must be evaluated to the extent that the evidence warrants.
Furthermore, the interpreter must be prepared to recognize that the agenda or
perspective of a redactional form of the text and a posited earlier text form may
not always be one and the same, even when the earlier text form is incorporated
into the later text. Redactors often understand or reinterpret the meanings of texts
very different from their earlier authors.

Finally, the rhetorical functions of the text also must be considered. This literature, whether in its final form or posited earlier forms, was written to have an
impact on an audience.[42] It may articulate a goal to be achieved, or it may attempt
to persuade its audience to make a choice or to take a particular course of action.
In these cases, the text may not describe historical reality as it is but as the author
of the text posits that it should or could be. Consequently, rhetorical aspects,
such as propagandistic or exhortational functions, must be identified and considered in relation to the interpretation of the text and its historical settings. In

40. For discussion of this methodological perspective, see Marvin A. Sweeney, "Formation
and Form in Prophetic Literature," in *Old Testament Interpretation: Past, Present, Future*, Fs. G. M.
Tucker, ed. J. L. Mays, D. L. Petersen, K. H. Richards (Nashville: Abingdon, 1995) 113–126;
Sweeney, *Isaiah 1–39, with an Introduction to Prophetic Literature*, FOTL 16 (Grand Rapids, Mich.
and Cambridge, U.K.: William Eerdmans, 1996), esp. 10–15; Sweeney, "Form Criticism," in *To
Each Its Own Meaning: Revised and Enlarged Edition*, ed. S. L. McKenzie and S. R. Haynes (Louisville, KY: Westminster John Knox, 1999) 58–89. Cf. Rolf Knierim, "Criticism of Literary Features,
Form, Tradition, and Redaction," in *The Hebrew Bible and Its Modern Interpreters*, ed. D. A. Knight
and G. M. Tucker (Chico, Calif.: Scholars Press, 1985) 123–165.

41. John Barton, *Reading the Old Testament: Method in Biblical Study* (Louisville, KY: Westminster John Knox, 1996) 56–58.

42. See esp. Phyllis Trible, *Rhetorical Criticism: Context, Method, and the Book of Jonah*
(GBS; Minneapolis: Fortress, 1994), and Patricia Tull, "Rhetorical Criticism," in *To Each Its Own
Meaning: Revised and Enlarged Edition*, ed. S. L. McKenzie and S. R. Haynes (Louisville, KY:
Westminster John Knox, 1999) 156–180, for discussion of this issue.

such cases, a full understanding of the social, political, and economic functions of the text must be considered alongside its theological, ideological, or historiographical perspective. In short, the interpreter must ask what the text is designed to accomplish.

As a result of the application of these methodological perspectives to the study of the literature identified above, I argue that biblical literature—including the Deuteronomistic History; the book of Deuteronomy; and the prophetic books of Jeremiah, Zephaniah, Nahum, Habakkuk, Isaiah, Amos, Hosea, and Micah—indeed points to the historical reality of Josiah's reform as a program that was designed to unify Israel and Judah around the Jerusalem Temple under Davidic rule. I argue that the DtrH presents an ideologically charged history directed particularly to the northern tribes of Israel. The DtrH maintains that, from the time of Joshua on, the northern tribes were never able to rule themselves according to the ideal Mosaic model of leadership and only King Josiah represented the proper Mosaic model of ideal centralized leadership over a united people of Israel. I argue that the book of Deuteronomy represents Josiah's attempt to revise the system of Israelite law in order to enhance the religious, economic, and political power of the centralized state and thereby to unite the people around the Jerusalem Temple and the house of David. Finally, I argue that prophetic literature was employed to carry out various aspects of the reform. Earlier traditions of Isaiah, Amos, and Micah were designed to portray Israel's downfall as an act of YHWH and show that Israel and Judah could be reunited under Davidic rule once the problems of both nations were addressed. Traditions of Jeremiah and Hosea were designed to convince the people of the former northern kingdom to return to Jerusalem and the House of David. Zephaniah was designed to call for the reform of religious and political practice in Judah in order to rally support for Josiah. Nahum points to the collapse of Assyria as an act of YHWH that prepares for a restored Israelite people. Finally, Habakkuk points to Judah's frustration with Babylon, apparently Josiah's primary ally, in the aftermath of Josiah's reign when Judah came under Babylonian hegemony.

Overall, Josiah emerges as a figure who attempted to restore the ancient Davidic empire by reuniting the collapsed former kingdom of Israel with Judah; but he failed in this endeavor as the Egyptians, and later the Babylonians, proved to be too strong to allow for the restoration of an independent Davidic state. Josiah apparently saw himself as the king or messiah of all Israel who could restore his people and enable them to achieve their full potential as the nation to which YHWH chose to reveal Torah. Nevertheless, his early death at Megiddo; the apparent demise of his program for reform and restoration; and the subsequent destruction of Judah, Jerusalem, and the Temple mark him as a failed or lost messiah. Despite his failure, however, Josiah emerges as a key figure in the composition of biblical literature and the development of Judean thinking concerning YHWH's intentions to return Israel and the Davidic dynasty to its former glory. Overall, the Josianic emphasis on the restoration of a unified Davidic kingdom of Israel following northern Israel's destruction at the hands of Assyria establishes a fundamental pattern of restoration in the aftermath of disaster. A recent study by Antti Laato demonstrates that this pattern plays a foundational role in the means by which later Judean prophets and writers addressed the issues posed by the Babylonian destruction of Judah, Jerusalem, the Temple, and the royal house of David—that is, the image of a restored Josianic/Davidic kingdom of Israel centered around the Jerusalem Temple provides the model for a restored people of Israel centered around the restored Jerusalem Temple in the postexilic period.[43] In this regard, Josiah lays the foundation for the exilic thinkers and movements that ultimately rescued Judaism from the obscurity and anonymity of Babylonian defeat and exile and saw to the restoration of the post-exilic Jewish community in the land of Judah. Although there may well have been "a conspiracy of silence" concerning the death of Josiah, there has been considerable conversation about the significance of this great monarch, both in antiquity and in the present.

---

43. *Josiah and David Redivivus: The Historical Josiah and the Messianic Expectations of Exilic and Postexilic Times*, ConBibOT 33 (Stockholm: Almqvist & Wiksell, 1992).

I

THE DEUTERONOMISTIC HISTORY

The Deuteronomistic History (DtrH) plays an important role in the biblical presentation of King Josiah of Judah. Originally identified in 1943 by Martin Noth as a coherent historiographical work, it comprises the books of Deuteronomy, Joshua, Judges, 1–2 Samuel, and 1–2 Kings.[1] Based on the theological principles that define the stipulations of the covenant between YHWH and the twelve tribes of Israel in the book of Deuteronomy, DtrH presents the history of the nation Israel from the time of the conquest of the land of Canaan under Joshua until the time of the collapse of the kingdom of Judah and the Babylonian exile. It is clearly an ideologically charged interpretation of Israel's and Judah's history in that it employs the theological perspectives of the book of Deuteronomy to explain Israel's and Judah's historical experience in the land of Israel. Essentially, it argues that the various problems manifested throughout Israel's history—including the disintegration of the tribal confederacy in the period of the Judges, the division of the united empire of David and Solomon into the separate kingdoms of Israel and Judah, the destruction of the Israelite kingdom by the Assyrian empire, and the exile of the Judean kingdom by the Babylonian empire—were the result of the people's failure to abide by the terms of the covenant with YHWH as articulated in the book of Deuteronomy. Although Deuteronomy contains a wide variety of legal material that is intended to define the relationship between YHWH and the tribes of Israel, the basic causes of Israel's problems as presented in the DtrH include its failure to accept YHWH alone as G-d and its pursuit of various pagan deities, the failure to establish a single sanctuary for the worship of YHWH in the land and the worship of other deities at various altars and high

---

1. See Noth, *Überlieferungsgeschichtliche Studien I*, 1–110, ET: *The Deuteronomistic History*.

places throughout the land, the failure to abide by the commandments of
YHWH's covenant, and the abuse of power by the kings who continually led
the people into apostasy by their failure to implement the stipulations of
YHWH's covenant. Altogether, the DtrH is a work of theodicy, in that it places
the blame for Israel's and Judah's collapse on the people themselves rather
than on YHWH. According to the presentation of the DtrH, YHWH fulfilled
the expectations of the covenant by enabling the people to take possession of
the land of Israel; the people, by contrast, failed to keep their part of the
covenant and thereby lost the land that YHWH provided.

Since Noth's initial identification and definition of the DtrH, a vigorous
discussion has ensued among scholars that raises questions concerning the
literary history and theological outlook of the work.[2] Noth maintains that the
DtrH is a unified work that stems from the hand of a single author working
during the period of the Babylonian exile. Although this author employed a
great deal of older material, the Dtr author provided the basic outline and
theological perspective of the work, which is especially evident in the various
Deuteronomistic "sermons" that define the stages in Israel's history and
provide the author with the opportunity to summarize each stage according to
the theological principles laid down in Deuteronomy. Altogether, the Dtr
author sought to explain the demise of the people of Israel for their failure to
maintain YHWH's covenant and thereby to close the book on Israel's history.
Thus, the Dtr author incorporated an earlier version of Deuteronomy to define
the theological principles by which the people would be judged. Speeches by
Moses and Joshua in Joshua 1 and 23, respectively, made it clear that the
people were to receive the land from YHWH in return for their obedience to
YHWH's commands. Speeches by Samuel (1 Sam 12) and Solomon (1 Kgs 8)
outline the problems posed by kingship and the Temple in Deuteronomistic
ideology. Likewise, the Dtr author presents summary reflections on Israel's
history in Joshua 12, which summarizes YHWH's granting of the land to Israel;
Judges 2:11ff, which defines the cycle of sin and deliverance in the book of
Judges; and 2 Kings 17, which presents the destruction of the northern kingdom of Israel as a consequence of the people's failure to live by YHWH's
expectations.

Other scholars note features of the DtrH that challenge Noth's view of a
single exilic work concerned entirely with Israel's sin and judgment. Von Rad,
for example, points to the release of the exiled King Jehoiachin from Babylonian
prison at the end of the work and its continuous attention to the royal promise
tradition as an indication that the DtrH was concerned with presenting some

---

2. For full discussions of the history research on the Deuteronomistic History, see Römer and
de Pury, "L'historiographie deutéronomiste (HD)"; McKenzie and Graham, eds., *The History of
Israel's Traditions*; Preuss, "Zum deuteronomistischen Geschichtswerk"; McKenzie, "Deuteronomistic
History"; McKenzie, *The Trouble with Kings: The Composition of the Book of Kings in the
Deuteronomistic History*, VTSup 42 (Leiden: E. J. Brill, 1991) 1–19; O'Brien, *The Deuteronomistic
History Hypothesis* 3–22; Knoppers, *Two Nations under G-d: The Deuteronomistic History of
Solomon and the Dual Monarchies. Volume 1* 1–56.

hope for the people of Israel rather than only a scenario of punishment.[3] Wolff likewise notes the importance of the theme of Israel's repentance in the historical presentation of the DtrH.[4] Based on the work of von Rad and others, McCarthy identifies 2 Samuel 7, which presents YHWH's promise of an eternal dynasty to King David, as one of the Deuteronomistic key texts that defines the theological perspective of the history.[5] Each of these studies points to elements of promise and return that challenge Noth's conception of a history dedicated only to understanding the judgment and end of the people of Israel. Literary critical concerns are evident in the work of Smend and Dietrich, who identify three different exilic literary layers in the DtrH: a legally oriented "nomistic" source from ca. 560 B.C.E. that dwells on the legal terms of the covenant; a "prophetic" source from 580 to 560 B.C.E. that emphasizes the roles of the prophets in the decline and fall of the biblical kingdoms; and the basic Deuteronomistic Historical source from shortly after the fall of Jerusalem, which presents the basic history of the decline of Israel from the time of Moses through the kings of Israel and Judah.[6] Weippert examines the regnal formulas that evaluate the reigns of the various kings of Israel and Judah. Based on their formulaic differences, she identifies three major stages of redaction in Kings: RI, which includes the reigns of the Judean kings Jehoshaphat to Ahaz and the Israelite kings Joram to Hosea; RII, which comprises the framework for RI with the reigns of the Judean monarchs Rehoboam to Asa and the Israelite monarchs Jeroboam I to Ahaziah prior to RI and the Judean kings Hezekiah to Josiah after RI; and, finally, RIII, which comprises the reigns of the last Judean monarchs Jehoahaz to Zedekiah.[7]

By far the most influential current model for understanding the literary composition and theological outlook of the DtrH is that of Cross and his followers.[8] This model has tremendous implications for understanding the presentation of Josiah in biblical literature in that it argues for an original Josianic edition of the DtrH that presents Josiah's reign as the culmination of Israel's history. Cross turns to an old literary critical hypothesis argued by Kuenen[9] that posits two editions of the Deuteronomistic historical work in which the basic preexilic edition was touched up and completed in its present form at some point during the exile. Cross's basic argument is thematic in that he traces the contrasting presentations in the DtrH concerning the monarchies of Israel and Judah. The DtrH presentation concerning the northern monarchies is entirely negative, in that all northern monarchs are judged to be evil because

3. Gerhard von Rad, *Old Testament Theology*, Vol. 1 (New York: Harper & Row, 1962) 334–347; von Rad, *Studies in Deuteronomy* 74–91.

4. Wolff, "The Kerygma of the Deuteronomic Historical Work."

5. Dennis J. McCarthy, "II Samuel 7 and the Structure of the Deuteronomic History," *JBL* 84 (1965) 131–138.

6. Smend, "Die Gesetz und die Völker"; Dietrich, *Prophetie und Geschichte*.

7. Weippert, "Die 'deuteronomistischen' Beurteilung."

8. Cross, "The Themes of the Book of Kings."

9. Abraham Kuenen, *Historisch-Kritische Einleitung in die Bücher des Alten Testaments* I (Leipzig: Otto Schulze, 1887) 88–100.

they perpetuate the "sin of Jeroboam" in their revolt against the house of David and their rejection of the Jerusalem temple. The DtrH presentation concerning the Davidic monarchy focuses on the "promise to David" in that YHWH promises David an eternal dynasty (2 Sam 7) in return for the faithfulness that David showed to YHWH. Therefore, David is the ideal monarch of the DtrH, and all Judean kings are judged in comparison to David and his faithfulness to YHWH. Those who walk in the path of David, such as Jehoshaphat, Hezekiah, and Josiah, are judged positively; those who deviate from David's adherence to YHWH are condemned. According to Cross, these themes define the overall presentation of the DtrH throughout the books of Kings and culminate in the reign of King Josiah of Judah. The presentation of Josiah's reform in 2 Kings 22–23 demonstrates his efforts to restore the former glory of the Davidic empire by purging the land of foreign worship, centralizing worship in the Jerusalem Temple, and reinstituting the celebration of Passover, all in accordance with the principles of the "book of Torah," undoubtedly an early version of Deuteronomy, found in the Temple during Josiah's early reign. The presentation of Josiah's reign and reform program to restore the Davidic empire in accordance with YHWH's wishes as articulated in Deuteronomy thereby represents the climax of the first edition of the DtrH, intended to point to the reign of Josiah as the fulfillment of YHWH's promise to the House of David. The unexpected death of Josiah at Megiddo and the subsequent collapse of Judah prompted a revision of the DtrH during the exilic period to account for the Babylonian exile. The accounts of both Manasseh's and Josiah's reigns were revised to assign Manasseh blame for the exile despite Josiah's righteousness. Likewise, the DtrH was brought up to date in 2 Kings 24–25, with accounts of the last kings of Judah and the Babylonian exile.

Cross's theory has been extended and modified by a number of his students and followers. Nelson, for example, provides detailed argumentation concerning the linguistic criteria that distinguish the later exilic edition of the DtrH from the original Josianic edition.[10] He likewise points to the differences in literary form evident in the accounts of the last four kings of Judah that mark 2 Kings 24–25 as a later supplement to the DtrH. Finally, his study of the DtrH presentation of Joshua points to an attempt to portray Joshua as a precursor to Josiah and thereby to foreshadow the ultimate climax of the DtrH in Josiah's reign.[11] Friedman notes the absence of the prophecy-fulfillment scheme in the last chapters of Kings as support for an original Josianic edition.[12] Levenson argues that the insertion of the Deuteronomic law code is the work of the exilic DtrH.[13] Mayes argues that the exilic DtrH edition resembles the "nomistic"

10. Nelson, *The Double Redaction of the Deuteronomistic History*.

11. Nelson, "Josiah in the Book of Joshua."

12. Richard E. Friedman, *The Exile and Biblical Narrative*, HSM 22 (Chico, Calif.: Scholars, 1981) 7–10; Friedman, "From Egypt to Egypt: Dtr[1] and Dtr[2]," in *Traditions in Transformation: Turning Points in Biblical Faith*, Fs. F. M. Cross, ed. B. Halpern and J. Levenson (Winona Lake, Ind.: Eisenbrauns, 1981) 167–192.

13. Jon D. Levenson, "Who Inserted the Book of the Torah?" *HTR* 68 (1975) 203–233.

edition posited by Smend and Dietrich.[14] Peckham attempts to argue that the exilic DtrH is the major edition of the work,[15] whereas McKenzie argues that the exilic material does not constitute a full edition of the DtrH but only disconnected supplements to the basic Josianic edition.[16] O'Brien builds on the Cross thesis in addition to that of Weippert and Campbell to argue for multiple redactions of the DtrH, including a Josianic redaction.[17] Studies by Halpern and Vanderhooft, and by Eynikel, employ arguments advanced by Weippert to argue for a preexilic Hezekian edition of the work in addition to the Josianic and exilic editions.[18] Knoppers argues that the DtrH presents Josiah as the figure who corrects the problems evident in the northern kingdom as well as in the south, and thereby represents the "David *redivius*" (II, p. 245) who promises to restore the unity of the people that was both promised in the model of Solomonic.rule and disrupted by his unfaithful conduct.[19]

The theory argued by Cross and his followers of a Josianic edition of the DtrH revised in an exilic edition clearly accounts for many features of the DtrH. One of the most fundamental themes is its emphasis on the Davidic promise together with the themes of judgment against both the northern kingdom and the south. The dynastic promise to David, in 2 Samuel 7, maintains that YHWH will guarantee the throne of the house of David forever, although it does stipulate that the house of David will be punished when the monarchs do wrong (vv. 14–15). This conditionalized view of the Davidic covenant is articulated subsequently in the narrative of Solomon's reign (1 Kgs 6:12–13; 8:25–26; 9:4–5), and it plays a role in the DtrH presentation of the revolt of the northern tribes. The oracle of Ahijah the Shilonite to Jeroboam emphasizes that the revolt is a punishment of the house of David, but that YHWH will stand behind the Davidic promise by leaving one tribe to the Davidic house (1 Kgs 11:26–40). This enables the DtrH to judge the later Davidic monarchs by measuring them against the actions of David. The theory of a Josianic redaction also emphasizes the role of King Josiah as the image behind the presentation of Joshua. As Nelson argues,[20] there are a number of parallels between the presentation of Joshua and that of Josiah, which point to the association between the two. Just as Josiah takes his directions from the "book of the Torah" found in the Temple (2 Kgs 22:8–13; 23:2–3), so Joshua writes and reads a "copy of the Torah" (Josh 8:32). This parallel is especially

14. A. D. H. Mayes, *The Story of Israel Between Settlement and Exile: A Redactional Study of the Deuteronomistic History* (London: SCM, 1983).

15. Brian Peckham, *The Composition of the Deuteronomistic History*, HSM 35 (Atlanta: Scholars, 1985).

16. McKenzie, *The Trouble with Kings*.

17. O'Brien, *The Deuteronomistic History Hypothesis*. O'Brien presupposes the work of his teacher, Campbell, who posits a ninth-century Prophetic History in 1 Samuel 1:1–2 Kings 10:28 as the basis for the DtrH. See Campbell, *Of Prophets and Kings*.

18. Halpern and Vanderhooft, "The Editions of Kings in the 7th–6th Centuries B.C.E."; Eynikel, *The Reform of King Josiah*.

19. Knoppers, *Two Nations under G-d* II; cf. Knoppers, *Two Nations Under G-d* I.

20. Nelson, "Josiah in the Book of Joshua."

noteworthy in that the "Torah of the King" in Deuteronomy 17:14–20 requires the king to write and read a "copy of the Torah."

Like Josiah, Joshua is the only other figure in the DtrH who "does not turn to the right or the left from the Torah of Moses" (2 Kgs 22:2; Josh 1:7), which likewise employs language from Deuteronomy 17:20. Like Joshua, Josiah is the only other figure in the DtrH who acts as a royal covenant mediator (Josh 8:30–35; 2 Kgs 23:1–3). Finally, Joshua and Josiah are the only figures in the DtrH who keep the Passover celebration (Josh 5:10–12; 2 Kgs 23:21–23). According to Nelson, these associations point to the fact that Joshua is presented in the image of Josiah, and thereby defines a model of ideal leadership for the DtrH. It is also noteworthy that Joshua presides over a unified Israel in a land free of Canaanite influence just as Josiah attempts to purify the land of pagan influence and unify the people around the worship of YHWH. This last point is particularly important because the narrative concerning Jeroboam's dedication of the Beth-El altar in 1 Kings 13 points to Josiah as the figure who will ultimately destroy the Beth-El altar and thereby put to an end the apostasy in Israel caused by Jeroboam.[21] Finally, Knoppers is quite correct to point to the fact that it is Josiah who rights the wrongs of the DtrH by eliminating the pagan installations in Jerusalem built by Solomon, destroying Jeroboam's altar at Beth-El, and thereby restoring the unity of the people that split as a result of Solomon's excesses.[22] Altogether, Josiah appears to be the climactic figure of the DtrH who sees to the realization of YHWH's promise to the house of David.

But several major problems continue to plague this theory and to prevent its full acceptance. The most fundamental problem is the failure to provide a full analysis of the conceptual plan of the Josianic edition of DtrH from beginning to end—that is, from Joshua to Josiah.[23] Nelson's and Knoppers's work represent important steps in this direction because they point to the image of Josiah in the presentation of Joshua, on the one hand, and to Josiah as the figure who resolves the problems created by Solomon and the subsequent dual monarchies, on the other. Although these analyses account for a great deal of material in the books of Joshua and Kings, they do not account for the role played by the presentations of Israel's premonarchic history in the book of Judges and of both Saul's and David's reigns in the books of Samuel. As indicated by the accounts of Gideon and Abimelech (Judg 6–8; 9) and of the people's request for a monarch (1 Sam 8–12), these materials are somewhat ambivalent, if not outright hostile, to the idea of kingship as a potentially abusive form of power that rejects YHWH's rule. They are especially hostile to Saul, who is presented as a member of a morally questionable tribe and community that is nearly destroyed for tolerating and defending the rape and

21. See Werner Lemke, "The Way of Obedience: 1 Kings 13 and the Structure of the Deuteronomistic History," in *Magnalia Dei/The Mighty Acts of G-d*, Fs. G. E. Wright, ed. F. M. Cross et al. (Garden City, N.Y.: Doubleday, 1976) 301–326.

22. Knoppers, *Two Nations Under G-d* II, 229–254.

23. O'Brien, *The Deuteronomistic History Hypothesis* 12.

murder of a Levite's concubine (Judg 19–21) and also as a king whose personal failings caused him to alienate supporters such as Samuel and David and ultimately to lose Israel's independence to the Philistines. Although David is presented as an ideal figure in much of this material, there is little indication that any of it is relevant to defining a Josianic edition of the DtrH.

O'Brien attempts to define the overall conceptual outlook and structure of the DtrH by arguing that it articulates a model of ideal leadership in Israel by means of a periodized view of Israel's history—that is, Moses and Joshua constitute models of ideal leadership in the premonarchic period, and David and Solomon constitute such ideal models in the period of the monarchy.[24] But this model does not account for the presentation of David in the so-called Succession Narrative (2 Sam 9–24; 1 Kgs 1–2), in which David commits adultery with Bath Sheba and then arranges for the murder of her husband Uriah to cover up the affair. This presentation is particularly pertinent in that it leads to the birth of Solomon and his accession to the throne in the midst of a bloodbath that eliminates his brother Adonijah and Adonijah's supporters. The result is a major shift in the identity of the Davidic house because all of David's supporters from his days in Hebron as king over the tribe of Judah alone are eliminated and replaced by a faction of the house that emerges only when David moves his capital to Jerusalem and assumes kingship over all twelve tribes.[25] David and Solomon are hardly ideal figures in this scenario, and this has prompted many to argue that the Succession Narrative is a later insertion in the DtrH that reflects hostility to the house of David.[26] But the removal of the Succession Narrative would leave a major gap in the DtrH that effects the transition between the reigns of David and Solomon. Its focus on David's abuse of royal power in his affair with Bath Sheba highlights themes that appear in Judges and 1 Samuel, on the one hand, and throughout the books of Kings on the other. Furthermore, Solomon ultimately causes the split in the united kingdom of Israel by his abuse of royal power, and he thereby provides the rationale for much of Josiah's program. If David's and Solomon's actions point to the abuse of royal power in the DtrH, then Josiah's attempted resolution of problems in the kingdom may well point to the fact that Josiah, and not David or Solomon, is the intended ideal monarch of the DtrH.[27] It is therefore essential that the role of the material in Judges and Samuel be incorporated into an overall understanding of the conceptual outlook of the DtrH and its presentation of David, Solomon, and Josiah.

A second major problem relates to the presentation of Manasseh's and Josiah's reigns in 2 Kings 21:1–18 and 2 Kings 22:1–23:30, respectively. The present forms of both narratives presuppose the final form of the DtrH, in that

24. O'Brien, *The Deuteronomistic History Hypothesis* 24–44.

25. Cf. Gwilym Jones, *The Nathan Narratives*, JSOTSup 80 (Sheffield: JSOT, 1990).

26. For example, John Van Seters, *In Search of History: Historiography in the Ancient World and the Origins of Biblical History* (New Haven: Yale University, 1983) 277–291.

27. Marvin A. Sweeney, "The Critique of Solomon in the Josianic Edition of the Deuteronomistic History," *JBL* 114 (1995) 607–622.

they point to Manasseh's sins as the ultimate cause of the destruction of Jerusalem and the Babylonian exile. 2 Kings 21:10–15 conveys YHWH's statement, through the prophets, that Manasseh's sins were greater than those of the Amorites and that he caused Judah to sin. As a result, YHWH will punish Jerusalem and Judah in a manner analogous to the punishment of Samaria; YHWH will give them into the hands of their enemies and cast off the remnant of the people. 2 Kings 23:26–27 reiterates this point in relation to the account of Josiah's reign. Despite the portrayal of Josiah's righteousness, YHWH remains firm in the decision to remove Judah, Jerusalem, and the Temple on account of Manasseh's wickedness. These pericopes thereby prepare for the final two chapters of the DtrH in which YHWH's punishment against Judah, Jerusalem, and the Temple is realized.

Although the present form of these narratives anticipates the Babylonian exile as the conclusion of the present form of the DtrH, the evidence amassed by Cross and his followers that points to Josiah's restoration as the original culmination of a Josianic edition of the DtrH is considerable. Weippert's observations concerning the differences in the regnal formulas in 2 Kings 23:31–25:30 for the last four monarchs of the Davidic dynasties likewise points to the likelihood that these accounts constitute a later addition to the original DtrH work designed to bring the history to a conclusion in the Babylonian exile rather than in the reign of Josiah.[28] Consequently, supporters of an original Josianic DtrH edition consistently argue that the present narratives concerning the reigns of both Manasseh and Josiah have been reworked as part of the process in which the original Josianic edition was reformulated to account for the Babylonian exile.[29]

But this contention suffers from the inability of scholars successfully to reconstruct the original edition of either narrative. The Manasseh narrative is the most problematic. Most scholars maintain that vv. 10–15 are a later supplement to the original account of the reign of Manasseh, but this contention leaves several difficulties unexplained. Cross and Nelson argue that the bulk of the narrative was essentially the creation of the exilic edition of the DtrH, but this leaves little grounds for reconstructing a Josianic account of the reign of Manasseh and prompts many scholars to contend that it is impossible to reconstruct an earlier version of the narrative.[30] Friedman, on the other hand,

---

28. Weippert, "Die 'deuteronomistischen' Beurteilung."

29. Cross, *Canaanite Myth* 285–286; Nelson, *The Double Redaction* 65–69; McKenzie, *The Trouble with Kings* 125–126, 142–143.

30. See, most recently, Percy S. F. van Keulen, *Manasseh Through the Eyes of the Deuteronomists: The Manasseh Account (2 Kings 21:1-8) and the Final Chapters of the Deuteronomistic History*, OTS 38 (Leiden: E. J. Brill, 1996), who employs both synchronic and diachronic literary analyses to argue that there was no preexilic edition of the Manasseh narrative in the DtrH. Instead, he argues that the image of Manasseh is linked to the narratives concerning Jeroboam, Ahab, and the fall of Israel. He identifies only two exilic editions—that is, the basic account in verses 1–7, 9aβ–14, and 16–18 from the early exilic period and a "nomistic" addition in verses 8–9aα and 15 from the late exilic period. Both editions posit that Josiah's actions were irrelevant, because the magnitude of Manasseh's sins had already prompted YHWH to condemn Jerusalemand Judah. For

points to the enumeration of Manasseh's sins in vv. 1–7, all of which are corrected by Josiah in the course of his reform.[31] Consequently, he argues that vv. 1–7 are part of an original Josianic account of Manasseh's reign and that vv. 8–15 are the work of the exilic DtrH. But this solution also leaves problems because it does not explain why Manasseh should revert to the sins of Ahab in building an Asherah in the Temple. This is especially pertinent when the narrative concerning YHWH's deliverance of Hezekiah and Jerusalem in 2 Kings 18–20 is taken into consideration. Following such a demonstration of YHWH's actions on behalf of the faithful Hezekiah, who in many respects serves as a model for Josiah, why should the Josianic DtrH include a narrative concerning Manasseh's reign that portrays him as a sinner on the magnitude of Ahab? Such a portrayal is hardly necessary to promote Manasseh as a foil to Josiah; rather, it points to an effort to portray Manasseh as the cause for Judah's destruction on analogy with Israel.

The narrative concerning Josiah's reign is less problematic because it is a simple matter to argue that 2 Kings 23:26–30 was appended to an original Josianic account of the reform in order to explain the unexpected early death of Josiah and the subsequent decline of Judah.[32] The primary difficulty comes in explaining the narrative of the oracle of Huldah in 2 Kings 22:14– 20.[33] For the most part, the oracle is consistent with the purposes of a proposed Josianic edition of the narrative in that it points to an interest in averting YHWH's wrath as a motivating force behind the reform. The primary consideration in relation to an exilic reworking of the narrative appears in v. 20, which points to Josiah's death prior to the evil that YHWH plans for Jerusalem. Verse 20 may represent a redactional updating of the Huldah oracle, but this must be demonstrated. In any case, these considerations point to the need to establish a secure redaction-critical analysis of the DtrH narratives concerning the reigns of Manasseh and Josiah as a necessary basis for establishing an original Josianic edition of the work.

The third major problem relates to the presentation of Hezekiah in 2 Kings 18–20 in that a great deal of evidence seems to point to Hezekiah rather than Josiah as the hero of the DtrH. Provan argues this case in detail based upon several lines of evidence.[34] The first is the continuous reference to the failure of Davidic kings who were otherwise judged as righteous—that is, Jehoshaphat

---

references to recent discussion prior to van Keulen's work, see O'Brien, *The Deuteronomistic History Hypothesis* 226–234.

31. Friedman, *The Exile and Biblical Narrative* 10–12.

32. For a redaction-critical treatment of the Josiah narrative, see Norbert Lohfink, "The Cult Reform of Josiah of Judah: 2 Kings 22–23 as a Source for the History of Israelite Religion," in *Ancient Israelite Religion*, Fs. F. M. Cross, ed. P. D. Miller et al. (Philadelphia: Fortress, 1987) 459–475.

33. For discussion of the treatment of this passage, see O'Brien, *The Deuteronomistic History Hypothesis* 243–249. See also Halpern and Vanderhooft, "The Editions of Kings," 221–230, who argue that the Huldah oracle is the product of the Josianic edition of DtrH, and serves the purposes of the reform in that it galvanizes Josiah into action.

34. Provan, *Hezekiah and the Books of Kings*.

(1 Kgs 22:44), Joash (2 Kgs 12:4), Amaziah (2 Kgs 14:4), Azariah (2 Kgs
15:4), and Azariah (2 Kgs 15:35), to remove the high places from the land.
Other Davidic monarchs are likewise judged for this shortcoming, including
both Solomon (1 Kgs 3:2–15; 11:1–8) and Asa (1 Kgs 15:11–15). This stands
in contrast to the condemnation of all the northern kings for walking in the sin
of Jeroboam. Interestingly enough, it is not Josiah who resolves this issue, but
Hezekiah who removes the high places from the land (2 Kgs 18:4). Furthermore, Hezekiah is the Davidic monarch to rule in the aftermath of the destruction of the northern kingdom, and therefore he is the first monarch who has the
opportunity to centralize worship in Israel in accordance with the centralization
concern of the DtrH. His Temple reforms certainly speak to this point (2 Kgs
18:1–8), and the DtrH presents him as doing what is right in the eyes of
YHWH according to all that David his father had done" (2 Kgs 18:3). It further
states that "there was none like him among all the kings of Judah after him, nor
among those who were before him" (2 Kgs 18:5). On the basis of these
considerations and because of Hezekiah's faithfulness toward YHWH and the
Davidic promise as expressed in the account of Sennacherib's siege of Jerusalem, Hezekiah serves as the model Davidic monarch in the DtrH. Likewise,
changes in the death and burial formulae for the kings of Judah following the
reign of Ahaz point to the possibility of redactional activity in the materials that
follow. Provan therefore argues that the Hezekiah narrative originally concluded a Josianic edition of the DtrH in which Hezekiah served as a model for
Josiah's reform program. The material following the account of Hezekiah is the
product of an exilic edition of the DtrH that takes the history through the
Babylonian exile.

Provan's work obviously raises a number of questions that need to be
addressed. First, it points to a correspondence with Weippert's work on the
regnal formulae in the books of Kings in which her second redaction concluded
with the reigns of Ahaz and Hoshea.[35] In such a scenario, the narrative of
Hezekiah's reign provides an appropriate conclusion to a block of material that
culminates in the destruction of the northern kingdom and the potential
reunification of the land around the Jerusalem Temple by Hezekiah. Second, if
Hezekiah represents the culmination of the Davidic promise in the DtrH, then
how is Josiah to be understood? Clearly, Hezekiah's faithfulness in 2 Kings
18–20 stands in striking contrast to the lack of faithfulness among the northern
monarchs as represented in 2 Kings 17. Both 2 Kings 17 and 2 Kings 18–20
point to two contrasting models of kingship that highlight the Dtr ideal of the
faithful king. Jeroboam and the other northern monarchs failed to meet that
ideal, and the northern kingdom was destroyed. Hezekiah displayed the proper
qualities of faithfulness, and the southern kingdom was delivered. Nevertheless, Hezekiah displays certain shortcomings; he submits to Sennacherib and
strips the Temple to pay tribute (2 Kgs 18:14–16), and he admits the Babylonian
embassy to the Temple storehouses and thereby earns the condemnation of

---

35. Weippert, "Die 'deuteronomistischen' Beurteilung."

Isaiah (2 Kgs 20:12–19). Together with the observations made above concerning the character of David in the DtrH, these considerations raise questions as to whether Hezekiah is in fact the ideal monarch of the DtrH or whether he plays some other role in preparation for Josiah. Hoffmann and Nelson argue that Josiah is presented as an ideal monarch on the model of Moses, Joshua, and Samuel, and continue to raise the possibility that Josiah is in fact the intended ideal monarch of the original DtrH.[36] Josiah's kingship would then have to be understood in relation to the period prior to the rise of David. Clearly, the role of the Hezekiah narrative in the DtrH and its relation to the narratives concerning Manasseh and Josiah deserve further consideration in defining the overall perspectives of the DtrH and the possibility of reconstructing a Josianic edition.

These considerations demonstrate the need for an overall evaluation of the hypothesis of a Josianic edition of the DtrH. A number of factors seem to point to the likelihood of such an edition, but a number of key questions remain open. Therefore, several issues require detailed treatment. The first is the possibility of reconstructing earlier forms of the narratives concerning the reigns of Josiah and Manasseh. This is clearly one of the most important issues in establishing the validity of the hypothesis. On the one hand, these narratives point toward an exilic edition of the DtrH by placing the blame for the Babylonian exile squarely on Manasseh. On the other hand, the account of Josiah's reforms points to the culmination of the entire DtrH in that Josiah resolves the problems caused by his royal predecessors and institutes a model of ideal leadership based on that of Moses and Joshua. The second is the role of Hezekiah as the ideal Davidic monarch. Although a great deal of evidence seems to identify Hezekiah as an ideal Davidic figure, questions must be raised as to whether this justifies naming him as the ideal monarch of the DtrH. The question is further complicated by the fact that Davidic kingship is not necessarily the model of ideal leadership in the DtrH. David, after all, was less than ideal because he committed adultery and murder while on the throne, thereby abusing his power as king. The fact that Solomon was the product of David's actions likewise raises questions about the nature of ideal Davidic kingship because Solomon's own abuse of his royal office was the immediate cause of the split in the monarchy that led ultimately to Jeroboam's idolatry and the destruction of the northern kingdom. This raises the possibility that the DtrH is concerned not merely with ideal Davidic kingship, but with ideal leadership in general that extends ultimately back to the time of Moses and Joshua. Indeed, it also suggests that an underlying Hezekian edition may be identified in the present form of the DtrH. The question of ideal leadership points to the third major issue—that is, the role of the period of the Judges and the kingship of Saul in the DtrH and their relationship to a projected Josianic edition. These narrative clearly raise the issue of proper leadership in that they point to the abuse of royal power as a major problem while at the same time pointing to the

36. Hoffmann, *Reform und Reformen* esp. 312–313; Nelson, "Josiah in the Book of Joshua."

need for proper leadership as the means by which Israel will cease to disintegrate and achieve its destiny in the history. This raises the possibility that the narratives in Judges and 1 Samuel play a role in presenting Josiah as the ideal monarch in the DtrH. Certainly the portrayal of Joshua as a leader based upon the model of Josiah and the portrayal of Josiah based upon the model of Moses and Joshua supports such a contention.

1

2 Kings 23:31–25:30 and the Exilic Edition of the DtrH

The present form of the DtrH is clearly written from the perspective of the Babylonian exile insofar as 2 Kings 24–25 includes accounts of the destruction of Jerusalem and the Temple, the exile of elements of the surviving population, and, ultimately, Jehoiachin's release from prison by the Babylonian King Evil-Merodach. To establish the validity of an earlier Josianic edition of the DtrH, justification must be provided for identifying this material and, indeed, the accounts of all events from Josiah's death on as the conclusion for a later exilic edition to the DtrH. Consequently, 2 Kings 23:31–25:30, which presents the final years of the kingdom of Judah beginning with the brief reign of Jehoahaz and concluding with the period of the Babylonian exile, must be included in the exilic edition. 2 Kings 23:26–30, which reiterate YHWH's decision to destroy Judah, Jerusalem, and the Temple on account of the sins of Manasseh together with the account of Josiah's death, also must be included.

In addition to these clearly exilic texts, Cross points to others that seem to presuppose the exile as the work of the exilic edition of DtrH. These texts include Deuteronomy 4:27–31, 28:36f, 29:27, 30:1–10; Joshua 23:11–13, 15f; 1 Samuel 12:25; 1 Kings 2:4, 6:11–13, 8:25b, 46–53, 9:4–9; and 2 Kings 17:19, 20:17f, 21:2–15.[1] He notes that other texts, such as Deuteronomy 30:11–20 and 1 Kings 3:14, may belong as well.[2] With the exception of 2 Kings 20:17f and 21:2–15, which refer explicitly to Babylonian captivity and YHWH's decision to destroy Jerusalem, Judah, and the Temple, these texts are ambiguous in that they mention the threat of exile as a potential punishment without specifically identifying the Babylonian exile as their referent. Deuteronomy 4:27–31, 28:36f, 30:1–10,11–

---

1. Cross, "Themes," 285–287.
2. Cross, "Themes," 287, n. 49.

20; Joshua 23:11–13, 15f; 1 Samuel 12:25; and 1 Kings 8:46–53 all refer to the
potential for exile, but do not specify whether this looks ahead to the possibility
of Babylonian exile for Judah or to the Assyrian exile of the northern kingdom of
Israel. This applies also to Deuteronomy 29:27, which indicates that the people
have been cast into another land, "as at this day." Deuteronomy 4:27–31, 30:1–
10, and 1 Kings 8:46–53 hold out the possibility that the people might repent while
in exile and be restored by YHWH to the land of Israel, but they do not indicate
whether they address the Babylonian or the Assyrian exile. Several texts refer
explicitly to the Davidic promise, including 1 Kings 2:4, 6:11–13, 8:25b, and
9:4–9, but they all do so in reference to a Davidic king sitting on the throne of Israel
if he observes YHWH's commandments. They do not indicate whether Israel refers
to the northern tribes or to the united kingdom that includes the tribe of Judah. This
is particularly important because 2 Samuel 7:16 states that David's kingdom will
be secure forever, but it does not specify that David's rule over the northern tribes
will be secure forever. This becomes clear in Ahijah's speech to Jeroboam in 1 Kings
11:34–39, which distinguishes carefully between the kingdom of Israel that is promised to Jeroboam and the one tribe that is left to the house of David. 1 Kings 9:4–9
also refers to the potential destruction of the Temple, which many take to be evidence of an exilic hand, but the account of Nathan's oracle to David in 2 Samuel
7:4–17 makes it very clear that YHWH does not want a "house" or Temple, nor
does it indicate that the security of the Temple is guaranteed forever, only the throne
of David. 1 Kings 3:14 only indicates that Solomon's days will be lengthened if he
observes YHWH's commands, and 2 Kings 17:19 only refers to Judah's wickedness in following the pattern of Israel. The former has nothing to do with exile, and
the latter easily serves as a premise for Hezekiah's, Manasseh's, and Josiah's reigns.
None of these texts refer clearly to the Babylonian exile, and therefore do not constitute clear evidence for an exilic redaction of the DtrH. This is not to deny that these
texts function easily in relation to an exilic edition of the DtrH. It simply demonstrates that they were not necessarily composed as part of such a work.

But several texts identified by Cross as evidence for an exilic edition of the
DtrH are unambiguous and point specifically to the Babylonian exile or to events
associated with the death of Josiah and its aftermath. These texts include 2 Kings
20:16–19 and 21:2–15 together with 23:26–25:30. The report of the prophecy of
Huldah in 2 Kings 22:11–20 must also come into consideration as it points to
Josiah's death prior to the great "evil," presumably destruction and exile, that
YHWH is bringing upon the land.

The first major text block to be considered is 2 Kings 23:31–25:30, which
contains the accounts of the kings of Judah who followed Josiah, including Jehoahaz
(2 Kgs 23:31–35), Jehoiakim (2 Kgs 23:36–24:7), Jehoiachin (2 Kgs 24:8–17,
25:27–30), and Zedekiah (2 Kgs 24:18–25:7). In addition, it reports the destruction of Jerusalem and the exile of the people as well as the revolt against Gedaliah
and his assassination (2 Kgs 25:8–26). Nelson summarizes the major arguments
for viewing this material as the product of an exilic edition of the DtrH.[3] First is

3. Nelson, *The Double Redaction* 89–90.

"the vague prophecy-fulfillment schema" in 2 Kings 24:2–4, which links these chapters to the prophecy concerning the destruction of Jerusalem and Judah in 2 Kings 21:10–15. Second is the "editorial link" between 2 Kings 25:21b, which states that Judah was exiled from its land, and 2 Kings 17, which provides the rationale for Israel's exile and states that Judah also did not keep YHWH's commandments (2 Kgs 17:19). Third is "the unifying formula" of 2 Kings 24:3, 20, "because of the anger of YHWH, he removed them/cast them out [i.e., Jerusalem and Judah] of his presence," which is unique in the DtrH and supersedes the regnal formula as the pattern of organization in 2 Kings 24. Fourth is the rigidification of the regnal formulae in 2 Kings 23:31–32, 36–37 and 24:8–9, 18–19. Fifth is the distinctive phraseology of 2 Kings 24:2, 3, 20, which corresponds to that of other major "exilic" texts, including "my servants the prophets (cf. 2 Kgs 17:23; 21:10), the above-mentioned "he removed them from his presence" (cf. 2 Kgs 17:18, 23; 23:27), and "Jerusalem and Judah" (2 Kgs 21:12; cf. 2 Kgs 18:22). Interestingly, arguments 1, 2, and 5 all point to links between these chapters and the preceding DtrH, which renders them subordinate to other arguments that establish the distinctive nature of this material. Argument 3 likewise is not decisive because of the shift in the rhetorical setting of the text that describes the Babylonian destruction of Jerusalem, and thereby renders the reference to YHWH's removal of Jerusalem and Judah comprehensible in relation to its immediate literary context. The potentially decisive argument is 4, insofar as the formulaic consistency of the regnal formulae in this material may well point to its distinctive nature.

In arguing for the existence of an exilic DtrH redactional layer in 2 Kings 23:31–25:30, Weippert notes the relative consistency of the formulas employed in this material to evaluate the reigns of the last kings of Judah:

Jehoahaz (2 Kgs 23:32): *wayya'aś hāra' bĕ'ênê yhwh kĕkōl 'ăšer 'āśû 'ăbōtāyw*
and he did evil in the eyes of YHWH according to all that his fathers did;

Jehoiakim (2 Kgs 23:37): *wayya'aś hāra' bĕ'ênê yhwh kĕkōl 'ăšer 'āśû 'ăbōtāyw*
and he did evil in the eyes of YHWH according to all that his fathers did;

Jehoiachin (2 Kgs 24:9): *wayya'aś hāra' bĕ'ênê yhwh kĕkōl 'ăšer 'āśû 'ābîw*
and he did evil in the eyes of YHWH according to all that his father did;

Zedekiah (2 Kgs 24:19): *wayya'aś hāra' bĕ'ênê yhwh kĕkōl 'ăšer 'āśâ yĕhôyāqîm*
and he did evil in the eyes of YHWH according to all that Jehoiakim did.[4]

---

4. See Weippert, "Die 'deuteronomistischen' Beurteilungen," 333–334. Note that the inconsistencies in the formulas for Jehoiachin and Zedekiah are due to an effort to emphasize the evil deeds of Jehoiakim. The plural references to the "fathers" in the formulas for Jehoahaz and Jehoiakim relate to previous Davidic and Omride monarchs who did evil in the eyes of YHWH. It should be noted that, from the reign of Joash ben Jehoram on, all Davidic monarchs are descended from the house of Omri, through Athaliah, the daughter of Ahab, who was married to Jehoram ben Jehoshaphat (cf. 2 Kgs 8:16–19; 11:1–20).

According to Weippert, these formulae are somewhat compatible with earlier regnal formulae employed in the DtrH that make reference to the evil or righteous deeds of the kings of Israel and Judah, but they are distinguished from all other formulae by their references to the "fathers," expressed as "his fathers" (23:32, 37), "his father" (24:9), and "Jehoiakim" (24:19). They are further distinguished by the gap between this material and the portrayal of other evil kings created by the righteous portrayal of Josiah in 2 Kings 22:3–23:30. Altogether, she maintains that these considerations demonstrate that the account of the post-Josiah Judean kings in 2 Kings 23:31–25:30 constitutes a single redactional layer within Kings, dated to the exilic period.[5] Nelson points to variations within the formulae, but supports Weippert in her claim that the consistency within these formulas identifies them as a characteristic of a distinctive exilic edition of the DtrH.[6]

Nevertheless, the weakness of this argument is similar to the others, in that the regnal formulas for the last four kings of Judah correspond to those of earlier kings, including the Judean kings Manasseh (2 Kgs 21:2; cf. 21:15) and Amon (2 Kgs 21:20) and all of the Israelite kings, all of which are based on the statement, *wayya ʿaś hāraʿ běʿênê yhwh*, "and he did what was evil in the eyes of YHWH."[7] Apart from Joram and Ahaziah, both of whom were married to daughters of Ahab, this formula is not applied to Davidic monarchs prior to Manasseh,[8] which suggests that the references to the sins of the "fathers" in the formulas for Jehoahaz and Jehoiakim apply specifically to Manasseh and Amon.[9] Given the fact that Manasseh is blamed for the destruction of Jerusalem (2 Kgs 21:12–16; 23:26–27; 24:3–4), the similarities in the evaluative formulas for the post-Josiah kings with those for Manasseh and Amon might well point to common authorship by an exilic hand.[10] Furthermore, the comparison of Manasseh with Ahab in 2 Kings 21:3, 13 demonstrates an interest in linking Manasseh and Amon to the sins of the northern kings as a means to justify the destruction of Jerusalem and Judah. The association of the last four kings of Judah with Manasseh—and thereby

---

5. Cf. Nelson, *The Double Redaction* 29–42, 85–90, who points to "the rigidification of the introductory regnal formulae in 2 Kings 23:31–32, 36–37; 24:8–9, 18–19" (p. 90) as a major criterion for the identification of this material as the product of an exilic editor.

6. Nelson, *Double Redaction* 29–42, esp. 36–41.

7. See also the formulas for the Judean kings Joram and Ahaziah (2 Kgs 8:18, 27), both of whom were married to daughters of Ahab of the northern house of Omri. Ahaziah is likewise the grandson of Ahab. Both kings are explicitly compared to Ahab and the kings of Israel.

8. In addition to Joram and Ahaziah cited above (2 Kgs 8:18, 27), the other exception appears in 1 Kings 14:22, which employs the formula in reference to Rehoboam, but supplies Judah as the subject of the verb.

9. Note that all other Davidic monarchs are said to have done "that which is right in the eyes of YHWH" with the exception of the account of Solomon, which lacks such a formula (but cf. 1 Kgs 11:33). See Weippert's tables, "Die 'deuteronomistischen' Beurteilungen."

10. Cf. Provan, *Hezekiah* 48–50, who critiques Weippert's and Nelson's positions by comparing the formula for the post-Josiah monarchs with those for the northern kings. He notes that Weippert's separation of RIII from RII is based entirely on the references to the "fathers" in the post-Josiah evaluative formulas, and questions whether they should thereby constitute a completely separate source (cf. Halpern and Vanderhooft, "The Editions," 208–212).

with the northern monarchs—likewise serves this interest and points to bridges between the accounts of the last four Judean kings and earlier elements of the DtrH that look to the downfall of the northern kingdom of Israel. Consequently, there is evidence of both disruption and continuity between the narratives of the last kings of Judah and the rest of the DtrH. The issue therefore cannot be decided without an evaluation of the narratives concerning the reigns of Manasseh, Amon, and Josiah, which will determine if these narratives have been updated to account for the Babylonian exile or if they were composed for this purpose from the outset.

The issue is further complicated by evidence for another shift in royal formulae culminating in the reign of Hezekiah (2 Kgs 18–20). Weippert notes that common patterns exist for the kings of Israel from Joram (2 Kgs 3:2) through Pekah (2 Kgs 15:28) based on formulaic elements such as, "and he did what was evil in the eyes of YHWH," "the sin(s) of Jeroboam ben Nebat which he caused to sin," and "he/they did not turn." Likewise, she identifies a common pattern for the Judean monarchs from Jehoshaphat (1 Kgs 22:43–44) through Ahaz (2 Kgs 16:2b, 4; cf. 17:22), based on the elements, "and he did what was right in the eyes of YHWH/ his G-d," and "only the high places were not removed, the people continued sacrificing and burning incense at the high places." These formal features form the basis for her "Redaktion I" (RI), which constitutes the first Dtr redaction of Kings. The second Dtr redaction (RII), which comprises accounts of Judean kings from Rehoboam through Asa and Hezekiah through Josiah and northern kings from Jeroboam I through Ahaziah, constitutes the framework for RI to which RIII is appended.

Various critiques of Weippert's work have appeared, which challenge the details of her identification of RI and RII.[11] One of the most important results of these critiques is the emerging view that the account of Hezekiah's reign constitutes the culmination of a major segment of the DtrH.[12] Provan, in particular, makes the case that an edition of the DtrH must conclude with the reign of Hezekiah. He argues this case on two grounds. The first is the notice in 2 Kings 18:4 concerning Hezekiah's removal of the high places, which provides the capstone to the many statements concerning the people's continued use of the high places that appear throughout the DtrH up to that point. The second is the portrayal of Hezekiah as a monarch like David, "and he did right in the eyes of YHWH according to all that David his father had done" (2 Kgs 18:3, cf. vv. 7–8). Other Judean monarchs had been given this praise, but it was always qualified by reference to the continued operation of the high places. In this regard, Hezekiah then appears as the exemplary monarch of the house of David who finally succeeds in removing the high places and in emulating the righteousness of David. Provan therefore argues

---

11. For example, Halpern and Vanderhooft, "The Editions," 199–208; Campbell, *Of Prophets and Kings* 139–202; Provan, *Hezekiah* 35–41, 48–55; Nelson, *Double Redaction* 29–42; W. B. Barrick, "On the 'Removal of the High Places' in 1–2 Kings," *Bibl* 55 (1974) 255–257. See also Eynikel, *The Reform of King Josiah* 33–135, who attempts to modify her proposal to demonstrate the existence of exilic, Josianic, and Hezekian editions of the DtrH.

12. Halpern and Vanderhooft, "The Editions," 208; Provan, *Hezekiah*; Eynikel, *The Reform of King Josiah*.

that the narrative in 2 Kings 18–20 concerning YHWH's deliverance of Jerusalem during the reign of Hezekiah constitutes the conclusion to the original preexilic edition of the DtrH, written during the reign of Josiah to provide a model for the reform of the latter monarch. 2 Kings 21–25 then constitutes the exilic edition of the DtrH. Halpern and Vanderhooft elaborate on Provan's case by pointing to changes in the death and burial formulas and the naming of queen mothers. Judean kings through Ahaz are buried "in the city of David," but this pattern is disrupted beginning with Hezekiah. There is no burial notice for Hezekiah, Manasseh and Amon are buried in the "garden of Uzzah," and kings from Josiah on show no consistent pattern. This corresponds roughly to the consistent identification of queen mothers by name, patronym, and place of birth from Amon on, whereas only one or two elements were available in the accounts of the Judean kings from Rehoboam through Hezekiah.[13] On the basis of this evidence and that of the regnal formulae, Halpern and Vanderhooft argue for a three-stage DtrH, in which a first edition concludes with Hezekiah, a second edition concludes with Josiah, and an exilic edition completes the entire book.

Both Provan's and Halpern/Vanderhooft's work clearly shows that there is a significant change in the DtrH centered around the account of the reign of Hezekiah. Nevertheless, the situation is analogous to that for the narratives concerning the last four kings of Judah; there is evidence of significant discontinuity between the Hezekiah narratives and the following material in the DtrH, but there is evidence of continuity as well. This is evident in the narrative concerning Merodach Baladan's embassy to Hezekiah in which Isaiah predicts that the Temple treasures and the sons of Hezekiah will be carried off to Babylon. This points to the possibility that the present form of the Hezekiah narratives reflects the work of an exilic edition of the DtrH, especially since 2 Kings 24:13 apparently refers back to Isaiah's prophesy as part of its description of the exile.

But the issue must be considered in relation to the evidence that the account of Josiah's reign also marks an important stage in the DtrH in which his actions eclipse those of Hezekiah.[14] Josiah effects a reform program that surpasses that of Hezekiah by dismantling the Beth-El altar and instituting the first Passover celebration since the time of the Judges (23:15–20, 21–23). Josiah not only removes the offensive cultic objects introduced by Manasseh (2 Kgs 23:12), he eliminates the various idolatrous constructions of Ahaz (23:12) and Solomon (23:13). Consequently, the narrative portrays Josiah as a monarch who resolves the major problems articulated in the DtrH: the idolatry that divides the tribes of Israel into the northern and southern kingdoms and the idolatry within Judah. Furthermore, although Hezekiah is portrayed as an ideal monarch on the model of King David, "and he did what was right in the eyes of YHWH according to all that David his father had done" (2 Kgs 18:3), Josiah is portrayed as an ideal leader on the model of Moses and Joshua as well as of David. Thus, 2 Kings 22:2 states, "and he did

---

13. Ahaz is an exception in that the narrative does not identify his mother (2 Kgs 16:2). Manasseh mother is Hephzibah, but her father and birthplace are not listed (2 Kgs 21:1).

14. Cf. Halpern and Vanderhooft, "The Editions," 208, n. 74, who point to the emerging scholarly consensus concerning a shift in authorship in the DtrH roughly at the point of Josiah's death.

what was right in the eyes of YHWH and walked in the way of David his father, and he did not turn aside to the right hand or to the left," which employs the Davidic formula like that of Hezekiah together with language drawn from Deuteronomy 17:20 and Joshua 1:7, which describe the ideal conduct of the monarch and the people respectively in the DtrH.[15] Likewise, the incomparability formula applied to Josiah in 2 Kings 23:25, "before him there was no king like him who turned to YHWH with all his heart and with all his soul and with all his might, according to all the Torah of Moses, nor did any like him arise after him," employs typical Dtr language for ideal conduct such as that of Deuteronomy 6:5, "and you shall love YHWH your G-d with all your heart and with all your soul and with all your might," together with the reference to the Torah of Moses.

The Josianic formula thereby surpasses the similar formula applied to Hezekiah in 2 Kings 18:5, "He trusted in YHWH, G-d of Israel, so that there was none like him among all the kings of Judah after him, nor among those who were before him." This leaves open the possibility that the narrative concerning Hezekiah was intended to conclude a major compositional block of the DtrH, insofar as it is difficult to imagine that the author of 2 Kings 18:5 had Josiah in mind.[16] In this scenario, the reference to Josiah would have been deliberately composed as a redactional expansion designed to justify the greater praise applied to Josiah. But it also points to the possibility that the progressive superlative applied to Josiah was deliberately composed for such a role as part of the same DtrH edition. In this scenario, Josiah's superiority to Hezekiah is established by comparing him to Moses and to Joshua, rather than only to David. Again, this points to the necessity to settle the character of the Manasseh, Amon, and Josiah narratives in the DtrH.

Obviously, the redaction-critical questions of the DtrH cannot be settled on the basis of regnal formulae, burial notices, and the designations of queen mothers alone, even though these factors provide important evidence. Each of the major royal narratives, including those of Josiah (2 Kgs 22:1–23:30), Manasseh (2 Kgs 21:1–18), and Hezekiah (2 Kgs 18–20), must be examined separately for evidence that will aid in establishing the literary history of the DtrH. Once it is determined whether earlier narratives can be reconstructed from the present forms of their respective texts, then decisions can be made about both the Hezekiah narratives and the narratives of the last four kings of Judah.

15. See also the exhortations to the people to abide by the covenant in Deuteronomy 5:30; 28:14; Joshua 23:6.

16. Cf. Gary Knoppers, "'There was None like Him': Incomparability in the Books of Kings," *CBQ* 54 (1992) 411–431, who notes that the three figures to whom the formula is applied, Solomon (1 Kgs 3:12), Hezekiah (2 Kgs 18:5), and Josiah (2 Kgs 23:25), represent different types of ideal figures in the DtrH. Alternatively, the repeated references to the incomparability formula merely indicate its superlative character.

2

The Regnal Evaluation of Josiah in 2 Kings 22:1–23:30

To establish whether an earlier Josianic text form stands behind the present form of the narrative concerning the reign of Josiah in 2 Kings 22:1–23:30, the basic structure of the text must first be established. This will determine its intention and outlook and will identify the criteria for redaction-critical reconstruction.[1] The narrative form is typical of the so-called regnal accounts (historical narratives) of the books of Kings, although the genre appears to require specification. As the following analysis demonstrates, it is not simply an "account" of the reign of King Josiah that relates the details of his rule, but an "evaluation" of his reign that characterizes Josiah as a righteous leader on a par with David, Moses, and Joshua. Therefore, it should be designated generically as a "Regnal Evaluation." The narrative is demarcated at the beginning by its introductory regnal resume in 2 Kings 22:1, which provides details of Josiah's life—including his age at accession, the length of his reign, and the identity of his mother. It is demarcated at the end by its concluding regnal resume in 2 Kings 23:28–30, which includes a notice that the rest of his acts are recorded in the chronicles of the kings of Judah, the details of his death and burial, and a notice concerning the accession of his successor, Jehoahaz.

---

1. For a discussion of the methodological principles employed in the redaction-critical interpretation of prophetic texts, see Marvin A. Sweeney, *Isaiah 1–39, with an Introduction to Prophetic Literature*, FOTL 16 (Grand Rapids, Mich.: Eerdmans, 1996) 10–15; Sweeney, "Formation and Form in Prophetic Literature," in *Old Testament Interpretation: Past, Present, and Future*, Fs. G. M. Tucker, ed. J. L. Mays, D. L. Petersen, K. H. Richards (Nashville: Abingdon, 1995) 113–126. For an alternative discussion of the structure and formal characteristics of this narrative, see Burke Long, *2 Kings*, FOTL X (Grand Rapids, Mich.: Eerdmans, 1991) 250–285; cf. Pierfelice Tagliacarne, *"Keiner war wie er": Untersuchung zur Struktur von 2 Könige 22–23*, ATSAT 31 (St. Ottilien: EOS, 1989).

The core of the narrative is a detailed presentation of Josiah's reign in 2 Kings 22:2–23:27 that begins and ends with statements that evaluate his reign. The introductory assessment in 22:2 comprises a standard DtrH formula concerning the righteous character of Josiah's reign, "and he did what was right in the eyes of YHWH, and he walked in all the path of David his father, and he did not turn right or left." This is followed by a specification of this assessment in 22:3–23:24, which provides a detailed account of Josiah's actions in ruling the kingdom and in carrying out a reform program based upon the commands of the Torah scroll found in the Temple that demonstrate his righteousness. This segment of the narrative begins with the formulation, *wayĕhî bišmōneh ʿeśrēh šānâ lammelek yōʾšîyāhû šālaḥ hammelek*, "and it came to pass in the eighteenth year of King Josiah that the king sent . . . ," which employs a typical narrative introduction to introduce the detailed account of Josiah's actions. It concludes in 2 Kings 23:24 with a final statement of Josiah's actions in clearing the land of improper cultic figures and abominations and a motivating clause, "in order to establish the words of the Torah that were written on the scroll which Hilkiah the priest found in the house of YHWH." This clause thereby returns the reader to the initial motif of the narrative, the discovery of the Torah scroll in the Temple, and so rounds out the account of Josiah's actions. The concluding evaluation of Josiah's reign then appears in 2 Kings 23:25–27, with the incomparability formula that presents Josiah as a righteous monarch who rules on the basis of Mosaic Torah (v. 25). The formula begins with the statement, *wĕkāmōhû lōʾ-hāyâ lĕpānāyw melek ʾăšer*, "and there was not a king like him, who . . . ," which disrupts the syntax of the preceding narrative sequence that portrays Josiah's actions and thereby indicates the beginning of the new subunit. Verses 26–27, joined to v. 25 by the introductory particle *ʾak*, "indeed," which establishes their syntactical dependence of vv. 26–27 on v. 25, reiterate YHWH's decision to destroy Judah, Jerusalem, and the Temple on account of the sins of Manasseh (cf. 2 Kgs 21:10–15), despite Josiah's actions. This demonstrates that the overall purpose of the present form of the evaluation of Josiah's reign in 2 Kings 22:2–23:27 is to reiterate YHWH's decision to destroy Judah, Jerusalem, and the Temple. The present form of the narrative thereby prepares for 2 Kings 23:31–25:30 and serves the interests of an exilic edition of the DtrH.

The internal structure of the detailed evaluation of Josiah's reign likewise demonstrates this intention. It is based on a combination of theme and a relatively consistent *waw*-consecutive verbal pattern that defines a basic narrative sequence. As noted, the general assessment of Josiah's reign in 22:2 stands apart from the detailed evaluation in 22:3–23:24, on the basis of both content and syntactical structure. The *waw*-consecutive sequence begins with the combination verbal statement *wayĕhî bišmōneh ʿeśrēh šānâ lammelek yōʾšîyāhû šālaḥ hammelek . . .* , "and it came to pass in the eighteenth year of King Josiah, that the king sent . . . "In this instance, the combination of the *waw*-consecutive *wayĕhî*, "and it came to pass," and the finite *šālaḥ*, "he sent," initiates the *waw*-consecutive sequence that defines the balance of the narrative through 23:24. There are disruptions in the sequence evident in the two statements that begin with *ʾak*, "indeed," in 22:7 and 9, but each is syntactically dependent on the preceding statement and represents an aside that does not disrupt the basic *waw*-consecutive narrative sequence. Likewise, 23:12 and 13 begin with direct objects rather than *waw*-consecutive verbs, and 23:15 and 19 begin with *wĕgam*, but in each case, the syntactical variation is subordinated into the *waw*-consecutive structure to highlight a special feature of the narrative that calls attention to particularly important features of Josiah's actions. The function of these materials in relation to the larger narrative structure are examined in more detail below.

Many scholars now follow Lohfink's analysis of the structure of this narrative, in which he argues that it includes five major subunits based on the interplay of the statements "King Josiah/the king sent" and "the king commanded."[2] Such a view is overly dependent on the repetition of the verbs *šālaḥ*, "sent," and *ṣiwwâ*," command," and the role of the king in the narrative. It highlights the decisive actions of the king, and perhaps suggests the deep structure of the narrative, but it does not account for the entire action or narrative structure of the text. Instead, the structure of the narrative appears to be based upon a progressive sequence of action, as defined by the *waw*-consecutive syntactical structure that governs the entire unit, and the successive subjects of the action conveyed by the verbs. Thus, the major subunits of the narrative are identified with the major subject of the verbal sequence. The first block appears in 22:3–7, which begins with the initial *waw*-consecutive verbal statement that initiates the action of the entire unit, "and it came to pass in the eighteenth year of King Josiah that the king sent . . ." The subject is the king, and the action is sending Shaphan the scribe to the Temple with a commission to go to the high priest Hilkiah in order to dispense funds to the workmen at the Temple. The next major subunit appears in 22:8, which begins with the *waw*-consecutive *wayyō᾽mer*, "and he said," for which Hilkiah is the subject. In this case, Hilkiah reports to Shaphan the discovery of a Torah scroll during the course of Temple renovation. The unit thereby introduces the Torah scroll into the narrative, where it will serve as the premise on which subsequent action builds. The narration of Shaphan's report to the king follows in 22:9–10, beginning with the *waw*-consecutive *wayyābō᾽*, "and he came," for which Shaphan is the subject.

The next major subunit appears in 22:11–13, which takes up Josiah's reaction to Shaphan's report. It begins with the *waw*-consecutive *wayĕhî kišmō῾a hammelek*, "and when the king heard," which identifies the king as the subject and conveys his sorrow by noting that he tears his garments in reaction to the words of the Torah scroll. Verses 12–13 continue the sequence with Josiah as the subject, in which he commands his officers to make an inquiry of the prophetess Huldah to determine the implications of this Torah scroll for Josiah, the people,

---

2. See Lohfink, "The Cult Reform of Josiah of Judah," esp. 460–465. Prior to Lohfink's study, many scholars were heavily influenced by Theodor Oestreicher (*Das deuteromistische Grundgesetz* [BFCT 27/4; Gütersloh: Bertelsmann, 1923] 12–55), who divides the narrative into the "report of the finding of the law" in 22:2–23:3, 16–18, 20–24, and the "report of the reform" in 23:4–14 (15–20). Nevertheless, Oestereicher's decision relies overmuch on the mention of the Torah scroll in the former but not in the latter and a supposed "abrupt" style of the "report of the reform" in relation to the "report of the finding of the law" (for full discussion of the issue, see Knoppers, *Two Nations* II 125–133).

and Judah. The account then employs the *waw*-consecutive *wayyēlek*, "and he went," to turn to its next major segment in 22:14–20, in which the subject Hilkiah, together with other officers of Josiah, goes to make an inquiry of Huldah. This segment includes the report of Huldah's oracle in vv.15–20a and the report that the officers delivered her oracle to the king in v. 22b. The subunit employs the oracle of Huldah to announce that YHWH has decided to bring "evil" on "this place" because of the idolatrous practices of the people, but that Josiah will die in peace because of his repentant attitude. This serves as the premise for the death of Josiah and the failure of his reform measures to alter Jerusalem's and Judah's fate.

The final segment of this text appears in 23:1–24, in which the king is the subject of the narrative. It begins with a *waw*-consecutive verb, *wayyišlaḥ hammelek*, "and the king sent," in 23:1, followed by two instances of *wayĕṣaw hammelek*, "and the king commanded," in 23:4, 21, which define the subunits of this block. This section begins with an account of Josiah's gathering the people at the Temple to establish a covenant based on the teachings of the Torah scroll (23:1–3), an account of Josiah's specific actions to remove various cultic installations that violate the covenant (23:4–20), and an account of Josiah's institution of the Passover celebration together with the concluding statement that indicates his motivation to establish the words of the Torah scroll (23:21–24). Each account of Josiah's specific actions to enact the covenant includes two basic components identified by their respective linguistic features—that is, the above-mentioned *waw*-consecutive sequence based on the verb *wayĕṣaw*, "and he commanded," followed by a series of statements introduced by *wĕ'et* or *wĕgam*, which disrupt that sequence in order to highlight a specific feature of the narrative. The account of Josiah's removal of objectionable cultic installations in 23:4–20 begins with a *waw*-consecutive narrative sequence in 23:4–11 that relates Josiah's commands to remove and destroy specific cultic items throughout Jerusalem and Judah and to disenfranchise the priests associated with them. This is followed by statements introduced by *wĕ'et* or *wĕgam*, which highlight Josiah's measures against various structures erected by Ahaz and Manasseh (altars, v. 12, *wĕ'et*), Solomon (high places, vv. 13–14, *wĕ'et*), Jeroboam (the Temple at Beth-El, vv. 15–18, *wĕgam*), and the people of Israel (the high places, vv. 19–20, *wĕgam*). In each case, the narrative calls attention to a specific figure or party that creates cultic problems in the preceding narratives of the books of Kings in order to present Josiah as the figure who removes major cultic abominations and thereby resolves problems in Judah and Israel identified in the DtrH. The second component is a narrative concerning Josiah's celebration of Passover (23:21–24), which includes the basic *waw*-consecutive narrative (vv. 21–23) followed by a summarizing statement of Josiah removal of improper cultic figures and abominations that begins with *wĕgam*.

The structure of the narrative concerning Josiah's reign may be outlined as in table 2.1. On the basis of this analysis of the structure of the regnal account of Josiah's reign in 2 Kings 22:1–23:30, some observations concerning the intention and outlook of the narrative are in order. It is clear that the purpose of this narrative is not simply to provide an account of Josiah's reign. Rather, the introductory evaluative comments in 22:2 and the concluding evaluative comments in 23:25–27 demonstrate that the narrative is designed to provide an evaluation of

TABLE 2.1   Reiteration or YHWH's devision to destroy Jerusalem and Judah

Regnal evaluation of the reign of King Josiah of Judah	*22:1–23:30*
I. Regnal information	22:1
II. Reiteration: Evaluation of Josiah's reign as righteous	22:2–23:24
A. Initial evaluation: righteous	22:2
B. Detailed evaluation: report of Josiah's righteousness	22:3–23
1. Josiah's commisson to Shaphan to dispense funds to Hilkiah at Temple	22:3–7
2. Hilkiah's reports discovery of Torah scroll in Temple to Shaphan	22:8
3. Shaphan reports discovery of Torah scroll to Josiah	22:9–10
4. Josiah's reaction to words of torah scroll: tears garment and commands inquiry to seek word of YHWH	22:11–13
5. Hilkiah et al's inquiry to the prophetess Huldah	22:14–20
a. Report of officers' approach to Huldah	22:14
b. Report of Huldah's words: prophecy of evil for Judah and peaceful death for Josiah	22:15–20a
c. Report of officers' report of Huldah's words to Josiah	22:20b
6. Account of Josiah's reforms	23:1–24
a. Concerning assembly of people for covenant	23:1–3
b. Concerning Josiah's specific measures to remove cultic abominations	23:4–20
i. Detailed account of reform measures in Jerusalem and Judah	23:4–11
ii. Specification concerning removal of installations built by Ahaz and Manasseh	23:12
iii. Specification concerning installations built by Solomon	23:13–14
iv. Specification concerning installations built by Jeroboam (Beth-El Temple)	23:15–18
v. Specification concerning installations built by Israel (high places)	23:19–20
c. Celebration of Passover	23:21–24
i. Basic account of command to celebrate Passover	23:21–23
ii. Concluding statements concerning Josiah: establish words of Torah scroll	23:24
C. Concluding evaluation: righteous beyond compare	23:25–27
1. Evaluation proper: incomparable in observing Torah of Moses	23:25
2. Reiteration of YHWH's decision to punish Jerusalem, Judah, and Temple despite Josiah's righteousness due to sins of Manasseh	23:26–27
III. Concluding regnal resume	23:28–30

Josiah's reign that demonstrates the king's righteousness. This purpose is further evident in the attempts to highlight Josiah's actions in relation to those of previous monarchs and the people of Israel. As noted above, the syntactical structure of the material in 23:12–20 calls attention to Josiah's removal of various cultic installations initiated by Ahaz and Manasseh, Solomon, Jeroboam ben Nebat, and the people of Israel. In this regard, the narrative points to almost all of the major problems in the cultic life of the people of Israel and the major figures responsible for them. It thereby ties the Josiah narrative into the overall presentation of the books of Kings insofar as it presents Josiah as the monarch who corrects the wrongdoings identified in Kings from Solomon on. The evaluative comments concerning his reign point to a relation between the Josiah narrative and the DtrH even beyond Kings, in that 2 Kings 22:2 compares Josiah to David who appears primarily in 1–2 Samuel, and 2 Kings 23:25 emphasizes Josiah's adherence to the Torah of Moses, which points to Deuteronomy and Joshua.

Nevertheless, the notice of YHWH's decision to destroy Judah, Jerusalem, and the Temple in 2 Kings 23:26–27 demonstrates that the purpose of the narrative goes beyond even a simple evaluation of Josiah. Rather, its purpose is to reiterate and perhaps to justify YHWH's decision to punish Judah, Jerusalem, and the Temple despite Josiah's exemplary behavior. From the perspective of the narrative, Josiah's actions are of absolutely no consequence for deciding the future of Judah and Jerusalem; the decision was already made in relation to Manasseh's actions.[3] This concern points beyond the immediate context to the Manasseh narrative in 2 Kings 21:1–18 and to the repeated notices throughout Samuel and Kings concerning the Davidic promise and the decision to establish Jerusalem as the site for the Temple to YHWH (2 Sam 7:1–29; 1 Kgs 6:11–13; 8:22–30; 9:1–9; 11:31–39).

But the intention to reiterate and justify YHWH's decision to destroy Judah also points to the grounds for a redaction-critical reconstruction of the Josiah narrative, primarily because it appears to be working at cross purposes.[4] Why should the narrator make the effort to portray Josiah's righteousness in such detail so that he potentially becomes the figure who resolves the major problems of the DtrH? It is possible that the narrator intended to present Josiah as a tragic figure like Moses who failed to see the promised land despite all his efforts, but the presentation of Moses in the DtrH never points to the futility of his life or actions. Moses' actions result ultimately in the establishment of the people of Israel in the promised land; Josiah's actions lead to no such conclusion in the DtrH. His actions have absolutely no bearing on the future of his people. Furthermore, the narrative presentation of the sequence of events indicates that Josiah is aware of the futility of his actions, at least from the perspective of the narrator. The prophecy of Huldah indicates to him prior to his reform measures that YHWH's decision is already made, and there is absolutely no indication that the decision can be reversed. Consequently, Josiah's reform measures are carried out with full knowledge that they will not affect the future of Jerusalem and Judah. In the present form of the narrative, they are completely useless, but if they were designed to correct Judah's behavior and thereby to avert a punishment, they would be eminently useful and well-motivated.

In this regard, an examination of the narrative concerning Huldah's oracle in 22:14–20 is imperative because, together with the notice of YHWH's decision in 23:26–27, it creates this anomaly in the narrative presentation of Josiah's reign by announcing to Josiah YHWH's decision to bring punishment and reward him with a peaceful death even before he begins his reform activities. In fact, the narrative tension could be resolved simply by the removal of the Huldah episode. YHWH's decision would still be announced in 23:26–27, but Josiah's reform actions would be consistent with his efforts to renovate the Temple and the dis-

---

3. Cf. van Keulen, *Manasseh Through the Eyes of the Deuteronomists* esp. 191–203.

4. For alternative reconstructions, see Lohfink, "The Cult Reform of Josiah"; O'Brien, *The Deuteronomistic History Hypothesis* 235–268; McKenzie, *The Trouble with Kings* 110–115; Halpern and Vanderhooft, "The Editions"; Knoppers, *Two Nations. Vol. 2* 121–228.

covery of the Torah scroll. The statement in 22:11 that Josiah "tore his garments"—that is, he went into mourning—on hearing the words of the Torah scroll would provide adequate motivation for his subsequent actions, especially since 23:1–3 indicates that they are undertaken on the basis of the newly discovered Torah.

But the issue is not quite so simple. Scholars have noted an important discrepancy in relation to Huldah's oracle in that her prophecy of Josiah's peaceful death appears to conflict with his seemingly violent death at the hands of Pharaoh Necho of Egypt (2 Kgs 23:29–30). The sources are not clear as to whether there was a battle between Necho and Josiah at Megiddo. 2 Chronicles 35:20–25 maintains that there was a battle in which Josiah was shot by Necho's archers, but 2 Kings 23:29 states simply that Necho "killed him in Megiddo when he saw him" (*wayĕmîtēhû bimegiddô kir'ōtô 'ōtô*).[5] Nevertheless, this unexpected death hardly corresponds to the peaceful death predicted for Josiah by Huldah, who delivers an oracle from YHWH to Josiah, "Therefore behold, I am gathering you to your fathers and you shall be gathered to your tombs in peace, and your eyes will not see all the evil that I am bringing upon this place" (22:20a). Scholars have noted that this statement could not have been written after the death of Josiah, because it simply is not aware of the circumstances of his death.[6] Therefore, it would not have been part of an exilic redactional updating of an original Josianic narrative designed to account for the failure of Josiah's reign in relation to the Babylonian exile. Rather, it must have been written prior to Josiah's death.

This suggests, of course, that Huldah's statement concerning Josiah's death could well have been part of an earlier edition of the narrative concerning the reign of Josiah that employed the prophecy to point to his anticipated peaceful death at the end of a successful and righteous reign. But such a contention is problematic when weighed against the contents of the rest of the oracle. The oracle is quite clear that YHWH is bringing evil upon this place on account of the sins of the people, and it is well aware of Josiah's righteousness. Nevertheless, the oracle makes it clear that YHWH has no intention of reversing the decision. No such conditions for a reversal are laid out, and the punishment will come despite Josiah's righteousness. If the entire oracle appears in its original form, it is difficult to understand how it could have served as part of a Josianic narrative designed to point to the king's success. Again, it would suggest that the entire Josianic reform program was futile and that it was undertaken in full knowledge of that futility.

Obviously, there is tension within the present form of the Huldah oracle. An examination of the tensions within the oracle, however, demonstrates that it has

5. 2 Chronicles 35:21–22 attempts to portray Josiah in a somewhat unfavorable light, and thereby perhaps to explain Josiah's death. It portrays Necho as stating that he is sent by G-d and that, in attempting to stop him from moving north to assist the Assyrians, Josiah opposes G-d's will. It also removes the statements that there was no king like Josiah in observing the Torah or Moses, and thereby deals with the problem of Josiah's seemingly unjustified death. The narrative does not mention YHWH's decision to destroy Jerusalem on account of Manasseh and thereby eliminates the problem of Josiah's useless reform actions. See Sara Japhet, *I and II Chronicles: A Commentary*, OTL (Louisville, KY: Westminster John Knox, 1993) 1042–1044, who notes the use of the elements from the death of Ahab in 2 Kings 22:30–37 as well as other accounts to portray Josiah as sinful.

6. See Halpern and Vanderhooft, "The Editions," 221–230, for a full discussion of this point.

been extensively reworked for its present role in the final form of the Josianic narrative. Furthermore, the tensions within the present form of the oracle are the result of an attempt to portray the upcoming demise of Judah, Jerusalem, and the Temple in relation to the fall of the northern kingdom of Israel as presented in the DtrH. In this regard, the oracle employs formulaic language that appears elsewhere in relation to the condemnation of Jeroboam ben Nebat and Ahab, the two most notorious monarchs of the northern dynasties, who are held to be responsible by the DtrH for the destruction of the northern kingdom of Israel (2 Kgs 17:21–23; 21:3, 13). Furthermore, the analogy with Ahab underlies the combination of an oracle against Judah, and so on, with an oracle that promises Josiah a peaceful death. Several factors support this conclusion: the formula "I am bringing evil unto/upon this place," in 2 Kings 22:16, 20, and its use in relation to Jeroboam ben Nebat and Ahab elsewhere in the DtrH; the appearance of the preposition *'el*, "unto," in 2 Kings 22:16; the seeming appearance of two oracle reports in 2 Kings 22:15–17 and 18–20; and the text-critical problem related to the phrase, "the words which you heard," in 2 Kings 22:18b.

The present form of the Huldah oracle appears in the context of a narrative that describes Josiah's commissioning of a delegation to inquire of the prophetess (vv. 12–13), a report of the delegation's approach to Huldah (v. 14), a report of her response in which she delivers the oracle (vv. 15–20a), and a brief notice that the delegation communicated the results to the king (v. 20b). The oracle itself appears in vv. 15aβ–20a, immediately following the speech formula in v. 15aα. Scholars generally maintain that it is formulated in two parts, vv. 15aβ–17 and vv. 18–20a, each of which is based on a distinct oracle in vv. 16–17 and 18b–20a introduced by a version of the standard messenger speech formula, *kōh 'āmar yhwh*, "thus says YHWH."[7] In the first case, v. 15aβ–b stands as an introduction that commissions Huldah to speak the following oracle in vv. 16–17 "to the man who sent you (i.e., plural in reference to Josiah's delegation) to me." In the second case, v. 18a serves a similar function in relation to what appears to be a second oracle in vv. 18b–20a in that it commissions Huldah to speak the oracle to "the king of Judah who sends you (again plural) to inquire of Me." The content of the two oracles is formulated similarly:

> vv. 16–17: Thus says YHWH, "Behold, I am bringing evil unto this place and upon its inhabitants, all the words of the scroll which the king of Judah has read. Because they have abandoned me and burned incense to other gods in order to provoke me in all the work of their hands, my anger is kindled against this place and it shall not be quenched."

> vv. 18b–20a: Thus says YHWH, G-d of Israel, the words which you have heard, "Because your heart has softened and you bowed down before YHWH when you heard that which I spoke about this place and about its inhabitants to become a desolation and a curse and you tore your garments and you wept before me and indeed I heard," oracle of YHWH.

---

7. For a discussion of the structure of this passage, see Long, *2 Kings* 260–265.

> "Therefore, behold, I am gathering you to your fathers and you shall be
> gathered to your tombs in peace and your eyes shall not see the evil that I
> am bringing upon this place."

In arriving at the conclusion that two oracles appear in this passage, scholars
have relied not only on the two versions of the messenger formula, but on other
formal features as well. These include the repeated references to the evil that
YHWH is bringing, the initial statement of the people's or Josiah's actions introduced by a causative formulation, and the resulting consequences that YHWH will
bring upon each party.

But several factors raise questions about this view and point to a different
understanding of the form and content of the Huldah oracle report. The first is the
text-critical problem of v. 18 that indicates literary tension within this oracle. The
introductory messenger formula in v. 18b reads, "Thus says YHWH, G-d of Israel,
the words which you have heard." The Hebrew of this verse is problematic in that
most interpreters take the statement, "the words which you have heard," to be the
beginning of the oracle by YHWH that extends through v. 20a. But the verse provides an awkward introduction for the oracle because it seems to have only a remote
connection to what follows and lacks any auxiliary words that might ease the
syntactical transition into vv. 19–20a. Consequently, BHS states that something
is apparently missing in this verse, and RSV supplies an auxiliary in its translation,
"Regarding the words which you have heard."

This understanding is undermined by the fact that there is no textual evidence
to indicate that anything has dropped out of this text. Consequently, the text must
stand as it is despite the difficulty that it seems to present. But other considerations suggest that v. 18b is intended to conclude the oracle of vv. 16–17 in the
present form of the text rather than to introduce the oracle in vv. 19–20a. The statement in v. 19 appears to be designed to reflect Josiah's reaction to hearing the
words of the Torah scroll when they were read. It therefore refers to Josiah's
softened heart, his prostrating himself before YHWH, his tearing of his garments,
and his weeping, but v. 11 mentions only that Josiah tore his garments. None of
the other actions appear in v. 11, they can only be inferred. Furthermore, the language employed in v. 19, which states that Josiah acts in reaction to "what I
spoke concerning this place and concerning its inhabitants," makes no reference to Josiah's hearing the scroll, but only to his hearing the words that YHWH
spoke about "this place." Apart from the oracle in vv. 16–17, there is no statement in the narrative concerning the discovery and reading of the Torah scroll
that "this place" will be destroyed. That language appear only in the oracle in v. 16,
"Behold I am bringing evil unto this place and upon its inhabitants." This
suggests that the mourning described in v. 19 appears better suited to the statement made by YHWH in v. 16 concerning "this place." Verse 19 would then be
a description of Josiah's reaction to YHWH's announcement in v. 16 rather than
to the reading of the Torah scroll in vv. 8–11. If this is the case, then a literary
transition must be missing between vv. 16–17 and v. 19 that would indicate that
the first oracle was already concluded and transmitted to Josiah so that he could
react.

This has implications for understanding the text critical problem of v. 18b. In the present form of the verse, the phrase "the words which you heard," stands as a direct object to the verb *'āmar*, rendering v. 18b as follows, "Thus YHWH, the G-d of Israel, said the words which you heard." It is an awkward transition, as one would expect the verb *dibber*, "he spoke," rather than *'āmar*, "he said," but it is the only conceivable way to read the present form of the verse. Despite the awkward nature of the verse, this points to the possibility that v. 18b is not intended to introduce a new oracle in the present form of the text, but to supplement and conclude the previous oracle by confirming that the message of impending evil was indeed from YHWH.

Even if v. 19 may be explained as a phrase that may once have described Josiah's reaction to the oracle in vv. 16–18, the problem of v. 20a still remains. Verse 20a promises a peaceful death to Josiah, which contradicts the balance of the narrative. In this regard, the phraseology of vv. 20a and 16, and the text-critical problem of v. 16a, come into play. Verse 20a states that Josiah will not see "the evil that I am bringing upon this place," which employs language nearly identical to that of v. 16, "behold, I am bringing evil unto this place and upon its inhabitants." The appearance of the preposition *'el*, "unto," has occasioned some comment because one would expect *'al*, "upon, against," in keeping with the following phrase, "and against (*wĕ'al*) its inhabitants" and that of v. 20a "against (*'al*) this place." BHS suggests that the correct reading should be *'al*, but again there is no secure text critical evidence. At this point, it is striking to note that the statement, "I am bringing evil *unto* (*'el*) this place," is especially significant in that it is used elsewhere in the DtrH only against Jeroboam ben Nebat and Ahab to express judgment. Thus, 1 Kings 14:10 reads, "Behold I am bringing evil *unto* (*'el*) the house of Jeroboam . . ." and 1 Kings 21:21 reads, concerning Ahab, "behold, I am bringing *unto you* (*'ēlêkā*) evil. . . ." It is clearly no accident that this phraseology is employed here in the Josiah narrative to describe the impending destruction of Jerusalem and the Temple and in relation to the two most notorious monarchs of the northern kingdom. Jeroboam is the figure most clearly identified as the cause of the destruction of the northern kingdom (cf. 2 Kgs 17:21–23), and Ahab serves as the model for Manasseh, on whom the destruction is blamed in 23:26–26 (cf. 1 Kgs 21:3).The phraseology of v. 16, with its use of the preposition *'el*, indicates that this association is deliberate. Furthermore, statements elsewhere in the DtrH employ similar phraseology, but with *'al* instead of *'el*, to describe the impending punishment of Judah, Jerusalem, and the Temple. Thus, 2 Kings 21:12 states, "Therefore I am bringing evil *against* (*'al*) Jerusalem. . . ." A slightly different rendering appears in relation to YHWH's statement to Solomon in 1 Kings 9:9: that the Temple will be destroyed if the Davidic kings are not righteous, "therefore YHWH has brought *upon them* (*'ălêhem*) all this evil."

The example of Ahab in 1 Kings 21:17–29 is especially important in that it supplies a model for understanding the use of the phrase, "I am bringing evil unto this place," in the present form of the Huldah oracle. Following Elijah's condemnation of Ahab for the murder of Naboth and the appropriation of his vineyard, Ahab went into mourning, tore his garments, fasted, and so on, to repent for what he had done (1 Kgs 21:28). Consequently, in 1 Kings 21:29, YHWH states, "Because he (Ahab) prostrated himself before me (*ya'an kî nikn'a mippānay*), I will not bring evil in his days, but in the days of his son I will bring this evil against his house." The language is very similar to that employed to describe Josiah's humbling himself in 2 Kings 22:19, "and you prostrated yourself before YHWH (*wattikkāna' mippĕnē yhwh*)." In this case, Ahab's repentance does not avert the evil, but it does delay it for at least a generation. The same thing takes place in relation to Josiah; his repentance does not avert the evil, it delays it until after his death. It would appear that the narrative concerning Ahab's repentance and the delay of judgment against the house of Omri in 1 Kings 21 played a role in shaping the present form of the Huldah oracle, with its announcement of judgment against Judah, Jerusalem, and the Temple, and the subsequent delay of that judgment because of Josiah's repentance.

At this point, it would appear that the present form of the Huldah oracle has been reworked for its present role in the narrative concerning the reign of King Josiah. It seems clear that the phraseology from the narratives condemning Jeroboam ben Nebat and Ahab, "behold I bringing evil unto this place," was employed in the reworking of this oracle in order to present the projected destruction of Judah, Jerusalem, and the Temple in relation to the destruction of the northern kingdom of Israel. This is evident in not only in the use of the phrase in the present context, but also in relation to the reign of King Manasseh, who is presented in analogy to Ahab (2 Kgs 21:3, 13) and who is ultimately blamed for the upcoming punishment in an oracle that employs the same phraseology, "behold I am bringing evil against Jerusalem and Judah" (2 Kgs 21:12; cf. 23:26–27; 24:3–4). Furthermore, the analogy with Ahab provides not only the rationale for Manasseh's reign, because Manasseh erected an Asherah in the Temple analogous to that of Ahab (2 Kgs 21:3; cf. 1 Kgs 16:33), but also the delay in the implementation of the punishment; just as Ahab repented of his evil and delayed the punishment of his house until the days of his son (1 Kgs 21:29), so Josiah's repentance delayed the punishment until after his death (2 Kgs 22:19–20). Such reworking would have to be the product of an exilic writer. It also points to a rather decisive role for Ahab and northern Israel as a model or predecessor for the sin and destruction of Judah in the overall conception of the exilic DtrH.

It is difficult to say what the original form of the Huldah oracle might have been, but several things do seem to be clear. First, the phrase, "behold, I am bringing evil unto/upon this place," holds the two parts of the Huldah oracle, vv. 16–17 and vv. (18b)19–20a, together in that it appears both at the beginning (v. 16aβ) and at the conclusion (v. 2aα²–β) of the present form of the oracle. Second, the conclusion that this phrase is the result of an exilic reworking of the oracle points to the fact that it was originally two oracles that were combined into their present form to explain the punishment of Judah following the death of Josiah in the DtrH. The first appears in vv. (16)17 and 18b, and appears to constitute a statement of YHWH's intention to punish "this place" (v. 17) because the people have gone after other gods. The second appears in vv. (19)–20a, as an oracle that promises Josiah a peaceful death for his repentance after the initial oracle. The two versions of the statement, "I am bringing evil unto this place," in vv. 16 and 20 appear then to be a later redactional envelope around two earlier oracle forms in vv. 17, 18b, and 19–20aα¹.

This, of course, has implications for the reconstruction of an earlier Josianic form of the Josiah narrative in that it points to the possibility that an earlier form of the Huldah oracle played a role in prompting not only Josiah's repentance but also his entire reform program. Obviously, the notice concerning YHWH's decision to destroy Judah, Jerusalem, and the Temple in 23:26–27 and the notice concerning the death and burial of Josiah in 2 Kings 23:28–30 cannot constitute part of an earlier Josianic edition as they presuppose the events of the Babylonian invasion and destruction of Judah in the years following Josiah's reign. The narrative would then proceed on the presumption that YHWH's decision to punish Judah, Jerusalem, and the Temple was reversible, and that Josiah's reform program, was undertaken in an attempt to purify the land of its cultic abominations and thereby to avert the punishment stated by YHWH in the Huldah oracle. In this case, the second oracle concerning Josiah's peaceful death would have little meaningful place in its present position in that Josiah's repentance on hearing the words of punishment would be fully realized in relation to his actions to reform the land. It seems best, then, to consider the second part of the Huldah oracle as an element that might originally have concluded an earlier form of the Josiah narrative. The promise of a peaceful death for the monarch would then serve as a reward to the monarch for his efforts to purify Judah, Jerusalem, and the Temple, and to institute righteous rule, as conceived by the DtrH.[8] In this regard, the proposed second Huldah oracle would then serve as a fitting conclusion to a Josianic version of the narrative concerning King Josiah's reign in that it would highlight his righteous actions during his lifetime and point to an expected peaceful death for a monarch who had secured the future of his country. Although the precise form of such a conclusion must remain an object of speculation at present, it seems that the portrayal of a secure land led by a monarch who rule on the basis of YHWH's Mosaic Torah fits the expectations of ideal leadership articulated in the DtrH (cf. Deut 17:14–20) and the evaluation of Josiah's reign presented in 2 Kings 23:24–25. Furthermore, it points to several characteristic features of a potential Josianic edition of the DtrH: the observance of YHWH's commands as expressed in the Torah of Moses by the king as well as by the people; the elimination of cultic abuses instituted by Solomon, Jeroboam ben Nebat, Ahab, and the entire people of Israel, particularly the Beth-El altar; the proper celebration of the Passover festival; the establishment of YHWH's one legitimate altar at Jerusalem; and the institution of the covenant between the people and YHWH.

---

8. Note that Josiah's actions, undertaken on the basis of his reading of the Torah scroll found in the Temple, would then correspond to the image of the righteous monarch presented in Deuteronomy 17:14–20, who rules on the basis of his reading a copy of the Torah.

3

The Regnal Evaluation of Manasseh in 2 Kings 21:1–18

The narrative concerning the reign of Manasseh in 2 Kings 21:1–18 is one of the key texts for establishing the possibility to reconstruct a Josianic version of the DtrH. Insofar as Manasseh is blamed for YHWH's decision to destroy Judah, Jerusalem, and the Temple in 2 Kings 21:10–15; 23:26–27; and 24:3–4, the presentation of Manasseh clearly plays a major role in the exilic edition of the DtrH. According to the DtrH presentation of his reign, Manasseh's sins are so great that even the righteous actions of Josiah are inadequate to persuade YHWH against carrying out the punishment.

There is quite a consensus, however, that this understanding of Manasseh is the product of a proposed exilic edition of the DtrH alone, which attempted to explain the reality of the Babylonian exile by choosing Manasseh as the scapegoat.[1] Several lines of evidence support this contention. First, there is the very clear buildup of Josiah as the culminating figure of the DtrH, evident in the presentation of Joshua as a model for Josiah, the prediction that Josiah would destroy the Beth-El altar (1 Kgs 13:2), and the presentation of Josiah as the ideal ruler after the model of Moses and Joshua (2 Kgs 23:24–25). Second, whereas Josiah has an extensive buildup in the DtrH, Manasseh has none.[2] There is perhaps some indication of an attempt to build toward Manasseh by comparing him with Ahab (2 Kgs 21:3, 13), because both monarchs caused their nations to sin and thereby played major roles in their punishment as articulated in the DtrH. But the association appears to be somewhat forced in that Jeroboam, and not Ahab, is blamed for the destruction of Israel (2 Kgs 17:21–23). Furthermore, the discus-

---

1. See McKenzie, *The Trouble with Kings* 142–143, for an overview of the discussion.

2. See van Keulen, *Manasseh*, who argues that Manasseh is presented in relation to the Israelite kings Jeroboam ben Nebat and Ahab, as well as the comments on Manasseh's relation to these monarchs below.

sion of the DtrH narrative concerning Josiah demonstrates that the model of Jeroboam and Ahab is applied to Josiah as well in an effort to support the contention of the exilic edition of the DtrH that YHWH would destroy Jerusalem and Judah despite Josiah's righteousness.[3] Third, Manasseh serves as a foil to Josiah in the present form of the DtrH in that Josiah reverses all the objectionable cultic measures instituted by Manasseh. Manasseh thereby enhances the presentation of Josiah and prepares the way for his restoration as a major goal in the historical presentation of the DtrH. Fourth, the report of YHWH's judgment speech against Jerusalem and Judah in 2 Kings 21:10–15 appears to be somewhat intrusive in the narrative concerning the reign of Manasseh in that it interrupts the narrative description of Manasseh's wrongdoing in vv. 3–9 and v. 16.

Despite these indications of the secondary nature of the Manasseh narrative in 2 Kings 21:1–18, scholars have faced tremendous difficulties in attempting to reconstruct a credible version of the narrative that might have formed part of the proposed Josianic edition of the DtrH. For the most part, they have proceeded by identifying vv. 10–15, which report YHWH's decision to destroy Jerusalem and Judah because of the sins of Manasseh, as the primary element of the exilic edition of the DtrH.[4] But differences emerge in the identification of exilic DtrH material beyond vv. 10–15. Cross identifies vv. 2–15 as the work of the exilic edition;[5] Nelson identifies vv. 3c–15;[6] Friedman identifies vv. 8–15;[7] O'Brien identifies vv. 2–7, 10–14;[8] and McKenzie identifies vv. 6, 8–15.[9]

The reason for the difficulty is that it is not so easy to remove vv. 10–15 and still have a coherent narrative that eliminates any reference to the blame assigned to Manasseh for the fall of Judah and Jerusalem in the DtrH. Verse 3 creates the analogy with Ahab, and thereby aids in building the case for Manasseh's extraordinarily evil character. Verse 6 likewise refers to Manasseh's increasingly evil character. Verse 9 refers to the people not listening to YHWH as a result of Manasseh leading them astray to do more evil than the nations whom YHWH destroyed before Israel. Verse 16 refers to Manasseh's causing Judah to sin, which builds toward the punishment of the kingdom. In other words, the extraordinary sin of Manasseh pervades this material to such an extent that simple removal of vv. 10–15 does not eliminate the motif. Furthermore, even if vv. 10–15 and other references to Manasseh's extraordinary evil could be successfully removed, the question would still remain as to why a Josianic edition of the DtrH would set up Manasseh as such an evil figure only to knock him down as a foil to Josiah. This

---

3. For recent studies that examine the analogy between Manasseh and Ahab, see Stuart Lasine, "Manasseh as Villain and Scapegoat," *The New Literary Criticism and the Hebrew Bible*, JSOTSup 143, ed. J. C. Exum and David J. A. Clines (Sheffield: JSOT Press, 1993) 163–183; William M. Schniedewind, "History and Interpretation: The Religion of Ahab and Manasseh in the Book of Kings," *CBQ* 55 (1993) 649–661.

4. For example, McKenzie, *The Trouble with Kings* 142–143.

5. Cross, "The Themes," 285–286.

6. Nelson, *The Double Redaction* 65–69.

7. Friedman, *The Exile* 10–11; "From Egypt to Egypt," 177–178.

8. O'Brien, *The Deuteronomistic History Hypothesis* 234.

9. McKenzie, *The Trouble with Kings* 143, cf. n. 5.

is especially pertinent in that the narrative concerning Manasseh appears immediately following the narrative concerning YHWH's deliverance of Jerusalem and
Hezekiah during the time of the Assyrian invasions in 2 Kings 18–20. According
to 2 Kings 18–20, Hezekiah displays extraordinary faith in YHWH that results in
the deliverance of Jerusalem and the defeat of the Assyrian empire. The defeat of
Assyria is especially remarkable in that it removes the primary motivation for
understanding Manasseh's actions as those of an Assyrian vassal who feared for
his life and the safety of his country (cf. 2 Chron 33:10–17). As portrayed in the
present form of the DtrH, Manasseh acts after the pattern of Ahab for no particular reason, and Josiah must step in to reverse his abominations. Although the presentation of Manasseh in this manner aids in enhancing the figure of Josiah, his
apostasy makes little sense in relation to a proposed Josianic edition of the DtrH.[10]

Clearly, a full analysis of the narrative concerning the reign of Manasseh in
2 Kings 21:1–18 is necessary, both to establish the possibility of reconstructing
an earlier Josianic edition of the narrative and to ascertain the role of Manasseh in
a projected Josianic edition of the DtrH. This requires a full analysis of the structure of the text and will provide the basis for understanding the character of the
presentation in its present form, as well as the basis for identifying criteria for
redaction-critical reconstruction.

The narrative concerning Manasseh's reign in 2 Kings 21:1–18 is formulated
typically as an example of the regnal evaluation genre in that it not only describes
the major events of Manasseh's reign but also evaluates his actions as evil (e.g.,
vv. 2, 16).[11] The narrative is demarcated initially by the typical regnal introduction in v. 1, which presents information about Manasseh, including his age at
accession to the throne (twelve years old), the duration of his reign (fifty-five years),
and the identity of his mother (Hephzibah). The core of the narrative is the evaluation of his reign in vv. 2–16, which includes the formulaic introduction in v. 2
that characterizes his rule, "and he did evil in the eyes of YHWH according to the
abominations of the nations which YHWH drove out from before the sons of
Israel," and the concluding evaluation of his reign in v. 16, "and also Manasseh
shed very much innocent blood until he filled Jerusalem end to end, apart from
his sin by which he caused Judah to sin to do evil in the eyes of YHWH." The
concluding regnal resume in vv. 17–18 employs typically formulaic language to
refer the reader to the Chronicles of the Kings of Judah for the remaining details
of his reign together with the notices of Manasseh's death, burial in the Garden of
Uzza, and the succession of his son Amon.

---

10. Several recent studies eschew attempts to reconstruct a Josianic edition, and, instead, focus
on synchronic literary study of the Manasseh narrative or on exilic redactional editions. For literary studies of 2 Kings 21, see Klaas A. D. Smelik, "The Portrayal of King Manasseh: A Literary
Analysis of II Kings xxi and II Chronicles xxiii," *Converting the Past: Studies in Ancient Israelite
and Moabite Historiography*, OTS 28 (Leiden: E. J. Brill, 1992) 129–189. For a study that emphasizes the exilic redactional formation of the Manasseh narrative, see Ehud Ben Zvi, "The Account
of the Reign of Manasseh in II Reg 21, 1–18 and the Redactional History of the Book of Kings,"
ZAW 103 (1991) 355–374.

11. For an alternative analysis of the structure and formal features of the Manasseh narrative,
see Long, *2 Kings* 246–250.

Although the evaluation of Manasseh's reign in vv. 2–16 begins with a *waw*-consecutive verbal form, this syntactical feature does not play a role in determining the overall structure of this particular textual unit as conjunctive perfect forms (e.g., vv. 4, 6, 9a, cf. v. 16) appear together with *waw*-consecutive forms (vv. 2, 3, 5, 7, 9b, 10) throughout. Instead, the structure of the evaluation narrative is determined by the shift in subject matter caused by the appearance of a report of YHWH's announcement of punishment against Jerusalem and Judah in vv. 10–15 in the midst of material that describes and evaluates Manasseh's reign in vv. 2–9 and 16. Whereas Manasseh's actions are the subject matter of vv. 2–9 and 16, YHWH's announcement is the subject of vv. 10–15. Consequently, the structure of the evaluation comprises three major parts: the initial evaluation of Manasseh's actions in vv. 2–9; the report of YHWH's announcement of judgment against Jerusalem and Judah in vv. 10–15, and the concluding evaluation of Manasseh's reign in v. 16.

The initial evaluation of Manasseh's reign in vv. 2–9 includes a general assessment of his reign in v. 2 that charges him with doing evil like that of the nations that YHWH drove out before Israel and a detailed description and evaluation of Manasseh's actions in vv. 3–9 that illustrates and confirms the general assessment in v. 2.[12] The structure of the initial evaluation is based on a combination of syntactical and thematic factors. It employs an alternating sequence of statements governed by initial 3ms *waw*-consecutive verbs (vv. 3, 5, 7) and conjunctive perfect 3ms verbs (vv. 4, 6), which describe the various actions judged by Manasseh judged to be evil. These include an overview of his actions in v. 3, which summarize what is to follow; a reference in v. 4 to his building altars in the Temple where YHWH places the divine name; a reference in v. 5 to his building altars for the Host of Heaven in the courtyards of the Temple; a reference in v. 6 to his passing his son through fire for Molech and practice of divination; and a more extensive discussion in vv. 7–9 of his building an Asherah in the Temple that causes Judah to sin. This last point is particularly important in that it merits a quotation of YHWH's promise never again to remove Israel from the land (vv. 7–8), a reference to Israel's failure to listen to YHWH (v. 9a), and a reiteration of Manasseh's role in leading the people astray (v. 9b). It also is significant in that it seems to be the cause of YHWH's decision to destroy Jerusalem and Judah as announced in vv. 10–15, and it is reiterated as a major sin of Manasseh in v. 16.

The report of YHWH's announcement of punishment against Jerusalem and Judah in vv. 10–15 begins with an introduction in v. 10 that identifies anonymous prophets as the source for YHWH's announcement. The speech by the prophets then appears in vv. 11–15, which are formulated in a modified form of the typical prophetic announcement of judgment. Verse 11, introduced by the particle *ya ʿan ʾăšer*, "because," identifies Manasseh's abominations as the cause of the punish-

---

12. Note the initial *wayyāšāb wayyiben*, "and he turned and he built," idiomatically translated as "and he again built," in v. 3. The combined *waw*-consecutive form both expresses Manasseh's return to actions of past monarchs and distinguishes formally v. 3 from the preceding v. 2. It thereby disrupts the normal *waw*-consecutive sequence initiated by *wayya ʿaś*, "and he did," and marks v. 3 as the beginning of new textual subunit.

ment. This announcement of the basis for punishment emphasizes that Manasseh's actions are worse than those of the Amorites and that he caused Judah to sin. Verses 12–15, introduced by the typical particle *lākēn*, "therefore," and an expanded form of the prophetic messenger formula, "thus says YHWH, G-d of Israel" (v. 12aα) then convey the consequences in a report of YHWH's announcement of punishment against Jerusalem and Judah. The report of YHWH's speech includes both the announcement of punishment proper in vv. 12aβ–14 and another statement of the basis for punishment in v. 15.

The concluding evaluation of Manasseh's reign appears in v. 16, which mentions the innocent blood spilt by Manasseh in Jerusalem (v. 16a) and reiterates his causing Judah to sin (v. 16b).

The structure of the regnal evaluation for Manasseh in 2 Kings 21:1–18 may be represented as in table 3.1. From this analysis of the structure and genre of 2 Kings 21:1–18, it is quite clear that the primary purpose of the narrative is to evaluate the reign of King Manasseh. It characterizes Manasseh's reign as evil, and charges that his actions are analogous to those of the nations that YHWH drove out from before the Israelites (v. 2) and worse than those of the Amorites (v. 11), because he caused Judah to sin. Furthermore, the interest in blaming Manasseh for the upcoming destruction of Jerusalem and Judah is not the primary purpose of the narrative, although it is important in the overall framework of the DtrH in 2 Kings 21–25. This is evident from the fact that the report of the decision to destroy Manasseh does not constitute the climax of either the narrative or of Manasseh's actions in their entirety. Verse 16a indicates that Manasseh spilled a great deal of innocent blood in Jerusalem, but this action is not equated with his causing Judah to sin in v. 16b; spilling innocent blood is listed alongside causing Judah to sin as a separate crime. Furthermore, v. 11 indicates that Manasseh's abominations and his causing Judah to sin are responsible for YHWH's decision to destroy Jerusalem and Judah. This would include all of the charges outlined in vv. 3–9, especially the building of an Asherah in the Temple, which constitutes the culmination of Manasseh's sins and prompts the comment in v. 9b that Manasseh "led them (the people) astray to do more evil than the nations that YHWH destroyed from before the sons of Israel." On the one hand, the report of YHWH's decision to destroy Jerusalem and Judah in vv. 10–15 represents the culmination of the evil actions described in detail in vv. 3–9; on the other hand, v. 16 indicates that Manasseh committed other crimes that did not play a role in prompting this decision but that did play a role in the evaluation of Manasseh's reign.

This observation points to the fact that the report of YHWH's decision to destroy Jerusalem and Judah does not constitute the centerpiece of the Manasseh narrative; rather, it interrupts the evaluation of his reign by appearing between the initial evaluation in vv. 2–9 and the concluding evaluation in v. 16. Although the narrative points to the unparalleled character of Manasseh's evil deeds in several places (i.e., vv. 2, 6, 9, 16), it does not refer to YHWH's decision to destroy Jerusalem and Judah outside of vv. 10–15. Verses 10–15, however, likewise emphasize the unparalleled nature of Manasseh's actions both at the beginning (v. 11) and end (v. 15). This suggests the possibility that vv. 10–15 could have been inserted secondarily into the narrative concerning Manasseh's reign.

TABLE 3.1   Structure and genre of 2 Kings 21:1–18

Regnal evaluation of the reign of King Manasseh	*21:1–18*
I. Regnal information	1
A. Age at accession: 12 years	1aα
B. Duration of reign: 55 years	1aβ
C. Identity of mother: Hephzibah	1b
II. Evaluation of Manasseh's reign: Evil, cause of Jerusalem's and Judah's punishment	2–16
A. Initial evaluation of Manasseh's reign	2–9
1. General assessment: evil like abominations of expelled nations	2
2. Detailed evaluation of Manasseh's reign	3–9
a. Overview of Manasseh's actions	3
b. Built altars in Temple where YHWH set name	4
c. Built altars for Host of Heaven in courtyards of Temple	5
d. Passed son through fire and practiced divination	6
e. Erected Asherah in Temple causing Judah to sin	7–9
i. Manasseh's action: place Asherah in Temple	7–8
ii. People's reaction: did not listen	9a
iii. Summation: led people astray to do more evil than nations	9b
B. Report of YHWH's announcement of punishment against Jerusalem and Judah by prophets	10–15
1. Narrative introduction: YHWH speech formula through prophets	10
2. Speech by prophets	11–15
a. Cause/basis for punishment: Manasseh did greater evil than nations and caused Judah to sin	11
b. Consequence: report of YHWH's announcement of punishment against Jerusalem and Judah	12–15
i. Introduction: messenger formula	12aα
ii. YHWH speech proper: prophecy of punishment	12aβ–15
a) Announcement of punishment	12aβ–14
b) Basis for punishment: people have done evil	15
C. Concluding evaluation of Manasseh's reign: spill blood apart from causing Judah to sin	16
1. Spill innocent blood	16a
2. Cause Judah to sin	16b
III. Concluding regnal resume	17–18
A. Rest of acts written in Chronicles of Kings of Judah	17
B. Death and succession formulae	18

In this regard, it is noteworthy that a number of literary tensions appear within the narrative. The first appears in v. 6, *wĕheʿĕbîr ʾet bĕnô bāʾēš wĕʿônēn wĕniḥēš wĕʿāśâ ʾôb wĕyiddĕʿōnîm hirbâ laʿăśôt hāraʿ bĕʿênê yhwh lĕhakʿîs*, "and he caused his son to pass through fire and he practiced soothsaying and augury and he dealt with mediums and wizards. He increased doing evil in the eyes of YHWH to provoke (him)." Apart from the correction of *lĕhakʿîs*, "to provoke," to *lĕhakʿîsô*, "to provoke him," in keeping with many Masoretic and versional manuscripts,[13] the major problem of this verse is the correct understanding of the verb *hirbâ*, "he increased." According to the punctuation of the Masoretic text, *hirbâ* is the initial

---

13. See BHS note. Apparently this reading is simply an error in the Leningrad Codex.

verb of v. 6b that begins a new clause following v. 6a. In this reading, *la'ăśôt* is the verbal object of *hirbâ*, and in v. 6a, the noun pair *'ôb wĕyiddĕ'ōnîm*, "mediums and wizards," constitute the direct object of the verb *wĕ'āśâ*, "and he made," here translated as, "he dealt (with)." Strictly speaking, this reading is correct; although *hirbâ* normally takes a noun as a direct object, it appears with a verbal indirect object in eight other instances,[14] but it is unusual in that it creates a hendiadys of *'ôb wĕyiddĕ'ōnîm* as direct objects of *w 'āśâ* in v. 6b which combines a singular *'ôb* with a plural *wĕyiddĕ'ōnîm*. This is especially noteworthy in that the corresponding statement in 2 Chronicles 33:6 corrects the plural *wĕyiddĕ'ōnîm* to the singular *wĕyiddĕ'ōnî* to match the singular *'ôb*.[15] But *hirbâ* may be understood differently as the concluding verb of v. 6a. In this case, only *'ôb* would serve as the object of *wĕ'āśâ*, and *wĕyiddĕ'ōnîm* would then serve as the object of *hirbâ*, thereby eliminating the problem of the discrepancy between the singular *'ôb* and the plural *wĕyiddĕ'ōnîm*, in that they would no longer constitute a pair of direct objects for the same verb. Verse 6b would then begin with *la'ăśôt*, which serves as the verbal object that would summarize all of the finite verbs in v. 6a. The entire verse would then be translated, "and he caused his son to pass through fire, and he practiced soothsaying and augury, and he made magicians and wizards he increased, to do evil in the eyes of YHWH to provoke (him)." Although it also unusual for *la'ăśôt* to have more than one verb antecedent, examples appear in Deuteronomy 6:3; 1 Kings 14:8; and 1 Kings 22:43. In this instance, the phrase *la'ăśôt hāra' bĕ'ênê yhwh* presents a problem in that it seems to displace *hirbâ* from its proper role in relation to *wĕyiddĕ'ōnîm*.

The second example appears in v. 9a, which reads *wĕlō' šāmē'û*, "and they did not listen." The problem occasioned by this phrase is to determine its syntactical relation to the statements that precede and follow it. In the first instance, vv. 7bβ–8 constitute a quotation of a statement by YHWH, which refers to Israel, the subject of the verb *wĕlō' šāmē'û* in v. 9a. Given the identification of Israel as the subject of the verbal phrase "and they did not listen," it would be reasonable to conclude that the phrase, *wĕlō' šāmē'û* constitutes the concluding statement made by YHWH. But the following statement in v. 9b includes the phrase *wayyat'ēm mĕnaššeh la'ăśôt 'et hārā' min-haggôyim 'ăšer hišmîd yhwh mippĕnê bĕnê yiśrā'ēl*, "and Manasseh led them astray to do more evil than the nations that YHWH destroyed from before the sons of Israel." The initial verb *wayyat'ēm*, "and he (Manasseh) led them astray" likewise presupposes the reference to Israel in the statement by YHWH in vv. 7bβ–8 as the antecedent to the suffix pronoun "them," but v. 9b clearly does not constitute a part of the speech by YHWH as indicated by the subject Manasseh and the third-person reference to YHWH's destruction of the nations. In this instance, the place of v. 9a is ambiguous, in that it could reasonably constitute a part of the statement by YHWH in vv. 7bβ–8 or it could just as reasonably constitute a part of the narrative material together with v. 9b.

---

14. Exodus 36:5; 1 Samuel 1:12; Isaiah 55:7; Hosea 8:11; Amos 4:11; Psalms 78:38; Ezra 10:13; 2 Chronicles [33:6 = 2 Kgs 21:6]; 36:14.

15. Note that 2 Chronicles 33:6 also corrects *lĕhak'îs* to *lĕhak'îsô*, as indicated above.

In this instance, the appearance of the phrase, "to do more evil . . ." is noteworthy in that, once again, it is involved in an apparently ambiguous text.

The third instance of disruption appears in v. 16b, which reads *lĕbad mĕḥaṭṭ'tô 'ăšer heḥĕṭî 'et yĕhûdâ la'ăśôt hāra' bĕ'ênê yhwh*, "apart from his sin by which he caused Judah to sin to do evil in the eyes of YHWH." The appearance of v. 16b interrupts the narrative syntax of v. 16a by use of the particle *lĕbad*. Strictly speaking, this is not incorrect as *lĕbad* frequently appears in the DtrH as a means to introduce distinct items or groups, often in the context of a list or categorization.[16] But it is unusual in that this is the only instance of *lĕbad* employed to interrupt the normal presentation of activities on the part of kings in the DtrH. Furthermore, it highlights Manasseh's role in causing Judah to sin, the crime that prompts YHWH's decision to destroy Jerusalem and Judah in vv. 10–15. Again, the presence of the phrase, "to do evil in the eyes of YHWH," is noteworthy in a statement that stands out syntactically as an unusual statement in the narrative sequence of the actions of a king.

These examples have an important bearing on the redaction-critical analysis of 1 Kings 21:1–18 in that they point to a common thread that both disrupts the narrative concerning Manasseh's reign and corresponds to the announcement of YHWH's decision to destroy Jerusalem and Judah in vv. 10–15. Each of these statements plays a role in building the case that Manasseh's sins are greater than those of the nations that populated the land of Israel prior to the arrival of the Israelites. Thus, v. 6 points to Manasseh's increasing sin by use of the verb *hirbâ*; v. 9 makes reference to Manasseh's doing more evil than the nations whom YHWH destroyed before Israel; and v. 16 refers to Manasseh's greatest evil in his causing Judah to sin. All three of these statements point to the two primary factors in YHWH's decision to destroy Jerusalem and Judah identified in 2 Kings 21:11: (1) Manasseh did more evil than all the Amorites before him, and (2) Manasseh caused Judah to sin. Both of these factors prompt the prophecy of punishment in vv. 12–15.

The redaction-critical implications of these observations may now be considered. Because of their syntactical peculiarities, vv. 6b, 9b, and 16b each constitutes a disruption within a literary context that is otherwise syntactically well ordered. Likewise, vv. 10–15 constitutes a disruption within the literary context of 2 Kings 21:1–18, in that it intrudes in a syntactically well-ordered description of Manasseh's wrongdoings to identify those listed in vv. 3–9, but not the shedding of innocent blood identified in v. 16, as the cause for YHWH's decision to destroy Jerusalem and Judah. Furthermore, vv. 7–9 appear to play a particularly important role in this decision because they describe Manasseh's building of an Asherah. This is particularly important because v. 3 compares Manasseh's Asherah with that of Ahab (cf. 1 Kgs 16:3), and v. 13 states that Jerusalem shall be judged with "the measuring line of Samaria and the plummet of the House of Ahab." Clearly, the Asherah built by Manasseh plays a major role in the narrative portrayal of the decision to destroy Jerusalem and Judah because of its associations

16. See Deuteronomy 3:5; 18:8; Joshua 17:5; Judges 8 :26; 20:15, 17; 1 Kings 5:3; 5:30; 10:15.

with Ahab and because it is the last item mentioned prior to the statement in v. 9 that Manasseh caused Judah to sin. This, of course, raises questions about vv. 3 and 7–9 in relation to a redaction-critical reconstruction of the Manasseh narrative.

Several observations are in order.[17] First, the reference to Ahab's Asherah is especially significant because 1 Kings 16:33 not only refers to Ahab's erection of an Asherah, but employs language similar to that 2 Kings 21:6, 9 in stating that "Ahab continued to do evil to provoke (*lĕhak'îs*) YHWH, G-d of Israel, more than all the kings of Israel who were before him (*mikkōl malkê yiśrā'ēl 'ăšer hāyû lĕpānāyw*)." Second, the statement that Manasseh caused Judah to sin takes up the same language applied to the northern kings of Israel who were said to have caused Israel to sin. This is especially significant in that it establishes an analogy between Manasseh and Jeroboam I as well. Jeroboam, of course, is the paradigmatic figure in the DtrH for causing Israel's destruction by causing Israel to sin; all of the northern kings are said to have followed him in causing Israel to sin (cf. esp. 2 Kgs 17:21–23).[18] It is also noteworthy that 2 Kings 13:6 associates Jeroboam's causing Israel to sin with the continued existence of Ahab's Asherah. Clearly, this material shows a marked interest in establishing an analogy between Manasseh, on the one hand, and Ahab and Jeroboam, on the other hand, by means of the Asherah and causing Judah to sin.[19]

A third element also must come into consideration. The reference to Manasseh's building an Asherah in the Temple in vv. 7–8 includes a quote of a statement by YHWH to David and Solomon in reference to the Temple:

> In this House and in Jerusalem which I have chosen from all the tribes of Israel, I will place my Name forever, and I will not again cause the foot of Israel to wander from the land which I gave to their fathers, only if they will be careful to act according to all that I have commanded them and (according) to all the Torah which My servant Moses commanded them.

This statement clearly plays an important role in the present context because it establishes the counterpoint for Manasseh's actions and thereby provides the rationale for the destruction of Jerusalem and Judah in that Manasseh does not follow YHWH's commandments. But it is remarkable in that it refers to YHWH's promise never again to remove Israel from the land. Throughout the DtrH, YHWH never causes Israel to depart from the land except in one instance, the exile of the northern Israelite tribes in the aftermath of the Assyrian invasion (2 Kgs 17:6, 7–23). Elsewhere, YHWH brings Israel back after the people leave the land of their own accord (e.g., Deut 26:5; Josh 24:4; 1 Sam 12:8). In 2 Samuel 7:10, YHWH promises David that a place is appointed for Israel, but there is no indication in

17. See also the studies by van Keulen, Lasine, and Schniedewind, cited above.

18. 1 Kings 14:16 (Jeroboam); 15:26 (Nadab), 30 (Jeroboam), 34; 16:2 (Baasha), 13 (Baasha and Elah), 19 (Zimri), 26 (Omri); 21:22 (Ahab), 53 (Ahaziah); 2 Kings 3:3 (Jehoram); 10:29, 31 (Jehu); 13:2 (Jehoahaz), 6 (Jeroboam), 11 (Jehoash); 14:24 (Jeroboam II); 15:9 (Zechariah), 18 (Menahem), 24 (Pekahiah), 28 (Pekah); 17:21; 23:15 (Jeroboam).

19. Cf. van Keulen, *Manasseh*, who comes to similar conclusions in his synchronic analysis of the Manasseh narrative.

the DtrH that YHWH had ever removed the people prior to this promise. Likewise, YHWH's statements to Solomon in the DtrH state that YHWH will place the divine name in Jerusalem and threaten exile if he and his descendants do not obey YHWH's commandments (1 Kgs 6:11–13; 8:14–30; 9:1–9; cf. 11:31–39), but they never indicate that YHWH had ever before removed Israel from the land. Within the context of the DtrH, the only possible antecedent for this statement is the exile of Israel in 2 Kings 17; in 2 Kings 21:7–8, YHWH's statement to David and Solomon can only mean that the exile will not happen again.

In the present form of the text, vv. 7–8 provide the rationale for the destruction of Jerusalem and Judah that is announced in vv. 10–15, but the combination of vv. 7 and 8 creates a major tension in the narrative. YHWH's promise to David and Solomon never again to remove Israel from the land makes little sense in the present form of the DtrH.[20] YHWH never makes such a promise to David and Solomon in the DtrH because it is impossible to do; YHWH does not remove the people from the land until the time of the Assyrian exile of the northern kingdom of Israel as stated in 2 Kings 17. Only the promise to set the divine Name in the Temple fits, because this promise is made repeatedly to David and Solomon in the DtrH. This suggests that v. 8 is a secondary addition to the narrative concerning Manasseh's erection of an Asherah in v. 7. It also demonstrates that v. 8 aids in establishing the analogy between Judah and the northern kingdom of Israel as a basis for the announcement concerning Jerusalem's and Judah's destruction in vv. 10–15.

These considerations indicate that vv. 6b, 8, 9, 10–15, and 16b are all redactional additions to the narrative concerning Manasseh's reign in 2 Kings 21:1–18 that are designed to transform a report of Manasseh's evil actions into a justification for the destruction of Jerusalem, Judah, and the Temple in an exilic edition of the DtrH. Once these verses are removed, the narrative constitutes a simple report of Manasseh's evil actions that is designed to serve as a foil for the reform of Josiah. In this regard, it is noteworthy that the narrative of Josiah's reforms refers to his removal of the courtyard altars built by Manasseh in 2 Kings 23:12, but the verse does not give special notice to the Asherah built by Manasseh.Likewise, 2 Kings 23:14, 15 mention Josiah's removal of Asherim and Asherah, respectively, but they include them with the destruction of other items and do not associate them with Manasseh.It would seem that the Asherah plays a major role in the present form of 2 Kings 21:1–18, but it does not play such a large role in the subsequent narrative of Josiah's reform. This provides further support to the argument that 2 Kings 21:1–18 has been reworked so that Manasseh's Asherah provides a major basis for the decision to destroy Jerusalem and Judah in the DtrH. Apart from this

---

20. In fact, it would best serve, together with the promise of a peaceful death in 22:20a, as a conclusion to a Josianic form of the Josiah narrative immediately following the destruction of the Beth-El altar. The Beth-El altar symbolizes the cultic division of the twelve tribes of Israel. By destroying it, Josiah removes the last major impediment to the reunification of the land. His concern then would have to be the return of the exiles taken away by the Assyrians, in keeping with statements elsewhere in the DtrH that YHWH would return exiles to the land following their repentance (cf. Deut 30:1–10; 1 Kgs 8:33–36).

agenda, the references to Manasseh's Asherah in 2 Kings 21:3 and 7 are only part of the inventory of Manasseh's wrongdoing. Even the reference to Ahab in v. 3 serves no other purpose than to call attention to a previous monarch in the earlier form of the text.

This leads to one last question: What role does the proposed Josianic edition of the account of Manasseh's reign play in a Josianic edition of the DtrH—that is, why does Josiah's reform require the reign of Manasseh to serve as a foil to Josiah's righteous actions? The narrative concerning Hezekiah already demonstrates ideal Davidic rule in that it portrays Hezekiah's faithfulness to YHWH and the promise to defend Jerusalem as a contrast to the apostasy displayed by Jeroboam and the other monarchs of the northern kingdom. In this regard, the narrative concerning Hezekiah in 2 Kings 18–20 stands as a foil to that concerning the collapse of the northern kingdom of Israel in 2 Kings 17. But despite Hezekiah's exemplary behavior, he still does not overcome the major problem in the DtrH that permeates the books of Kings from the reign of Solomon on—that is, he does not reunite the twelve tribes of Israel around the one legitimate sanctuary in Jerusalem. This applies both to the present form of the Hezekiah narrative and any projected Josianic form. Only Josiah has the potential to resolve this issue in the DtrH as indicated by his destruction of the Beth-El altar, the cultic symbol of division within the tribes of Israel and the source of the condemnation of Jeroboam and the northern kings throughout the books of Kings. Had Josiah reunited the tribes of Israel, he would have resolved the most important problem presented in the books of Kings and reinstituted kingship such as that of David and Solomon.

In this regard, several observations are now pertinent. First, the narrative has to account for the monarchs between Hezekiah and Josiah. Narratives concerning the reigns of Manasseh and Amon are therefore necessary, although they do not advance an agenda that will see the reunification of the people.

Second, the end of the Assyrian threat to Judah (and Israel), in the eyes of the DtrH, takes place in relation to YHWH's deliverance of Jerusalem in the Hezekiah narrative. Manasseh and Amon must therefore be presented as wicked of their own accord because the Assyrians are no longer available to act as villains in the DtrH narrative. Despite his lengthy reign of fifty-five years, longer than any other Davidic monarch, Manasseh necessarily reverts to northern patterns of evil behavior. This not only marks time between the reigns of Hezekiah and Josiah, it apparently plays a role in explaining the coup d'etat against Amon that ultimately results in Josiah's accession to the throne. The notice of Manasseh's shedding innocent blood in 2 Kings 21:16 would likely motivate a coup against his son. Although the coup was not designed to bring Josiah to the throne, it points to internal problems in Judah that Josiah must resolve by instituting just rule.

Third, whereas Hezekiah is presented as an ideal Davidic monarch, Josiah is presented as an ideal monarch after the model of Moses as indicated by 2 Kings 23:25. Whereas Hezekiah follows the commands given by YHWH to Moses, Josiah reads the Torah of Moses in accordance with the description of the DtrH's ideal monarch in Deuteronomy 17:14–20. At this point, the reference to David and Solomon in 2 Kings 21:7 is relevant. Throughout the DtrH, the promise of eternal rule to David and Solomon by YHWH is always presented conditionally—that is, the Davidic line will rule so long as it observes YHWH's commandments. But as the DtrH makes clear, neither David nor Solomon observes YHWH's commands in their entirety. In Solomon's case, his marrying foreign wives and building cultic installations for their gods stands as the basic cause of the division of the kingdom in the DtrH (cf. 2 Kgs 11)—that is, Solomon is the cause of the most fundamental problem in Israel's history according to the DtrH. David likewise commits adultery and murder in his affair with Bath Sheba, the mother of Solomon. Although David and Solomon are considered ideals in the DtrH, the narratives point to problems in relation to each. This suggests that the portrayal of Josiah as an ideal monarch who meets not only the Davidic ideal but the Mosaic as well must be taken into consideration. In this case, Josiah may well have been intended as a monarch who surpassed David and Solomon in the DtrH, insofar as each played a role in the division of the Israelite kingdom. David fathered Solomon after an adulterous affair with Bath Sheba that saw the murder of her husband, and Solomon's marriage to foreign women led directly to the revolt against Rehoboam that established the northern kingdom and the idolatrous sanctuaries at Beth-El and Dan.

This indicates the need to reassess several aspects of the DtrH narrative. First, the Hezekiah narrative requires analysis, not only to determine if there is a prior Josianic form that predates the reference to the upcoming Babylonian exile in 2 Kings 20:12–19 but also to assess Hezekiah's role in the DtrH. Hezekiah constitutes an example of the Davidic ideal in the narrative, but is this sufficient in the eyes of the DtrH narrative? It obviously is not in the present or exilic form of the narrative, but these considerations suggest that it may not have been sufficient in the eyes of a Josianic edition as well. Second, this points to the need to reassess the role of both Solomon and David in the narrative. Although Solomon is assigned primary responsibility for the division of the kingdom in 1 Kings 11, David may well play a role because his adultery with Bath Sheba and murder of Uriah the Hittite pave the way for Solomon's birth and accession to the throne. David is not presented in ideal terms in the DtrH, and this may well inform the presentation of both Hezekiah, as the ideal Davidic monarch, and Josiah, as the ideal Mosaic monarch, in the DtrH. Finally, David is presented in ideal terms up to the point of his affair with Bath Sheba in the DtrH. Not only does he replace the tragically failed figure of Saul, he institutes well-ordered rule in Israel for the first time since Joshua. This indicates that the traditions in Judges and 1 Samuel also must be examined in order to determine their role in presenting the rise of David, who not only creates the kingdom of Israel, but lays the seeds for its dissolution after Solomon's reign.

4

The Regnal Evaluation of
Hezekiah in 2 Kings 18–20

The narrative concerning the reign of Hezekiah in 2 Kings 18–20 plays an important role in discussion concerning a potential Josianic edition of the DtrH for several reasons. First, the present form of the narrative clearly points to exilic concerns as indicated by the narrative concerning the Babylonian embassy to Hezekiah in 2 Kings 20:12–19.[1] When Hezekiah receives the Babylonians as part of his preparations for revolt against Assyria and shows them his storehouses and treasuries, the prophet Isaiah condemns Hezekiah's actions and states that ultimately the goods that Hezekiah has shown to the delegation will be carried off to Babylon together with Hezekiah's own sons. In the view of most scholars, this represents a prediction of the Babylonian exile. Second, as noted previously, Provan builds on the arguments of Weippert in an attempt to demonstrate an edition of the DtrH that culminates in the narrative concerning the reign of Hezekiah.[2] He argues that Hezekiah's removal of the high places (2 Kgs 18:4) brings to a conclusion a major theme of the DtrH that condemns previous monarchs for their failure to remove the high places. He further argues that Hezekiah represents the ideal monarch of the DtrH insofar as he acts in accordance with the righteousness of David, and thereby represents the fulfillment of the Davidic promise for righteous rule in Jerusalem. Third, many scholars, including Provan, maintain that the narrative concerning YHWH's deliverance of Jerusalem from Sennacherib's siege is the product of a Josianic edition of the DtrH insofar as it portrays YHWH's defeat of Assyrian power.[3]

---

1. See esp. Peter Ackroyd, "An Interpretation of the Babylonian Exile: A Study of II Kings 20 and Isaiah 38–39," *Scottish Journal of Theology* 27 (1974) 329–352, reprinted in his *Studies in the Religious Traditions of the Old Testament* (London: SCM, 1987) 152–171, 282–285.
2. Provan, *Hezekiah*; cf. Weippert, "Die 'deuteronomistischen' Beurteilung."
3. For example, Ronald E. Clements, *Isaiah and the Deliverance of Jerusalem: A Study of the Interpretation of Prophecy in the Old Testament*, JSOTSup 13 (Sheffield: JSOT Press, 1980).

The narrative presents a model of Assyrian collapse that is certainly relevant in the reign of King Josiah. It further highlights the model of Davidic faithfulness to YHWH and YHWH's actions to defend both the monarchy and the city of Jerusalem in keeping with the Davidic promise tradition. In this case, Hezekiah serves as a model for Josiah. This is in striking contrast to the kings of the northern dynasties who led their country to destruction at the hands of the Assyrians (2 Kgs 17).

These considerations indicate the need to establish the literary history of the Hezekiah narratives. This requires an attempt to determine whether or not it is possible to establish an exilic edition of the Hezekiah narrative distinct from an earlier form. It also requires an attempt to determine the character of any potential earlier editions of the narrative, including a Josianic form of the narrative or an even earlier form. In all cases, it is necessary to establish the relationship between the narrative and the literary context of the DtrH. This requires consideration of the overall structure and outlook of the present form of the narrative in 2 Kings 18–20 and its relation to its literary context. The issue is further complicated by the fact that the narrative appears, albeit in a slightly different form, in Isaiah 36–39. Most scholars correctly maintain, however, that the Isaiah version of the narrative is derived from that in 2 Kings 18–20.[4]

The basic structure of the Hezekiah narrative in 2 Kings 18–20 is determined by its generic character as a regnal evaluation.[5] In keeping with the typical features of the form, it is demarcated initially by its introductory regnal resume in 2 Kings 18:1–2, indicating that Hezekiah's accession took place during the third year of Hoshea's reign in Israel, Hezekiah's age at accession, the duration of his reign, and the identity of his mother. The concluding regnal resume, which specifies the rest of his acts to be found in the Chronicles of the Kings of Judah, and which provides the notification of his death and the succession of his son Manasseh, appears in 2 Kings 20:20–21.

The evaluation of Hezekiah's reign, which constitutes the core of the narrative, appears in 2 Kings 18:3–20:19. It begins in typical form with the general assessment of his reign in 2 Kings 18:3, "and he did what was right in the eyes of YHWH according to all that David his father did." The detailed evaluation of his reign follows in 18:4–20:19, which comprises three basic units as indicated by the references to events in the fourth and fourteenth years of Hezekiah's reign, respectively, in 18:9 and 18:13. The first subunit in 18:4–8 contains a detailed summary of Hezekiah's actions that emphasizes his removal of objectionable cultic installations, his adherence to YHWH's expectations, YHWH's support for his activities, and his subduing of the Philistines. 2 Kings 18:9–12 then makes reference to the fall of Samaria to the Assyrian monarch Shalmanezer and the subsequent exile of Israel in the fourth to sixth years of Hezekiah. A highly detailed account of events that take place in relation to Hezekiah's revolt against Assyria and Sennacherib's invasion of Judah is then provided in 2 Kings 18:13–20:19.

---

4. For a full discussion of this issue, see Sweeney, *Isaiah 1–39* 476–485.

5. For an alternative analysis of the structure and generic characteristics of this narrative, see Long, *2 Kings* 190–246.

As indicated by the temporal formulae in 18:13, 20:1, and 20:12, three major episodes comprise this section: 2 Kings 18:13–19:37 relates Sennacherib's invasion of Judah and YHWH's deliverance of Jerusalem following Hezekiah's supplication through Isaiah; 2 Kings 20:1–11 relates Hezekiah's illness and cure through Isaiah; and 2 Kings 20:12–19 relates Isaiah's condemnation of Hezekiah following his reception of the Babylonian embassy sent to Jerusalem by the Chaldean prince Merodach-Baladan.

The narrative concerning Sennacherib's invasion of Judah in 2 Kings 18:13–19:37 is frequently divided into three major segments: account A in 2 Kings 18:13–16, which relates Hezekiah's submission to Sennacherib; account B[1] in 2 Kings 18:17–19:9a, 36–37, which contains the first account of Sennacherib's negotiations with Hezekiah during the siege of Jerusalem; and account B[2] in 2 Kings 37:9b–35, which contains the second account of Sennacherib's negotiations. These divisions do not constitute the structure of the narrative, however, but an analysis of the literary sources that underlie the present form of the narrative.[6] The structure of the narrative is determined on other grounds. Its generic character is based in the prophetic confrontation story, which posits a conflict between a prophet and those who challenge the prophet as a means to demonstrate the legitimacy or validity of the prophet's message. Other examples appear in Amos' confrontation with the high priest Amaziah at Beth-El in Amos 7:10–17 and Jeremiah's confrontation with the prophet Hananiah in Jeremiah 27–28. In all instances of the genre, the narrative points to the death of the prophet's opponent(s) as a means to demonstrate the validity of the prophet's message.[7] In the present instance, the confrontation is not centered on the prophet Isaiah, however, but on YHWH for whom Isaiah acts as spokesman. The narrative disguises this initially by positing first a confrontation between Sennacherib's officers (the Tartan, the Rab Saris, and the Rab Shakeh), and Hezekiah's officers (Eliakim ben Hilkiahu the Chief Steward, Shebna the Scribe, and Yoah ben Asaph the Secretary), in which the numbers are evenly matched, three versus three. The narrative then shifts to the confrontation between Sennacherib and Hezekiah, as the negotiations actually take place between the two monarchs through their officers, and Sennacherib demands Hezekiah's surrender. But the final episodes of the narrative make it clear that the confrontation is actually between Sennacherib—who blasphemes against YHWH by stating that YHWH deceived Jerusalem by promising to deliver the city when in fact YHWH could not oppose the power of the Assyrian monarch (2 Kgs 18:35, 19:10)—and YHWH. As a consequence of this challenge, YHWH returns a message to Sennacherib condemning him for his arrogance and promising to defeat him and send him back to his home country. The confrontation is completed and YHWH's power vindicated when an angel of YHWH strikes down 185,000 Assyrian troops and Sennacherib returns home only to be struck down by his own sons in the temple of his own god.

6. For the identification of these sources, see B. Stade, "Anmerkungen zu 2 Kö 15–21," *ZAW* 6 (1886) 172–186; cf. Brevard S. Childs, *Isaiah and the Assyrian Crisis*, SBT II/3 (London: SCM, 1967) 69–103; Long, *2 Kings* 198–202.

7. For a full discussion of the genre, see Sweeney, *Isaiah 1–39* 471–476.

Because the prophetic confrontation story is a subgenre of the prophetic narrative, the major episodes of the plot determine the narrative structure. The narrative begins with a report of Sennacherib's invasion of Judah and Hezekiah's initial attempt to appease Sennacherib by stripping the Temple to pay tribute (2 Kgs 18:13–16). The arrogance of the Assyrian monarch is highlighted by the fact that he then sends his representatives to negotiate Jerusalem's surrender even after Hezekiah has already submitted to him. Consequently, the next major episode is the report concerning Sennacherib's first message to Hezekiah in 2 Kings 18:14–38, in which the Assyrian monarch demands Hezekiah's unconditional surrender. Hezekiah's reaction to this initial demand when he sends a delegation to Isaiah, who assures them that YHWH will return Sennacherib to his own land where he will fall by the sword is reported in 2 Kings 19:1 7. Sennacherib's second message to Hezekiah, in which his messengers attempt to dispute Hezekiah's trust in YHWH's promise of deliverance, is then reported in 2 Kings 19:8–13. Hezekiah's prayer to YHWH, in which he beseeches YHWH to save Jerusalem, is reported in 2 Kings 19:14–19. YHWH's response to Hezekiah through Isaiah, in which YHWH renews the promise to deliver the city and to defeat Sennacherib, is reported in 2 Kings 19:20–34. Finally, 2 Kings 19:35–37 reports the destruction of the Assyrian army by the angel of death, Sennacherib's return to Nineveh, and his assassination by his own sons in the Temple of Nisroch.

The narrative concerning Hezekiah's illness and recovery appears in 2 Kings 20:1–11, introduced by the formula *bayyāmîm hāhēm*, "in those days." The narrative is formulated as a royal novelle about Hezekiah's sickness and recovery.[8] Again, the structure of the narrative is determined by the major episodes of the plot.[9] It begins in 20:1–3 with an initial discussion of Hezekiah's mortal illness,

---

8. For an alternative analysis of the genre and structure of this narrative, see Long, *2 Kings* 235–241.

9. Note that this version of the narrative differs considerably from its counterpart in Isaiah 38, and therefore displays a very different structure. For a full discussion of the version of the narrative in Isaiah 38 and its relation to the narrative in 2 Kings 20:1–11, see Sweeney, *Isaiah 1–39* 488–505. Contra Seitz, *Zion's Final Destiny* 149–191, esp. 162–182, who argues that the version in Isaiah 38 is original, and that the version in 2 Kings 20:1–11 is derived from the Isaiah narrative on three grounds: (1) the narrative concerning Hezekiah's illness is not concerned with exile, like the account of Merodach Baladan's embassy, but associates YHWH's decision to cure Hezekiah with the defense of Jerusalem outlined in the account of Sennacherib's siege (cf. 2 Kgs 20:6; Isa 38:6). It must therefore be considered together with the Sennacherib narrative that Seitz argues is originally part of a seventh-century edition of Isaiah; (2) the Kings narrative conflates the reports of two signs that were originally distinct in the Isaiah narrative, that concerning Hezekiah's recovery (Isa 38:7–8) and that concerning his visit to the Temple (Isa 38:22); and (3) associations between the Isaiah version and other portions of Isaiah, including the reference to illness (Isa 1:5b–6) and the placement of poetic compositions, such as the Psalm of Hezekiah that is unique to the Isaiah version, at the end of major tradition blocks. These arguments do not hold up, however. As indicated below, the Hezekiah narrative is in fact concerned with exile. The association between Hezekiah's illness and his visit to the Temple are to be expected, as a boil would render him unfit to enter the Temple (cf. Lev 13:18–23). The associations with other portions of Isaiah and the practice of concluding major blocks of tradition with a poem are irrelevant, in that Isaiah 38 lacks specific citation of other texts in Isaiah and the placement of poems is an editorial decision that may or may not be the work of an original author. Furthermore, the narrative form of Isaiah 36–39 points to an original setting

in which the monarch weeps and prays after learning from Isaiah that he will die. 2 Kings 20:4–7 then presents YHWH's commission to Isaiah that the prophet convey YHWH's decision to cure Hezekiah and extend his life because of his piety. This segment of the narrative highlights the association of Hezekiah's cure with YHWH's decision to save Jerusalem from the King of Assyria for the sake of David (v. 6), prior to narrating Isaiah's compliance with YHWH's commission. 2 Kings 20:8–11 then narrates Hezekiah's request for a sign confirming that he will be healed and therefore be able to go up to the Temple. After discussing the matter with Hezekiah, Isaiah calls on YHWH to reverse the shadow on the dial of Ahaz by ten steps, thereby confirming that Hezekiah will be healed.

The narrative concerning Merodach Baladan's embassy to Hezekiah in 2 Kings 20:12–19 begins with the introductory formula *bāʿēt hahî*, "at that time," which coordinates it with the narratives concerning Sennacherib's siege of Jerusalem and Hezekiah's illness. The narrative is a prophetic story concerning Isaiah's announcement of punishment against Hezekiah on the occasion of Merodach Baladan's embassy.[10] Again, the episodes in the plot sequence govern the structure of the narrative. 2 Kings 20:12–13 sets the stage for the confrontation between Isaiah and Hezekiah by reporting the King's reception of an embassy from Merodach Baladan in which he showed them the Temple and his various storehouses and treasuries. The main portion of the narrative appears in 2 Kings 20:14–19, which reports the ensuing dialogue between Isaiah and Hezekiah. The first exchange between the two appears in v. 14, in which Isaiah asks where the men are from and Hezekiah replies that they are from Babylon. The second exchange in v. 15 reports Isaiah's request to know what they saw and Hezekiah's response that they saw all that was in the house and all that was in the treasuries. The third exchange in vv. 16–19 includes Isaiah's announcement of punishment against Hezekiah, stating that all that is in his house, including his sons, will be carried off to Babylon. The third exchange concludes with Hezekiah's response that YHWH's word is good and his rhetorical question that asserts that there will be peace and truth in his days.

The structure of the Hezekiah narrative may be portrayed as in table 4.1. Overall, this analysis of the structure and generic character of the Hezekiah narrative demonstrates that its present form displays an interest in Hezekiah's actions as a partial cause for the Babylonian exile. This is indicated most clearly by the presence of the narrative concerning Isaiah's condemnation of Hezekiah for receiving the delegation from the Babylonian prince Merodach Baladan, which points ultimately to the Babylonian exile. Although Hezekiah is righteous, and YHWH delivers Jerusalem because of Hezekiah's piety, his reception of the

---

in Kings, and the differences between the Isaiah and Kings versions of the narrative point to an effort to "whitewash" Hezekiah by eliminating potentially negative representations of the monarch in Kings so that he would serve as a model of piety for the balance of the book of Isaiah in chapters 40–66. For full discussion of this issue, see Sweeney, *Isaiah 1–39* 476–485.

10. For a full analysis of the genre and structure of this narrative, see Sweeney, *Isaiah 1–39* 505–511. Cf. Long, *2 Kings* 241–246.

TABLE 4.1   Structure of the Hezekiah narrative

Regnal evaluation of Hezekiah's reign	*2 Kings 18–20*
I. Introductory regnal resume	18:1–2
II. Evaluation of Hezekiah's reign	18:3–20:19
A. General evaluation: righteous like David	18:3
B. Detailed evaluation	18:4–20:9
1. Detailed summary of Hezekiah's actions	18:4–8
2. Report of fall of Samaria and exile of Israel in 4th–6th years of Hezekiah's reign	18:9–12
3. Report of events related to Hezekiah's revolt against Assyria and Sennacherib's invasion of Judah in Hezekiah's 14th year	18:13–20:19
a. Report of Sennacherib's invasion of Judah and YHWH's deliverance of Jerusalem	18:13–19:37
i. Initial report of Sennacherib's invasion and Hezekiah's attempt at appeasement	18:13–16
ii. Sennacherib's first message to Hezekiah demanding unconditional surrender	18:17–38
iii. Hezekiah's delegation to Isaiah resulting YHWH's assurance of salvation	19:1–7
iv. Sennacherib's second message to Hezekiah disputing Hezekiah's trust in YHWH's promise of deliverance	19:8–13
v. Hezekiah's prayer to YHWH to save Jerusalem	19:14–19
vi. YHWH's renewed promise through Isaiah to deliver Jerusalem and defeat Sennacherib	19:20–34
vii. YHWH's destruction of Assyrian army and subsequent assassination of Sennacherib by his own sons	19:35–37
b. Royal novelle concerning Hezekiah's illness	20:1–11
i. Report concerning Hezekiah's mortal illness	20:1–3
ii. Report concerning YHWH's commission to Isaiah to deliver oracle conveying YHWH's decision to cure Hezekiah	20:4–7
iii. Report concerning the sign to Hezekiah confirming that he will be cured	20:8–11
c. Prophetic story concerning Isaiah's announcement of punishment against Hezekiah on the occasion of Merodach Bulletin's embassy	20:12–19
i. Report concerning Hezekiah's reception of the Babylonian embassy	20:12–13
ii. Report of dialogue between Isaiah and Hezekiah resulting in Isaiah's condemnation of Hezekiah	20:14–19
a) 1st exchange: men are from Babylon	20:14
b) 2nd exchange: men saw house and treasuries	20:15
c) 3rd exchange: Isaiah's announcement of punishment against Hezekiah	20:16–19
III. Concluding regnal resume	20:20–21

Babylonian embassy becomes cause for condemnation by YHWH through Isaiah and a prediction that the Babylonian exile would be the ultimate result of his actions. Furthermore, the narrative displays an interest in comparing the events related to Sennacherib's siege of Jerusalem with the fall of Samaria, in that it highlights each with an introductory reference to the years of Hezekiah's reign in which each occurred. The fall of Samaria and the exile of Israel would then form an analogy with the impending Babylonian exile announced in 2 Kings 20:12–19, which is associated with Sennacherib's siege in the present form of the narrative. Overall, Judah's fate will mirror that of Israel in the perspective of the present form of the narrative.

But there are two major indications that this perspective is not integral to the text as a whole, and that its present form represents the product an exilic redaction that redefined its perspective. First, the general assessment of Hezekiah in 18:3 identifies him as righteous like David, and vv. 4–8 illustrate his righteousness by pointing to his removal of the high places, a problem that plagued the Judean kings from Solomon's time on (cf. 1 Kgs 3:2, 3). As Provan indicates, Hezekiah's removal of the high places brings a major problem among the kings of Judah to an end, and thereby it indicates that the narrative concerning Hezekiah's reign represents the culmination of a Josianic edition of the DtrH.[11] Apart from the narrative of Merodach Baladan's embassy, Hezekiah's actions are never criticized. Second, the narratives concerning YHWH's deliverance of Jerusalem at the time of Sennacherib's siege and the corresponding narrative concerning YHWH's cure of Hezekiah point to Hezekiah's righteousness as a primary motivation for YHWH's actions. In the former case, the Deity responds only after Hezekiah prays for deliverance thereby pointing to Hezekiah's piety, together with Sennacherib's arrogance, as a primary cause for YHWH decision to defeat the Assyrians. Likewise, Hezekiah's prayer to YHWH on learning that his illness is mortal constitutes the primary cause for YHWH's decision to save Hezekiah. In neither case is there any hint of wrongdoing on Hezekiah's part. The primary concern of both narratives seems to point to YHWH's interest in delivering Jerusalem and Hezekiah, not in bringing about exile.

This discrepancy in the perspective of the narrative demonstrates that it has been reworked from a narrative that portrays the righteous acts of Hezekiah as a cause for YHWH's deliverance to one that attempts to employ Hezekiah's image to point to the coming Babylonian exile.[12] In this regard, it seems quite clear that the narrative concerning Hezekiah's reception of Merodach Baladan's embassy in 2 Kings 20:12–19 is the product of an exilic reworking of this text. The introductory temporal formula in v. 12 sets it off as a distinct narrative, and the reference to the embassy's intention to bring gifts to Hezekiah at the time of his illness ties it into the overall narrative context. Although it is likely that Hezekiah did receive such an embassy as part of his preparations for revolt against Sennacherib, insofar as the revolt was a coordinated effort between Hezekiah and Merodach Baladan, the present form and placement of the narrative must be attributed to an exilic redaction of the DtrH. Clements is correct to argue that the present form of the narrative was likely composed between the years 597 and 587 B.C.E. as a means to come to terms with the deportation of Jehoiachin by the Babylonians in that the narrative only deals with the deportation of Davidic sons and not with the destruction of Jerusalem or the Temple.[13] Nevertheless, there is no evidence of a

11. Provan, *Hezekiah and the Books of Kings*.
12. See esp. Ackroyd, "An Interpretation of the Babylonian Exile."
13. Ronald E. Clements, "The Isaiah Narrative of 2 Kings 20:12–19 and the Date of the Deuteronomic History," in *Isac Leo Seeligmann Volume*, ed. A. Rofé and Y. Zakovitch (Jerusa-

DtrH edition dated to these years, but the evidence for an exilic edition is quite clear, given the report of Jerusalem's fall and Jehoiachin's release from prison in 2 Kings 24–25.

It is noteworthy that the narrative concerning Hezekiah's illness in 2 Kings 20:1–11 shares several features with that concerning Merodach Baladan's embassy. It, too, is connected to the preceding narrative concerning YHWH's deliverance of Jerusalem by a temporal formula, "in those days," that associates Hezekiah's illness with the siege of Jerusalem. But like the narrative concerning the Babylonian embassy, the events reported in the narrative concerning Hezekiah's illness also must take place prior to Sennacherib's invasion. This is clear in the case of the embassy narrative in that Hezekiah's display of wealth and preparations obviously predates the invasion when he was forced to strip the Temple to pay off the Assyrian monarch. This is also clear in relation to the illness narrative in that the embassy arrives, ostensibly to comfort Hezekiah on account of his illness (2 Kgs 20:12), and because 2 Kings 20:6 refers to YHWH's deliverance of Hezekiah and Jerusalem from the hand of the Assyrian monarch as future events. But the Sennacherib narrative shows no awareness of either the illness narrative or the embassy narrative, even though both events take place prior to the siege.

This in itself, of course, is not enough to establish the secondary character of either narrative. But several other features of the illness narrative also must be taken into consideration. First is the fact that Hezekiah receives only a temporary reprieve from death. Naturally, the limits of human existence preclude his eternal deliverance from death, but the fact remains that his reprieve is only temporary. The placement of this narrative immediately following the Sennacherib narrative then takes on added importance as it points to the temporary nature of YHWH's actions with regard to Hezekiah and thereby influences the reading of the narrative concerning YHWH's deliverance of Jerusalem. If Hezekiah's reprieve is temporary, then what about Jerusalem? Such a concern is not evident in the Sennacherib narrative, but the illness narrative introduces an element that builds toward the judgment announced in the embassy narrative. Like Hezekiah's reprieve from illness, the reprieve of Jerusalem from destruction is only temporary. Moreover, the illness narrative establishes an analogy between Hezekiah and Ahab. Just as Ahab won a reprieve from death in 1 Kings 21:17–29 when he weeps and repents over his actions in the Naboth affair upon hearing the judgment against him conveyed by Elijah, so Hezekiah wins a reprieve from death when he weeps upon hearing of his impending death as conveyed by Isaiah. The inclusion of this motif thereby plays upon the reference to the fall of Samaria and exile of Israel in 2 Kings 18:9–12. Just as Ahab of Israel is reprieved, so is Hezekiah of Judah, but both Israel and Judah will ultimately succumb to YHWH's punishment. These considerations demonstrate that, like the narrative concerning Merodach Baladan's embassy in 2 Kings 20:12–19, the narrative concerning Hezekiah's illness in

---

lem: E. Rubenstein, 1983) 209–220; cf. Christof Hardmeier, *Prophetie im Streit vor dem Untergang Judas: Erzählkommunikative Studien zur Entstehungssituation der Jesaja- und Jeremiaerzählungen in II Reg 18–20 und Jer 37–40*, BZAW 187 (Berlin and New York: Walter de Gruyter, 1990).

2 Kings 20:1–11 is placed in its present position by the exilic redaction of the DtrH as a means to point to the coming Babylonian exile. Because it employs motifs from the narrative concerning King Ahab in its portrayal of Hezekiah as a means to point to the Babylonian exile, it stands in analogy to the present forms of the narratives concerning Manasseh and Josiah, which also employ the image of Ahab to portray these monarchs and thereby build toward the Babylonian exile.

This leaves the narrative concerning YHWH's deliverance of Jerusalem from Sennacherib's siege. Although it, too, appears in the exilic edition of the DtrH, it seems to derive from the Josianic period and thereby would play a role in a postulated Josianic edition of the DtrH. Several features of the narrative speak in favor of such a hypothesis. The portrayal of the defeat of Sennacherib in the narrative certainly conflicts with other sources, such as Sennacherib's annals, which point to a different outcome for the siege in which Sennacherib received tribute from Hezekiah (cf. 2 Kgs 18:13–16), but was unable to take Jerusalem or dislodge Hezekiah from his throne.[14] The result was that both monarchs could claim victory. Furthermore, Sennacherib's assassination by his sons is a known fact, but it occurred in 681 B.C.E. some twenty years after his siege of Jerusalem in 701. It is noteworthy that the narrative concerning YHWH's defeat of Sennacherib's army marks the end of Assyria as a threat to Judah in the DtrH, despite the fact that Assyria continued to rule Judah through the early reign of Josiah, and even conquered Egypt during the reign of Manasseh. These factors, along with the strong stamp of YHWH's promise to the house of David and the restoration of Jerusalem, point to the Josianic period as the time of the composition of this narrative.[15]

In this regard, the function of the Hezekiah narrative in relation to the literary context of the DtrH must be considered. The narrative obviously plays a role in relation to the final exilic edition of the DtrH in that the narratives concerning Merodach Baladan's embassy to Hezekiah and Hezekiah's illness point forward to the Babylonian exile. They thereby temper the very optimistic outlook of the narrative concerning YHWH's defeat of Sennacherib by pointing out that YHWH's deliverance of Jerusalem (and Hezekiah) is only temporary because the city will ultimately succumb to the Babylonians. At the same time, the Hezekiah narrative prepares the way for the notice concerning Jehoiachin's release from prison, insofar as it emphasizes the Davidic theme with its promise of eternal rule for the house of David if the monarchs continue to observe YHWH's commands. The narrative concerning Jehoiachin's release does not refer to the Davidic tradition, but when it is read in relation to the Hezekiah narrative, the DtrH Davidic promise tradition anticipates the possibility of Davidic restoration based on YHWH's past fidelity to righteous Davidic monarchs such as Hezekiah.

The Hezekiah narrative also must be read in relation to the material that precedes in the DtrH in that Hezekiah serves as both a positive and a negative role

14. See James Pritchard, *Ancient Near Eastern Texts Relating to the Old Testament* 3rd edition (Princeton: Princeton University Press, 1969) 287–288. For a full analysis of the historical setting and problems of this narrative, see Sweeney, *Isaiah 1–39* 476–485.

15. See Clements, *Isaiah and the Deliverance of Jerusalem* for a full discussion of the reasons for dating this narrative to the Josianic period. See also Sweeney, *Isaiah 1–39* 476–485.

model in the exilic edition of the DtrH. He is positive, as he removes the high places (2 Kgs 18:4) and thereby resolves one of the major problems among the kings of Judah who failed to remove the high places. The fact that the high places are initially mentioned in relation to Solomon's reign (1 Kgs 3:2, 3) further highlights Hezekiah's positive image as Solomon ultimately causes one of the major problems of the DtrH—the split of the people Israel into the kingdoms of Israel and Judah—on account of his marriages to foreign women and the cultic apostasy that he initiated on their behalf. The placement of the narrative concerning Hezekiah's reign immediately following the DtrH commentary in 2 Kings 17 on the fall of the northern kingdom of Israel automatically highlights the differences between the righteous Hezekiah and the apostate kings of northern Israel. This issue is further highlighted by the inclusion of the notice concerning Israel's fall in the midst of the Hezekiah narrative (2 Kgs 18:9–12), which enables the narrative to contrast Hezekiah's faithful dependence on YHWH in the Assyrian crisis over against the faithless kings of northern Israel.

But Hezekiah is a negative role model as well, because he succumbs to faithlessness in YHWH's promises in a manner reminiscent of many of his predecessors. When Sennacherib initially invades Judah, Hezekiah's first act is to surrender immediately to the Assyrian monarch and to strip the Temple in order to pay tribute. The futility of this action is highlighted in the present form of the narrative by virtue of the fact that Sennacherib besieges Jerusalem anyway and announces his blasphemy against YHWH's power and promises during the course of his negotiations for Hezekiah's unconditional surrender of the city of Jerusalem. This issue is revisited in 2 Kings 20:11–19. Although the reception of Merodach Baladan's embassy precedes the Assyrian invasion and Hezekiah's ultimate turn to YHWH for deliverance, the placement of the narrative at the end of the complex emphasizes Hezekiah's initial lack of faith in YHWH's promises as demonstrated by his efforts to secure an alliance with the Babylonians. In this regard, his actions are similar to those of Ahaz, who refused to rely on YHWH's promises of security and turned to the Assyrians for support at the time of the Syro-Ephraimitic invasion of Judah (2 Kgs 16). Ahaz stripped the Temple and his treasuries to send Tiglath Pileser a "present" (*šōḥad*, lit. "bribe"). Following the Assyrian defeat of Israel and Aram, Ahaz was compelled by Tiglath Pileser to build an altar in the Temple courtyard according to the pattern of the one he saw in Damascus and made other innovations in the Temple and his own palace on account of the Assyrian monarch. The fact that Hezekiah displays the wealth of the Temple and his treasuries to the Babylonians while courting them for a military alliance, and that he strips the Temple to pay off Sennacherib, establishes the analogy between Hezekiah and Ahaz that ultimately plays a role in justifying the Babylonian exile in the final form of the DtrH. As noted earlier, the portrayal of Hezekiah in relation to Ahab—insofar as Hezekiah is reprieved from death like Ahab so that he will not see the disaster overtake his people—likewise builds the case for the Babylonian exile in a manner analogous to that of Manasseh and Josiah.

The narrative plays a somewhat different role in a Josianic edition of the DtrH. In the absence of the narratives concerning Hezekiah's illness and the embassy of Merodach Baladan, Hezekiah becomes an entirely positive role model who paves the way for Josiah. Hezekiah's reform measures point to those enacted by Josiah nearly a century later, and his faithful turning to YHWH during the Assyrian crisis points to Josiah's turning to YHWH at the time of his own reforms. Likewise, the contrast between Hezekiah and the northern kings of Israel continues to play a major role in that Hezekiah exemplifies righteous Davidic kingship as demonstrated by the statements that "did what was right in the eyes of YHWH according to all that David his father had done" (2 Kgs 18:3) and that "he removed the high places" (2 Kgs 18:4). Again, these statements demonstrate the contrast between Hezekiah and Solomon as well as with the northern kings, as Solomon is the one who initiates the high places in the DtrH and thereby leads to the split within Israel and the establishment of the northern kingdom.

Nevertheless, the portrayal of Hezekiah's reign in a Josianic edition of the DtrH does not complete the history in that Hezekiah leaves much undone. This is not to condemn Hezekiah, but to point to Josiah as a monarch who surpassed his great-grandfather in resolving the problems of the people of Israel. Hezekiah is able to achieve the deliverance of Jerusalem through his piety, but he is not able to reunite the people of Israel. Josiah's destruction of the Beth-El altar points to this possibility, thereby portraying him as the monarch who would have resolved Israel's greatest problems: the division of the people into two kingdoms and the continued estrangement of the north from the Jerusalem Temple. The Hezekiah narrative points to this possibility by its reference to the remnant of Judah taking root to grow once again (2 Kgs 19:29–34), but this takes up the fate of Jerusalem and Judah alone and does not refer to the reunification of the people. Likewise, the Josiah narrative highlights Josiah's removal of Ahaz's altars (2 Kgs 23:12) and Solomon's high places (2 Kgs 23:13), indicating that Hezekiah's reform was not sufficiently comprehensive. Furthermore, Hezekiah's comparison with David points to Hezekiah as preparatory figure in that David's actions in the DtrH are not entirely commendable. As mentioned, Solomon came to the throne as the ultimate result of David's adulterous affair with Bath Sheba and the murder of Bath Sheba's husband, Uriah the Hittite. All of these factors must be considered in assessing the role of the Hezekiah narrative as part of the Josianic edition of the DtrH. In initiating his reform measures and in playing his role in bringing the Assyrian threat to an end in the DtrH, Hezekiah points to the possibility of righteous Davidic rule. But Josiah realizes the full measure of such rule, not simply on the basis of the Davidic model, but on the model put forward by Moses and Joshua.

Finally, one must be prepared for the possibility of a DtrH edition that concluded with the reign of Hezekiah. Indications of such an edition include several factors. First, there is the reference to Hezekiah's righteousness in accordance with the actions of David (2 Kgs 18:3), whereas Josiah is judged both in relation to David (2 Kgs 22:2) and in relation to the Torah of Moses (2 Kgs 23:25). Second, there is the reference to Hezekiah's removal of the high places initiated by Solomon (2 Kgs 18:4). This is especially curious in relation to the notice concerning Josiah's removal of Solomon's altars (2 Kgs 23:13). Third, there is the incomparability formula applied to Hezekiah in 2 Kings 18:5, "In YHWH, G-d of Israel, he trusted, and after him there was none like him among all the kings of Judah." On the one hand, this could be considered hyperbole, but, on the other hand, it does not leave much room for Josiah. who is described in similar terms in 2 Kings 23:25, "and before him there was not like him a king who turned to YHWH with all his heart and with all his soul and with all his might according to all the Torah of Moses and after him there did not arise one like him." Fourth, there is the portrayal of Hezekiah's actions that see not only the deliverance of Jerusalem but also the possibility of new growth for Jerusalem and Judah (2 Kgs 19:29–34).

These factors indicate the likelihood that the Hezekiah narratives present Hezekiah as the ideal monarch of the DtrH, and that YHWH's defense of Jerusalem and the possibility of the restoration of Jerusalem and Judah concluded an earlier edition of the DtrH. In such a model, the Josiah narrative (including those of Manasseh and Amon) would have been added as a means to expand the DtrH so that it would point to Josiah as the ideal monarch of the history. A Hezekian edition would have been written in the aftermath of Sennacherib's siege when Hezekiah remained on the throne and Jerusalem would have to serve as the center for the rebuilding of Judah. During this period, Sennacherib was occupied with the task of chasing down Merodach Baladan, and this continued through 689 B.C.E. It would have to follow Sennacherib's assassination in 681. It also would have to coincide with the period during the reign of Manasseh in which Assyria asserted full control over Judah in its efforts to conquer Egypt during the first half of the seventh century or, perhaps, with the aftermath of Assyria's loss of control over Egypt in 664.[16] Such an edition would point to Hezekiah as the model of the faithful monarch who turned to YHWH and thus demonstrated the efficacy of the Davidic promise tradition. In this respect, he would stand in contrast not only to the kings of northern Israel who brought their kingdom to ruin (2 Kgs 17) but also to Solomon, whose acts of apostasy on behalf of his foreign wives brought about the split in the people of Israel to begin with. In such a scenario, Manasseh's actions to suppress dissent in the kingdom would be directed against those who looked to Sennacherib's withdrawal as an Assyrian defeat and who propagated literature that would portray it as such. A Hezekian edition of the DtrH and the circles who wrote and promoted it may well have been among the targets of Manasseh's actions.

But major problems remain in establishing the possibility of a Hezekian edition of the DtrH and indeed of the Josianic edition as well. As noted, both Hezekiah and Josiah are portrayed in contrast to Solomon, as well as in contrast to the northern monarchs. On the one hand, Hezekiah removes the high places initiated by Solomon; on the other hand, Josiah attempts to reunite the people split apart by Solomon's actions. Furthermore, the role of David also must be considered.

---

16. Note the tradition in 2 Chronicles 33:10–13, that Manasseh was dragged in hooks and fetters to Babylon by the Assyrian king. Such a tradition suggests that Manasseh had to be subdued before the Assyrians could begin their efforts to conquer Egypt under Esarhaddon, Sennacherib's successor. For a discussion of the potential historical background to this event and the Chronicler's use of this tradition in shaping the account to meet a unique theological concern, see Sara Japhet, *I and II Chronicles: A Commentary*, OTL (Louisville, KY: Westminster John Knox, 1993) 1008–1009.

Although he is portrayed as an ideal ruler who serves as a model in relation to Hezekiah and even to Josiah, his affair with Bath Sheba must be examined in relation to the DtrH, as this calls his righteousness into question. This requires a full examination of the role of Solomon in the DtrH (as he creates the problems that both monarchs attempt to resolve) and the role of David's affair with Bath Sheba (as this brings Solomon to the throne). Insofar as Josiah's reign points beyond David to Moses and Joshua as ideal models of rule, it could suggest that the Succession Narrative in 2 Samuel 9–1 Kings 2 was part of a Josianic edition of the DtrH, but that it was not included in a Hezekian edition.

5

The Presentation of the Northern Kingdom of Israel in 1 Kings 12–2 Kings 17

The narratives concerning the northern kingdom of Israel in 1 Kings 12– 2 Kings 17 clearly constitute a key element in the overall presentation of the history of the people of Israel and Judah in the DtrH. Following the narratives concerning King Solomon in 1 Kings 1–11, they dominate the historical account of the books of Kings in that the bulk of the narrative's attention is devoted to the Elijah/Elisha narratives in 1 Kings 17–2 Kings 13, which relate the fall of the northern dynasty of Omri and the rise of the house of Jehu. In contrast, the narrative pays relatively less attention to the founding dynasty of Jeroboam and the other short-lived northern dynasties that followed or even to the kings of the southern house of David. Indeed, without the Elijah/Elisha narratives, there would be relatively little substance to the DtrH presentation of the northern kingdom of Israel or to the presentation of the history as a whole. Although many correctly argue that the Elijah and Elisha narratives apparently constitute self-contained narrative traditions that likely had their own literary prehistories prior to their inclusion in the DtrH,[1] it does serve DtrH historiographical and theological interests. It

---

1. For overviews of discussion, see Rolf Rendtorff, *The Old Testament: An Introduction*, translated by J. Bowden (Philadelphia: Fortress, 1986) 178–183; J. A. Soggin, *Introduction to the Old Testament*, OTL, 3rd edition, translated by J. Bowden (Louisville, KY: Westminster John Knox, 1989) 229–230, 234. See esp. Antony F. Campbell, *Of Prophets and Kings: A Late Ninth Century Document* (*1 Samuel 1–2 Kings 10*), CBQMS 17 (Washington, D.C.: The Catholic Biblical Association of America, 1986); A. J. Hauser and R. Gregory, *From Carmel to Horeb: Elijah in Crisis*, JSOTSup 85, BLS 19 (Sheffield: Almond, 1990); Georg Hentschel, *Die Elijaerzählungen: Zum Verhältnis von historischem Geschehen und geschichtlicher Erfahrung* (Erfurter Theologische Studien 33; Leipzig: St. Benno, 1977); Hans-Christoph Schmitt, *Elisa: Traditionsgeschichtliche Untersuchungen zur vorklassischen nordisraelitischen Prophetie* (Gütersloh: Mohn, 1972); Odil Hannes Steck, *Überlieferung und Zeitgeschichte in den Elia-Erzählungen*, WMANT 26 (Neukirchen: Neukirchener Verlag, 1968).

demonstrates the decline of a dynasty that derived its power from the intermarriage of its primary king Ahab to the Phoenician princess Jezebel, in violation of Deuteronomic injunctions concerning intermarriage with the pagan nations. As a result, this marriage played a major role in introducing pagan religious worship into the lives of the people of Israel. As noted, Ahab's actions in establishing an Asherah for worship by the people serves as a model for the condemnation of Manasseh at a later time, and the subsequent but temporary reprieve of the nation's judgment as a result of his repentance plays a role in the formulation of the exilic editions of both the Hezekiah and Josiah narratives.

Despite the important role played by the Elijah/Elisha cycle in the overall DtrH historical narrative, it is clear that the DtrH narrator focuses especially on the figure of Jeroboam in the presentation of the northern kingdom of Israel. As noted already by Cross and others before him,[2] all of the kings of northern Israel are judged in relation to the sins of King Jeroboam ben Nebat, who not only served as the founding monarch of the northern kingdom but established the state sanctuaries at Dan and Beth-El in opposition to Jerusalem and placed images of the golden calf in each. These actions clearly violate Deuteronomic injunctions against idolatry and the establishment of more than one legitimate worship site among the people. Although the golden calves were likely not to be identified as representations of YHWH, but as mounts for YHWH analogous to the ark in Jerusalem that functioned as a divine throne,[3] the DtrH narrative makes it very clear that it regards this action as a deliberate establishment of idolatry and, therefore, grounds for the condemnation of both Jeroboam and the northern kingdom of Israel. Likewise, the sanctuaries at Dan and Beth-El appear in the narrative prior to this point and likely served as sanctuaries for the people of Israel for centuries prior to the reign of Jeroboam, but in the context of the DtrH narrative they serve as indicators of Jeroboam's and Israel's rebellion against the commandments of YHWH as set down in the Mosaic Torah of Deuteronomy. By stating that each of the northern kings followed in the sin of Jeroboam, the DtrH makes it very clear that Jeroboam sets the pattern for the entire northern kingdom and thereby provides the grounds for which it is condemned and destroyed.

The DtrH concern with Jeroboam is highlighted, however, not only by his presence in the regnal summaries of the northern kings of Israel but by the role that he plays at the beginning and end of the narrative concerning the northern kingdom of Israel as well. He is introduced during the account of the reign of Solomon in 1 Kings 11 as one of the adversaries raised by YHWH against Solomon's rule when Solomon is said to have turned away from YHWH on account of his pagan wives and concubines. Jeroboam is introduced as an Ephraimite officer of Solomon who had charge over the forced labor imposed upon the northern tribes and who "raised his hand against the king"—that is, revolted against Solomon. As a result of his revolt, he flees Jerusalem to take sanctuary in Egypt. While on the road to Egypt, the Shilonite prophet Ahijah encounters him and promises him

2. Cross, "Themes in the Books of Kings."

3. L. R. Bailey, "The Golden Calf," *HUCA* 42 (1971) 97–115; Otto Eissfeldt, "Lade und Stierbild," *ZAW* 58 (1940–41) 190–215.

kingship over the northern tribes of Israel on account of Solomon's sins. Jeroboam returns to Israel when the northern tribes revolt against Solomon's son Rehoboam in 1 Kings 12 and is subsequently declared king over the northern kingdom of Israel. Once he is declared king, he establishes the sanctuaries at Dan and Beth-El. While officiating over the dedication of the altar at Beth-El, he is condemned in 1 Kings 13 by an unnamed prophet of G-d, who declares that the Beth-El altar shall ultimately be destroyed by King Josiah. Following the Beth-El narrative, the account of Jeroboam's reign quickly winds down in 1 Kings 14 with a notice that his dynasty is condemned for his idolatry; in 1 Kings 15:25–32, his son Nadab is assassinated by Baasha and the dynasty comes to a speedy end in the second generation.

Jeroboam appears once again at the conclusion of the narrative concerning the northern kingdom of Israel in 2 Kings 17, which comprises a deuteronomistic sermon concerning the causes for Israel's destruction by the Assyrian empire during the reign of Hoshea. Although the historic reasons for Israel's destruction have to do with Assyria's superior military power and its interests in extending its trade network west and south toward Egypt, the DtrH narrative argues that Israel's idolatry in violation of YHWH's commands, including its observance of the golden calves and the Asherah among other abominations, are the cause for YHWH's decision to bring the Assyrians to destroy the northern kingdom. Jeroboam and Ahab are not named in 2 Kings 17:7–18, which describes Israel's cultic abominations in detail as the cause of the destruction, although they are respectively responsible for the golden calves and the Asherah according to the DtrH narrative. Nevertheless, vv. 21–23 focus on Jeroboam as the fundamental cause of Israel's sins, "When he (YHWH) had torn Israel from the house of David they made Jeroboam ben Nebat king. And Jeroboam drove Israel from following YHWH and made them commit great sin. The people of Israel walked in all the sins which Jeroboam did; they did not depart from them, until YHWH removed Israel out of his sight as he had spoken by all his servants the prophets. So Israel was exiled from their own land to Assyria until this day."

This statement is remarkable, not only because it places the entire blame for the destruction of the northern kingdom of Israel on the shoulders of Jeroboam ben Nebat but also because it points to a continuing situation of exile "until this day." What day? Scholars have discussed the meaning of this reference extensively, arguing that it must point to a reality of the period of the Babylonian exile or its aftermath when the present form of the DtrH was produced, or perhaps to a time in the preexilic period following the destruction of the northern kingdom of Israel, perhaps in the time of Josiah or even during the reign of Hezekiah.[4] Several factors enter in to this discussion. First, 2 Kings 17:19–20 appears to refer to the Babylonian exile of Judah, "Judah also did not keep the commandments of YHWH their G-d, but walked in the customs which Israel had introduced. And YHWH rejected all the descendants of Israel, and afflicted them, and gave them into the hand of spoilers, until he had cast them out of his sight." Second, vv. 24–41 refer to the decision by the Assyrian king to introduce foreign peoples into the

---

4. For an overview of discussion, see Nelson, *Double Redaction* 23–25.

land of Israel and his subsequent decision to bring an Israelite priest to Beth-El in order to instruct the people in the laws of YHWH so that they might avoid the lions that YHWH sent to kill those who ignored his requirements. Overall, the narrative provides an account of how the people of the land mixed their pagan worship practice with that devoted to YHWH and thereby produced a syncretistic religious situation that persists "until this day" (vv. 34, 41).

Many take this as a reference to the origins of the Samaritan community and thereby consider the narrative to be postexilic,[5] but the role played by the sanctuary at Beth-El in bringing about this syncretism also deserves attention. Beth-El is the source of the continuing syncretism in Israel in the perspective of the writer of 2 Kings 17, and thereby brings about an unsatisfactory situation that requires resolution in the DtrH. Like Jeroboam, Beth-El appears at the beginning and end of the DtrH narrative concerning the northern kingdom of Israel and plays a substantial role in conjunction with Jeroboam in establishing the grounds for Israel's destruction. As noted, the initial account of the dedication of the Beth-El altar in 1 Kings 13 points to Josiah as the one who will ultimately destroy the Beth-El altar, and 2 Kings 23 makes it clear that Josiah fulfills this aim, thereby taking a step toward the resolution of the continuing syncretism in the land. This suggests that Beth-El is of interest to a Josianic writer of the DtrH, but it is not clear how Beth-El would fit into the interests of an exilic DtrH writer, especially since the DtrH does not return to the issue of Beth-El or the syncretism of the northern population following its presentation of the reign of Josiah. Furthermore, the only clear indication of exilic concerns appears in the notice in vv. 19–20 that YHWH also would remove Judah on account of its sins. But even this conclusion is questionable in that it is not entirely clear that Judah is to be included as part of Israel in v. 20 and because Judah's continuing sins provide the premise for King Josiah's reforms. Finally, Provan notes the contrast between the experience of Israel and Judah in the face of Assyrian invasion.[6] Whereas Israel is destroyed because of its lack of faith in YHWH in 2 Kings 17, the remnant of Judah in Jerusalem is spared when Hezekiah turns to YHWH in faith in 2 Kings 18–20. Insofar as the Hezekiah narrative appears to have associations with the exilic, Josianic, and the potential Hezekian editions of the DtrH, it is possible that the concerns raised in 2 Kings 17 might well relate to any one or more of these potential editions.

The figures of Jeroboam and Beth-El clearly play constitutive roles in the DtrH presentation of the northern kingdom of Israel at both the beginning and the end. They therefore form particularly important elements in the framework of the DtrH presentation of the northern kingdom of Israel and aid in defining the DtrH perspective on the north. Furthermore, their respective or combined roles may well provide further evidence that will aid in defining the settings and perspectives of the various proposed editions of the DtrH, including the exilic, Josianic, and Hezekian editions of the work. It is therefore necessary to examine both 2 Kings

---

5. For example, James A. Montgomery and Henry Snyder Gehman, *The Books of Kings*, ICC (Edinburgh: T & T Clark, 1951) 471–477.
6. Provan, *Hezekiah*.

17 and 1 Kings 11, 12–13 in order to clarify the historiographic perspectives and literary history of the DtrH.

2 Kings 17 is demarcated initially by the formula, *bišnat šĕtêm 'eśrēh lĕ'āḥāz melek yĕhûdâ mālak hôšē'a ben-'ēlâ bĕšōmrôn 'al-yiśrā'ēl tēša' šānîm*, "in the twelfth year of Ahaz, King of Judah, Hoshea ben Elah ruled in Samaria over Israel nine years."[7] In addition to this introductory form, it is distinguished from the preceding evaluation of King Ahaz in 2 Kings 16 by content, in that it focuses on Hoshea rather than on Ahaz, and by the lack of syntactical conjunction at the beginning of 2 Kings 17:1. The unit focuses on the evaluation of Hoshea's reign and events during his reign. It contains a standard regnal evaluation in vv. 1–2, which includes the date and duration of Hoshea's reign in v. 1 and an evaluation of the character of his reign as evil in v. 2. Verses 3–5 comprise an account of actions taken by Shalmanezer, King of Assyria, against Hoshea, beginning with a syntactically independent statement in v. 3 that Shalmanezer "went up against him," and subjugated him by requiring tribute. Verses 4 and 5 continue with successive *waw*-consecutive statements that Shalmanezer imprisoned Hoshea for treachery in attempting an alliance with Egypt and that Shalmanezer assaulted the land of Israel and besieged Samaria for three years.

Scholars generally maintain that v. 6 concludes the account of Hoshea's reign and that vv. 7–41 then follow with the DtrH sermon concerning the fall of Israel and its aftermath so that all of 2 Kings 17:1–41 form single, coherent unit.[8] But several factors indicate that vv. 6–41 form a second unit, related to but distinct from the regnal evaluation of Hoshea in vv. 1–5. First, although v. 6 mentions that Samaria was captured in Hoshea's ninth year, Hoshea's reign was concluded by v. 5 so that the capture took place after his reign had ended. Second, Hoshea is never mentioned again after v. 6, so the subsequent material has nothing to do with his reign. Third, v. 6 begins with a formula that is syntactically independent and parallel to that of v. 1, *bišnat hattĕšî'ît lĕhôšē'a lākad melek-'aššûr 'et-šōmrôn wayyegel 'et-yiśrā'ēl 'aššûrâ wayyōšeb 'ōtām baḥlaḥ ûbĕḥābôr nĕhar gôzān wĕ'ārê mādāy*, "in the ninth year of Hoshea, the king of Assyria captured Samaria and he exiled Israel to Assyria and he settled them in Halah and in Habor, Nehar Gozan, and the cities of the Medes." This formula marks v. 6 as the beginning of a unit that is coordinated with that of vv. 1–5 but that is a distinct unit with a different set of concerns. Fourth, the introductory *wayĕhî*, "and it came to pass," in v. 7 follows up v. 6 syntactically and begins a discussion as to why the exile mentioned in v. 6 came to pass. Fifth, the balance of the unit in vv. 7–41 continues to focus on the theme of Israel's exile, including its causes and the situation in the land of Israel in the aftermath of the Assyrian action. Sixth, the regnal evaluation of Hezekiah's reign in 2 Kings 18–20 is linked syntactically to 2 Kings 17:6–41 by

---

7. For an overview of discussion concerning 2 Kings 17, see Long, *2 Kings* 180–190; Nelson, *Double Redaction* 53–69. See also Marc Brettler, "Text in a Tel: 2 Kings 17 as History," in *The Creation of History in Ancient Israel* (London and New York: Routledge, 1995) 112–134, 208–217; P. A. Viviano, "2 Kings 17: A Rhetorical and Form-Critical Analysis," *CBQ* 49 (1987) 548–559.

8. See Long, *2 Kings* 181.

the *waw*-consecutive formulation, "and it came to pass in the third year of Hoshea ben Elah, King of Israel, that Hezekiah ben Ahaz ruled as king of Judah." Insofar as 2 Kings 18:1 begins with *wayĕhî* and relates Hezekiah's reign to that of Hoshea, it provides a second narrative that follows from 2 Kings 17:6 in a manner analogous to that of 2 Kings 17:7–41. Both 2 Kings 18–20 and 2 Kings 17:7–41 discuss the situation of the land of Israel/Judah in the aftermath of the Assyrian deportation of the people of northern Israel, and this reinforces Provan's conclusion that the DtrH intends to provide a contrast in the experience of faithless Israel versus that of Judah and its eventually faithful monarch Hezekiah.

Verse 6 provides the introductory statement that begins the new unit in 2 Kings 17:6–41 that is concerned with the exile of the people from the land of Israel and its aftermath. Following the initial notice of the exile, v. 7 begins a section that discusses the causes of the exile by pointing to the various iniquities committed by the people of Israel in vv. 7–12, YHWH's warning to the people and their persistence in iniquity in vv. 13–19, and the concluding section in vv. 20–23, which states YHWH's rejection of the people of Israel culminating in their exile from the land "until this day." Verses 24–41 shifts attention away from the causes of the exile, and focuses on the circumstances in the land of Israel in the aftermath of the people's exile from the land. It begins with a statement in v. 24, "and the King of Assyria brought (people) from Babylon and from Kuthah, and from Avva, and from Hamath, and Sepharvaim, and he settled (them) in the cities of Samaria in place of the sons of Israel, and they possessed Samaria and they dwelt in its cities." This statement is followed in v. 25, introduced by the *waw*-consecutive formation *wayĕhî*, "and it came to pass," which describes the consequences or aftermath of this action, viz., the new population does not fear YHWH and thereby suffers attacks by lions sent by YHWH to punish them for their lack of observance of YHWH's laws. Within this section, v. 25 describes the slaying of the people by the lions, vv. 26–33 describes the continuing syncretism of the people despite the efforts of the king of Assyria to bring an Israelite priest to Beth-El to teach the laws of YHWH to the people, and vv. 34–41 describe the continuing state of corruption that persists in the land "until this day." This last section is particularly important in that it shifts from the past perspective of vv. 24–33 to a portrayal of circumstances in the present. This is evident from the initial statement of the subunit in v. 34, which employs participles instead of *waw*-consecutive and perfect verb forms

> until this day they do (*hēm 'ōśîm*) according to the former laws, but they do not fear YHWH (*'ēnām yĕrē'îm 'et-yhwh*) and they do not do (*wĕ'ēnām 'ōśîm*) according to their statutes and according to their law and according to the Torah and according to the commandment which YHWH commanded the sons of Jacob whose name is Israel.

The narrative states that YHWH made a covenant with these people, but they would not listen and acted according to their former manner. By v. 41, the narrative employs participial forms once again to describe the persistent syncretism of the people living in the land of Israel, "so these nations feared YHWH and also served their graven images; their children likewise, and their children's children— as their fathers did, so they do to this day."

The structure of 2 Kings 17, and its relation to 2 Kings 18–20, may be portrayed as in table 5.1. As the structural discussion indicates, the narrative in 2 Kings 17 must be considered together with 2 Kings 18–20 so that it presents the contrast in the experience of the northern kingdom of Israel and the southern kingdom of Judah when faced with Assyrian invasion. 2 Kings 17:1–5 makes it clear that the Assyrians invaded Israel as a result of King Hoshea's "conspiracy" or alliance with Egypt. This is of particular note in the context of the DtrH in that the Torah of the King in Deuteronomy 17:14–20 states that the king is not to cause the people to return to Egypt to multiply horses for himself. Although the Deuteronomic law is apparently concerned with a trading relationship with the Egyptians, it nevertheless expresses its disapproval of any relationship with Egypt in that Egypt was the source of Israelite slavery. In addition, Egypt played a role in bringing about the split of the kingdom and Jeroboam's kingship in that Solomon married the daughter of Pharaoh, bearing in mind that Solomon's pagan wives played a major role in turning Solomon's heart from YHWH, thereby bringing about the split in the kingdom according to the DtrH narrative. Furthermore, Egypt

TABLE 5.1   Structure of 2 Kings 17 and its relation to 2 Kings 18–20

Regnal evaluation of Hoshea and contrast of Israel and Judah under Assyrian assault	*2 Kings 17–20*
I. Regnal evaluation of the reign of Hoshea	2 Kings 17:1–5
A. Introductory regnal summary	17:1–2
1. Date and duration of reign: nine years from 12th year of Ahaz	17:1
2. Character of reign: evil	17:2
B. Report of Assyrian actions against Hoshea	17:3–5
1. Shalmanezer's subjugation of Hoshea	17:3
2. King of Assyria's arrest of Hoshea for conspiracy	17:4
3. King of Assyria's assault against Israel and siege of Samaria	17:5
II. Contrasting portrayal of Israel and Judah under Assyrian assault	17:6–20:21
A. Concerning Israel: exile of people and persistent corruption of land	17:6–41
1. Concerning exile	17:6–23
a. Report of King of Assyria's exile of Israel in ninth year of Hoshea	17:6
b. Explanation for exile: Israel's sins against YHWH	17:7–23
i. Concerning sins of Israel	17:7–12
ii. Concerning YHWH's warning to Israel and Judah and people's persistent sinning	17:13–19
iii. Concerning YHWH's rejection of Israel	17:20–23
2. Concerning current corruption of land by new inhabitants	17:24–41
a. Report of King of Assyria's resettlement of foreigners in land	17:24
b. Results: continued corruption of land until this day	17:25–41
i. Concerning slaying of people by lions due to their failure to fear YHWH	17:25
ii. Concerning continuing corruption of land following bringing of Israelite priest to Beth-El by King of Assyria	17:26–33
iii. Concerning current situation of land: corruption because people attempt to serve YHWH and their own gods and therefore do not fear YUHWH	17:34–41
B. Concerning Judah under Hezekiah	18–20

offered haven to Jeroboam after he raised his hand against Solomon, and later invaded the land of Israel, stripping the gold shields from the Temple, in the aftermath of the northern revolt against the house of David. Hence, the DtrH portrays the cause of Israel's exile as its lack of faith in YHWH and failure to observe YHWH's commandments. Jeroboam is given the primary share of the blame in 2 Kings 17:6–41 for leading the people astray. 2 Kings 18–20, by contrast, portrays Judah as suffering punishment like Israel at the hands of the Assyrians, but Hezekiah's turn to YHWH in faith spares Jerusalem and the House of David full destruction. Nevertheless, it is only a temporary reprieve as Hezekiah's reception of the Babylonian delegation becomes cause for Isaiah's prophecy that the treasures of the Temple and the king's sons would be carried off as captives to Babylon.

But the narrative is not only concerned with explaining the causes of Israel's exile and contrasting Israel's experience with that of Judah. As the discussion of 2 Kings 17:24–41 indicates, it is also concerned with explaining the current situation of the land of Israel, viz., cultic apostasy on the part of the inhabitants of the land who attempt to serve both YHWH and their own pagan gods. Many take this as an explanation of the origins of the Samaritan community that is portrayed as opposing Ezra and Nehemiah in the postexilic period, and thereby date the final form of the 2 Kings 17 narrative to an exilic edition of the DtrH.[9] The clear concern with pointing to the sins of Judah together with those of Israel in 2 Kings 17:13, 18, and 19, plays a role in this discussion as well, as these references are frequently understood in relation to the Babylonian exile of Judah. The statement in 2 Kings 17:19–20, which follows the reference to Judah's sins in v. 19 with a statement that YHWH rejected "all the seed of Israel, and afflicted them, and gave them into the hand of spoilers, until he had cast them out of his sight," is frequently noted in this regard as a statement of YHWH's rejection of all Israel, including Judah as well as the northern kingdom.[10] Certainly, when read in relation to 2 Kings 18–20, 21, 22–23, and 24–25, which point to the Babylonian exile, these references aid in preparing the reader for this eventual outcome.

But a number of observations raise questions as to whether this narrative, or any part of it, was written to address the Babylonian exile. First, there is no explicit statement concerning the Babylonians or the Babylonian exile. The enemy throughout the entire passage is consistently portrayed as Assyria, not Babylon. Second, the portrayal of the current situation in the land that persists "until this day" does not take account of Jerusalem (or Judah) at all, but focuses entirely on Samaria and Beth-El. This is all the more striking in that Beth-El does not seem to have been involved in the interrelationship between the so-called Samaritans and the Jewish community under Ezra and Nehemiah in the postexilic period, but it is of central concern in the narrative concerning Josiah's reign and reform. Third,

---

9. See n. 5, this chapter.

10. See Brettler, "Text in a Tel," 182; Nelson, *Double Redaction* 56; Provan, *Hezekiah* 70, n. 35. The other occurrences of "seed" in reference to all Israel, including Judah, cited by the studies do not determine the meaning of the expression in this instance, in that none of them appear in Kings.

2 Kings 21:10–15, 23:26–27, and 24:3–4 make it very clear that Manasseh is to blame for the exile of Judah. At this point in the exilic version of the narrative, Manasseh has not appeared and the decision to exile Judah has not yet been made.

Finally, scholars have taken the reference to "all the seed of Israel" in v. 20 as a reference to all the tribes of Israel, since Judah's sins are mentioned in v. 19.[11] In this interpretation, they also note that the term "Israel" can apply either to the northern kingdom or to the totality of the twelve tribes as suggested by the phrase *kol zer'a*, "all the seed."[12] But it is not entirely clear that this statement understands Israel in reference to all twelve tribes. Israel throughout the rest of the passage must be read in relation to the northern kingdom, especially when one considers the immediately following statements in vv. 21–23 concerning YHWH's tearing Israel from the house of David so that they made Jeroboam king. This can hardly include Judah. Likewise, the references to Judah in vv. 13, 18, and 19 also must be examined more closely as the narrative has a clear interest in portraying the sins of Judah as well in order to set up the Assyrian invasion of Judah in 2 Kings 18–20 and the need for Josiah's reforms in 2 Kings 22–23. Verse 13 merely states that Judah was warned together with Israel, which points to a very clear distinction between the terms so that Israel cannot be understood to include Judah. Verse 18 merely states that Judah was left alone after the exile of Israel, again pointing to the distinction between the terms.

The key statement appears in vv. 19–20. Syntax and structure play a determinative role in establishing the meaning of these verses. As noted in the preceding discussion, the structure of this text is governed by the *waw*-consecutive verbal formations that convey the basic narrative sequence of events. Verse 18 is tied into this narrative structure, "and YHWH was provoked (*wayyit'annap*) very much by Israel, and he removed them from his presence; none was left but the tribe of Judah alone." Verse 20 likewise begins with a *waw*-consecutive statement, "and YHWH rejected (*wayyim'as*) all the seed of Israel, and afflicted them, and gave them into the hand of spoilers, until he had cast them away from his presence." Interestingly, v. 19, which mentions Judah's sins, is not tied into the *waw*-consecutive narrative structure at all, but it begins with the conjunctive particle *wĕgam*, "and also (*wĕgam*) Judah did not observe the commandments of YHWH their G-d, and they walked in the statutes of Israel which they did." Given the conjunctive character of the particle *wĕgam*, v. 19 cannot be considered as the grammatical and syntactical antecedent to v. 20, which takes up the exile of all the seed of Israel; rather, it follows up the statement in v. 18, which states that Judah was left alone but not destroyed. When considered in relation to the syntax of these verses, and the considerations brought forward above, v. 19 must only be understood in relation to v. 18 as an incidental statement concerning Judah's sinfulness, but not in relation to v. 20 as a statement concerning its exile. Within the structure of 2 Kings 17:6–41, vv. 13–19 speak of Israel's and Judah's persistence in sins despite YHWH's warning, but vv. 20–23 speak only of Israel's exile. In this manner, the narrative explains the exile of Israel, and prepares the reader

---

11. See n. 10, this chapter.
12. Cf. Brettler, "Text in a Tel," 121.

for the Assyrian invasion of Judah in 2 Kings 18–20 and the reforms of Josiah in 2 Kings 22–23. When read in relation to the exilic edition of the DtrH and its concern for Judah's exile, it also can point forward to that reality as well, but it does not seem to have been written for that purpose.

This points to the likelihood that the present form of the narrative in 2 Kings 17 functions as part of the Josianic edition of the DtrH.[13] This seems clear from the emphasis on the sins of Jeroboam and their impact upon the people of Israel as the cause for the northern kingdom's defeat and exile to Assyria. As Cross aptly demonstrates, the theme of Jeroboam's sins provides the counterpoint to the faithfulness of David and YHWH's promise of an eternal house for David as a basic motif of the Josianic edition of the DtrH.[14] This argument is further buttressed by the portrayal of Josiah as a righteous monarch who corrects the wrongs of his predecessors, including Jeroboam.

The concern with Beth-El in 2 Kings 17:24–41 calls for particular attention in relation to a proposed Josianic edition of the DtrH, particularly because Jeroboam's major sin, corrected by Josiah in 2 Kings 23:15–20, is identified as the building of the Beth-El altar. According to 2 Kings 17:24–41, Beth-El plays a special role in bringing about the situation of apostasy in the land of Israel that persists "until this day" (vv. 34, 41; cf. v. 23). In an effort to educate the newly settled pagan inhabitants of the land of Israel in the laws of YHWH, the king of Assyria commands that an Israelite priest be brought to the land for this purpose. He settles at Beth-El, and teaches the people to fear YHWH. But the narrative reports that the people continue to observe their pagan customs as well as the teachings that emanate from Beth-El. The result is the situation of apostasy described in vv. 29–41, in which the people would serve both YHWH and their own gods. The narrative portrays this as a situation that obviously requires correction, and it portrays Beth-El as the source of the problem. In the context of the Josianic DtrH, this is the situation corrected by King Josiah's destruction of the Beth-El altar.

But questions also may be raised as to whether all of 2 Kings 17 was written in relation to a Josianic edition of the DtrH. The concern with Beth-El and the continued cultic apostasy in the land of Israel enters the narrative only in v. 24 at a relatively late point. This concern plays no role in the narrative through v. 23, which focuses on Israel's apostasy on account of Jeroboam as the cause for the destruction and exile of the northern kingdom. The narrative outlines all the abominations of Israel in relation to the high places, pillars and asherim, incense like the nations, idols, the two calves, the Asherah, the host of Heaven, Baal, burning sons and daughters, divination, sorcery, and so on, but Beth-El does not enter the picture in any explicit way. Only the oblique reference to the molten calves (v. 16) provides any hint of a reference, but only in the context of a catalogue of numerous other sins. The focus is not on Beth-El, but on Jeroboam and his sins. In vv. 20–23, Jeroboam is presented in relation to the separation of the northern tribes from the house of David. Furthermore, the syntax of the narrative changes at v. 24. The

---

    13. Cf. Mordechai Cogan and Hayim Tadmor, *II Kings*, AB 11 (New York: Doubleday, 1988) 241; Cogan and Tadmor, "Israel in Exile—The View of a Josianic Historian," *JBL* 97 (1978) 40–44.
    14. Cross, "Themes."

syntax of the narrative was based upon the *waw*-consecutive verbal formations through v. 23, but the syntax begins to change in vv. 24ff, which indicates a change in writing style. At first, a number of statements employ a combination of a *waw*-consecutive formation of the verb *hāyâ*, "to be," with a participle, viz., "and they were slaying them" (*wayyihĕyû hōrĕgîm bāhem*) in v. 25; "and he was teaching them" (*wayĕhî môreh 'ōtām*) in v. 28; "and each nation was doing" (*wayyihĕyû 'ōśîm gôy*) in v. 29; "and they were fearing YHWH" (*wayyihĕyû yĕrē'îm 'et-yhwh*) in v. 32. Other statements employ perfect verbs (vv. 30–31) or a combination of perfect verbs and participles (v. 33). Verse 34 is formulated completely with participles, "To this day they do (*'ōśîm*) according to the former laws; they do not fear (*yĕrē'îm*) YHWH and they do not do (*'ōśîm*) according to the statutes and the laws and the Torah and the commandment which YHWH commanded the sons of Jacob whose name is Israel." Verses 35–39 employ a combination of *waw*-consecutive and other formations. Verse 40 combines perfect and participle forms, and v. 41 returns to the initial pattern a *waw*-consecutive form of *hāyâ* combined with a participle and combined participle and perfect forms:

> And these nations were fearing (*wayyihĕyû haggôyim hā'ēlleh yĕrē'îm*) YHWH, and their images they were serving (*hāyû 'ōbĕdîm*), also their sons and their daughters just as their fathers did (*'āśû*), they are doing (*hēm 'ōśîm*) until this day.

Although Cross points to the sins of Jeroboam as a major theme of the Josianic DtrH, one must note that Jeroboam plays a relatively minor role in the account of Josiah's reign in that he is mentioned together with the various other kings who committed abominations that Josiah corrected, viz., Solomon, the kings of Judah, Manasseh, Ahab, and so on. Beth-El is a major concern of Josiah's reform, and insofar as Beth-El is established by Jeroboam in the DtrH narrative, Jeroboam becomes a manner of concern in the account of Josiah's reform. But otherwise, Jeroboam receives very little mention in 2 Kings 22–23. With the exception of the Beth-El altar, Jeroboam is of very little concern following 2 Kings 17; he and his dynasty are long gone, and the kingdom that he created is finished. Indeed, 2 Kings 17:1–23 is concerned primarily with the destruction of northern Israel, not with Beth-El.

It is at this point that the relationship between 2 Kings 17 and 2 Kings 18–20 must be considered. As noted previously, 2 Kings 18–20 functions as part of the exilic and Josianic editions of the DtrH, but it also appears to have been written initially as part of a Hezekian edition of the narrative. Insofar as 2 Kings 17 focuses on the demise of the northern kingdom "until this day" (v. 23), it is of importance for comparison with the fate of Judah in 2 Kings 18–20. But 2 Kings 18–20 holds no interest in Beth-El; such interest emerges only in the Josiah narrative. This would suggest that the narrative in 2 Kings 17:1–5, 6–23 is written in relation to the proposed Hezekian edition of the DtrH, but that it was updated for the Josianic edition of the DtrH by the addition of 2 Kings 17:24–41. With the addition of 2 Kings 17:24–41, the Josianic DtrH elaborated on the theme of Jeroboam's sins as the cause for northern Israel's destruction by pointing to the continued influence of Beth-El in bringing about cultic apostasy in the land, and thereby establishing the need for Josiah's destruction of the altar in order to rid the land of this influence. The Hezekian edition is interested in the destruction of northern Israel on account of sins introduced by Jeroboam, and points to Judah as the remnant (2 Kings 17:18) that would be delivered by Hezekiah's faithfulness.

The two major themes of 2 Kings 17, the concern with Jeroboam and the concern with Beth-El and their relation to the proposed Hezekian and Josianic editions of the DtrH, has obvious implications for understanding the narratives concerning the establishment of Jeroboam as king of Israel and his establishment of Beth-El (and Dan) as the state sanctuaries of the northern kingdom in 1 Kings 12 and 13. Insofar as 2 Kings 17 concludes the DtrH presentation of the northern kingdom of Israel and the narratives concerning Jeroboam introduce it, such a relationship will obviously play an important role in determining the overall outlook of the DtrH, in all of its various proposed editions, concerning the character of the northern kingdom of Israel and its place and function in the history of the people of Israel.

The narratives concerning Jeroboam and Beth-El in 1 Kings 12–13 are part of a larger narrative complex that presents the reigns of Rehoboam and Jeroboam in 1 Kings 12:1–14:31.[15] This complex follows immediately upon the narrative concerning the reign of Solomon in 1 Kings 1–11, where the figure of Jeroboam has already been introduced as an opponent of Solomon who was forced to flee to Egypt as a result of his "raising his hand" against Solomon.-1 Kings 11 relates that the prophet Ahijah the Shilonite has conveyed a promise by YHWH that Jeroboam would rule over the northern tribes of Israel as a result of Solomon's apostasy in worshiping foreign gods. Finally, the narrative points to Rehoboam's failure properly to assess the discontent of the northern tribes, thereby leading to the revolt against the house of David, and his failure to contain the revolt once it had broken out. As a result, the primary concern of the narrative appears to be a presentation of Israel's division into two kingdoms.

The structure of this narrative is relatively straightforward. It begins in 1 Kings 12:1 with a notice that Rehoboam ben Solomon traveled north to Shechem to become king of all Israel, and it concludes with the regnal summary concerning Rehoboam in 1 Kings 14:29–31. The overall structure of the narrative is based upon the presentation of Rehoboam's reign, as the presentation of Jeroboam's reign is subordinated to that of Rehoboam. The first major block of the narrative appears in 1 Kings 12:1–14:20, which is tied together by a *waw*-consecutive syntactical sequence and which describes Rehoboam's loss of the northern tribes and the resulting reign of Jeroboam. The second major block is 1 Kings 14:21–28, which interrupts the preceding *waw*-consecutive sequence with the introductory regnal evaluation, "And Rehoboam ben Solomon ruled in Judah." This segment recounts the reign of Rehoboam over Judah following the revolt.-The third major block is 1 Kings 14:29–31, which again interrupts the *waw*-consecutive formulation with a concluding regnal formula for Rehoboam.

---

15. For overviews of the narratives concerning Jeroboam and Rehoboam in 1 Kings, see Long, *1 Kings* 131–165; Simon J. De Vries, *1 Kings*, WBC 12 (Waco, Tex.: Word, 1985) 152–185. See esp. Jörg Debus, *Die Sünde Jerobeams: Studien zur Darstellung Jerobeams und der Geschichte des Nordreichs in der deuteronomistischen Geschichtsschreibung*, FRLANT 93 (Göttingen: Vandenhoeck & Ruprecht, 1967); Knoppers, *Two Nations Under G-d* II 13–120; Lemke, "The Way of Obedience."

Based on the shift of subject matter from Rehoboam to Jeroboam, the presentation of the establishment of the northern kingdom in 1 Kings 12:1–14:20 comprises two basic components: the narrative concerning Israel's revolt against Rehoboam in 1 Kings 12:1–24 and the narrative concerning Jeroboam's reign in 1 Kings 12:25–14:20. The narrative concerning Israel's revolt against Rehoboam proceeds according to the stages of a progressive plot sequence that culminates in the revolt itself. 1 Kings 12:1–5 relates the initial meeting between Rehoboam and the people of Israel at Shechem in which the people question the would-be king concerning his policies. 1 Kings 12:6–11 relates Rehoboam's taking counsel first with his older advisors who tell him to speak softly to the people and win them over and second with his younger companions who tell him to speak harshly and demonstrate that he is in full control of the people. 1 Kings 12:12–17 relate the results of Rehoboam's response to the people. When he informs them that he will increase their burdens from those of his father, they inform him that they have no portion in the house of David and they reject him as king. Finally, 1 Kings 12:18–24 relates Rehoboam's inability to quell the revolt by force, and his decision to accept the revolt after hearing from the Shemaiah that this is the will of YHWH.

The narrative concerning Jeroboam's reign in 1 Kings 12:25–14:20 comprises three basic components: (1) the account of Jeroboam's actions as king in 1 Kings 12:25–13:34, including his establishment of the sanctuary at Beth-El for which he is condemned; (2) the account of Ahijah's announcement of judgment against the house of Jeroboam in 1 Kings 14:1–18 for serving other gods; and (3) the concluding regnal evaluation of Jeroboam in 1 Kings 14:19–20. There is no introductory regnal evaluation for Jeroboam, which is likely due to its subordination to the Rehoboam narrative. 1 Kings 14:19–20 fills this role by noting the duration of Jeroboam's reign, and 1 Kings 12:29 and 13:33–34 point to Jeroboam's sins in order to establish the evil character of his reign.

The account of Jeroboam's actions as king in 1 Kings 12:25–13:34 focuses especially on his establishment of the altar at Beth-El as a demonstration of the sinful character of his reign. It comprises four basic components that focus increasingly upon his actions at Beth-El as a basis for condemnation. The first, 1 Kings 12:25, laconically notes his building Shechem, which served as his residence, and Peniel. The second, 1 Kings 12:26–30, reports his establishment of cultic centers at Beth-El and Dan, beginning with his thoughts that the sanctuary at Jerusalem might undermine his kingdom (vv. 26–27), a report of his building the golden calves at Dan and Beth-El (vv. 28–29), and a concluding statement that this constituted a sin for Israel (v. 30). The major portion of the narrative appears in the third subunit, 2 Kings 12:31–13:32, which relates Jeroboam's actions and experience at Beth-El. 1 Kings 12:31a reports his making Beth-El a high place; 1 Kings 12:32b reports his making priests from the common people who were not Levites; and 1 Kings 12:32–13:32 relates his celebration of Sukkot at Beth-El. 1 Kings 12:32 reports his instituting the celebration of Sukkot in the eighth month, a month after the time when Sukkot is supposed to be observed, and 1 Kings 12:33–13:32 relates what takes place when he ascends the altar to celebrate Sukkot and to dedicate the altar. Following the initial notice of his ascent of the altar, two interrelated stories follow. The first, 1 Kings 13:1–10, relates the condemnation of Jeroboam by an unnamed man of G-d who informs the king that Josiah will one day destroy the illicit altar and sacrifice upon it the illegitimate priests of the high places. The story also relates YHWH's command to the man of G-d not to eat bread or drink water in this place. The second, 1 Kings 13:11–32, relates the man of G-d's encounter with a prophet from Beth-El, who lies to him by stating that YHWH has commanded him to feed the man of G-d.-He thereby tricks the man of G-d into sharing a meal and then condemns him for disobeying the command of YHWH not to eat or drink in this place. The narrative then relates the slaying of the man of G-d by a lion on the road and his burial in the tomb of the Beth-El prophet who would one day be buried there himself. Following the narrative concerning Jeroboam's actions during Sukkot at the Beth-El altar, the fourth major section of 1 Kings 12:25–13:34 appears in 1 Kings 13:33–34, which provides a summation or reprisal of Jeroboam's sinful actions that reiterates his making priests from the common people and thereby causing Israel to sin.

The structure of the narrative may be portrayed as in table 5.2. Within the overall DtrH, 1 Kings 12:1–14:31 relates the origins of the northern kingdom of Israel and establishes the basis by which all of the kings of the north will be condemned as following in the sins of Jeroboam. In addition, it points to the downfall of the house of Jeroboam, whose son Nadab would be assassinated and replaced as king by Baasha ben Ahijah of Issachar (1 Kings 15:25–32). Although the narrative clearly must function as a component of the exilic DtrH, there is no evidence that it was written for this role in that it only lays the basis for the eventual destruction of the northern kingdom of Israel. Although the exile of northern Israel serves as a model for that of Judah in the exilic DtrH, the Jeroboam narratives do not appear to presuppose this goal, and point only to the continuation of the house of David in its rule over the tribe of Judah (1 Kgs 12:20).

As the preceding discussion demonstrates, the present form of the narrative clearly looks forward to the reign of King Josiah as the time when the prophecies of the unnamed man of G-d will be fulfilled, viz., the destruction of the altar at Beth-El by Josiah. In addition, the narrative explains the background for the tomb of the unknown man of G-d that Josiah noted during his destruction of the Beth-El altar in 2 Kings 23:15–20. The Josiah narrative specifically mentions that the man of G-d prophesied Josiah's actions, and it takes care to explain that his bones and those of the northern prophet buried with him were not burned on the altar together with the bones from other tombs in order to desecrate it. Many scholars suspect that the narratives concerning the man of G-d and the Beth-El prophet have an extensive prehistory,[16] but their present forms indicate that they have been formulated and placed in the present context in order to anticipate the narrative concerning Josiah's reforms in 2 Kings 22–23. In this regard, the motif of the lion attacking the man of G-d on the road also recalls the narrative in 2 Kings 17:24–41 concerning the attacks of lions against the newly settled pagan inhabitants of the land of Israel following the Assyrian exile. Insofar as this narrative appears to be the product of the Josianic edition of the DtrH, the narratives in 1 Kings 13:1–32 would also relate to this edition. Furthermore, the narrative concerning the lying

16. Long, *1 Kings* 151–152.

TABLE 5.2 Narrative account concerning the division of the kingdom

The reigns of Rehoboam and Jeroboam	*1 Kings 12:1–14:31*
I. Concerning the establishment of the northern Israelite kingdom	12:1–14:31
A. Israel's revolt against Rehoboam	12:1–24
1. Initial exchange between Rehoboam and Israel at Shechem: question posed to Rehoboam concerning nature of his rule	12:1–24
2. Rehoboam's counsel with older advisors and younger companions	12:6–11
3. Results of Rehoboam's harsh response to people: revolt	12:12–17
4. Rehoboam's inability to quell revolt	12:18–24
B. Jeroboam's reign over northern Israel	12:25–14:20
1. Account of Jeroboam's actions as king: causing Israel to sin	12:25–13:34
a. Building of Shecham and Peniel	12:25
b. Establishment of cultic centers at Dan and Beth-El	12:26–30
i. Jeroboam's thoughts: Jerusalem Temple could undermine rule	12:26–27
ii. Building calves of gold at Dan and Beth-El	12:28–29
iii. Result: sin for Israel	12:30
c. Actions and experience at Beth-El	12:31–13:32
i. Makes Beth-El a high place	12:31a
ii. Makes priests from common people who are not Levites	12:31b
iii. Celebration of Sukkot at Beth-El	12:32–13:32
a) Institutes celebration of Sukkot in eighth month	12:32
b) Ascent of Beth-El altar for Sukkot and results	12:33–13:32
1) Ascent of altar	12:33
2) Condemnation by man of G-d: altar will be destroyed by Josiah	13:1–10
3) Death and burial of man of G-d due to encounter with lying prophet of Beth-El	13:11–32
d. Summation/reprisal of Jeroboam's actions: causes Israel to sin	13:33–34
2. Concerning Ahijah's announcement of judgment against house of Jeroboam for serving other gods	14:1–18
3. Concluding regnal evaluation of Jeroboam	14:19–20
II. Concerning the reign of Rehoboam over Judah	14:21–28
III. Concluding regnal evaluation of Rehoboam	14:29–31

prophet at Beth-El would raise questions concerning the validity of the royal promise made by Ahijah to Jeroboam ben Nebat in 1 Kings 11, and aid in preparing the reader for the reversal of Ahijah's promise in 1 Kings 14.[17] From the perspective of the Josianic DtrH, prophecy in support of Jeroboam is a questionable enterprise and Beth-El is a source of falsehood.

But the question must be posed as to whether the entirety of the present form of the Jeroboam narrative is the product of the Josianic DtrH. There are some

17. For discussion of the issues pertaining to true and false prophecy in this narrative, see Simon J. De Vries, *Prophet against Prophet* (Grand Rapids, Mich.: Eerdmans, 1978); W. Gross, "Lying Prophet and Disobedient Man of G-d in 1 Kings 13: Role Analysis as an Instrument of Theological Interpretation of an Old Testament Narrative Text," *Semeia* 15 (1979) 97–135; F. L. Hossfeld and I. Meyer, *Prophet gegen Prophet; eine Analyse der alttestamentlichen Texte zum Thema: Wahre und falsche Propheten*, BibB 9 (Freibourg: Schweizerisches Katholisches Bibelwerk, 1973).

noteworthy tensions in the narrative. The narrative in 1 Kings 12:31–13:24 focuses especially on the role of Beth-El as the basis for Jeroboam's causing Israel to sin. It is in the context of this narrative that he appoints non-Levitical priests from among the people, initiates the celebration of Sukkot in the eighth month in violation of southern tradition, and receives the condemnation of the unnamed man of G-d, all of which build toward Josiah's reform in 2 Kings 23:15–20. Elsewhere in the narrative, the concerns with Beth-El do not play such a central role. Although Beth-El is mentioned in the summary of Jeroboam's actions in 1 Kings 12:25, 26–30, it appears together with his establishment of Dan, his making of the two golden calves, and his building of Shechem and Peniel. Indeed, the statement concerning Jeroboam's causing Israel to sin in 1 Kings 12:30 notes Dan. Here, Beth-El is not the central issue but one among other concerns. Likewise, when Ahijah delivers the oracle to Jeroboam's wife concerning the impending overthrow of Jeroboam's house, he charges Jeroboam with making other gods and molten images, but he does not mention Beth-El at all. If the narratives in 1 Kings 12:31–13:34 were to be removed, there would remain a coherent narrative that points to Jeroboam's actions as the cause for northern Israel's sin. Beth-El would not play a central role in the narrative, but the essential points would be made just the same.

As noted, the proposed Hezekian edition of the DtrH emphasizes the role of Jeroboam in its account of the collapse of the northern kingdom (2 Kings 17:1–23), and shows an interest in contrasting the experience of the faithless Israel with Judah led by the faithful Hezekiah (2 Kings 18–20). In this regard, it is noteworthy that the Ahijah prophecy in 2 Kings 14:15–16 points forward to the Assyrian exile of Israel as part of its condemnation of Jeroboam. Ahijah's prophecy also takes note of David's righteousness, a theme that is emphasized in the Hezekiah narrative when Hezekiah is compared to his righteous father David. These factors suggest that the basic form of the Jeroboam (and Rehoboam) narrative was written as part of a Hezekian edition of the DtrH that was designed to portray the northern kingdom of Israel as a sinful nation, due to the influence of its founding monarch Jeroboam who led the country into sin by his observance of foreign gods. The narrative apparently was updated and reformulated by the authors of the Josianic edition of the DtrH, who introduced the traditions concerning Jeroboam's experience at the Beth-El altar in 1 Kings 12:31–13:34 in order to point forward to the Josianic destruction of the Beth-El altar as presented in 2 Kings 23:15–20.

Overall, this analysis of 2 Kings 17, 18–20, and 1 Kings 12–14 points to the role played by the presentation of the northern kingdom of Israel in the exilic, Josianic, and Hezekian editions of the DtrH. But the issue is already anticipated in the narrative concerning Solomon in 1 Kings 1–11. As noted, Jeroboam was already introduced into the narrative as an opponent of Solomon who was forced to flee after his treasonous actions against the king. Likewise, the revolt of the northern tribes is clearly motivated by Solomon's unfair treatment of the north in placing the obligation of a state corvée on the northern tribes. This stands in contrast to the narrative in 1 Kings 11, which points to Solomon's apostasy against YHWH as the cause for the split in the kingdom. Clearly, the Solomon narrative also requires examination in order to determine its role and place within the larger DtrH and its various editions.

6

The Critique of Solomon in 1 Kings 1–11 and 2 Samuel 9/11–24

The narrative concerning the reign of King Solomon in 1 Kings 1–11 is especially important in defining the overall perspective of the DtrH.[1] Although it lauds Solomon extensively for his wisdom, power, wealth, and role in building the Temple in Jerusalem, it points to his reign as the ultimate cause of the revolt against the house of David by the northern tribes of Israel and their estrangement

---

1. For overviews and recent discussion of the Solomon narratives, see Long, *1 Kings* 33–131; De Vries, *1 Kings* 1–151; Knoppers, *Two Nations Under G-d* I 57–168; Sweeney, "The Critique of Solomon." See also David A. Glatt-Gilad, "The Deuteronomic Critique of Solomon: A Response to Marvin A. Sweeney," *JBL* 116 (1997) 700–703, who offers his own critique of my study of the presentation of Solomon cited above. Glatt-Gilad questions whether the references to Solomon's marriage to the daughter of Egypt and the role that Egypt plays in undermining the Israelite kingdom by giving shelter to Jeroboam ben Nebat and by Shishak's subsequent invasion of the land consistute a conscious historiographical agenda that presents Solomon in a negative fashion. He is quite correct to note that the various notices concerning Solomon's treatment of the northern tribes do not constitute critique of Solomon in and of themselves and may represent historical reality. But they must be read in relation to the literary framework in which the notices concerning Solomon's marriage to the Egyptian princess and the Pharaoh's sheltering of Jeroboam function as part of the overall DtrH presentation and evaluation of Israel's history, in which Deuteronomy 17:14–20 prohibits intermarriage with the pagan nation. 2 Samuel 7–1 Kings 2 also demonstrate the consequences of the king's failure to live according to divine expectations as articulated throughout the DtrH. Glatt-Gilad misses an essential methodological point, that is, that literary context plays a constitutive role in determining the overall interpretation of text, especially when the literary setting is the result of a redactional reworking of an earlier text (see my *Isaiah 1–39*; *Isaiah 1–4 and the Postexilic Understanding of the Isaianic Tradition*, BZAW 171 [Berlin and New York: de Gruyter, 1988]; and numerous other publications on prophetic literature for extensive discussion of this point). Although the marriage to Pharaoh's daughter was initially intended to demonstrate Solomon's greatness, like his construction of the palace and the Temple, they become elements of critique when read in relation to a literary framework that points to the downfall of the kingdom as a result of his own excesses with foreign women who reportedly turn his heart away from YHWH. Much the

from the Jerusalem Temple. It seems clear that Solomon's abusive policies toward the northern tribes and his inability properly to manage the finances of the
kingdom are causes of the revolt against his son Rehoboam. 1 Kings 1–11 focuses
especially on Solomon's love for foreign women and his willingness to tolerate
and even promote their pagan religious practices as the primary cause for YHWH's
decision to split the kingdom. Because the DtrH identifies Solomon's own religious apostasy as the cause for the split, Solomon thereby bears ultimate responsibility for the religious apostasy of the northern kingdom as well, even though it
is Jeroboam who actually erects the golden calves at the sanctuaries at Dan and
Beth-El. The DtrH maintains that all northern monarchs walk in the sin of Jeroboam,
but Solomon's actions set the stage for those of Jeroboam. Furthermore, Solomon
tolerates the high places and thereby initiates a source of criticism for the Judean
monarchs as well. In short, Solomon's actions cause the fundamental problems
addressed in the DtrH presentation of the history of the people of Israel—that is,
the division of the people into two kingdoms and the apostasy of both the northern and southern kings.

This critique is somewhat anomalous, however, when one considers that
Solomon is the true founder of two of the most important institutions in Israel's
history as portrayed by the DtrH, the Davidic dynasty and the Jerusalem Temple.
He is the true founder of the House of David in that he is the first monarch to
succeed his father and thereby stands as the one who establishes the dynastic succession of the line. The constant references to the Davidic promise of eternal rule
by both YHWH and Solomon in the narrative (1 Kgs 3:3–10; 6:11–13; 8:14–26;
9:1–9; 11:9–13; 11:29–40) demonstrates the importance of this theme in the DtrH
presentation of Solomon. Indeed, the emphasis on the Davidic theme throughout

---

same may be said about the narrative concerning Solomon's worship and vision of YHWH at Gibeon
in 1 Kings 3. Although it appears to have been written as a laudatory narrative, it associates Solomon
with the Canaanite inhabitants of the land when read in relation to Joshua 9–10. Why does Solomon
worship at a Canaanite enclave in Gibeon when the ark is already in Jerusalem? When read in relation to the literary context of the DtrH, the Gibeon narrative points to a flaw in Solomon in that he
tolerates and even endorses a worship site with pagan associations, much as he marries pagan women.
Such a literary association shifts the function of this narrative from praise to critique. Similar observations may be made concerning Solomon's use of the corvée. Although it enables him to build
the Temple, it provides the basis for the revolt of the northern tribes as Jeroboam ben Nebat,
Solomon's overseer for forced labor in the house of Joseph, attempts to revolt against a monarch
who treats his people much as the Pharaoh did in the Exodus tradition. As for Glatt-Gilad's contention that the people participate in the choice of Solomon by acclamation, he fails to note that the
people's acclamation comes only after David chooses Solomon over Adonijah. David makes
the choice, not the people. The dynastic principle is in effect, but David chose a younger son over
the elder without apparent justification and thereby circumvented the normal dynastic succession.
In contrast to Josiah who was placed on the throne by the people of the land, David chooses Solomon
as the next monarch after having fathered him in a very questionable relationship with Bath Sheba.
Unlike Solomon, who worships at Gibeon, engages in various forms of relations with Egypt (and
even acts like the Pharaoh in imposing the corvée), and marries pagan women, Josiah closes sanctuaries outside of Jerusalem, reinstitutes the observance of Passover with its anti-Egyptian overtones, and marries only Israelite women. These considerations demonstrate that Solomon, like other
figures in the DtrH such as Jeroboam, Ahab, or Manasseh, indeed serves as a foil for Josiah.

the DtrH demonstrates its importance to the outlook of the work as a whole.[2] Solomon also is the true founder of the Jerusalem Temple, even though David establishes Jerusalem as the cultic center of Israel by bringing the ark to Jerusalem (2 Sam 6) and selects the site of the Temple (2 Sam 24:18–25). Insofar as the Jerusalem Temple stands as the only legitimate worship site for YHWH in the eyes of the DtrH, Solomon's role is especially significant as founder of the Temple and the dynasty that sponsors it.[3]

The issue is further compounded by the fact that Solomon seems to serve as the model for improper kingship in the "Torah of the King" (Deut 17:14–20) as well.[4] The Torah of the King identifies the qualities of a proper monarch: He should be chosen by YHWH from among the people; he should not multiply horses for himself nor cause the people to return to Egypt for such a purpose; he should not multiply wives for himself because they might turn him from YHWH; he should not multiply silver and gold for himself; and he should read YHWH's Torah. Interestingly, the narrative in 1 Kings 1–11 portrays Solomon as violating every one of these guidelines. He is not chosen by YHWH from among the people, but by David under the influence of Bath Sheba (1 Kgs 1). His great wealth is based in part on his trade with Egypt and Kue in horses and chariotry (1 Kgs 10:26–29). His many foreign wives are the source of his turning away from YHWH (1 Kgs 11:1–8). His ceding twenty Galilean cities to Hiram of Tyre in payment for Phoenician assistance in building the Temple places Israelites under the control of a foreign king (1 Kgs 9:10–14). The narrative throughout stresses Solomon's great wealth, especially in silver and gold gained by trade with foreign nations (1 Kgs 10:1–25). At no point does the narrative ever mention that Solomon reads the Torah, even when he dedicates the Temple during the festival of Sukkot in 1 Kings 8. Although he refers to YHWH's commandments, the dedication speech makes it clear that he depends on YHWH's promise to David as the basis for his relationship with the Deity. Solomon clearly stands as the royal (Davidic) antitype in the Torah of the King and indeed in the DtrH.

Why then should Solomon be subject to such serious criticism in the DtrH? Many have argued that the critique of Solomon in the DtrH stems ultimately from northern sources that were hostile to the Davidic dynasty and brought south in the wake of the northern collapse.[5] But the collapse of the northern kingdom would undermine northern ideology and lend credence to the Davidic traditions, insofar as Judah survived the Assyrian onslaught with the monarchy and Temple intact.

2. Cf. McCarthy, "II Samuel 7"; G. E. Gerbrandt, *Kingship According to the Deuteronomistic History*, SBLDS 87 (Atlanta: Scholars Press, 1986).

3. Cf. Cross, "Themes," 278–285.

4. Cf. Gary Knoppers, "The Deuteronomist and the Deuteronomic Law of the King: A Reexamination of a Relationship," *ZAW* 108 (1996) 329–346, who argues that Deuteronomy 17:14–20 circumscribes the power of the king and that the positive presentation of Solomon is then revised when he is evaluated negatively in relation to this law. See also Baruch Halpern, *The Constitution of the Monarchy in Israel*, HSM 25 (Chico, Calif.: Scholars Press, 1981) 225–232, who argues that the Torah of the King was written at the inception of the monarchy.

5. For example, Nicholson, *Deuteronomy and Tradition* esp. 58–82.

This experience would affirm Judean ideology, not call it into question. The DtrH is fundamentally a Judean work with vested interests in the Davidic dynasty and Jerusalem Temple.[6] The critique of Solomon might well serve an exilic edition of the work that looked to the northern experience as a means to understand the Babylonian exile, but this would require that the critique of Solomon only entered the DtrH at the end of the compositional process. In such a scenario, it would be difficult to explain why northern traditions critical of Solomon would lie dormant for over a century before entering the DtrH. It would be equally difficult to explain the revolt of the northern tribes in earlier editions of the history without Solomon's actions to blame. Although Hezekiah removes the high places tolerated by Solomon, and Josiah resolves many of the other problems created by Solomon, the critique of Solomon in the DtrH must be accepted as a Judean work.

When viewed in relation to the entire DtrH, it is clear that the critique of Solomon functions in relation to exilic and Josianic editions of the DtrH, and possibly in relation to the proposed Hezekian edition as well. Not only do Solomon's actions lead the way to the establishment of the northern kingdom, which dominates the presentation of the DtrH through the commentary on the collapse of the north in 2 Kings 17, but also they prepare the way for the final destruction of the Jerusalem Temple and the exile of the people. Thus, 1 Kings 9:1–9 makes it very clear that if Solomon and the house of David do not observe YHWH commandments, then Israel shall be cut off from the land (v. 7) and the Temple will be destroyed (v. 8). It thereby prepares for the exile of the northern kingdom of Israel (2 Kings 17), as well as for the exile of the southern kingdom of Judah, the destruction of the Jerusalem Temple, and the overthrow of the house of David (2 Kgs 24–25). But the critique of Solomon also functions in relation to the Josianic edition of the DtrH. This is clear from the narrative concerning Jeroboam's dedication of the Beth-El altar (1 Kgs 13) in which a man of G-d comes to Jeroboam and prophesies that eventually King Josiah of Judah will destroy the altar. The narrative concerning Solomon's reign identifies Jeroboam as one of the figures who revolted against the king prior to his death and thereby links the critique of Solomon to the establishment of Jeroboam's kingdom. The fact that a Josianic theme enters into the critique of Jeroboam necessarily ties the critique of Solomon to Josianic interests, insofar as Jeroboam's rise to power presupposes problems in Solomon's reign. This means that the critique of Solomon must either have been written as part of the Josianic DtrH or it was at least presupposed by the Josianic DtrH. In this regard, the notice of Solomon's worship at the high places, which plays such an important role in arguments for an edition that concludes with the reign of Hezekiah who removes the high places, suggests that the latter is the case. This, of course, does not exclude the possibility that the Solomon narrative was elaborated on by both Josianic and exilic DtrH writers. Nevertheless, it points to the critique of Solomon as a foundational account in any edition of the DtrH because it defines the cause of primary problems in all editions of the history. In

---

6. Cf. Clements, "Deuteronomy and the Jerusalem Cult Tradition," who argues that Deuteronomy reflects Judean interests.

considering the role of the critique of Solomon within the DtrH in all of its editions, one must ask why a Judean work would present the founder of the Davidic dynasty and the Jerusalem Temple in such a negative light.

An analysis of the structure and genre of the Solomon narrative is fundamental to determining its overall outlook and role in the final form of the DtrH, and to identifying criteria for the reconstruction of earlier editions. Although the narrative formally begins in 1 Kings 3:1, immediately following the notice in 2 Kings 2:46 that the kingdom was established in Solomon's hands, the account of Solomon's succession to the throne in 1 Kings 1–2 must be considered as well. These chapters, of course, form part of the so-called Succession Narrative in 2 Samuel 9/11–20, 1 Kings 1–2, which describe the circumstances that lead to Solomon's birth and accession to the throne over his older brothers, but they also include important aspects of Solomon's early reign as he established his power. The narrative concludes in 1 Kings 11:41–43 with a typical concluding regnal resume that refers to the reader to the Book of the Acts of Solomon, the duration of his reign, his burial, and the succession of his son Rehoboam.

The overall structure and genre of the narrative is more complicated than usual because it lacks the typical introductory regnal resume. Nevertheless, a sequence of topical concerns appears to define the structure of the narrative, and constant references to the character of Solomon's actions demonstrate its interest in evaluation. At the most basic level, the narrative contains two major portions. The first is the account of Solomon's accession to the throne in 1 Kings 1–2, which focuses on the transition between David and Solomon and culminates in the full establishment of Solomon's rule. The second is the evaluation of Solomon's reign proper, which relates the major events and evaluates Solomon's reign once he is established in power. It is noteworthy that it begins and ends with references to Solomon's marriages to foreign women and his own religious apostasy that results from his marriages (1 Kgs 3:1–2, 3; 11:1–8), which ultimately play the primary role in dividing his kingdom according to the DtrH presentation (1 Kgs 11:9–40). But it is also noteworthy that this section begins and ends with elements that are typical of the introductory and concluding regnal resumes of the books of Kings. Although it lacks a reference to Solomon's age at accession, the duration of his reign, and the identity of his mother,[7] 1 Kings 3:3 describes Solomon as "walking in the statutes of David his father; only he sacrificed and burnt incense at the high places," a familiar characteristic of the initial evaluation of the kings of Judah. As noted, the concluding regnal resume appears in 1 Kings 11:41–43, which also contains the reference to the duration of his reign that is characteristic of the introductory regnal resumes.

Although many scholars group 1 Kings 3:1–3 together as a single unit,[8] v. 3 must be considered separately from vv. 1–2. Verses 1–2 are concerned primarily with Solomon's marriage to the daughter of Pharaoh and the people's worship at

---

7. The duration of his reign appears in the concluding regnal resume (1 Kgs 11:42), and the account of his accession to the throne identifies Bath Sheba as his mother.

8. See Long, *1 Kings* 61–62.

the high places as a means to criticize Solomon's reign in keeping with the criticisms leveled against him in 1 Kings 11. Verse 3 also makes reference to the high places, but its reference to Solomon's walking in the statutes of David enables the verse to function as an introduction to the narrative concerning Solomon's wisdom. It thereby serves as a means to praise Solomon, not to condemn him. In this case, the reference to Solomon's worship at the high places explains his presence at Gibeon where YHWH appears to him in a dream, and thereby serves as the introduction to Solomon's display of wisdom that results in YHWH's blessings. Consequently, 1 Kings 3:1–2 serves as the initial evaluation of Solomon's reign, 1 Kings 11:1–40 serves as the concluding evaluation of Solomon's reign, and 1 Kings 3:3–28, which contains various illustrations of Solomon's wisdom, then forms a unit concerned with depicting Solomon's wisdom. Interestingly enough, the narrative in 1 Kings 10 concerning the Queen of Sheba's visit to Solomon revisits this theme as she comes to test his wisdom.

Following the narrative concerning Solomon's wisdom in 1 Kings 3:3–28, the account of Solomon's reign continues with a progressive description of Solomon's power and activities through 1 Kings 5:14. Thus, 1 Kings 4:1–20 begins with a statement that "King Solomon was king over all Israel," and continues with a description of his administrative officers and their functions before concluding with the statement, "Judah and Israel were as many as the sand of the sea; they ate and drank and were happy." 1 Kings 5:1–14 begins with the statement that "Solomon was ruler over all the kingdoms from the Euphrates to the land of the Philistines and until the border of Egypt, they were bringing tribute and serving Solomon all the days of his life." Verses 9–14 then describe Solomon's wealth, concluding with an extensive description of his wisdom that culminates in the statement, "and there came from all the peoples to hear the wisdom of Solomon from all the kings of the land who heard his wisdom." This statement thereby returns to the wisdom theme of 3:3–28 and defines 3:3–5:14 as a single section concerned with Solomon's wisdom and power.

1 Kings 15:15–32 then begins a series of subunits concerned with the building of the Temple by describing the relationship between Solomon and Hiram of Tyre, who provided Solomon with the expertise to build the Temple. 1 Kings 6–7 describe the details of Solomon's building operations, including both the Temple and his own palace. 1 Kings 8 describes the dedication ceremony for the Temple. 1 Kings 9 concludes the section on the building of the Temple by turning to the aftermath of Solomon's building operations. YHWH appears to him a second time in vv. 1–9 to warn him that Israel will be exiled and the Temple destroyed if he and his successors do not observe YHWH's commandments. Verses 10–22 describe the measures that Solomon took to pay off his debts for his building operations, and vv. 23–25 relate other details of Solomon's subsequent activities, concluding with the statement that "he completed the house (Temple)."

1 Kings 9:26–28 describes Solomon's fleet. 1 Kings 10:1–13 describes the visit of the Queen of Sheba, who is greatly impressed by Solomon's wealth and wisdom. 1 Kings 10:14–29 concludes the section with further descriptions of Solomon's wealth and wisdom. 1 Kings 11:1–40 resumes the concern with Solomon's marriages to foreign women and his cultic apostasy as the cause

for the breakup of the kingdom after his death. It thereby takes up the concerns of 1 Kings 3:1–2. Finally, 1 Kings 11:41–43 constitutes the concluding regnal resume.

The structure of the narrative concerning Solomon's reign in 1 Kings 1–11 may be outlined as in table 6.1. This analysis of the structure, genre, and outlook of the Solomon narrative makes several things clear. First, the critique of Solomon appears to be placed primarily at the beginning and end of the narrative. It appears initially in the account of Solomon's accession to the throne in which Bath Sheba, supported by Nathan, sees to her son's accession by manipulating the aged David into agreeing that he had promised the throne to Solomon rather than to Adonijah. Likewise, she seems to play a role in the killing of Solomon's rival Adonijah when she conveys to Solomon his request for Abishag, the concubine of David, which is understood to be a claim on the throne. The narrative does not criticize Solomon for this action, or for his role in the killings of Shimei and Joab and the expulsion of Abiathar, but these actions raise questions about the righteousness of a monarch who comes to the throne in the midst of a bloody purge. Otherwise, the notices concerning Solomon's marriage to the daughter of Pharaoh in 1 Kings 3:1, in violation of fundamental Dtr commands against returning the people to Egypt (Deut 17:16), and his worship at the high places (1 Kgs 3:3;

TABLE 6.1   Structure of the narrative concerning Solomon's reign in 1 Kings 1–11

Regnal account of Solomon's reign	*1 Kings 1–11*
I. Regnal account of Solomon's succession to the throne	1-2
II. Regnal evaluation of Solomon's reign	3–11
A. Initial notice of Solomon's marriage to the daughter of Pharaoh and the people's worship at the high places	3:1–2
B. Concerning Solomon's wisdom and power	3:3–5:14
1. Concerning Solomon's wisdom	3:3–28
2. Concerning Solomon's rule over all Israel	4:1–20
3. Concerning Solomon's rule over all kingdoms from the Euphrates to the border of Egypt	5:1–14
C. Concerning Solomon's building of the Temple and his palace	5:15–9:25
1. Concerning Solomon's preparations with Hiram of Tyre	5:15–9:25
2. Concerning the building of the Temple, Palace, and environs	6–7
3. Concerning the dedication ceremony for the Temple	8
4. Concerning the aftermath of the building	9:1–25
a. YHWH's warning to obey commandments	9:1–9
b. Solomon's payment of debts	9:10–22
c. Miscellaneous details	9:23–25
D. Concerning Solomon's wealth and power	9:26–10:29
1. Solomon's fleet at Ezion Geber that brings gold from Ophir	9:26–28
2. The visit of the Queen of Sheba	10:1–13
3. Further descriptions of Solomon's wealth and wisdom	10:14–29
E. Concerning opposition to Solomon's rule	11:1–40
1. Solomon's foreign wives and religious apostasy	11:1–8
2. YHWH's anger and raising of adversaries	11:9–40
F. Concluding regnal resume	11:41–43

cf. 3:2), in violation of the Dtr centralization law (Deut 12:1–14), introduce the narrative, but they play little role in the overall presentation of his reign.[9] Both issues also reappear at the end of the narrative in 1 Kings 11:1–8, thereby provoking YHWH to raise adversaries against Solomon in preparation for taking the bulk of the kingdom away from the Davidic house following Solomon's death. It is noteworthy that both concerns appear to come together in the Dtr law prohibiting marriage to the daughters of the Canaanite nations because such unions lead to apostasy (Deut 7:1–6). Although Egypt is not one of the seven Canaanite nations mentioned in the law, the consequences are identical as presented in the DtrH. There is, however, very little critical material in the narrative concerning Solomon's reign. 1 Kings 5:27–32 makes reference to Solomon's raising a corvée of forced labor in Israel to assist in building the Temple, but this does not appear designed to criticize Solomon; it is only a description of the means by which he carried out the building activities. The notices concerning Solomon's ceding of twenty Galilean cities to Hiram as a means to pay his bills (1 Kgs 9:10–14), and the second notice concerning Solomon's use of forced labor (1 Kgs 9:15–22), which emphasizes that Israelite were not employed as slaves, again does not appear to be critical, but simply describes the means by which Solomon accomplished his goals. The portrayal of Solomon in 1 Kings 3:3–10:29 is laudatory and emphasizes his wisdom, power, and great wealth.

Second, it is noteworthy that although the framework of the narrative emphasizes Solomon's love of foreign women and his resulting cultic apostasy as the cause for the division of the kingdom, the narrative concerning the revolt of the northern tribes against Rehoboam seems to stress Solomon's treatment of the northern tribes. When Rehoboam comes to Shechem in 1 Kings 12 to have his kingship confirmed by the northern tribes, the people ask him to lighten the burden that Solomon imposed on them. When Rehoboam states that he will be even harsher than Solomon, the people revolt and Rehoboam is unable to regain control. This highlights issues raised above in the central core of the Solomon narratives as the true cause of the revolt even though the DtrH attempts to point to Solomon's marriages to foreign women and religious apostasy. Thus, Solomon's forced labor in Israel (1 Kgs 5:27–32) appears in fact to be a primary cause of the revolt. Although the phrase "all Israel" in 1 Kings 5:27 appears to include Judah, the employment of the corvée in Lebanon would suggest that the northern tribes would bear a disproportionately greater share of the burden. Likewise, Solomon's ceding twenty Galilean cities to Hiram to pay his debts imposes a burden on the northern tribes once again, as these cities were located in the general vicinity of the territories of Asher, Zebulun, and Naphtali. Finally, the description in 1 Kings 4:7–19 of the support given by the tribes to Solomon's court indicates that the northern tribes again bore a disproportionate share of the burden of supporting the monarchy. Eleven of the twelve tax districts were from the northern tribes, whereas only one was from Judah. Solomon's kingdom was supposedly a two-

---

9. Other references to Solomon's marriage to the daughter of Pharaoh appear in 1 Kings 7:8, 9:16, and 9:24, but they seem to play little role in the overall critique of Solomon.

part federation of Judah and Israel (1 Kgs 11:20; cf. 2 Sam 5:1–5),[10] but the northern tribes paid eleven shares of support to every one share paid by Judah. Given Solomon's Judean tribal affiliation, this could hardly have endeared the monarch to his constituents north of Jerusalem. Furthermore, the account of Jeroboam's opposition to Solomon appears to turn on the king's unfair treatment of the northern tribes, as Jeroboam is identified as an officer of Solomon in charge of forced labor by the house of Joseph (1 Kgs 11:28). Perhaps Jeroboam had his fill of serving a Judean king who abused his own people.

Third, the concerns of the exile seem to play very little role in the overall presentation of Solomon's reign. Exilic concerns appear in only one place in the narrative, in the account of YHWH's second appearance to Solomon in 1 Kings 9:1–9, which threatens the exile of the people of Israel from the land and the destruction of the Temple if Solomon and his descendants do not observe YHWH's commands. Many view the present form of this narrative as the product of an exilic writer in that its reference to the potential destruction of the Temple anticipates the latter parts of the history, which take up the theme of the Babylonian exile in accounts of the reigns of Hezekiah (2 Kgs 20:12–19), Manasseh (2 Kgs 21:10–15), Josiah (2 Kgs 23:26–27), and the last four kings of Judah (2 Kgs 24–25).[11] Nevertheless, the statement only anticipates the potential destruction of the Temple; it does not presuppose that such destruction actually takes place. In this respect, the statement is entirely in keeping with the narrative concerning YHWH's promise of an eternal dynasty to David in which it is made clear that YHWH does not need the Temple, nor does YHWH guarantee its eternal security. Otherwise, the reference to the removal of "Israel" from the land (1 Kgs 9:7) could very easily refer to the northern tribes in the context of an earlier edition of the DtrH. The narrative does after all stress YHWH's interest in maintaining fidelity to the Davidic promise by leaving one tribe in the hands of David's descendants even when the northern tribes are wrested from Davidic hands and given to Jeroboam (1 Kgs 11:9–13, 29–39). Otherwise, the threatened exile of Israel makes perfect sense in relation to the exile of the northern kingdom outlined in 2 Kings 17. Once the northern tribes revolted from Rehoboam and turned to Solomon, the DtrH stresses that they were lost as every monarch followed in the paths of Jeroboam and caused Israel (the northern kingdom) to sin. The fact that the narrative concerning YHWH's anger at Solomon in 1 Kings 11:9 points out that YHWH appeared to Solomon twice demonstrates that 1 Kings 9:1–9 is integrated into the overall narrative of the critique of Solomon.

Fourth, the critique of Solomon in 1 Kings 1–11 is tied closely to Jeroboam's attempted revolt and his subsequent flight to Egypt for sanctuary. In this regard, the notices concerning Solomon's marriage to the daughter of Pharaoh cannot be ignored. Solomon's marriage to the daughter of Pharaoh leads him to apostasy, his apostasy leads YHWH to raise adversaries against him. Jeroboam, one of his key adversaries, flees to Egypt for protection, and Egypt thereby plays an impor-

---

10. For a discussion of the organization of the Davidic kingdom, see Albrecht Alt, "The Monarchy in the Kingdoms of Israel and Judah," in *Essays on Old Testament History and Religion*, translated by R. A. Wilson (Garden City, N.Y.: Doubleday, 1967) 311–335.

11. For example, Long, *1 Kings* 108–111.

tant role both in causing the both apostasy that leads to the collapse and protecting a revolutionary who eventually becomes king of the rebellious new kingdom. The significance of this perspective also must be weighed against the fact that Pharaoh Shishak of Egypt then attacks Rehoboam following the revolt of the northern tribes, and forces him to pay a heavy tribute from the treasuries of the Temple and the king's house (1 Kgs 14:25–28). Considering that Shishak is reported to have given Jeroboam sanctuary during the reign of Solomon (1 Kgs 11:40), the irony of Solomon's marriage to the daughter of Pharaoh is complete, especially when considered against the Dtr injunction against the king's leading the people to Egypt and multiplying wives for himself (Deut 17:16–17). The fact that Jeroboam serves as such a foil to Josiah in the DtrH, insofar as Jeroboam's dedication of the Beth-El altar becomes the occasion for the prediction of Josiah's reforms (1 Kgs 13), suggests that the theme of the critique of Solomon for his cultic apostasy and marriage to the daughter of Pharaoh may well be attributed to a Josianic redaction. The fact that Egypt was one of Josiah's primary enemies, as indicated by his death at the hands of Necho and by his emphasis on the anti-Egyptian Passover tradition, suggests that this is a likely possibility.

Overall, these considerations point to a narrative that does not stand as a fundamental core to an exilic edition of the DtrH; 1 Kings 9:1–9 can certainly be read in relation to the concerns of the exile, but it contains reference only to the potential destruction of the Temple. Otherwise, the threat of exile could certainly apply to the northern kingdom of Israel, and thereby serves preexilic Judean interests.[12] Instead, they point to a narrative that, in its present form, serves the interests of a Josianic edition of the DtrH, because it is organized to point to the accession of Jeroboam, who serves as a primary foil to Josiah in the DtrH. In this case, the critique of Solomon in the DtrH plays a major role in preparing the reader for the accession of Jeroboam as king of northern Israel. This is especially noteworthy in that the presentation of the critique of Solomon as a religious apostate who was unduly influenced by his foreign wives appears to have been composed as a frame for an earlier edition in 3:3–10:29 that lauded Solomon for his wisdom and wealth, but pointed to certain problems in his economic management and treatment of the northern tribes that seem actually to have caused the northern revolt.

Likewise, these factors point to a narrative concerning Solomon's reign that has been framed. Insofar as 1 Kings 3:3–10:29 present Solomon in largely laudatory terms but identify his economic policies as the cause of the split in the northern kingdom, the framework material in 1 Kings 1–2; 3:1–2; and 11:1–40 appears to be the work of a later redaction that reworked an earlier Solomon narrative.[13]

---

12. Scholars sometimes point to 1 Kings 8:25–26, 46–51 as exilic additions in that they refer to the conditional nature of Davidic rule over Israel and the potential for the exile of Israel from the land and their return after repentance. But these statements can easily apply only to Judean perspectives concerning the northern kingdom and the possibility of the north's return to the south. These texts therefore do not require an exilic setting.

13. Cf. Knoppers, *Two Nations Under G-d* I 137–139, who notes the transition evident in 1 Kings 11, but argues throughout his study that the basic DtrH account of Solomon's reign stems from the time of King Josiah.

In this regard, it is important to consider the role that the account in 1 Kings 1–2 of Solomon's accession to the throne plays in relation to the critique of Solomon that frames the regnal evaluation of his reign in 1 Kings 3–11 and points to the rise of Jeroboam. Scholars do not normally treat this narrative in relation to 1 Kings 3–11 because it forms the conclusion to the Succession Narrative or Court History in 2 Samuel 9/11–20, 1 Kings 1–2, which constitutes a completely different literary source from that of the rest of Kings. Nevertheless, it must be considered in relation to 1 Kings 3–11. It stands in place of the normal introductory regnal resume that identifies the mother of the new king, Bath Sheba in the case of Solomon, and it demonstrates the role that she plays in bringing her son to the throne. Furthermore, the questionable means by which this decision is made— certainly Solomon is not the choice of YHWH or the people, but of an aged and senile David, manipulated by Bath Sheba—must be considered in relation to the critical portrayal of Solomon that frames 1 Kings 3–11. Likewise, the slaughter or removal of his opponents, Adonijah, Shimei, Joab, and Abiathar, often on rather trumped up charges, hardly inspires confidence in Solomon as a just monarch. The narrative of Solomon's succession in 1 Kings 1–2 thereby prepares the reader for the critique of his reign that follows. Insofar as it forms the conclusion to the Succession Narrative, the role of 2 Samuel 9–20 must be considered as well.

Beginning with Rost's initial identification and study of the work,[14] scholars have generally maintained that the purpose of the Succession Narrative is to legitimize Solomon's accession to the throne in place of his older brothers. But this is somewhat anomalous in that it does so by presenting Solomon's accession as the ultimate result of David's adulterous affair with Bath Sheba; the murder of her husband Uriah the Hittite to cover up the affair; and David's inability to control the impetuous actions of his sons Amnon, Absalom, and Adonijah. Ironically, the turmoil among the Davidic sons is also caused by sexual misconduct, in that Amnon rapes his half sister Tamar, and is killed for this crime by her brother Absalom when David fails to discipline his miscreant son appropriately. Absalom's resentment against his father leads in turn to his revolt against David, and the near destruction of the empire. When Absalom is killed by David's soldiers, his mourning for his son nearly causes another revolt among his soldiers and demonstrates his inability to appreciate the sacrifices made for him by his supporters. Nevertheless, the deaths of Amnon and Absalom remove two major obstacles to Solomon's accession to the throne. The portrayal of Solomon's parents in such a manner hardly does credit to Solomon, even though he was legitimately born after the marriage of David and Bath Sheba. Likewise, Bath Sheba's and Nathan's manipulation of David to put Solomon on the throne does not enhance his reputation. Altogether, the Succession Narrative explains how Solomon came to the throne, but it does

---

14. Leonhard Rost, *Die Überlieferung von der Thronnachfolge Davids*, BWANT 42 (Stuttgart: Kohlhammer, 1926); ET: *The Succession to the Throne of David*, translated by M. D. Rutter and D. Gunn, HTIBS 1 (Sheffield: Almond, 1982). For the history of scholarship since Rost's study, see P. Kyle McCarter, *II Samuel*, AB 9 (Garden City, N.Y.: Doubleday, 1984) 9–11; Walter Dietrich and Thomas Naumann, *Die Samuelbücher*, ErFor 287 (Darmstadt: Wissenschaftliche Buchgesellschaft, 1995) 169–295.

so in a manner that raises many questions about his parents, the Davidic dynasty in general, and indeed of Solomon himself.

To understand the reasons for such questions, it is necessary to consider the major changes that take place among the key personnel of the Davidic court as a result of Solomon's accession to the throne. Obviously, Solomon comes to the throne in place of his older brothers, Amnon, Chileab, Absalom, Adonijah, Shephatiah, and Ithream, all of whom were born in Hebron, David's first capital during his rule over the tribe of Judah alone (2 Sam 3:2–5). The Succession Narrative accounts for the deaths of Amnon, Absalom, and Adonijah, but it is silent concerning Chileab, Shephatiah, and Ithream; apparently the writer of the narrative did not consider them to be factors in the succession. Likewise, Bath Sheba becomes queen mother when Solomon ascends the throne, and displaces potential rivals among David's earlier wives from his Hebron days—Ahinoam, Abigail, Maacah, Haggith, Abital, and Eglah. Joab, David's military commander from his early days at Ziklag and Hebron who played such a major role in bringing David to power and even in capturing Jerusalem, is killed and replaced by Benaiah. The High Priest Abiathar, who escaped from the massacre of the priests at Nob and supported David throughout his rise to power in Jerusalem, is expelled and replaced by Zadok. Finally, the prophet Gad, who assisted in David's escape from Saul (1 Sam 22) and who advised David to build an altar at the threshing floor of Araunah, the future site of the Temple, disappears whereas the prophet Nathan comes to prominence. A very clear pattern emerges in relation to this shift in personnel in that all of those who are removed from the scene are David's family and supporters from his days prior to his ascent to power in Jerusalem. All of those who emerge in power following Solomon's accession to the throne are people who seem to appear only after David's transfer of the throne to Jerusalem. Benaiah served David as commander of the Cherethites and Pelethites (2 Sam 8:18; 20:23), perhaps to be identified as David's bodyguard (2 Sam 23:20–23), but he plays no role in David's Hebron period. Nathan and Zadok appear only after David arrives in Jerusalem. David sees Bath Sheba only after he is established in Jerusalem, and of course, Solomon is born in Jerusalem. It would appear that the death of Adonijah brought to an end a power struggle within the house of David between a faction centered around Adonijah and consisting of David's supporters from his Hebron days and another faction centered around Bath Sheba and Solomon consisting of new Davidic supporters from the time following his move to Jerusalem.

This shift is noted by G. Jones, who attempts to argue that the Jerusalem faction is a Jebusite group that gained control of the house of David and set the course for the future of the Davidic dynasty.[15] Although his contention that Bath Sheba is the center of a Jebusite group cannot be sustained for lack of evidence, it does point to the Succession Narrative's portrayal of a very substantial change that takes place in the house of David that sees the elimination of the entire Hebron-based faction of the Davidic line. The significance of this change for the overall portrayal of the Davidic house in the DtrH becomes clear when one notes that the

---

15. Jones, *The Nathan Narrative*.

means by which David became king over both Judah and Israel during his time at Hebron. According to 2 Samuel 2:1–4, the "men of Judah" anointed him as king when he came to Hebron, and 2 Samuel 5:1–5 states that "all the tribes of Israel" came to David at Hebron and requested that he become their king. In the latter instance, the "elders of Israel" acted on behalf of the people to conclude a covenant with David that made him king of all Israel in Hebron. David shifted his rule to Jerusalem only after he was anointed king over all the tribes in order to appease both segments of his kingdom: Judah and the northern tribes of Israel. Solomon, by contrast, is never designated king by the people; he is designated only by David and announces to the people that he rules as a result of YHWH's promise to establish the Davidic house. Ironically, the revolt against Rehoboam took place when "all Israel" came to Shechem to make Rehoboam king. Apparently, Rehoboam was still subject to popular approval and failed to gain it when he refused to lighten the burden imposed by his father on the people of the northern tribes. Instead, they designated Jeroboam as their monarch (1 Kgs 12:20). The DtrH presents appointment by the people as an important element in the legitimate selection of kings, but Solomon's selection by David clearly disrupts this principle and thereby calls his rule into question.

The significance of this disruption is best understood in relation to the DtrH presentation of the selection of Josiah as king. As noted, 2 Kings 22–23 idealizes Josiah with unqualified and unparalleled praise as the greatest of all the Davidic monarchs who not only walks in the ways of David, but fills a model of ideal Mosaic rule as well (2 Kgs 22:2; 23:25). In addition, Josiah sets right the major shortcomings of monarchs in the DtrH including those of Ahaz, Manasseh, Jeroboam, and Solomon. He also reinstituted the celebration of Passover, which had not been celebrated since the days of the Judges (2 Kgs 23:21–23). This action very pointedly bypasses the periods of both David and Solomon, and extends back to Joshua (Josh 5:10–12).

It is therefore noteworthy that the *'am hā'āreṣ* "people of the land" bring Josiah to the throne following a failed attempt at a coup d'état against the Davidic house that saw the assassination of his father Amon (2 Kgs 21:23–24). As portrayed in the DtrH, the *'am hā'āreṣ* generally acted in times of crisis to install a Davidic monarch on the throne following the assassination of his predecessor.[16] Although the people of the land do seem to act in time of political crisis, this observation obscures the fact that popular legitimization of the monarch appears to be foun-

---

16. S. Talmon, "The Judaean 'Am ha'Ares' in Historical Perspective," *Fourth World Congress of Jewish Studies. Papers. Volume I* (Jerusalem: World Union of Jewish Studies, 1967) 71–76. The *'am hā'āreṣ* also acted to install Joash following the assassination of Ahaziah (2 Kgs 11:17–20), Azariah/Uzziah following the assassination of Amaziah (2 Kgs 14:21), and Jehoahaz following the death of Josiah (2 Kgs 23:30). See further, H. Tadmor, "'The People' and Kingship in Ancient Israel: The Role of Political Institutions in the Biblical Period," *Cahiers d'histoire mondiale* 11 (1968) 3–23; T. Ishida, "'The People of the Land' and the Political Crises in Judah," *AJBI* 1 (1975) 23–38; T. N. D. Mettinger, *King and Messiah: The Civil and Sacral Legitimation of the Israelite Kings*, ConBibOT 8 (Lund: Gleerup, 1976) 111–150, esp. 124–129; C. R. Seitz, *Theology in Conflict: Reactions to the Exile in the Book of Jeremiah*, BZAW 176 (Berlin and New York: Walter de Gruyter, 1989) 42–65.

dational to the concept of legitimate kingship in the DtrH. Both Saul and David
were selected by the people as well as by YHWH, and Rehoboam was rejected by
the people of the northern tribes in favor of Jeroboam. Solomon was not selected
by the people. But the northern tribes were not condemned for their rejection of
the house of David; this was divinely legitimized by the oracle of Ahijah the
Shilonite to Jeroboam in the DtrH presentation (1 Kgs 11:29–39). Rather, they
were condemned for cultic apostasy and rejection of the Jerusalem Temple (1 Kgs
12:25T–14:20; 2 Kings 17). Although kings prior to Josiah were selected by the
people, ideal kingship did not follow. Both Joash and his son Ahaziah were
assassinated in attempted coups (2 Kgs 12:19–21; 14:17–22), and Azariah's
kingship was impaired by his leprosy. In the eyes of the DtrH, any potential gains
by these monarchs were negated by Ahaz's acceptance of Assyrian patronage
and his building of a foreign altar in the Jerusalem Temple (2 Kgs 16:10–20).
In short, although David serves as the model against whom the righteousness of
the Davidic kings is measured, Josiah is the ideal monarch in the DtrH who institutes leadership like Moses and Joshua. Josiah is legitimated by the people,
and his reforms correct the problems manifested throughout Israel's history in
the eyes of the DtrH.

This raises some rather obvious considerations concerning the redactional
character of the DtrH narrative concerning the reign of Solomon and the Succession Narrative. First, it seems clear that the entire Succession Narrative, including 2 Samuel 9/11–20 and 1 Kings 1–2, must be read in relation to the narrative
concerning Solomon's reign in 1 Kings 3–11. The Succession Narrative provides
the background for understanding the critique of Solomon, in that it points to a
shift in the monarchy that sees the elimination of the entire Hebron-based faction
of the Davidic house, that was legitimately chosen by the people of both the southern and northern tribes, in favor of a Jerusalem-based faction that appears only
after David unites the country and that was not chosen by the people. Furthermore, it points to David's affair with Bath Sheba, including his sexual misconduct and his commission of murder, as the ultimate cause of a course of events
that leads to Solomon's accession to the throne. This must be read in relation to
Solomon's actions as king, viz., he puts to death or expels all of his major opponents in securing his position on the throne, and his passion for foreign women
leads him into apostasy. In short, Solomon's actions as monarch mirror in character those of his father David in the Succession Narrative. As in the case of
David, Solomon's conduct presents problems for both the monarch and the kingdom. Ultimately, David's actions with Bath Sheba stand behind the critique of
Solomon in 1 Kings 3–11 and therefore play a role in the present form of the
DtrH in prompting the problems that lead to the division of the kingdom after
Solomon's death.

Not only does the Succession Narrative play an important role in leading to
the DtrH presentation of the critique of Solomon and the division of the kingdom,
it is also well integrated into the material concerning the rise of David that precedes it. Although most scholars tend to interpret the Succession Narrative in isolation from its immediate literary context in the DtrH, Van Seters points to a number
of associations that demonstrate that the Succession Narrative builds upon prior

DtrH traditions, especially those concerning David and Saul in 1–2 Samuel.[17] It thereby effects the presentation of a coherent transition from David's rise to Solomon's reign that explains the demise of the house of Saul and points to David's corrupt nature. He notes, for example in relation to the conclusion of the Succession Narrative, that the portrayal of David's instructions to Solomon in 1 Kings 2:1–4 follows the typical Dtr pattern of Moses instructing Joshua (Deut 31:7–8), Joshua instructing the people (Joshua 23), and Samuel warning the king and people about the potential abuses of royal power (1 Samuel 12).[18] Whereas each of the previous figures counsels his listeners to follow Deuteronomic commandments, David advises Solomon to kill or banish his opponents, which hardly presents either David or Solomon as an ideal leader in the perspective of the DtrH. Likewise, the statement in 1 Kings 2:10–12 that David "lay down with his fathers . . . and Solomon sat upon the throne of David his father and his kingdom was firmly established" (cf. 1 Kgs 2:24) reflects the language of the dynastic promise in 2 Samuel 7:12 and further demonstrates the relationship between the Succession Narrative and the larger context of the DtrH.

Van Seters also points to problems at the beginning of the Succession Narrative, especially with regard to its relation to prior traditions concerning the house of Saul.[19] He notes, for example, that the initial statements concerning Saul's son Mephibosheth in 2 Samuel 9:3, 13 refer back to earlier statements in 2 Samuel 4:4 that explain how he become lame. David's humane treatment of Mephibosheth, insofar as he gave him a place at the royal table, masks the fact that David was able to control one of Saul's last surviving sons who might have presented a challenge to his rule. Furthermore, Solomon's killing of Shimei (1 Kgs 2:36–46), a member of the family of Saul who cursed David during Absalom's revolt (2 Sam 16:5–8), likewise speaks to the legitimacy of the Davidic house over that of Saul. Because Shimei is the last surviving member of the house of Saul mentioned in the DtrH, it is probably no accident that Solomon instructs him to "build a house in Jerusalem" (1 Kgs 2:36)—mirroring language used for the establishment of a dynasty—and reiterates the divine promise to the Davidic house (2 Kgs 2:45) immediately before ordering his execution. These features have an impact on the reading of other DtrH traditions concerning the descendants of Saul, including the death of Ish-boshet (2 Sam 2 4) and David's shunning of Michal so that she would not have children (2 Sam 6). In both cases, no further descendant of Saul would emerge to challenge David, and the Succession Narrative continues this perspective with relation to Mephibosheth and Shimei. When Shimei dies by Solomon's order, Solomon's throne is secure.

Van Seters is quite correct to point to the Succession Narrative as an attack on the royal ideology of sure house for David.[20] It points to the turmoil in David's house that stands behind the foundation of the Davidic dynasty with Solomon's

17. Van Seters, *In Search of History* 277–291.
18. Van Seters, *In Search* 278–279.
19. Van Seters, *In Search* 280–285.
20. Van Seters, *In Search* 290.

succession, and it points to David's cowardice in his affair with Bath Sheba and Solomon's inability to rule without a bloodbath that sees the elimination of his opponents, many of whom were loyal supporters of David from his Hebron days. This is in striking contrast to the earlier traditions about David, which present him in ideal terms as the monarch chosen by YHWH, and later traditions that measure the righteousness of the Judean kings against the actions of David. According to the Succession Narrative, neither David nor Solomon is an ideal leader, and yet the narrative has clearly been integrated into the DtrH in that it follows up the elimination of the house of Saul and plays a role in justifying the criticism of Solomon. Overall, the contrast in the presentation of David beginning in 2 Samuel 11 (or 9) and the shift to religious apostasy in the criticism of Solomon beginning at 1 Kings 3 demonstrate that the Succession Narrative was written independently of these other materials. Obviously, it was written by someone with a stake in criticizing the Davidic house; however, attempts to identify its authors in northern circles fail to realize that the Davidic dynasty would be relatively unimportant in northern circles as a short-lived dynasty that continued as the rulers of a small vassal state that was dominated by northern Israel throughout most of its history. Rather, the Succession Narrative would have to come from a party connected with Judah and with an interest in the House of David and the actions portrayed in the narrative. The high priest Abiathar is the only major figure to survive the Solomonic purge. Because of Abiathar's expulsion to Anathoth and the continued role of the Elide house in Israelite and Judean history, the Elide house might be a potential source for the composition of this narrative.[21] Such a contention would account for a narrative that portrays a shift in the power structure of the Davidic house as the cause of its own expulsion from Jerusalem after enjoying the favor of King David during the period of his rise over against Saul. The Elide priests of Nob were slaughtered under Saul; Abiathar was eventually installed as high priest by David.

It is also noteworthy that the DtrH as a whole portrays Josiah as the first major monarch to be selected by the people after David. The Succession Narrative would thereby serve Josiah's interests because it portrays Solomon as a ruler who came to the throne not as a monarch who was chosen by the people, but as the result of adultery, bloodshed, senility or incompetence, and manipulation. The resulting problems in the kingdom of Israel that eventually saw the split of the people into two kingdoms and the ultimate demise of the northern kingdom are thereby attributed to Solomon. Given Josiah's role in resolving all the major problems of the DtrH, including Solomon's high places, Jeroboam's altar at Beth-El, and the cultic

---

21. Note that Ahijah the Shilonite commissions Jeroboam to be the next king of Israel in 1 Kings 11. His Shilonite background may well indicate his association with the Elide house in Anathoth to which Abiathar was expelled. Likewise, Jeremiah's associations with Anathoth, the Elide house, and Dtr literary style indicate the possibility that the Elides played some role in the composition of the DtrH traditions during the later monarchy. Certainly the Elides would have an interest in criticizing the house of David for the transition from the Hebron-based faction to the Jerusalem faction and in setting the situation straight with the selection of Josiah by the people. Josiah's reforms may well have led to the Elide Jeremiah's appearance in Jerusalem.

installations of other kings, Josiah emerges as the monarch who sets aright all of the problems that Solomon set in motion. The fact that Josiah is chosen by the people, whereas Solomon is not, prepares him for such a role insofar as he acts to correct the shortcomings of the Davidic line descended from Solomon. The fact that Josiah is idealized as a leader on a par with Moses and Joshua, as well as with David, enables him to act as a monarch who sets aright problems that ultimately stem from David and points to Josiah as the ideal monarch of the entire Davidic monarchy. Had he been able to follow through on his program of reunifying north and south, he certainly would have deserved such a reputation.

All of this suggests that the Josianic redaction was responsible for the inclusion of the Succession Narrative in the DtrH and for the framing of 1 Kings 3–11 with the portrayal of Solomon's lust for foreign women as the causes for the dissolution of the united kingdom of Israel. In framing the Solomon narrative in this manner, the Josianic redaction took up an earlier tradition that presupposed David as the ideal monarch and lauded Solomon to a large extent, but pointed to economic issues in his treatment of the northern tribes as the true cause of the revolt. Insofar as the core material in 1 Kings 3–10 presupposes Solomon's and David's righteousness, it would seem that this material must be identified with the proposed Hezekian edition of the DtrH. 2 Kings 18–20 presents David as the ideal model to whom Hezekiah is compared, and asserts that Hezekiah removes the high places that first come to notice in Solomon's reign. By adding the Succession Narrative and the traditions concerning Solomon's marriages to foreign women, the Josianic DtrH presented David and Solomon as the ultimate causes of Israel's problems and Josiah as the ideal monarch who would resolve them and thereby fulfill the Davidic promise. Nevertheless, it still remains to determine the role of the idealized David in the traditions concerning Saul and David and the role of the narrative concerning the judges in the overall presentation of the DtrH.

7

David, Saul, and the Presentation of the Judges

Scholars generally recognize that the DtrH presentation of the traditions concerning David and Saul in 1–2 Samuel are designed to legitimize the kingship of David over that of Saul and thereby to legitimize the rule of the House of David.[1] Several major literary sources that stand behind the present form of the text have been identified, including the Succession Narrative or Court History (2 Sam 9/11–20; 1 Kgs 1–2); the History of the Rise of David (1 Sam 16–2 Sam 5); the Saul Cycle (1 Sam 1–15); and the Ark Narrative (1 Sam 4–6; 2 Sam 6). In addition, several minor literary sources also appear, including the Dynastic Oracle (2 Sam 7); the summary of David's victories and administration (2 Sam 8); the Ammonite Wars of David (2 Sam 10); and various miscellaneous texts concerning the execution of Saul's sons, poetic traditions concerning David's kingship, and the selection of Araunah's threshing floor as the site of the altar (2 Sam 21–24). Although scholars generally argue that these narrative were originally independent, it is clear that they are organized in the present form of the text to present a coherent account of David's kingship.

The history of David's rise plays a particularly important role in the DtrH presentation of this period because it points to YHWH's favor for David in place of Saul.[2] It thereby leads the reader to the dynastic oracle in 2 Samuel 7, which promises David an eternal dynasty, but warns him that his sons will be punished if they fail to live according to YHWH's expectations. This stands in contrast to the Saul cycle, which presents the failure of Saul's kingship due to his inability to cope with

---

1. For recent overviews of the study of 1–2 Samuel, see James W. Flanagan, "Samuel, Book of 1–2," *ABD* V 957–965; P. Kyle McCarter, Jr., "The Books of Samuel," in *The History of Israel's Traditions*, ed. McKenzie and Graham, 260–280; Dietrich and Naumann, *Die Samuelbücher*.

2. See esp. Jakob H. Grønbæk, *Die Geschichte vom Aufstieg Davids (1. Sam. 15–2. Sam. 5). Tradition und Composition*, Acta Theologica Danica X (Copenhagen: Munksgaard, 1971).

the Philistines and his troubled personality. Overall, the narrative points out that all Israel favors David, including Saul's children, who help him escape the wrath of their father. Jonathan, the heir apparent to Saul, becomes David's best friend, and Michal, Saul's daughter, becomes his wife. The Ark Narrative highlights Saul's failure against the Philistines, and points out that the ark, representing the presence of YHWH among the people, is absent from Israel during the entire course of Saul's kingship. David's return of the ark in 2 Samuel 6 coincides with his announcement that he will shun Michal, thereby securing his kingship by ensuring that no descendants of Saul will be born. It is therefore no accident that the dynastic oracle immediately follows in 2 Samuel 7. As noted, the Succession Narrative tempers the assessment of David by pointing to his personal weaknesses that affect the character of the dynasty and the future course of Israel's history, but it never denies David's legitimacy as king. In doing so, it prepares for the kingship of Josiah, who will correct the problems brought about by David and Solomon. When read in relation to the exilic edition of the DtrH, it aids in explaining the downfall of the house of David. When the Succession Narrative is removed, David emerges as an ideal figure who resolves the problems of Israel evident during Saul's kingship and provides the model for Hezekiah's kingship in the proposed Hezekian edition of the DtrH.

Although the role of the David and Saul traditions in the proposed Hezekian, Josianic, and exilic editions of the DtrH seems relatively clear, that of the Judges narrative is not. The book of Judges is generally treated separately from 1–2 Samuel because of its focus on premonarchic Israel.[3] Most studies tend to focus on Judges as a narrative source relevant for the reconstruction of early Israelite history and social structure, whereas literary study tends to lag behind that of Samuel and Kings. Nevertheless, it is clear that the Judges narrative plays a role in introducing the question of kingship in ancient Israel, and thereby serves as an introduction to the Samuel narratives. This is evident from the repeated formula, "there was no king in Israel" (Judg 17:6; 18:1; 19:1; 21:25), which demonstrates the need for kingship as a means to restore order among the tribes, and the Gideon and Abimelech narratives (Judg 6–8, 9), which portray kingship as a Canaanite institution and a potential source for the abuse of power among the tribes. In this regard, Judges points to both the necessity for kingship and its potential problems in the framework of DtrH ideology, which both lauds David and blames the kings for the ultimate collapse of Israel and Judah. The introductory material in Judges 1:1–3:6 likewise serves the interests of DtrH ideology in that it points to the continued apostasy of the people and thereby prepares the reader for the collapse of Israel and Judah in Kings. In the ideology of the DtrH, this collapse was due to the people's apostasy, prompted in large measure by the actions of the kings of both nations.[4]

3. For overviews of the study of Judges, see A. D. H. Mayes, *Judges*, OT Guides (Sheffield: JSOT Press, 1985); Rüdiger Bartelmus, "Forschung am Richterbuch seit Martin Noth," *TRu* 56 (1991) 221–259; Robert G. Boling, "Judges, Book of," *ABD* III 1107–1117; Mark O'Brien, "Judges and the Deuteronomistic History," *The History of Israel's Traditions*, ed. McKenzie and Graham, 235–259.

4. For full discussion of the following, see Marvin A. Sweeney, "Davidic Polemics in the Book of Judges," *VT* 47 (1997) 517–529. See also Tammi J. Schneider, *Judges*, Berit Olam: Studies in Hebrew Narrative and Poetry (Collegeville, MN: Liturgical, 2000).

There are several further indications that the Judges narrative is well integrated into the overall structure and perspective of the DtrH. The narratives concerning individual Judges are each introduced by the formulae *wayyaʿăśû běnê yiśrāʾēl ʿet-hāraʾ běʿênê yhwh*, "and the sons of Israel did evil in the eyes of YHWH" (Judg 3:7), *wayyōsipû běnê yiśrāʾēl laʿăśôt hāraʿ běʿênê yhwh*, "and the sons of Israel continued to do evil in the eyes of YHWH" (Judg 3:12), or a variant, which corresponds to the formulae employed for the evaluation of wicked kings in the Kings narratives.[5] Likewise, Judges 17–18 portrays the foundation of the sanctuary at Dan, one of Jeroboam's two altars associated with the golden calves, as a site for the worship of a graven image, and notes that descendants of the first priest Jonathan served at the sanctuary until "the day of the captivity of land" (Judg 18:30), an apparent reference to the conquest of the region and deportation of its population by Tiglath Pileser in the late eighth century (2 Kgs 15:29). Judges 19–21 likewise notes the role of Beth-El, the site of Jeroboam's main sanctuary, as the site where the tribes of Israel decided to embark upon a civil war against the tribe of Benjamin and nearly destroyed it (Judg 20:18, 26; 21:2). Neither sanctuary is portrayed in positive terms; Dan is a source of idolatry and Beth-El is associated with the potential destruction of one of the twelve tribes. In both cases, the negative portrayal of the sites appears to serve as polemics that anticipate their future role in the DtrH as sanctuaries for the northern kingdom of Israel.[6]

By far, the most important indicator of the role of Judges in relation to its immediate literary context is the polemic against Saul that appears in the narrative concerning the war against Benjamin in Judges 19–21.[7] Saul's name is never mentioned in the narrative. Nevertheless, the various elements of the narrative point to characteristic features of Saul and his activities in 1 Samuel that demonstrate his role as the target of the narrative. It begins with a portrayal of a major crime in the city of Gibeah in the tribal territory of Benjamin, later to become Saul's capital. A Levite traveling with his Bethlehemite concubine is invited to spend the night in Gibeah by an anonymous old man. In addition to setting the initial episodes in the city of Gibeah, the narrative takes special pains to note that the Levite is traveling with two asses and a servant, calling to mind the asses for which Saul and his servant searched in 1 Samuel 9:1–10:16. It likewise highlights Ramah, which figures prominently in the lost asses narrative as the place where Saul lodged for the night with Samuel and became king, as a potential place to spend the night.

---

5. Cf. Frederick E. Greenspahn, "The Theology of the Framework of Judges," *VT* 36 (1986) 385–396; Marc Brettler, "The Book of Judges: Literature as Politics," *JBL* 108 (1989) 395–418, esp. 417; Robert O'Connell, *The Rhetoric of the Book of Judges*, VTSup 63 (Leiden: E. J. Brill, 1996) 112–134, 208–217, all of whom note the analogy but argue that the differences in formulation undermine any attempt to identify the redaction of Judges with that of Kings.

6. See Yairah Amit, "Hidden Polemic in the Conquest of Dan: Judges xvii–xviii," *VT* 40 (1990) 4–20; idem," Literature in the Service of Politics: Studies in Judges 19–21," in *Politics and Theopolitics in the Bible and Postbiblical Literature*, JSOTSup 171, ed. H. Graf Reventlow and B. Uffenheimer (Sheffield: Sheffield Academic Press, 1994) 28–40.

7. For overviews of Judges 19–21, see Amit, "Literature in the Service of Politics"; Robert G. Boling, *Judges*, AB 6A (Garden City, N.Y.: Doubleday, 1975) 271–294; J. A. Soggin, *Judges: A Commentary*, OTL, translated by J. Bowden (Philadelphia: Westminster, 1981) 279–305.

During the night, men of the city demanded that the Levite be brought out so that they might "know" him, and when the old man refused to hand over the Levite, the men of the city raped the concubine all night until she died. This of course calls to mind the narrative concerning the two angels who visited Lot in Sodom (Gen 19), and serves as a means to characterize the people of the city of Gibeah in less than flattering terms. The concubine's body is then cut into twelve pieces to call the crime to the attention of the twelve tribes of Israel, an act which recalls Saul's cutting up his oxen into twelve pieces to call out the tribes to battle in support of the beleaguered men of Jabesh Gilead (1 Sam 11). After the Benjaminites are nearly destroyed and Israel has vowed not to give its daughters to the surviving Benjaminites, four hundred virgins from Jabesh Gilead are found to serve as wives for them. This, of course, was after the city was destroyed because its people did not respond to the call for war against Benjamin. The remaining Benjaminite men are left to seize their wives in the vineyards as they dance during the course of a festival celebration at the Shiloh sanctuary. The narrative emphasizes the small size of the tribe of Benjamin, which is a key element in 1 Samuel 10:17–27, in which Saul was selected by lot from the smallest tribe. Likewise, the "base fellows" of the city of Gibeah (Judg 19:22) call to mind the "base fellows" who raise questions about Saul in 1 Samuel 10:27. Overall, the many associations with Saul prepare the reader for the coming narrative in 1 Samuel. Naturally, such a background cannot help but sway the reader's opinion that Saul could not possibly succeed as a just monarch over the people of Israel. In this regard, Judges serves as the introduction to the failed kingship of Saul and the consequent rise of David.

The polemics against the sanctuaries at Dan and Beth-El and against Saul clearly indicate that the book of Judges does not constitute a discrete literary composition in and of itself,[8] but that it plays a role within the larger DtrH narrative that requires further consideration. In order to establish the historiographical and theological perspectives of the book of Judges as well as its literary history as part of the overall DtrH narrative, it is necessary to examine its literary structure, generic character, and the means by which it presents its material. The narrative is easily demarcated in Judges 1:1 by the initial statement, "and it came to pass after the death of Joshua," that introduces a new period in Israel's history following the conquest under Joshua. The narrative is demarcated at the end by its use of the formula, "in those days there was no king in Israel, and each man would do what was right in his eyes," and the introduction of a new narrative concerning the birth of Samuel, the next leader of Israel, in 1 Samuel 1:1. The overall genre of the book of Judges is historical evaluation of Israel in the period of the Judges. This is evident by several features of the narrative, including its historical perspective and presentation, its interest in evaluating the behavior of Israel throughout the narrative, its focus on the Judges who led Israel during this period as a barometer for the character of the people, and the repeated use of the formula, "and the sons of Israel did/continued to do evil in the eyes of YHWH," corresponding the regnal evaluation formulae of Kings.

---

8. Cf. Brettler, "Judges," 316–318, who argues that the book of Judges was edited as a distinct book.

Most scholars argue that the structure of the book falls into three major sections:[9] Judges 1:1–3:6, which serves as the introduction to the narrative that outlines its major concerns; Judges 3:7–16:31, which serves as the body of the narrative that conveys the narratives concerning the individual Judges and their activities; and Judges 17–21, which defines the overall goal of the Judges narrative in that it points to the potential dissolution of the tribes of Israel for lack of a king. Unfortunately, this consensus is based not on consideration of the literary features of the present form of the text, but on redaction-critical considerations that define the above components in relation to the literary history of the text. Thus, Judges 1:1–3:6 includes both the revised presentation of the allotment of the land in Judges 1:1–2:5, which points to the failure of the tribes to expel the Canaanites, and the Deuteronomistic "introduction" in Judges 2:6–3:6, which points to the standard pattern of apostasy, punishment, outcry, and deliverance that governs the presentations of the individual Judges throughout the book. Judges 3:7–16:31 includes the narratives pertaining to the individual Judges. Judges 17–21 contains two "appendices" that appear to have little to do with the preceding Judges narratives.[10] This structural model presupposes that Judges 1:1–3:6 was added to the previously existing narratives of the Judges as part of a Deuteronomistic redaction that attempted to correct the portrayal of a complete conquest in the book of Joshua and to provide a theological introduction for the Judges. The previously independent narratives in Judges 17–18 and 19–21 were simply added to fill out the chronology of the period.

Unfortunately, this view of the structure of the book of Judges overlooks or misconstrues several key literary features of the present form of the text. Consideration of the literary, syntactical, and formal features of the present form of the text points instead to a basic two-part structure for the book that focuses especially on the role of Israel's intermarriage with the nations and the consequences that holds for the welfare of the people.[11]

The first major unit of the book is Judges 1–2. The syntactical structure of this unit is defined by a consistent *waw*-consecutive formulation that governs the overall presentation of this text. It continues until Judges 3:1, which disrupts the *waw*-consecutive sequence with the statement, *wĕ'ēlleh haggôyim 'ăšer hinnîaḥ yhwh lĕnassôt bām 'et-yiśrā'ēl*, "These are the nations which YHWH left to test Israel." The unit is concerned throughout with YHWH's decision to "test" Israel

---

9. See Brevard S. Childs, *Introduction to the Old Testament as Scripture* (Philadelphia: Fortress, 1979) 256–261. For an alternative three-part structure comprising Judges 1:1–3:6; 3:7–15:20; and 16–21, see Boling, "Judges," *ABD* III 1107–1117. For full discussion of the redaction critical issues in the study of the book, including the distinction between the Deuteronomistic framework and the individual "savior" or Judges narratives, see Wolfgang Richter, *Traditionsgeschichtliche Untersuchungen zum Richterbuch*, BBB 18 (Bonn: Peter Hanstein, 2nd ed., 1966); Richter, *Die Bearbeitungen des "Retterbuches" in der Deuteronomischen Epoche*, BBB 21 (Bonn: Peter Hanstein, 1964).

10. For the identification of these narratives as "appendices," see Martin Noth, "The Background of Judges 17–18," *Israel's Prophetic Heritage*, Fs. J. Muilenberg, ed. B. W. Anderson and W. Harrelson (London: SCM, 1962) 68–85.

11. For a full study of this issue, see Sweeney, "Davidic Polemics."

by afflicting them with the nations that Israel failed to drive out during the conquest of the land. It begins with a detailed account in Judges 1:1–36 of the conquests by the tribes of Israel, which highlights areas in which the Canaanites were not destroyed or expelled and therefore continued to live among the tribes of Israel. Judges 2:1–23, which is linked to Judges 1:1–36 by the *waw*-consecutive statement "and the angel of YHWH went up (*wayya'al*) from Gilgal to Bochim," clearly portrays this situation as a source of difficulty for Israel. It begins by presenting an assembly of the people at Bochim in which the angel of YHWH calls attention to YHWH's command to drive out the Canaanites, and portrays Israel's failure to do so as a violation of YHWH's will. Consequently, the angel states that YHWH will not drive out the Canaanites and that they and their gods will become adversaries and snares for Israel. Although many scholars consider the report in Judges 2:6–11 of Joshua's dismissal of the people and his subsequent death as a misplaced conclusion to the narrative concerning Joshua's assembly of the people at Shechem in Joshua 24,[12] it serves as a report of Joshua's dismissal of the people from Bochim. In the context of the present form of the DtrH, this narrative indicates that a second assembly took place at Bochim prior to Joshua's death, and it introduces the theme of Israel's apostasy both in the period of the Judges and in the DtrH as a whole. The report of this incident then serves as the introduction to Judges 2:7–23, which outlines the overall pattern of apostasy, punishment, repentance, and deliverance that governs the presentations of the individual Judges throughout the book, viz., Israel will do evil by turning to the pagan gods, YHWH will raise an oppressor to punish them for their apostasy, Israel will repent, and YHWH will raise a deliverer for the people to remove the oppressor. Insofar as Bochim is identified with Beth-El,[13] this points to an effort on the part of the narrator to associate this apostasy with Beth-El.

The second major structural block of Judges appears in Judges 3–21. It begins in Judges 3:1–6 with a brief section that summarizes the nations left in the land to test Israel, and it provides the premise for the rest of the book. Although scholars generally view Judges 3:1–6 as a section independent from the following narratives concerning the individual Judges,[14] this view overlooks the syntactical and thematic features of the present form of the narrative. As noted, Judges 1:1–2:23 is governed throughout by a *waw*-consecutive syntactical structure that includes both the notice of the failure to drive out the Canaanites in Judges 1:1–36 and the narrative concerning the assembly at Bochim and its results in Judges 2:1–23. It is only at Judges 3:1–6, introduced by the statement *wě'ēlleh haggôyim 'ăšer hinnîaḥ yhwh lěnassôt bām 'et-yiśrā'ēl*, "and these are the nations that YHWH left to test Israel . . . ," that the sequence is disrupted.

Although Judges 3:1–6 is generally considered to be independent of the following material in Judges 3:7ff, the *waw*-consecutive formulation of Judges 3:7, *wayya 'ăśû běnê yiśrā'ēl 'et-hāra' bě'ênê yhwh*, "and the sons of Israel did evil in

12. For discussion, see Boling, *Judges* 29–38, 72.
13. Cf. LXX and Boling, *Judges* 62.
14. Boling, *Judges* 78–79.

the eyes of YHWH . . ." indicates that the narratives devoted to the Judges beginning in Judges 3:7 are tied structurally to Judges 3:1–6. Judges 3:1–6 identifies
the nations that YHWH left to test Israel and notes that Israel intermarried with
the nations and served their gods. It thereby introduces the theme of Israel's
Canaanization or deterioration in that narratives concerning the individual Judges
in Judges 3:7–16:31 point to the increasing "Canaanization" of the people and increasing conflict, both between Israel and its enemies and among the tribes of Israel
themselves.

Judges 3:7–16:31 therefore constitutes the second major subunit of Judges 3–
21, which comprises the narrative evaluations of Israel during the period of each
of the individual Judges. Although the individual narratives clearly take up the
Judges in relation to rather localized events involving only one or two tribes, or
at most six in the case of Deborah, the narrative framework of this section emphasizes that the individual episodes involve all Israel. Consequently, each episode is formulated in a relatively consistent fashion in keeping with the pattern
laid out in Judges 2:1–23. It begins with the formula, "and the sons of Israel did/
continued to do what was evil in the eyes of YHWH." The account of the oppression of Israel follows together with the narrative concerning the means by which
the Judge defeated the oppressor and restored Israel's security. Each narrative then
characteristically concludes with a notice concerning the duration of the Judge's
rule or the length of time that the land had rest. The narratives concerning the
individual Judges include Othniel of Judah and his defeat of Cushan Rishathaim,
king of Mesopotamia (3:7–11); Ehud of Benjamin and his defeat of Eglon of Moab
(3:12–30); Deborah of Ephraim and her defeat (with Barak) of Sisera of Hazor
(4–5); Gideon/Jerubbaal of Manasseh and his defeat of the Midianites (6–8);
Jephthah of Gilead/Gad and his defeat of the Ammonites and Ephraimities (10:6–
12:7); and Samson of Dan and his humiliation of the Philistines (13–16). Various
appendices that address the consequences or aftermath of the careers of the individual Judges also appear, including the narrative concerning Abimelech,
Gideon's son, who seized kingship in Shechem (9); and the notices concerning
the minor Judges (3:31; 10:1–5; 12:8–15). Consequently, the structural subunits
of Judges 3:7–16:31 comprise the individual evaluations of Israel in the time of
each Judge, introduced by the formula, "and the people of Israel did/continued to
do evil in the eyes of YHWH," together with any associated appendices. These
subunits include the presentations of the careers of Othniel (Judg 3:7–11); Ehud
(Judg 3:12–31); Deborah (Judg 4–5); Gideon (Judg 6–9); Jepthah (Judg 10:6–
12:15); and Samson (Judg 13–16).

Overall, the structure of Judges 3:7–16:3 presents a scenario in which Israel's
position deteriorates over the course of time. At the beginning of the narrative,
Israel's enemies are the nations that continue to inhabit the land; by the end of the
narrative, Israelites are fighting among themselves as the tribes attempt to punish
Benjamin for the rape and murder of the Levite's concubine and for Benjamin's
refusal to accept the authority of the other tribes when Benjamin refuses to hand
over the perpetrators of the crime for punishment. The gradual deterioration of
the tribes is likewise represented by the fact that Othniel, the first of the major Judges,
leads a unified people in fighting against Cushan-Rishathaim of Mesopotamia, an

enemy who comes from outside of the land of Israel. Ehud likewise leads a unified people against Eglon of Moab, an enemy who is somewhat closer to home
than Cushan-Rishathaim. But the unity of the people begins to unravel in the narrative concerning Deborah. Not only does Deborah's enemy come from Hazor, a
city within the land of Israel that supposedly was conquered by Joshua in the DtrH
(Joshua 11), but also several Israelite tribes or clans are cursed for their failure to
participate in the war, including Reuben (5:15b–16), Gilead (5:17), Dan (5:17),
Asher (5:17), and Meroz (5:23). The situation deteriorates further in the Gideon
narrative when the tribe of Ephraim threatens Gideon for failing to call them out
in the war against the Midianites (8:1–4). Likewise, when Gideon's son Abimelech
assumes kingship in Shechem, he sparks a civil war among the people that leads
to the deaths of many Israelites, including Abimelech. The tribe of Ephraim enters the picture again and actually goes to war against Jephthah for his failure to
call them out against the Ammonites. The result is Ephraim's defeat by Jepthah
and the deaths of some forty-two thousand Ephraimites. Finally, Samson humili-
ates the Philistine on several occasions, but he is never able to defeat them, and
he dies when he uses his great strength to collapse a building on top of himself
and the Philistines after they captured him, blinded him, and put him in bonds for
their own amusement.

The deterioration of the tribes in Judges 3:7–16:31 includes not only their
internal unity and their position vis-à-vis their enemies, but their integrity as a
people dedicated to YHWH as well. Throughout this section, it is evident that the
people increasingly take up Canaanite practices, which contribute to the portrayal
of their deterioration. This issue is introduced in the introduction to the book in
Judges 1–2 and in the introduction to the Judges narratives in Judges 3:1–6 when
Israel's failure to drive out the Canaanites is turned against them by YHWH who
determines that the continued presence of the Canaanites would form a snare for
Israel. The issue seems to be tied up with kingship, which elsewhere in the DtrH
is identified as an institution characteristic of the nations that surround Israel (cf.
Deut 17:14; 1 Sam 8). The issue first emerges in the narrative concerning Gideon.
Gideon is also identified in the narrative as Jerubbaal, a Canaanite name that means,
"Baal contends." Although the narrative in Judges 6:32 attributes the name to
Gideon's willingness to pull down an altar dedicated to Baal, the fact that the
altar was erected by Gideon's father together with an Asherah (Judg 6:25–32) indicates the extent to which Canaanite practice had already permeated the tribes of
Israel. Likewise, when the people ask Gideon to become king and to establish a
dynasty, he refuses and states that YHWH should rule over the people (Judg 8:22–
23). Nevertheless, he asks the people to give him earrings from the spoil, which
he uses to make an ephod, here portrayed as an idolatrous cultic object, which the
people worship after the pattern of pagan Canaanite worship (Judg 8:24–28). After
Gideon's death, his son Abimelech kills the seventy sons of Gideon, apparently a
reference to the ruling council of elders in Israel at the time, and attempts to assume kingship for himself. The Abimelech narrative consistently identifies his
father by his Canaanite name Jerubbaal, and it identifies the god worshiped in the
Temple at Shechem as Baal Berith (Judg 9:4) or El Berith (Judg 9:46), apparently
a Canaanite name. Jephthah emulates practices attributed to the Canaanites and

Moabites throughout the Hebrew Bible when he vows to sacrifice the first person he sees after his victory of the Ammonites. The fact that it is his daughter apparently reflects Israelite perceptions of human sacrifice by the Canaanites. The lamentations associated with her death (Judg 11:40) call to mind the lamentations associated with Ishtar's attempts to raise Tammuz from the dead (cf. Jer 44) and Canaanite attempts to raise Baal or Aqhat. Samson's marriages to Philistine women stand in direct violation of the Dtr command against marrying the women of foreign nations as they might lead the people into apostasy (Deut 7:1–6). In the Judges narrative, it is Samson's marriage to the Philistine Delilah that leads him to his demise.

The Samson narrative is particularly important within the overall structure and historiographical and theological outlook of Judges 3–21 in that it points to the narratives in Judges 17–21 as the third structural element of Judges 3–21. Like the narratives concerning the individual Judges, these chapters also take up the themes of Israel's Canaanization and deterioration in that they present the loss of Dan's tribal inheritance to the Philistines, the origins of the idolatrous sanctuary at Dan, the civil war among the tribes that nearly sees the destruction of Benjamin, and the introduction of marriage practices for Benjamin at Shiloh that hints at rape.[15] Furthermore, the entire sequence is presented as the consequence of Samson's failure as a Judge. He is the only Judge who dies at the hands of his enemies. He is the only Judge who fails to secure the safety of his people. He is the only Judge to marry among the pagans of the land. Finally, his failure as a Judge is presented as the direct result of his betrayal by his Philistine wife. In short, Samson violates the prohibition against intermarriage stated in Judges 1–2 and 3:1–6, and this in turn leads to the problems outlined in Judges 17–21. In the end, Israel's Canaanization and deterioration in Judges is the direct result of Israel's failure to observe YHWH's commands to drive out the Canaanites and to avoid intermarriage with them.

As noted, the variations of the formula, "there was no king in Israel, and every man did what was right in his own eyes," ties Judges 17–21 together as a single block. In addition, the occurrences of this formula define the major structural blocks of Judges 17–21. Following Samson's demise, Judges 17:1–5 reports that an Ephraimite named Micah returned money to his mother that he had previously stolen from her. In turn, she uses part of the money to make a graven image that is set up in their house. Judges 17:6–13, which is introduced by the formula, "in those days there was no king in Israel, and each man would do what was right in his own eyes," relates that Micah hired a Levite from Bethlehem to serve as a priest for his idolatrous shrine. Judges 18:1–31, introduced by the formula, "In those days there was no king in Israel," relates how the tribe of Dan is forced to move north for lack of a tribal inheritance, indicating that one of the tribes of Israel was displaced by the Philistines as the result of Samson's failure. When the tribe moves north, they steal Micah's graven image and his priest, and they eventually set them up in a new shrine devoted to the worship of YHWH at Dan when they conquer

---

15. See Schneider, *Judges* 271–285.

the city from its "quiet and unsuspecting" inhabitants. Finally, the narrative in Judges 19–21 concerning the war against Benjamin is tied syntactically and structurally to Judges 18 by the introductory *waw*-consecutive formulation of the formula, "and it came to pass (*wayĕhî*) in those days that there was no king in Israel," and the concluding formula, "In those days, there was no king in Israel and every man would do what was right in his own eyes" (Judg 21:25). The narrative relates how the rape and murder at Gibeah in Benjamin, later Saul's capital, of the Bethlehemite concubine of a Levite, Benjamin's refusal to give up the culprits for justice, the war of the Israelite tribes against Benjamin, the near destruction of Benjamin, and the decision to allow them to take wives from the survivors of the sacked city of Jabesh Gilead, kidnapping them from among the maidens who would dance at the sanctuary at Shiloh during the "festival" (Sukkot). Altogether, these narratives continue the themes of Israel's Canaanization and deterioration that were evident in the narratives concerning the individual Judges. Micah's theft of his mother's money, his worship of a graven image, his corruption of a Bethlehemite Levite, and the establishment of his shrine in the sanctuary at Dan testifies to moral corruption and Canaanite influence among the people. The treatment of the Levite's Bethlehemite concubine by the men of Gibeah points again to corruption that mirrors the behavior of the men of Sodom as portrayed in Genesis 19. Likewise, war against Benjamin and the Benjaminite practice of seizing wives in the vineyards during a grape harvest festival indicates Israel's internal deterioration and the possibility of a background in Canaanite fertility worship. Altogether, Judges 17–21 provides the capstone to the individual Judges narratives in Judges 3–21 and to the themes of intermarriage and corruption laid out at the beginning of the book in Judges 1–2.

The structure of the Judges narrative may be represented as in table 7.1. In considering the progressive deterioration of the tribes of Israel in the DtrH portrayal of the period of the Judges, it is important to recognize the polemical nature of the presentation. The attempt to discredit Dan, Beth-El, and Saul in Judges 17–21 was noted above, but this does not account for the entire book. Rather, these polemics are only the culmination of the deterioration of the tribes as a whole. In this respect, it is noteworthy that Othniel, the first of the Judges, encounters very little difficulty in overcoming, Cushan-Rishathaim of Mesopotamia, the oppressor of Israel from his time. In fact, the narrative concerning Othniel presents only the most basic elements of the situation, and defines the basic structure of all of the narratives concerning individual Judges. The other Judges encounter difficulties. Eglon ruled Israel for eighteen years. Furthermore, Ehud must resort to subterfuge by relying on his left-handedness to hide a sword so that he might kill Eglon during the course of a private audience; he is unable to organize Israel for open combat until Eglon is dead. Not all of the tribes came out to join Deborah. The Ephraimites threatened Gideon, and actually attacked Jephthah. Samson was unable to overcome his enemies except by his own suicide.

The fact that Othniel is Judean is significant, because it portrays a Judean Judge as the model for establishing stability without great difficulty in the period of the Judges. All of the other major Judges are from the northern tribes; Ehud from Benjamin, Deborah from Ephraim, Gideon from Manasseh, Jepthah from Gilead,

TABLE 7.1   Narrative evaluation of Israel in the period of the judges

Israel's Canaanization and degeneration during the pre-monarchic period	*Judges 1–21*
I. Introduction	1–2
A. Concerning the inability of israel to drive out the Canaanites	1:1–36
B. Concerning YHWH's decision to make the Canaanites adversaries and snares to test Israel	2:1–23
II. Presentation of Israel's degeneration and Canaanization proper	3–21
A. Basic problem: intermarriage with pagan nations	3:1–16
B. Evaluation of Israel in the time of each judge	3:7–16:31
1. Othniel of Judah: defeat of Cushan Rishathaim, king of Mesopotamia	3:7–11
2. Ehud of Benjamin: defeat of Eglon of Moab	3:12–31
a. Concerning Ehud proper	3:12–30
b. Concerning the minor Judge: Shamgar	3:31
3. Deborah of Ephraim (with Barak): defeat of Sisera/Jabin of Hazor	4–5
4. Gideon of Manasseh: defeat of the Midianites	6:1–10:5
a. Concerning Gideon proper	6–8
b. Concerning Abimelech's assumption of kingship	9
c. Concerning the minor judges: Tola and Jair	10:1–5
5. Jephthah of Gilead/Gad: defeat of Ammonites and Ephraimites	10:6–12:15
a. Concerning Jephthah proper	10:6–12:15
b. Concerning the minor judges: Ibzan, Elon, Abdon	12:8–15
6. Samson of Dan: humiliation of the Philistines	13–16
C. Consequences of Israel's Canaanization	17–21
1. Micah's creation of a graven image	17:1–5
2. Micah acquires priest from Bethlehem	17:6–13
3. Establishment of idolatry and injustice in Israel	18–21
a. Establishment of idolatrous cultic site at Dan	18
b. Establishment of injustice in Benjamin	19–21

and Samson from Dan. Likewise, the tribe of Ephraim is presented as a continuing source of difficulty among the tribes in that it attempts to assert its leadership by threatening Gideon and Jephthah and thereby making their task of protecting the people that much more difficult. The role of the Danites in setting up a pagan sanctuary also points to problems in a northern tribe. By contrast, Judah is selected as the first tribe to go out against Benjamin in an attempt to see that justice is done in the matter of the Levite's concubine (Judg 20:18). Overall, the tribe of Judah is a source of order among the tribes, but the northern tribes demonstrate that they are unable to govern or even to organize themselves effectively. The result is chaos among the tribes by the end of the narrative.

This interest in portraying Judah as a successful and stabilizing force in contrast to the northern tribes is evident in the introduction to the book as well.[16] As in the case of the war against Benjamin, Judah is identified as the first tribe to go up against the Canaanites at the very beginning of the book (Judg 1:2). Further-

16. See Moshe Weinfeld, "Judges 1.1–2.5: The Conquest under the Leadership of the House of Judah," in *Understanding Poets and Prophets*, Fs. G. W. Anderson, ed. A. G. Auld, JSOTSup 152 (Sheffield: JSOT Press, 1993) 388–400.

more, Judah takes Simeon under its wing and enables the Simeonites to conquer
their own territory as well as that of Judah. Overall, Judges 1:1–20 presents the
Judeans very positively. They are successful in driving out the Canaanites from
their territory, taking the Judean hill country, Jerusalem, the Negeb, Hebron, Jericho (the city of palms), Arad, Hormah, Gaza, Ashkelon, and Ekron. They failed
only to take the coastal plain, which lay outside of Judean territory anyway. This
stands in striking contrast to the experiences of the northern tribes. Benjamin was
unable to drive out the Jebusites who inhabited Jerusalem, and were forced to dwell
there with them (v. 21), even though v. 8 had earlier stated that Judah took and
destroyed Jerusalem. The house of Joseph took Beth-El, but it could do so only
by deceiving the inhabitants into thinking that their intentions were peaceful (vv.
22–26). Manasseh was unable to drive out the Canaanites from its land (vv. 27–
28), the Ephraimites failed to drive out the inhabitants of Gezer (v. 29). Asher did
not drive out Canaanites from their cities by the sea (vv. 31–32). Naphtali did not
drive out the inhabitants of Beth Shemesh or Beth Anat (v. 33). Finally, the
Amorites drove the Danites away from the coastal plain, and remained there (vv.
34–36). In all cases, the northern tribes are unable to dislodge Canaanites from
their territories and therefore are left to dwell together with them. Judah, on the
other hand, succeeds in a way that the northern tribes do not.

This points to a narrative that stems from Judean sources with an interest in
discrediting the leadership capabilities of the northern tribes of Israel. Saul and
Benjamin are very clearly targets by the end of this narrative, and the special
position of Benjamin in Judges 1:20 indicates that the polemic against Benjamin
actually begins immediately after the notice concerning Judah's successes in driving out the Canaanites. Ephraim also receives special attention as the tribe that
foments civil war at a time when the people's efforts need to be directed to defending themselves. Likewise, the Ephraimite city of Shechem, where the kings
of northern Israel are ratified (1 Kgs 12) and covenants are concluded for the people
as a whole (Deut 27; Josh 24), becomes a source of turmoil during Abimelech's
attempt to establish his own kingship. The sanctuaries at Dan and Beth-El present
their own problems to the life of the people, and the other northern tribes seem to
be incapable of putting together a full tribal coalition, unless it is to exterminate
one of their own members.

The present form of the book of Judges is clearly a Judean composition. When
read in the context of the DtrH, it prepares the reader for the failure of Saul's kingship; after all, what kind of a king could come from a city like Gibeah or a tribe
like Benjamin? But it likewise prepares the reader for the failures of the northern
kingdom; Ephraim is an abusive tribe, the people are naturally idolatrous, and the
sanctuaries at Dan and Beth-El promote idolatry and intertribal warfare. What kind
of leadership could come from Ephraim or the other northern tribes? In both cases,
subsequent narratives in the DtrH demonstrate what is postulated in the Judges
narrative—that is, the northern tribes are incapable of governing themselves. They
need Judah to establish order, security, and justice.

This obviously prepares the reader for the rise of David, and, given the polemic
against Saul, suggests that the narrative could stem from the court of David or
Solomon themselves. A Davidic or Solomonic setting could explain these inter-

ests insofar as Ephraim and the northern tribes came to David only after Saul and Ish-Bosheth/Eshbaal failed to provide security against the Philistines. But the polemics against Ephraim, Dan, and Beth-El suggest that a later agenda may be at work behind this narrative. Although many scholars see exilic concerns at work here,[17] in that the portrayal of Israel's decline in the period of the Judges points forward to the final destruction of the land in the Babylonian period, the positive portrayal of Judah suggests that the present form of the narrative is intended to serve Judean interests. The narrative thereby presupposes a setting in which Judah exists in some form as a viable entity, and it has an agenda to serve in pointing to the failure of the northern tribes with their sanctuaries at Dan and Beth-El. This precludes the exilic period or any later time as the collapse of Israel was hardly an issue unless it pointed to the collapse of Judah as well. Rather, the narrative seems to presuppose a setting in which Judah attempts to assert its ability to maintain order and security and to promote justice over against Israel.

The reference to the captivity of the land in Judges 18:30, which marks the duration of the priests at the sanctuary at Dan, is indicative in this regard in that it points to the latter part of the eighth century B.C.E. as the earliest possible setting for the present form of this narrative.-The captivity to which Judges 18:30 refers could be Tiglath-Pileser's early invasions of Israel in 734–732 during the course of the Syro-Ephraimitic War. During these campaigns, Tiglath Pileser stripped away various outlying territories of the northern kingdom of Israel, including the Galilee, the Coastal Plain, and the Trans-Jordan, naming them Duru (Dor), Magidu (Megiddo), and Gal'azu (Gilead). This left Israel as a rump state that comprised only the hill country of Ephraim.[18] Alternatively, the comment could presuppose the final collapse of the northern kingdom of Israel in 722/1 B.C.E. In either case, the suggests a possible setting for this narrative anytime between the late eighth century and the time of King Josiah's reign. During this period, Judah would have quite an interest in asserting the right of the Davidic monarchy to rule over the former northern kingdom of Israel. By pointing to the failures of the northern tribes to govern themselves in contrast to Judah, which always plays a role in establishing order and justice, the narrative attempts to make the case that Judean rule is preferable and even justified. In this regard, the portrayal of Ephraim as a tribe that attempts to intimidate Gideon and Jephthah and nearly blocks their efforts to defeat the enemies of Manasseh and Gilead is especially pertinent in the aftermath of the loss of these territories to the Assyrians. Likewise, the polemic against Saul and Benjamin is pertinent in the aftermath of the full Israelite collapse, which Benjamin apparently survived, driving it into the orbit of Judah. The fact that David emerges in 1 Samuel 1–2 Samuel 8 as the only monarch to unite the tribes and defeat their enemies drives these points home. An interest in asserting the legitimacy of the Davidic house to rule over the north is evident already on the part of

---

17. Boling, *Judges* 278–279, although he places Judges 17–18 in relation to the Assyrian invasions of the eighth century (pp. 258–259).

18. For a discussion of the details of these campaigns and the source material involved, see Herbert Donner, "The Syro-Ephraimitic War and the end of the Kingdom of Israel," in *Israelite and Judaean History*, ed. J. H. Hayes and J. M. Miller (Philadelphia: Westminster, 1977) 421–434.

Isaiah in the time of Ahaz and beyond.[19] It extends through the period of Josiah's reforms, as indicated by his destruction of the Beth-El altar (2 Kgs 23:15–20). The completely positive portrayal of David through 2 Samuel 8 suggests that this narrative is the product of the Hezekian edition of the DtrH. The Josianic edition would have employed these traditions to assert Davidic rule over the north, but the more nuanced presentation of David in the Succession Narrative would serve Josianic interests in presenting Josiah as the ideal monarch of the Josianic DtrH.

There are, however, indications of Josianic interests in this material in that both the beginning and end of the Judges narrative demonstrate special efforts to point to Beth-El as a focal point for Israel's problems in this period. As noted earlier, Judges 1–2 identifies Bochim or Beth-El as the site in which YHWH declares through an angel that the nations will remain in the land as adversaries and snares for the people because of their failure to drive them out. Furthermore, the narrative concerning the war against Benjamin points to Beth-El as the site where the Israelites make the decision to go to war against one of their own tribes. Later in the narrative Beth-El is the site at which Israel decides to attack Jabesh Gilead in order to procure wives for the surviving Benjaminites and, later, to institute the practice at Shiloh whereby the men of Benjamin would kidnap maidens who dance in the vineyards during the festival of Sukkot.

The presence of Beth-El in Judges 19–21 certainly raises questions as to whether this narrative is the product of the Josianic DtrH, especially because the tribes of Israel meet initially at Mizpah and then shift to Beth-El where they make their final preparations for war with Benjamin. Whereas Mizpah is the site where the people of Israel conducts its investigation of the crime at Gibeah and demands justice from Benjamin (Judg 20:1–17), Beth-El is the site at which they make their final preparations for war with Benjamin, where they weep after their initial defeat and then renew their efforts, and where they decide to provide wives for Benjamin by destroying Jabesh Gilead in order to give the surviving maidens to Benjamin and by allowing the Benjaminites to kidnap maidens dancing in the vineyards at Shiloh, which Judges 21:19 notes is in the vicinity of Beth-El, during the festival of Sukkot. In all cases, Beth-El plays a very unfavorable role in the narrative, which indicates a secondary interest in targeting Beth-El as well as Saul. Insofar as Beth-El is not entirely necessary to the polemic against Saul, but the polemic against Saul is necessary to establish the role of Beth-El, this would suggest that an early narrative that targeted Saul was reworked to target Beth-El as well. Such reworking would clearly serve the interests of the Josianic DtrH. It also might serve the interests of a Hezekian DtrH by providing background for Jeroboam's decision to make Beth-El (and Dan) into state sanctuaries.

This, of course, raises the question of the composition and role of Judges 1–2, which outlines the failures of the tribes to expel the Canaanites from their territories and the consequences of this failure when YHWH decides to leave the nations

19. See Stuart A. Irvine, *Isaiah, Ahaz and the Syro-Ephraimitic Crisis*, SBLDS 123 (Atlanta: Scholars Press, 1990); Marvin A. Sweeney, "A Philological and Form-Critical Reevaluation of Isaiah 8:16–9:6," *HAR* 14 (1994) 215–231; Sweeney, *Isaiah 1–39* 175–188.

as adversaries and snares for Israel. Many scholars see this pericope as an exilic redaction of the DtrH that attempts to correct the portrayal of a full conquest of the land under Joshua by working Judges 1:1–2:5 into the narrative.[20] The continued presence of the Canaanites would then become a means to explain the apostasy of Israel presented throughout the DtrH and the ultimate collapse of both Israel and Judah, which the DtrH attributes to apostasy from YHWH due to continued Canaanite influence. As indicated above, however, the positive portrayal of Judah in this section precludes such a setting in that it demonstrates the continuing polemical interests of Judah to assert its leadership position over that of the northern tribes. Furthermore, the discussion presented points to the role that Beth-El, identified here as Bochim, plays in this scenario. Overall, the present form of the narrative presents a rereading of the book of Joshua that makes several points. First, it highlights the role of Judah as the only tribe able to fulfill YHWH's commands to drive out the Canaanites from its midst. This is in contrast to the narratives in Joshua 1–12 that point to the destruction of nearly all the Canaanites throughout the land. Second, it points to the continuing presence of Canaanites among the tribal allotments, much like Joshua 13–22, but it emphasizes the Canaanite presence among the northern tribes, whereas Joshua 13–22 emphasizes the territories that are allotted to the tribes. Third, it represents the narrative in Joshua 24 concerning the assembly at Shechem prior to Joshua's death as an assembly at Beth-El that sees the condemnation of the people for their failure to expel the Canaanites. Again, the emphasis on the role of Beth-El in this scenario points to the interests of the Josianic DtrH.

Clearly, this discussion demonstrates that the book of Judges is to be read in relation to the book of Joshua in the present form of the DtrH. Whereas Joshua presents the ideal vision of a united Israel occupying the entire land, Judges 1–2 shows the reality of a disunited Israel that was unable to drive out the Canaanites and thereby began to disintegrate as a result of its Canaanization. Joshua represents the goal of the DtrH, but Judges represents the problems that prevent the realization of that goal. To clarify the historiographical and theological perspective of the DtrH and its literary history, analysis must now turn to Joshua.

8

Joshua

One of the major results of Noth's Deuteronomistic History hypothesis was to challenge the notion that the book of Joshua should be read as a continuation of the Pentateuchal sources, particularly J, E, and P, and to define it instead as the introduction to the Deuteronomistic presentation of the history of Israel in Joshua-Kings.[1] Scholars had already agreed that much of Joshua's framework in Joshua was Deuteronomistic and thereby related to the book of Deuteronomy or the D source of the Pentateuch, but Noth pointed to the programmatic historiographic character of the book in relation to the following books of Judges-Kings. In arguing his case, Noth maintained that framework texts, such as the introduction in Joshua 1, the account of Joshua's initial covenant ceremony at Mt. Ebal and Mt. Gerizim in Joshua 8:30–35, the summary of Israel's conquests in Joshua 12, and the account of Joshua's summation speech in Joshua 23, played major roles in defining the historiographic perspective of the book as an account of Israel's conquest of the land and covenant with YHWH. Although the hand of the Deuteronomistic Historian was evident elsewhere as well, the rest of the book was largely traditional material that the Deuteronomistic Historian had taken up and incorporated into the overarching historical framework. Subsequent scholarship has continued to assert that J, E, and P material is present in the work, particularly in the materials concerning the allotment of the land in Joshua 13–22,[2] but such contentions

---

1. For an overview of research concerning the relationship between Joshua and the DtrH, see Brian Peckham, "The Significance of the Book of Joshua in Noth's Theory of the Deuteronomistic History," in *The History of Israel's Traditions*, ed. McKenzie and Graham, 213–234. See also Robert Boling, "Joshua, Book of," *ABD* III 1002–1015, for an overview of research in general.

2. For example, Enzo Cortese, *Josua 13–21: Ein priesterschriftlicher Abschnitt im deuteronomistischen Geschichtswerk*, OBO 94 (Freiburg: Universitätsverlag; Göttingen: Vandenhoeck & Ruprecht, 1990).

do not undermine the role defined by Noth for Joshua in relation to the DtrH. Instead, it provides evidence that Joshua constitutes an important link in the overall "primary history" of Genesis–Kings and demonstrates that this interrelationship must be explored.[3]

Nevertheless, the book of Joshua has received relatively less attention as a component of the DtrH than books such as 1–2 Kings or Judges, as scholars have chosen instead to focus especially on attempts to reconstruct the historical events portrayed within the book or the social character of the Israelite tribes in the premonarchic period.[4] Various attempts have been made to establish exilic and Josianic Deuteronomistic redactions of Joshua, but for the most part they have allowed views of the earliest layers of the text to set the terms by which the DtrH material is interpreted. This results in treatment of the posited DtrH material as supplementary to earlier layers of tradition, which gives relatively less attention to the shape and ideology of the book as a whole. As Peckham points out in his discussion of Joshua in relation to Noth's DtrH hypothesis, there is a need to recognize Noth's fundamental insight that the DtrH writer of Joshua is an author, despite the extensive use of earlier traditional material, who shapes the entire work according to a well-conceived historiographic plan for the work as a whole.[5] Joshua thereby requires treatment as literature and as a component of the overall DtrH. This is of particular importance for establishing the existence of a Josianic edition of the work insofar as the preceding analysis notes that Joshua stands as a model for Josiah.[6]

Such an attempt requires assessment of Joshua's literary form. For the most part, scholars have come to accept a basic three-part division for the book based largely on the major themes of its components—that is, Joshua 1–12 relates the conquest of the entire land; Joshua 13–21/3 relates the division of the land among the tribes; and the appendix in Joshua 24 (or 22/23–24) concludes the book with an account of Joshua's final speech to the people in a covenant ceremony at Shechem.[7] But such a scheme also needs to account for some of the fundamental formal and thematic features of this text,[8] such as the major syntactical disjunction at Joshua 13:13; the report of the initial Shechem covenant ceremony at Mt. Ebal and Mt. Gerizim in Joshua 8:30–35; the repeated references to the kings

3. For the thesis of a "primary history" that comprises Genesis–2 Kings, see David Noel Freedman, "Deuteronomic History," *IDB[S]* 226–228.

4. See Boling, "Joshua, Book of"; Robert G. Boling and G. Ernest Wright, *Joshua*, AB 6 (Garden City, N.Y.: Doubleday, 1982) 1–108, for discussion of these issues.

5. Peckham, "The Significance of the Book of Joshua," 213.

6. For discussion of the analogy between Joshua and Josiah, see Nelson, "Josiah in the Book of Joshua."

7. Cf. Noth, *The Deuteronomistic History* 36–41; Boling, "Joshua, Book of," 102; J. A. Soggin, *Joshua: A Commentary*, OTL, translated by R. A. Wilson (Philadelphia: Westminster, 1972) 1–3; Otto Kaiser, *Introduction to the Old Testament*, translated by J. Sturdy (Minneapolis: Augsburg, 1975) 134–135; Rolf Rendtorff, *The Old Testament: An Introduction*, translated by J. Bowden (Philadelphia: Fortress, 1986) 165.

8. N.B. the alternative structures laid out by Peckham, "The Significance," 229–232, and Boling, "Joshua, Book of," 1002.

of Canaan hearing about Joshua and Israel in Joshua 5:1, 9:1, 10:1, and 11:1; the concluding statements of Israel's possession of the whole land in Joshua 11:23 and 21:43–45; the references to Joshua's advanced age in Joshua 13:1 and 23:1; and the interrelationship between the accounts of Joshua's final speeches to the people in Joshua 23 and 24. All of these features must be considered in an assessment of the literary form of the book.

Overall, the book of Joshua comprises an account of YHWH's granting possession of the land to Israel.[9] The basic structure of the book comprises two major portions: the account of YHWH's enabling Joshua and Israel to conquer the land from its previous inhabitants in Joshua 1–12 and the account of the apportionment of the land to the tribes of Israel in Joshua 13–24.[10] There are several bases for this division, including the syntactical differentiation between Joshua 1–12 and 13–24, in which Joshua 13 begins with the statement, "And Joshua was old, advanced in days." This statement does not begin with the normal *waw*-consecutive narrative tense that appears throughout the entire book, but it begins with a combination of a conjunction and Joshua's name prior to the verb, *wîhôšuʿa zāqēn bāʾ bayyāmîm*. Although Joshua 12:1 also begins with a somewhat similar construction, "And these are the kings of the land (*wĕʾelleh malkê hāʾāreṣ*) whom the sons of Israel smote and took possession of their lands . . . ," the initial demonstrative pronoun "these" requires a syntactical antecedent, which is to be found in the repeated formulas concerning the kings of Canaan who heard about Joshua and Israel in Joshua 5:1, 9:1, 10:1, and 11:1.[11] Joshua 12 closes the account of the conquest, but Joshua 3 opens

---

9. The literary form appears to be based in part on Neo-Assyrian campaign reports and grant treaties from the eighth–seventh centuries B.C.E. For discussion of the relationship of the book of Joshua to these forms, see John Van Seters, "Joshua's Campaign of Canaan and Near Eastern Historiography," *SJOT* 4/2 (1990) 1–12; Moshe Weinfeld, "The Covenantal Aspect of the Promise of the Land to Israel," in *The Promise of the Land: The Inheritance of the Land of Canaan by the Israelites* (Berkeley: University of California, 1993) 222–264; Richard Hess, "A Typology of West-Semitic Place Name Lists with Special Reference to Joshua 13–21," *BA* 59 (1996) 160–170. See also Lori L. Rowlett, *Joshua and the Rhetoric of Violence: A New Historicist Analysis*, JSOTSup 226 (Sheffield: Sheffield Academic Press, 1996), who argues that the book of Joshua employs Assyrian language concerning violence and conquest as part of its own effort to assert Judean identity and interests during the Josianic period in the aftermath of the Assyrian collapse and thereby to differentiate itself from the oppressor. Volkmar Fritz (*Das Buch Josua*, HAT I/7 [Tübingen: J. C. B. Mohr (Paul Siebeck), 1994] 17) attempts to deny this hypothesis on the grounds that Joshua excludes common Assyrian elements, such as the appeal to the gods. His position is based in large measure on his view that Joshua employs earlier material that reflects a concern with occupation of the land, analogous to the J traditions of the Pentateuch. He also appears to allow his views of the literary presentation of Israel's early history to influence his assessment of the later book of Joshua. His criteria appear to be far too rigid, in that he expects nearly exact correspondence in the formal elements of Joshua and the Assyrian accounts, and thereby overlooks the role that Assyrian concepts and writing practices play in influencing the form of the Joshua tradition rather than in dictating their overall form.

10. Cf. Fritz, *Josua* 2–9, 14–17, who comes to similar conclusions, but on literary historical grounds.

11. For a recent assessment of the notices in Joshua concerning the Canaanites' hearing of Joshua and Israel, see Lawson G. Stone, "Ethical and Apologetic Tendencies in the Redaction of the Book of Joshua," *CBQ* 53 (1991) 25–36. He is correct to note the role that the formulas in Joshua

the account of the apportionment. The account of the apportionment continues
through Joshua 24. The notice of Joshua's advanced age in Joshua 23:1, formulated in *waw*-consecutive form, ties the account of Joshua's summation speech to
the accounts of land distribution in Joshua 13–22 and provides an exhortation to
the people to keep YHWH's commandments in order that they might keep the land.
Furthermore, the account of the covenant ceremony at Shechem and the death and
burial notices concerning Joshua, Joseph, and Eleazar are tied to Joshua 23 by the
introductory *waw*-consecutive formulation of Joshua 24:1 and by the concern to
ratify the terms of the covenant by which the land is granted to the people.

The structure of the account concerning YHWH's enabling Israel to conquer
the land in Joshua 1–12 is fundamentally determined by the report of YHWH's
instructions to take possession of the land in Joshua 1:1–9 and the report of Joshua's
successful compliance with that instruction in Joshua 1:10–12:24. In the first subunit, the narrative conveys YHWH's instructions to be strong and of good courage, as YHWH will give to Israel all portions of the land on which it treads.
YHWH's speech provides several fundamental premises that underlie the entire
presentation of Joshua—that is, that YHWH is granting the land to Israel as promised to the ancestors; that YHWH is fulfilling YHWH's portion of the covenant
with Israel; that Israel is obligated to serve YHWH in return; and that the land of
Israel will extend through the entire Syro-Israelite corridor from Mesopotamia to
Egypt and from the Trans-Jordan to the Mediterranean Sea.

The report of Joshua's compliance with YHWH's instructions is more complex. It begins in Joshua 1:10–18 with a report of Joshua's instructions to the people
to begin preparations for the conquest of the land, including the need to gather
provisions and instructions to the Trans-Jordanian tribes to join in the conquest
of the land of Canaan proper west of the Jordan River. The second subunit follows in Joshua 2:1–23 with an account of Joshua's sending spies into the city of
Jericho and their experience with Rahab, who hid them from the king's soldiers,
thereby saving their lives and securing an oath that she and her family would be
spared when Israel conquered the city. The subunit concludes with the spies statement in Joshua 2:24, "Indeed YHWH has given into our hands all the land, and
all the inhabitants of the land are dismayed before us." The third subunit in

---

9:1, 10:1, and 11:1 play in organizing Joshua 9–11, but he allows thematic considerations to over-
ride the formal features of the text in Joshua 2–5. In short, he sees the sequence of action in crossing the Jordan and preparing for the campaign against Jericho as criteria to define Joshua 2–5. He
is correct to note the lexical parallels between Rahab's statement in Joshua 2:10–11 concerning the
fear of the Canaanites and Joshua 5:1, but fails to note that the notice in Joshua 5:1 functions as an
introduction to the following material concerning the conquest of Jericho and Ai in a manner analogous to that of Joshua 9:1–2, 10:1–2, and 11:1–5. As noted in the discussion of the structure of
Joshua 5–8 below (cf. Peckham, "The Significance," 229, 231, for a similar assessment of the structure of Joshua 5–8), the ritual acts of circumcision and observance of Passover and the encounter
with YHWH's military commander are essential to portraying the conquests of Jericho and Ai as
acts of holy war. The reference to the fear of the Canaanite kings in Joshua 5:1 thereby aids in presenting the conquest of these cities as acts of YHWH in which Canaanite resistance is virtually
meaningless in these narratives, apart from the initial success at Ai due to the sin of Achan. It also
points forward to Joshua 9–11, and thereby prepares the reader for these narratives as well.

Joshua 3:1–4:24 relates the miraculous crossing of the Jordan River in 3:1–17, in which YHWH divides the water so that the people walk across dry land as in the crossing of the Red Sea, and Joshua 4:1–24, which relates the establishment of twelve stones in the Jordan while the people passed in order to commemorate the event. The result was the establishment of a camp at Gilgal.

The balance of the subunit in Joshua 5–12 relates the campaigns against the major cities and regions of Canaan. It is demarcated by its concern with the kings of Canaan, including the formulaic statements concerning their hearing of YHWH's and Israel's actions in Joshua 5:1, 9:1, 10:1, and 11:1, and the summation of the kings who were defeated and dispossessed by Joshua and Israel in Joshua 12:1–24. Each of the formulaic statements marks the beginning of a new subsection. Thus, Joshua 5:1–8:35[12] relates the conquest of the central region in four basic episodes: the circumcision of the men and the observance of Passover at Gilgal in Joshua 5:1–12, which culminates in the people's eating the fruit of the land; the account of Joshua's encounter with YHWH's angelic commander, which designates the land as holy ground, and the conquest of Jericho in Joshua 5:13–6:27; the account of the conquest of Ai near Beth-El in Joshua 7:1–8:29, including the initial defeat due to Achan's theft from the proscribed spoils of Jericho and the victory over Ai once the evil had been removed with the punishment of Achan and his family; and, finally, the account in Joshua 8:30–35 of the covenant made by Joshua at Mt. Ebal and Mt. Gerizim near Shechem, in which he wrote a copy of the Torah of Moses and read it before the people. Joshua 9:1–11:23 relates the conquest of the balance of the land in several episodes.[13] This section begins with an initial statement in Joshua 9:1–2 concerning the gathering of the kings of Canaan for war against Israel after hearing of Joshua's and Israel's victories. It continues with an account in Joshua 9:3–27 of the ruse by Gibeon, beginning with an initial statement in Joshua 9:3 that the people of Gibeon heard about Joshua's victories at Jericho and Ai, in which the Gibeonites deceived Israel into making a covenant with them. The account in Joshua 10:1–43 of the conquest of the southern region, including the defeat of a coalition of the kings of Jerusalem, Hebron, Yarmuth, Lachish, and Eglon who attempted to attack Gibeon, begins with the initial statement in Joshua 10:1–2 that Adoni-Zedek, King of Jerusalem, had heard of Joshua's victories and covenant with Gibeon. The account in Joshua 11:1–15 of the conquest of the northern region centered around Hazor, begins with the initial statement in Joshua 11:1–5 that King Jabin of Hazor heard of Israel's victories and assembled a coalition of kings to oppose them. Joshua 11:16–23 provides a summation of Joshua's and Israel's conquest of the entire land with the exception of the Philistine cities of Gaza, Gath, and Ashdod. Finally, Joshua 12:1–24 enumerates the kings of Canaan who were defeated and dispossessed by Israel to conclude the account of YHWH's granting the land to Israel.

The account of the apportionment of the land then follows in Joshua 13–24. The basic structure of this subunit is determined by the notices of Joshua's advanced

---

12. Cf. Peckham, "The Significance," 229, 231.
13. Cf. Stone, "Ethical and Apologetic Tendencies," 31–34.

age in Joshua 13:1 and 23:1, which mark the two major stages of this narrative and its subsections in Joshua 13–22 and 23–24. The subunits of Joshua 13–22 are evident by the geographical and tribal divisions of the land, and by the opening and closing statements for each section. The first section is Joshua 13:1–33, which takes up the western and eastern portions of the land. The report of YHWH's speech in Joshua 13:1–7 states that YHWH will eventually drive out the Philistines who occupy the western region, and the narrative in Joshua 13:8–33 takes up the distribution of the Trans-Jordanian lands to Manasseh, Reuben, and Gad. The unit closes in Joshua 13:32–33, which sums up Moses' distribution of the eastern land, and reports that Levi would receive Israel as an inheritance rather than land. The second section is Joshua 14:1–21:45, which takes up the distribution of the western lands. The subunit begins with an introduction in Joshua 14:1–5, which relates that Joshua and Eleazar the priest would distribute the western lands. It continues with an account of the distribution of land from Gilgal to Caleb (Josh 14:6–15); Judah (Josh 15:1–63); and the Joseph tribes Ephraim and Manasseh (Josh 16:1–17:18). Joshua 18:1–19:15 relate the distribution of land by lot to the remaining seven tribes, including Benjamin, Simeon, Zebulun, Issachar, Asher, Naphtali, Dan, and finally to Joshua, from Shiloh. Joshua 20:1–21:42 relates the distribution of Levitical cities to the tribe of Levi. The subunit concerning distribution of the western lands in Joshua 14:1–21:45 closes with a summary statement in Joshua 21:43–45 that YHWH gave the land to Israel, gave them rest from enemies, and fulfilled all promises for good. Finally, Joshua 22:1–34 relates the resolution of the dispute between the western tribes and the Trans-Jordanian tribes concerning the existence of a Trans-Jordanian altar. When the eastern tribes indicated that it was merely a witness to their intention to serve YHWH and not a declaration of independence from the west, the issue was settled.

The second major subunit of Joshua 13–24 is the account of the ratification of the covenant by which land is granted to Israel in Joshua 23:1–24:33. It includes three basic components that close out the account of the distribution of the land and the book as a whole. The first is Joshua 23:1–16, which presents Joshua's exhortation speech to the people that aims to persuade them to observe YHWH's covenant and commandments in order to maintain possession of the land that YHWH has granted. Chief among the commands that Joshua relates in this speech are the commands to follow only YHWH and to avoid marrying into the Canaanite nations and thereby turning to their gods. The second is Joshua 24:1–28, which provides an account of the covenant made between Israel and YHWH at Shechem, in which Joshua relates YHWH's actions on behalf of Israel from the time of Abraham to the present, and the people swear to adhere only to YHWH. The third section in Joshua 24:29–33 relates the death and burial of Joshua in Timnath Serah (Josh 24:28–31), the burial of Joseph in Shechem (Josh 24:32), and the death and burial of Eleazar in Gibeah (Josh 24:33).

The structure of the book may portrayed as in table 8.1. This analysis of the structure and generic character of the book of Joshua reveals two important features of the book that must be considered. First, it portrays the conquest of the land of Israel as the result of YHWH's decision to grant the land to the people in

TABLE 8.1   Structure and genre of the Book of Joshua

Narrative account of YHWH's granting land to Israel	*Joshua 1–24*
I. Concerning YHWH's enabling Joshua and Israel to conquer the land	1:1–12:24
A. Report of YHWH's instructions to Joshua to take possession of land	1:1–9
B. Report of Joshua's successful compliance with YHWH's instruction	1:10–12:24
1. Report of Joshua's instructions to people concerning campaign	1:10–18
2. Report of Joshua's sending spies to Jericho and experience with Rahab	2:1–23
3. Report of miraculous crossing of Jordan	3:1–4:24
a. Crossing of Jordan	3:1–17
b. Establishment of twelve stone in Jordan by Gilgal	4:1–24
4. Report of campaigns against Canaan	5:1–12:24
a. Conquest of central region	5:1–8:35
i. Circumcision and observance of Passover at Gilgal	5:1–12
ii. Encounter with divine commander and conquest of Jericho	5:13–6:27
iii. Conquest of Ai near Beth-El	7:1–8:29
iv. Covenant at Shechem and reading of Torah	8:30–35
b. Conquest of balance of the land	9:1–11:23
i. Gathering of Canaanite kings of war	9:1–2
ii. Covenant with Gibeon	9:3–27
iii. Conquest of southern region	10:1–43
iv. Conquest of northern region	11:1–15
v. Summation of Joshua's and Israel's conquest of the land	11:16–23
c. Enumeration of Canaanite kings defeated and dispossessed by Israel	12:1–24
II. Concerning apportionment of land to Israel	13:1–24:33
A. Distribution of the land to the tribes	13:1–22:34
1. Overview concerning distribution of western and eastern portions of land	13:1–33
a. Report of YHWH speech promising to drive out Philistine in west	13:1–7
b. Distribution of Trans-Jordanian lands to Manasseh, Reuben, and Gad	13:8–33
2. Concerning distribution of western lands	14:1–21:45
a. Concerning disribution by Eleazar and Joshua to Caleb, Judah, and Joseph from Gilgal	14:1–17:18
i. Introduction	14:1–5
ii. Distribution to Caleb	14:6–15
iii. Distribution to Judah	15:1–63
iv. Distribution to Joseph tribes	16:1–17:18
b. Concerning distribution of land by lot to seven tribes from Shiloh	18:1–19:15
c. Concerning distribution of Levitical cities to Levi	20:1–21:42
d. Summation statement concerning fulfillment of YHWH's promises	21:43–45
3. Resolution of status of eastern tribes as part of Israel	22:1–34
B. Ratification of covenant by which YHWH grants land to Israel	23:1–24:33
1. Report of Joshua's exhortation speech to promote YHWH's covenant	23:1–16
2. Report of covenant at Shechem	24:1–28
3. Concluding death and burial notices	24:29–33
a. Joshua	24:29–31
b. Joseph	24:32
c. Eleazar	24:33

return for Israel's fidelity to YHWH's expectations.[14] Overall, it presents Israel's possession of the land as the result of a covenant or agreement with YHWH in which both parties have a certain set of defined expectations, viz., YHWH is expected to provide the land, and Israel is expected to accept YHWH as the only G-d and to observe YHWH's commandments. Interpretation of the book of Joshua generally focuses on either one of these themes—Israel's conquest of the land and the questions raised by violence and dispossession of the Canaanite people or YHWH's "gift" of the land to Israel—but the two must be considered together. Although Israel fields an army of warriors who carry out the actual combat, the book of Joshua presents the conquest of the land of Israel as an act of G-d in which YHWH essentially grants victory to Israel. This is evident from the repeated notices of divine involvement in the conquest, such as the initial parting of the Jordan River so that the people could cross over into the land, the appearance of YHWH's army commander to Joshua at Jericho, the miraculous collapse of Jericho's walls as a result of a cultic procession around the city, the initial defeat of Israel at Ai as a result of Achan's theft from the booty of Jericho and the subsequent victory once Achan was punished and the evil was removed from Israel, the miracle of the stones from heaven and the sun's standing still that enabled Israel to defeat the southern Canaanite kings at Gibeon, and YHWH's statement to Joshua that Hazor would be given to Israel. Divine intervention is evident at every stage of the conquest; indeed, only thirty-six Israelites die in the conquest of Canaan, and this takes place only because of the sin of Achan. But whereas the course of the campaign is clearly the result of YHWH's intervention, the conclusion of the book demonstrates that this is no free "gift." Rather, the presentation of the covenant between Israel and YHWH in Joshua 24 (cf. Josh 8:30–35) demonstrates that the conquest of the land represents YHWH's fulfillment of the terms of the relationship with Israel. Israel has requirements to fill as well.[15] This, of course, is not portrayed in the book of Joshua, which focuses on YHWH, but it is the subject of the balance of the DtrH. Insofar as Joshua portrays YHWH's fulfillment of the terms of the covenant and then looks forward to Israel's fulfillment of the agreement, Joshua sets the terms by which the DtrH historical account is to be read, and thereby stands as the introduction to the DtrH.

Second, although the narrative clearly portrays Israel as the totality of the twelve tribes, the imagery portrayed throughout points especially to the northern kingdom as the center of Israel. Joshua, for example, is a member of the tribe of Ephraim, who serves as the central leader of all twelve tribes, including Judah, and who is ultimately buried in Timnath Serah in the land of Ephraim. Eleazar ben Aaron is buried in Gibeah in Benjamin. Major sites in the narrative empha-

---

14. Cf. the discussion by Weinfeld of the interrelationship between Joshua and Assyrian treaty forms that grant land to vassals ("The Covenantal Aspect of the Promise of the Land to Israel").

15. Cf. the discussion by Harry Orlinsky of the land promise motifs in the Bible, in which he demonstrates the contractual nature of YHWH's granting land to Israel in return for observance of YHWH's requirements ("The Biblical Concept of the Land of Israel: Cornerstone of the Covenant Between G-d and Israel," in *The Land of Israel: Jewish Perspectives*, ed. L. A. Hoffman [Notre Dame: University of Notre Dame, 1986] 27–64).

size northern or Benjaminite locales. Both narratives concerning the covenant between YHWH and Israel are set at Shechem in Ephraim, again in keeping with Deuteronomy 27, but this feature points to the north as the center of the people. Gilgal in the territory of Ephraim near Benjamin serves as the central base for the people during the conquest. It serves together with Shiloh in Ephraim as a central location for the distribution of land among the tribes. Major cities conquered by the people include Jericho in Benjamin near Ephraim, Ai in Ephraim near Beth-El and Benjamin, Gibeon in Benjamin, and Hazor in Naphtali. Overall, the central areas of Israel in Ephraim/Manasseh and Benjamin receive a great deal of attention, whereas outlying regions are defined in relation to this central area. Thus, the initial covenant in Joshua 8:30–35 is concluded following the conquest of Jericho and Ai in Benjamin. The Trans-Jordanian tribes, subject to northern control or contention at various points in subsequent Israelite history, submit to Joshua and Israel after the people gather at Shiloh in Ephraim to force their hand. The southern regions of Judah are conquered by Joshua and Israel only as a result of the relationship with Gibeon in Benjamin. Indeed, the only point at which the tribe of Judah receives special recognition is in the distribution of the land, in which Caleb and Judah receive land first, followed by the Joseph tribes, and subsequently the remaining seven tribes on the peripheries of the land. This is clearly in keeping with the presentation of Deuteronomy, which also focuses on northern locations and personalities even when the message of cultic centralization seems to have Jerusalem in mind. Overall, northern locales, figures, and power relationships among the twelve tribes predominate in the Joshua account. The book of Joshua portrays Israel according to a northern model.

Both of these factors must be considered in the interpretation of Joshua, not only in and of itself, but in relation to the DtrH as well. Joshua presents YHWH's fulfillment of the covenant with Israel, and looks forward to Israel's fulfillment of its obligations, but through the course of the historical presentation of the DtrH, Israel fails to fulfill its obligations. This is evident immediately following Joshua in the book of Judges and continues through 2 Kings. At this point, the emphasis in Joshua on northern locales and figures is important in that the theme of Israel's failure to fulfill its covenant obligations extends only through the presentation of Israel's downfall to Assyria in 2 Kings 17. When Hezekiah turns to YHWH in 2 Kings 18–20, he and Jerusalem are saved. When Manasseh sins in 2 Kings 21, YHWH decides to destroy Jerusalem and Judah, not because of the sins of the people, but because of the sins of Manasseh. Afterwards, the righteous actions of Josiah and the wicked actions of Jehoiakim and Zedekiah are irrelevant to YHWH's decision and to the course of Israel's/Judah's history. The northern kingdom falls because it fails to fulfill its covenant obligations; Judah falls because its Davidic king Manasseh fails to adhere to YHWH.

These considerations suggest that the book of Joshua is not designed to anticipate the exile of all Israel from the land at the end of the book. Indeed, the general theme of a covenant between all Israel and YHWH for possession of the land of Israel may be read in relation to the destruction of Jerusalem and the exile of Judah to Babylon, but there is no indication of specific anticipation of such a scenario in Joshua other than the general concern with the loss of land if Israel does not fulfill the terms of the covenant (Josh 23:14–16). Rather, Joshua points to Ephraim and Benjamin as central regions and the Ephraimite Joshua as a central figure in the book, all of which relate to the subsequent northern kingdom of Israel. Insofar as Joshua portrays Israel largely in relation to northern Israelite images, this would suggest that the book of Joshua anticipates the failure and exile of the northern Israelite kingdom.

It is at this point that Nelson's observations concerning the portrayal of Joshua as an ideal monarchic leader and model for King Josiah become pertinent.[16] Nelson points to several factors that demonstrate that Joshua is "a thinly disguised Josianic figure who acts out the events of Dtr's own day on the stage of the classical past."[17] YHWH's instructions to Joshua in Joshua 1:7–8 call for Joshua to meditate night and day on the Torah that Moses commanded and to act upon it, not turning to the right or left. The language of this verse clearly recalls the language employed in the Torah of the King in Deuteronomy 17:18–20 and the language applied to the evaluation of Josiah's reign in 2 Kings 22:2 and 23:25. This language appears once again in Joshua's exhortation speech to Israel in Joshua 23, in which he counsels the people "to keep and do all that is written in the book of the Torah of Moses, turning from it neither to the right hand nor to the left" (v. 6) in the context of a speech that exhorts the people not to intermarry with the Canaanites and thereby adopt their gods. The Torah motif appears once again in the account of the covenant ceremony between Israel and YHWH at Shechem in Joshua 8:30–35, in which Joshua writes a copy of the Torah of Moses, employing the same language as Deuteronomy 17:18, and reads it before the people in keeping with Josiah's actions in 2 Kings 23:1–3 and the instructions to read the Torah to the people in Deuteronomy 31:9–14. In this regard, Joshua's covenant ceremony at Shechem stands as a model for Josiah's covenant ceremony at Jerusalem. Nelson notes that scholars have puzzled over the inclusion of this narrative insofar as Joshua 24 also presents a covenant ceremony at Shechem, and concludes that it is the result of Dtr's willingness to break into a source in order to facilitate the analogy between Josiah and Joshua. In this regard, the association of the covenant narrative with the conquest of Ai is important. Ai is associated with Beth-El, later the royal altar of the northern kingdom of Israel which Josiah destroyed as part of his reform program. By placing a covenant ceremony at Shechem modeled on that of Josiah, in which Joshua and the people read and hear the Torah of Moses as the basis for their covenant with YHWH, the book of Joshua points both to the failure of the north to fulfill this covenant and the attempt by Josiah to do so. Finally, Nelson notes that Josiah's observance of the Passover (2 Kgs 23:21–23) was the first since the time of Joshua's observance at Gilgal (Josh 5:10–12). Clearly, Joshua 1, 5, 8, and 23 play key roles in establishing the analogy between Joshua and Josiah.

It appears likely that the present form of Joshua is designed to establish the analogy between Joshua and Josiah, although it does not appear that the basic form of the book was originally composed for this purpose. Smend has already argued

16. Nelson, "Josiah in the Book of Joshua."
17. Nelson, "Josiah in the Book of Joshua," 540.

for the existence of a "nomistic" redactional layer in Joshua from the exilic period, which he identifies in Joshua 1:7–9, 13:1bβ–6, and 23, and which he associates with the redactional reworking of Judges 2:17, 20–21, 23 and the insertion of 1:1–2:9.[18] He views this as an updating of the basic Deuteronomistic source that emphasizes the theme of obedience to the "law" as a means to explain the exile of Israel to Babylonia in the DtrH. Many of his presuppositions may be questioned, but his fundamental insights concerning the literary tension between Joshua 1:7–9 and its context and between Joshua 23 and 24 stand. Joshua 1:7–9 repeats the fundamental instruction of Joshua 1:6 to "be strong and of good courage" and emphasizes that instruction by focusing on the need for observance of Torah as the means for continued possession of the land. Joshua 23 is frequently viewed as a doublet with Joshua 24, or vice versa, although it merely prepares for the formal conclusion of the covenant by presenting an exhortation for the people to do so. Nevertheless, the presentation of first one assembly followed by a second is noteworthy in that one would expect both to take place together. Furthermore, the theme of Mosaic Torah is key here in that it is presupposed throughout Joshua on the basis of Joshua 1:7–9, 8:30–35, and 23, but Joshua writes the "Torah of G-d" in Joshua 24:26 and makes it the basis of the covenant between Israel and YHWH at Shechem. Why should this Torah be written when it was already commanded in Joshua 1 and 23 and both written and read to the people in Joshua 8:30–35?[19] Given the Josianic associations of the language in these chapters established above, this would suggest that Joshua 1 and 23 are the product of redaction that is designed to establish the analogy between Joshua and Josiah. Likewise, Joshua 8:30–35 also appears to be the product of such redaction, insofar as it seems to be somewhat out of place in its present location and provides an alternative account of a Shechem covenant. As noted, the association of this narrative with the conquest of Ai near Beth-El facilitates critique of Beth-El and the analogy between Josiah and Joshua.

As part of a Josianic edition of the DtrH, the book of Joshua points to Israel's covenant with YHWH as the basis for its possession of the land, and it maintains that the covenant is based upon the Torah of Moses. It portrays Joshua as an ideal leader who observes Torah and reads it to the people as expected in Deuteronomy, but it also portrays Israel along the lines of the later northern kingdom and thereby lays the foundation for an explanation of its fall. Insofar as the northern kingdom did not observe the covenant in the presentation of the DtrH, it was exiled from the land by the Assyrians. Insofar as Josiah observed the Torah as did Joshua, the possibility for the continuation of the covenant by Judah alone or Israel's restoration to the land might be entertained.

Finally, the question concerning the provenance of a pre-Josianic form of the book must be raised. Apart from the references to Mosaic Torah and the analogy

18. "Das Gesetz und die Völker."

19. N.B. the term Torah appears elsewhere in Joshua only in Joshua 22:5, in which the Trans-Jordanian tribes are instructed to observe the commandment and the Torah. Here it functions not as a general term for Mosaic Torah but as a term for a specific type of instruction analogous to *miṣwâ*, "commandment."

between Joshua and Josiah, Joshua otherwise presents a scenario in which Israel is granted the land by YHWH in return for observance of the covenant at Shechem as expressed in Joshua 24. Again, it portrays Israel largely in northern terms and thereby prepares the reader for Israel's failure to observe the covenant and retain the land as expressed in 2 Kings 17. In this regard, the narrative also appears to form a component of a potential Hezekian edition of the DtrH, insofar as it points to the failure of the north. Furthermore, the conclusion of the covenant at Shechem points forward to the split of the kingdom as presented in 1 Kings 12, which also takes place at Shechem, and thereby raises the issue of Israel's unity and its view of proper kingship. As noted in the preceding discussion, the book of Judges demonstrates the north's inability to establish effective leadership, 1 Samuel 8 points to the request for kingship like the nations and the warning that a king will entail certain obligations for finances and service on the part of the people, and 1 Kings 12 demonstrates the people's willingness to revolt when those expectations are realized under Solomon. Overall, Joshua plays a role in laying the foundation for the critique of northern Israel in the Hezekian DtrH. The people are granted the land by YHWH, but their failure to observe YHWH's expectations and their failure to govern themselves or to accept proper leadership results in their destruction and exile. In the end, only Judah remains to carry on.

9

Deuteronomy

B ecause it serves as the literary and theological basis from which the DtrH is composed, the book of Deuteronomy is generally considered to predate the composition of the DtrH. Nevertheless, it has long occupied an important place in scholarly discussion of the DtrH, particularly because it is believed to have provided the literary and conceptual foundations on which the DtrH is composed. The basis for this interest is the account of King Josiah's reign and reform program in 2 Kings 22:1–23:30.[1] According to this narrative, Josiah's reform program was based on the discovery of an unnamed book of the Torah during the course of Temple renovations that were undertaken in the eighteenth year of Josiah's reign. Because the measures enacted by Josiah, especially the centralization of worship at the Jerusalem Temple and the removal of alternative worship installations in Jerusalem and elsewhere throughout the land, correspond so closely to the requirements of the Deuteronomic lawcode, scholars by and large maintain that the book of the Torah found during Josiah's reign must represent some form of the book of Deuteronomy, perhaps an earlier version that preceded the present form of the book.[2]

---

1. See esp. the first three essays in N. Lohfink, ed., *Das Deuteronomium: Entstehung, Gestalt und Botschaft*, BETL 68 (Leuven: Peeters, 1985), viz. M. J. Paul, "Hilkiah and the Law (2 Kings 22) in the 17th and 18th Centuries: Some Influences on W. M. L. de Wette" (pp. 9–12); J. Lust, "A. Van Hoonacker and Deuteronomy" (pp. 13–23); and N. Lohfink, "Zur neuer Diskussion über 2 Kön 22-23" (pp. 24–48).

2. For surveys of the current state of research on Deuteronomy, see M. A. O'Brien, "The Book of Deuteronomy," *CR:BS* 3 (1995) 95–128; H. D. Preuss, "Zum deuteronomistischen Geschichtswerk," *TRu* 58 (1993) 229–264, esp. 230–245; Preuss, *Deuteronomium*, ErFor 164 (Darmstadt: Wissenschaftliche Buchgesellschaft, 1982); R. E. Clements, *Deuteronomy*, OTG (Sheffield: JSOT Press, 1989); N. Lohfink, "Deuteronomy," *IDB[S]* 229–232; M. Weinfeld, "Deuteronomy, Book of" *ABD* II 168–183; see also M. Weinfeld, Deuteronomy 1–11, AB 5 (New York: Doubleday, 1991) 1–122.

Despite this close association between Deuteronomy and the policies of the Judean monarch Josiah, scholars generally argue that Deuteronomy owes its composition to circles that were rooted in the religious traditions of the northern kingdom of Israel.[3] The hypothesis generally takes one of two forms: either (1) an early edition of the book was composed in the north and later brought south after the collapse of the northern kingdom of Israel in 721 B.C.E.,[4] or (2) the book was composed in Judah by prophetic disciples or Levitical priests who had fled the northern kingdom in the aftermath of its destruction by the Assyrians[5] or by Judean scribes who employed northern traditions.[6] In both cases, scholars point to the characteristically northern motifs that appear throughout the book: the focus on Shechem rather than on Jerusalem as the location for the ratification of the covenant with YHWH; the emphasis on Mosaic rather than on Davidic tradition to express the relationship between the people and YHWH; and the promulgation of Levitical and prophetic figures as models of authority rather than the monarch. A number of motifs that are characteristic of the southern tradition do appear in the book, such as the ark, the concern with a single central sanctuary, the idea of election, and YHWH's "gift" of land, but they are subsumed into the framework of the Mosaic tradition and redefined so that they conform to northern norms.[7]

In the view of most scholars, Deuteronomy therefore represents an attempt to reform the Judean monarchy and cult, which was rooted in the southern tradition of monarchic rule in Jerusalem based on YHWH's selection of the House of David and Mt. Zion, with northern perspectives that focus on adherence to the principles of social justice and religious fidelity expressed in the Mosaic covenant tradition.[8] Insofar as the "book of the Torah" found in Josiah's Temple restoration is identified as a form of the book of Deuteronomy, scholars maintain that Josiah tempered the Judean ideology of unconditional monarchic authority based on divine election with the northern ideology of divine favor conditioned by adherence to Mosaic law—that is, Josiah's reform was intended to limit the power of the monarchy by subjecting it to Mosaic law.[9]

A number of considerations regarding the political ideology of the Josianic reform and the socioeconomic implications of the laws of Deuteronomy raise questions that may challenge this consensus. The narrative concerning Josiah's

3. See Adam C. Welch, *The Code of Deuteronomy: A New Theory of its Origin* (London: James Clarke, [1924]; more recently, H. Louis Ginsberg, *The Israelian Heritage of Judaism* (New York: Jewish Theological Seminary, 1982).

4. A. Alt, "Die Heimat des Deuteronomiums," *KS II* (1953) 250–275.

5. E. W. Nicholson, *Deuteronomy and Tradition: Literary and Historical Traditions in the Book of Deuteronomy* (Philadelphia: Fortress, 1967).

6. Weinfeld, *Deuteronomy 1–11* 44–57; cf. idem, *Deuteronomy and the Deuteronomic School* (Oxford: Oxford University Press, 1972).

7. See R. E. Clements, "Deuteronomy and the Jerusalem Cult Tradition," *VT* 15 (1965) 300–312.

8. For example, Nicholson, *Deuteronomy and Tradition*; G. von Rad, *Deuteronomy: A Commentary*, OTL, translated by D. Barton (London: SCM, 1966) 23–30.

9. See, for example, E. W. Nicholson, "Deuteronomy's Vision of Israel," in *Storia e Tradizioni di Israele*, Fs. J. A. Soggins, ed. D. Garrone and F. Israel (Brescia: Paideia, 1991) 191–203.

reign in 2 Kings 22:1–23:30 indicates that one of the goals of Josiah's reform was to reestablish the old Davidic/Solomonic empire by extending Davidic rule over the former northern kingdom of Israel. Such a policy is firmly rooted in the ideology of the Davidic/Jerusalem covenant tradition. Likewise, recent studies of the Deuteronomic concept of centralization demonstrate that it includes not only a requirement for cultic centralization, but the centralization of tax collection and administration of justice that places greater power in the hands of the monarch.[10] Furthermore, Deuteronomy contains a number of legal provisions, such as the law for cultic centralization in Deuteronomy 12:2–31 (cf. Exod 20:21–26), that appear to be alternate versions of laws in Exodus and Numbers that reflect a less centralized religious and socioeconomic power structure.[11] Again, such centralization would serve the interests of the Davidic monarchy. Both of these issues suggest that Deuteronomy was composed to enhance and not to limit the power of the Davidic monarchy; consequently, the question of the provenance and purpose of the book must be reopened. This requires a reexamination of the literary form of Deuteronomy as a basis for a reconstruction of its historical setting and its religiopolitical and socioeconomic outlook. Such considerations demonstrate that the book of Deuteronomy employs various means, such as the call for religious centralization and the reformulation of earlier northern traditions and motifs, to place greater political and socioeconomic power in the hands of the Davidic king. Because Deuteronomy defines ideal kingship in terms that anticipate Josiah's policies, Deuteronomy was apparently composed to support King Josiah's program of religious reform and national restoration.[12]

10. W. Eugene Claburn, "The Fiscal Basis of Josiah's Reforms," *JBL* 92 (1973) 11–22; Naomi Steinberg, "The Deuteronomic Law Code and the Politics of State Centralization," *The Bible and the Politics of Exegesis*, Fs. Norman K. Gottwald, ed. D. Jobling, P. L. Day, and G. T. Sheppard (Cleveland: Pilgrim, 1991) 161-170, 336-339; Y. Suzuki, "Deuteronomic Reformation in View of the Centralization of the Administration of Justice," *AJBI* 13 (1987) 22-58. For an overview of historical and archeological issues relevant to Josiah's reign, see Na'aman, "The Kingdom of Judah Under Josiah."

11. For a discussion of the relation of Deuteronomic laws to other legal traditions, see Bernard M. Levinson, *Deuteronomy and the Hermeneutics of Legal Innovation* (New York and Oxford: Oxford University Press, 1997). Levinson argues that many of the Deuteronomic laws are rewritten versions of earlier laws in Exodus and Numbers. See also Bernard Levinson, "The Case for Revision and Interpolation in within the Biblical Legal Corpora," in *Theory and Method in Biblical and Cuneiform Law: Revision, Interpolation and Development*, JSOTSup 181, ed. B. M. Levinson (Sheffield: Sheffield Academic Press, 1994) 37–59; Eckart Otto, "Aspects of Legal Reforms and Reformulations in Ancient Cuneiform and Israelite Law," in *Theory and Method in Biblical and Cuneiform Law: Revision, Interpolation and Development*, JSOTSup 181, ed. B. M. Levinson (Sheffield: Sheffield Academic Press, 1994) 160–196; Otto, "Vom Bundesbuch zum Deuteronomium: Die deuteronomistische Redaktion in Dtn 12–26," in *Biblische Theologie und gesellschaftlicher Wandel*, Fs. N. Lohfink S.J., ed. G. Braulik, W. Gross, and S. McEvenue (Freiburg, Basel, Vienna; Herder, 1993) 260–278.

12. Cf. Weinfeld, *Deuteronomy 1–11* 44–57; Weinfeld, *Deuteronomy and the Deuteronomic School*, who also maintains that Deuteronomy was composed to support Josiah's reform. In his view, however, the reform was intended to modify Judean religious and political concepts so that they would conform to northern prophetic perspectives.

Deuteronomy occupies a pivotal position in the narrative presentation of the history of Israel and Judah. In its present position at the conclusion of the Pentateuch, Deuteronomy reprises the themes of the earlier books of Genesis–Numbers by reiterating YHWH's promises of land and covenant to Israel's ancestors, the exodus from Egypt and the revelation of YHWH's Torah through Moses, and the journey through the wilderness that brought the people to the eastern banks of the Jordan River prior to their taking possession of the promised land. Insofar as Deuteronomy reiterates YHWH's Torah from Sinai/Horeb, it provides the foundation for understanding the narrative history of Joshua–Kings or the Deuteronomistic History, especially because that history is presented in relationship to Israel's and Judah's adherence to YHWH's Torah as a basis for their possessing the promised land. Overall, the DtrH attempts to demonstrate that the later Assyrian exile of northern Israel and the later Babylonian exile of Judah were due to the people's neglect of YHWH's requirements as expressed in Deuteronomy, especially those of cultic centralization and the prohibition of interrelationships with the Canaanites.

The overarching literary form of Deuteronomy is prose narrative report or account, insofar as the book provides a narrative report or account of Moses' last speeches to the people of Israel on the day of his death, immediately prior to their entry into the land of Canaan. The book therefore also contains a great deal of material formulated as speeches by Moses, but these speeches are subsumed structurally and generically into the overall narrative report/account form of the book. Consequently, the literary structure and genre of the book is constituted by the narrative report/account of Moses' last speeches to the people of Israel on the day of his death, prior to Israel's taking possession of the promised land.

The overall structure of Deuteronomy includes two basic components: the report in Deuteronomy 1:1–30:20 of the words that Moses spoke to the people on the east bank of the Jordan River on the first day of the eleventh month in the fortieth year, and the report in Deuteronomy 31:1–34:12 of Moses' transfer of leadership to Joshua and his death.

The first component is distinguished by the superscription in Deuteronomy 1:1–4, which identifies the following material as "the words that Moses spoke to all Israel" on the east bank of the Jordan River, on the first day of the eleventh month of the fortieth year. It is also distinguished by its conveyance of four speeches by Moses to the people in Deuteronomy 1:5–30:20, each of which is introduced by a narrative speech report form that introduces the speech by Moses per se. The speech report form in Deuteronomy 1:5, "Beyond the Jordan in the land of Moab, Moses began explaining this Torah, saying . . . ," introduces the report of Moses' first speech in Deuteronomy 1:5–4:40. This speech focuses especially on an exhortational resume of Israel's journey from Egypt through the wilderness. Its basic functions are (1) to explain how Israel arrived at its present situation to possess the promised land and to hear the Torah as the basis for that possession, and (2) to provide motivation for the observance of Torah on the part of the people, whether those directly addressed in the book or those readers addressed by the book. The formulation in Deuteronomy 4:44–49, "And this is the Torah that Moses set before the Children of Israel; these are the testimonies and the statutes, and the cases that Moses spoke unto the Children of Israel when they went out from Egypt . . . ," introduces the report of Moses' second speech in Deuteronomy 4:44–26:19. This is the core of the book that focuses especially on conveying the Torah or legal instruction for the people's life in the land that is laid out in great detail. This material apparently constitutes the basis for the fundamental purpose of the book of Deuteronomy. It will be treated in greater detail below. The speech report form in Deuteronomy 27:1, "and Moses and the elders of Israel commanded the people saying . . . ," introduces the report of Moses' third speech to the people in Deuteronomy 27:1–28:69. The basic concern of this speech report is to convey the blessings and curses that are designed to motivate observance of the legal instruction that appears in Moses' second speech to the people. Finally, the speech report form in Deuteronomy 29:1, "and Moses called unto all Israel and he said to them . . . ," introduces the report of Moses' fourth speech to the people in Deuteronomy 29:1–30:20. This speech constitutes the final exhortation to the people to observe YHWH's Torah in the promised land.

The second major component of Deuteronomy in Deuteronomy 31:1–34:12 is distinguished by its introductory statement in Deuteronomy $31:1–2a\alpha^{1-2}$, "And Moses continued and he spoke these words unto all Israel and he said to them . . . ," which reprises the wording, "these are the words that Moses spoke to all Israel," in Deuteronomy 1:1 that introduce the first major section of the book. This section includes speeches by Moses, but they are no longer the lengthy exhortational addresses of Deuteronomy 1:1–30:20; rather, they are shorter speeches and blessings or songs that are subsumed into an overall narrative concerned with the transfer of leadership from Moses to Joshua and Moses' death. The section includes three basic episodes: the report of Moses' writing of the Torah and his transmission of the Torah and leadership to Joshua in Deuteronomy 31:1–29; the report of Moses' final song to Israel in Deuteronomy 31:30–32:47, in which he charges that Israel's rebellion is the reason that he is unable to enter the promised land; and the report of Moses' death in Deuteronomy 32:48–34:12, in which YHWH tells Moses that his own rebellion is the cause of his failure to enter the promised land. On this basis, Moses blesses Israel before he ascends to Nebo to die.

Although the overall form of Deuteronomy is that of a narrative report/ account of Moses' last addresses to Israel, the generic character of Moses' speeches must be considered further in that they contain a number of other generic elements that appear to be included within the more general generic framework. The core of the speeches comprise legal forms, such as variations of the case law form, as their basic element, but the presence of a great deal of 2mp/ 2ms address forms throughout the legal material indicates its generic character not simply as law, but as legal instruction. Not only are the case law forms employed together with second-person address forms to produce the "if-you" forms and the like, but various other instructional forms, such as commands, prohibitions, and orders, appear together with the case forms as legal instruction. In addition, parenetic or exhortational elements aid in motivating the addressees to observe the legal instruction of the book.

In addition to elements of legal instruction and parenesis, suzerain-vassal treaty forms play an important role in defining the language and presentation of the book of Deuteronomy.[13] Attempts to correlate the structure of such treaties with the structure of Deuteronomy have generally proved to be unwarranted, but standard elements from the form appear throughout Deuteronomy. These elements include the identification of the partners to the agreement—that is, YHWH and Israel; the historical prologue expressed through the summaries of YHWH's promises to the ancestors and guidance from Egypt through the wilderness; the stipulations expressed in the form of the book's legal instruction; blessing and curses that appear especially in Deuteronomy 27–30; provisions for the public reading of the agreement that appears in the instructions to read the Torah every seven years at Sukkot (Deut 31); and witnesses to the agreement that are sometimes identified with heaven and earth from Deuteronomy 32:1. The "if-you" instructional form is particularly important here in that it plays an important role in the formulation of stipulations for the vassal in the treaties.[14] Furthermore, the provision that prevents adding or subtracting from the terms of the treaty appears in the so-called canonization formula of Deuteronomy 13:1, "Everything that I command you, you shall be careful to do; you shall not add to it or take from it." Likewise, the following call in Deuteronomy 13:2–19 for the destruction of individuals or cities that rebel from the commands of YHWH correspond to treaty stipulations that call for the destruction of those who would violate the terms of the treaty.

Weinfeld argues that Deuteronomy is heavily influenced by the "testament" form that is especially prominent in Egypt in which kings and viziers convey instructions to their successors.In this instance, the transmission of Torah and leadership from Moses to Joshua plays a prominent role.[15] Although the form may have some influence, it cannot account for the generic character of the entire book. It must be kept in mind that the people of Israel are the primary addressees of the book of Deuteronomy and that Joshua is generally addressed as one of the people.

The Levitical sermon form also appears to play a role in defining the generic character of the book.[16] The Levitical sermon is an exhortational or parenetic speech or preaching form that attempts to convey cultic or legal instruction to the people. Festival occasions, such as Sukkot, would be a likely setting for such speeches as that would be time when the people were gathered to engage in cultic

13. For a summary of the discussion, see Clements, *Deuteronomy* 20–22; see esp. Weinfeld, *Deuteronomy and the Deuteronomic School* 59–157.

14. For a study of the "If-you" form, see H. Gilmer, *The If-You Form in Israelite Law*, SBLDS 15 (Missoula, Mont.: Scholars Press, 1975).

15. Weinfeld, *Deuteronomy 1–11* 4–6.

16. G. von Rad, *Studies in Deuteronomy*, SBT I/9, translated by D. M. G. Stalker (London: SCM, 1953) 11–24. See also Rex A. Mason, *Preaching the Tradition: Homily and Hermeneutics after the Exile* (Cambridge, U.K.: Cambridge University Press, 1990), who objects to von Rad's designation of the speeches in Chronicles as "Levitical sermons," because they are neither Levitical nor sermons. Instead, he sees them as a series of "addresses" that reflect temple preaching by various figures in the post exilic Judean community. Although he is correct to maintain that Levitical is not inherent in the genre, the addresses must be considered as sermons because of their parenetic character. The identification of this form as Levitical sermon presupposes Moses' institutional identification as a Levite and the typical role of Levites in Temple-based instruction (see Jer 7; Neh 8:7–8).

activity that would require or provide the occasion for instruction in such matters. Here Moses "repeats" what the people have experienced or been taught before, which of course calls to mind the repetitive nature of cultic or liturgical instruction in a Temple-based context, in that festivals provide the occasion for the yearly repetition of the same instruction. Some might object that the loss of status and privilege suffered by the Levites throughout the book of Deuteronomy might well challenge the generic identification of Moses' speeches as Levitical sermons, but this would miss an essential point—that is, the Levitical sermon form is used in Deuteronomy expressly for the purpose of challenging Levitical rights. By casting the material in such a form, the author of Deuteronomy employs the Levitical sermon form to add authority to the diminution of Levitical rights as a statement from the epitome of the Levitical role, Moses.[17] Overall, the use of the Levitical sermon form in Moses's speeches aids in characterizing them as Levitical Instruction or Levitical Torah.

Having characterized the whole as a Narrative Account of Moses' Levitical Instruction, analysis may now turn to the organization of Moses' second speech in Deuteronomy 4:44–26:19, which conveys the basic Levitical Torah or instruction of the book. Based on the form of the narrative material, the passage breaks down into two major components. Deuteronomy 4:44–49 employs the statement, "and this is the Torah which Moses set before the children of Israel . . . ," as a means to identify his following speech as (Levitical) Torah and to define historical-narrative setting in which the speech is delivered in the aftermath of Israel's journey through the Trans-Jordan region that brought them to their present possession "beyond the Jordan." The speech form in Deuteronomy 5:1aα^{1-2}, "and Moses called unto all Israel and he said unto them . . . ," introduces the report of Moses' Levitical Torah speech to Israel in Deuteronomy 5:1–26:19.

The organization of the Levitical Torah speech in Deuteronomy 5:1aα^{3-6}–26:19 clearly breaks down into three basic components. The introductory exhortation, which begins with the exhortational statement, "Hear, O Israel, the statutes and the laws that I am speaking in your ears today so that you will learn them and you shall be careful to do them," appears in Deuteronomy 5:1aα^{3-6}–b. The exhortational character of the unit continues through the concluding statements in Deuteronomy 11:31–32, "For you are crossing the Jordan to enter to take possession of the land which YHWH your G-d is giving to you, and you shall possess it and you shall dwell in it and you shall be careful to do all of the statutes and the laws which I am placing before you today." The Torah proper, which conveys the actual statutes and laws referred to in the introductory exhortation, appears in Deuteronomy 12:1–26:15. It is introduced by the statement, "These are the statutes and the laws which you shall be care to do in the land which YHWH, the G-d of your ancestors, has given to you to possess all the days which you are alive upon the earth." The actual statutes and ordinances then follow through Deuteronomy 26:15.

---

17. Moses is identified as a Levite in Exodus 2:1–4; 6:14–25; and Numbers 26:59. Moses' Levitical identity is not mentioned in Deuteronomy, although he is identified as a prophet in Deuteronomy 18:15 and 34:10.

Finally, the concluding exhortation appears in Deuteronomy 26:16–19. It begins with Moses' statement, "Today, YHWH your G-d commands you to do these statutes and the laws and you shall be careful and you shall do them with all your heart, and with all your being," and concludes with statements in Deuteronomy 26:18–19 that identify Israel as a "treasured people," a "holy people," and so on, to YHWH.

Following the above-mentioned superscription in Deuteronomy 12:1, the organization of the actual legal instruction or Levitical Torah has been the subject of a great deal of discussion.[18] Difficulties in specifying the organizational principles of this material have prevented the emergence of a full consensus, but a number of scholars, including Kaufman, Braulik, and Olson, have recently revived a proposal that the decalog provides the organizational principles by which this material is presented.[19] Essentially, these scholars maintain that the legal instruction is structured according to the organizational principles of the decalog, so that each block of Deuteronomy 12–26 elaborates successively on each of the ten commandments. The specific identification of each text varies among these scholars, but in general the proposal runs as follows. The prohibition against other gods is expressed in Deuteronomy 12:1–13:18, which calls for centralized worship and prohibits apostasy. The prohibition against desecrating G-d's name corresponds to Deuteronomy 14:1–21, which specifies the conduct of a holy people. The command to observe the Shabbat corresponds to Deuteronomy 14:22–16:17, which presents the festival calendar. The command to obey parents corresponds to Deuteronomy 16:18–18:22, which specifies legal and religious authority. The prohibition against murder corresponds to Deuteronomy 19:1–22:8, which takes up issues of justice, especially involving the taking of human life. The prohibition against adultery corresponds to Deuteronomy 22:9–23:18, which takes up laws pertaining to sexual relations. The prohibition against stealing corresponds to Deuteronomy 23:19–24:7, which focuses especially on property issues. The prohibition against false witnesses corresponds to Deuteronomy 24:8–25:4, which takes up issues of legal procedure among other matters. The prohibition against coveting a neighbor's wife corresponds to Deuteronomy 25:5–12, which deals with Levirite marriage and a wife who injures a man's genitals. The prohibition against coveting a neighbor's property corresponds to Deuteronomy 25:13–26:15, which among other things takes up proper weights for commercial exchange. Essentially, these correspondences indicate that the legal instruction or Levitical Torah of Deuteronomy 12–26 constitutes "an expanded decalog."[20]

Although there does appear to be some broad points of correspondence between the decalog and the legal instruction presented in Deuteronomy 12–26, there are many problems associated with this proposal. First, there is no clear agree-

18. See O'Brien, "Deuteronomy," 105–108, 110–112, for a summary of the discussion.

19. S. A. Kaufman, "The Structure of the Deuteronomic Law," *Maarav* 1–2 (1978-79) 105–158; G. Braulik, *Die deuteronomistischen Gesetze und der Dekalog: Studien zum Aufbau von Deuteronomium 12–26*, SBS 145 (Stuttgart: Katholisches Bibelwerk, 1991); D. T. Olson, *Deuteronomy and the Death of Moses: A Theological Reading*, OBT (Minneapolis: Fortress, 1994).

20. Kaufman, p. 147.

ment as to what actually constitutes the ten commandments as presented in the Bible.[21] The statements, "I am YHWH your G-d . . ." (Deut 5:6), or "You shall not make for yourselves a graven image . . ." are sometimes taken as independent commandments, and the prohibitions against coveting a neighbor's wife and property (Deut 5:21) are frequently considered as one. Second, there is no formal structural indication that the legal material in Deuteronomy 12–26 is organized according a ten-part thematic sequence. Instead, the formal features of this material shift between two basic types: apodictic instructions or prohibitions and case-law based instructional materials. Third, many of the individual laws that are grouped into the ten basic components identified above simply do not correspond to the respective command or prohibition from the decalog. Deuteronomy 21:15–17 takes up inheritance by the sons of a man with two wives, but it is only loosely related to the prohibition against murder in that it is subsumed under killing in general and reflects a situation that follows from war when a man takes a wife from among war captives. Deuteronomy 22:1–8 takes up issues of the care of a neighbor's sheep and cattle, cross-dressing, the protection of a mother bird and her nest, and a parapet on a house. These laws are likewise identified as expressions of the prohibition against murder, but they have little to do with murder. The laws of Deuteronomy 22:9–23:18 are associated with the prohibition against adultery, but many issues can hardly be characterized as sexual, such as the prohibition against mixing two types of seeds in a vineyard, the prohibition against garments of mixed material, the requirement to wear tassels, the command to maintain proper toilet practices in camp, and the prohibition against returning an escaped slave.

These considerations indicate that there is not a full correspondence between the elements of the decalog and the organization of the Deuteronomic legal instruction; rather, there seems to be a more generalized correspondence between them. Therefore, it is not possible to argue that the Deuteronomic legal instruction is patterned after the rubrics of the decalog. It is possible, however, to argue that the decalog is drawn from major concerns expressed in the Deuteronomic legal instruction in that the decalog seems to express principles that are addressed much more specifically in the Deuteronomic legal material. In this case, the decalog expresses some sense of the deep structure of the legal material, but it does not express the formal structure of the text. The decalog therefore serves as part of the introduction to the Deuteronomic legal instruction in that it articulates fundamental concerns or principles expressed by the code.

Attention to the formal features of the Deuteronomic legal instruction, however, does provide criteria for establishing the formal structure and organization of the text. As noted, there is a consistent interplay between two basic generic entities throughout the Deuteronomic Torah—that is, the apodictic commands and prohibitions or order forms, which express categorical expectations or legal instructions, and the casuistic instructional forms that posit a legal situation or case

---

21. For discussion of the problems associated with identifying the individual commandments, see M. Greenberg, "Decalog," *EncJud* 5, 1435-1449; H. Cazelles, "Ten Commandments," *IDB[S]* 875–877.

and then express the means for its resolution. In this regard, it is noteworthy that both the superscription to the Deuteronomic legal instruction in Deuteronomy 12:1 and the opening and closing exhortations for the Deuteronomic legal instruction in Deuteronomy 5–11 and 26:16–19 consistently identify the contents of the Deuteronomic code as *ḥuqqîm*, "statutes," and *mišpāṭîm*, "law cases," terms that are generally employed respectively for the identification of apodictic commands or prohibitions and legal cases. In short, these terms identify generically the contents of the Deuteronomic legal instruction, and point to its basic principle of organization. For the most part, these genres of legal instructional material are grouped together; for example, Deuteronomy 22:9–12 contains a series of three apodictic elements, a prohibition against mixing seed in a vineyard (v. 9), a prohibition against plowing with two types of animals (v. 10), a prohibition against mixing material in a garment (v. 11), and a command to make tassels for one's garments. This is followed by a series of four casuistically formulated instructions in Deuteronomy 22:13–29—that is, a case in which a husband spurns his wife (vv. 13–21), a case in which a man lies with a married woman (v. 22), a case in which a man lies with a betrothed woman (vv. 23–27), and a case in which a man lies with a nonbetrothed woman (vv. 28–29). Although there are instances in which individual apodictic (e.g., the prohibition against taking millstones in pledge in Deut 24:6) or casuistic (e.g., the case in Deut 23:10–15, in which an "evil thing" or impurity might come upon a man in camp) elements appear alone, for the most part they appear together in series of two or more elements.

An examination of the contents of the individual legal instructions, both in and of themselves and in relation to their respective literary contexts, helps to establish the interrelationship between apodictic and casuistic legal instruction as the basic structural principle of the Deuteronomic Torah in that it points to an intentional, rather than a haphazard, organization that serves specific legal or instructional purposes. In his recent study of the principles that stand behind biblical law and aid in determining the modes of its expression, J. J. Finkelstein demonstrates that in some cases, biblical laws or instructions are not always to be taken literally according to the plain meaning or surface meaning of the text; rather, they frequently express a legal principle that is to be applied or expressed in the material that follows and thereby determines the interpretation of laws that are grouped together.[22] Finkelstein notes, for example, that the goring ox laws appear frequently in both biblical and Mesopotamian law codes, but that the likely occurrence of such a situation in reality is not very great. In asking why such provisions appear so frequently, he argues that they do not pertain to the specific case of an ox that gores a human being, but that they express basic legal principles of property damage, legal responsibility, and compensation that are applied to other situations, but that are not always spelled out. For example, when an ox gores another human being to death, the ox is considered to be responsible, but the owner is clear because he was not aware that the ox might kill (Exod 21:28). But if the ox is known to

---

    22. J. J. Finkelstein, *The Ox That Gored*, TAPS 71/2 (Philadelphia: The American Philosophical Society, 1981) esp. 5–47.

gore, the owner is responsible and may be held responsible for the deaths caused by his ox (Exod 21:29). Although the ox or the owner is subject to a death penalty in such instances, Exodus 21:30 stipulates that the owner can substitute a cash or property fine in place of his life. The following verses specify the legal responsibilities of the owner is a series of different cases. Overall, these laws express the legal responsibility of the owner of an animal that causes death, injury, or damage. The principles can be easily applied to other situations as well.

Indeed, examination of the apodictic instructions of Deuteronomy indicate that a similar understanding may apply. The prohibition against moving boundary markers in Deuteronomy 19:14, for example, establishes a principle that appears in the following cases in Deuteronomy 19:16–21:23, all of which involve some sort of boundary issue in that all discuss the disposition of cases that arise from a situation of war. The prohibitions against mixing seed in a vineyard (Deut 22:9), plowing with two types of animals (Deut 22:10), mixing material in garments (Deut 22:11), and the instruction to wear tassels (Deut 22:12) all address the need to prevent the mixing of two entities that do not belong together; the instruction concerning tassels distinguishes Israelites/Judeans from pagans in keeping with the prohibition of relations with the Canaanites in Deuteronomy 7:1–11. The following cases then take up issues pertaining to mixing, all of which involve sexual relations between men and women, including a husband who spurns his wife (Deut 22:13–21), a man who lies with a married woman (Deut 22:22), a man who lies with a betrothed woman (Deut 22:23–27), and a man who lies with a nonbetrothed woman (Deut 22:28–29). Likewise, the prohibitions against relations with a father's wife (Deut 23:1); entry into the congregation by a man with damaged genitals (Deut 23:2), a mamzer (Deut 23:3), and an Ammonite or Moabite (Deut 23:4–7); and abhorring an Edomite (Deut 23:8a) or an Egyptian (Deut 23:8b) all address the problems of impurities that appear in the case concerning protection from an "evil thing" or uncleanness in the camp (Deut 23:10–15).

Indeed, these examples point to an organizational principle in the Deuteronomic legal instruction that first presents basic principles in the form of apodictic instruction that are then applied to specific cases formulated as casuistic instruction. The principle is already evident in the initial segment of the Deuteronomic Torah in Deuteronomy 12:2–13:19 that addresses the issue of Israel's cultic differentiation from the nations in keeping with the principles earlier articulated in the exhortational material of Deuteronomy 7:1–11. Deuteronomy 12:2–31 contains a detailed instruction, formulated in apodictic style, that calls for the worship of YHWH exclusively at the one altar that YHWH chooses for the presence of the Divine Name. The passage begins in vv. 2–19 with apodictic language drawn from that of Deuteronomy 7:1–11, which calls for the destruction of pagan worship installations and the worship of YHWH exclusively at YHWH's chosen altar. A series of qualifications follows in vv. 20–31, formulated initially in casuistic language, but each is composed primarily with apodictic commands that lay out YHWH's instructions. Verses 29–31 are particularly noteworthy, in that they summarize the basic concern that Israel is not to be ensnared by the pagan practices of the nations. Deuteronomy 13:1–19 then presents a series of cases that are designed to ensure Israel's distinctive character. The canonization formula in v. 1

introduces a series of cases that pertain to issues of cultic apostasy among the people, whether by a prophet or dream interpreter (vv. 2–6), an individual family member (vv. 7–12), or an entire city (vv. 13–18). In each case, the evil is to be purged, and the concluding case instruction in v. 19 reiterates the command to do what is right in the eyes of YHWH.

Essentially, the instructions concerning for cultic centralization around YHWH's altar in Deuteronomy 12:2–13:19 constitute the basis for the balance of the Deuteronomic Torah in Deuteronomy 14:1–26:15, in that it defines the fundamental basis for Israel's identity as a distinctive people. This becomes clear when one notes that Deuteronomy 14:1–2, a basic instruction that identifies Israel as the children of YHWH, forbids them to cut their flesh or make themselves bald for the dead like the nations, and states that they are to be a holy people, distinct from the pagan nations. Specific instructions then follow throughout the balance of the Deuteronomic Torah concerning what constitutes the proper behavior of such a people. Apodictic instruction then follows concerning the proper eating of meat (Deut 14:3–21). Mixed apodictic and casuistic instruction then follows concerning the payment of tithes (Deut 14:22–29), the payments of debts (Deut 15:1–18), and the offering of the firstborn (Deut 15:19–23). Apodictic instruction concerning the observance of festivals (Deut 16:1–17) precedes mixed apodictic and casuistic instruction concerning the establishment of judicial and political authority (Deut 16:18–17:20), religious authority (Deut 18:1–19:13), territorial and boundary issues (Deut 19:14–21:23), treatment of what pertains to others (Deut 22:1–8), mixing what does not belong together (Deut 22:9–29), impurities (Deut 23:1–15), improper transactions among human beings (Deut 23:16–24:5), improper financial or lending transactions (Deut 24:6–13), justice to the poor (Deut 24:14–25:3), rights to sustenance or continuity (Deut 25:4–12), and the obligation to give what is due (Deut 25:13–26:15).

Altogether, the categories of legal instruction in the Deuteronomic Torah define proper conduct among a people that is designated as "a holy people" to YHWH. It clearly is not a full law code, in that it does not address every situation that might arise in the life of the people. The instructional form and the organization by which issues are presented first by apodictic instruction concerning principles followed by casuistic instruction concerning the application of those principles indicates that it serves as a guidebook for legal reasoning. The basic structure of the book of Deuteronomy may be presented as in table 9.1.

In addition to the overall form of Deuteronomy, it is also necessary to examine the specific contents of the legal instruction. The preceding analysis points to the principle of cultic centralization as a key element in the presentation of the Deuteronomic Torah, which is confirmed by the appearance of this motif throughout the Deuteronomic legal instruction. A number of studies already examine the pervasive role that cultic centralization occupies in the formulation of the Deuteronomic Torah.[23] In addition, these and other studies examine

23. See E. Reuter, *Kultzentralization: Entstehung und Theologie von Dtn 12*, BBB 87 (Frankfurt/Main: Anton Hain, 1993), who points to the appearance of centralization formulae throughout the Deuteronomic code, but explains the appearance of this material as the result of the redactional

TABLE 9.1 Basic structure and genre of the Book of Deuteronomy

Narrative account of Moses' last address to Israel: Deuteronomic Torah	*Deut 1–34*
I. Narrative report of Moses' last speeches to Israel	1:1–30:20
A. Report of Moses' first speech: exhortational resume of Israel's journey	1:1–4:43
B. Report of Moses' second speech: exhortational summary of YHWH's Torah	4:44–26:19
1. Introduction: setting of speech and identification as Torah	4:44–49
2. Report of speech proper: Levitical Torah	5:1–26:19
a. Speech formula	$5{:}1a\alpha^{1-2}$
b. Speech proper: Levitical Torah	$5{:}1a\alpha^{3-6}$–26:19
i. Introductory exhortation	$5{:}1a\alpha^{3-6}$–11:32
ii. Torah proper: statutes and cases	12:1–26:15
a) Superscription	12:1
b) Statutes and ordinances proper	12:2–26:15
1) Concerning cultic differentiation from the nations	12:2– 13:19
A) Instructions concerning exclusive worship at YHWH's chosen altar	12:2–31
B) Cases concerning cultic/national apostasy	13:1–19
2) Concerning holy conduct of treasured people	14:1–26:15
A) Basic instruction: holiness of people	14:1–2
B) Specific instruction	14:3–26:15
I) Eating of meat	14:3–21
II) Tithes	14:22– 29
III) Debt issues	15:1–18
IV) Offering of first born	15:19–23
V) Observance of holidays	16:1–17
VI) Judicial and political authority	16:18–17:20
VII) Religious authority	18:1–19:13
VIII) Territorial/boundary issues	19:14–21:23
IX) Treatment of what pertains to others	22:1–8
X) Mixing what does not belong together	22:9–29
XI) Impurities	23:1–15
XII) Improper transactions with human beings	23:16–24:5
XIII) Improper financial/lending transactions	24:6–13
XIV) Justice to the poor	24:14–25:3
XV) Rights to sustenance/continuation	25:4–12
XVI) Obligation to give what is due	25:13–26:15
iii. Concluding exhortation	26:16–19
C. Report of Moses' third speech: blessings and curses	27:1–28:69
D. Report of Moses' fourth speech: final exhortation to observe covenant	29:1–30:20
II. Report of Moses' transfer of leadership and death	31:1–34:12

the use of earlier legal traditions in Exodus (and Numbers) in the reformulation of the Deuteronomic Torah's own provisions. The Covenant Code of Exodus 20–23 is generally identified as an independent literary source or as part of the Elohistic or northern Israelite source of the Pentateuch, and many scholars identify it as the

formation of the code. See also, Weinfeld, *Deuteronomy 1–11*; Weinfeld, *Deuteronomy and the Deuteronomic School*; Levinson, *Deuteronomy and the Hermeneutics of Legal Innovation*; Jan Christian Gertz, *Die Gerichtsorganization Israels im deuteronomischen Gesetz*, FRLANT 165 (Göttingen: Vandenhoeck & Ruprect, 1994). For an overview of the issue, see O'Brien, "Deuteronomy," 99–100.

law code of the northern kingdom of Israel.[24] Scholars have long noted the interrelationship between the Deuteronomic law code and the Covenant Code of Exodus 20–23.[25] Von Rad provides a long list of parallel passages from Deuteronomy
and the Covenant Code in which the content and formulation of the laws are similar.[26] In many cases, Deuteronomy modifies the provisions of the Covenant Code;
as noted above, for example, Deuteronomy allows for only one legitimate sanctuary, whereas the Covenant Code allows more than one. Various scholars, therefore, have argued that the Deuteronomic code was intended to replace the older
Covenant Code.[27] Others point out that Deuteronomy does not modify or replace
all of the laws of the Covenant Code; rather, it must be read together with the
Covenant Code in that it represents a revision of the older code that allows the
unmodified laws in Exodus 20–23 to stand as written.[28] This conclusion may be
confirmed by the observation that Deuteronomy frequently specifies the procedures or rationales for laws that appear in the Covenant Code, but the Covenant
Code does not specify the procedures for laws found in Deuteronomy. As the
following discussion demonstrates, these features point to a comprehensive reform program in which cultic centralization stands as the basis for a much more
highly centralized socioeconomic and political power structure than that which
previously existed. Furthermore, the Levites suffer loss of status and power in this
reformulated system, the people of the land gain greater rights, and the monarchy
emerges as the ultimate power behind the system.

The principle of cultic centralization in Deuteronomy 12:2–13:19 permeates
the book of Deuteronomy, and it has a major impact on the collection and distribution of the economic resources of the land. Its primary feature is the command
to worship YHWH exclusively at the one place where YHWH chooses to cause
the divine name to dwell and the closure of all other sanctuaries.[29] Although
Deuteronomy never identifies the site for worship with Jerusalem, scholars have
recognized the requirement for cultic centralization as a feature of the Jerusalem
cult tradition which identifies Zion as the only legitimate worship site.[30] Indeed,
the language employed for the altar designated by YHWH, "the place where

24. For the character of the Covenant Code in Exodus 20–23, see O. Eissfeldt, *The Old Testament: An Introduction*, translated by P. R. Ackroyd (Oxford: Blackwell, 1965) 212–219; H.-J.
Boecker, *Law and the Administration of Justice in the Old Testament and Ancient East*, translated
by J. Moiser (Minneapolis: Augsburg, 1980) 135–175, esp. 141–4; R. Westbrook, "What is the Covenant Code?" *Theory and Method in Biblical and Cuneiform Law* 15–36.

25. See Eissfeldt, *Introduction* 220–223; R. Rendtorff, *The Old Testament: An Introduction*,
translated by J. Bowden (London: SCM, 1985) 153–154; G. von Rad, *Deuteronomy* 13–15.

26. *Deuteronomy* 13.

27. For example, Eissfeldt, *Introduction* 222.

28. Rendtorff, *Introduction* 154. Contra John Van Seters, "Cultic Laws in the Covenant Code
(Exodus 20, 22–23, 33) and their Relationship to Deuteronomy and the Holiness Code," *Studies in
the Book of Exodus*, BETL 126 (Leuven: Leuven University Press/Peeters, 1996) 319–345, who
attempts to argue on the basis of his late dating of the Pentateuchal narrative and a comparative
study of selected laws that the laws of the Covenant Code and the Holiness Code must presuppose
the laws of Deuteronomy.

29. See Nicholson, *Deuteronomy and Tradition* 1–17.

30. Cf. Clements, "Deuteronomy and the Jerusalem Cult Tradition," 303–305.

YHWH chooses to cause his name to dwell," employs the language of the Davidic/ Zion tradition in which David is "chosen" by YHWH and Zion is the place where YHWH "dwells."[31] This identification is reinforced by the fact that the northern kingdom of Israel designated two sites for the worship of YHWH, viz. Dan and Beth-El, and never seems to have pursued a policy of cultic centralization.It represents a modification of the older Covenant Code law in Exodus 20:21–26, which allows for the existence of multiple altars "in every place where I cause My name to be remembered" (Exod 20:24).

Furthermore, the instruction calls for the eating of tithes and other offerings at YHWH's central altar. The importance of this requirement is highlighted by its appearance at the beginning of the legal instruction in Deuteronomy 12:1–31 and again at the end in Deuteronomy 26:1–15, which articulates the ritual by which the people offer their firstfruits offerings at the central sanctuary as part of a larger section in Deuteronomy 25:13–26:15 that is concerned with the obligation to give what is due. But Deuteronomy 12:15–19 allows for the secular slaughter and eating of meat within the towns. This has a major impact on the Levites, in that such meat is not considered to be a part of the tithe, which normally constitutes a part of the Levites' income, nor does it need to be slaughtered by Levites. To collect a share of the tithe, this instruction calls for the Levite to travel to the central sanctuary, where he eats it together with the people. The Levite thereby has no guaranteed professional role or source of income in the towns outside of the central altar. The section concerning centralization includes a special instruction in v. 19 to take care of the Levites.

Although the requirement for cultic centralization appears at first sight to be strictly religious, recent studies have pointed to its economic and administrative implications, especially with regard to the collection of tithes, in that it enhances the monarch's control over the economic resources of the land.[32] Such a perspective corresponds well to the authority exercised in Judah by the House of David, which justified its economic and administrative control over the country by the right of divine election based upon David's establishment of Jerusalem as the site for the sanctuary of YHWH. It is noteworthy therefore that, following the basic instructions for the holiness of the people in Deuteronomy 14:1–2, the Deuteronomic Torah focuses first of all on the eating of meat in Deuteronomy 14:3–21. This section appears as apodictic instruction that defines all of the basic categories of clean meat that may be eaten and unclean meat that is prohibited for consumption by Israelites. As noted above, the slaughter and eating of meat has a major impact on the roles and income of the Levites in that the basic instruction for cultic centralization specifies that tithes may be eaten only at the central altar, but that secular

---

31. Cf. R. E. Clements, "Deuteronomy and the Jerusalem Cult Tradition," 303–304; Clements, *G-d's Chosen People: A Theological Interpretation of the Book of Deuteronomy* (Valley Forge: Judson, 1969) 45–49, who notes the association with Davidic/Zion language, but argues that Deuteronomy transforms the concept from the Davidic/Zion sphere to that of the entire nation, expressed through the covenant at Horeb—that is, Sinai.

32. For example, Claburn, "The Fiscal Basis of Josiah's Reforms"; M. Weinfeld, "Tithe," *Encyclopaedia Judaica* 15 (1971) 1156–1162.

slaughter could take place in the towns. It is likely no accident then that the following sequence of concerns in the Deuteronomic Torah includes tithes in Deuteronomy 14:22–29, the treatment of debt issues in Deuteronomy 15:1–18, the offering of the firstborn in Deuteronomy 15:19–23, and the observance of Temple or altar festivals in Deuteronomy 16:1–17, as each of these issues is bound up with the role and status of the Levites. The Levites are especially dependent upon tithes for support, debt is a necessary reality for those who lack support, the tithes are taken from the firstborn animals, and the tithes are eaten at the altar festivals.

Deuteronomy 14:22–29 requires payment of a yearly tithe of grain, wine, and oil, as well as the firstborn of herd and flock "before YHWH your G-d, at the place which (YHWH) will choose (Deut 14:23). In essence, the tithe constitutes the tax upon the produce of the land that is collected at the major Temple festivals.[33] Because the Deuteronomic law code requires the closing of all sanctuaries except for the one place that YHWH will choose, the collection of the tithe will be centralized in one location. This eliminates outlying sanctuaries as collection points; consequently, the centralized collection of tithes appears to place greater control over the economic resources of the land into the hands of Temple priesthood.

But this is not entirely the case. The Deuteronomic law of the tithe apparently reduces the amount of income due to the Levites who live outside of the central sanctuary. Deuteronomy 14:22–29 modifies earlier practice whereby the tithe was brought to the sanctuary where it was given to the priests.[34] It is not entirely certain whether the law of the tithe in Numbers 18:21–32, which grants the entire tithe to the Levites, reflects preexilic practice,[35] but statements concerning the preexilic collection and distribution of the tithe in Genesis 14:18–20, 28:18–22, 1 Samuel 8:15, and Amos 4:4–5 indicate that it was brought to the sanctuary to be used either by the priests or by the king. Deuteronomy 14:22–29 does not grant the entire tithe to the Levites nor even to the king; rather, it stipulates that the tithe must be taken to the central sanctuary, where it will be eaten before YHWH at the festivals. Here, the people, not the Levites or the king, eat the tithe; the requirement to give also to the Levite (v. 27) indicates some consideration must be given to the priests, but this hardly constitutes the entire tithe represented in other texts that was collected at the sanctuary. Instead, the Levites must rely on the offerings that are made at the sanctuary (Deut 18:1–8) and the leftovers of the tithe that might be given to them by the people (Deut 12:18–19; 14:27).

33. See Weinfeld, "Tithe."

34. A. D. H. Mayes, *Deuteronomy*, NCeB (London: Marshall, Morgan and Scott; Grand Rapids: Eerdmans, 1979) 244–245; J. Milgrom, *Numbers*, JPS Torah Commentary (Philadelphia and New York: Jewish Publication Society, 1990) 432–436.

35. Cf. J. G. McConville, *Law and Theology in Deuteronomy*, JSOTSup 33 (Sheffield: JSOT Press, 1984) 70–87, who maintains that Deuteronomy 14:22–29 reflects awareness of the priestly law of the tithe in Numbers 18:21–32 and that both laws presuppose that the tithe is a tax for the Levites. Although he is correct to consider the tithe to be a tax to support the Levites in both texts, his argument that Deuteronomy 14:22–29 is aware of Numbers 18:21–32 is weak; it is perhaps aware of the practice of granting the tithe to the Levites, but there is no proof that it is aware of the text.

This loss is also evident in the command to store the tithe in the cities every third year for the use of the Levites, aliens, orphans, and widows (vv. 28–29). Although the law at first sight appears to be designed to support the Levites, it actually undermines them again. Unless the Levites travel to the central sanctuary, they are not entitled to a yearly tithe, but only to that of every third year; and they must share it with the disadvantaged classes of the land, the alien, orphan, and widow. In short, the Deuteronomic law of the tithe reduces the income of the Levites by placing a substantial amount of the tithe in the hands of the people. Texts in the Covenant Code do not specify distribution of the tithe other than to state that the "fullness of your harvest," the "outflow of your press," and the first-born of your sons, as well as your cattle, and your sheep must be given to YHWH (Exod 22:28–30) or that the firstfruits of your land must be brought to the house of YHWH your G-d (Exod 23:19). Deuteronomy 15:19 specifies that the cattle and sheep mentioned in Exodus 22:29 also must be firstborn.

The interrelationship between cultic and economic centralization is evident insofar as the celebrations of the major temple festivals serve as the occasions on which the tithe is delivered to the central sanctuary. Deuteronomy 16:1–17 specifies the celebration of the three major festivals at "the place which YHWH will choose to cause the divine name to dwell" (v. 2). The three festivals include Pesach, Shavuot, and Sukkot. Each of these festivals is one of the three major Temple festivals, and each is associated with a different phase of the agricultural year. The festival calendar concludes with the statement: "Three times in the year, each of your males shall appear before YHWH your G-d in the place which YHWH will choose, at the festival of Matzot, at the festival of Shavuot, and at the festival of Sukkot, and each shall not appear before YHWH empty handed; each according to the gift of his hand, according to the blessing of YHWH your G-d which YHWH has given to you" (vv. 16–17). In sum, each male is required to bring to the sanctuary a portion of the produce which YHWH has given to him. Deuteronomy 16:1–17 differs from its counterpart in the Covenant Code, Exodus 23:14–19, in three major respects: First, Deuteronomy 17:1–17 calls specifically for the sacrifice and eating of meat at Pesach, whereas Exodus 23:14–19 refers to it only elliptically; second, Deuteronomy 16:1–17 specifies that the celebration of festivals be observed at the place that YHWH chooses, whereas Exodus 23:14–19 refers generally to the "house of YHWH your G-d," without specifying how many such houses might exist; and third, Deuteronomy 16:1–17 gives great emphasis to including the poor or disadvantaged among the celebrants—that is, "your manservant, your maidservant, the Levite who is within your towns, the sojourner, the fatherless, and the widow who are among you" (v. 11)—whereas Exodus 23:14–19 does not specify the celebrants other than as all the males.

Nevertheless, the central sanctuary serves as the primary focus for the collection and distribution of the tithe in Deuteronomy. Insofar as this represents a specification and modification of previous practice, one may legitimately ask who benefits from the centralization of the collection and distribution of the tithe. Obviously, the Levites do not, and the people do. But the matter is not quite so simple in that some authority must be responsible for such change. Although the priests officiate at the Temple, they would hardly be the party responsible for the reduction of their income. In this regard, two factors suggest that royal authority may be the source of this modification. First, the law of the tithe gives special consideration to the disadvantaged—that is, the alien, the orphan, and the widow. In the ancient Near East, the care of the orphan and the widow in particular, and the justice due to them, is the responsibility of the king, and his fitness to rule is measured by his care for these disadvantaged parties.[36] Second, the central sanctuary is also the royal sanctuary, and the tithe of the produce of the land is generally regarded as the due of the king in the ancient near-eastern world and in Israel, which he may distribute to support his political or his religious establishment.[37] Because the distribution of the tithe is a royal prerogative, the Deuteronomic modification of the law of the tithe may well be traced to royal authority, especially insofar as it benefits the alien, the orphan, and the widow. It enhances the king's standing, at the same time weakening the position of the Levitical priesthood and benefiting the people. In this regard, the centralization of the collection and the redistribution of the tithe functions as an economic and political tool that strengthens the position of the monarch who employs it as a means to gain popular support.

In addition to its interest in cultic centralization, it is apparent that the book of Deuteronomy also centralizes the administration of justice, especially with regard to the centralization of legal authority and the modification of prior legal practice in relation to socioeconomic issues and family relationships.[38] This is evident in several major features of the Deuteronomic law code pertaining to these issues: (1) it modifies prior legal tradition, especially the Covenant Code of Exodus 20–23; (2) it grants greater legal and economic rights to disadvantaged classes, especially indebted Israelites and women; and (3) it grants greater authority to the state to regulate the economic and family life of the people.

Such concerns appear in the provisions concerning debt issues in Deuteronomy 15:1–18. This section comprises a basic apodictic instruction concerning the release of debt in vv. 1–6, followed by two casuistically formulated instructions that address the requirement to loan to the poor in vv. 7–11 and the release of Hebrew slaves in vv. 12–18. The placement of this section immediately following the instructions concerning the tithe in Deuteronomy 14:22–29 apparently envisions the reduced economic circumstances of the Levites and the instruction to lay up the tithe in the towns every three years for the Levites and other classes of the poor. Nevertheless, Deuteronomy 15:1–18 applies not only to the Levites, but to all the poor within Israelite society, which demonstrates the interrelationship between Deuteronomy's cultic and socioeconomic concerns.

36. See F. C. Fensham, "Widow, Orphan, and the Poor in Ancient Near Eastern Legal and Wisdom Literature," *JNES* 21 (1962) 129–139; L. Epsztein, *Social Justice in the Ancient Near East and the People of the Bible*, translated by J. Bowden (London: SCM, 1986) 105.

37. See 1 Samuel 8:15 and Genesis 14:18–20; Weinfeld, "Tithe."

38. See Steinberg, "The Deuteronomic Law Code and the Politics of State Centralization," and Gertz, *Die Gerichtsorganization*, who attributes the centralization of justice in Deuteronomy to Josianic redaction.

The first major concern of this passage is the year of release in vv. 1–6 and 7–11.[39] Verses 1–6 provide the basic instruction concerning the release of debt every seven years, and vv. 7–11 require that loans be given to the poor. Exodus 23:10–11 contains only brief statements concerning the use of agricultural land— that is, land may be farmed for a period of six years but it is to lie fallow during the seventh year. The rationale provided is that the poor among the people may eat from whatever grows wild during the seventh year. Deuteronomy 15:1–6, 7– 11 modifies this law substantially, however, in that it completely ignores the issue of the agricultural use of the land in order to focus on the maintenance and rights of the poor.It defines the seventh year as the year of "release" (*šĕmiṭṭâ*), and it presents the issue in terms of the forgiveness of loans that are made to the poor—that is, all loans made during the previous six years shall be forgiven during the year of release. The issue of the land appears only in the motivation statement of v. 4, "but there will be no poor among you for YHWH will bless you in the land which YHWH your G-d gives you for an inheritance to possess." This law represents a substantial improvement in the lot of the poor as well, in that it provides a means of support for the duration of each six-year cycle; whereas Exodus 23:10–11 only provides support during the seventh year, Deuteronomy 15:1–6, 7–11 provides a means of support for all seven years through a loan.

A similar concern for the welfare of the poor motivates the modification of the slave law in Deuteronomy 15:12–18.[40] The analogy between the stipulations of the Covenant on this issue and the Deuteronomic year of release indicates that such slavery is undertaken to repay a debt—that is, slavery is essentially a debt issue in that one becomes a slave when one is unable to maintain oneself economically. Exodus 21:1–11 states the provisions of the Covenant Code for the treatment of an Israelite slave. A male slave shall serve for six years, and he shall be released in the seventh year. The Covenant Code stipulates that the slave is not entitled to compensation; if he is given a wife and has children during the term of his service, the wife and children remain the property of the master. A procedure is defined if he chooses to remain a slave permanently. A female Israelite slave is designated for marriage, and she may be released only if her marriage rights are compromised. The Deuteronomic slave law, on the other hand, makes several major modifications to the Covenant Code law. First, when the male Hebrew slave is released after six years, he is compensated from the property of his master because the master has prospered from the slave's work. Second, the female slave is given the same right of release as the male slave; after six years, she, too, is entitled to release on the same terms as those of the male. Presumably, this allows the slave wife of a male slave to be released following the completion of her term of service. In this case, the Deuteronomic

---

39. For a recent study of the law of release in Deuteronomy 15, see J. M. Hamilton, *Social Justice and Deuteronomy: The Case of Deuteronomy 15*, SBLDS 136 (Atlanta: Scholars, 1992).

40. See Hamilton, *Social Justice*; G. C. Chirichigno, *Debt-Slavery in Israel and the Ancient Near East*, JSOTSup 141 (Sheffield: JSOT Press, 1993) 256–301; cf. I. Cardellini, *Die biblischen "Sklaven" Gesetze im Lichte de keilschriftlichen Sklavenrechts: Ein Beitrag zur Tradition, Über-lieferung und Redaktion der alttestamentlichen Rechtstexte*, BBB 55 (Bonn: P. Hanstein, 1981).

law modifies the older Covenant Code law in order to give greater rights to the poor and to women.[41]

Similar concern for the rights of the poor and women are evident elsewhere in the Deuteronomic Torah. An important example appears in Deuteronomy 22:28–29, a revision of the Covenant Code law concerning the seduction of an unbetrothed virgin.[42] As already noted, this instruction is part of the larger section in Deuteronomy 22:9–29, which takes up problems concerning mixing what does not belong together, especially as it pertains to sexual relations between men and women. According to Exodus 22:15–16, if a man seduces and lies with an unbetrothed virgin, he is required to pay the marriage price for her and make her his wife. If her father refuses to give her to the man, however, he is still required to pay the marriage price to the father. Deuteronomy 22:28–29 modifies this law with several stipulations: (1) the man must marry the woman, and he may never divorce her; (2) although he must pay the marriage price to the father, the father has no right to withhold his daughter from the man; (3) the marriage price is set at fifty shekels; and (4) the man must seize the woman, not seduce her. First and foremost, this law offers greater protection to the woman, but it also protects the interests of the father and the man. With regard to the father, it stipulates the marriage price at fifty shekels, and leaves no room for negotiation as to what the marriage price for a virgin might be. With regard to the man, he must be guilty of seizing the woman— that is, of raping her, and this protects him from the ambiguity involved in establishing the meaning of the term for seduction in the Covenant Code. As for the woman, she is protected economically. The man is required to marry her, and he may not divorce her. This obviously does not address the issue of marriage to a rapist, but it does offer her the economic support due to a wife, and it forbids the man from withdrawing that support by divorcing her at a later time. Furthermore, it protects her from the economic disadvantage of remaining in her father's house where she would always be dependent upon him. Upon his death, she would not be eligible for a share of the inheritance. Without her own sons, she would be dependent upon her brothers. Concern with provision for the poor appears elsewhere in the Deuteronomic Torah, including the prohibition against returning an escaped slave (Deut 23:16–17), the prohibition against loaning money at interest (Deut 23:20–21), eating grapes in a vineyard (Deut 23:25), eating grain in a field (Deut 23:26), the overall concern with improper financial or lending transactions (Deut 24:6–13), and the overall concern with justice for the poor (Deut 24:14–25:3). In general, these cases are not addressed in the Covenant Code, or they provide greater rights to the poor by specifying procedures in a manner that favors those who have little.

Although the major concern of Deuteronomy 22:28–29 appears to be with the economic welfare of the nonbetrothed woman, the context in which this pas-

---

41. Cf. Mayes, *Deuteronomy* 250, who maintains that Deuteronomy 15:12–18 is not an independent law, but constitutes an example of the application of the law in Exodus 23:10–11.

42. See C. Pressler, *The View of Women Found in the Deuteronomic Family Laws*, BZAW 216 (Berlin and New York: Walter de Gruyter, 1993) esp. 35–41.

sage appears indicates a major concern with protecting the family structures of Israelite/Judean society in that the preceding instructions take up cases in which a man spurns his wife (Deut 22:13–21), a man lies with a married woman (Deut 22:22), or a man lies with a betrothed woman (Deut 22:23–27), all of which stem from the basic concern articulated in the apodictic prohibitions in Deuteronomy 22:9–12 with mixing what does not properly belong together. Essentially, these provisions are designed to protect marriage relationships and the family ties, thereby created by specifying the means by which a man may reject his newly married wife and by prohibiting the violation of a marriage relationship. Deuteronomy 22:13–21 allows a man to reject his new wife on a charge of unchastity, but it protects the woman and her family from unwarranted charges by specifying the means by which such a charge will be proved. At the same time, it protects the marriage relationship by specifying severe punishment whether the charge is true or not: A man who brings a false charge against his wife will be flogged and prevented from divorcing his wife in a manner similar to one who rapes an unbetrothed woman; a woman who is guilty of unchastity will be put to death. Clearly, such a charge can not be made lightly. Likewise, Deuteronomy 22:22 stipulates that a man who lies with a married woman will be put to death, as will the woman. There are no qualifications to this case as the matter is unambiguous. Deuteronomy 22:23–27 stipulates the same punishment for a man who lies with a betrothed woman, although it allows for the possibility of rape and excuses the woman in such a circumstance. Interestingly, these provisions have no parallels in the Covenant Code, other than the basic commands of the decalog that adultery is prohibited. This suggests that the Deuteronomic Torah takes up these provisions in order to provide greater protection for women and for family lines than was available in other legislation. Such concern with the protection of women and family lines is evident elsewhere in the Deuteronomic provisions concerning the treatment of female captives (Deut 21:10–14), the resulting cases of men with two wives and the inheritance rights of their sons (Deut 21:15–17), remarriage after divorce (Deut 24:1–4), the exemption from military service of a newly married man (Deut 24:5), Levirite marriage (Deut 25:5–10), and damage to a man's genitals or reproductive capacity (Deut 25:11–12).

Deuteronomy's interest in women and family lines appears to express a related concern with the protection of property rights, especially in relation to the protection of rights to property within a family unit. This is evident in the case in Deuteronomy 21:15–17 concerning a man with two wives. The instruction is a part of a larger unit in Deuteronomy 19:14–21:23 concerned with territorial or boundary issues, particularly those that arise from situations of war. It follows an instruction concerning the treatment or female captives and apparently envisions a situation in which a man might marry a female captive as a second wife. In such a case, questions of favoritism are naturally bound to arise as one wife might be preferred over the other, most likely the later wife over the former. The present instruction addresses this situation as it relates to the inheritance rights of the sons of each woman. It specifies that, regardless of the father's preferences for either wife, the rights of the firstborn son are to be acknowledged and the appropriate share of the inheritance assigned to him. This provision thereby protects the transmission of property within the family. The firstborn son is more likely to be the son of the man's first wife to whom he would have been contracted to marry with the woman's family rather than the son of a war captive whom the man would likely marry after having already married a first wife. A similar concern underlies the instructions concerning the Levirite marriage in Deut 25:5–10. The Levirite marriage specifies the procedure by which a man who dies with no heir may obtain one; his brother is to father a child with the dead man's widow, thereby ensuring his brother an heir. It also includes a ritual in which the brother who refuses such an obligation is to be humiliated publicly, thereby providing a strong incentive to carry out the Levirite marriage, even though the brother will not realize any material gain for his action. Finally, the instructions concerning eating in a neighbor's vineyard or grain field (Deut 23:25, 26) apparently express concern for the poor by allowing the consumption of grapes or grain until one is full, but they protect the owner's rights by prohibiting carrying off grapes in a vessel or taking a sickle to harvest the grain.

The greater provision for the poor and for women and the concern for the protection of family lines and property rights have generally been recognized in previous studies of the Deuteronomic law code.[43] But these examples are important for understanding the role that the Deuteronomic law code plays in establishing the centralization of justice in ancient Israel. It grants greater decision-making power to the centralized authority that stands behind the Deuteronomic law code. In these cases, the state takes upon itself greater authority in defining and asserting the rights of the disadvantaged in the regulation of loan, the compensation and terms of release for slaves, and the provision for a woman who is raped, and the protection of family lines of inheritance. Under the terms of the Covenant Code, no regulation was apparent for the provision of the poor other than slavery or the right to glean a fallow field in the Sabbatical year; the owner of slaves bore no responsibility for their welfare after they were released, and they were not even required to release the women. Furthermore, a raped woman could be denied the economic benefits of marriage that were so necessary in ancient Israelite society, and a widow without sons was left to the mercy of the street. In each case, the state steps in and defines what should be done, thereby denying the advantaged the ability to decide. Thus, the lender no longer decides when a debt is forgiven; the owner of a slave no longer decides whether or not to compensate a male slave or release a female slave; the father of a raped woman no longer decides her fate; and the brother is obligated to see to his dead brother's family continuity or suffer public disgrace. The ability to make decisions is removed from the local sphere and assigned to the state.[44]

The Deuteronomic modifications of the Covenant Code clearly have an impact upon the means and authority for making legal decisions, but they have an eco-

---

43. For example, Pressler, *The View of Women*, who attributes concern with women in Deuteronomy to an interest in preserving the patriarchal structure of Israelite society; B. Halpern, "Jerusalem and the Lineages in the Seventh Century BCE: Kinship and the Rise of Individual Moral Liability," *Law and Ideology in Monarchic Israel*, JSOTSup 124, ed. B. Halpern and D. W. Hobson (Sheffield: JSOT, 1991) 1–107.

44. Cf. Steinberg, "The Deuteronomic Law Code."

nomic impact as well. In assigning to itself greater legal authority in each of the afore-mentioned cases, the state also reserves for itself the right to assign the economic resources of the parties involved. In the case of the law of the year of release, the party making the loan no longer has the right to expect repayment of the loan after a period of six years, and Deuteronomy 15:7–11 stipulates that such a loan may not be withheld at the approach of the seventh year. Here, the state assumes control of the resources of one who makes a loan, although Deuteronomy does not specify how the need for such a loan is to be established. In the case of the manumission law, the state assumes the right to determine at least part of the distribution of the master's property, although it does not stipulate the amount that is to be given to the released slave. In the case of the raped woman, the state assumes the authority to assign the economic resources of the rapist; he must pay the father the set amount of fifty shekels, and he must marry the raped woman without the right of divorce, thereby providing her with the support due to a wife for the rest of his life. In each case, economic resources are taken from the hands of people in positions of power, and placed in the hands of the those who lack power. But in each case, it is the state that decides.

Again, one may ask about the identity of the authority that stands behind the Deuteronomic code, and again, the question of who benefits and who does not is relevant. Obviously, disadvantaged people especially benefit from these laws; property owners are protected, but only after the disadvantaged are addressed. The situation is analogous to that observed above in relation to cultic centralization. The disadvantaged classes—that is, the poor and women—benefited from the loss of economic resources by the Levites as a result of cultic centralization. Likewise, the disadvantaged—that is, the poor and women—receive benefits from the wealthier or more powerful parties among the people as a result of the centralization of state authority.

The monarchy appears to be the party responsible for such change. As noted, it is the monarch who is ultimately held responsible for the care of the disadvantaged in ancient near eastern societies, and the Deuteronomic law code addresses precisely their situation. But the monarch is also responsible for the promulgation of law, including the regulation of criminal and civil affairs, in ancient neareastern societies. The monarchy generally ascribes the authority to promulgate such law to the deities of the state, but the monarch nevertheless serves as the mouthpiece for the deity, and by necessity must be the final authority for interpreting what the deity intends.[45] In this regard, it is noteworthy that the Deuteronomic law code places both the Levites and the wealthy who might make loans at an economic disadvantage, and it protects lines of inheritance. This would suggest that it is indeed the monarch who stands behind the promulgation of this law code in that he would be the only authority capable of such action.

It remains then to examine the role of the monarch in the administration of justice in the book of Deuteronomy. At first sight, Deuteronomy does not appear

45. See, for example, the introduction to the law code of Hammurapi, in which the monarch claims that his authority to establish law is granted by the gods Enlil and Marduk who rule humankind and Babylon respectively (see *ANET* 164–5).

to assign specific judicial functions to the king, nor does it indicate that the monarch bears any responsibility for the appointment of the judges. Likewise, the "Torah of the King" in Deuteronomy 17:14–20 appears to place restrictions on the authority of the king by requiring him to abide by the laws of "this Torah," which he is to copy before the priests and read all the days of his life. A number of scholars, therefore, have argued that the king is a relatively weak figure who is subject to the legal authority of the priests in the book of Deuteronomy.[46]

But consideration of the "Torah of the King" in relation to its literary context provides the basis for a different understanding of the role of the King as a major power figure in the Deuteronomic Torah. Deuteronomy 17:14–20 appears within the larger context of the Deuteronomic Torah concerning judicial and political authority in Deuteronomy 16:18–17:20. In keeping with the organizational principles of the Deuteronomic Torah identified here, this section begins with apodictic instruction concerning the establishment of proper judicial authority in Deuteronomy 16:18–17:1 and follows with casuistic instructions concerning the procedure for convicting and punishing a violator in Deuteronomy 17:2–7, the procedure for referring cases to a higher court in Deuteronomy 17:8–13, and the procedure for establishing the king, the highest political and judicial authority in the land in Deuteronomy 17:14–20.

The conceptual progression of thought in this unit is clear. The basic requirements concerning the appointment of judicial authority in Deuteronomy 16:18–17:1 include apodictic instructions concerning the appointment of judges and judicial officers in the towns (Deut 16:18–20). The prohibition of an Asherah and Matzevah (Deut 6:21) aids in establishing the authority of those judicial figures in that the central YHWHistic altar provides the authoritative basis for judicial action in ancient Israel and Judah. The prohibition against sacrificing a defective animal (Deut 17:1) demonstrates the interrelationship between cultic sacrifice of pure animals at the altar and the need to establish "purity" in the life of the people—that is, a means to remove "impurity" through judicial action is thereby mandated by the presence of the altar in the midst of the people. The following cases then establish the spheres of judicial authority from the most basic elements of the system to the overarching judicial authority. Basic procedures for conviction and punishment by the aforementioned judges in the towns is addressed in Deuteronomy 17:2–7, higher courts of appeal are addressed in Deuteronomy 17:8–13, and the appointment of the king, who always stands as the highest court of appeal in ancient Israel and Judah, is then addressed in Deuteronomy 17:14–20.

---

46. For example, von Rad, *Deuteronomy*, 118–120; C. Carmichael, *The Laws of Deuteronomy* (Ithaca and London: Cornell University Press, 1974) 105. Cf. Gary Knoppers, "The Deuteronomist and the Deuteronomic Law of the King: A Reexamination of the Relationship," *ZAW* 108 (1996) 329–346, who argues that the Torah of the king circumscribes the powers of the king, but that the DtrH presentation of Solomon, for example, endorses substantial royal powers. Knoppers overlooks the critical effect of the redactional framework in the Solomon narrative is placed, and reads the accounts of Solomon's building the Temple, and so on, as laudatory accounts, apparently in keeping with the intent of their composition. See my analysis of the Solomon traditions above and in my "Critique of Solomon."

Further examination of the contents of this section points to the central role played by the king. According to Deuteronomy 16:18–20, legal authority is in the hands of the "judges" (*šōpěṭîm*) and "officers" (*šōṭěrîm*), who are to be appointed to administer justice at the law courts in the gates of the city. Various passages in Deuteronomy demonstrate that the Levites also played a role in the administration of justice together with *šōpěṭîm* and *šōṭěrîm*. Although some scholars argue that the judicial system reflected in Deuteronomy reflects priestly control over the administration of justice, Weinfeld's studies of judicial terminology and roles in the Hebrew Bible and ancient Near East indicate that the administration of justice was a royal function. His studies of the terms *šōpēṭ* and *šōṭēr* indicates that *šōpēṭ* refers to a royal judicial functionary throughout the ancient Near East who decides matters of legal principle or matters that pertain to the crown, such as land rights. Likewise, *šōṭēr* refers to an administrative assistant to a higher ranking official, who functions as "a secretary for recording, a constable for executive-punitive measures, and a messenger or attendant for rendering service to the court."[47] Furthermore, it was not unusual to have priests serve together with the royal judges in the ancient Near East. The description of Jehoshaphat's legal reform in 2 Chronicles 19:4–11 demonstrates that the appointment of judges was understood by the Chronicler to be the king's prerogative.[48] Likewise, the narratives in 2 Samuel 12:1–6 and 1 Kings 3:16–28 demonstrate that the king may serve as the ultimate legal authority of the land. Jehoshaphat also authorizes the Levites to act as judges in matters concerning YHWH—that is, concerning the Temple and cultic propriety—as opposed to the matters of the king, which were supervised by a subordinate royal official.

Given the commonly accepted principle of royal authority in the administration of justice, it is noteworthy that the Deuteronomic law code diminishes the economic rights and power of both the Levitical priests and the advantaged classes among the people. As the preceding analysis demonstrates, disadvantaged classes among the people, the poor and women in particular, are given greater economic rights in relation to both of these groups. Furthermore, this reallocation of resources occurs in a context that emphasizes the need for greater cultic and administrative centralization. As noted, the monarch normally is charged with the care of such disadvantaged classes in ancient near-eastern societies. Furthermore, the Davidic monarchy in particular would benefit from greater cultic centralization, since it authorized only one royal sanctuary in Jerusalem that served as the basis for defining the Davidic monarchy's concept of divine election. The northern monarchies maintained two such royal sanctuaries in Dan and Beth-El.

These factors have some important implications for understanding the so-called Torah of the King in Deuteronomy 17:14–20. Scholars normally point to its provisions and portrayal of the king as a basis for arguing that Deuteronomy

---

47. See Moshe Weinfeld, "Judge and Officer in Ancient Israel and in the Ancient Near East," *IOS* 7 (1977) 65–88, 84.

48. See Gary Knoppers, "Jehoshaphat's Judiciary and "the Scroll of YHWH's Torah," *JBL* 113 (1994) 59–80.

stems originally from northern Israelite circles.[49] It appears to restrict the power
of the king in that it defines a number of stipulations by which the king must abide.
He must not be a foreigner; he may not amass horses to himself nor lead the people
back to Egypt for such a purpose; he may not amass wives to himself nor silver
and gold; and he must write a "copy of this Torah" for himself in the presence of
the Levitical priests and read all the days of his life. The monarch portrayed here
appears to be Solomon, who violated every one of these provisions.[50] Insofar as
Solomon's policies led to the revolt of the northern tribes against the house of
David, and insofar as the northern kingdom never seems to have developed the
centralized monarchic concept that characterized the southern kingdom of Judah,
scholars conclude that the "Torah of the King" reflects northern attitudes that would
restrict the power and role of the monarch.

But two considerations must be born in mind. First, the "Torah of the King"
does not restrict royal authority; it merely defines the conditions by which it may
be exercised. It does not compromise the judicial role of the king;[51] rather, it testifies to it by requiring the monarch to write and observe a copy of "this Torah"—
that is, the lawcode that defines the legal system administered of the land. Although
the king is to copy it in the presence of the Levitical priests, they do not make the
final legal decisions; that is the prerogative of the king. Second, scholarly contentions that a relatively weak model of kingship prevailed in the northern kingdom
of Israel rely on Alt's erroneous conception of "charismatic kingship" in the north
versus the more stable dynastic kingship of the House of David in Judah. Alt
maintains that northern kingship was based on a model of charismatic leadership
in which the king was legitimated by the people, rather than by dynastic birth,
and expressed by the notion that the "spirit of YHWH" had descended on him in
a manner analogous to the portrayal of prophetic activity.[52] But Buccelatti's analysis of kingship in Israel demonstrates that no such charismatic principle is evident in the north.[53] Northern kingship is based on the same model of dynastic
succession employed in the south; the House of David was simply much more
successful in maintaining its power than the northern dynasties. The northern kings
clearly act as central authorities, and a number of coup d'états are attempted against
the House of David, but in contrast to those against the northern dynasties, they fail.

In this regard, the Deuteronomic Torah concerning religious authority in
Deuteronomy 18:1–19:13 is especially noteworthy in that it points to the dimin-

---

49. For example, K. Galling, "Das Königsgesetz im Deuteronomium," *TLZ* 76 (1951) 133–
138; von Rad, *Deuteronomy* 118–120.

50. Note that his ceding of twenty cities in the Galilee to Hiram of Tyre established a foreigner as king over people of Israel (1 Kgs 9:10–14).

51. See Knoppers, "The Deuteronomist," who argues that the Torah of the King circumscribes
his powers by prescribing only one positive commandment, the reading of the Torah, but this allows him a great deal of leeway in interpreting the extent to which he might exercise power under
the cloak of Levitical supervision.

52. A. Alt, "The Formation of the Israelite State in Palestine," in *Essays in Old Testament
History and Religion* (Oxford: Blackwell, 1966) 171–237.

53. G. Buccellati, *Cities and Nations of Ancient Syria: An Essay on Political Institutions with
Special Reference in the Israelite Kingdoms* (Rome: University of Rome, 1967).

ished role of the Levites and thereby provides for a more powerful role by the monarchy. Again, it begins with apodictic instruction to establish the principles employed in the following cases. Deuteronomy 18:1–8 thereby employs apodictic instruction to stipulate that the fire offerings and firstfruits are the priestly due from the people, but it also stipulates that the Levites may come to the central sanctuary and serve at the altar. This provision is especially interesting in the context of Deuteronomy in that such offerings by fire and the firstfruits offerings are to be presented at the central sanctuary; if Levites do not come to the sanctuary, it is not clear how they are to collect this portion of their income. This obviously serves as a powerful incentive for the Levites to come to the central sanctuary in order to serve at the altar. The following case in Deuteronomy 18:9–22 concerning prophets from YHWH also provides an interesting perspective in that it presents the prophets, not the priests, as the legitimate spokespersons for YHWH; the prophets thereby become the primary authority figures who represent the presence of YHWH to the people and communicate to them YHWH's will. Throughout the traditions in Exodus, Leviticus, and Numbers, it is the priests who occupy this role—that is, Moses is the prophet par excellence in Deuteronomy, but in Exodus–Numbers, he is the priest. Finally, the casuistic instruction in Deuteronomy 19:1–13 concerning cities of refuge is pertinent in that such cities are not associated with the Levites. Such cities are established to provide protection for persons who commit unintentional manslaughter, as opposed to premeditated murder. Elsewhere in the tradition (Number 35; Joshua 20), cities of refuge are identified as *Levitical* cities of refuge, and Exodus 21:12–14 indicates that YHWH's altar will serve as the place of refuge.[54] Insofar as the altar is under the supervision of the priests, the Covenant Code presupposes that the establishment of a place of refuge is a Levitical or priestly role. Deuteronomy, on the other hand, makes no mention of the Levites in this role and thereby represents another case in which Levitical power is diminished. Insofar as the central altar provides the only legitimate place for the Levites to carry out their professional functions, it would seem that the centralization of worship in Deuteronomy also has an impact on the judicial powers of the Levites in relation to the cities of refuge. The role of the Levites is diminished, but the king stands at the head of the judicial system.

Overall, Deuteronomic Torah presupposes that the monarch is a strong central authority who stands behind and enforces its provisions as the chief judicial and political figure in the land, but it attempts to portray that power discreetly as an expression of YHWH's will exercised through the authority granted it by the presence of the central sanctuary. Clearly, the centralization of the altar in Deuteronomy is a major factor in diminishing the power and role of the Levites and in establishing the king as the central authority figure in the land.

54. Cf. 1 Kings 2:28–35, in which Joab seeks sanctuary at the altar when Benaiah attempts to kill him. Interestingly, the sanctuary at the altar is overridden by the authority of Solomon the king, who instructs Benaiah to kill Joab at the altar. Solomon hardly feels constrained against such action by Levitical presence.

These considerations have important implications for establishing the literary, social, and historical setting and function of the Deuteronomic Torah. In its present form, the Deuteronomic Torah is part of the larger book of Deuteronomy and the Deuteronomistic History as a whole. It is tied into the narrative framework of the earlier books of the Pentateuch so that Deuteronomy plays a key role in tying the various elements of the narrative history of the people of Israel and Judah together. Insofar as the final form of the DtrH dates to the exilic period, as indicated by its concluding narrative concerning the release of King Jehoiachin from prison by Evil Merodach, the Deuteronomic Torah functions as part of an exilic literary work that addresses the problems of the exile of the Jewish community from its homeland and looks forward to its eventual restoration.

Nevertheless, literary study of the book of Deuteronomy and the DtrH has consistently indicated that Deuteronomy does not appear to have been composed for its role as the introduction to the DtrH; rather, the DtrH presupposed Deuteronomy or at least an earlier form of the book. This, of course, raises the question of the literary integrity of the book. Most scholars maintain that Deuteronomy is an edited book, in which a core of Deuteronomic law has been expanded into the present form of the book as a whole. Especially pertinent to this discussion is the generic distinction between the exhortational framework of the book in Deuteronomy 1–11 and 27–34 and the Deuteronomic lawcode in Deuteronomy 12–26. Within the exhortational material, scholars have noted that repetitions in form and content point to the existence of two introductory speeches in Deuteronomy 1:1–4:40 and 4:44–11:32.[55] Likewise, the closing chapters in Deuteronomy 27–34 appear to contain two basic elements, the closing portions of Moses' speech to the people in Deuteronomy 27–30 and the report of Moses' death in Deuteronomy 31–34.[56] Deuteronomy 1:1–4:40; 31–34 tie Deuteronomy into the overall framework of the Pentateuch in that these sections bring closure to the period of wilderness wandering and the life of Moses, and Deuteronomy 4:44–11:32 and 27–30 sets the basic themes of the DtrH, such as observance of YHWH's Torah as the condition for continued possession of the land and the prohibition against mixing with the Canaanites. It would appear that these sections point to the two major stages of Deuteronomy's redactional incorporation first into the Deuteronomistic History (Deut 4:44–11:32; 27–30) during the period of the exile and second into the Pentateuch (Deut 1:1–4:40; 31–34) at some point in the early postexilic period. Obviously, the issue is much more complicated as the interchange between 2mp and 2ms address forms in Deuteronomy 4:44–11:32 indicates, but this model accounts for the most basic literary history of the present form of Deuteronomy.

The question of the setting of the Deuteronomic Torah in chapters 12–26 remains. In this regard, the interchange between 2mp and 2ms address forms is especially noteworthy. The forms are thoroughly mixed throughout Deuteronomy 4:44–11:32, which has prompted any number of marginally successful attempts to disentangle them and thereby clarify the redactional history of these chapters.

---

55. Rendtorff, *The Old Testament* 150–151.
56. Rendtorff, *The Old Testament* 154–155.

But the Deuteronomic Torah displays a relatively consistent preference for 2ms address form throughout Deuteronomy 12–26, with the exception of the initial instructions concerning cultic centralization in Deuteronomy 12:1–31. Scholars have already raised questions concerning the literary integrity of this text in that three versions of the centralization law appear to be extant in vv. 2–7, 8–12, and 13–19 (20–28), respectively.[57] Such a view overlooks the rhetorical perspective of the text, which does not repeat the centralization instruction gratuitously, but successively builds toward the disenfranchisement of the Levites. Nevertheless, it is noteworthy that vv. 2–12 are formulated in 2mp address style, whereas vv. 13–31 are formulated in 2ms address style. It also noteworthy that vv. 2–12 appear to tie the centralization instruction into the overall framework of Deuteronomy. Verses 2–3 presuppose language and themes from Deuteronomy 7:16, which calls for the destruction of Canaanite cultic installations and prohibits intermarriage with the Canaanites. Verses 4–7 take up motifs from vv. 13–31 concerning the centralization of YHWHistic sacrifice. Verses 8–12 presuppose the narrative setting of Deuteronomy on the plains of Moab. Verses 13–31, by contrast, do not tie into the literary framework of Deuteronomy in the manner of vv. 2–12; they could easily be set within the land of Israel. Furthermore, they convey the basic centralization instructions, including the disenfranchisement of the Levites, themes that permeate the Deuteronomic Torah. Insofar as Deuteronomy 12:13–31 share these motifs and the 2ms address form with the rest of the Deuteronomic Torah, it would appear that these verses constitute the introduction to a self-standing Deuteronomic Torah; vv. 2–12 represent an expansion of this Torah that is designed to tie it into the overall literary framework of the present form of the book. It is possible that 2ms elements of the exhortational framework in Deuteronomy 4:44–11:32 and 27–30 accompanied this Deuteronomic Torah at some point, but this must remain hypothetical until the issue of the interrelationship of the 2mp and 2ms address forms in these sections is resolved.

Various features of the Deuteronomic Torah point to the preexilic period, especially the period of King Josiah's late-seventh-century reign and perhaps the late-eighth-century reign of Hezekiah as the historical setting in which it functioned and was composed. First and foremost is the role of the monarch, whose political, judicial, and economic power is enhanced by the centralization of the cult and the corresponding centralization of the legal functions and economic resources of the land. Such a model might presuppose the late-sixth-century attempts to install Zerubbabel as the new Davidic monarch in Jerusalem, but such an attempt required the support of the priesthood, which would have little to gain from the model put forward in Deuteronomy. Rather, the model fits the description of Josiah's reforms as articulated in 2 Kings 22–23, in which cultic worship of YHWH was centralized at the Jerusalem Temple and in which Josiah attempted to secure his hold on at least the territory of the former northern kingdom of Israel. As the narrative in 2 Kings 23:9–10 indicates, Josiah brought out the priests of the various high places in the countryside destroyed during the course of his reform,

---

57. See von Rad, *Deuteronomy* 89.

but they declined to come to the Jerusalem altar and serve there. Such a move reflects the disenfranchisement of the Levites, who chose not to serve in Jerusalem, a disenfranchisement that is evident throughout the Deuteronomic Torah. Such concerns also appear to pertain to the reign of King Hezekiah, who attempted to centralize worship in Jerusalem and through his revolt against Sennacherib attempted to reestablish Davidic control over the former northern kingdom and other surrounding states, such as the Philistine city Ekron. The relationship between the portrayal of the monarch in the Torah of the King in Deuteronomy 17:14–20 and in the DtrH is especially instructive. Solomon is the model against whom a righteous monarch is measured in the Deuteronomic "Torah of the King." Scholars have frequently viewed this as an indication of the northern provenance of the book of Deuteronomy, insofar as the northern kingdom of Israel was formed by means of a revolt against Solomon and his abusive policies toward the northern tribes. But it is noteworthy that in the view of the Deuteronomistic History, no northern monarch ever meets the standards for righteous kingship that are defined in the "Torah of the King." Instead, every northern monarch is condemned for acting contrary to the will of YHWH. Worship of YHWH was never centralized at one location in the northern kingdom and pagan cults were allowed to exist; these appear to be the primary bases for condemning the northern monarchs throughout the Deuteronomistic History.

The contrast between Solomon and Josiah also highlights other major concerns of the Deuteronomic Torah, the protection of family lines of inheritance and the care for the poor of the land. Solomon was well known for the extravagant lifestyle of his court and his extensive building projects, all of which were supported by the people of Israel who lived throughout the land. Insofar as Solomon went into debt to Hiram the King of Tyre, it is likely that such debts would be passed on to the people, with the potential consequence that people in the land would be unable to pay their obligations to the state and thereby suffer loss of land, slavery, or both. Indeed, the narratives concerning Solomon's reign indicate that he imposed a state corvée on the people and ceded twenty cities to Hiram. Furthermore, unlike David, Solomon was not chosen to be king by the people but by David his father. With the exception of Joash, who was later assassinated, and Azariah, who was unable to rule independently due to his leprosy, Josiah was the first King of Judah to be placed on the throne by the people of the land. Insofar as the Deuteronomic Torah protects the rights of the family lines, it protects the rights of family inheritance and possession of land. Furthermore, the various measures pertaining to debt and slavery make it easier for those who find themselves in economic trouble to get out of it and to have a basis on which to rebuild their lives. It would appear that the Deuteronomic Torah addresses the needs of the people of the land, the very group that put Josiah into power after the assassination of his father Amon. This would suggest that the Deuteronomic Torah played a role in supporting Josiah's reign and reform program.

Several other features also support this conclusion. First is the use of Assyrian treaty forms and language in Deuteronomy. The provisions concerning cultic apostasy in Deuteronomy 13:1, 2–19 by a prophet or dreamer of dreams (vv. 2–6), a relative or neighbor (vv. 7–12), or a city (vv. 13–19) are especially noteworthy in that they establish an analogy between the Deuteronomic Torah and neo-Assyrian treaties. The so-called canonization formula in Deuteronomy 13:1, "Everything that I command you, you shall be careful to do; you shall not add to it or take from it," corresponds to similar statements in neo-Assyrian treaties that prohibit any change in the treaty's provisions, for example, "That the word of Esarhaddon, king of Assyria, you will neither change nor alter."[58] Weinfeld likewise notes a number of parallels between Deuteronomy 13:2–19 and the neo-Assyrian treaties, especially in relation to the calls for loyalty to the Assyrian monarch.[59] The fullest analogies appear in the vassal treaties of Esarhaddon. The provision concerning incitement to religious apostasy by a prophet or dreamer of dreams in Deuteronomy 13:2–6 corresponds to provisions in Esarhaddon's treaties that warn against sedition by various mantic figures, such as a *rāgimu*, "oracle priest," *maḫḫû*, "ecstatic priest," or "the son of the divine word/prophet (*DUMU ša a-mat DINGIR*)," which Weinfeld identifies as a šā'ilu or divination prophet.[60] The prohibition against sedition by family members or neighbors corresponds to the provisions of Esarhaddon's treaty that prohibits sedition "from the mouth of your brothers, your sons, your daughters."[61] The phrase *dibber sārâ*, "has spoken rebellion," in Deuteronomy 13:6 corresponds to the phrase *dabab surrāte*, "speaking treason," from Esarhaddon's treaties.[62] Finally, the provisions for the destruction of an apostate city in Deuteronomy 13:13–19 correspond to the provisions of the eighth-century Sefire treaty, which calls for the destruction of a rebellious city: "And if it be a city, you shall smite it by the sword."[63] Such treaties by the neo-Assyrian empires were very common throughout the eighth and seventh centuries, and point to a potential historical model for the formulation of the provisions in Deuteronomy. Furthermore, the extensive use of language throughout Deuteronomy requiring that the people "love YHWH" (e.g., Deut 13:3) likewise reflects the language of neo-Assyrian treaties.[64]

Other indications of neo-Assyrian influence include the prohibition against destroying trees in time of war (Deut 20:19–20), a common Assyrian practice; the prohibition against returning escaped slaves (Deut 23:16–17), as the return of fugitives was a prominent feature of Assyrian treaties; and the prohibition against hanging a criminal on a tree (Deut 21:22–23), a common Assyrian practice.[65] As

58. Vassal treaty of Esarhaddon with Ramataia, city ruler of Urakazabanu, col. i, ll. 57–58, cited in D. J. Wiseman, *The Vassal Treaties of Esarhaddon* (London: British School of Archaeology in Iraq, 1958) 33–34; republished from *Iraq* 20 (1958), Part I.

59. Weinfeld, *Deuteronomy and the Deuteronomic School* 91–100.

60. Cf. col. ii, ll. 116-117, Wiseman, *Vassal-Treaties* 37–38.

61. Col. ii, ll. 115–116, Wiseman, *Vassal-Treaties* 37–38. Cf. S. Parpola, "Neo-Assyrian Treaties from the Royal Archives of Nineveh," *JCS* 39 (1987) 161–189, esp. 167, who cites a treaty made by Queen Zakatu on behalf of her son Assurbanipal, which calls for the client to turn in brothers and friends who speak rebellion against Assurbanipal.

62. Col. vii, l. 502, Wiseman, *Vassal-Treaties* 67–68.

63. Sefire III 12–13, *ANET* 661.

64. W. L. Moran, "The Ancient Near Eastern Background of the Love of G-d in Deuteronomy," *CBQ* 25 (1963) 77–87.

65. See also Eckart Otto, "Rechtsreformen in Deuteronomium xii-xxvi und im Mittelassyrischen Kodex der Tafel A (KAV 1)," *Congress Volume: Paris 1992*, VTSup 61, ed. J. A. Emerton (Leiden:

many have noted before, Deuteronomy portrays the relationship between YHWH and Israel/Judah essentially along the lines of a suzerain-vassal relationship as articulated in the neo-Assyrian vassal treaties. In essence, this portrays Israel's/Judah's subservience to YHWH, but it also expresses Israel's/Judah's independence from foreign political control. In the aftermath of the collapse of Assyrian hegemony over Judah, this demonstrates the coordination of religious and political factors in Josiah's program of restoration. Deuteronomy's concern with offensive warfare also comes into play, as Josiah's reign would present the first opportunity to expand Davidic influence over neighboring territories in the aftermath of Assyria's collapse.

All of these factors point to Josiah's reign as the setting for the Deuteronomic Torah in that it appears to function as the authoritative basis for the reform measures articulated in the account of his reign. Altogether, it presents a model of a powerful monarch, who centralizes the cultic establishment, the economic resources, and the judicial power of the land under the auspices of the king, who is presented as operating strictly in accordance with YHWH's instruction. Therefore, it is important to note that the only monarch who meets the requirements for a righteous monarch as defined in Deuteronomy 17:14–20 is King Josiah of Judah. Although several other monarchs are praised, Josiah is the only king described in the Deuteronomistic History who "walked in all the path of David his father, and who did not turn to the right or to the left" (2 Kings 22:2). The formulation that requires one not to turn to the right or to the left (*sûr yāmîn ûśĕmō'l*) is used throughout Deuteronomy and the DtrH to describe righteous conduct and obedience to YHWH's commands;[66] it is the formulation used to describe the righteous monarch in Deuteronomy 17:20, "so as not to turn from the command to the right or to the left in order that he may lengthen his days upon his throne." According to 2 Kings 22–23, Josiah's policies are based on a "book of Torah" found during the renovation of the Temple; his major actions include the centralization of Temple worship; the prohibition of pagan worship; emphasis on the celebration of Passover with its anti-Egyptian viewpoint; and other measures, all of which are in keeping with the commands of Deuteronomy. Furthermore, he is placed into power by the "people of the land," best understood to represent the farming classes outside of Jerusalem who would benefit most from the Deuteronomic policies that favor the disadvantaged.[67] Thus, Josiah is the one king in the DtrH who fulfills

---

Brill, 1995) 239–273, who points to legal reform measures undertaken by Neo-Assyrian monarchs that parallel that postulated for Josiah, and Hans Ulrich Steymans, *Deuteronomium 28 und die adê zur Thronfolgeregelung Asarhaddons: Segen und Fluch im Alten Orient und in Israel*, OBO 145 (Fribourg: Éditions universitaires; Göttingen: Vandenhoeck & Ruprecht, 1995), who establishes an analogy between the curses of Deutereonomy 28:20–44 and those of Esarhaddon's vassal treaties.

.   66. Deuteronomy 5:29; 17:11, 20; 28:14; Joshua 1:7; 23:6; 2 Kings 22:2.

67. See Halpern, "Jerusalem and the Lineages in the Seventh Century BCE," who argues that Josiah intended to rebuild the tribal structure of the land following its destruction by Hezekiah's reforms and the Assyrian invasions. In this case, laws favoring the disadvantaged classes, as opposed to those resident in the city of Jerusalem, would presumably enable the farming classes to reestablish themselves with less potential of losing their lands during periods of economic hardship.

the requirements for a righteous monarch as defined in Deuteronomy 17:14–20. By destroying the altar at Beth-El, Josiah provides the basis for returning the former northern kingdom to Davidic rule and reuniting the twelve tribes of Israel. In this regard, Josiah repairs the damage to the people of Israel caused by Solomon's policies; Solomon therefore provides a fitting foil to the image of the righteous monarch, which the DtrH identifies as Josiah.

This has implications for understanding the overall perspective of Deuteronomy in that it points to an interest in addressing not only the people of Judah, but the people of the former northern kingdom of Israel. By employing traditional images of authority in the former northern kingdom, the figure of Moses, the location of Shechem as the site of covenant ratification, and elements from the old Covenant Code, Deuteronomy appeals especially to the people of the former northern kingdom to accept the program for national constitution articulated herein.[68] The formulation of the book as a Levitical sermon certainly facilitates such an appeal. The curses of Deuteronomy point to the past, and thereby address the destruction and exile suffered by the people of the former northern kingdom of Israel. The blessings of Deuteronomy, by contrast, point to the future, and raise the possibility that the people and state just might succeed. In making this appeal, Deuteronomy avoids explicit identification of the Davidic monarchy as the power that stands behind the Deuteronomic Torah, insofar as northern memories of Davidic kingship under Solomon are likely not very fond. Nevertheless, it employs the concept of altar centralization to present the Davidic model of a strong central authority, and it does so in a manner that acknowledges the abuses of northern Israel by the house of David in the past. The king is presented as a figure who stands under the authority of YHWH and YHWH's altar, rules under the supervision of YHWH's Torah as mediated by the Levitical priests, and is chosen from among the people of Israel. At the same time, it undermines the role of the Levites, who were likely the only remaining Israelite authority in the territory of the former northern kingdom, and assures the continuity of family lines of inheritance and the economic welfare of those in need. The monarchy is thereby presented as an institution that is consistent with the will of YHWH and the values and institutions of the former northern kingdom of Israel. Thus Deuteronomy presents the monarchy as part of an overall program to rebuild the nation on a secure foundation of YHWH's Torah.

---

68. See esp. S. Dean McBride, Jr., "Polity of the Covenant People: The Book of Deuteronomy," *Int* 41 (1987) 229–244.

10

Conclusion to Part I

The preceding discussion demonstrates that it is possible to identify both an exilic and a Josianic redaction in the present form of the DtrH. It also points to the likelihood that a Hezekian redaction can be identified within the text. It is now possible to define the literary character of each edition and its overall ideological or historiographical perspective.

The final form of the DtrH constitutes the exilic redaction of the DtrH. It appears to have reworked an earlier Josianic edition of the history by adding or rewriting several key texts. 2 Kings 23:31–25:30 is an addition of the exilic DtrH, which relates the reigns of the last four kings of Judah following the death of Josiah, that is, Jehoahaz, Jehoiakim, Jehoiachin, and Zedekiah. Following a description of the fall and destruction of Jerusalem, it continues through the middle of the Babylonian exile, when Jehoaichin is released from prison. The exilic DtrH has reworked the Josiah narrative in 2 Kings 22:1–23:30 by adding the notices concerning Josiah's death and YHWH's decision to destroy Jerusalem, Judah, and the Temple in 2 Kings 23:26–30. It also has reworked the Huldah oracle in 2 Kings 22:14–20 so that it would draw an analogy between King Ahab and King Josiah in pointing to judgment against Judah following Josiah's peaceful death. Like Ahab, who repented concerning his actions against Naboth in 1 Kings 21:27–29 and thereby did not see evil realized against his house during his lifetime, Josiah repented concerning the deeds of his people and was allowed to die without seeing the punishment that would come upon them. The exilic DtrH reworked the Manasseh narrative by adding notices in 2 Kings 21:6b, 8, 9, 10–15, and 16b that would highlight Manasseh's unrivaled sins and thereby assign responsibility to him for YHWH's decision to destroy Jerusalem, Judah, and the Temple. As in the account of Josiah's reign, it highlights the parallel between Manasseh and Ahab. It reworked the Hezekiah narrative by adding the stories concerning Hezekiah's recovery from illness and Isaiah's condemnation of Hezekiah for receiving the

Babylonian embassy in 2 Kings 20:1–19. In this manner, the Hezekiah narratives point to the Babylonian exile and present Hezekiah's illness as an indication that YHWH's deliverance of Jerusalem and Hezekiah is only a temporary measure.

As Noth and many scholars since have argued, the exilic edition of the DtrH is primarily concerned with explaining the tragedy of the Babylonian exile. It focuses specifically on the leadership of Israel, especially the kings of both Israel and Judah, as the primary parties responsible for leading Israel into the apostasy and abandonment of YHWH's commandments that ultimately cause the exile of the people from the land. It begins with the book of Deuteronomy, which lays out the basic requirements of the covenant between YHWH and Israel for possession of the land, as a means to define the criteria by which YHWH and Israel are measured in the history. The book of Joshua presents YHWH's adherence to the covenant by granting the land promised to Israel in three easy campaigns that result in Israel's conquest of the entire land. Divine assistance is evident throughout: YHWH divides the waters of the Jordan River to let the Israelites pass through on dry land; the walls of Jericho fall in a conquest that is portrayed as a cultic procession around the city; Ai falls only after the people purify themselves of a thief who attempted to steal part of the booty dedicated to YHWH; the sun stands enabling Israel to destroy the south Canaanite coalition; and YHWH states to the people that Hazor is delivered into their hand. Only thirty-six Israelites die in the conquest of the entire land, and these because Israel had failed to eliminate the impurity of a thief in its midst. Following the apportionment of the land to the twelve tribes, Joshua gathers the people together at Shechem where they reaffirm the covenant with YHWH. Altogether, the exilic DtrH portrays YHWH as trustworthy covenant partner who provides what is promised to the Israelites.

But following the portrayal of YHWH's covenant fidelity in Joshua, the books of Judges, 1–2 Samuel, and 1–2 Kings turn to an evaluation of the people in relation to the covenant established with YHWH. Overall, the narrative points to Israel's failure to abide by the terms of the covenant as the means to explain the exile of the people from the land. The book of Judges portrays the people as a loose tribal alliance that lacks a clear central authority such as a king. The people are ruled instead by a succession of judges who arise to defeat various enemies that threaten Israel, but the judges create no ongoing means to insure stable rule among the people. After they die, leadership does not pass on to anyone until another judge arises to deal with the next crisis. Although the tribes appear to function as a unity at the beginning of the book, the continued influence of Canaanites who live among them plays a role in the disintegration of the tribal system. The narrative portrays the people as increasingly susceptible to Canaanite religious influence and abusive political relationships that lead to tensions among the tribes. By the end of the narrative, the tribes are engaged in a civil war caused by an outrageous rape and murder of a Levite's concubine, which nearly wipes out the tribe of Benjamin that perpetrated the crime. The books of Samuel relate the rise of kingship in Israel. 1 Samuel 8–12 plays an especially important role in defining kingship as a foreign institution characteristic of the nations that represents a rejection of YHWH's rule and a potential source of abuse and hardship for the people. Because of his personal failings, the first king, Saul, is unable to defeat

the Philistines or unite the people behind him, and eventually falls as a suicide in
a hopeless attempt to save the land from Philistine domination. Because of his
skills and the favor of YHWH, David is able to defeat and subjugate the Philistines after Saul's death, and he thereby creates a secure kingdom with its capital
and religious center in Jerusalem. Despite his personal failings in the affair with
Bath Sheba and his inability to control his children, David establishes a dynasty
that is guaranteed by YHWH's promise of an eternal house if his sons will observe
the commandments.

The books of Kings then take up the primary portion of the task to explain
the exile of the people from the land. They relate the history of the monarchy from
Solomon to the Babylonian exile. Building on 2 Samuel's portrayal of David's
affair with Bath Sheba and its consequences for the stability of the kingdom,
1 Kings presents Solomon's reign as a continuing example of violence, poor judgment, and apostasy that ultimately leads to the split of the kingdom into northern
Israel and southern Judah. Jeroboam, the founding monarch of the northern kingdom, sets a pattern for idolatry with his erection of golden calves at the sanctuaries at Dan and Beth-El. Because the northern monarchs all follow in the path of
idolatry set by Jeroboam, the northern kingdom is destroyed by the Assyrian empire
in an act of divine punishment outlined in 2 Kings 17. The Judean monarchs receive
a more nuanced treatment. Many are judged to be righteous although they fail to
remove the high places; others, such as Hezekiah and Josiah, receive a great deal
of praise for their righteous actions, although they are unable to avert the final
disaster.-Ultimately, the exilic DtrH blames Manasseh for the fall of Jerusalem,
the Temple, and Judah because of his actions in causing Judah to sin. Despite his
exemplary righteousness, Josiah is unable to save the kingdom and is granted the
right to die peacefully without witnessing the catastrophe.

The ideology of the exilic DtrH is especially evident in its presentation of
Manasseh's guilt. Overall, the narrative does not build toward this theme well, in
that the decision to destroy Jerusalem and the Temple seems to be somewhat of
an afterthought in the wake of the destruction of northern Israel. Only Solomon's
second vision of YHWH in 1 Kings 9:1–9, which points to the possible destruction of the Temple, and the narrative concerning Hezekiah's reception of the
Babylonian embassy prepare the reader explicitly for this result. It thereby demonstrates the redactional character of the exilic DtrH, but it also demonstrates the
means by which the exilic DtrH incorporated this theme into the overall history
of Israel and Judah. The exilic DtrH takes special care to establish a parallel between Manasseh and the northern Omride king Ahab in its portrayal of Manasseh's
guilt. This is especially important in that from Ahaziah on, all of the Davidic kings
are descendants of the house of Omri as well as of the house of David. This was
the result of the marriage between Jehoram, son of the Judean Jehoshaphat, and
Athaliah, daughter (or granddaughter) of the Israelite Ahab. Like Ahab, Manasseh
shed innocent blood, but, most important, he built an Asherah that caused the
people to sin. Josiah is drawn into the parallel as well. Just as Ahab repented of
his actions and avoided judgment on the land during his lifetime, so Josiah's actions
constituted repentance on the part of the house of David that delayed punishment
until after his death. But just as Ahab's repentance only delayed punishment against

Israel until the reigns of his descendants, so Josiah's repentance only delayed the destruction of Jerusalem until after his death.

This preserves some tension in the exilic DtrH presentation of the monarchies. On the one hand, the prophecy against the house of Ahab (1 Kgs 21:20–24) is fulfilled in relation to the northern kings, and Manasseh's actions demonstrate the continuing influence of the Omride line within the house of David. On the other hand, YHWH's promise of a secure house to David sees the preservation of the Davidic line in Jehoiachin even though Jerusalem and the Temple are destroyed and the people are exiled. Overall, it points to the Dtr call for repentance on the part of the people when they are exiled from their land. Deuteronomy 30:1–10 makes it clear that the people may repent after their exile and return to the land. The continued influence of the Omride house in Manasseh explains their exile; the release of Jehoiachin from Babylonian prison points to the possibility of their restoration. In this regard, the DtrH is clearly focused on the future of the people of Israel and Judah; it does not simply write their epitaph by focusing exclusively on the past.

The ideology of the Josianic edition of the DtrH is quite different from that of the exilic DtrH, even though they are virtually identical until the narratives concerning Hezekiah and his successors. Unlike the exilic edition, the Josianic DtrH is not designed to explain the exile of the people from the land, but to point to the realization of the Deuteronomic covenant under the leadership of King Josiah of Judah. It presents Josiah as the greatest of all the monarchs who resolves the problems of the people of Israel, including both the northern tribes of Israel and southern tribe of Judah, and reunites them around the Jerusalem Temple. In describing Josiah as a king who "did what was right in the eyes of YHWH, and walked in all the way of David his father, and . . . did not turn aside to the right hand or to the left" and "who turned to YHWH with all his might, according to all the Torah of Moses," the DtrH employs language that points to Josiah as a leader on a par with Moses and Joshua. He thereby surpasses David as an exemplary monarch among the entire people of Israel.

A number of features in the Josianic DtrH demonstrate this overall ideology. First is the presentation of Joshua as a leader who appears to be patterned upon Josiah. The Josianic DtrH portrays Joshua as an exemplary leader of a unified Israel who rules in accordance with the requirements of Deuteronomic law. He directs a campaign that sees the conquest of the entire land of Israel and the removal of Canaanite/pagan influence. He serves as covenant mediator and observes the festival of Passover. Although the image of Joshua appears to be modeled on that of Josiah, it serves as the paradigm for Josiah's rule in the Josianic DtrH and thereby points to Josiah as an ideal monarch on the pattern of Joshua. Furthermore, the emphasis on Joshua's northern or Ephraimite identity aids in establishing the Judean Josiah as an ideal ruler for both the northern and southern tribes.

Second, the book of Judges points to the inability of the people to rule themselves without a monarch. It thereby aids in preparing the way for the institution of monarchy, but it does so in a manner that subtly questions the ability of the northern tribes to rule themselves and to establish proper worship of YHWH. It thereby paves the way for the emergence of the Davidic dynasty. In contrast to

Judah, which secures its own land, the northern tribes are unable completely to remove the Canaanites from the land so that they stand as a continuing source of apostasy among the people. Likewise, in contrast to the Judean Judge Othniel who expels his enemy easily, the Judges from the northern tribes find various problems in defeating their enemies, uniting the people, preventing Canaanite religious influence, and establishing justice in the land. Especially problematic is the tribe of Ephraim, which continually provokes tension and civil war by attempting to assert its leadership over the other tribes. The tribe of Benjamin, which later produces Saul, is shown to be an unworthy tribe that produces and harbors men who will rape and murder without cause. The sanctuaries at Dan and Beth-El serve as centers for idolatrous worship and the corruption of Levites originally associated with Bethlehem. Beth-El in particular also serves as a gathering point for war among the tribes and the potential destruction of Benjamin. Overall, the Judges narrative is designed to demonstrate that Ephraim, Benjamin, Dan, and Beth-El are all faulty in some way or another. It thereby polemicizes against the leading tribes and sanctuaries of the northern kingdom of Israel, and it prepares the reader for the emergence of the House of David and the Jerusalem Temple. The narrative concerning the kingship of Saul and the rise of David then demonstrate Saul's inadequacies as a ruler over against David. Again because of his personal shortcomings, Saul is unable to defeat the Philistines or to capture the loyalty of the people. David, who counts as his supporters Saul's son and likely successor Jonathan and Saul's daughter Michal, is able to defeat the Philistines and to secure his position as king over both Judah and the northern tribes of Israel by popular approval. He not only supplants the dynasty of Saul, he establishes Jerusalem as his political and religious capital. As a result, the narrative presents YHWH's promise to David of an eternal house dynasty. David thereby becomes the model by which the later Davidic kings are measured.

The narrative concerning the reign of Solomon is especially important in the Josianic DtrH because it points to Solomon as the cause of most of the problems that Josiah must resolve. It builds on the Succession Narrative of 2 Samuel 9/11–20, which presents David's adulterous affair with Bath Sheba and his murder of her husband Uriah as the background for Solomon's birth. It further presents the turmoil within his own house, as David is unable to control his sons, whose capacity for sexual misbehavior and violence match that of their father. The deaths of David's older sons Amnon and Abshalom prepare the way for Bath Sheba's efforts to secure the throne for her son Solomon. By the time Solomon has full control of the kingdom, the entire Hebron-based faction of the Davidic house has been eliminated and replaced by a faction centered around Solomon and Bath Sheba that emerges only after David moves his capital from Hebron to Jerusalem. In contrast to David, Solomon is not chosen by the people, but by David who is manipulated by Bath Sheba and Nathan. In his rule of the kingdom, Solomon displays the same capacities for violence and sexual excess characteristic of his father in the Succession Narrative.-Although Solomon is unable to control the finances of his kingdom properly or to establish just rule over the northern tribes, the Josianic DtrH focuses especially on his love for foreign women, especially his marriage to the daughter of Pharaoh, as the reason for the split within the kingdom that occurs after his death. According to the Josianic DtrH, Solomon's apostasy, a result of his attempts to accommodate the religious impulses of his pagan wives, prompts YHWH to split the kingdom by giving ten tribes to Jeroboam ben Nebat. The retention of one tribe by the house of David upholds YHWH's promise of an eternal dynasty to David. The Josianic DtrH also highlights Solomon's involvement with Egypt, in clear contradiction to the interests of Deuteronomy, which ultimately plays a major role in fomenting revolt by giving asylum to Jeroboam and later invades and subdues the separated kingdoms.

The Josianic DtrH in Kings then proceeds by focusing especially on the reigns of the northern monarchs as the cause for the eventual collapse of the northern kingdom and exile of its people. Building on the Judges narrative, which points to the continuing influence of the Canaanites on the northern tribes, the inadequacies of Ephraim as a ruling tribe, and the problems of the sanctuaries at Dan and Beth-El, it presents Jeroboam as the paradigmatic sinful monarch of the northern kingdom who leads his people to disaster. Jeroboam erects golden calves at the Dan and Beth-El sanctuaries and thereby earns the condemnation of the Josianic DtrH, which points to Josiah as the one who will ultimately destroy Jeroboam's idolatrous altar at Beth-El. Not only is Jeroboam and his house condemned, all of the northern monarchs are judged to have followed in the path of Jeroboam in causing Israel to sin. Overall, the Josianic DtrH presents the northern monarchy as a complete failure in that the Assyrian destruction of the northern kingdom is attributed to the people's sins in following in the path of Jeroboam.

Again, the Josianic DtrH treats the southern monarchs in a more nuanced manner. As in the exilic edition, many are judged to be righteous although they do not remove the high places. Hezekiah in particular is singled out for praise. His Temple reforms are a model of proper Davidic action in the Josianic DtrH, although his attempted revolt against Assyria results in the devastation of the entire land when Sennacherib's army invades. When Hezekiah's military options fail, his turn to YHWH in prayer at the Temple likewise serves as a model of proper Davidic action that sees the destruction of the Assyrian army and the assassination of Sennacherib by his own sons, as YHWH takes action to save Jerusalem for the sake of David. This brings the Assyrian period to a close in the DtrH, but leaves plenty of room for Josiah to enact his reforms that will see the reestablishment of a people reunited around the Jerusalem Temple in the land of Israel.

Manasseh's reign constitutes a brief interlude in which the sins of the house of Omri/Ahab emerge in the form of an Asherah and the shedding of innocent blood to serve as a foil for Josiah's reform measures. When Josiah is brought to power by the people of the land, reinstituting the principle of popular selection of the monarch abandoned by Solomon, the young king embarks upon a reform program that will implement the commandments of Deuteronomy as the basis for a revitalized state centered solely around a purified Jerusalem temple. The narrative highlights Josiah's resolution of various problems created by sinful kings—that is, he reconstitutes the covenant based on the Torah scroll (Deuteronomy) discovered in the course of Temple renovation; he removes various high places throughout the land and pagan installations in the Temple and Jerusalem, including the altars of Ahaz and Manasseh; the installations Ashtoreth, Chemosh, and

Milcom built by Solomon; and the Beth-El altar built by Jeroboam. Although the narrative does not mention it in its present form, the destruction of the Beth-El altar paved the way for the reunification of the people around the Jerusalem Temple. Likewise, the reinstitution of the Passover, last celebrated by Joshua and a united people of Israel, prepared for the reunification of the people under Josiah's rule. As noted in the discussion of the Manasseh narrative, the promise by YHWH not again to let the people of Israel wander from the land given to their ancestors apparently was intended to serve as part of the Josiah narrative in that it expresses Josiah's interest in restoring the former northern kingdom of Israel to its land and to Davidic rule under Josiah.

The interest in the restoration of the northern kingdom to Davidic rule in the Josianic DtrH aids in explaining the often noted focus by the DtrH on the northern kingdom of Israel. Scholars have always noted that the DtrH in all editions emphasizes the need for centralized worship on the part of Israel exclusively at the Jerusalem Temple. Furthermore, despite the criticism leveled against most of the Davidic monarchs, the DtrH acknowledges the legitimacy of the house of David. But it is also noteworthy that in presenting the history of Israel, the Josianic DtrH takes special care to demonstrate that the northern tribes are not able to rule themselves effectively. It points not only to the failings the various northern dynasties that ruled the kingdom, but to the failings of the House of David as well. In this regard, it is important to acknowledge that from the perspective of the northern kingdom, the house of David was only one of the series of dynasties that rule the kingdom of Israel. Although David represents a model of ideal rule up to the point that he established his capital in Jerusalem, his actions as portrayed in the Succession Narrative portray a kingdom that is dissatisfied with Davidic rule and that is ready to revolt under Abshalom and later Sheba. Likewise, Solomon's unfair treatment of the northern tribes leads directly to their revolt against Rehoboam. From the perspective of the Josianic DtrH, Davidic rule had failed in the north as well as that of all the various northern dynasties. Josiah's reign represented an opportunity to rectify the mistakes of the past.

This demonstrates that the Josianic DtrH is not only an ideologically charged presentation of the history of Israel and Judah, it is a propagandistic work as well, insofar as it attempts to justify the reinstitution of Davidic/Josianic rule over the former northern kingdom of Israel. Essentially, the Josianic DtrH presents Josiah as the monarch who not only rules on the basis of the promise made by YHWH to David, formerly the king of the northern tribes, but as the monarch who rectifies the problems of the past created by both David and Solomon. Overall, it is designed to demonstrate that the northern tribes are not capable of ruling themselves, as demonstrated by their many failures to do so throughout their history, but that Davidic rule under Josiah represents their only chance to achieve the promises of the Deuteronomic covenant of a secure people, centered around the worship of YHWH at the central shrine (Jerusalem). In this regard, the Torah of the King in Deuteronomy 17:14–20 points to Solomon as the quintessential example of improper monarchic rule; Josiah represents the example of the monarch who implements proper rule as conceived in Deuteronomic law.

This points to the role that Deuteronomy 30:1–10 plays in the overall conception of a Josianic DtrH. Deuteronomy 30:1–10 calls for the people to repent once they have been exiled from the land so that YHWH might forgive them and return them to the land from exile. In the context of the Josianic DtrH, such a call is constitutive of the overall purpose of the work; it is designed to convince the exiles of the northern kingdom—and those that remained behind—that it is possible to return to Israel and to restore their land and kingdom under proper Davidic rule. Overall, the Josianic DtrH lays out the rationale and program for the restoration of the northern kingdom of Israel to Davidic rule under King Josiah. The result would be a unified people, centered around the Jerusalem sanctuary, living under the Deuteronomic law code as the basic law of the land propagated by the house of David.

Finally, it appears that the Josianic edition of the DtrH may well have built on an earlier edition of the DtrH that culminated in the account of YHWH's deliverance of Jerusalem during the reign of Hezekiah. Although it is not possible to reconstruct an entire Hezekian DtrH, the analysis of the DtrH presented above points to Hezekiah as the righteous monarch who rules according to the model of David and who removes the high places instituted by Solomon and maintained by his successors in both the north and the south. Overall, the Hezekian DtrH presents David as the ideal monarch, and thereby lacks the Succession Narrative that casts David in such an unfavorable light. It presents Solomon in a relatively ideal light as the builder of the Temple and successor to David. It portrays his abusive economic treatment of the northern tribes, but it also indicates that the northern tribes were warned in 1 Samuel 8 that this is precisely what they should expect from kingship. It further castigates the northern monarchs for their inability to provide effective rule and for their rejection of YHWH. By pointing to the collapse of northern Israel as a judgment by YHWH, it provides an appropriate foil for presenting Hezekiah as a model of a faithful Davidic monarch, who saves his city by turning to YHWH. The fact that it presents the collapse of Assyrian rule over Judah and Sennacherib's assassination by his own sons as points to the mid-seventh century as the time of its composition. Its emphasis on Hezekiah's turn to YHWH as the key to his deliverance suggests that it may well have played a role in forming the outlook of the young king Josiah and in motivating him to pursue his program of religious reform and national restoration.

II

PROPHETIC LITERATURE AND JOSIAH'S REIGN

E ven a perfunctory reading of the account of King Josiah's reign in
2 Kings 22:1–23:30, and indeed of the DtrH as a whole, demonstrates
that prophets and prophecy play a major role in conveying the DtrH
presentation of history. Josiah's actions in reforming the religious practice of
Judah, for example, is motivated in large measure by Huldah's prophecy,
which announced doom to the nation for not observing YHWH's requirements
as articulated in the Torah scroll found during the course of the king's Temple
renovation. Likewise, the early death of Josiah is not only characterized by
Huldah as a merciful gesture by YHWH toward the monarch so that he would
not have to witness the disaster that would overtake the people, but YHWH's
decision to destroy Jerusalem and Judah is articulated as an announcement by
the prophets in relation to the reign of King Manasseh as a means to punish the
people for the sins of Manasseh and for their actions throughout the history.
Apart from specific concerns with Josiah and his reign, prophets appear
throughout the history as key characters. Moses is portrayed as the prophet
par excellence of the book of Deuteronomy and the DtrH as a whole (cf.
Deut 18:15–22), who founds the nation and leads it through the wilderness to
the promised land, provides it with YHWH's guidance in the form of the
Deuteronomic Torah, and who serves as the ideal role model for subsequent
leaders such as Joshua (Josh 1:7–8; 8:30–35; 23:6) and Josiah (2 Kgs 23:25).[1]
Samuel sees the people through the transition from tribal leadership to monarchy,

---

1. For studies of the role of Moses as exemplar for Joshua and Josiah in the DtrH, see Hoffmann,
Reform und Reformen; Christa Schäfer-Lichtenberger, *Josua und Salomo: Eine Studie zu Autorität
und Legitimität des Nachfolgers im Alten Testament*, VTSup 58 (Leiden: Brill, 1995) 177–224
(Joshua); Nelson, "Josiah in the Book of Joshua" (Joshua and Josiah); Sweeney, "The Critique of
Solomon" (Josiah).

anointing both Saul and David as the first kings of Israel. Nathan conveys YHWH's promise of an eternal dynasty to David, and facilitates Solomon's accession to the throne. Ahijah the Shilonite legitimizes the establishment of the northern kingdom of Israel by granting the right of kingship to Jeroboam, and then removes it when Jeroboam proves to be inadequate. An unnamed man of G-d condemns Jeroboam at Beth-El, and predicts that Josiah will one day destroy the Beth-El altar. Elijah and Elisha condemn the Omride dynasty for its alliance with Phoenicia and its apostasy to foreign gods and support the coup that leads to the establishment of a new dynasty by Jehu. Isaiah conveys YHWH's expectations to Hezekiah, and thereby plays a key role in defining the Assyrian threat against Jerusalem and the deliverance of the city as acts of YHWH in the DtrH. Clearly, prophecy is a major force in the historical presentation of the DtrH, in that prophets generally give voice to the DtrH interpretation of Israel's and Judah's history and to its overall theological viewpoint.

Nevertheless, the study of prophecy and prophetic literature in relation to Josiah's reign has lagged behind that devoted to the DtrH. This lag is the result of theological presuppositions and methodological standpoints that have informed the modern critical study of prophecy throughout the nineteenth and twentieth centuries.[2] Earlier scholarship tends to portray prophets in light of the founders of the early Protestant reformation, as iconoclastic rebels who stood above the particular concerns of Israelite national life to denounce the political and religious establishments of their day for their lack of moral and spiritual commitment to the expectations of YHWH. Overall, the prophets are portrayed as universalistic and eschatological in perspective; they would hardly be bound by the national concerns of the Judean monarchy or the Jerusalem Temple, but would consistently point to the eschatological age in which all nations together with Israel would recognize YHWH as L-rd over all the earth. Thus, the reign of King Josiah, with its interests in centralizing worship in the Jerusalem Temple would hardly be a matter in which the prophets of the Bible would be concerned; instead, the issue of the exile and its implications for the universal recognition of YHWH take center stage throughout most of the nineteenth and twentieth centuries. Consequently, prophecy in the seventh century B.C.E. receives relatively little treatment in modern scholarship when compared to the major prophetic figures of the eighth-century period of Assyrian invasion and those of the sixth-century period of exile.[3]

But more recent scholarly perspectives tend to stress the social character of the prophets as figures who were well connected to the political and religious

---

2. For an overview of the history and presuppositions of modern literary-critical study of prophetic literature, see Joseph Blenkinsopp, *A History of Prophecy in Israel*, revised edition (Louisville, KY: Westminster John Knox, 1996) 16–26.

3. Cf. Gerhard von Rad, *Old Testament Theology. Volume II. The Theology of Israel's Prophetic Traditions*, translated by D. M. G. Stalker (New York: Harper and Row, 1965), who devotes considerable attention to the theological significance of eighth-century prophecy as well as that pertaining to the Babylonian exile, but treats seventh-century prophecy with a perfunctory three and one half pages as a transitional phase between the Assyrian and Babylonian periods.

institutions of their time and who spoke out from their individual perspectives in attempts to convince their peers of the validity of their particular view-points.[4] Thus, Isaiah emerges as a royalist figure who views Judah's relationship with Judah and Israel in relation to the traditions of the Davidic monarchy. Based on the Davidic view of YHWH's promise of eternal protection for the monarchy, the Temple, and Jerusalem, he opposes alliances with foreign nations that are designed to protect Judah from foreign invasion (Isa 7; 28–31). He presses his royalist ideology to such an extent that he portrays YHWH as a monarch on the throne, holding court before the Seraphim and autocratically declaring that the role of the prophet is to prevent the people from seeing and hearing lest they repent and be healed (Isa 6). Jeremiah is an Elide priest whose ancestors served at the Shiloh sanctuary before being deposed from the high priesthood in the time of Solomon. His viewpoint is formed in relation to the traditions of Mosaic Torah and a distinctly anti-Egyptian perspective. He therefore questions the Davidic viewpoints that postulate YHWH's absolute guarantee of security for Jerusalem (Jer 7), and argues that the nation should submit to Babylonian power rather than to Egypt as an expression of the will of YHWH (Jer 27-28). Ezekiel is a Zadokite priest in Babylonian exile who sees a vision of YHWH's throne chariot that appears to be modeled on the image of the ark in the holy of holies of the Jerusalem Temple, and thereby attempts to establish the holiness of the Temple as a basis for Jewish life in a foreign land (Ezek 1; 18). He looks forward to the restoration of creation that is signaled when Israel, the Temple, and its ritual are restored at the center of the nations and the natural world (Ezek 40–48). Essentially, the prophets do not stand apart from the political and religious institutions of their own societies. They are closely tied into such institutions and attempt to argue for their respective viewpoints within the societies in which they live. They therefore represent partisan perspectives derived from these ties which inform their portrayals of YHWH, Israel/Judah, and the events that serve as the basis for their particular messages.

These advances have tremendous implications for the study of prophecy and prophetic literature in relation to the reign of King Josiah. The interrelationship between prophecy and both cultic and political institutions in ancient Israel and Judah demonstrates the need to reassess prophecy in relation to the seventh century B.C.E., particularly in relation to Josiah's program of national reform, including both its political and its religious aspects. The superscriptions of Jeremiah and Zephaniah explicitly associate these prophetic figures with the

---

4. See Blenkinsopp, *History of Prophecy*, 26–39; Robert Carroll, "Prophecy and Society," in *The World of Ancient Israel: Sociological, Anthropological, and Political Perspectives*, ed. R. E. Clements (Cambridge, U.K.: Cambridge University Press, 1989) 203–225; Patrick D. Miller, Jr., "The World and Message of the Prophets: Biblical Prophecy in its Context," in *Old Testament Interpretation: Past, Present, and Future*, Fs. G. M. Tucker, ed. J. L. Mays, D. L. Petersen, and K. H. Richards (Nashville: Abingdon, 1995) 97–112; Marvin A. Sweeney, "The Latter Prophets: Isaiah, Jeremiah, Ezekiel," in *The Hebrew Bible Today: An Introduction to Critical Issues*, ed. S. L. McKenzie and M. P. Graham (Louisville, KY: Westminster John Knox, 1998) 69–94.

reign of King Josiah, and Nahum clearly addresses the fall of Nineveh, which took place late in Josiah's reign. Habakkuk treats the period following Josiah's reign when the Babylonians asserted their power over Judah. Obviously, these books are potentially very useful in establishing prophetic perspectives on Josiah's reign and reform, but the introduction to this volume points to the various issues in the literary-historical or redaction-critical study of the prophets that have raised questions concerning their applicability to the Josianic reform. Nevertheless, the awakening interest in Zephaniah, Nahum, Habakkuk, and renewed efforts in the redaction-critical study of Jeremiah indicate that such work is currently under way.

In addition to the changing perspectives concerning the social and political roles of the prophets and the impact of these roles in defining their theological perspectives, methodological advances in the study of prophetic literature throughout the twentieth century also must be considered.[5] Throughout the late nineteenth and twentieth centuries, modern literary-critical study of the prophetic books has been dominated by an interest in reconstructing an image of the prophetic figures themselves, the events in which they participated, and the words that they spoke. Consequently, a great deal of modern scholarship emphasizes attempts to reconstruct the earliest forms of the prophetic literature that stand behind the final forms of the prophetic books insofar as these books show clear evidence of having been edited by later hands during the postexilic period. Such attempts generally presuppose that authentic prophetic utterances from the monarchic period were short, self-contained, generic statements, that were spoken by the prophet in a state of ecstatic trance possession. This view of prophetic speech presupposes that the ancient prophets were primitive figures incapable of formulating long, complex original texts and ideas. Consequently, the short generic statements were collected by other writers, who frequently made mistakes in recording and arranging the prophet's words, and who failed to provide an adequate description of the historical context and setting in which the prophet spoke. Furthermore, later writers added their own interpretative comments and other materials that addressed concerns from much later periods, particularly that of the exile of Judah and the potential restoration of the Jewish people in the postexilic era, and that distorted the original message of the preexilic prophet. The task of the scholar, then, is to strip away extraneous later material, so that the original words of the prophet could be recovered, and to reconstruct the social and historical setting in which the prophet spoke. Prophetic books are therefore frequently treated as collections of short prophetic utterances that were spoken at various times and places in the prophet's careers. Many modern scholars in the nineteenth-to-

---

5. For overviews and discussion of methodology in the study of prophetic literature, see Gene M. Tucker, "Prophecy and Prophetic Literature," in *The Hebrew Bible and its Modern Interpreters*, ed. D. A. Knight and G. M. Tucker (Chico, Calif.: Scholars Press, 1985) 325–368; Marvin A. Sweeney, "Formation and Form in Prophetic Literature," *Old Testament Interpretation: Past, Present, and Future* 113–126; Sweeney, *Isaiah 1–39, with an Introduction to Prophetic Literature*, FOTL 16 (Grand Rapids, Mich. and Cambridge, U.K.: Eerdmans, 1996) 1–30.

mid-twentieth centuries therefore consider the later work of redactors or editors to be unimportant and generally set it aside.

The years since World War II, however, have seen a shift in scholarly thinking from concern in the personalities of the prophets or great figures of the past to concern with literature in and of itself, including the specific literary characteristics of a work, the sociopolitical background that shaped its expression and ideas, and the social world in which it is read and interpreted.[6] The result is a renewed interest in the study of prophetic books as literature, including both the "original" words of the prophets and the later literary additions that shape and define the present forms of prophetic books. Scholars now recognize that later readers of prophetic literature provide the lenses or theological perspective through which it is read. Thus, the redactors or later editors of a prophetic book are now seen not simply as literary mechanics who assembled the creative works of others without really understanding it or contributing to its ideas but as creative writers and theologians in their own right who employed the earlier works of others in creating their own compositions. Scholars have begun to consider redactional work to be theologically significant, not only because it pointed to the creative process by which the prophetic literature and ideas were formulated, but because it pointed to the hermeneutical process by which earlier prophetic works were read and reinterpreted in relation to much later historical and social settings and in relation to entirely different sets of interpretative concerns.[7] Thus, the words of the eighth-century prophet Isaiah ben Amoz, who promised the establishment of an ideal Davidic king in the Assyrian period (e.g., Isa 9:1–6), could be read as a prophecy concerning the future kingship of Josiah in the seventh century, or Cyrus in the sixth century, or even of YHWH's kingship in a future period.

Such methodological advances in the study of prophetic literature point to the possibility that earlier prophetic works may well have been read in relation to Josiah's reform or supplemented and updated to addresses the concerns of the Josianic period. As noted in the introduction to this volume, prophetic books that present eighth-century prophets such as Isaiah, Hosea, Amos, and Micah also must be considered because of their potential relevance to Josiah's reform. Insofar as redaction-critical scholarship points to the reformulation and resignification of these prophets in relation to later periods, scholars must be prepared to examine these writings in order to determine if they have been reformulated and read in relation to later periods, such as the period of King

6. See especially, Knierim, "Criticism of Literary Features, Form, Tradition, and Redaction"; Robert Morgan with John Barton, *Biblical Interpretation* (Oxford: Oxford University Press, 1988); John Barton, *Reading the Old Testament: Method in Biblical Study*, revised edition (Louisville, KY: Westminster John Knox, 1996).

7. In addition to the works cited above, see Terence Collins, *The Mantle of Elijah: The Redaction Criticism of the Prophetical Books*, BibSem 20 (Sheffield: JSOT Press, 1993); Klaus Koenen, *Heil den Gerechten—Unheil den Sündern: Ein Beitrag zur Theologie der Prophetenbücher*, BZAW 229 (Berlin and New York: Walter de Gruyter, 1994); Simon J. De Vries, *From Old Revelation to New: A Tradition-Historical and Redaction-Critical Study of Temporal Transitions in Prophetic Prediction* (Grand Rapids, Mich.: William Eerdmans, 1995).

Josiah's reign and reform. Given the potential for contemporary prophetic involvement and influence in Josiah's reform and the use of prophetic figures to convey the historiographical perspective of the DtrH, it is reasonable to ask whether or not earlier prophetic writings might be included among those that provided prophetic legitimation to the king's program.

These considerations call for an investigation of the prophetic books mentioned above—those that clearly derive from the period of King Josiah's reign and its aftermath, as well as those that appear to derive from earlier periods—in an attempt to gain some understanding of prophetic perspectives on Josiah and his reform and the role of prophecy in relation to his program. Obviously, this requires a redaction-critical method that can take seriously the literary character of the present form of the prophetic books and probe behind their present forms in order to recover earlier statements and perspectives. Insofar as the prophetic books are the products of their final redactors, who selected, arranged, supplemented, rewrote, and composed the final form of the prophetic books, redaction-critical questions must be addressed from the outset.[8] .Consequently, analysis must begin with the present form of the text, including an assessment of its literary structure, generic characteristics, ideological perspectives, and contents. These serve as the basis for a reconstruction of the historical and social setting from which the present form of the text derives as well as the setting that it portrays and the issues that it addresses. Once the character and interpretation of the final form of the text is established, it may then be probed for evidence that earlier material may somehow be present in the final form of the text. Literary and ideological tension provides criteria that may well point to the presence of earlier material that has been taken up and reformulated in the present form of the text. Likewise, the contents of the text may well relate to an earlier historical or social setting, for example, the concern with exile may relate to the Babylonian exile of Judah or the Assyrian exile of the northern kingdom of Israel. Concern with the restoration of the monarchy may well relate to the postexilic restoration of kingship in Judah or to the preexilic restoration of Davidic rule over the north. Each case must be assessed individually, and the exegete must be prepared to determine how a shift in the interpretation of the text might occur as the literary and sociohistorical settings of the text change.

With these considerations in mind, I turn my analysis to prophetic books that may have some bearing on the reign of Josiah. Those that relate directly to Josiah's reign include Zephaniah, Nahum, and Jeremiah, whereas Habakkuk portrays the situation in Judah following Josiah's death when the Babylonian empire took control of the country. Isaiah, Hosea, Amos, and Micah must be considered as earlier prophetic writings that may well have been read or reformulated in relation to the concerns of the Josianic period.

---

8. Knierim, "Criticism of Literary Features," 150–158, esp. 156; Sweeney, "Formation and Form," 115–117.

11

Zephaniah

T he book of Zephaniah is potentially one of the most important prophetic
sources for the study of the reign of King Josiah. It is the only prophetic book
in which the superscription states that the word of YHWH came to the prophet
exclusively during the reign of Josiah, "The word of YHWH which was to
Zephaniah ben Cushi ben Gedaliah ben Amariah ben Hizkiah in the days of Josiah
ben Amon King of Judah." This superscription is unusually informative concerning the prophet's genealogy, and it has therefore provoked considerable discussion concerning Zephaniah's ancestry.[1] Many take the reference to his father Cushi
as an indication of Ethiopian descent, and others take the reference to his great-
great-grandfather Hizkiah as an indication that he is descended from King Hezekiah
of Judah. Neither hypothesis can be confirmed for lack of further information,[2]
but Ethiopian descent would help to explain the prophet's interest in the downfall
of Cush (Zeph 2:12) and the return of Judean exiles "from beyond the rivers of
Cush" (Zeph 3:10). The reference to descent from Hezekiah would likewise call
to mind King Hezekiah's alliance with Egypt, which was ruled by the 25th Ethiopian dynasty in the late eighth century B.C.E., as well as the king's attempts to
remove foreign influences from the Jerusalem Temple and to free Judah from
Assyrian control.

---

1. For discussion of the issue, see Ehud Ben Zvi, *A Historical-Critical Study of the Book of
Zephaniah*, BZAW 198 (Berlin and New York: Walter de Gruyter, 1991) 41–51; Roger W. Anderson, Jr., "Zephaniah ben Cushi and Cush of Benjamin: Traces of Cushite Presence in Syria-Palestine,"
in *The Pitcher is Broken: Memorial Essays for Gösta W. Ahlström*, JSOTSup 190, ed. S. W. Holloway
and L. K. Handy (Sheffield: JSOT Press, 1995) 45–70.

2. Cf. J. J. M. Roberts, *Nahum, Habakkuk, and Zephaniah: A Commentary*, OTL (Louisville,
KY: Westminster/John Knox, 1991) 164–166; Adele Berlin, *Zephaniah*, AB 25A (New York:
Doubleday, 1994) 63–69.

Despite the testimony of the superscription, there is a great deal of disagreement concerning the literary character and message of the book of Zephaniah and its relation to King Josiah's reign.[3] The present form of the book focuses on the coming "Day of YHWH" as a time for the overturning of the present world order.[4] Those in Judah and Jerusalem who have followed foreign cults and practices will be punished together with the nations prior to the final exaltation of Jerusalem and the return of her captives. Although the motif of cultic purification and the exaltation of Jerusalem could easily relate to Josiah's policies, many scholars have argued that various features of the present form of the book point not to a Josianic composition, but to a postexilic redaction that arranged and extensively supplemented the words of the prophet in order to address later concerns from the postexilic era.[5] The first is the supposed tripartite structure of the present form of the book, which takes up concern with the punishment of Jerusalem and Judah (Zeph 1:2–2:3), the punishment of the nations of the earth (Zeph 2:4–3:8), and promises of salvation to both Judah/Jerusalem and the nations, in a worldwide eschatological scenario that could only have emerged in the postexilic period. The second is the dichotomy between the concern with universal eschatological punishment and restoration in 1:2–3, 17–18, 2:4–15, 3:6–8, 9–20 versus the specific concern with Jerusalem/Judah in 1:4–16, 2:1–3, 3:1–5. The third is the concern with the destruction of Moab and Ammon (Zeph 2:8–9a), which were destroyed only in the sixth century B.C.E. The fourth is the concern with "the remnant of the house of Judah" (Zeph 2:7), "the remnant of my people/remainder of a nation" (Zeph 2:9), "the remnant of Israel" (Zeph 3:13), and the return of the exiles (Zeph 3:10, 19–20), which presupposes the period of the Babylonian exile and the postexilic restoration. Furthermore, those passages that are considered to be authentic to Zephaniah portray the people of Jerusalem and Judah engaging in foreign worship practices that are opposed to Josiah's reforms. Many scholars take this as an indication that the prophet addressed the failure of Josiah's reforms.

Nevertheless, there are various problems with these views that hold open the possibility that the present form of the book of Zephaniah can and should be read in relation to Josiah's reign.[6] My recent study of the structure and generic charac-

3. For surveys of research on Zephaniah, see Rex Mason, *Zephaniah, Habakkuk, Joel*, OT Guides (Sheffield: Sheffield Academic Press, 1994) 16–58; Michael Weigl, *Zefanja und das "Israel der Armen": Eine Untersuchung zur Theologie des Buches Zefanja*, ÖBS 13 (Klosterneuburg: Österreichisches Katholisches Bibelwerk, 1994) 230–242; Marvin A. Sweeney, "Zephaniah: A Paradigm for the Study of the Prophetic Books," *CR:BS* 7 (1999) 119–145.

4. Cf. B. Renaud, "Le livre de Sophone: Le jour de YHWH thème structurant de la synthèse rédactionelle," *RevScRel* 60 (1986) 1–33; Renaud, *Michée—Sophone—Nahum. Sources bibliques* (Paris: J. Gabalda, 1987) 175–259.

5. For example, Otto Kaiser, *Introduction to the Old Testament: A Presentation of its Results and Problems*, translated by J. Sturdy (Minneapolis: Augsburg, 1977) 230–231; Brevard Childs, *Introduction to the Old Testament as Scripture* (Philadelphia: Fortress, 1979) 458. Cf. most recently the essays in Walter Dietrich and Milton Schwantes, eds., *Der Tag wird kommen: Ein interkontextuelles Gespräch über das Buch des Propheten Zefanja*, SBS 170 (Stuttgart: Katholisches Bibelwerk, 1996), which continue to reflect such a perspective.

6. Contra Ehud Ben Zvi, "History and Prophetic Texts," in *History and Interpretation*, JSOTSup 173, Fs. J. H. Hayes, ed. M. P. Graham et al. (Sheffield: JSOT Press, 1993) 106–120,

ter of Zephaniah demonstrates that it is not organized according to the standard tripartite principle articulated above, but according to a two-part scheme that points to the coming "Day of YHWH" (Zeph 1:2–18) and then calls on the people to repent (Zeph 2:1–3:20).[7] The supposed dichotomy between the "postexilic" universal eschatological concerns of the final redactional form of Zephaniah and the specifically Judean concerns of the "authentic" words of the prophet is based to a large degree on the tripartite scheme mentioned above. In turn, this influences interpretation of the interrelationship of language pertaining to humanity or creation in general and the nations with that pertaining to the specific nations mentioned in the book. Likewise, it is based in large measure on an exegetical approach that focuses only on the short, self-contained units of the text and interprets them in isolation from their literary context. When one considers that the nations mentioned in Zephaniah 2:4–15 do not constitute a universal listing of all the nations of the earth, but a list of nations that would be of particular interest to Josiah,[8] the claims that the book of Zephaniah constitutes a postexilic scenario of universal eschatological judgment and restoration begin to come into question. Finally, concern with the "remnant" of the people and the return of exiles to Jerusalem and Judah can hardly be assigned exclusively to the postexilic period. The Assyrian destruction of the northern kingdom of Israel, the subjugation of Judah in a diminished territory, and the continued Assyrian demands for manpower produced a large number of Israelites and Judeans living in exile in foreign lands during the eighth to seventh centuries B.C.E.[9]

These considerations call for a reevaluation of the book of Zephaniah in relation to the reign of Josiah. Three major issues require discussion: (1) the structure and form of the book of Zephaniah as a whole; (2) the literary integrity of the book of Zephaniah; and (3) the message of the book of Zephaniah in relation to its historical setting.

An analysis of the structure of the book of Zephaniah, and indeed of prophetic literature in general, must take account of its various literary features.[10] Fundamentally, the interrelationship between form and content plays a major role in

---

who appropriately raises questions concerning a too facile identification of prophetic texts with historical contexts, but errs in his assessment of the Josianic period by assuming that Judah actually succeeded in expanding his kingdom. For overviews of texts and issues relevant to the history of this period, see Bustenay Oded, "Judah and the Exile," in *Israelite and Judaean History*, OTL, ed. J. H. Hays and J. M. Miller (Philadelphia: Westminster, 1977) 435–488; Na'aman, "The Kingdom of Judah under Josiah."

7. Marvin A. Sweeney, "A Form-Critical Reassessment of the Book of Zephaniah," *CBQ* 51 (1991) 388–408; Sweeney, *The Book of the Twelve Prophets*, Berit Olam: Studies in Hebrew Narrative and Poetry (Collegeville, MN: Liturgical, 2000); cf. Renaud, "Le livre de Sophonie," 1–3, who likewise rejects the tripartite scheme.

8. Cf. Duane Christensen, "Zephaniah 2:4–15: A Theological Basis for Josiah's Program of Political Expansion," *CBQ* 46 (1984) 669–682.

9. Cf. G. W. Anderson, "The Idea of the Remnant in the Book of Zephaniah," *ASTI* 11 (1977–78) 11–14; Anderson, "Some Observations on the Old Testament Doctrine of the Remnant," *Transactions of the Glasgow University Oriental Society* 23 (1969–70) 1–10.

10. For the methodological perspectives employed here, see Sweeney, "Formation and Form in Prophetic Literature"; Knierim, "Criticism of Literary Features, Form, Tradition, and Redaction."

defining textual structure and outlook, but these basic categories must be refined by attention to particular features of literary expression and rhetorical setting. Syntactical structure or arrangement constitutes a fundamental aspect of textual organization that must be considered together with the semantic contents of the material that the text conveys. Likewise, basic attention to the speakers and addressees of the text must be considered at various levels within the text as a means to determine its organization and the means by which it presents its contents. Fundamentally, the contents of the text are conveyed by a narrator to the reader. But in addition to its own perspectives, the narrative at various points conveys speeches by the prophet, by YHWH, or by other figures that appear in the text, to a variety of addressees that may or may not be identified. Furthermore, these subordinate speakers in the text may likewise convey the speech of others, such as the prophet who presents a speech by YHWH. Close attention to the forms of address, such as the pronouns, are essential to such analysis. Genre or literary type is an important indicator as well, but the exegete must recognize that genres function within uniquely formulated texts and frequently play a major role in determining the presentation of the text. They do not constitute the text as many past interpreters have assumed.

The book of Zephaniah begins with a narrative superscription in Zephaniah 1:1 that identifies the following material as the "word of YHWH" that came to Zephaniah in the days of King Josiah of Judah. Although the balance of the book in Zephaniah 1:2–3:20 is presented as the words of the prophet Zephaniah, this segment of the book essentially constitutes the second part of the narrative begun in 1:1.[11]

Overall, Zephaniah 1:2–3:20 may be identified generically as a "prophetic exhortation to seek YHWH," in that it attempts to persuade its audience to adapt a specific course of action—that is, adherence to YHWH as opposed to adherence to foreign deities—in light of the fundamental changes that are now taking place in the world at large, for example, upheaval among the nations that will result ultimately in the return of Jewish exiles and the exaltation of Jerusalem.

The first basic segment of the prophet's exhortation is a "prophetic announcement of the day of YHWH" in Zephaniah 1:2–18. The prophet is the basic speaker throughout this section, and addresses his words to an unnamed audience, presumably the people of Jerusalem and Judah (cf. 1:7). The fundamental genre of this section is "prophetic announcement" in that the prophet simply conveys information to the audience in 1:2–18, whereas Zephaniah 2:1–3 begins a syntactically independent section that calls on the audience to make a decision. The prophetic announcement comprises two basic parts. The prophet conveys two words by YHWH in vv. 2–6, as indicated by the oracular formula *nĕ'um yhwh*, "oracle of YHWH," in vv. 2 and 3. Verses 2–3a comprise the prophet's report of YHWH's speech concerning the punishment of all creation, and vv. 3b–6 comprise the prophet's report of YHWH's speech concerning the punishment of those in Judah

11. For detailed discussion of the structure of Zephaniah, see Sweeney, "Form-Critical Reassessment."

and Jerusalem who worship foreign deities. The prophet then turns to announcement of the "Day of YHWH" in vv. 7–18. First, he announces YHWH's statements concerning the significance of the day in vv. 7–13—namely, that the "Day of YHWH" is a day of sacrifice for YHWH's victims. Afterward, the prophet explains the consequences of the "Day of YHWH" in vv. 14–18—namely, it is a day of wrath in which those who have sinned against YHWH will be punished.

The second basic segment of the prophet's exhortation appears in Zephaniah 2:1–3:20, which constitutes the "Prophet's exhortation to seek YHWH proper." This clearly constitutes the main segment of the book that was introduced by the announcement of the day of YHWH in 1:2–18. It begins with the prophet's "exhortation address" in Zephaniah 2:1–3, in which the prophet calls on the nation of Judah, here identified as a humble or worthless nation, to seek YHWH and do YHWH's commands before the divine wrath comes upon them.

The specific basis for this exhortation then follows in Zephaniah 2:4–3:20, in which the prophet points to specific events that are affecting various nations in the world as a means to call attention to the implications of these events for Jerusalem and Judah. Although many scholars have attempted to argue that the introductory *kî* of v. 4 is merely emphatic,[12] the causative function of *kî*, "for, because," must be recognized in relation to the rhetorical setting of this text which attempts to persuade the audience to adopt a specific course of action, and then provides evidence as to why it should do so. Overall, 2:4–3:20 provides specific evidence that the general claims of 1:2–18 will in fact take place, and thereby supports the exhortation of 2:1–3. The primary basis for the exhortation appears in Zephaniah 2:4, which points to disasters that are overtaking four major Philistine cities: Gaza, Ashkelon, Ashdod, and Ekron. The text then moves in 2:5–3:20 to an extended elaboration on 2:4 that explains YHWH's purposes in relation to both the nations and to Jerusalem and Israel. Each section begins with an introductory *hôy*, "woe!" that calls attention to each major segment of this subunit. Zephaniah 2:5–15 focuses on the disasters that will overtake various nations, including Philistia (2:5–7), Moab and Ammon (2:8–11), Cush/Ethiopia (2:12), and Assyria (2:13–15), as evidence of YHWH's action. Zephaniah 3:1–20 then turns to consideration of Jerusalem and Israel by first announcing salvation for Jerusalem following a period of punishment and cleansing in which YHWH "gathers" or punishes the nations and removes the wicked from Jerusalem (3:1–13) and then summons Jerusalem and Israel to rejoice at YHWH's restoration of Jerusalem and Israel and the return of the exiles. The positive note on which the book ends provides further motivation to the audience to accept the prophet's exhortation to seek YHWH.

The structure of Zephaniah may be presented as in table 11.1 Altogether, the present form of the book of Zephaniah displays a coherent literary structure. Nevertheless, scholars have challenged the literary unity of the book on a number of grounds, including a universalist perspective that would be impossible in the preexilic period; references to the "remnant" of Judah, and so on, and the return of captives or exiles that would only presuppose the Babylonian exile; and oracles

12. For example, Weigl, *Zefanja* 242, n. 54; Ben Zvi, *Zephaniah* 150.

TABLE 11.1   Structure of the Book of Zephaniah

Prophetic exhortation to seek YHWH	*Zephaniah 1:1–3:20*
I. Superscription: Word of YHWH to Zephaniah in the days of Josiah	1:1
II. Prophetic exhortation to seek YHWH	1:2–3:20
A. Prophetic announcement of the day of YHWH	1:2–18
1. Report of YHWH's oracular speeches	1:2–6
a. Concerning punishment of creation	1:2–3a
b. Concerning punishment of Jerusalem and Judah for apostasy	1:3b–b
2. Announcement of the day of YHWH	1:7–18
a. Report of YHWH's announcement concerning significance of the day: day of sacrifice for YHWH's victims	1:7–13
b. Prophetic explanation of the day's consequences	1:14–18
B. Prophetic exhortation to seek YHWH proper	2:1–3:20
1. Prophetic exhortation address: seek YHWH	2:1–3
2. Basis for exhortation	2:4–3:20
a. Exhortation basis proper: disaster for Philistine cities	2:4
b. Explanatory elaboration	2:5–3:20
i. Concerning punishment of nations	2:5–15
a) Philistia	2:5–7
b) Moab and Ammon	2:8–11
c) Cush/Ethiopia	2:12
d) Assyria	2:13–15
ii. Concerning Jerusalem and Israel	3:1–20
a) Announcement of salvation for Jerusalem following punishment and cleansing	3:1–13
b) Prophetic summons to rejoice directed to Jerusalem and Israel	3:14–20

of salvation that would be unlikely in preexilic setting.[13] On various manifestations of these grounds, several passages are frequently considered to be postexilic additions: Zephaniah 1:2–3, 17–18; 2:7, 8–11; and 3:1–13, 14–20.

Zephaniah 1:2–3, 17–18 are frequently cited as a postexilic redactional framework for the initial words of judgment directed by Zephaniah against Jerusalem and Judah.[14] The basic reason for this view is the universal language of the passages, which posits judgment against the entire earth, humanity, and the animals of all creation in a manner reminiscent of the flood story in the P account of Genesis 6–9:

> I will surely gather all from upon the face of the earth, oracle of YHWH;
> I will gather human and beast, I will gather the birds of the heavens and the fish of the sea;
> and those who cause the wicked to stumble;
> and I shall cut off humanity from upon the face of the earth, oracle of YHWH.

Similar motifs appear in Zephaniah 1:17–18:

13. For an overview of this issue, see Mason, *Zephaniah* 44–54.
14. Renaud, "Sophonie," 6–10.

And I shall afflict humanity, and they shall walk like the blind,
because they have sinned against YHWH;
and their blood shall be spilled out like dust, and their entrails like dung;
even their silver and their gold will not be able to save them;
on the day of the wrath of YHWH;
and in the fire of his jealousy all the earth will be consumed;
for complete destruction, indeed terror, he shall render for all the
    inhabitants of the earth.

Scholars who maintain this view argue that such language stands in contrast
to the specific threats leveled against Jerusalem and Judah throughout vv. 4–16,
and that Judah developed such a universalist perspective in its experience of
Babylonian exile when Deutero-Isaiah began to place Judean/Jerusalemite experience into worldwide perspective. But other prophetic texts indicate that such
"universalist" language is not unusual in a preexilic context that addresses the
specific experience of Judah or Jerusalem. For example, the prophet Hosea who
was active in the northern kingdom of Israel during the late eighth century B.C.E.,
employs the motif of worldwide destruction in his indictment of the people of
northern Israel in Hosea 4:1–3:

Hear the word of YHWH, O Sons of Israel;
for YHWH has a controversy with the inhabitants of the land;
for there is no truth, nor fidelity, nor knowledge of G-d in the land;
swearing, lying, murder, stealing, and adultery have broken out;
and bloodshed follows upon bloodshed;
therefore, the earth mourns, and all the inhabitants in it languish;
among the animals of the field and the birds of the heavens,
and even the fish of the sea are gathered.

In addition to the general association of worldwide or cosmic suffering that
appears together with alleged wrongdoing among the people of Israel, several
lexical/semantic features must be noted. First, the terminology employed to
describe the entire world in both Zephaniah and Hosea, "from upon the face of
the land" (*mēʿal pĕnê hāʾădāmâ*; in 1:2a and 1:3b), "all the earth" (*kol hāʾāreṣ*;
Zeph 1:18a), and "in the land" (*bāʿāreṣ*; Hos 4:1b), can be used for either "earth"
at large or "land" in particular. Second, both passages refer to the inhabitants of
the world/land in similar terms—that is, "all the inhabitants of the earth" (*kol yōšĕbê
hāʾāreṣ*) in Zephaniah 1:18b, and "with the inhabitants of the earth" (*ʾim yōšĕbê
hāʾāreṣ*) in Hosea 4:1b and "all who dwell in it" (*kol yôšēb bāh*) in Hosea 4:3a.
Third, both passages employ a similar sequence of living creatures in their respective portrayal of the impact of human action on the created world—that is, beasts,
birds, and fish in Zephaniah 1:3 and animals of the field, birds, and fish in Hosea
4:3. Finally, forms of the same verb *ʾsp*, "to gather," is employed in both passages
to describe YHWH's actions against people and creation in both passages—that
is, *ʾāsōp ʾāsēp*, "I will surely gather," in Zephaniah 1:2 and two occurrences of
ʾāsēp, "I shall gather," in Zephaniah 1:3 and *yēʾāsēpû*, "they shall be gathered,"
in Hosea 4:3b.

Similar observations can be made in Jeremiah 4:23–26, which is frequently attributed to Zephaniah's contemporary, Jeremiah:[15]

> I looked at the earth, and behold, absolute chaos, and to the heavens, and their light was gone;
> I looked to the mountains, and behold, quaking, and all the hills were shaking;
> I looked, and behold, there was no human being, and all the birds of the heavens had fled;
> I looked, and behold, the Carmel was desert and all its cities torn down;
> from before YHWH, from before the anger of his wrath;
> for thus says YHWH,
> "All the earth shall be desolate, and complete destruction I will make for it;
> therefore the earth shall mourn and the heavens above shall become dark,
> for I have spoken, I have considered, and I shall not repent, and I shall not reverse it."

As in the previous passages, the fate of birds is compared with that of human beings, and language pertaining to "all the earth" is employed. Again, a general correlation is made between human wrongdoing and the cosmic realm when this passage is read in relation to the larger context of Jeremiah 4, which speaks of the foolishness of the people of Judah (Jer 4:22).

On the basis of these comparisons with the work of the eighth-century prophet Hosea and the late-seventh-/early-sixth-century prophet Jeremiah, it becomes very difficult to argue that Zephaniah 1:2–3, 17–18 must be the work of a postexilic author. Rather than pointing to a postexilic redaction that formulates the work of Zephaniah in relation to a new concern with universal eschatology, they point instead to Zephaniah's attempt to express his message concerning the significance of the difficulties faced by Jerusalem and Judah in relation to the overall state of being of the world or cosmos at large. Such a conception is entirely consistent with other preexilic prophetic traditions, such as those of Hosea and Jeremiah.

Various challenges have also been made against the authenticity of the oracles against the nations in Zephaniah 2:4–15. The present arrangement and formulation of the oracles is frequently taken as the product of later redaction that attempted to point to the universal or worldwide significance of Zephaniah's message. There are two basic grounds for this view. First, the oracles against the nations are not formulated in a uniform manner, indicating that they were originally formulated at different times and for different occasions, but were brought together by a later hand. Second, the selection of nations includes one for each cardinal direction of the compass—that is, Philistia is west, Moab and Ammon are east, Cush is south, and Assyria is north—indicating a universalist concern to represent all the nations of the earth. Neither of these arguments demonstrates postexilic redaction, however. The uniform arrangement of the oracles against the nations in Amos 1:3–

---

15. See William Holladay, *Jeremiah I*, Hermeneia (Philadelphia: Fortress, 1986) 152, 163–167.

2:6, for example, points to a single setting or occasion for their composition, but those in Isaiah 13–23, Jeremiah 46–51, and Ezekiel 25–32 are clearly redactionally formulated for placement in their respective literary settings. The common super-scription *maśśāʿ PN*, "pronouncement concerning PN," in Isaiah, and the varia-tions of the YHWH word formulas in Jeremiah and Ezekiel merely provide an introduction to oracles that are inconsistently formulated, apparently for a variety of settings and concerns. Furthermore, in no case does one of the major oracle collections include a universal scenario of all the nations of the earth. Amos 1:3–2:6 omits Assyria and Egypt and includes only those nations that were once a part of Jeroboam II's sphere of influence as a means to convey coming judgment against northern Israel. Ezekiel 25–32 includes Egypt and Israel's immediate neighbors but does not include Babylon, as YHWH's judgment against these nations is iden-tified with the rise of the Babylonian empire. Isaiah 13–23 and Jeremiah 46–51 both include Babylon and Egypt among other nations but omit Persia/Media, as they attempt to identify YHWH's judgment of these nations with the rise of the Achaemenid empire.[16]

A recent article by Christensen points to a similar principle for the enumera-tion of the nations in Zephaniah 2:4–15: that is, these nations were all of interest to Josiah as they were either major enemies of the Josianic kingdom (Assyria and Cush/Egypt) or areas into which Josiah intended to expand (Philistia and Moab/Ammon).[17] This principle appears to hold for Assyria, as Assyria was the former overlord of Judah against whom Josiah would have established Judean indepen-dence. It also appears to hold for Philistia and Moab/Ammon, as both areas ap-parently were once part of the Davidic/Solomonic empire and both areas held substantial numbers of Israelites and Judeans. In the case of Philistia, the Assyrians had taken Judean territory in the Shephelah during the eighth century and turned it over to the Philistines. Furthermore, excavations at Tel Miqne/Ekron indicate that the Assyrians turned Philistia into a major area for olive oil production and moved substantial numbers of Israelites to the area to support this industry.[18] In the case of Moab and Ammon, the Moabites had taken substantial amounts of Israelite territory east of the Jordan during the ninth century B.C.E., and this pro-cess continued during the eighth-century Assyrian invasions when Assyria stripped all territory east of the Jordan from Israel,[19] leaving it open to the Ammonites and Moabites in the aftermath of Assyria's late-seventh-century collapse.

The primary problem appears to be the mention of Cush, which many take as a reference to Egypt, the country that eventually killed Josiah and destroyed Judean hopes for independence.[20] A recent study by Haak notes that Cush cannot simply

16. See Sweeney, *Isaiah 1–39* 216–217.

17. Christensen, "Zephaniah 2:4–15."

18. See Seymour Gitin, "Tel Miqne-Ekron: A Type Site for the Inner Coastal Plain in the Iron Age II Period," in *Recent Excavations in Israel: Studies in Iron Age Archaeology*, AASOR 49, ed. S. Gitin and W. G. Dever (Winona Lake, Ind.: Eisenbrauns, 1989) 23–58.

19. Sweeney, *Isaiah 1–39* 246–249.

20. For the various options on the identification of Cush in Zephaniah 2:12, see Berlin, *Zephaniah* 111–114.

be identified as Egypt in that the 25th Ethiopian dynasty that ruled Egypt during the eighth and early seventh centuries, was defeated and overthrown by the native Egyptian Saite dynasty in 664 B.C.E., long before Josiah's birth.[21] He attempts to relate the mention of Cush to Cushite settlements in southern Judah, but this solution is inadequate in that the identification of Cushites along the southern border of Judah is hardly conclusive.[22] It seems best to recognize that the mention of Cush in this context refers to Ethiopia, and indicates that the overall concern of this passage is to identify YHWH's punishment of these nations is equated with the rise of Saite Egypt in the seventh century. The first Saite Pharaohs, Necho I and Psamtek, had driven the Assyrians out of Egypt after having defeated the Ethiopians on Assyria's behalf.[23] Psamtek is reported to have been very active along the coastal plain of Philistia, laying siege to Ashdod for twenty-nine years and bribing the Scythians to leave the land after they plundered Ashkelon.[24] The rise of Saite Egypt would likewise present a threat to Moab and Ammon, former Assyrian clients who controlled the "King's Highway," the trade route from Aram to the Red Sea and Arabia. In the aftermath of Assyria's collapse, these countries would be prime targets for the Egyptians. Like Philistia, they would also be prime targets for Judah. In this regard, it must be kept in mind that the Egyptians did not openly support the Assyrians until 616 B.C.E., when they sent an expeditionary force to support the Assyrians against Judah's ally Babylonia.[25] Up until this point, the possibility of a Judean Egyptian alliance could well have been open as both nations had a common interest in the downfall of Assyria. After 616 B.C.E., such an alliance would be unlikely.

Challenges also have been made against individual verses in the oracles against the nations. The first is Zephaniah 2:7, which concludes the oracle against the Philistines. Several reasons lie behind efforts to identify v. 7 as later redaction. The form of the verse changes from that of a speech by YHWH in vv. 4/5–6, but the statement that "the word of YHWH is against you" in v. 5bα indicates that the entire oracle is conveyed by the prophet. The reference to "the remnant of the house of Judah" and the statement that YHWH "will return their captivity" likewise are taken as indications of postexilic authorship. The expression "remnant of Judah" appears elsewhere only in Jeremiah 40:15; 42:15, 19; 43:5; 44:12, 14, 28 (cf. 40:11), where it refers to the Judean community governed by Gedaliah in the aftermath of the Babylonian destruction of Jerusalem. The reference to the return of the captivity is generally taken as a reference to the Babylonian exile. But these views overlook the losses sustained by Judah during the eighth-century Assyrian invasions. As noted above, substantial amounts of Judean territory in the Shephelah was handed over to the Philistines by the Assyrians, and substantial numbers of

---

21. Robert D. Haak, "'Cush' in Zephaniah," in *The Pitcher is Broken* 238–251.

22. Cf. Berlin, *Zephaniah* 112.

23. For an account of the rise of the Saite dynasty and its impact on the Syro-Israelite corridor, see Donald Redford, *Egypt, Canaan, and Israel in Ancient Times* (Princeton: Princeton University Press, 1992) 430–469.

24. See Herodotus, *History* I. 105; II. 157.

25. Redford, *Egypt* 446.

the Judean population were deported by the Assyrians. Furthermore, archeological surveys of the land of Judah during the seventh century point to a substantial drop in population, and shift away from the Shephelah toward the central hill country of Judah around Jerusalem.[26] During a period of Assyrian collapse, it makes a great deal of sense for a seventh-century Judean oracle against Philistia to speak of the "remnant of Judah" and the "return of the captivity." This is especially important to note in relation to the rebuilding of Lachish, Judah's primary city in the Shephelah, during the latter part of the seventh century B.C.E. Such a move would have to be understood in relation to Josiah's interest in reestablishing a Judean presence in the region.

Challenges have likewise been leveled against various elements of the oracle against Moab and Ammon in Zephaniah 2:8–11. Some claim that the oracle is later in that Moab was only invaded by the Babylonians in the sixth century B.C.E., but the projection of Moabite and Ammonite punishment need not be related to its actual occurrence. In the present instance, the oracle charges Moab and Ammon with expanding their territory at the expense of the people of Israel (i.e., "my people," cf. v. 9). As noted above, Moab and Ammon were able to take over much of the Israelite territory east of the Jordan during the ninth century B.C.E., and the eighth-century Assyrian invasions resulted in the creation of an Assyrian province, Galazu, out of this land. In the aftermath of both the collapse of Israel and of Assyria, this land would be wide open to Moabite and Ammonite expansion. Despite Assyrian deportation, it is likely that some elements of an Israelite population would remain there. This and the remaining population of northern Israel west of the Jordan would explain the statements in v. 9 that "the remnant of my people shall plunder them (i.e., Moab and Ammon), and the remainder of a nation will inherit them." Overall, the oracle looks to the reestablishment of Israelite control in this region when "Moab will become like Sodom and the sons of Ammon like Gomorrah" (v. 9). Finally, the references to YHWH's diminishing "all the gods of the earth" and the worship of YHWH by "all the coastlands of the nations" simply refers to worldwide recognition that YHWH is responsible for the defeat of Moab and Ammon. Such recognition does not require a setting in the postexilic period as manifestations of YHWH's power before the eyes of the nations is a common motif in the Zion tradition that underpinned the ideology of the Davidic monarchy.

Zephaniah 3 presents a number of problems, as interpreters have had a great deal of difficulty in defining the constituent subunits of this passage and their interrelationship and interpretation within the larger structure of the text. Furthermore, a number of passages within Zephaniah 3 are viewed as postexilic, especially vv. 8, 9–10 and 14–20, due in part to these difficulties and in part to their concerns with the nations at large and the restoration of Judean/Israelite exiles.

---

26. For an overview of archeological study of the land of Israel during the seventh century B.C.E., see Israel Finkelstein, "The Archaeology of the Days of Manasseh," in *Scripture and Other Artifacts*, Fs. P. J. King, ed. M. D. Coogan et al. (Louisville, KY: Westminster John Knox, 1994) 169–187; cf. Na'aman, "The Kingdom of Judah under Josiah."

First of all, it is essential to understand the overall structure and argument of this chapter. It points to the restoration of Jerusalem and Israel, but it does so by first taking up YHWH's punishment of both Jerusalem and the nations as a prelude to its comments on the restoration of the exiles and the recognition of YHWH's power by the nations. Verses 1–13 announce salvation for Jerusalem. The woe speech in vv. 1–4 begins by pointing to Jerusalem's current state of corruption, which is clearly in need of change. Verses 5–13 then take up the process by which the change will occur. Verse 5 states the basic principle that YHWH is righteous and that YHWH's law or justice brings light to the world. The details of the process are then laid out in vv. 6–13. Verses 6–7 point to YHWH's defeat of nations as a basis for a command to "wait for me" in vv. 8–13. The command points to YHWH's future actions that appear in a series of statements, introduced by causative *kî*, "because," that provide the reasons why the people should wait for YHWH to act. YHWH will gather nations (v. 8bα); YHWH's jealous wrath will consume all the earth (v. 8bβ); YHWH will therefore cause the nations to recognize his power by praising him, thereby resulting in the return of exiles from beyond the rivers of Cush (vv. 9–10a); and YHWH will remove the arrogant from Jerusalem to make way for the humble and poor remnant of Israel who will call on YHWH's name (vv. 10b–13). Following this announcement of salvation for Jerusalem, Zephaniah 3:14–20 call upon Jerusalem and Israel to rejoice at the restoration. Verses 14–15 call for rejoicing because YHWH the king has removed the judgment against the people. Verses 16–19 point to the future when Jerusalem will fear no more because YHWH is in her midst to gather her exiles and turn their shame into praise. Verse 20 reiterates the theme of YHWH's return of the exiles as a demonstration to all the peoples of the earth.

Again, the supposed universalism of elements in chapter 3 and the theme of the return of exiles have prompted scholars to argue that these verses are postexilic additions that have affinities to the work of Deutero-Isaiah. Two major factors must be considered that point to a preexilic setting for this chapter. First, the universalism of the passage is directed specifically to the worldwide recognition that YHWH has defeated Judah's/Israel's enemies and is restoring the exiled people to their homeland. The impending downfall of the Assyrian empire and its clients during the latter part of the seventh century B.C.E. provides appropriate background for the assertion that YHWH is acting in the world to restore Jerusalem and Israel/Judah. Second, the assertion that exiles will return from beyond the rivers of Cush is likewise appropriate to this setting. As noted previously, the rise of Saite Egypt and its defeat of both the 25th Ethiopian dynasty and the Assyrian empire provides the opportunity for Judah to reassert its independence. Contrary to many scholars who maintain that Jewish exiles could not be in Cush, Cush is precisely the place where many Jewish exiles would have fled during the course of the Assyrian invasions as the Ethiopian dynasty, although ineffective, supported both northern Israel and Judah in their respective revolts against Assyria. King Manasseh of Judah supported Assyria in its campaigns to subdue Egypt, thereby preventing Jewish exiles who sided with the Ethiopian/Egyptian dynasty from returning home. But the Saite defeat of Assyria and the deaths of Manasseh and Amon opened the way for a new relationship between Egypt and Judah that would allow for the return of exiles. In this regard, the oracle against Jerusalem in Zephaniah 3:1–4 and the statements in Zephaniah 3:11–13 that the arrogant of Jerusalem would be removed and replaced by the humble and poor remnant of Israel would presuppose the actions of Manasseh and perhaps Amon. Manasseh is known for his suppression of dissent in Jerusalem during the course of his reign, and his actions may be explained as those of a fearful but loyal Assyrian vassal who supported his over-lords during the course of their Egyptian campaigns. But the obvious failure of the Assyrian empire to control Egypt and its subsequent reverses elsewhere led to the recognition in Judah that a new age had dawned in the Near East and that Manasseh and his policies were now obsolete. With the downfall of Assyria and the rise of Saite Egypt, Judah now has the opportunity to restore itself. But, first, Assyrian supporters must be cleared out.

This analysis of Zephaniah provides the basis for assessing the book in rela-tion to Josiah's reign. It clearly calls for change in Judah based upon the recogni-tion of the changes that are taking place among the nations of the world with the impending downfall of the Assyrian empire and the rise of Saite Egypt. Zephaniah 1:2–18 announces the "Day of YHWH" as a day of wrath in which the nations of the world are being judged, as well as those in Judah who adhere to foreign gods. The upheaval taking place among the nations has its implications for Judah; those who worship Baal and the Host of Heaven, those who wear foreign garments and cross the threshold (perhaps of foreign gods or service to Assyria) are finished. A new order is coming, and Zephaniah 2:1–3:20 calls on the people to be a part of it. The impending downfall of the Philistines, Moab and Ammon, Cush, and Assyria all provide motivation for the people to make the correct choice. The downfall of these nations also provides the background for the changes taking place in Jerusalem; a corrupt element is being removed, the nations will recog-nize YHWH's power, the exiles will return home, and Jerusalem and Israel will be restored when a poor and humble element of the population (cf. Zeph 2:1, 3; 3:11–12) are restored to their proper position in Jerusalem in place of the arro-gant who had turned to foreign gods and Assyria in place of YHWH.

Overall, the scenario corresponds precisely to the early years of Josiah's reign. Amon had been assassinated, apparently in reaction to the discredited policies of Manasseh who suppressed dissent and submitted to Assyria throughout his reign. Although the revolt was put down and the conspirators from among the servants of the king were put to death, the young King Josiah was placed into power by the "people of the land." Such a move set the course of the Davidic monarchy in a new direction to reject the old policy of submission to Assyria, to reassert an indepen-dent Judean/Israelite state, to restore the lands and exiles that had formerly consti-tute the kingdom of the Davidic dynasty, and to point to the power of YHWH in the world as the author of events that would lead to an Israelite/Davidic restoration.

12

Nahum

T he book of Nahum is another potentially important prophetic source concerning the reign of King Josiah. The superscription of the book makes no reference to the reign of Josiah, or any other Judean or Israelite king, but it employs
the title, "Pronouncement concerning Nineveh: Book of the Vision of Nahum the
Elqoshite." The book then proceeds to lay out a scenario concerning the downfall
of Nineveh, the capital of the Assyrian empire, which was defeated and destroyed
by the Babylonians and Medes in 612 B.C.E. This would suggest that the book was
composed late in Josiah's reign in relation to the fall of Nineveh, perhaps in the
aftermath of the city's destruction or in anticipation of the event.

Nevertheless, a number of problems have confounded the interpretation of
Nahum and raised questions as to whether the book may be properly set in relation to the late-seventh-century destruction of Nineveh.[1] Scholars have faced tremendous difficulties in attempting to define the overall structure and coherence
of the book, due in large measure to its enigmatic language in Nahum 1:9–2:1.[2]

---

1. For an overview of research on the book of Nahum, see R. Mason, *Micah, Nahum, Obadiah*,
OT Guides (Sheffield: JSOT Press, 1991) 57–84, esp. 73–79.

2. See the comments by R. J. Coggins in R. J. Coggins and S. P. Re'emi, *Israel Among the
Nations: Nahum, Obadiah, Esther*, International Theological Commentary (Grand Rapids, Mich.:
Eerdmans, 1985) 6–8. For recent discussions of the literary structure of Nahum, see D. L. Christensen,
"The Book of Nahum: The Question of Authorship and the Canonical Process," *JETS* 31 (1988)
51–58; Christensen, "The Book of Nahum as a Liturgical Composition," *JETS* 32 (1989) 159–169;
Marvin A. Sweeney, "Concerning the Structure and Generic Character of the Book of Nahum,"
ZAW 104 (1992) 364–377; K. Spronk, "Synchronic and Diachronic Approaches to the Book of
Nahum," in *Synchronic or Diachronic? A Debate on Method in Old Testament Exegesis*, OTS 34,
ed. J. C. De Moor (Leiden: E. J. Brill, 1995) 159–186; Bob Becking, "Divine Wrath and the Con-
ceptual Coherence of the Book of Nahum," *SJOT* 9 (1995) 277–296; idem, "Passion, Power, and
Protection: Interpreting the G-d of Nahum," in *On Reading Prophetic Texts: Gender-Specific and*

The issue is further exacerbated by the presence of a partial acrostic in Nahum 1:2–8, which presents difficulties as scholars attempt to reconstruct a supposed full form and to explain its relationship to the balance of the book.[3] As a result, many scholars have argued that the book is composed of a number of originally independent textual subunits that have been redactionally placed together into their present order.[4] Furthermore, various other features have prompted scholars to argue that the present form of the book must be placed in the postexilic or Persian period.[5] First are the references to Belial in Nahum 1:11 and 2:1, which appears as a personified satanic figure in many texts from the late Second Temple period. Insofar as the figure of Belial is equated with Assyria in the minds of many scholars, the portrayal of Assyria in the book of Nahum thereby becomes a cipher for the condemnation of Babylon or other enemies as an apocalyptic symbol of cosmic evil in the postexilic period following the model of the Belial figure in the War Scroll from Qumran or the Babylon figure in Revelation 18. The associations between Nahum 2:1 and Isaiah 52:7 are likewise cited as evidence that the present form of Nahum dates to the Persian period, insofar as many scholars argue that the present text of Nahum draws on the exilic writings of Deutero-Isaiah.

There are several problems with the view that Nahum is the product of the Persian or postexilic period, however. First, it is somewhat surprising to see Assyria identified as a symbol of cosmic evil during this time when Babylon, and not Nineveh, is the city responsible for the destruction of Jerusalem and the Temple. In fact, biblical tradition elsewhere indicates that Assyria was soundly punished for its threats against Jerusalem (e.g., Isa 5–12, 36–37; 2 Kgs 18–19) even prior to its actual destruction, and even portrays the city as repentant (Jonah). The argument depends on the supposition that postexilic Jews would be afraid to refer openly to Babylon, either because Babylon was still the ruling power at the time or because Persia employed Babylon as an administrative center for ruling its western empire, but other texts mention Babylon explicitly without any suggestion of fear (e.g., Isa 13–14, 47; Jer 50–51; Zech 6).

Related Studies in Memory of Fokkelien van Dijk-Hemmes, BibInt 18, ed. B. Becking and M. Dijkstra (Leiden: E. J. Brill, 1996) 1–20.

3. For a discussion of the problems posed by Nahum 1:2–8, see Michael Floyd, "The Chimerical Acrostic of Nahum 1:2–10," *JBL* 113 (1994) 421–437.

4. For current redaction-critical approaches, see Bernard Renaud, "La composition du livre de Nahum," *ZAW* 99 (1987) 198–219; Renaud, *Michée—Sophonie—Nahum*, Sources bibliques (Paris: Gabalda, 1987) 261–323; Klaus Seybold, *Profane Prophetie: Studien zum Buch Nahum*, SBS 135 (Stuttgart: Katholisches Bibelwerk, 1989); Seybold, *Nahum, Habakuk, Zephanja*, ZBK (Zürich: Theologischer Verlag, 1991) 11–41; J. J. M. Roberts, *Nahum, Habakkuk, and Zephaniah: A Commentary*, OTL (Louisville, KY: Westminster John Knox, 1991) 35–77; James Nogalski, *Redactional Processes in the Book of the Twelve*, BZAW 218 (Berlin and New York: Walter de Gruyter, 1993) 93–128.

5. See esp. the works listed in n. 4, above. For detailed discussion of the following problems and the overall structure of Nahum presented here, see Sweeney, "Concerning the Structure and Generic Character."

Second, Belial (or Beliar) certainly appears as a personified Satanic figure in the late Second Temple period,[6] but there is little evidence that Belial functioned in this capacity prior to the Hellenistic period. A recent study by Emerton demonstrates that the term is not employed in relation to Sheol, and simply serves as a general term that denotes evil or disorder.[7] Another study by Rosenberg indicates that the term serves as a reference to behavior that violates the covenant relationship between YHWH and the people.[8]

Third, the argument that Nahum 2:1 is a postexilic midrash on Isaiah 52:1, 7 fails on several grounds.[9] The formulation of Nahum 2:1b, *kî lō' yôsîp 'ôd la'ăbor-bāk bĕlîya'al kullōh nikrāt*, "for never again shall evil (Belial) pass by you, it is entirely cut off," is awkward, which indicates that Nahum 2:1b is the original reading and not the smoothly flowing reading of Isaiah 52:1bβ, *kî lō' yôsîp yābō'-bāk 'ôd 'ārēl wĕṭāmē'*, "for not again shall the uncircumcised and unclean come into you." The author of Nahum 2:1 would have no reason to formulate an awkward text when such a clear model is available in Isaiah 52:1 (cf. Isa 10:20). Furthermore, the enigmatic reference to Assyria in Isaiah 52:4, which never appears elsewhere in Deutero-Isaiah, indicates that Isaiah borrowed from Nahum in that the reference to Assyrian oppression of the people in Egypt indicates Deutero-Isaiah's dependence on other traditions that refer to Assyria, such as Nahum 2:1 and Isaiah 10:20–26.

Finally, scholars have abandoned attempts to reconstruct a full alphabetic acrostic beyond Nahum 1:2–8.[10] The text only contains evidence of an acrostical pattern from aleph to kaph, and even that is disrupted by the appearance of *'umlal*, "withered," in 1:4b in place of a word that begins with daleth, such as *dālĕlû*, "languished," and *lipnê*, "before," prior to *za'mô*, "his anger," in 1:6a. The frequent appearance of nun in 1:2 likewise causes confusion. Questions have been raised as to whether even a partial acrostic actually exists in this text.[11] There seems to be sufficient evidence for the existence of at least a partial acrostic, although its significance continues to escape interpreters. As a result of these difficulties, scholars have turned to attempts to explain the relationship of Nahum 1:2–8 to its literary context.

Of course, this raises the question of the literary structure of the book. A number of proposals have been put forward, but scholars have been unable to come to a consensus because of difficulties in establishing the interrelationships between

6. For surveys of Belial in ancient sources, see T. H. Gaster, "Belial," *EncJud* 4:428–429; idem, "Belial," *IDB* I:357.

7. J. A. Emerton, "Sheol and the Sons of Belial," *VT* 37 (1987) 214–218.

8. R. Rosenberg, "The Concept of Biblical 'Belial,'" *Proceedings of the Eighth World Congress of Jewish Studies. Division A: The Period of the Bible* (Jerusalem: World Union of Jewish Studies, 1982) 35–41.

9. See J. Jeremias, *Kultprophetie und Geschichtsverkündigung in der späten Königszeit Israels*, WMANT 35 (Neukirchen-Vluyn: Neukirchener, 1970) 13–15.

10. See Floyd, "The Chimerical Acrostic."

11. Floyd, "Chimerical Acrostic," argues that the whole concept of acrostic in these verses should be abandoned.

the various subunits that constitute the book.[12] Recent studies by Becking and me,[13] however, point to the significance of the various address forms evident throughout the book, including second masculine plural (1:9), second feminine singular (1:11; 1:12–13; 2:1; 2:2; 2:14; 3:5–17), and second masculine singular (1:14; 3:18–19) forms. The referents of several of these forms are clear. The 2ms forms in 3:18–19 clearly refer to the Assyrian king, who is explicitly identified as "King of Assyria" in 1:18. The 2fs forms of 2:–3:17 likewise clearly refer to the city of Nineveh as indicate the general depiction of attack against a city throughout these verses, explicitly named as Nineveh in 2:9 and 3:7. Finally, the 2fs address forms of 2:1 refer to Judah, explicitly named in 2:1aβ. This leaves the 2mp form in 1:9, the 2fs forms in 1:11, 12–13, and the 2ms forms in 1:14.

Several observations and conclusions are in order. To begin with, Nahum 1:14 is syntactically connected to Nahum 1:12–13 by conjunctive *waw*, "and," which helps to portray a contrast between the respective addressees of each section. The 2ms addressee of 1:14 is portrayed as under judgment by YHWH—that is, "And YHWH has commanded concerning you, 'there shall not be planted/propagated from your name again, from the house of your gods I will cut off idol and image, I shall appoint your grave because you have cursed.'" Prior to this, the 2fs addressee in 1:12–13 is portrayed as the recipient of YHWH's protection following a period of oppression by a party who will now be punished, "Thus says YHWH, 'Although complete and many, they are mowed down and pass away, and I have afflicted you; I will afflict you no more, and now I will break his rod from upon you, and your bonds I will tear away.'" Clearly, the fate of the 2fs addressee improves as YHWH takes action against the 2ms addressee. Given the overall portrayal of judgment against Nineveh and the Assyrian king in Nahum 2:2–3:19 and the call for Judah to rejoice at the end of oppression in Nahum 2:1, it seems best to conclude that the 2ms addressee of Nahum 1:14 is the Assyrian king (cf. Nah 3:18–19) and that the 2fs addressee of Nahum 1:12–13 is Judah.

This has implications for understanding the 2fs addressee of Nahum 1:11 as well. Some read this verse as an address to Belial,[14] but the lack of correspondence between the 2fs address form and the ms *bĕlîyā'al* demonstrates that this cannot be the case. Otherwise, the 2fs addressee must be Judah as in 1:12–13 and 2:1. But this creates problems in that Judah appears to be charged with plotting against YHWH, insofar as the verse is frequently translated, "Did not one come out from you, who plotted evil against the L-rd, and counselled villainy?" (RSV).

12. See esp. Spronk, "Synchronic and Diachronic Approaches," 165, who points to the lack of consensus among scholars concerning the structure of the book. Spronk's own proposal for the structure of Nahum is completely unworkable, as it is based on the Masoretic divisions of the text. Unfortunately, there is no evidence that these divisions were introduced by the authors of the text; rather, they represent the interpretative efforts of later Jewish interpreters that were presented in the current text by the Masoretes in eighth–tenth centuries C.E.

13. See Bob Becking, "Is het boek Nahum een literaire eenheid?" *NTT* 32 (1978) 107–124; Sweeney, "Concerning the Structure and Generic Character."

14. For example, Kevin Cathcart, *Nahum in the Light of Northwest Semitic*, BO 26 (Rome: Biblical Institute Press, 1973) 33, 62–63.

Certainly, the use of the verb *ḥōšēb*, here translated as "plotted," does not support such a contention as the meaning "plot" generally requires a piel conjugation, whereas *ḥōšēb* is qal, and means simply "to think." Furthermore, the verb *yōʿēṣ*, here translated as "counseled," must be considered in relation to *bĕlîyāʿal*, which does not connote villainy in the sense of treachery, but foolishness or worthlessness. The sense of *yōʿēṣ bĕlîyāʿal* is therefore foolish or worthless advice. This likewise has an impact on the understanding of *ʿal yhwh*, here translated as "against the L-rd," in that *ʿal*, which literally means "on" or "over," can also mean "against" or "concerning." Clearly a situation of plotting calls for the translation "against," but mere thinking calls for the translation "concerning." When these considerations are taken to together, the verse does not portray some sort of plot against YHWH, but foolish thinking concerning YHWH—that is, "from you has gone forth evil/wrong thinking about YHWH, worthless counsel." Obviously, the 2fs addressee of Nahum 1:11 is accused of erroneous thinking about YHWH, not plotting against YHWH. Given the situation articulated in Nahum 1:12–13, that YHWH will cease oppressing Judah and break "his rod" from upon Judah, it become clear that the wrong thinking about YHWH in Nahum 1:11 refers to Judah's erroneous assumption that YHWH was either powerless or unwilling to stop Assyria's oppression. In this case, the focus on YHWH's power to defeat enemies in Nahum 1:2–8 indicates that the text challenges a prevailing belief that YHWH was unable to defeat the Assyrians who subjugated Judah.

Finally, the 2mp addressee of Nahum 1:9–10 must be considered. Verse 9 is generally translated as an indication of plotting against YHWH, "What do you plot against the L-rd? He will make a full end, he will not take vengeance (lit., rise up) twice against his enemies." (RSV). This time, the verb *ḥšb* is conjugated as piel, which many take to be an indication of plotting, but even the piel formulation of the verb means merely "to consider," "to reckon," or "to devise." The last meaning is sometimes considered to be an indication of plotting, but the verb *qšr* in biblical Hebrew is generally employed for conspiracy or plotting. Furthermore, v. 9b, *lōʾ tāqûm paʿămayim ṣārâ*, is mistranslated in that the feminine conjugation of *tāqûm*, "she shall rise," and the absence of *ʿal* demonstrates no indication that YHWH rises *against* his enemies. Rather, *ṣārâ*, "adversary," is the subject of the verb *tāqûm*. Consequently, the verse should read, "an adversary does not arise twice." When considered in context, this statement does not indicate a continuing threat against a party that "plots" against YHWH. Instead, it represents a situation in which a threat is coming to an end and will not be manifested again. Verse 10, "in thorns, they are entangled; like strong drink, they are drunk; they are consumed like chaff, fully dried," continues the theme of a threat that will be manifested no more. When one considers that the balance of the text addresses two basic parties, Judah and the Assyrians, the conclusion is clear that the 2mp address form in Nahum 1:9–10 likewise addresses both Judah and Assyria (i.e., Nineveh and the Assyrian king). Both the oppressed and the oppressor are asked, "What do you consider/reckon unto YHWH?" now that Assyria is about to fall and Judah is about to be delivered.

These considerations demonstrate that the book of Nahum presupposes three sets of addressees: Judah and Assyria in Nahum 1:9–10; Judah in Nahum 1:11–

2:1; and Nineveh/Assyrian king in Nahum 2:2–3:19. The address to both Judah and Assyria asks how these parties consider YHWH. Following the acrostic material in Nahum 1:2–8, it is clear that the question is concerned with perceptions of YHWH's power and capacity to defeat enemies. Given that an adversary is stated not to rise twice, and the portrayal of impending downfall, the text prepares the reader for what is to come—a portrayal of Judean deliverance and Assyrian downfall. Nahum 1:11–2:1 then addresses Judah and posits that Judah thought erroneously about YHWH. The contrast between deliverance of the oppressed and the downfall of the oppressor makes it clear that the text presupposes the end of Assyria's oppression of Judah. It is clear from the text that YHWH is the party responsible for this change of events, and indeed for Judah's oppression in the first place, but the command to rejoice further indicates that the time of oppression is at an end. Finally, Nahum 2:2–3:19 addresses Nineveh (2:2–3:17) and the Assyrian king (3:18–19). The text portrays graphically the downfall of Nineveh and rhetorically questions whether Nineveh actually believed whether she was any different from Thebes, which also was destroyed (Nah 3:8–10). The repeated statements, "behold, I am against you," in Nahum 2:14 and 3:5 make it clear that YHWH is the source of Nineveh's downfall. The address to the Assyrian king in Nahum 3:18–19 makes it clear that Assyria is finished for bringing evil upon others.

These considerations make it possible to define the overall structure and generic character of the book of Nahum. Following the superscription in Nahum 1:1, which identifies the book as Nahum's pronouncement concerning Nineveh, the body of the book in Nahum 1:2–3:19 constitutes a prophetic refutation speech. As indicated by the rhetorical question in Nahum 1:9 and the statement that Judah thought wrongly about YHWH in Nahum 1:11, it is evident that the book is designed to challenge a prevailing notion that YHWH is or was powerless to protect Judah against the Assyrian empire. To the contrary, the book asserts that YHWH is not only capable of defeating the Assyrians, but that YHWH was responsible for Judah's oppression by Assyria in the first place. The refutation speech is a part of the overall disputation genre, which is designed to challenge a particular thesis or viewpoint. The disputation has been studied by Graffy, who argues that the genre comprises two basic elements—a quotation of the thesis to be refuted and the refutation of the thesis.[15] It is further refined by Murray, who argues that three basic elements appear in the pattern: thesis, counterthesis, and dispute (or refutation).[16]

The surface structure of the text differs from this basic pattern, but all three of Murray's elements appear in the deep structure of Nahum 1:2–3:19.[17] The

---

15. A. Graffy, *A Prophet Confronts His People: The Disputation Speech in the Prophets*, AnBib 104 (Rome: Biblical Institute Press, 1984).

16. D. F. Murray, "The Rhetoric of Disputation: Re-examination of a Prophetic Genre," *JSOT* 38 (1987) 95–121.

17. Cf. Spronk, "Synchronic and Diachronic," 165, who fails to understand the distinction between the surface structure and the deep structure of the text.

counterthesis appears in Nahum1:2–10, which includes both the acrostic material that asserts YHWH's power and the rhetorical question, addressed to Judah and Assyria, that asserts YHWH's bringing about destruction. The rhetorical question thereby inaugurates a challenge to an unstated thesis that YHWH is not powerful and that the Assyrian empire subjugated Judah by its own initiative and strength.

Nahum 1:11–2:1 then makes the challenge clear. It is formulated predominantly as an address to Judah throughout, that begins in 1:11 with an assertion that Judah has thought wrongly about YHWH. The evidence for this assertion appears in 1:12–14, which state first that YHWH is ending the oppression that YHWH brought about in the first place, and that YHWH will defeat the oppression. Nahum 1:14 makes it clear that the oppressor is non-YHWHistic as it changes address forms and states that the oppressor's images and idols will be destroyed together with the oppressor's legacy. Nahum 2:1 then calls on Judah to rejoice because it is now redeemed from oppression. Both the thesis to be disputed and the counterthesis are present here: Assyria is not responsible for Judah's oppression, YHWH is, and YHWH is bringing that oppression to an end by bringing down Assyria.

Finally, Nahum 2:2–3:19 expresses the refutation or disputation elements very clearly. Formulated as address to Nineveh and the Assyrian king, they argue that YHWH is bringing about the impending or realized Assyrian downfall. The reality of Assyria's fall, whether impending or realized, is an important aspect of the argumentation, in that it provides an objective demonstration that the claims of Nahum 1:2–10 and 1:11–2:1 are in fact true.

The structure of Nahum may be portrayed as in table 12.1. The present form of the book of Nahum displays a unified and coherent literary structure and message. Overall, it presupposes the downfall of the Assyrian empire and argues that the Assyrian collapse is an act of YHWH. This has important implications for establishing the historical setting of the book of Nahum in relation to the reign of King Josiah and his program of religious reform and national restoration.

The presupposition of an Assyrian downfall is a key element in establishing the historical setting of the book.[18] In this sense, the argumentation of the book of Nahum requires a demonstrable event that can validate the claims made in the book concerning YHWH's power to act. The clearest example of such an event of course would be the actual fall of Nineveh to the Babylonians and Medes in 612 B.C.E., but it must be kept in mind that a perception of the impending fall of Nineveh also would serve this purpose. Practically speaking, a variety of events could serve this function and thereby provide a wide historical range for the background of the book. The first major event would be the decline of Assyria's power in Egypt following the sack of Thebes by Assurbanipal's army in 663 B.C.E. The

---

18. For discussion of the problems pertaining to the historical setting of the book, see Mason, *Micah, Nahum, Obadiah* 59–61. For historical surveys relevant to the background of Nahum, see W. W. Hallo and W. K. Simpson, *The Ancient Near East: A History* (New York: Harcourt, Brace, Jovanovich, 1971) 138–143; Hayes and Miller, eds., *Israelite and Judaean History* 435–488; Redford, *Egypt, Canaan, and Israel in Ancient Times* 351–364, 430–453.

TABLE 12.1   Structure of the Book of Nahum

Prophetic refutation speech	Nahum 1:1–3:19
I. Superscription	1:1
II. Prophetic refutation speech concerning YHWH's overthrow of Assyria and deliverance of Judah	1:2–3:19
A. Address to Judah and Assyria challenging view that YHWH is powerless against Assyria	1:2–10
1. Partial acrostic assertion of YHWH's power to punish enemies	1:2–8
2. Rhetorical question asserting YHWH's power to punish enemies	1:9–10
B. Address to Judah asserting that the redemption from Assyrian oppression is an act of YHWH	1:11–2:1
1. Initial assertion: Judah is mistaken in thinking that YHWH is powerless	1:11
2. Prophetic YHWH speech reports concerning end of Judah's oppression and punishment of the oppressor	1:12–14
a. Concerning Judah's relief from oppression	1:12–13
b. Concerning YHWH's defeat of oppressor	1:14
3. Concluding statement: command to Judah to rejoice at cessation of oppression	2:1
C. Address to Assyria asserting that fall of Assyria is an act of YHWH	2:2–3:19
1. Address to Nineveh	2:2–3:17
2. Address to Assyrian king	3:18–19

book of Nahum clearly presupposes this event, as indicated by the question as to whether Nineveh thought it was any better than Thebes in Nahum 3:8–10. Many have argued that the fall of Thebes provides the setting for the composition of Nahum.[19] The emergence of a relatively independent Saite dynasty in the aftermath of the Assyrian withdrawal from Egypt could well serve as a signal of Assyria's decline, but the lack of a decisive defeat of Assyria by Egypt at this time would undermine attempts to see the Assyrian withdrawal from Egypt as the historical setting of the book of Nahum.

The second major series of events would begin with the war in 652–648 between Assurbanipal, who ruled Assyria from Nineveh, and his brother, Shamash-shum-ukin, who ruled Babylonia as an Assyrian vassal state. Although Shamash-shum-ukin was defeated, Assyria was seriously weakened as a result of the war. The war thereby stood as a clear signal that Assyrian power was on the decline. Assyria subsequently undertook raids against Arabs in the Trans-Jordan region, and resumed an earlier war against Elam. But by the time of the Assyrian victory over Elam in 639, Assurbanipal's armies were exhausted. Nevertheless, Assyrian victories in all of these campaigns suggest that they do not constitute the setting for the composition of the book of Nahum.

The third series of events begins in 627 with the deaths of Assurbanipal of Assyria and Kandalanu, the regent appointed by Assurbanipal to rule Babylon following the defeat and death Shamash-shum-ukin. A year later, in 626, the Chaldean prince Nabopolassar seized the throne of Babylon and rebelled against

19. For example, Roberts, *Nahum* 38.

Assyrian suzerainty. After several Assyrian counterattacks were defeated, it was clear in 623 that the revolt had succeeded. In the years following 623, the Babylonians, supported by the Medes, began to push against Assyria in a counterattack of their own. By 616, if not before, Psamtek of Egypt campaigned in support of Assyria against the Babylonians in the middle Euphrates region. In 614, the Medes conquered the city of Ashur, and formally allied with the Babylonians against Assyria. A combined Median and Babylonian army laid siege against the palace of the Assyrian monarch Sin-shar-ishkun in Nineveh and conquered the city in 612. By 609, the last remnants of the Assyrian army were defeated at Haran.

This last sequence of events appears to provide the most likely setting for the composition of the book of Nahum, as the destruction of the city of Nineveh, whether anticipated or actual, could well be presupposed from the time of the Babylonian revolt on. In this regard, various scholars[20] have noted that the portrayal of Nineveh's destruction in Nahum 2:7–9 includes reference to the role of water in the destruction of the city, "the gates of the rivers are opened and the palace melts, (its mistress/idol) is stripped, it is carried off, her maidens lamenting, moaning like doves and beating their breasts. Nineveh is like a pool of water from those days, and they have fled." It corresponds to a notice in the History of Diodorus Siculus (History 2.26, 27) that Nineveh was taken when flood waters washed away part of its defenses (cf. Xenophon, Anabasis 3.4.12, who attributes the fall of Nineveh to fear of Zeus). There are problems with this interpretation, however, in that there is no evidence that Nineveh was destroyed by flood; there is a great deal of evidence of fire damage.[21] It should be kept in mind, however, that Nineveh's defenses included a series of moats that helped to protect the walls when filled with water. Tampering with the flood water gates of the Khusur River, which flows through the city and fills these moats, may well have contributed to its fall without leaving clear archeological evidence. Furthermore, the imagery associated with the fall of Thebes in Nahum 3:8, "are you better than Thebes that sat by the Nile, with water round about her, her rampart a sea, and water her wall?" contributes to this interpretation. In a manner analogous to Nineveh, the Nile flowed through the center of Thebes, although there is no indication that it contributed to Thebes's defenses. Nevertheless, the author of Nahum apparently chose to employ this imagery to make a point. Just as the powerful Thebes fell to the Assyrians under Assurbanipal in 663, so Nineveh is conquered a half century later. The use of the water imagery in the portrayal of the destruction of both Thebes and Nineveh points to the likelihood that the author of Nahum presupposed the circumstances of the actual fall of Nineveh. It also points to the likelihood that the author of Nahum deliberately employed part of a previously existing acrostic hymn that praised YHWH's power, insofar as the acrostic is incomplete and ends

20. See esp. the comments of J. M. P. Smith in J. M. P. Smith, W. H. Ward, and J. A. Bewer, *A Critical and Exegetical Commentary on Micah, Zephaniah, Nahum, Habakkuk, Obadiah, and Joel*, ICC (Edinburgh: T & T Clark, 1985) 318–324; Coggins, *Israel Among the Nations* 40–41.
21. Smith, *Nahum* 319; cf. S. Lloyd, *The Archaeology of Mesopotamia from the Old Stone Age to the Persian Conquest* (London: Thames and Hudson, 1984) 197–201, esp. 198.

in Nahum 1:8 with the imagery of YHWH employing flood waters to bring about the complete destruction of enemies.

Nevertheless, whether the argumentation of Nahum presupposes the actual destruction of Nineveh or merely anticipates it, the book appears to be set at some point between 627 and 612 B.C.E., when the destruction of Nineveh, whether real or anticipated, can reasonably be assumed by both the author and the audience of this text. This period corresponds to the years of Josiah's reign from the beginning of his reforms to shortly prior to his death. In this regard, the argument that YHWH is responsible for the destruction of Nineveh and that YHWH is likewise responsible for the subjugation of Judah to Assyrian power takes on special significance. Overall, it points to the power of YHWH to control events in the world at large, including both the natural world of the cosmos (Nah 1:2–8) and the human world of nations (Nah 1:9–3:19), and it provides some sense of a rationale for Judah's subjugation to Assyria prior to Josiah's reform. It employs empirical events to make its point and thereby provides support for Josiah's efforts to reform the religious establishment of Judah and to restore the nation—that is, just as YHWH had previously seen to the subjugation of Judah, so now YHWH was acting to bring down the oppressor and restore Judah's fortunes. Now that Assyria is fallen, Judah will rise. By making these points, the book of Nahum attempts to convince its audience—the people of Jerusalem and Judah—to support Josiah's efforts to reform the religious establishment dedicated to YHWH and to restore the state.

13

Jeremiah

The book of Jeremiah presents a potentially fruitful source for the study of the presentation of King Josiah and his reign in the Hebrew Bible. The superscription of the book in Jeremiah 1:1–3 places the beginning of Jeremiah's career in the thirteenth year of King Josiah's reign (627 B.C.E.), and traces it through the reigns of Jehoiakim and Zedekiah until the exile of Jerusalem (587 B.C.E.), "The words of Jeremiah ben Hilkiah from the priests who were in Anathoth in the land of Benjamin to whom the word of YHWH came in the days of Josiah ben Amon, King of Judah, in the thirteenth year of his rule, and it came in the days of Jehoiakim ben Josiah, King of Judah, until the completion of eleventh years to Zedekiah ben Josiah King of Judah until the exile of Jerusalem in the fifth month." The identification of the thirteenth year of Josiah as the beginning of Jeremiah's career appears again in Jeremiah 25:3 as part of the presentation of the prophet's speech concerning the projected seventy years of Babylonian exile. References to Jeremiah's speaking in the days of Josiah appear again in Jeremiah 36:2, which reports the prophet's instructions to record his words during the fourth year of Jehoiakim's reign, and Jeremiah 3:6, which presents a word of YHWH to Jeremiah during the reign of Josiah concerning the analogy between the faithlessness of Israel and that of Judah.

Although it would seem that the book of Jeremiah should contain a wealth of material pertaining to the reign of Josiah, scholars have pointed to the difficulties involved in employing the book of Jeremiah to reconstruct the historical background of the prophet.[1] The matter is complicated by the fact that two forms of

---

1. For surveys of the current discussion of Jeremiah research, see R. P. Carroll, *Jeremiah*, OT Guides (Sheffield: JSOT Press, 1989); Siegfried Herrmann, *Jeremia: Der Prophet und das Buch*, ErFor 271 (Darmstadt: Wissenschaftliche Buchgesellschaft, 1990); Jack Lundbom, "Jeremiah (Prophet)," *ABD* III, 684–698; Lundbom, "Jeremiah, Book of," *ABD* III, 706–721; Lundbom, *The Early Career of the Prophet Jeremiah* (Lewiston: Mellen Biblical Press, 1993) 1–66; Leo Perdue,

the book of Jeremiah are extant in the Masoretic and Septuagint versions, and that both were clearly composed into their present forms in the aftermath of the Babylonian exile. Scholars have noted that the books are heavily influenced by later theological or ideological viewpoints that play major roles in the presentation of the book and the prophet. There is extensive evidence of redaction and composition by hands that appear to be closely associated with or influenced by Deuteronomistic circles and outlooks.[2] Overall, the present form of the book is shaped by a concern to address the problem of the Babylonian exile. In this context, the people of Jerusalem and Judah are portrayed as disobedient to Mosaic Torah in a manner analogous to the rebelliousness of the wilderness murmuring traditions of the Pentateuch or the apostate northern kingdom of Israel of the Deuteronomistic history. Indeed, scholars have argued that Jeremiah is presented as a prophet like Moses, who attempts to lead the people during forty years of backsliding.[3] When confronted with the evidence that later theology and ideology have played such a pervasive role in the presentation of Jeremiah, many scholars have argued that it is simply impossible to try to reconstruct the historical Jeremiah or the specific historical backgrounds and "early" forms of the prophet's oracles contained within the book.[4]

Even if one grants the possibility that historical reconstruction is possible in the book of Jeremiah, the problem of establishing the prophet's activities and message during the reign of King Josiah looms large.[5] Apart from the oracle conveyed by Jeremiah 3:6, there are no indications that any of the material in the book of Jeremiah stems from the time of Josiah. The book consistently places Jeremiah's oracles in the reigns of Jehoiakim, Zedekiah, and the aftermath of the Babylonian destruction of Jerusalem. Indeed, scholars have raised questions concerning the extent to which Jeremiah 3:6 conveys material that can be placed during the reign of Josiah. Some identify only a very brief text in Jeremiah 3:6–11, and others question whether any of this material can stem from the time of Josiah at all.[6] Again, an important factor in this question is the overall perspective of judgment against Jerusalem and Judah evident in the material conveyed by Jeremiah 3:6. Such con-

---

"Jeremiah in Modern Research: Approaches and Issues," in *A Prophet to the Nations: Essays in Jeremiah Studies*, ed. L. G. Perdue and B. W. Kovacs (Winona Lake, Ind.: Eisenbrauns, 1984) 1–32; Klaus Seybold, *Der Prophet Jeremia: Leben und Werk* (Stuttgart: W. Kohlhammer, 1993).

2. See the essays published in Walter Gross, ed., *Jeremia und die "deuteronomistische Bewegung,"* BBB 98 (Weinheim: Belz Athenäum, 1995).

3. For example, Christopher Seitz, "The Prophet Moses and the Canonical Shape of Jeremiah," *ZAW* 101 (1989) 3–27.

4. See esp. Carroll, *Jeremiah* 9–16, 31–40.

5. See esp. Herrmann, *Jeremia* 1–37; Seybold, *Der Prophet Jeremiah* 37–67.

6. See Lundbom, *Early Career* 20, n 30; Mark Biddle, *A Redaction History of Jeremiah 2:1–4:2*, AThANT 77 (Zürich: Theologischer Verlag, 1990) 93–97; Nelson Kilpp, *Niederreissen und aufbauen: Das Verhältnis von Heilsverheissung und Unheilsverheissung bei Jeremia und im Jeremiabuch*, BTS 13 (Neukirchen-Vluyn: Neukirchener, 1990) 172–176. See also the commentaries: Robert P. Carroll, *Jeremiah: A Commentary*, OTL (Philadelphia: Westminster, 1986) 144–146; William L. Holladay, *Jeremiah 1*, Hermeneia (Philadelphia: Westminster, 1986) 116–118; William McKane, *Jeremiah 1*, ICC (Edinburgh: T and T Clark, 1986) 64–69.

demnation of Jerusalem and Judah in the material conveyed by Jeremiah 3:6 and throughout the rest of the book raises questions concerning Jeremiah's stance toward Josiah and his policies. The condemnation of Jerusalem and Judah during the days of Josiah in Jeremiah 3:6–6:30 for rejecting YHWH's Torah (Jer 6:19); the condemnation of the Temple in Jeremiah 7:1–8:3, which was the centerpiece of Josiah's reform program; the condemnation of those who are wise in Torah in Jeremiah 8:8–9, when Torah provided the basis for Josiah's program; and the general charges that the people have violated YHWH's covenant (Jer 11:1–17), all suggest that Jeremiah was hostile to Josiah's program if in fact he spoke during Josiah's reign at all.

The issue is complicated, however, by a number of indications throughout the book of Jeremiah's admiration for Josiah, his association with many key figures who were important to Josiah's administration and program, his identification with Deuteronomic Torah, and his support for Judean alliance with or submission to Babylon, which appears to have been a key ally of Judah during the reign of Josiah.[7] Indeed, many of these factors point to the possibility that a historical picture of the prophet can be constructed, at least to some extent, because many of these factors do not lend themselves entirely to the concerns with the Babylonian exile in the final forms of the book. They point to the possibility that Jeremiah may well have had an association with King Josiah's reform, or at least a viewpoint concerning Josiah's policies, and that it might be possible to reconstruct something of the prophet's outlook or message in this period.

Jeremiah's admiration for Josiah is made very clear, for example, in his condemnation of Jehoiakim in Jeremiah 22:1–23 for building a sumptuous palace for himself in Jerusalem while neglecting the welfare of his people. The oracle employs a pun on the word "house" to make clear Jeremiah's perspective that the king will secure his throne and dynasty/house by seeing to the welfare of the people:

> Thus says the L-rd, "Do justice and righteousness,
> and deliver from the hand of the oppressor him has been robbed.
> And do no wrong or violence to the alien, the fatherless, and the widow,
> nor shed innocent blood in this place. For if you will indeed obey this
>   word,
> then there shall enter the gates of this house kings who sit on the throne of
>   David,
> riding in chariots and on horses, they and their servants, and their people.
> But if you will not heed these words, I swear by myself, says the L-rd,
> that this house shall become a desolation." (RSV)

In vv. 10–12, the oracle makes reference to the Egyptian deportation of Josiah's son Jehoahaz, here identified by his personal name Shallum, whom the Egyptians removed in order to place Jehoiakim, who was apparently more favorably inclined

---

7. For a discussion of the political background of Jeremiah's preaching, see Jay Wilcoxen, "The Political Background of Jeremiah's Temple Sermon," in *Scripture in History and Theology*, Fs. J. C. Rylaarsdam, ed. A. L. Merrill and T. W. Overholt (Pittsburgh: Pickwick, 1977) 151–166.

to Egypt, on the throne. The prophet's oracle against Jehoiakim compares him to his father, Josiah:

> Woe to him who builds his house by unrighteousness, and his upper
>   rooms by injustice;
> who makes his neighbor serve him for nothing, and does not give him his
>   wages;
> who says, "I will build myself a great house with spacious upper rooms,"
> and cuts out windows for it, panelling it with cedar, and painting it with
>   vermilion.
> Do you think that you are a king because you compete in cedar?
> Did not your father eat and drink and do justice and righteousness?
> Then it was well with him.
> He judged the cause of the poor and needy; then it was well.
> Is this not to know me? says the L-rd.
> But you have eyes and heart only for your dishonest gain, for shedding
>   innocent blood,
> and for practicing oppression and violence. (RSV)

This brief reference to Josiah makes it very clear that Jeremiah held Josiah in high regard, which makes it somewhat difficult to maintain that Jeremiah opposed Josiah's reforms. Furthermore, the prophet cites concerns with the welfare of the poor, including the righteousness due to the resident alien, widow, and orphan, as well as proper payment of wages to workmen, all of which are characteristic of the law code of Deuteronomy, which scholars generally maintain stands at the basis of Josiah's reform.[8]

It is noteworthy that Jeremiah cites or presupposes Deuteronomic laws in other contexts as well. One example appears in Jeremiah 3:1–5, in which the prophet cites the case of a man who attempts to remarry his divorced wife after she has been married to another man.[9] The case appears in Deuteronomy 24:1–4 as part of the Deuteronomic lawcode where it is stipulated that such a remarriage is forbidden as an abomination. It likewise appears to be presupposed in Hosea 2, when YHWH, portrayed as a cuckolded husband, attempts to win back Israel, portrayed as his estranged wife. In keeping with the perspective of Deuteronomy 24:1–4, Jeremiah 3:1–5 portrays such an action as one that would pollute the land. Given the place of the Deuteronomic lawcode in the reform of Josiah, many have argued that the citation of such a case would help to establish some relationship between Jeremiah and Josiah's reforms.[10] Others have argued that Jeremiah 3:1–5 need not

---

8. For a discussion of the sociopolitical outlook of Deuteronomy and its relation to Josiah's reform, see Halpern, "Jerusalem and the Lineages in the Seventh Century B.C.E.: Kinship and the Rise of Individual Moral Liability"; Steinberg, "The Deuteronomic Law Code and the Politics of State Centralization"; Weinfeld, *Deuteronomy and the Deuteronomic School.*

9. For discussion of Jeremiah 3:1–5, see the commentaries, esp. Holladay, *Jeremiah 1* 112–116; McKane, *Jeremiah 1* 58–64.

10. For example, James D. Martin, "The Forensic Background to Jeremiah III 1," *VT* 19 (1969) 82–92.

presuppose the Deuteronomic version of this law per se, as the principle may well be derived from the sphere of wisdom or other sources.[11] In any case, knowledge of this particular law or tradition provides little solid evidence of Jeremiah's relationship to Josiah's reform, as the example from Hosea indicates that it appears to be a commonly accepted legal practice apart from the reform. Furthermore, if this law was in fact promulgated during the reign of Josiah, there is no reason why Jeremiah could not cite it at a later time.

The famous Temple Sermon of Jeremiah 7 provides another primary case in point.[12] After calling upon the people to mend their ways because the Temple in Jerusalem will not save them from YHWH's judgment, the prophet returns to characteristic Deuteronomic themes, such as prohibitions against oppressing the resident alien, the orphan, and the widow, and serving other gods. The text then presents Jeremiah's rhetorical questions posed to his audience, "will you steal, murder, commit adultery, swear falsely, burn incense to Baal, and go after other gods that you have not known, and then come and stand before me in this house, which is called by my name, and say, 'we are delivered!'—only to go on doing all these abominations?" Although many scholars have argued that this represents a later Deuteronomistically influenced composition that does not reflect the views of the prophet,[13] the reference to the destruction of the sanctuary at Shiloh as a basis for the claim that the Temple will provide security provides evidence that the speech does go back to the prophet in some form. The DtrH does not indicate that the sanctuary at Shiloh was destroyed, and yet Jeremiah cites it as an example. When one considers that Jeremiah is a priest from Anathoth, however, it makes perfect sense for him to cite this example as he apparently is descended from the priestly line of Eli, who previously served as priest at Shiloh, through Abiathar who was expelled to Anathoth from Jerusalem by Solomon and replaced by Zadok and his descendants. This speaks to the personal background of Jeremiah, but not to the DtrH.

This raises an important question pertaining to Jeremiah's potential relationship to Josiah's reform: How then is one to understand the rejection of the Jerusalem Temple, which stood as the centerpiece of Josiah's program together with Deuteronomic Torah? According to the narrative in Jeremiah 26, which presents Jeremiah's trial for sedition as a result of his Temple Sermon, the incident took place at the beginning of the reign of Jehoiakim. At this point, it must be kept in mind that Josiah had already been killed by the Egyptians, and Jehoahaz had been deported to Egypt. Several factors thereby come into play. Josiah's program had clearly failed—certainly it had failed to protect the monarch himself—and people would have been looking for explanations or drawing conclusions as to the meaning of this event. One possible conclusion, apparently articulated in Jeremiah 7, is that the Temple alone would not suffice to ensure the security of the nation; adher-

---

11. For example, T. R. Hobbs, "Jeremiah 3, 1–5 and Deuteronomy 24, 1–4," *ZAW* 86 (1974) 23–29.

12. See the commentaries and Winfried Thiel, *Die deuteronomistische Redaktion von Jeremia 1–25*, WMANT 41 (Neukirchen-Vluyn: Neukirchener, 1973) 103–135.

13. For example, Thiel, *Jeremiah 1–25*.

ence to YHWH's expectations as expressed in Deuteronomic Torah was also necessary, just as it is explicitly expressed throughout the law code of Deuteronomy.
Jeremiah's response to this situation is that the people had not adhered to YHWH's
expectations as required. Just as Josiah had perished, so the Temple in Jerusalem
could come to an end as well. Jeremiah's Temple Sermon does not represent
opposition to Josiah or to his reform; it represents the prophet's recognition that
Josiah's death signaled the failure of the reform.

This perspective is supported by several additional lines of evidence. First,
when Jeremiah is put on trial for sedition in Jeremiah 26, he is saved only by the
intervention of Ahikam ben Shaphan. Ahikam ben Shaphan was apparently a rather
important official in the administration of King Josiah.[14] He was the son of Shaphan,
Josiah's secretary, who read the Torah scroll found by the high priest Hilkiah in
the Temple, and brought it to the attention of the King in 2 Kings 22:8–10.
According to 2 Kings 22:12, 14, he was included together with his father among
the delegation of officials sent by Josiah to request an oracle from YHWH by the
prophetess Huldah concerning the significance of the book of Torah that was found
in the Temple during the course of Josiah's renovations. Although Ahikam had
served Josiah, the narrative in Jeremiah 26 indicates that he apparently still held
some clout during the reign of Jehoiakim, at least enough to save Jeremiah. His
brothers also played roles in Jeremiah's activities. According to Jeremiah 29, the
prophet sent his letter to the exiles, urging them to submit to Babylonia, to build
houses there, and so on, by the hands of Elasah ben Shaphan and Gemariah ben
Hilkiah. According to Jeremiah 36:9–18, when Jeremiah's scribe Baruch ben
Neriah read the prophet's scroll to the people in the fifth year of Jehoiakim's reign
(605 B.C.E.), he did so at the house of Gemariah ben Shaphan in the presence of
Gemariah, his son Micaiah, and others including the son of one other minister of
Josiah, Elnathan ben Achbor. Later at the fall of Jerusalem to the Babylonians,
Gedaliah, the son of Ahikam ben Shaphan, was appointed governor by the victo-
rious Babylonians, and Jeremiah was placed in his charge.

Jeremiah received a great deal of support from the Shaphan family, which
was clearly identified with Josiah and his reform, and which seems to have come
into conflict with Jehoiakim. When one considers that both the Shaphan family
and the prophet Jeremiah represent a consistently pro-Babylonian political stance,
in opposition to Jehoiakim's pro-Egyptian policies, it becomes clear that the Shaphan
family and Jeremiah represent elements of political opposition to Jehoiakim.
Jehoiakim was placed on the throne by Pharaoh Necho, after he had exiled
Jehoahaz, because Jehoiakim was better attuned to serving Egyptian interests.
The position of the Shaphan family, by contrast, is made clear by the Babylonian
appointment of Gedaliah as governor, and by the timing of the reading of Jeremiah's scroll to Jehoiakim in the fifth year of his reign. The scroll was dictated
in the fourth year—that is, 605 B.C.E., the year that Babylonia defeated Egypt at
Carchemesh and thereby supplanted Egypt as Judah's overlord. The Babylonian

14. On the role of the Shaphan family in Jeremiah's career, see Wilcoxen, "Political Background."

threat is made clear in Jeremiah 36:29. Furthermore, Jeremiah's consistently pro-Babylonian stance is clear from his actions in Jeremiah 27–28, when he walked about Jerusalem wearing a yoke to urge the people to submit to Babylon, and by his letter to the exiles in Jeremiah 29, urging them to accept life in Babylonia. In this regard, it is important to note that although there is no clear evidence that Josiah was allied with Babylon, his death at Megiddo, which delayed the northward march of the Egyptians to support the Assyrians in their last stand against the Babylonians at Haran, clearly served Babylon's interests. Such an alliance between Babylon and Judah at this time would mirror that between Hezekiah and Merodach-baladan a century earlier, which was undertaken to revolt against Sennacherib, and provide background to the similar policies of Temple purification and the establishment of political independence from Assyria enacted by both Hezekiah and Josiah. These signs point to an interrelationship between the Shaphan family and Jeremiah as supporters of the pro-Babylonian policy of King Josiah (and Jehoahaz) in opposition to the pro-Egyptian policy of Jehoiakim.

A further element involves Jeremiah's priestly identity and his presence in Jerusalem. Jeremiah 1:1 states that Jeremiah is the son of Hilkiah. This happens to be the name of the high priest in the Jerusalem Temple who found the Torah scroll that served as the basis for Josiah's reform in 2 Kings 22–23. There is no clear evidence that Jeremiah's father and the high priest are one and the same person, especially since Jeremiah is from the Elide line at Anathoth and the high priest is from the Zadokite line.[15] Nevertheless, it is noteworthy that Jeremiah is an Elide priest from Anathoth is serving in Jerusalem at this time. According to 2 Kings 23:8–9, Josiah closed all of the altars outside of Jerusalem and brought their priests out, but they refused to come to Jerusalem to serve at the altar there. Jeremiah appears to be an exception to this, however, and this may well explain several aspects of his career and message. It helps explain the conflict he has with the men of Anathoth who are plotting to kill him in Jeremiah 11:18–23 and those identified as his familiar friends in the other Jeremianic laments (cf. Jer 20:10). As an Elide priest, Jeremiah's proper place is in Anathoth, but he appears in Jerusalem and incurs the wrath of his counterparts in Anathoth. This would suggest that Jeremiah came to Jerusalem as part of Josiah's reform and suffered opposition for this action by his counterparts in Anathoth. His access to the Temple, his vision of a blossoming almond rod, his vision of a boiling pot from the north, his access to the Shaphan and Neriah families, and his identification with Deuteronomic Torah suggest that he was active as a priest in Jerusalem and that he came to Jerusalem in conjunction with Josiah's reform.

Indeed, either one or both of these elements of opposition in Jeremiah's life—either against the pro-Egyptian policies of Jehoiakim or against the priests of Anathoth who rejected Josiah's invitation to serve in Jerusalem—could well explain his diatribe against those who consider themselves wise in Torah in Jeremiah 8:8–12. In the case of the former, the shift in policy and power within the Davidic house, which became apparent with the accession of Jehoiakim to the

---

15. See 1 Chronicles 5:39; Ezra 7:1–5.

throne, could well explain the prophet's charges that the country would come to ruin. It is unlikely that a new king would declare a policy that would be overtly touted as opposed to YHWH's Torah; rather, Jehoiakim would have promulgated his actions as consistent with YHWH's Torah. In the case of the latter, the prophet could well charge that the priests of Anathoth, who like all priests were charged with the teaching of Torah, whatever that Torah might be, had misrepresented Torah and led the country to ruin by failing to recognize Josiah's reform. In any case, Jeremiah's criticism of those who consider themselves wise in Torah in Jeremiah 8:8–12 do not indicate the prophet's opposition to the principle of Torah per se; it indicates his opposition to the application of Torah by a specific group to which he is opposed.

These considerations point to the possibility and, indeed, the likelihood that Jeremiah had some relationship to Josiah's reform. Scholars have pointed to several texts that might yield some indication of the prophet's words or outlook during the reign of King Josiah.[16] Among the most commonly noted are Jeremiah 2–6 and 30–31, in that both of these text blocks employ language that appears to call for the return of the former northern kingdom of Israel to YHWH and Zion. Insofar as Josiah apparently attempted to bring the former northern kingdom of Israel back under Davidic rule, these texts require examination to determine if in fact they can point to Jeremiah's views on this issue.

Jeremiah 2–6

Many scholars have argued that Jeremiah 2–6, at least in part, contains material that stems from the prophet's earliest period.[17] There are a variety of reasons for this contention: (1) the assumption of a chronological arrangement for the book that would place earlier material near the beginning; (2) the reference to YHWH's speech to Jeremiah in the days of King Josiah (Jer 3:6); (3) the criticism of the kingdom for vacillating in its alliances between Assyria and Egypt rather than relying upon YHWH (Jer 2:14–19, 36–37); (4) the theme of the "foe from the north," which many see as a foundational theme for the prophet's early preaching (Jer 6:22–30; cf. 1:13–16); (5) the theme of rejection of YHWH's Torah, which many understand as a reference to the failure of Josiah's reform (Jer 6:19); and

---

16. See the surveys listed in n. 1 above.

17. For a discussion of Jeremiah 2–6, see the commentaries and R. Albertz, "Jer 2–6 und die Frühzeitverkündigung Jeremias," *ZAW* 94 (1982) 20–47; R. Liwak, *Der Prophet und die Geschichte. Eine literar-historische Untersuchung zum Jeremiabuch*, BWANT 121 (Stuttgart: W. Kohlhammer, 1987); Karl-Friedrich Pohlmann, *Die Ferne G-ttes—Studien zum Jeremiabuch*, BZAW 179 (Berlin and New York: Walter de Gruyter, 1989) 113–192; S. Herrmann, *Jeremia*, BKAT XII/2 (Neukirchen-Vluyn: Neukirchener, 1990) 93–109; Biddle, *Jeremiah 2:2–4:2*; Seybold, *Der Prophet Jeremia* 68–80; C. Hardmeier, "Die Redekomposition Jer 2–6: Eine ultimative Verwarnung Jerusalems im Kontext des Zidkijaaufstandes," *Wort und Dienst* 21 (1991) 11–42; Hardmeier, Geschichte und Erfahrung in Jer 2–6: Zur theologischen Notwendigkeit einer geschichts- und erfahrungsbezogenen Exegese und ihrer methodischen Neuorientierung," *EvTh* 56 (1996) 3–29. See also Dieter Böhler, "Geschlechterdifferenz und Landbesitz: Strukturuntersuchungen zu Jer 2, 2–4, 2," in *Jeremia und die "deuteronomistische Bewegung,"* ed. W. Gross, BBB 98 (Weinheim: Belz Athenäum, 1995) 91–127.

(6) a persistent contention that an earlier text form in Jeremiah 2:2–4:2, addressed to the former northern kingdom of Israel, underlies the present form of the text in Jeremiah 2–6, which is addressed to Jerusalem and Judah.

This last point is particularly important in the present context in that it raises the possibility that the prophet addressed a major concern of Josiah's reform: the return of the former northern kingdom of Israel to Davidic rule. The basis for this contention appears in the references to the prophet's audience throughout this material. Although the present form of Jeremiah 2–6 is clearly addressed to Jerusalem and Judah or a combination of Israel and Judah (cf. Jer 2:2; 3:6– 10, 11; 4:3–4, 5–6; 5:10–11; 6:1, 8, 9, 23), Jeremiah 2:2–4:4 frequently addresses only "Israel" (Jer 2:3, 14, 31; 3:23; 4:1); "the House of Jacob/Israel" (Jer 2:4, 26; 3:20); "apostate Israel" (Jer 3:12); and "the sons of Israel" (Jer 3:21). It emphasizes themes that typically pertain to the northern kingdom of Israel in Judean thought—that is, the wilderness tradition (Jer 2:2, 6, 17, 31); the return of the "rebellious children" to Zion (Jer 3:14, 17); the "walking together" of the "House of Judah" and the "House of Israel" (Jer 3:18); and it compares the apostasy of Israel with that of Judah (Jer 3:6–10, 11). Beginning in Jeremiah 4:3, the text consistently addressees Jerusalem and Judah, although the northern kingdom also may be included. On this basis, many scholars contend that Jeremiah composed an earlier form of Jeremiah 2:2–4:2, addressed to the former northern kingdom of Israel, in an effort to persuade the people to return to Davidic rule.[18]

Nevertheless, scholars have faced a number of difficulties in their attempts to reconstruct an earlier form of this text. Most fundamental are the problems noted above, concerning the difficulties in demonstrating that the prophet spoke during the reign of Josiah at all, and the problems associated with attempts to distinguish earlier oracles from a redactionally formulated text that is so heavily concerned with issues posed by the Babylonian exile. Other problems appear in the lack of clear historical information that might aid in dating this material. Scholars have been unable to resolve successfully the identification of the "foe from the north," which might be the Scythians, the Babylonians, the Medes, or some mythical enemy.[19] Furthermore, the references to alliances with either Egypt or Assyria present problems, in that alliance with Assyria would clearly presuppose a period prior to the final fall of Assyria in 609, but alliance with Egypt would likely presuppose a period following 609, when Pharaoh Necho II installed Jehoiakim as an Egyptian vassal. As a result of these difficulties, a number of scholars argue that although earlier Josianic material may appear in these chapters, the present form of the text addresses a much later situation.[20] Others argue that no clear Josianic text basis can be identified at all.[21]

18. For example, Holladay, *Jeremiah 1* 62–81.

19. For discussion of the "foe from the north" in relation to historical sources, see Henri Cazelles, "Sophonie, Jérémie, et les Scythes en Palestine," *RB* 74 (1967) 24–44.

20. For example, Liwak, *Der Prophet und die Geschichte* 304, 312; Hardmeier, "Die Redekomposition Jer 2–6"; Hardmeier, "Geschichte und Erfahrung in Jer 2–6."

21. For example, Biddle, *Jeremiah 2:2–4:2* 19–20, n. 53.

Nevertheless, several major grounds justify an attempt to reconstruct such an earlier text form. First is the consistent address to the former northern kingdom of Israel and the themes of a return to Zion that is expressed throughout Jeremiah 2:2–4:2 in contrast to the addresses to Jerusalem and Judah evident in Jeremiah 2:2 and 4:3–6:30. Second is the fact that Egypt would have easily presented itself as an ally to the former northern kingdom prior to 609 B.C.E.[22] The extant text of the Babylonian Chronicle makes it clear that the Egyptian army was operating along the Euphrates River in support of the Assyrians as early as 616 B.C.E., if not before.[23] In order to reach this region, the Egyptians would have to pass through the Jezreel Valley and move up through Damascus. This would require some arrangement with the former northern kingdom, which of course was an Assyrian province during this period, as Israel controlled passage through the Jezreel. It is unlikely that the governor of Samaria/Israel, an Assyrian appointee, would object to Egyptian passage through the Jezreel, especially since Assyria seemed to be in such dire straits during this period. Given Assyrian weakness at this point, this would suggest that Samaria/Israel would naturally begin to gravitate to the Egyptian orbit and perhaps become a formal vassal or protectorate of Egypt. A similar arrangement or alliance with Judah would not be necessary at this point, as Judah did not control access to the coastal highway or other routes that would be necessary for the Egyptians to move in support of Assyria.[24] Third is the clear effort to employ the case of northern Israel as an example for Judah in Jeremiah 3:6–10, 11, and throughout Jeremiah 4:3–6:30, which suggests that the hypothesized earlier text form was reworked to account for Judah's submission to Egypt following Josiah's death in 609. Fourth is the fact that the threat of the "enemy from the north" appears only in relation to the material addressed to Jerusalem and Judah in Jeremiah 4:3–6:30; it does not appear in relation to the material addressed solely to Israel. It is not necessary to demonstrate a Scythian invasion or another historical referent for this enemy in order to establish an earlier text form addressed to Israel alone.

To determine whether it is possible to reconstruct an earlier text form from Jeremiah 2–6, it is necessary first to examine the structure, generic character, setting, and outlook of the present form of the text.[25]

Jeremiah 2–6 is demarcated initially by the YHWH-word transmission formula in Jeremiah 2:1, "and the word of YHWH was unto me saying."[26] It is syn-

22. See Abraham Malamat, "The Kingdom of Judah Between Egypt and Babylon: A Small State Within a Great Power Confrontation," in *Text and Context*, JSOTSup 48, Fs. F. C. Fensham, ed. W. Claassen (Sheffield: JSOT Press, 1984) 117–129, esp. 119; cf. Herrmann, *Jeremia* 134–136.

23. For a translation of the relevant portion of the Babylonian Chronicle, see J. Pritchard, ed., *Ancient Near Eastern Texts Relating to the Old Testament* (Princeton: Princeton University Press 1969) 303–304; cf. Redford, *Egypt, Canaan, and Israel in Ancient Times* 441–469, esp. 446.

24. Contra J. Maxwell Miller and John H. Hayes, *A History of Ancient Israel and Judah* (Philadelphia: Westminster, 1986) 377–402, esp. 388–390, who argue that Josiah must have been an Egyptian vassal during this period.

25. For a full discussion of these issues, see my "Structure and Redaction in Jeremiah 2–6," in *Troubling Jeremiah*, JSOTSup 260, ed. A. R. Diamond, L. Stuhlman, and K. O'Connor (Sheffield: Sheffield Academic Press, 2000) 200–218.

26. Cf. Theodor Seidl, "Die Worterreignisformel in Jeremia," *BZ* 23 (1979) 20–47.

tactically linked by its *waw*-consecutive formulation to a series of prior examples of this formula in Jeremiah 1:4 and 1:11. In turn, these are tied to the superscription of the book in Jeremiah 1:1–3, making Jeremiah 2–6 the third in a series of textual blocks in Jeremiah 1–6 that are introduced by the superscription in Jeremiah 1:1–3. A syntactically independent example of the YHWH word transmission formula appears in Jeremiah 7:1 where it introduces an entirely new textual block—that is, "The word which was unto Jeremiah from YHWH, saying." This marks Jeremiah 6:30 as the conclusion of the textual block in Jeremiah 2–6. In addition to these formal features, Jeremiah 2–6 is demarcated thematically by its concern with impending punishment for both Israel and Judah and by its concern to call for the return of both Israel and Judah to YHWH in order to avoid this punishment.

The internal structure of Jeremiah 2–6 presents a number of problems. Several observations are therefore in order. First, the various address forms (i.e., 2ms, 2fs, 2mp) employed throughout this text cannot serve as adequate criteria by which to determine the structure, or even the redactional history, of Jeremiah 2–6. No clear pattern emerges, which suggests that the address forms shift as necessary in order to meet the rhetorical requirements of the text. This is evident already at the beginning of the text; the people can be addressed en masse as "the House of Israel/ Jacob" with 2mp (Jer 2:4–10), collectively as "Israel" with 2ms (Jer 2:3), or metaphorically as the bride of YHWH with 2fs (Jer 2:2). These references indicate neither structural nor redactional criteria; they simply reflect the different images of Israel employed by the author to make a point.

Second, the shift in addressee from Israel, and so on, in Jeremiah 2:2–4:2 to Jerusalem and Judah in Jeremiah 4:3–6:30 does not constitute a criterion for the structure of this text.[27] It may well constitute a criterion for the reconstruction of the redactional history of the text, but redactional criteria do not inherently constitute structural criteria. This is evident in the mixed address forms evident throughout Jeremiah 2–6. Jeremiah 2:2 begins by identifying the addressee as "Jerusalem," even though the bulk of material in Jeremiah 2:2–4:2 is directed to Israel, and so on, as noted above. An anomalous reference to Judah as an addressee also appears in Jeremiah 2:28, but this may well be a gloss that reflects the final form of the text as it apparently replicates a portion of Jeremiah 11:13, which is concerned with Judah's rebellion against YHWH. Jeremiah 5:14–19 is addressed directly to the "House of Israel" (v. 18) even though the context is directed Jerusalem and Judah. The apostasy of Judah is compared with that of Israel in Jeremiah 3:6–10, 11 in an effort to demonstrate that Judah is worse than Israel. Both Israel and Judah are addressed together in Jeremiah 5:20 (cf. 5:11), Jeremiah 6:8–9 defines Jerusalem as "the remnant of Israel." Finally, the material addressed to Jerusalem and Judah in Jeremiah 4:3–4 is linked directly to material addressed to Israel in Jeremiah 4:1–2 by the syntactical connective, *kî*, "because," which demonstrates a deliberate effort to create an analogy between Israel and Judah. In this case, a deliberate transition from Israel to Judah is fundamental to the concerns of this

---

27. Contra Biddle, *Jeremiah 2:2–4:2* 36.

text, insofar as the experience of Israel serves as a model for that of Judah, but it does not constitute a criterion for establishing the structure of Jeremiah 2–6.

Third, this effort to create an analogy between Israel and Judah points directly to Jeremiah 3:6–10, 11, where this analogy is stated explicitly. At this point, a formal observation is necessary in that Jeremiah 3:6–10, 11 are formulate as narrative, whereas the surrounding material is formulated as poetry. The only other narrative material in this text is the YHWH word transmission formula of Jeremiah 2:1. This is noteworthy in that Jeremiah 2:1 establishes the generic character of this text as a report of YHWH's word to Jeremiah concerning *Jerusalem*, not Israel or Jacob. Furthermore, both Jeremiah 2:1 and 3:6–10, 11 are formulated in a 1cs autobiographical perspective as statements by the prophet himself. In keeping with this perspective, Jeremiah 2:2 and 3:12 contain commissioning formulae that indicate instructions by YHWH to the prophet to convey YHWH's statements to the people. Altogether, these observations indicate that Jeremiah 2:1; 3:6–10, 11, mark the basic structural divisions of this text. Together, they define the overall text as an autobiographical report of YHWH's words to Jeremiah, instructing him to convey YHWH's words to the people. They define the basic concern of the text with Jerusalem and Judah, but they employ addresses to Israel as a means to establish an analogy between Israel and Judah: that is, just as Israel suffered by neglecting YHWH's requirements, so Judah will suffer punishment for the same reason.

This points to the identification of three basic structural elements within Jeremiah 2–6 (i.e., Jer 2:1–3:5, 3:6–10, and 3:11–6:30), each formulated in autobiographical narrative form that conveys words by YHWH to be spoken to the people. The thematic interrelationship between these subunits also must be considered. The material in Jeremiah 3:6–10 plays a key role in facilitating the transition from concern with Israel to concern with Judah within the larger framework of a text that is directed to Jerusalem and Judah. Obviously, Jeremiah 3:6–10 plays a constitutive role in establishing the structure and concerns of this text. Following the establishment of this analogy in Jeremiah 3:6–10, 11, the text turns immediately to a concern with the repentance of Israel that continues throughout the material addressed to Israel in Jeremiah 3:12–4:2. In contrast, the material addressed to Jerusalem and Judah in Jeremiah 4:3–6:30 is not explicitly concerned with repentance, but with the threat posed by "the enemy from the north."

This would appear to be unrelated to the repentance motif, but the nature of the analogy established between Israel and Judah in Jeremiah 3:6–10, 11 requires that the interrelationship of these themes be considered in relation to the larger literary context. Prior to the establishment of the analogy between Israel and Judah, the material directed to Israel in Jeremiah 2:2–3:5 focuses especially on YHWH's judgment and punishment of Israel expressed metaphorically in terms of a husband who divorces his philandering wife. Israel's guilt is thereby established as the basis for the divorce or punishment. Jeremiah 4:5–6:30 likewise focuses on Jerusalem's and Judah's guilt as the basis for YHWH's punishment by means of the "enemy from the north." In this regard, the calls for Israel's repentance in Jeremiah 3:12–4:2 play an important role in relation to the following announcements of punishment directed against Judah and Jerusalem in that they provide the context for understanding the purpose of such judgment. Based on the analogy of Israel, which YHWH calls to repentance following its "divorce," Judah and Jerusalem will likewise be called to repentance by YHWH in light of the upcoming punishment. This concern is hardly evident from Jeremiah 4:5–6:30; only the slightest hint of Jerusalem's repentance appears in Jeremiah 6:8, "be warned, O Jerusalem, lest my soul be thrust from you, lest I make you a desolation, an uninhabited land." Rather, it is evident from the literary context and structure of Jeremiah 2–6, in which Israel serves as an analogy for Jerusalem and Judah. Consequently, the call for repentance to Israel in Jeremiah 3:12–4:2 also serves as an indication of what YHWH expects from Jerusalem and Judah.

The result is a three-part structure for Jeremiah 2–6. Jeremiah 2:1–3:5 constitutes "the Prophet's report of YHWH's word concerning the punishment of Israel" in the form of a trial speech or divorce proceeding.[28] Jeremiah 3:6–10 constitutes "the Prophet's report of YHWH's word concerning both Israel's and Judah's unfaithfulness in the days of Josiah." Jeremiah 3:6–10 merely states the comparison or analogy between Israel and Judah—that is , both are unfaithful. Jeremiah 3:11 then asserts that the unfaithfulness of Judah is worse than that of Israel as the premise on which the following material will proceed. Jeremiah 3:11–6:30 therefore constitutes "the prophet's report of YHWH's word concerning Judah," which employs the analogy of Israel and Judah to call for repentance. (Jer 3:12–4:2) as the basis for defining the purpose of the punishment announced in Jeremiah 4:5–6:30.

The setting for the present form of this material, apart from the literary setting of the book of Jeremiah, appears to be placed in relation to the aftermath of Josiah's death in 609 B.C.E., when Pharaoh Necho of Egypt removed Jehoahaz from the throne and replaced him with his brother Jehoiakim, who apparently would be more inclined to serve Egyptian interests. This is indicated by the theme of a shift from alliance with Assyria to alliance with Egypt and the prophet's severe criticism of such a move. The marriage imagery plays naturally into the overall concern with Judah's and Jerusalem's political alignment, and it melds well with the pro-Babylonian stance consistently articulated by the prophet throughout the book. In this regard, alliance with Egypt represents a rejection of YHWH that will bring about YHWH's punishment of Judah. The threat of the "enemy from the north" would easily refer to the Babylonians and/or their Median allies who were responsible for the destruction of Assyria, Egypt's erstwhile ally.

This historical setting likewise influences interpretation of the present form of the text in that it demonstrates the role of historical retrospective in the criticism leveled against Israel. Insofar as the criticism of Israel serves as paradigm for that of Judah in the final form of the text, it employs the past experience of Israel's destruction and continued occupation by the Assyrians as a model for the punishment to be visited upon Judah for similar actions. In this regard, the attempts by eighth-century Israel to shift its alliances from Assyria during the reigns of Jeroboam II and, later, Menahem to alliances with Egypt during the reign of Hoshea provided the background—and, in the minds of many, the cause for—the Assyrian invasions that ultimately destroyed Israel as an independent state and reduced it

---

28. For a discussion of the trial genre in Jeremiah 2:2–3:5, see Holladay, *Jeremiah 1* 73–77.

to the status of a diminished Assyrian province. Likewise, any potential relationship between the seventh-century Assyrian province of Samaria and Egypt would emerge as part of the religiopolitical perspective articulated here; just as Samaria's relationship with Egypt rather than with YHWH (i.e., Jerusalem) would lead to ruin, so Judah's alliance with Egypt under Jehoiakim would lead to invasion by the anonymous "enemy from the north." For Israel, it was Assyria; for Judah, it could be the Babylonians, the Medes, the Scythians, or any combination of these parties. The Mesopotamian powers had demonstrated their ability to destroy Assyria. Egypt was an Assyrian ally and had failed to stop the Median-Babylonian alliances. From Jeremiah's perspective, reliance on Egypt represented a political and religious dead end. The Egyptians were no match for the Medes and Babylonians, and the rise of the Medes and Babylonians represented the will of YHWH.

On the basis of this analysis of the present form of Jeremiah 2–6, it is now possible to attempt a redaction-critical reconstruction of an earlier text form. As noted above, the evidence that such an attempt is justified appears in an apparent shift in addressees, from the northern kingdom of Israel to the southern kingdom of Judah or simply Jerusalem. The specific pattern of the respective addressees bears this out. The northern kingdom appears in the form of "Israel" (2:3, 14, 31; 4:1), the "house of Israel" (2:4, 26; 3:18, 20; 5:11, 15), the "sons of Israel" (3:21), the "house of Jacob" (2:4; 5:20), "apostate Israel" (3:6, 8, 11, 12), and "repentant Israel" (3:23). The southern kingdom or Jerusalem appears as "Judah" (3:18; 5:11), "treacherous Judah" (3:7, 8, 10, 11), "Jerusalem" (2:2; 4:3, 4, 5, 10, 11, 14, 16; 5:1; 6:6, 8), "Zion" (4:6), the "daughter of Zion" (4:31; 6:2, 23), and the "remnant of Israel" (6:9). A general pattern emerges in that, with the exception of Jeremiah 5:15, the direct references to northern Israel as the addressee appear only in Jeremiah 2:2–4:2; indirect references to the northern kingdom appear, however, in Jeremiah 5:11, 20, but these statements are not addressed to Israel. This relatively consistent address to Israel is set in a framework that is addressed to Judah and/or Jerusalem at the beginning (Jer 2:2), end (Jer 4:3ff), and at various points within Jeremiah 2:2–4:2 (viz., Jer 3:6–10, 11); Jeremiah 3:18 is an indirect reference to Judah. This suggests that a text originally addressed to the former northern kingdom of Israel in Jeremiah 2:2–4:2 was reworked into a text addressed to Jerusalem/Judah in Jeremiah 2–6. The survey of addressees indicates that such reworking should be sought in Jeremiah 2:2; 3:6–10, 11; and 4:3–6:30.

Further evidence for the redactional character of this text appears in the interrelationship between the prose material in Jeremiah 3:6–10, 11 that establishes the analogy between the unfaithfulness of "apostate Israel" and that of "treacherous Judah" and the surrounding poetic material that is addressed to the former northern kingdom of Israel. Based on the source-critical distinctions proposed by Mowinckel, scholars have generally identified poetry in Jeremiah as the work of the prophet (Mowinckel's source A) and the prose material as the work of a deuteronomic redaction (Mowinckel's source C).[29] Although the identification of

---

29. Sigmund Mowinckel, *Zur Komposition des Buches Jeremia*, Videnskapsselskapets skrifter 4, Hist.-Filos. Klasse, 1913 No. 5 (Oslo: Kristiana, 1914).

the prose material with Deuteronomistic circles is frequently questioned, a study by McKane adds further evidence to the source-critical distinction between the prose material in Jeremiah 3:6–10, 11 and the surrounding poetic context.[30] McKane demonstrates an exegetical relationship between Jeremiah 3:6–11 and Jeremiah 3:1–5, 12–13 in that the prose material of 3:6–11 takes up vocabulary and develops themes from the poetic material, thereby demonstrating a redactional relationship between the two sets of texts. Specifically, Jeremiah 3:6–11 takes up the divorce theme from Jeremiah 3:1–5 and develops it into a portrayal of both Israel's and Judah's harlotry; it employs the designation *mĕšubâ yiśrāʾēl*, "apostate Israel," from Jeremiah 3:12 as the designation for Israel throughout; and it employs the phrase *taḥat kol ʿēṣ raʿănān*, "under every green tree," from Jeremiah 3:13 to describe "apostate Israel's" harlotry in Jeremiah 3:6. By employing these themes and phrases, the author of Jeremiah 3:6–11 created a text that established the analogy between the actions of Israel and those of Judah in an effort to argue that the guilt of Judah is greater than the guilt of Israel; Judah had a prior example of the consequences of such actions, but Israel did not. By this means, Jeremiah 3:6–11 presents the premise for the final form of Jeremiah 2–6 as a whole, which warns Judah of the coming punishment from YHWH in the form of the unnamed "enemy from the north." It thereby calls for Judah's repentance, just as Israel was called to repent.

Similar concerns are evident in the framework material that appears at the beginning (Jer 2:1–2) and end (Jer 4:3–4) of the material addressed to the northern kingdom of Israel. Following the YHWH word transmission formula in v. 1, Jeremiah 2:2 contains a commissioning formula in which YHWH commissions the prophet to speak the following words "in the ears of Jerusalem." This is remarkable in that the following material does not speak directly about Jerusalem at all, but it speaks explicitly about Israel as indicated above. Apparently, this dichotomy was so striking that it influenced the Greek translator to omit the reference to Jerusalem in the LXX version of this text.[31] Nevertheless, such a distinction serves the purposes of the redaction evident in Jeremiah 3:6–11; the experience of the northern kingdom of Israel will serve as an example for Judah.

The same may be said for the juxtaposition of the address to Israel in Jeremiah 4:1–2, which states the conditions and resulting blessings for Israel's return to YHWH, and the address to Judah in Jeremiah 4:3–4, which is linked syntactically to 4:1–2 by the particle *kî*, "for, because." The address to Judah cannot be considered in isolation from that to Israel. The command for Judah and Jerusalem to "plow its own field" and to "circumcise itself" must be read in relation to the instructions to Israel to remove its filth and to restore righteousness

---

30. William McKane, "Relations between Poetry and Prose in the Book of Jeremiah with Special Reference to Jeremiah III 6–11 and XII 14–17," *VTSup* 32 (1981) 220–237, esp. 229–233.

31. See BHS note. LXX eliminates Jeremiah 2:1–2aα1, and reads simply *kai eipen tadei legei kurios*, "and he said, Thus says the L-rd." For a summary of various interpretative possibilities, see McKane, *Jeremiah 1* 26–27.

and justice; just as Israel must repent, so Judah and Jerusalem must likewise repent. Again, Israel provides the model for Jerusalem and Judah.

These considerations indicate the redactional character of Jeremiah 2:1–2, 3:6–11, and 4:3–4 in relation to Jeremiah 3:2–4:2, in that they transform an address to Israel into an address to Jerusalem and Judah. Two major exceptions to this pattern remain to be examined. The first occurs in Jeremiah 2:28 as an address to Judah that appears rather unexpectedly in the midst of an address to Israel (cf. Jer 2:26, 31), *kî mispar 'āreykā hāyû 'ĕlōheykā yĕhûdâ*, "for the number of your cities were as the number of your gods, O Judah." But this text appears to be a gloss in that it duplicates exactly the same phrase of Jeremiah 11:13, which addresses Judah's revolt against YHWH. It appears that a glossator or redactor employed this phrase to strengthen the overall context of an address to Judah in keeping with the outlook of the redactional form of this text throughout chapters 2–6. The second example appears in Jeremiah 3:18, which looks forward to the time when the "house of Judah" will walk together with the "house of Israel." But this statement is consistent with expectations that the northern kingdom would reunite with Judah under Davidic rule as a result of its repentance and return to YHWH in Zion (cf. Jer 3:14–17). It is not a secondary addition to this text.

These considerations demonstrate that a redaction has transformed a text addressed to the former northern kingdom of Israel to one addressed to Jerusalem and Judah. It employs the model of Israel's failure to repent and to return to YHWH as the premise for what will befall Jerusalem and Judah if they fail to do so. It is only the redactional material in Jeremiah 2:1–2aα[1], 2:28, 3:6–11, and 4:3–6:30 that establishes this analogy between Israel and Judah. If this material is removed, a relatively coherent text remains in which the northern kingdom of Israel is called to repentance and to return to YHWH at Zion. The text begins with a trial speech or divorce proceeding in Jeremiah 2:2aα[2–3]–3:5, which identifies Israel as YHWH's bride. It continues with YHWH's statements concerning the grounds for the divorce proceeding—that is, Israel has abandoned YHWH for other gods, and it contends that Israel has no basis to challenge the charges. A call for repentance follows in Jeremiah 3:12–4:2, in which Israel is given the chance to return to YHWH at Zion, provided the filth is removed and Israel is circumcised or purified from wrongdoing.

The setting for the earlier text addressed to Israel in Jeremiah 2:2–4:2* must be placed in the reign of King Josiah insofar as Josiah attempted to bring the former northern kingdom back under Davidic rule. The call for Israel to return to YHWH at Zion in Jeremiah 3:12–20 is key to this understanding in that it points to such an effort to bring the former northern kingdom back into the Davidic fold. Apart from Josiah's efforts, no Judean monarch is known to have attempted such a return from the time of Jeremiah on. Likewise, the charges that Israel is shifting its alliances from Assyria to Egypt are relevant. Although this can be understood in relation to the past historical experience of the northern kingdom during the eighth century, the late-seventh-century context is also relevant. As noted, Samaria was an Assyrian province during the seventh century B.C.E., but as Assyrian power weakened during the later years of Assurbanipal's reign and beyond, the Egyptians emerged as a major power in the Syro-Israelite corridor.[32] Insofar as Pharaoh Psamtek sent an army to the Euphrates region in support of Assyria by 616 B.C.E. at the latest, he would have to pass through the Jezreel Valley, as this represented the only reasonable means to move troops and equipment from Egypt to Mesopotamia at this time. In such a situation, Samarian/Israelite cooperation would be absolutely necessary, as Samaria was in a position to control access to the Jezreel. Such cooperation would be expected, not only because Egypt likely possessed the means to force Samaria to submit, but because Samaria would naturally be expected to step in to aid Egypt in its efforts to support the Assyrian overlord. A confrontational relationship is not necessary in these circumstances; the Assyrian appointed governor of Samaria, the Egyptians, and the Assyrians would all share a common interest in Assyria's survival.

Judah under the rule of Josiah, however, would share no such interest. Assyria had been Judah's overlord, but the demise of Assyrian power would represent the opportunity for Josiah to reassert Judah's independence to resume Davidic control over the former northern kingdom. This would provide the basis for calls to Israel to return to YHWH at Zion/Jerusalem. In such a scenario, Egypt stood as an obstacle to such goals. Hence, criticism of Israel for its shifting alliances from Assyria to Egypt are germane to the situation. In such a case, Jeremiah, a consistent supporter of a pro-Babylonian policy, could point to the experience of the formerly independent northern kingdom with both Assyria and Egypt; association with both of these countries led to disaster for Israel. Jeremiah's northern Benjaminite background would prove useful as well. He was a "homegrown" priest and prophet with roots in the ancient northern sanctuary at Beth-El, from a priestly family that had been expelled by Solomon. He employs characteristic northern themes, the portrayal of Israel as the bride of YHWH in the wilderness period, to express his views. His word would add credibility to a call to Israel to return to Jerusalem.

Likewise, the redaction that transformed the original address to Israel in Jeremiah 2:2–4:2* to the full address to Jerusalem and Judah in Jeremiah 2–6 would be the product of the prophet Jeremiah. In the aftermath of the death of Josiah in 609 and the submission of Judah to Egypt, the prophet could be expected to continue his criticism of alliance with Egypt. Certainly, the example of northern Israel's experience would be pertinent to Judah in this setting as alliance with Egypt had already led Israel to destruction during the eighth century and beyond. In this case, the shift in alliance from Assyria to Egypt reflects the realities of Judah under Jehoiakim's rule. The king was installed by Pharaoh Necho himself to be a compliant vassal. Jeremiah's opposition to such a pro-Egyptian monarch would aid in explaining the conflict that ensued between the prophet and the king during the course of his reign. Jeremiah's articulation of a message of punishment brought against Judah by means of an "enemy from the north" would fit in well with the

---

32. For discussion of the historical background for this period, see Hallo and Simpson, *The Ancient Near East: A History* 138–149; Hayes and Miller, eds., *Israelite and Judaean History* 435–476; Redford, *Egypt, Canaan, and Israel* 430–469.

rise of the Babylonian empire during this period and mirror the experience of Israel which was destroyed by an "enemy from the north," while allied with Egypt.

Jeremiah 30–31

Jeremiah 30–31 generally plays a major role in attempts to reconstruct the words of the prophet from the time of Josiah.[33] Although it appears to be a component of a larger "Book of Consolation" in Jeremiah 30–33 that presupposes the destruction of Jerusalem and the demise of the Davidic dynasty, chapters 30–31 stand as a distinct block within the larger unit and display evidence that an earlier text form may stand behind the present form of the text. The present form of Jeremiah 30–31 calls for the restoration of Israel and the rebuilding of Jerusalem following the Babylonian exile. But, whereas this text calls for the restoration of *both* "the House of Israel" and "the House of Judah" at its beginning and end (Jer 30:2–3, 4; 31:27–30, 31–34; cf. 31:37–40), the bulk of the central portion of these chapters calls only for the restoration of a devastated Israel to Judah and the royal house of David (Jer 30:5–11; 31:7–14; cf. 30:18–31:1; 31:16–22).

Although some scholars argue that the term "Israel" in this text is a postexilic designation for the restored people of Israel and Judah,[34] scholars have persistently attempted to reconstruct an earlier text form that calls for the restoration of Israel. The motive for such an attempt lies not only in the evidence presented above that points to an address to Israel alone, but in concerns to establish a basis for the contention that Jeremiah spoke during the reign of Josiah and supported Josiah's attempts to restore the former northern kingdom to Davidic rule. Although numerous attempts of this nature have been made, they have been plagued by various problems, including difficulties in establishing the structure and outlook of the present form of the text, inconsistent literary criteria for the identification of redactional material within the text, difficulties in reconciling the prophet's message of judgment with the message of salvation contained within this text, and difficulties in distinguishing Jeremianic material from that considered to be Deuteronomistic.[35]

33. For a current discussion of Jeremiah 30–31, see the commentaries and Herrmann, *Jeremia* 146–163; Seybold, *Der Prophet Jeremia* 80–87; S. Böhmer, *Heimskehr und neuer Bund. Studien zur Jeremia 30–31* (Göttingen: Vandenhoeck & Ruprecht, 1976); N. Lohfink, "Der junge Jeremia als Propagandist und Poet. Zum Grundstock von Jer 30–31," *Le livre de Jérémie: Le prophète et son milieu, les oracles et leur transmission*, BETL LIV (Leuven: Peeters, 1981) 351–368; Barbara Bozak, *Life "Anew": A Literary-Theological Study of Jer. 30–31*, AnBib 122 (Rome: Pontifical Biblical Institute, 1991); Georg Fischer, *Das Trostbüchlein: Text, Komposition und Theologie von Jer 30–31*, SBB 26 (Stuttgart: Katholisches Bibelwerk, 1993); Marvin A. Sweeney, "Jeremiah 30–31 and King Josiah's Program of National Restoration and Religious Reform," *ZAW* 108 (1996) 569–583.

34. Paul Volz, *Der Prophet Jeremia*, KAT X (Leipzig: A. Deichert, 1922) 281; Volz, *Der Prophet Jeremia*, KAT X (Leipzig: A. Deichert, 1928) 284, who sees a Jeremianic core addressed to the northern kingdom that was expanded to include Judah in the postexilic period; see also William McKane, "The Composition of Jeremiah 30–31," in *Texts, Temples, and Traditions*, Fs. M. Haran, ed. M. V. Fox et al. (Winona Lake, Ind.: Eisenbrauns, 1996) 187–194.

35. For a full discussion of the problems in these chapters, see Herrmann, *Jeremia* 146–162.

Despite these problems, there does appear to be a clear formal criterion with Jeremiah 30–31 that can serve as the key for establishing the structure and interpretation of the text in its present form and for reconstructing an earlier text form within it.[36] Two characteristic formulas of this text introduce most of its constituent subunits, and, together, they establish the basic structure of the whole. The first, *kōh 'āmar yhwh*, "thus says YHWH," appears in Jeremiah 30:2, 18; 31:2, 15, 16, 23, 35, 37, and its variant, *kî kōh 'āmar yhwh*, "for thus says YHWH," appears in Jeremiah 30:5, 12; 31:7. The second, *hinnēh yāmîm bā'îm*, "behold, the days are coming," appears in Jeremiah 30:3; 31:27, 31, 38. Several observations are in order. First, *hinnēh yāmîm bā'îm* appears only at the beginning and end of this text; it does not appear in its central portions. Second, *hinnēh yāmîm bā'îm* consistently appears in contexts that address the fate of *both* Israel and Judah; it never introduces material that is concerned only with Israel. Third, passages introduced by (*kî*) *kōh 'āmar yhwh* address the situation of the former northern kingdom of Israel in a relatively consistent fashion. There are some exceptions, however, but these appear to conform to the general pattern of a text based on the formula (*kî*) *kōh 'āmar yhwh* and concern with the northern kingdom of Israel to Zion/David that has been redactionally expanded by material at the beginning and end based on the formula *hinnēh yāmîm bā'îm* and a concern for the restoration of both Israel and Judah. Thus, both formulas appear together in Jeremiah 30:1–4, but this subunit serves as an introduction to the final form of the text as a whole and lays out the basic premises of its structure and outlook. Jeremiah 30:12–17 addresses a wounded Zion rather than Israel, but this appears to be the result of a text-critical emendation in v. 17, in which the original reading *ṣêdēnû hî'* was altered to *ṣîyôn hî'* in keeping with the overall Judean orientation of the final form of the text, thereby producing its only reference to Zion.[37] Finally, Jeremiah 31:23–26 appears to address the restoration of Judah, but examination of this passage in context demonstrates that the restoration of Judah constitutes the culmination of Israel's return to Zion and thereby serves the interests of a text that calls for Israel's return.

Jeremiah 30–31 is demarcated initially by the formula, "the word which was unto Jeremiah from YHWH, saying. . . ." The conclusion of this text is marked by the appearance of similar formula in Jeremiah 32:1, "the word which was unto Jeremiah from YHWH," which marks the beginning of a new textual block. As noted, Jeremiah 30 and 31 are united formally by the appearances of the formulas *hinnēh yāmîm bā'îm* and (*kî*) *kōh 'āmar yhwh* at key points within the text and thematically by the concern with the restoration of Israel and Judah. Because the superscription in Jeremiah 30:1 introduces the entire text and identifies it as the word of YHWH to Jeremiah, the initial superstructure of Jeremiah 30–31 comprises the superscription in 30:1 and the report of YHWH's word in 30:2–31:40.

Because Jeremiah 30:2–31:40 is defined generically as a report of YHWH's word to Jeremiah, the basic structure of the passage is constituted by the formula

---

36. For a full discussion of these issues, see my "Jeremiah 30–31 and King Josiah's Program of National Restoration and Religious Reform."

37. See BHS note.

kōh 'āmar yhwh, "thus says YHWH," in Jeremiah 30:2, 18; 31:2, 15, 16, 23, 35, 37, which introduces each individual component of YHWH's word. Several other generic elements of the text are subordinated to this basic structure. Jeremiah 30:3 begins with the formula *kî hinnēh yāmîm bā 'îm*, "for behold the days are coming," but the introductory *kî*, "for, because," establishes its syntactic dependence on 30:2 and indicates that YHWH's word is directed toward the future restoration of Israel and Judah in the land. The report of YHWH's command to Jeremiah in Jeremiah 30:2–3 that he write the words in a book is followed by an introductory statement in 30:4 that identified the following words as those of YHWH to Israel and Judah. Nevertheless, this statement is linked syntactically to 30:2–3 by a conjunctive *waw*—that is, "and these are the words which YHWH spoke to Israel and to Judah"—which indicates that 30:4 is included structurally within the unit introduced by 30:2–3. Furthermore, the formula *kî kōh 'āmar yhwh*, "for thus says YHWH," appears in Jeremiah 30:5 and 12, but the initial particle *kî* is both causative and conjunctive in nature. These formulas thereby introduce textual subunits that are included structurally within the material introduced by 3:4; they are thereby worked into the general framework established by Jeremiah 3:2–3.

The initial report of YHWH's word therefore comprises Jeremiah 30:2–17. It begins in Jeremiah 30:2–3 with a report of YHWH's instructions to Jeremiah to write YHWH's words concerning the future restoration of Israel and Judah in a book. Jeremiah 30:4–17 constitutes the actual report of YHWH's initial words. Jeremiah 30:4 introduces the words and identifies them as YHWH's to Israel and Judah. Individual prophetic words then appear in Jeremiah 30:5–11 and 30:12–17, each introduced by the formula, "for thus says YHWH." Jeremiah 30:5–11 indicates Jacob's/Israel's present situation of distress, but announces that YHWH will save Israel from its captivity. Verses 8–11 indicate that Israel's deliverance will be realized in a return to YHWH and to the Davidic king. Jeremiah 30:12–17 reiterates the theme of Israel's punishment and captivity but announces that YHWH will punish those who torment Israel with an exile of their own. Each of these prophetic words may therefore be further defined generically as announcements of salvation for Israel.

The report of YHWH's second word appears in Jeremiah 30:18–31:1. Again, this word announces salvation for Israel in the form of restored fortunes and restored leadership by an Israelite prince. Likewise, v. 22 contains a version of the covenant formula, "and you shall be a people to me, and I shall be G-d to you," that indicates the restoration of Israel's fortunes and relationship with YHWH. In context, this word affirms YHWH's prior statements in 30:5–17 that Israel will be restored.

The report of YHWH's third word in Jeremiah 31:2–14 contains two basic components, each introduced by the formula (*kî*) *kōh 'āmar yhwh*. The first, Jeremiah 31:2–6, includes a 2fs address by YHWH to *bĕtûlat yiśrā'ēl*, "the maiden Israel," that focuses on the theme of Israel's restoration with the imagery of a bride dancing at the planting of vineyards. Again, the theme of a return to Zion enters with the concluding statement by the watchmen, "Arise, and let us go up to Zion, unto YHWH our G-d." The second is Jeremiah 31:7–14, which announces YHWH's restoration of Israel to the land from its captivity in the "land of the north." The passage is directed to the nations, and it reiterates the themes of a return to Zion, the fertility of the crops and animals, the dancing maidens, and general rejoicing.

The report of YHWH's fourth word appears in Jeremiah 31:15. It simply describes Rachel's weeping for her lost sons and thereby returns the theme of Israel's punishment as Rachel is the mother of Joseph (i.e., Ephraim and Manasseh) and Benjamin, the key tribes of the northern kingdom. In this manner, it aids in providing the basis for the call to repentance that follows.

The report of YHWH's fifth word in Jeremiah 31:16–22 focuses on the theme of Israel's repentance. It begins with the word report proper in vv. 16–20, which includes commands to cease weeping, reports of Ephraim's decision to repent of return, and assertions by YHWH that the relationship with Ephraim, YHWH's "dear" son, is secure. As indicated by the 3ms references to YHWH in vv. 21–22, the prophet interjects with an address to the maiden Israel to return by highway to her cities.

The report of YHWH's sixth word in Jeremiah 31:23–34 begins with a word report in vv. 23–25 that emphasizes the restoration of Judah. Here, YHWH is identified as "YHWH Sebaot, G-d of Israel," employing a title that emphasizes YHWH's role over Israel as over Judah and that suggests the restoration of Israel to Zion. Verses 26–34 then supply the prophet's own words that build upon the imagery of vv. 23–25 to portray a new covenant between YHWH and a reunited Israel and Judah. Three basic subunits appear within the prophet's report. The prophet reports his visionary experience in v. 26, which presumably indicates the setting in which the words of YHWH were communicated to him. Verses 27–30, introduced by the formula *hinnēh yāmîm bāʾîm*, portray the future restoration of Israel and Judah with the imagery of a replanted land. Verses 31–34, likewise introduced by the formula *hinnēh yāmîm bāʾîm*, announces a new covenant between YHWH, here self-identified as husband, and Israel/Judah in which YHWH's Torah will be written upon the heart.

The report of YHWH's seventh word in Jeremiah 31:35–36 focuses on YHWH's eternal promise to Israel. It employs the imagery of YHWH as creator to indicate that YHWH's promise of security to Israel is as secure as the created order of the universe.

Finally, the report of YHWH's eighth word in Jeremiah 31:37–40 focuses on YHWH's promise to Jerusalem. The word report in v. 37 reiterates the theme of the previous subunit in that YHWH promises not to cast off the descendants of *Israel* as long as the created order is in place. The prophet's announcement of the future, introduced by the formula *hinnēh yāmîm bāʾîm*, then focuses on the future restoration of Jerusalem, especially the rebuilding of three of its major districts.

The structure of Jeremiah 30–31 may be portrayed as in table 13.1. As indicated by the references to the rebuilding of Jerusalem in Jeremiah 31:38–40 and the concern with the restoration of both Israel and Judah, the setting for the present form of Jeremiah 30–31 clearly lies in the aftermath of the Babylonian destruction of Jerusalem in 587 B.C.E. Although these chapters presuppose a distinction between Israel and Judah throughout, they clearly presuppose that the fate of both countries is interrelated in that the restoration of Israel is presented coterminously with the restoration of Judah. Insofar as the restoration is presented in terms of Israel's return to Zion, the restoration of Jerusalem appears to constitute the rhetorical goal of

TABLE 13.1   Structure of Jeremiah 30–31

Prophet's report of YHWH's word: Restoration of Israel and Judah	*30:1–31:40*
I. Superscription	30:1
II. Prophet's report of YHWH's words	30:2–31:40
A. Initial word: instruction to write YHWH's words in a book	30:2–17
1. Report of instruction: future restoration of Israel and Judah	30:2–3
a. Report of instruction proper	30:2
b. Basis for instruction: future restoration of Israel and Judah	30:3
2. Report of YHWH's word concerning Israel and Judah	30:4–17
a. Introduction: identification as YHWH's word	30:4
b. First word concerning Jacob: prophetic announcement of salvation	30:5–11
c. Second word concerning Zion: prophetic announcement of salvation	30:12–17
B. Second word: salvation for Israel	30:18–31:1
C. Third word: restoration of Israel to Zion	31:2–14
1. Initial word report: description of Israel's restoration	31:2–6
2. Second word report: announcement of Israel's restoration	31:7–14
D. Fourth word: portrayal of Rachel weeping for lost sons	31:15
E. Fifth word: repentance of Israel	31:16–22
1. Word report proper	31:16–20
2. Prophet's exhortation to Ephraim to return	31:21–22
F. Sixth word: announcement of new covenant	31:23–34
1. Word report proper: restoration of Judah	31:23–25
2. Prophet's announcement of future vision	31:26–34
a. Report of prophet's vision	31:26
b. First announcement: restoration of Israel and Judah	31:27–30
c. Second announcement: new covenant	31:31–34
G. Seventh word: eternal promise to Israel	31:35–36
H. Eighth word: eternal promise to Jerusalem	31:37–40
1. Word report proper: eternal promise to seed of Israel	31:37
2. Prophet's announcement of future: restoration of Jerusalem	31:38–40

the text. In the present instance, the restoration of Israel and Judah at Zion is presented as the establishment of a new covenant with YHWH, which is clearly required in the aftermath of the Babylonian destruction of Jerusalem and the Temple that called the old relationship between YHWH and the people into question.

Overall, the scenario is presented as a vision or dream of the prophet, but it is not entirely clear that Jeremiah is the author of the final form of Jeremiah 30–31. The reference in Jeremiah 31:29–30 to the proverb concerning the fathers' eating sour grapes so that the children's teeth are set on edge in relation to the assertion of individual moral responsibility corresponds much more closely to Ezekiel 18 than it does to Jeremiah, who tends to focus on the moral responsibility of the nation as a whole. Likewise, the references to a new covenant inscribed upon the heart in Jeremiah 31:31–34 correspond to the statements in Ezekiel 18:30–32 that the house of Israel needs a new heart and a new spirit to return from transgression.[38] Finally,

---

38. Cf. Holladay, *Jeremiah 2* (Hermeneia; Minneapolis: Fortress, 1989) 163–164, who argues that the theme of individual moral responsibility is secondary to Ezekiel 18.

the verbs employed in Jeremiah 31:28 (cf. v. 40) to describe both the destruction and rebuilding of the land are the same verbs employed in the prophet's vocation account in Jeremiah 1:10, which suggests redactional activity by a later hand interested in tying the present chapters into the overall framework of the book. On the basis of these references, it would seem that the present form of Jeremiah 30–31 dates to some time during the Babylonian exile and addresses the restoration of Israel and Judah to the land, but it is unlikely that Jeremiah is responsible for the final form of this text.

As noted, there is considerable evidence that the present form of Jeremiah 30–31 is the product of redactional activity that reworked a text concerned with the return of northern Israel to YHWH, Zion, and Davidic rule into a text concerned with the restoration of Israel and Judah to the land, the rebuilding of Jerusalem, and the establishment of a new covenant between YHWH and the people. The interrelationship between the two formulas characteristic of this text appears to provide a primary criterion for this view in that (*kî*) *kōh 'āmar yhwh* constitutes the basic structure of the text and addresses the concern with Israel's return to Zion, and so on, whereas *hinnēh yāmîm bā'îm* appears only at the beginning and end of the text and consistently addresses a concern with the restoration of both Israel and Judah. In all cases, texts introduced by the latter formula appear to supplement and draw out the meaning of texts introduced by the former. This is clear in Jeremiah 30:2–3, 4 where v. 2, introduced by *kî kōh 'āmar yhwh*, conveys an instruction to Jeremiah by YHWH, G-d of Israel, to write YHWH's words in a book, whereas v. 3, introduced by *hinnēh yāmîm bā'îm*, points to the future realization of these words in the return of Israel's and Judah's captivity to the land. Verse 4 immediately follows and identifies the subsequent words as those of YHWH concerning Israel and Judah. The feature is likewise apparent in Jeremiah 31:37–40. Whereas v. 37 is introduced by *kōh 'āmar yhwh* and addresses the security of the descendants of Israel, vv. 38–40, introduced by *hinnēh yāmîm bā'îm*, focuses on the future restoration of Jerusalem.

Two potential exceptions to this pattern appear in Jeremiah 30:12–17 and 31:23–25, in that they constitute texts introduced by (*kî*) *kōh 'āmar yhwh* that address the situation of Jerusalem or Judah rather than Israel. The first appears to be the result of a text-critical emendation. The only reference to Jerusalem in Jeremiah 30:12–17 appears in v. 17, which reads *ṣîyôn hî'*, "it is Zion," in reference to the wounded outcast for whom YHWH cares. The LXX, however, reads *thēreuma hēmōn*, "our prey," in place of *ṣîyôn*, which presupposes Hebrew *ṣēdēnû*, "our prey, game."[39] A reference to our prey makes perfect sense in the context of a text that speaks of YHWH's care for a victim wounded by devouring and plundering foes.[40] If the text is read with LXX, it corresponds well to an immediate context that addresses YHWH's concern for Israel and its restoration. If it is read with MT, it fits well with an overall context that addresses the restoration of Zion. It would appear that the LXX reading reflects an earlier text form and that the MT

---

39. See BHS note.
40. Cf. Holladay, *Jeremiah 2* 176.

reading represents a scribal emendation in keeping with a reading of the final form of Jeremiah 30–31.

Jeremiah 31:23–25 likewise seems to be an exception in that it addresses the restoration of Judah, but the formulation of this text and its position within the overall structure of the "words of YHWH" indicates that it plays a role in establishing Judah as the goal of Israel's return and restoration. It is introduced by an expanded version of the formula that appears in prior texts, *kōh 'āmar yhwh ṣĕbā'ôt 'lhy yiśrā'ēl*, "thus says YHWH of Hosts, G-d of Israel." Several observations are in order. First, the reference to YHWH as "G-d of Israel" corresponds to the similar reference to YHWH in Jeremiah 30:2, "Thus says YHWH, G-d of Israel," which indicates a concern to identify YHWH with the northern kingdom in both texts. Second, Jeremiah 31:23–25 follows immediately upon Jeremiah 31:21–22, which calls for the maiden Israel to return by highway to her cities. Jeremiah 31:23–25 identifies these cities as the cities of Judah, and thereby serves the earlier interest expressed in Jeremiah 30:8–9; 31:6, 12 that Israel return to David and Zion. Furthermore, the reference in Jeremiah 31:22 to a female who will "encompass a man" recapitulates the gender role reversal evident at the beginning of the sequence of texts concerned with the restoration of Israel in Jeremiah 30:5–7, which portrays men screaming as if they were in childbirth as a means to illustrate Israel's distress.[41] Third, Jeremiah 31:23–25 appears in sequence prior to Jeremiah 31:35–36; 31:37, which portray YHWH's relationship with the descendants of *Israel* as secure as the created order of the cosmos. In the current order of texts introduced by the formula "Thus says YHWH . . . ," Jeremiah 31:23–25 occupies a penultimate position that brings to a close the cycle of disruption and the call for return evident from Jeremiah 30:2 on. Following its portrayal of a secure pastoral setting in the cities of Judah, the goal to which the maiden Israel travels, Jeremiah 31:35–36, 37 portray a secure Israel. It also suggests that by the end of the sequence, "Israel" does not refer only to the northern kingdom, but to the united people of Israel.

These considerations indicate that Jeremiah 30:3, 4; 31:27–34; 31:38–40 are the result of a later redaction that reworked an earlier text that appears in Jeremiah 30:1–2; 30:5–31:26; 31:35–36; 31:37. Naturally, it cannot be absolutely certain that these verses represent the full original text form, as other material may have been eliminated or existing material may have been modified. Nevertheless, a relatively coherent text emerges, which articulates a coherent message concerning the return of the former northern kingdom of Israel to YHWH, Zion, and the Davidic king. The text is formulated as a series of statements by the prophet of YHWH's word, introduced by a form of the messenger formula, "(for) thus says YHWH . . . ," in Jeremiah 30:1–2; 30:5–11; 30:12–17; 30:18–31:1; 31:2–6; 31:7–14; 31:15; 31:16–22; and 31:23–25. The prophet's statements in Jeremiah 31:3, 26 that he awoke from a sleep in which he "saw," provides a visionary context for the following promises of YHWH's security to Israel in Jeremiah 31:35–36 and 31:37.

---

41. Cf. Holladay, *Jeremiah 2* 194–195; cf. Bernard W. Anderson, "The L-rd has Created Something New," *CBQ* 40 (1978) 463–478; Phyllis Trible, *G-d and the Rhetoric of Sexuality*, OBT (Philadelphia: Fortress, 1978) 40–50.

The setting for this text must be placed in relation to King Josiah's reforms, particularly his destruction of the Beth-El altar during the early years of the reform. Overall, the message of this text that Israel's welfare lies in its return to YHWH and the Davidic monarch at Zion corresponds well to the goals of Josiah's actions in relation to the northern kingdom. By destroying the altar at Beth-El, Josiah destroyed the primary religious symbol of northern Israel's revolt against the house of David (and the Jerusalem Temple). He likewise destroyed a primary symbol of Assyrian domination of Israel as 2 Kings 17:27–28 indicates that the Assyrians installed a priest at Beth-El to teach the people the law of the land and thereby to secure their hold on Israel by identifying themselves with the local cultic establishment. By destroying Beth-El, Josiah demonstrated that Assyrian power had passed, and that YHWH, through the resurgence of Judah and the Davidic dynasty in the aftermath of the Assyrian collapse, was acting to restore Israel's fortunes. Clearly, Israel had suffered as a result of the policies of its own monarchs. By calling on Israel to return to Zion, Jeremiah, a priest and prophet from the northern territory of Benjamin whose ancestors were deposed by Solomon, lent a certain native authority or justification to the call to return to Jerusalem. Israel had been wounded, but the danger had passed and it was now time for Israel to restore herself.

Employing characteristically northern traditions that portrayed Israel as a maiden who had wandered or as Rachel who mourned for her lost children, Jeremiah could call for the return of the northern tribes. Jeremiah's portrayal of Israel as wandering or returning to her home enabled the people of Israel to associate the prophet's message traditions of a redeemed Israel wandering through the wilderness to return to their land or Jacob returning from Aram to the land of Israel. Likewise, the motif of Rachel mourning for her lost children calls to mind Jacob's mourning for his beloved Rachel and his lost son Joseph. Furthermore, whereas later traditions associate Rachel's tomb with Ephrath, near Beth-lehem in the territory of Judah, earlier traditions place her tomb in the vicinity of Beth-El in an area that seems to be associate with weeping or mourning rituals.[42] This is particular important in relation to the portrayal of the maiden Israel returning by highway to Zion. There was a major highway in antiquity from Beth-El to Jerusalem that would serve as the conduit for the northern tribes to come to Jerusalem in the aftermath of Josiah's destruction of Beth-El. Furthermore, the references to the highway signposts, *ṣiyunîm* and *tamrûrîm* in Jeremiah 31:21, are important. The term *ṣiyûn*, "monument or roadmarker," associates assonantally with *ṣiyôn*, "Zion," and is employed in 2 Kings 23:17 to designate the tomb of the man of G-d at Beth-El who predicted Josiah's destruction of the Beth-El altar in 1 Kings 13:1–3. The term *tamrûr*, "pillar, waypost," alludes to the "tamarisk" (*tōmer*) of Deborah in Judges 4:5 and the "oak of weeping" associated with Rachel's nurse Deborah in Genesis 35:8, located south of Beth-El and north of Rachel's tomb.

Altogether, these factors point to Jeremiah's use of Israelite tradition to call on the people of northern Israel to return to Jerusalem and the house of David in

---

42. Cf. Judges 2:1–5; L. Luker, "Rachel's Tomb," *ABD* V, 608–609.

support of Josiah's efforts to reunite the people of Israel and Judah into one kingdom. The underlying text in Jeremiah 30–31* therefore corresponds to that of Jeremiah 2:2–4:2* insofar as both share the same concern to return the northern tribes to Jerusalem and Davidic rule. Nevertheless, the text in Jeremiah 30–31* must predate that of Jeremiah 2:2–4:2*. Whereas Jeremiah 2:2–4:2* presupposes a very real threat that Israel will turn to Egypt, Jeremiah 30–31* presupposes no such threat but simply calls for the return of Israel to Judah. Jeremiah 30–31* therefore must date to the early period of Josiah's reforms—that is, 621 B.C.E. and afterward. At this point, Babylon's revolt against Assyria had succeeded and the Assyrians were clearly falling back as Babylon advanced against them from the east. The likelihood of Assyrian defeat naturally opened the way for Josiah to act to recover Israel from its status as an Assyrian province and to return it to the Davidic fold. Although Egypt was already active in the Syro-Israelite corridor at this time, it was only later, in 616 B.C.E., that it appears to have secured its position in this area to the extent that it could send troops in support of Assyria against the Babylonians. The turn of Israel to Egypt at this time would have prompted the concerns expressed in Jeremiah 2:2–4:2*—that is, that Israel turn from Egypt and return to YHWH and David at Zion, as previously anticipated.

Overall, Jeremiah emerges as a prophet who was active during the course of King Josiah's reign. From the evidence presented above, it appears that the prophet supported Josiah's reform measures and called for the return of the former northern kingdom of Israel to the Jerusalem Temple and the house of David. It was only after Josiah's untimely death at the hands of Pharaoh Necho of Egypt in 609, and Judah's subsequent submission to Egypt, that Jeremiah began to conclude that, like Israel, Judah would suffer punishment for rebellion against YHWH's will at the hands of northern powers. Nevertheless, this analysis indicates that the seeds for a message of restoration also are evident in the earliest preaching of Jeremiah.[43] Just as the prophet envisioned the restoration of Israel in earliest work, so that message of restoration influenced the message of later forms of the book Jeremiah and its promises of a restored Jerusalem, Israel, and house of David in the aftermath of the Babylonian exile.

43. Cf. Kilpp, *Niederreissen und aufbauen* 177–182, who argues that Jeremiah was a theologically reflective prophet who proclaimed salvation to Judah and the former northern kingdom of Israel.

14

Isaiah

A lthough the prophet Isaiah ben Amoz lived during the latter part of the eighth century B.C.E. when the Assyrian empire first asserted its control over the Syro-Israelite region, the book of Isaiah constitutes an important source for the study of King Josiah's reign and its presentation in biblical literature. Scholars have long noted that the present form of the book of Isaiah is the product of extensive redactional activity that expanded the earliest forms of the oracles of Isaiah ben Amoz into a sixty-six-chapter book that contains the works of prophet writers from the preexilic, exilic, and postexilic periods, and presents a theological interpretation of some four hundred years of Judean historical experience and expectations for the future.[1] The present form of the book dates to the period of Ezra's reforms in the late fifth century B.C.E., and employs the figure and words of Isaiah ben Amoz, as well as the words of later prophets or writers that appear in the book, as a means to legitimize Ezra's measures and plans as the object of YHWH's intentions for Jerusalem, the people of Israel and Judah, and the world.[2]

A great deal of scholarly effort has been directed to the study and reconstruction of the literary history of the book. The most commonly known paradigm for the literary history remains Duhm's classic identification of three major bodies of

---

1. For a survey of recent discussion on the formation of the book of Isaiah as a whole, see Marvin A. Sweeney, "The Book of Isaiah in Recent Research," *CR:BS* 1 (1993) 141–162. For surveys of research on Isaiah 1–39, see J. Vermeylen, *Du prophète d'Isaïe à l'apocalyptique*, 2 vols., EB (Paris: Gabalda, 1977–78) 1–31; Hans Wildberger, *Jesaja 28–39*, BKAT X/3 (Neukirchen-Vluyn: Neukirchener, 1982) 1529–1547; Rudolph Kilian, *Jesaja 1–39*, ErFor 200 (Darmstadt: Wissenschaftliche Buchgesellschaft, 1983); J. Barton, *Isaiah 1–39*, OT Guides (Sheffield: JSOT Press, 1995); Marvin A. Sweeney, "Isaiah 1–39 in Recent Critical Research," *CR:BS* 4 (1996) 79–113.

2. See Sweeney, *Isaiah 1–39* esp. 31–62.

prophetic material within the book: (1) Isaiah 1–39, which reflects the oracles and life of the eighth-century prophet Isaiah ben Amoz; (2) Isaiah 40–55, which constitutes the writings of an anonymous prophet from the period of the sixth-century Babylonian exile; and (3) Isaiah 56–66, which contains the writings of an individual prophet or a group of prophet who wrote during the period of the Judean restoration from the late sixth through the end of the fifth century B.C.E.[3] The issue is complicated by the appearance of a great deal of later material in Isaiah 1–39, for example, the exilic oracle against Babylon in Isaiah 13; the so-called Isaiah apocalypse in Isaiah 24–27 and the "little apocalypse" in Isaiah 34–35 from the exilic or postexilic periods; and other texts throughout First Isaiah (Isaiah 1–39) that demonstrate the redactional shaping and presentation of First Isaiah according to the theological and hermeneutical perspectives of writers from much later times. The result has been a variety of interpretations of the literary history of the book of Isaiah, especially of Isaiah 1–39, together with a variety of viewpoints concerning the message and activities of Isaiah ben Amoz. Because of the complexity of the issues involved, scholars frequently raise questions as to whether it is even possible to attempt such literary-historical reconstruction.[4]

Despite the difficulties involved in the reconstruction of the literary history of the book of Isaiah, the nature of the literature, and indeed theological exegesis, demands such efforts. This literature was produced by Judean writers, including Isaiah ben Amoz and those who followed him, who addressed the concerns and issues of their respective historical contexts, and thereby articulated their understandings of YHWH's activities in the world and intentions for its future in relation to those specific historical contexts.[5] Those historically rooted viewpoints may or may not have been shared by the later writers and readers of the Isaiah tradition, but they played a major role in shaping the literary traditions that provided the basis for later Isaianic writers and communities of readers who understood the Isaiah tradition as sacred scripture, interpreted it according to their own historically conditioned needs and viewpoints, and transmitted it through the generations. Altogether, this points to a prophetic book that is formed by real people in relation to real historical experience and future expectation. To be sure, the historical dimension is not the only means to approach the book and it may well result in mistaken historical reconstructions and interpretations; after all, all scholarly reconstructions are inherently hypothetical and their validity must be continually tested as new information or perspectives become available. But to ignore this dimension of the book of Isaiah would result in fundamental misunderstanding of the nature and message of the book, including its presentation of Isaiah ben Amoz, the experience of Jerusalem, Judah, and Israel articulated within, and its understanding of G-d.

With this in mind, it is important to note for the present concern with Josiah that a significant number of scholars have argued for the existence of an edition of the book of Isaiah that was produced in the seventh century during the reign of

3. Bernard Duhm, *Das Buch Jesaia* (Göttingen: Vandenhoeck & Ruprecht, 1968) esp. 7–22.

4. For example, Edgar Conrad, *Reading Isaiah*, OBT (Minneapolis: Fortress, 1991) esp. 3–33.

5. See Sweeney, *Isaiah 1–39* 10–15.

King Josiah of Judah.[6] Given the above-mentioned problems in the literary-historical reconstruction of biblical literature, the hypothesis is not accepted by all scholars in the field nor do all those who hold to the hypothesis agree on the definition of the texts included within the proposed Josianic edition of Isaiah. Nevertheless, those who do argue for such an edition, Barth, Vermeylen, Clements, L'Heureux, Sheppard, and the present writer, among others, agree that some form of the book was produced in the late seventh century to justify and to articulate King Josiah's reform measures as the goal of Isaiah ben Amoz's prophet message. To this end, Isaiah's calls for the downfall of the Assyrian empire (e.g., Isa 10:5–34) and the rise of the house of David (e.g., Isa 9:1–6; 11:1–9) were to be realized in the reign of Josiah, who freed Judah from its status as an Assyrian vassal and attempted to reestablish an independent Davidic monarchy. Further elements of the Isaiah tradition also play a role. The criticism of Israel and Judah and their punishment at the hands of the Assyrians (e.g., Isa 5:1–30; 9:7–10:5; 28–31) were acts of punishment authorized by YHWH for the people's and the king's lack of faith in YHWH as their G-d. But once the punishment had accomplished its goals of humbling the people and expressing YHWH's power, Judah and Israel would be restored under a righteous Davidic monarch and the people who had been exiled by the Assyrians would return to their homeland (e.g., Isa 11:10–16; 27:1–13; 32:1–20). Likewise, the nations would suffer YHWH's punishment as well as means for them to recognize YHWH's mastery of the world; the Assyrians would receive particular attention in this regard for their arrogance in failing to acknowledge YHWH as the source of their power (e.g., Isa 10:5–34; 14:24–27), but other nations, Philistia, Moab, Aram/Israel, Egypt, the Arabian desert tribes, and Tyre, also would come to recognize YHWH's power (Isa 14–23). Overall, the figure of Isaiah is employed in this edition to call for a return to YHWH by the king and the people as the means to see to a secure future (cf. Isa 36–37; contra Isaiah 7).

The Josianic edition of the book of Isaiah represents a combination of materials that stem from the eighth-century prophet Isaiah ben Amoz and materials that were composed specifically for the seventh-century edition of the book.[7] The purpose of the seventh-century material is to define the Josianic agenda and to shape the entire tradition so that it can be read in relation to the Josianic historical context and hermeneutical perspective. Several major blocks of material emerge. Isaiah 5–12 provides an overview of the destruction of Israel and the subjugation

---

6. Vermeylen, *Du prophète*; H. Barth, *Die Jesaja-Worte in der Josiazeit*, WMANT 48 (Neukirchen-Vluyn: Neukirchener, 1977); Ronald E. Clements, *Isaiah 1–39*, NCeB (Grand Rapids, Mich.: Eerdmans; London: Marshall, Morgan, and Scott, 1980); Conrad L'Heureux, "The Redactional History of Isaiah 5.1–10.4," in *In the Shelter of Elyon*, JSOTSup 31, Fs. G. W. Ahlström. ed. W. B. Barrick and J. R. Spencer (Sheffield: JSOT Press, 1984) 99–119; Gerald T. Sheppard, "The Anti-Assyrian Redaction and the Canonical Context of Isaiah 1–39," *JBL* 104 (1985) 193–216; F. Gonçalves, *L'expédition de Sennachérib en Palestine dans la littérature hébräique ancienne*, PIOL 34, Louvaine-la-neuve: Institut orientaliste (Université de Louvain, 1986); Sweeney, *Isaiah 1–39* passim; Sweeney, "Jesses New Shoot in Isaiah 11: A Josianic Reading of the Prophet Isaiah," in *A Gift of G-d in Due Season*, JSOTSup 225, Fs. J. A. Sanders, ed., D. M. Carr and R. D. Weis (Sheffield: Sheffield Academic Press, 1996) 103–118.

7. For an overview, see Sweeney, *Isaiah 1–39* 57–59.

of Judah by the Assyrians and calls for the punishment of Assyria and the rise of a righteous Davidic monarch who will restore the nation. Isaiah 14–23* contains the oracles against the nations that will suffer punishment from YHWH and thereby demonstrate YHWH's power in the world. Isaiah 27 takes up the punishment of Israel and calls for the restoration of the exiles to the homeland following the punishment of the oppressor, portrayed in mythological terms as the chaos monster Leviathan. Isaiah 28–32 presents oracles concerning the punishment of Jerusalem and the consequent emergence of the righteous Davidic monarch. Isaiah 36–37 constitutes an apocryphal tradition drawn from the book of Kings that portrays Hezekiah's (and Isaiah's) actions during the Assyrian monarch Sennacherib's siege of Jerusalem in 701 B.C.E. It is only when Hezekiah turns to YHWH in full piety and trust that the Assyrian army is destroyed and Jerusalem liberated. Overall, the narrative presents Hezekiah as a model of piety to be followed by the Davidic kings (and people) of the future.

Isaiah 5–12

Isaiah 5–12 is the first major textual of the book of Isaiah that contains material from the Josianic redaction.[8] Although Isaiah 1 and Isaiah 2–4 contain a great deal of material that stems from Isaiah ben Amoz, they are presently arranged to address the punishment and subsequent restoration or purification of Jerusalem and Judah, and therefore they presuppose the Babylonian exile.[9] There is no evidence of Josianic redaction in either text. Many scholars likewise argue that major elements of Isaiah 5–12 are also the product of the postexilic period, especially the royal oracles of Isaiah 11:1–16 (cf. Isa 9:1–6), which presents a scenario of a righteous Davidic monarch who will restore Israel from exile, but this view must be rejected.[10] It is based in large measure on the supposition that oracles of restoration for Israel and Judah or the house of David would presuppose the need for such restoration once the nation and the house of David had been destroyed by the Babylonians. A particularly important element in this thinking is the portrayal of the return of Israel's captives from exile in Assyria and Egypt in that such exile is conceived in relation to the Babylonian exile.

   This view sidesteps the language of the text by arguing that it must be understood allegorically. At no point is Babylonia ever mentioned in these chapters; the enemy who oppresses Israel/Judah is consistently portrayed as the Assyrian empire and the Assyrian monarch. Likewise, the captives do not return from exile in Babylonia, but from Assyria and Egypt, a situation fully in keeping with the results of the Assyrian destruction of Israel and subjugation of Judah. The Babylonian exile greatly influenced the worldview and writings of ancient Judah, but the Babylonian exile was not the only major exile experienced by the people

---

8. See esp. L'Heureux, "Isaiah 5.1–10.4"; Sweeney, "Jesse's New Shoot."

9. See Sweeney, *Isaiah 1–39* 112–211.

10. For example, Wildberger, *Jesaja 1–12*, BKAT X/1 (Neukirchen-Vluyn: Neukirchener, 1972) 438–446, 465–467, who argues that Isaiah 11:1–9 is Isaianic and 11:10–16 is postexilic; Otto Kaiser, *Isaiah 1–12: A Commentary*, OTL (Philadelphia: Westminster, 1983) 252–268.

of Israel and Judah in ancient times. Prior to the Babylonian exile, the Assyrian destruction of northern Israel and the deportation or flight of a great deal of its population constituted the greatest tragedy and challenge yet experienced by the people of Israel and Judah in their self- conception and understanding of G-d. Grappling with the problem of exile did not begin in the Babylonian period; it began in the aftermath of Israel's exile to Assyria, Egypt, and elsewhere in the ancient near-eastern world of the eighth and seventh centuries B.C.E. The projected restoration of Davidic rule over a reunited and restored people of Israel and Judah represented one means for addressing this problem. The likely setting for such thinking is King Josiah's program of national restoration and religious reform.

To establish the perspective of this text and its historical setting, it is first necessary to examine its structure and generic character. Isaiah 5–12 is defined thematically by its overall concern with the destruction of the northern kingdom of Israel by the Assyrians and the consequences of this destruction for Assyria, Judah, and the house of David. It is thereby distinguished from Isaiah 1 and Isaiah 2–4, which both focus on the punishment and projected restoration of Jerusalem (and Judah) as the center for YHWH's rule over the world, and from Isaiah 13–23 and Isaiah 24–27, which focus on the punishment of the nations or the world at large and the recognition by the nations of YHWH's worldwide sovereignty centered on Zion. Although distinct from the surrounding material, Isaiah 5–12 plays a crucial role in relation to these textual blocks. It argues that as a result of the destruction of Israel, a punishment brought about by YHWH for Israel's rejection of YHWH's Torah, the Assyrian monarch will display unbridled arrogance against YHWH by claiming world power for himself and by threatening Jerusalem. Consequently, YHWH will bring down the Assyrian monarch like an over-ripe olive tree that must be beaten and pruned of its extending branches and raise a righteous Davidic monarch, portrayed as a new root or shoot, that will restore the people of Israel and Judah in the aftermath of Assyria's fall. Isaiah 5–12 thereby explains the punishment suffered by Israel and Judah and prepares for the judgment against the nations and the restoration of Jerusalem in preparation for its role as the seat of YHWH's worldwide sovereignty that is articulated throughout the balance of the book.

The structure of Isaiah 5–12 illustrates this role.[11] The first major section of this textual block begins with an oracular sequence in Isaiah 5:1–30 that announces YHWH's judgment against both Israel and Judah. The premise for this announcement is the vineyard allegory of Isaiah 5:1–7 that establishes the guilt of the people by portraying them as a well-cared-for vineyard that, despite its owner's (i.e., YHWH's) best efforts to care for it, continually produces sour grapes. A series of woe oracle follows in Isaiah 5:8–24 that provide the details of the people's wrong-doings that justify punishment together with an announcement in Isaiah 5:25–30 that YHWH is summoning a foreign army (i.e., the Assyrians) to carry out the punishment.

---

11. For detailed discussion of the structure and interpretation of Isaiah 5–12, see Sweeney, *Isaiah 1–39* 112–211.

The second major section of this textual block appears in Isaiah 6–12, which elaborates on the preceding announcement of judgment against Israel and Judah by laying out the rationale for that judgment in terms of Isaiah's presentation of YHWH's plans for the punishment of the people and their consequent restoration. The narrative material in Isaiah 6:1–8:15 presents the rationale for YHWH's punishment of Israel and Judah in a manner that highlights the role of the prophet, both in relation to G-d and in relation to the Judean monarch Ahaz. The autobiographical vocation account of Isaiah 6 presents the prophet's vision of YHWH, in which YHWH announces the decision to punish the people until only a small remnant of the people, portrayed as a burning tree stump, remains. The narrative material in Isaiah 7:1–8:15 presents Isaiah's encounter with Ahaz, in which Ahaz rejects Isaiah's/YHWH's signs that YHWH will protect Jerusalem and the house of David if only the monarch will have faith in YHWH. As a result, Ahaz's and Jerusalem's fate is sealed. The second major subunit of Isaiah 6–12 appears in Isaiah 8:16–12:6 in the form of oracular material that articulates projected outcome of YHWH's plans. Isaiah 8:16–9:6 articulates the prophet's instructions concerning YHWH's signs and his decision to withdraw from public life and wait for the fulfillment of YHWH's plans. This appears in the form of a royal oracle that announces the birth of a righteous Davidic monarch. The oracular material in Isaiah 9:7–12:6 then takes up the question of Israel's, Assyria's, and Judah's respective fates as fulfillment of YHWH's signs. Isaiah 9:7–10:4 presents the prophet's warnings of judgment against Israel. Isaiah 10:5–12:6 then contrasts the downfall of the arrogant Assyrian monarch who blasphemes YHWH and threatens Jerusalem with the rise of the righteous Davidic monarch who will restore the people of Israel and Judah, establish sovereignty over various neighboring nations, and bring about the praise of YHWH in Zion as deliverer of the people.

Overall, Isaiah 5–12 constitutes prophetic instruction concerning the Assyrian judgment against Israel in that it points to the restoration of the Davidic empire as the outcome of the punishment. The structure of Isaiah 5–12 may be presented as in table 14.1. Isaiah 5–12 clearly portrays a scenario of judgment against the northern kingdom of Israel and the southern kingdom of Judah. But whereas the text presupposes the realities of Israel's destruction, as indicated by the very real images of Isaiah 9:7–10:4 and the Assyrian king's references to his conquest of Samaria, it only presents the threat of destruction against Jerusalem and Judah in the form of the signs that project punishment in Isaiah 7:18–25; 8:1–15; and 10:5–34. This is not to say that Jerusalem and Judah escape punishment as portrayed in this material; rather it points to the portrayal of Jerusalem (and Judah) as the remnant of Israel that will survive YHWH's punishment as articulated in Isaiah 6:11–13. This conception is resumed in Isaiah 10:20–26 that points to the people of Zion/Jerusalem as the remnant of Israel that will survive the punishment and turn to YHWH. This then prepares for the fall of Assyria and the restoration of the Davidic empire that follows.

For the most part, Isaiah 5–12 contains material that stems from the eighth-century prophet Isaiah ben Amoz, but it is organized and presented by the introduction of two major textual units that were written for this purpose as part of the

TABLE 14.1   Structure of Isaiah 5–12: Concerning the significance of the Assyrian punishment of Israel

Prophetic instruction: Restoration of the Davidic empire	*Isaiah 5:1–12:6*
I. Announcement of judgment against Israel and Judah	5:1–30
A. Allegorical announcement: vineyard allegory	5:1–7
B. Prophetic announcement of punishment against Israel and Judah	5:8–30
II. Explanation of punishment of Israel and Judah: establishment of renewed Davidic empire	6:1–12:6
A. Account concerning basis for punishment of Israel and Judah by Assyria	6:1–8:15
1. Autobiographical account of Isaiah's vision of YHWH	6:1–13
2. Narrative concerning Isaiah's encounter with faithless Ahaz	7:1–8:15
B. Announcement concerning fall of Assyria and restoration of Davidic empire	8:16–12:6
1. Prophetic instruction concerning YHWH's signs: birth of righteous Davidic monarch	8:16–9:6
2. Prophetic announcement concerning fulfillment of YHWH's signs	9:7–12:6
a. Concerning judgment against Israel	9:7–12:6
b. Concerning restoration of Davidic empire in aftermath of Assyria's fall	10:5–12:6

Josianic redaction of Isaiah. The first is Isaiah 11:1–12:6.[12] This text's portrayal of the Josianic concerns for the restoration of the exiles from Assyria and Egypt was already noted above, but several other factors confirm the Josianic authorship of this passage. The first is the portrayal of a reunited Israel and Judah that establishes its authority over the Philistines, Edom, Moab, and Ammon, and that presupposes the punishment of Egypt and Assyria. Egypt and Assyria were not only the locations to which many Israelites and Judeans fled or were deported in relation to the Assyrian invasions of the land, they were the major enemies of Judah in the late seventh century that blocked the possibility of a full Judean restoration under Josiah. Although the possibility of an alliance with Egypt may well have presented itself early in Josiah's reign as a result of a shared experience of Assyrian vassaldom, by 616 B.C.E. Egypt had clearly sided with Assyria against Babylon,[13] which placed it in opposition to Judah's interests in establishing its own independence. The portrayal of YHWH's punishment of Egypt with the imagery of a smitten sea or river and the dryshod crossing of the returning exiles certainly calls to mind the traditions of the Exodus from Egypt and the crossing of both the Red Sea and the Jordan River that would feed into Josiah's emphasis on Passover as a major celebration to renew the covenant with YHWH.

The second is the portrayal of Davidic dominance over Philistia, Edom, Moab, and Ammon. Such a concern naturally recalls the former Davidic empire that exercised suzerainty over these nations, but it also points to Josianic interests in

12. For detailed discussion of this passage, see Sweeney, *Isaiah 1–39* 196–211; Sweeney, "Jesse's New Shoot."

13. See the notice in the Babylonian Chronicle that places the Egyptian army as allies of Assyria against Babylon in 616 B.C.E. (*ANET* 304). See also Redford, *Egypt, Canaan, and Israel in Ancient Times* 446.

restoring that sovereignty.[14] This was not simply a matter of imperialistic ambition, although such concerns naturally form a part of the scenario. By the late seventh century B.C.E., each of these nations occupied territory and controlled populations of native Israelites that had once constituted a part of the united tribes of Israel and Judah. As archeological surveys of the land of Israel have demonstrated, Judah's population shifted away from the Shephelah during the seventh century B.C.E. as the Assyrians placed this region under the control of Philistia. Furthermore, as excavations at Tel Miqne, Philistine Ekron, demonstrate, the Assyrians established Ekron as a major center for the production of olive oil and moved large segments of the Israelite population to the site in order to facilitate that production.[15] The portrayal of the Assyrian monarch as an overripe olive tree that must be beaten and pruned and the consequent portrayal of the Davidic monarch as a shoot that grows out of the stump or branch of Jesse may well play on this feature as well. Both Moab and Ammon occupied territory east of the Jordan River that had once constituted the tribal territories of the half-tribe of Manasseh, Gad, and Reuben. Although this area had been contested and sometimes lost in the ninth century,[16] Tiglath Pileser's invasion of the region in 734–732 finally stripped this territory and its population from Israel and reformed it into an Assyrian province administered in cooperation with the Ammonites and Moabites who did not join the revolt.[17] The Edomites were able to take Eilat from Judah during the course of the Syro-Ephraimitic War in 735–734 B.C.E.,[18] and following Sennacherib's invasion of Judah in 701, the opportunity to encroach on Judean territory in the Negev was available. The scenario of Davidic dominance over these nations in Isaiah 11:11–16 simply testifies to the fact that Josiah wanted Israelite/Judean land and people back under Davidic rule.

The third factor is the portrayal of the righteous Davidic monarch in Isaiah 11:6–9 as a small child. Josiah, after all, was only eight years old when he assumed the throne in the aftermath of his father Amon's assassination.

Finally, the liturgical character of Isaiah 12:1–6 makes any secure dating extremely difficult, but its use of language from the Song of the Sea in Exodus 15 suggests some association with Passover, which played such an important role in Josiah's program.[19]

---

14. Cf. Christensen, "Zephaniah 2:4–15: A Theological Basis for Josiah's Program of Political Expansion," who makes similar points concerning the nations listed in Zephaniah 2:4–15.

15. On the excavations at Tel Miqne (Ekron), see Gitin, "Tel Miqne-Ekron: A Type Site for the Inner Coastal Plain in the Iron Age II Period"; Gitin, "Seventh Century B.C.E. Cultic Elements at Ekron," in *Proceedings of the Second International Congress on Biblical Archaeology, June 1990* (Jerusalem: Israel Exploration Society, 1993) 248–258.

16. See the Moabite Stone, which indicates Moabite control over the formerly Israelite territories east of the Jordan in the ninth century B.C.E. (*ANET* 320–321; see also the essays on the Moabite Stone in A. Dearman, ed., *Studies in the Mesha Inscription and Moab*, ABS 2 [Atlanta: Scholars Press, 1989]).

17. See my comments on the setting of the pronouncement concerning Moab in Isaiah 15–16 (Sweeney, *Isaiah 1–39* 246–249).

18. 2 Kings 16:6.

19. For a discussion of the citations from the Song of the Sea in Isaiah 12, see Sweeney, *Isaiah 1–39* 118.

The second major text within Isaiah 5–12 that apparently was composed as part of the Josianic redaction is Isaiah 7:1–25. This text plays a role in the larger structure of the book of Isaiah as well in that, together with Isaiah 36–37, it establishes the contrast between the model of the faithless Ahaz and the faithful Hezekiah.[20] Isaiah 7:1–9:6 and 36–37 portray both kings in similar situations of crisis as they prepare to meet an anticipated invasion of the land by a foreign army, the Syro-Ephraimitic coalition in the time of Ahaz and the Assyrian army in the time of Hezekiah. The comparison is highlighted by the prominent mention of the location of conversation at the upper pool on the highway to the fullers' field. But, whereas Hezekiah eventually gives up his attempt at self-reliance on his own military power and turns to YHWH for protection, Ahaz rejects the various signs of YHWH's protection offered by Isaiah and apparently chooses to call on Assyria for help instead. The results are predictable: the city of Jerusalem is delivered because of Hezekiah's piety, whereas Judah is forced to submit to Assyria as a result of the Assyrian invasion. The importance of the portrayal of the faithless versus the faithful monarch is highlighted by the question posed to Ahaz in Isaiah 7:9, "If you will not believe, surely you will not be established," a pun on the verb *'mn*, "to believe" (*hiphil*) or "to be established" (*niphal*), which conveys the Davidic ideology of YHWH's promise of security to Jerusalem and the House of David. Within the Josianic version of Isaiah, this theme helps to characterize Josiah as a righteous and faithful monarch like Hezekiah, who restores Jerusalem and the people of Israel, in contrast to other monarchs, such as Ahaz or Manasseh, who submitted to the Assyrians and thereby lost Judah's independence.

Several features of this text indicate that it has been edited as part of the Josianic redactions.[21] First, Isaiah 7:1, "In the days of Ahaz ben Jotham ben Uzziah, king of Judah, Rezin the king of Aram and Pekah ben Remaliah the king of Israel came to Jerusalem to wage war against, but they could not conquer it," appears to be drawn from 2 Kings 16:5, which introduces the Ahaz narrative concerning the Syro-Ephraimitic War in the DtrH, "Then Rezin king of Aram and Pekah ben Remaliah, king of Israel, came to wage war on Jerusalem and they besieged Ahaz but could not conquer him." The report form of Isaiah 7:1ff, together with its dependence on the DtrH, immediately establishes a relatively late date for this narrative as the DtrH looks back chronologically on the events it presents. Furthermore, the version of the statement in Isaiah 7:1 contains variations that indicate that the verse was edited to bring it into line with its context in Isaiah; the reference to Ahaz as the grandson of Uzziah, for example, relates the episode to the preceding portrayal of Isaiah vision in the year of Uzziah's death (Isa 6:1). Likewise, the reference to making war against "it" in Isaiah 7:1 marks a change from 2 Kings 16:5, which reports that Rezin and Pekah were besieging Ahaz. This is in keeping with the interest of the Isaiah narrative to focus not so much on the

---

20. See especially Peter Ackroyd, "Isaiah 36–39: Structure and Function," in *Studies in the Religious Traditions of the Old Testament* (London: SCM, 1987) 105–120, 274–278; originally published in *Von Kanaan bis Kerala*, AOAT 211, Fs. J. P. M. van der Ploeg, ed., W. C. Delsman et al. (Neukirchen-Vluyn: Neukirchener, 1982) 3–21.

21. See Sweeney, *Isaiah 1–39* 143–175.

individual king Ahaz as on the house of David as a whole (cf. Isa 7:2, 9, 13, 17) as opposed to the Kings narrative, which focuses on Ahaz. This interest in the house of David permeates the entire book of Isaiah, but it also prepares the reader for the Davidic oracles in Isaiah 9:1–6 and 11:1–16 in particular. The Josianic interest appears in relation to the restoration of the house of David in both of these oracles.

Second, the narrative clearly shifts from a first person autobiographical style in Isaiah 6:1–13 and 8:1–15 to a third-person style in 7:1–25. Upon closer inspection, this shift is apparent only in Isaiah 7:1–9, as the only indication of third-person style in vv. 10–25 appears at the beginning in v. 10. Many scholars have argued that Isaiah 7:1–25 constitutes an original autobiographical narrative by the prophet that was transformed into a third-person narrative by redactional activity. The appearance of Isaiah 7:1, derived from 2 Kings 16:5, and the links between Isaiah 7:2–9, which establish the contrast between the portrayal of Ahaz and that of Hezekiah in Isaiah 36–37 bear this out. It would appear that Isaiah 7 was deliberately modified to create the contrast between Ahaz and Hezekiah in Isaiah by the introduction or reworking of Isaiah 7:2–9 in the context of an original autobiographical narrative; the use of a modified version of 2 Kings 16:5 in Isaiah 7:1 and the reference to YHWH's speaking to Ahaz in Isaiah 7:10, whereas the balance of the text fits well into an autobiographical context, indicate editorial adjustment to accommodate vv. 2–9. Insofar as the Hezekiah narrative was likely employed in the Josianic period, and perhaps composed at that time or during the preceding reign of Manasseh as means to encourage change in the house of David's policy of submission to Assyria, it would appear that this redaction took place in the Josianic period as well. As noted, it highlights a view of proper Davidic action that is consonant with the interests of Josiah's restoration program.

There is some evidence of additional redactional activity in Isaiah 7:18–19 and 7:21–25, insofar as both of these passages represent instances of inner biblical exegesis on earlier Isaianic texts—that is, Isaiah 5:26 and 5:1–7, 28; 7:13–17, respectively. The inclusion of these verses thereby further ties the passage into the scenario of judgment against Israel and Judah that is articulated in Isaiah 5:1–30, and it changes the function of the sign of Immanuel in Isaiah 7:13–17 that specifies the time before the Assyrians would come anyway to attack the Syro-Ephraimitic coalition to an indication of the Assyrian threat against Judah.

This redactional composition of Isaiah 5–12 indicates an interest on the part of the Josianic writers to employ earlier Isaianic tradition as a means to address the concerns of their own times. Overall, it points to an understanding of the original Isaianic oracles as statements from the prophet, representing the will of YHWH, that anticipated the measures undertaken by Josiah in the late seventh century in his efforts to restore Judah and Israel as an independent state under Davidic rule. It especially points to the former northern kingdom of Israel as an important catalyst for YHWH's decision to bring the Assyrian empire as a vehicle of punishment, but it also points to faulty decisions and actions on the part of the House of David, represented by Ahaz, that brought Judah into the orbit of Assyria, thereby demonstrating a lack of faithfulness in YHWH and costing the nation its independence. The passage argues, however, that this situation of punishment is not permanent. With the introduction of a righteous Davidic monarch, who ruled with wisdom and the fear of YHWH, the fortunes of the state and the dynasty could be restored, in keeping with YHWH's promise to the House of David and the city of Jerusalem. As understood and presented by the Josianic writers, that righteous monarch was Josiah ben Amon.

Isaiah 14–23; 27*

The oracles against the nations in Isaiah 13–23 and the so-called Announcement of YHWH's New World Order in Isaiah 24–27 together form a major component of the final form of the book of Isaiah in that, together with Isaiah 5–12, they lay out YHWH's plans for exercising judgment against both Israel and the nations as a means to bring about a new world order based on YHWH's kingship in Zion.[22] In their present forms, both Isaiah 13–23 and 24–27 thereby function as part of the fifth-century edition of the book, and they address the perspective on YHWH's actions in the world articulated in relation to Ezra's reforms. The oracles against the nations are laid out as a series of prophetic "pronouncements" (*maśśā'ôt*), a generic form that identifies and elaborates on YHWH's actions in human affairs.[23] The current arrangement of "pronouncements," beginning with Babylon (and Philistia) in Isaiah 13–14, and continuing with Moab (Isa 15–16); Israel and Aram (Isa 17–18); Egypt (Isa 19–20); the Wilderness of the Sea or Chaldea (Isa 21:1–10); Duma (Isa 21:11–12); the Arabian desert (Isa 21:13–17); the Valley of Vision or Jerusalem (Isa 22); and Tyre (Isa 23) presupposes the conquest of territories comprising the Babylonian empire to the Persians in the late sixth century B.C.E. Nevertheless, both textual blocks show evidence that they are the products of earlier redaction. The oracle concerning Babylon in Isaiah 13:1–14:23, for example, is the product of the sixth-century edition of the book of Isaiah that posited YHWH's judgment against the Babylonian empire as part of a scenario in which YHWH's sovereignty would be manifested throughout the world. The passage thereby took up an earlier eighth-century oracle against the Assyrian monarch Sargon II in Isaiah 14:4b–21 and recontextualized it to address the downfall of the Babylonian monarch by adding the sixth-century oracle against Babylon in Isaiah 13:1–22 and transitional material in Isaiah 14:1–4a, 22–23, that was designed to tie the Sargon oracle into its new literary context. The eighth-century summary appraisal in Isaiah 14:24–27 was added at this point to establish the analogy between Babylon and Assyria in the sixth-century edition of Isaiah, and the eighth-century oracle concerning Philistia in Isaiah 14:28–32 highlights the need to rely on YHWH alone by pointing to the futility of Hezekiah's alliance with the Philistines. Altogether, the present form of Isaiah 13:1–14:32 emphasizes YHWH's sovereignty and power to destroy enemies who challenge that sovereignty. Earlier

---

22. For detailed discussion of Isaiah 13–23 and 24–27 and the individual texts contained within, see Sweeney, *Isaiah 1–39* 212–353.

23. On the *maśśā'* form, see Richard D. Weis, "A Definition of the Genre *Maśśā'* in the Hebrew Bible," Ph.D. Dissertation (Claremont, Calif.: Claremont Graduate School, 1986).

material in Isaiah 27 concerning Israel and its restoration by YHWH was taken up in the sixth-century composition of Isaiah 24–27, again to address the issue of YHWH's worldwide sovereignty by demonstrating that the oracles against Israel and the nations would result in YHWH's punishment of Israel/Judah and the Babylonian empire as a prelude to YHWH's world wide rule and restoration from Zion.

Apart from the sixth-century material evident in these chapters, it seems that a seventh-century Josianic edition of the oracles against the nations appears in Isaiah 14–23* and the oracle concerning Israel in Isaiah 27. It is difficult to specify the exact boundaries of the beginning of this text unit in that the oracle against Sargon in Isaiah 14:4b–21 and the material concerning the destruction of Assyria in Isaiah 14:24–27 and the Philistines in Isaiah 14:28–32 was so heavily reworked as part of the sixth-century oracle concerning Babylon. The issue is complicated by the fact that this material may well have followed directly upon the oracles in Isaiah 10:5–34 originally addressed to Sargon II in an eighth-century edition of Isaiah. In any case, an oracle portraying the downfall of the Assyrian monarch in Isaiah 14:4b–21 and a statement that YHWH would destroy Assyria in Isaiah 14:24–27 would form a fitting introduction to a Josianic edition of the oracles against the nations in Isaiah. Such an oracle would follow upon and contrast appropriately with the portrayal of the rise of a righteous Davidic monarch and the restoration of the nation Israel and Judah in Isaiah 11:1–12:6. The statements in Isaiah 14:26–27 that the downfall of Assyria represented YHWH's intentions concerning the entire earth would likewise provide a fitting introduction to the following oracles against the nations in a Josianic context. The oracle concerning Philistia, with its introductory reference to the death of Ahaz in Isaiah 14:28, would likewise contrast with the similar reference to the death of Uzziah in Isaiah 6:1, the narratives concerning Ahaz in Isaiah 7:1–8:15, and the material concerning a new Davidic monarch in Isaiah 8:16–12:6.

The balance of the oracles concerning the nations in Isaiah 15–23 contains material that dates largely to the eighth-century prophet Isaiah ben Amoz, but at several key points, the hand of a seventh-century Josianic writer is evident, viz., in Isaiah 16:13–14; 19:18–25[20:1–6]; and 23:15–18. Each of these passages plays a role in reinterpreting the previously existing Isaianic material in relation to the concerns of the Josianic edition of Isaiah.

The oracle concerning Moab in Isaiah 15–16 includes an eighth-century oracle by Isaiah ben Amoz in Isaiah 15:1–16:12 that portrays the Assyrian conquest of formerly Israelite territories east of the Jordan that had fallen to Moabite rule. Overall, it portrays an Assyrian advance at the time of the Syro-Ephraimitic War (734–732 B.C.E.) as far as the wadi Arnon, the former northern border of Moab prior to conquest of Israelite territory, and the consequent threat that the Assyrian move presented to the Moabites. The prophet apparently counseled Moabite cooperation with the Davidic monarch of Judah, upon whose request the Assyrians had entered the region in the first place, as means to preserve Moabite self-interest. Such a view would make a great deal of sense in 734–732. Although Judah would emerge from the Syro-Ephraimitic War as an Assyrian protectorate, its alliance with the Assyrians would give Judah and the Davidic monarch a great deal of leeway in dealing with its neighbors as it would emerge as the key Assyrian ally in the region, thereby presenting an opportunity to reestablish Judean and Davidic control over elements of the former Davidic empire.

This dimension of Isaiah 15–16 is very important to keep in mind when considering the summary appraisal that appears in Isaiah 16:13–14 in that it points to a Josianic interest in interpreting the oracle against Moab in relation to Josianic ambitions to bring Moab under Davidic control in the late seventh century B.C.E.[24] The passage begins with a statement that summarizes the preceding material as "the word which YHWH spoke concerning Moab in the past" and continues with a statement that projects Moab's ill fortune in three years. This statement clearly presupposes the oracle against Moab as a past reality, and, in projecting the upcoming misfortune of Moab, it does not presuppose the actual destruction of Moab by the Babylonians in 582 B.C.E. It does presuppose the interests of Josiah in the late seventh century, however, to reestablish Davidic authority over the Moabites and thereby to return the former Trans-Jordanian territories of Israel, and their Israelite inhabitants, back under Israelite/Davidic control. In this regard, the Josianic addition of Isaiah 16:13–14 to Isaianic material in Isaiah 15:1–16:12 indicates that the Josianic redaction of Isaiah anticipated fulfillment of Isaiah's oracles concerning Moab in the reign of Josiah, insofar as Josiah was expected to reestablish the former Davidic state and restore all of Israel's exiles to their homeland and to Davidic rule.

Although the oracle in Isaiah 17–18 concerning the Syro-Ephraimitic coalition, viz., Israel and Aram, and its efforts to secure support from the Ethiopian dynasty that ruled Egypt stems entirely from Isaiah ben Amoz, it plays a role in the Josianic edition of the oracles against the nations in that it portrays the submission of Israel and Aram to YHWH and futility of looking to an outside power, Cush or Ethiopia. This latter point would be reinforced in the late seventh century by the fall of the Ethiopian dynasty in 664.

The oracle concerning Egypt in Isaiah 19–20, however, demonstrates evidence of Josianic redactional work. It builds on an original oracle by Isaiah ben Amoz concerning the futility of an Israelite alliance with Egypt at the time of its revolt against Assyria in 724 B.C.E., due to the infighting that was taking place within Egypt at that time. It concludes in Isaiah 19:16–17 with a projection that even tiny Judah would provoke fear within Egypt because of its internal weakness. This last statement, however, becomes the basis on which the Josianic redaction builds in Isaiah 19:18–25 and 20:1–6. Isaiah 19:18–25 apparently reflects the mid-seventh century, when Judah was firmly aligned with both Egypt and Assyria, and Judean mercenaries had set up various military colonies in Egypt at Memphis, Pathros, Tahpanhes-Daphnae, Migdol (cf. Jer 44:1), and Elephantine.[25] The apocryphal narrative in Isaiah 20:1–6 concerning Isaiah's symbolic actions during the Assyrian

---

24. On the summary-appraisal form, see Brevard S. Childs, *Isaiah and the Assyrian Crisis*, SBT 2/3 (London: SCM, 1967) 128–136; J. W. Whedbee, *Isaiah and Wisdom* (Nashville: Abingdon, 1971) 75–79.

25. Contra most scholars, for example, Hans Wildberger, *Jesaja 13–27*, BKAT X/2 (Neukirchen-Vluyn: Neukirchener, 1978) 727–746, who place this material in the postexilic period.

siege of Ashdod, however, highlights the defeat of Egypt once again in keeping with the perspective of the original oracle in Isaiah 19:1–17. Such a condemnation of Egypt in association with the imagery of a siege of Ashdod must be considered in relation to the twenty-nine-year siege of Ashdod carried out by the Egyptian Pharaoh Psamtek I in the late seventh century B.C.E. (cf. Herodotus 2.157). Such an action on the part of Egypt signaled Egyptian intentions to assert their control over the Syro-Israelite corridor and thereby identified the Egyptians as a power inimical to Judean/Josianic interests. By placing this narrative in its present position, the Josianic redaction highlights the theme of Egyptian weakness and defeat and projects Judah as the beneficiary of such weakness as the Egyptians (and Assyrians) come to recognize YHWH (and Israel).

The oracles concerning the wilderness of the sea—that is, Chaldea in Isaiah 21:1–10; Dumah in Isaiah 21:11–12; the Arabian desert in Isaiah 21:13–17; and the Valley of Vision or Jerusalem in Isaiah 22—all stem from Isaiah ben Amoz. In the context of the Josianic edition of the oracles against the nations, they testify to YHWH's power over the Babylonians and their allies in the north Arabian regions, who were allied with Josiah against Assyria (and Egypt) during the course of his reign. All highlight the suffering of these nations at the hands of the Assyrians.

The oracle concerning Tyre in Isaiah 23:1–18 likewise demonstrates the influence of Josianic redaction. It is based on an eighth-century oracle in Isaiah 23:1–14 by Isaiah ben Amoz that portrays Phoenicia's defeat by the Assyrian monarch Sennacherib in 701 B.C.E. that broke the back of Hezekiah's alliance against Assyria and brought his allies scurrying to Sennacherib to demonstrate their loyalty.[26] Isaiah 23:15–18 presents a very different picture, however, of a restored Tyre resuming its commercial contacts. The reference to a seventy-year period for such restoration and the notice that Tyre's merchandise and hire will be dedicated to YHWH indicate the work of the Josianic writer. The seventy-year period brings the date to 631 B.C.E., well within the reign of Josiah; coincidentally, it corresponds to the eighth year of Josiah's reign when, according to 2 Chronicles 34:3, the young monarch began to seek YHWH. The dedication of merchandise and hire as "holy to YHWH" calls to mind the resumption of the commercial relationship between David/Solomon and Hiram of Tyre from the days of the united Davidic empire. The resumption of such a relationship would clearly benefit Josiah's attempts to restore Israel/Judah in the late seventh century. It likewise points to an effort to demonstrate that Isaiah ben Amoz addressed the Josianic restoration of Israel and Judah.

Finally, Isaiah 27:1–13 appears to be the product of Josianic redaction as well. Although it is firmly integrated into Isaiah 24–27, scholars have continually noted its distinctive perspective in relation to chapters 24–26 in that it focuses on Israel and Jacob rather than up the nations and Zion. Several other features are noteworthy. First, it reverses the imagery of the original vineyard allegory in Isaiah 5:1–7

---

26. For an overview of Sennacherib's invasion of Judah, see Miller and Hayes, *A History of Ancient Israel and Judah* 353–363.

that pointed to judgment against Israel and Judah by portraying a new vineyard with which YHWH is greatly satisfied. Second, it employs the vineyard imagery to portray the restoration of Israel and Jacob after a period of smiting in which they had been punished for their idolatry. Third, it highlights the theme of the restoration of Israel's captives from both Egypt and Assyria. Judean captives are not mentioned, but the restored captives return to Zion where they worship YHWH. Altogether, the imagery and themes of this passage correspond to the restoration of the program of Josiah. It is difficult to be certain concerning the placement of this passage in the Josianic edition of Isaiah, but it would provide a fitting conclusion to the oracles against the nations, in that it would presuppose the manifestation of YHWH's power throughout the world and conclude with a reversal of the vineyard theme of punishment in Isaiah 5:1–7 and a reiteration of the restoration of Israel's captives from among the nations that is articulated in Isaiah 11:10–16. Such a capstone to a Josianic block in Isaiah 5–27* would once again demonstrate a concerted effort to relate the oracles of Isaiah ben Amoz to the restoration program envisaged in the time of Josiah.

Isaiah 28–32

Although Isaiah 28–33 forms a distinct textual unit within the larger structure of the fifth-century edition of the book of Isaiah, a block of material from the Josianic redaction of Isaiah appears in Isaiah 28–32.[27] As indicated by its citations and allusions to other texts and themes throughout the book of Isaiah, Isaiah 33 is a fifth-century composition that portrays the downfall of the anonymous oppressor and the rise of YHWH as king as means to summarize the first half of the book of Isaiah in Isaiah 1–33 and prepare for the second half in Isaiah 34–66.[28] It appears to have been added onto the basic structure of Isaiah 28–32, which is defined by the introductory *hôy*, "woe!" exclamations in Isaiah 28:1; 29:1; 30:1; 31:1 and the climactic *hēn*, "behold!" of Isaiah 32:1. The introductory *hôy* of Isaiah 33:1 resumes the earlier exclamations of the unit in a passage that draws out the meaning of Isaiah 32 by contrasting the downfall of the oppressor with the king of Isaiah 32 and identifying that king as YHWH.

With the absence of Isaiah 33, the Josianic edition of Isaiah 28–32 presents a sequence of passages that focus especially on YHWH's plans for the fate and future of Jerusalem, which follows naturally on the material concerned with Israel/Judah and the nations in Isaiah 5–12; 13–27/14–27*. Overall, these chapters provide the rationale for Jerusalem's experience. Isaiah 28 employs the analogy of the northern kingdom of Israel to argue that YHWH brought the Assyrians against Jerusalem as a means to remove the corrupt leadership of the city and thereby to prepare it for its future role in the world. Isaiah 29 argues that YHWH is the ultimate cause of the assault leveled against Ariel—that is, Jerusalem as symbolized by the presence of the Temple altar—and that the danger posed to Jerusalem will ultimately

27. For detailed discussion of Isaiah 28–33, see Sweeney, *Isaiah 1–39* 353–433.
28. See esp. W. A. M. Beuken, "Jesaja 33 als Spiegeltext im Jesajabuch," *ETL* 67 (1991) 5–35.

bring about the deliverance of Jacob. Isaiah 30 maintains that YHWH's deliverance of Jerusalem will be delayed but that, ultimately, the Assyrian oppressor will be brought down. Isaiah 31 employs parenesis to argue that it is futile to turn to Egypt for help, again because the threat against Jerusalem ultimately stems from YHWH. Isaiah 32 provides the climax for the entire sequence by pointing to the emergence of righteous king in an era of peace and righteousness following the period of oppression.

For the most part, the Josianic redaction in Isaiah 28–32 employs material that stems from Isaiah ben Amoz and that addresses the problems posed by the Assyrian threat against Jerusalem during the reign of Hezekiah and his revolt against the Assyrians in 705–701 B.C.E. Evidence of composition by the Josianic redaction of Isaiah appears only in Isaiah 30:19–33 and 32:1–20. In contrast to the Isaianic material that focuses on the futility of opposing YHWH's plans to bring the Assyrians against Jerusalem, the Josianic material emphasizes the contrasting themes of the downfall of Assyria and the rise of the righteous Judean monarch.

The present form of Isaiah 30:1–33 constitutes a prophetic instruction speech concerning YHWH's delay in delivering the nation from Assyrian oppression. The basic instruction speech in vv. 1–26 emphasizes both an oracular report of YHWH's dissatisfaction with Hezekiah's delegations to Egypt that are designed to ensure Egyptian support for the revolt (vv. 1–11) and the prophet's announcement concerning the consequences of YHWH's dissatisfaction: that YHWH will delay the deliverance of Jerusalem (vv. 12–26). The announcement includes three elements: an announcement of punishment introduced by a messenger formula in vv. 12–14; an announcement of the basis for the punishment again introduced by a messenger formula in vv. 15–17; and an announcement concerning the delay of YHWH's future deliverance in vv. 18–26. A theophanic announcement that YHWH will ultimately strike down the Assyrian oppressor appears in vv. 27–33, which describes YHWH's approach (vv. 27–28) and a description of YHWH's victory over the Assyrians (vv. 29–33) in keeping with the typical elements of a theophany report.[29] The structure of this text may be portrayed as in table 14.2. Several features of this text indicate its composite nature. The first is the abrupt shift from a theme of condemnation in vv. 1–17 to one of deliverance in vv. 18–33. Although this is in and of itself is an insufficient basis conclude that the text is composite, it is noteworthy that the two sections appear to have relatively little to do with each other. Verses 1–17 focus primarily on a political situation of a diplomatic embassy to Egypt and the corresponding religious perspective of YHWH's dissatisfaction. Verses 18–33 focus instead on the cosmic dimensions of YHWH's deliverance from oppression, such as the bringing of rains and produce, as well as on the theophanic description of YHWH's defeat of Assyria. The explicit reference to Assyria in v. 31 constitutes the second major feature of the text's composite nature. The identity of the oppressor that motivated the delegation to Egypt had been

---

29. For discussion of the theophany report genre, see J. Jeremias, *Theophanie: Die Geschichte einer alttestamentliche Gattung*, WMANT 10 (Neukirchen-Vluyn: Neukirchener, 1965).

TABLE 14.2   Structure of Isaiah 30: Concerning YHWH's delay in delivering the people from Assyria

Prophetic instruction speech	*Isa 30:1–33*
I. Prophetic instruction speech proper	30:1–26
A. Oracular report concerning YHWH's dissatisfaction concerning embassy to Egypt	30:1–11
B. Prophetic announcement of consequences: YHWH will delay deliverance	30:12–26
1. Announcement of punishment	30:12–14
2. Basis for punishment	30:15–17
3. Prophetic announcement concerning delay of YHWH's future deliverance	30:18–26
II. Theophanic announcement that YHWH will strike down Assyria	30:27–33
A. Description of YHWH's approach	30:27–28
B. Description of YHWH's victory over Assyria	30:29–33

relatively unimportant; rather vv. 1–17 apparently considers the important issue to be the rejection of YHWH's protection. Indeed, vv. 18–33 do not even mention Egypt but focus on Assyria instead. It is noteworthy, however, that in portraying YHWH's theophanic defeat of Assyria, vv. 29–33 employ themes and imagery from the festival of Passover: v. 29 mentions a festival that is celebrated at night, a characteristic feature of Passover; vv. 31–32 mention YHWH's smiting with a rod, which recalls the rod motif of the Exodus traditions; and the imagery of burning fire and wood calls to mind the imagery of the roasting of the Pesach offering that is to be consumed by the people on the night of Passover.

A final consideration is the syntactical structure of vv. 18 and 19. Despite the above-listed indications of discontinuity between vv. 1–17 and vv. 18–33, it is noteworthy that v. 18 begins with *wĕlākēn*, "and therefore," which constitutes a logical syntactical connections between the two units. It thereby presents YHWH's decision to delay showing favor as a consequence of the embassy to Egypt. But the appearance of two phrases introduced by causative *kî*, "because," in vv. 18b and 19 is noteworthy, especially since each verse introduces the basis for YHWH's decision to delay favor. Verse 18b merely states that YHWH is a G-d of justice and those who wait for YHWH are blessed; it does not specify for what the people are to wait. Verse 19, however, introduces an extended elaboration on this theme, employing the above-mentioned motifs of cosmic activity, YHWH's theophanic action against Assyria, and the motif of the Passover celebration.

It would appear that the syntactical features of v. 19 indicate the source of literary discontinuity within this text that indicates its composite nature. Although the association between Egypt and Passover would tend to draw the two major parts of the chapter together, the discontinuities mentioned above suggest that this material is composed to draw out a new theme that differs from that of vv. 1–17, namely, the punishment of Assyria on the model of Egyptian punishment at the time of the Exodus. In this regard, it is noteworthy that although Passover seems to play relatively little role in the work of Isaiah ben Amoz, it plays a substantial role in Josiah's reforms as Passover is the primary Temple holiday celebrated by Josiah to mark the renewed covenant between YHWH and the people and to renew the Temple as the religious center of the kingdom. Passover marks the renewal of the natural world as it marks the beginning of the agricultural harvest in the spring. Likewise, the themes of the outcry of the people and the eating of the bread of adversity and the water of affliction are also Passover themes. When the themes of rejection of idols and the deliverance of the people Jerusalem are read together with the themes of the manifestation of YHWH's power against the Assyrians, it becomes clear that vv. 19–33 recast an earlier oracle concerning YHWH's dissatisfaction with a Judean embassy to Egypt into a Passover-based scenario of YHWH's deliverance of the people after a period of delay. Such a presentation corresponds well with the outlook of the Josianic reform. It also presents the fall of Assyria and the rise of an independent Judah as the outcome of Isaiah's earlier oracle against the embassy to Egypt.

Isaiah 32 is a composition of the Josianic edition of Isaiah. It is formulated as a prophet instruction speech that concerns the announcement of a royal savior.[30] It comprises three basic elements. Verses 1–8 constitute a disputational announcement of the royal savior who will rule in righteousness and open eyes and ears so that none will utter folly or devise evil. Verses 9–19 constitute a prophetic announcement concerning the character of the king's reign in that salvation will emerge from disaster, resulting in the transformation of nature and peace and security for the people. A beatitude concerning the happiness of the righteous concludes this idyllic depiction of the rule of the righteous king.

Several features of Isaiah 32 indicate its Josianic provenance. First is the portrayal of an actual monarchic restoration, which places the text prior to 587 B.C.E. Exilic material in Isaiah, especially that beginning in chapter 40, never posits the restoration of a Judean monarch, but looks to Cyrus as YHWH's chosen king (Isa 44:28, 45:1) or points to YHWH as the king (Isa 65–66). The depiction of the city—that is, Jerusalem—and palace as forsaken and deserted are very unusual for Isaiah ben Amoz. Elsewhere, the prophet is highly critical of royal actions and announces punishment against Jerusalem, but he never portrays Jerusalem or the Davidic monarch in such a desolate state, although the coup that saw the assassination of Josiah's father Amon would present the possibility of an empty royal palace and the devising of evil by fools or knaves. Furthermore, the reference to the "spirit" or "wind" poured out upon the people from on high that accompanies the king's righteous rule is a motif that also appears in the portrayal of the righteous monarch in Isaiah 11:1–16, a text earlier identified as a Josianic composition. The emphasis on the wisdom themes, such as the references to good judgment of the mind of the rash, the contrast between the fool or knave and those who are noble or honorable, and so on, also correspond to the wisdom themes of Isaiah 11, which speak of the wisdom, understanding, and righteousness of the projected Davidic monarch.

In sum, a depiction of such a monarch and his reign concludes Isaiah 28–32 in a manner analogous to that of Isaiah 5–12. In both cases, the redaction employs past oracles by Isaiah ben Amoz as the basis for its projection of the future. As in Isaiah 5–12, the righteous monarch in Isaiah 28–32 emerges after a period of

---

30. On the announcement of a royal savior, see Wildberger, *Jesaja 1–12* 438–442.

punishment against the people. In this regard, the depiction of the monarch evident in Isaiah 5–12 and 28–32 corresponds to the ideology of the Josianic reign, which posited a reign of righteousness and peace in the aftermath of Judah's subjugation to Assyria. But in this instance, the focus is on the city of Jerusalem. After having outlined the future of Israel/Judah and the nations, the Josianic edition of Isaiah here focuses on Jerusalem as the centerpiece of YHWH's plans for Israel/Judah, the Davidic monarchy, and the nations at large.

Isaiah 36–37

The last textual block that stems from the Josianic redaction is the narrative concerning YHWH's deliverance of Jerusalem and Hezekiah from Sennacherib's siege in Isaiah 36–37.[31] This narrative is part of a larger textual block in Isaiah 36–39 that relates various narratives concerning Isaiah's interaction with Hezekiah. Together with Isaiah 34–35, these narratives introduce the second half of the book of Isaiah, which presents the projected outcome of YHWH's plans for establishing sovereignty over the world at Zion in the aftermath of the Assyrian period. As earlier studies have indicated, this section plays a key role in establishing a transition between the two halves of the book in that it contrasts Hezekiah's actions with those of Ahaz in a similar situation of crisis as presented in Isaiah 7:1–9:6, and thereby portrays Hezekiah as model for a faithful relationship with YHWH that the book attempts to promote.[32] The present form of Isaiah 36–39 thereby functions as part of the fifth-century edition of the book of Isaiah.

Nevertheless, it is clear that the present form of Isaiah 36–39 is a redactionally formulated text that addresses the problem of the initial Babylonian incursions against Judah and the deportation of King Jehoiachin and others in 597 B.C.E. The original setting of these chapters is the DtrH, where they form a part of the narrative concerning Hezekiah in 2 Kings 18–20. Insofar as the narrative ends with Isaiah's announcement that the Temple treasures and stores shown by Hezekiah to the visiting Babylonian delegation of Merodach-baladan would someday be carried off to Babylon together with Hezekiah's sons, the narrative addresses the issue of the Babylonian exile that concludes the DtrH.[33] Nevertheless, the fact that this narrative does not take up the destruction of Jerusalem demonstrates that it was composed in relation to the earlier deportation of Jehoiachin by the Babylonians.

---

31. For a detailed discussion of these chapters, see Sweeney, *Isaiah 1–39* 454–511. See also R. E. Clements, *Isaiah and the Deliverance of Jerusalem. A Study of the Interpretation of Prophecy in the Old Testament*, JSOTSup 13 (Sheffield: JSOT Press, 1980); Christof Hardmeier, *Prophetie im Streit vor dem Untergang Judas: Erzählkommunikative Studien zur Entstehungssituation der Jesaja- und Jeremiaerzählungen in II Reg 18–20 und Jer 37–40*, BZAW 187(Berlin and New York: Walter de Gruyter, 1990); Christopher R. Seitz, *Zion's Final Destiny: The Development of the Book of Isaiah. A Reassessment of Isaiah 36–39* (Minneapolis: Fortress, 1991).

32. For example, Ackroyd, "Isaiah 36–39."

33. Cf. R. E. Clements, "The Isaiah Narrative of 2 Kings 20:12–19 and the Date of the Deuteronomic History," in *Isac [sic] Leo Seeligmann Volume*, ed. A. Rofé and Y. Zakovitch (Jerusalem: E. Rubenstein, 1983) 209–220.

Furthermore, the various modifications that appear in the Isaiah form of the narrative indicate that the image of Hezekiah was whitewashed in order to emphasize his role as an ideal model of royal/human faithfulness to YHWH in the context of the book of Isaiah.[34]

It is also clear that the narratives concerning Hezekiah's illness (Isa 38/2 Kgs 20:1–11) and the embassy of Merodach-baladan (Isa 39/2 Kgs 20:12–19) are later expansions of an earlier narrative that treats Sennacherib's siege of Jerusalem. Scholars have already noted the temporal formulas that tie these narratives to the siege narratives—that is, *bayyāmîm hāhēm*, "in those days," in Isaiah 38:1/2 Kings 20:1 and *bā'ēt hahî'*, "at that time," in Isaiah 39:1/2 Kings 20:12.[35] Although these formulas tie both episodes into the overall narrative structure of the whole, each episode has its own distinctive characteristics and concerns that demonstrate its compositional independence. The narrative concerning Merodach-baladan's embassy apparently portrays Hezekiah's diplomatic efforts to secure an alliance with Babylon in preparation for the revolt that prompted Sennacherib's invasion. The chronological sequence is thereby inverted, as the narrative presents events from a retrospective viewpoint. But, whereas the narrative concerning Sennacherib's siege emphasizes YHWH's deliverance of Jerusalem and Hezekiah as a result of Hezekiah's pious turn to YHWH, the Merodach-baladan episode qualifies YHWH's deliverance of the city and destruction of the Assyrians by positing a renewed threat by a different power—that is, Babylon. Hezekiah no longer appears as a model of piety, but as an errant monarch whose actions laid the basis for the later Babylonian threat against Jerusalem and the House of David. The two versions of the king's response to Isaiah's word of judgment in Isaiah 39:8 and 2 Kings 20:19 likewise reinforce this perspective in that they indicate Hezekiah's concern that the kingdom be safe in his own days. The version in Isaiah 39:9, in which Hezekiah asserts that "the word of YHWH is good because there will be peace and security in my days," is somewhat more favorable to the character of Hezekiah because he at least takes concern for the welfare of his kingdom in his own time. The version in 2 Kings 20:19, however, appears to be somewhat flippant in that Hezekiah accepts the word of judgment with the question, "Why not if there will be peace and security in my days?" indicating his lack of concern for the future. In both cases, however, the Merodach-baladan narrative counters the promise of security in the Sennacherib narrative and thereby addresses a very different concern. Rather than assert YHWH's protection of Jerusalem and the House of David, the Merodach-baladan narrative points to a basis for compromising that promise.

---

34. Contra Seitz, *Zion's Final Destiny*, who argues that the Isaiah version of the narrative is the earlier one on which 2 Kings 18–20 depends. Seitz draws heavily from the work of K. A. D. Smelik, "Distortion of Old Testament Prophecy: The Purpose of Isaiah xxxvi and xxxvii," *OTS* 24 (1989) 70–93, later republished in revised form as "King Hezekiah Advocates True Prophecy. Remarks on Isaiah xxxvi and xxxvii//II Kings xviii and xix," *Converting the Past: Studies in Ancient Israelite & Moabite Historiography*, OTS 28 (Leiden: Brill, 1992) 93–128.

35. For example, Peter Ackroyd, "An Interpretation of the Babylonian Exile: A Study of II Kings 29 and Isaiah 38–39," *Studies in the Religious Tradition of the Old Testament* 152–171, 282–285, originally published in *Scottish Journal of Theology* 27 (1974) 329–352.

The narrative concerning Hezekiah's illness presents a more complicated scenario, in that the two versions of the narrative are very different. Again, the version in Isaiah 38 emphasizes Hezekiah's piety by restructuring the version of 2 Kings 1–11 with the addition of Hezekiah's prayer and other modifications. The narrative does build upon the message of the Sennacherib narrative, however, in that it points to YHWH's efforts to protect Hezekiah at a time of illness. Again, it reverses the chronology in that Hezekiah's illness appears to occur well before the siege of Jerusalem, but there is no hint that the illness narrative in any way contradicts the message of YHWH's protection that is articulated in Isaiah 36–37/2 Kings 18:14–19:37. Rather, it reinforces the message that YHWH will act to protect the faithful monarch by pointing explicitly to the analogy in Isaiah 38:5–6/2 Kings 20:5–6, which reiterate YHWH's promise to the house of David and YHWH's promise to defend the city. Despite the retrospective perspective, the narrative appears to have been composed together with the Sennacherib siege narrative. It does not challenge its fundamental premises; rather, it supports them with a somewhat more personal perspective.

Indeed, the concern with the protection of the house of David and the city of Jerusalem indicate the narrative's provenance in relation to the reign of King Josiah. The narrative clearly cannot have emerged in the immediate aftermath of Hezekiah's revolt as it portrays the assassination of Sennacherib by his sons, an event that actually took place in 681, some twenty years after the revolt. Instead, the narrative must be considered in relation to the threat posed to the House of David by the assassination of Amon, Josiah's father, in 640 B.C.E. Although the motives for this attempted coup are not entirely clear, it appears to have been an attempt to supplant the Davidic dynasty in light of Assyria's apparent declining hold over the Syro-Israelite region. Insofar as Manasseh apparently served as a loyal Assyrian vassal throughout his reign, the House of David would have been identified with Assyrian suzerainty; indeed, the narratives concerning Ahaz's reign in Isaiah 7:1–8:15 and 2 Kings 16 indicate that the House of David was responsible for Judah's vassal status. Josiah was brought to the throne only after the conspiracy had been wiped out; otherwise, he also might have been targeted as a member of the Davidic house. The countercoup preserved the Davidic dynasty and brought Josiah to the throne.

The narrative portrayal of Assyria's defeat is also an important element. It is noteworthy that this narrative marks the end of the Assyrian empire in the historiographical viewpoint of the DtrH. Afterward, the Assyrians are no longer a threat against Judah or Jerusalem; only Babylon fills this role. The realization of the significance of Assyria's downfall for Judah would hardly have occurred during the reign of Manasseh, at least not in the centers of ruling power, and it appears to have been a factor in the assassination of Amon. But by the time Josiah began to exercise his own authority on the throne, perhaps as early as his eighth year (631 B.C.E.) and certainly by his twelfth year (627 B.C.E.)—that is, the year of Assurbanipal's death—the implications for Judah would be clear. Judah would have the opportunity to reassert its independence. YHWH's promise of security to the city of Jerusalem and the House of David, especially when articulated in relation to the Assyrian threat, would carry a great deal of significance in the reign of Josiah because it would point to the post-Assyrian period as the time when YHWH's promises would be realized. Those who had been patient and held firm to YHWH were now experiencing the rewards of their faithfulness in a manner not unlike that of Hezekiah.

Although it is difficult to specify the literary form of the Josianic book of Isaiah, the placement of the Sennacherib narrative, together with that pertaining to Hezekiah's illness immediately following the Josianic edition of Isaiah 28–32, would make a great deal of sense. These narrative provide a concrete illustration of the message articulated in the various oracles concerning the future of Jerusalem; those who wait patiently for YHWH's future deliverance will see their hopes realized in the defeat of the Assyrians and the emergence of the righteous king. The Sennacherib and Hezekiah illness narratives thereby form the capstone to the entire Josianic edition posited here. YHWH's deliverance of Jerusalem and the House of David and the defeat of Assyria are the projected outcomes of the oracle concerning Israel/Judah in Isaiah 5–12; those pertaining to the nations in Isaiah 14–27*; and those concerning Jerusalem in Isaiah 28–32. Altogether, they point to the reign of Josiah as the time of promise in which the oracles of Isaiah ben Amoz would be fulfilled. The prophet had looked forward to and predicted the reign of King Josiah.

15

Hosea

Although there are many differences in viewpoint concerning the literary struc-ture, compositional history, and theological outlook of the book of Hosea, scholars generally agree in reading Hosea's message against the background of the rise of Assyria and the internal politics and social setting of the northern king-dom of Israel in the mid-eighth century B.C.E.[1] This is due in large measure to the superscription of the book, which places the prophet's activity in the reign of King Jeroboam ben Joash of Israel (786–746 B.C.E.) and the Judean kings Uzziah (783–742 B.C.E.), Jotham (742–735 B.C.E.), Ahaz (735–715 B.C.E.), and Hezekiah (715–687 B.C.E.). Furthermore, the internal references of the book address the concerns of the mid-eighth century as Assyria loomed on the horizon and tensions appeared within Israel concerning the activities of its kings and its relationship with Judah. Hosea's critique of Israel and its kings fits easily into a mid-eighth-century frame-work and provides a window into the internal situation of Israel during the period preceding its destruction by the Assyrians. The book thereby portrays the decline of Israel from a powerful state, ruled by Jeroboam ben Joash of the Jehu dynasty, that controlled an empire extending from Lebo Hamath in Syria to the Sea of the Arabah or the Gulf of Aqabah (2 Kgs 14:25) to a disorganized rump state that saw six new kings during the twenty-two years following Jeroboam's death, four of whom were assassinated by their successors and the last of whom, Hoshea, was carried off into exile by the Assyrians.

An earlier and condensed version of this chapter was published as "A Form-Critical Rereading of the Book of Hosea," *Journal of the Hebrew Scriptures* 2 (1998) article 2.

1. For surveys of current research on the book of Hosea, see C. L. Seow, "Hosea, Book of," *ABD* III, 291–297; Graham I. Davies, *Hosea*, OTG (Sheffield: Sheffield Academic Press, 1993); Gale A. Yee, *Composition and Tradition in the Book of Hosea: A Redaction-Critical Investiga-tion*, SBLDS 102 (Atlanta: Scholars Press, 1987) 1–25.

Nevertheless, the book of Hosea is generally recognized as one of the most difficult prophetic books in the entire Hebrew Bible. The text is considered to be highly corrupted due in large measure to the fact that, as the only unambiguously northern prophet whose work is preserved in the Hebrew Bible, Hosea's dialect is that of the northern kingdom of Israel rather than that of the more commonly known southern kingdom of Judah.[2] There is a great deal of disagreement in the overall interpretation of the book as scholars have arrived at various conclusions concerning its literary structure, its traditiohistorical and literary transmission history, and its historical and social setting.[3] In interpreting the message of the book, scholars have focused especially on Hosea's marriage to Gomer, described as a prostitute or woman of harlotry, and the birth of their children, Jezreel, Lo Ruhamah, and Lo Ammi, all of which carry symbolic names in reference to Hosea's message of judgment against the northern kingdom of Israel.[4] The book presents Hosea's marriage as a paradigm for YHWH's relationship with Israel, in which Israel is presented as a woman who pursues lovers other than her long-suffering and devoted husband, who continually attempts to win her back following a period of punishment. The theological theme of "knowledge of G-d" plays an important role in this discussion because of its sexual overtones in relation to Hosea's marriage to Gomer and because it expresses the intimate relationship with the Deity that Israel rejects in pursuing the Baal deities known for their role in Canaanite pagan fertility religion. Scholars are divided as to whether Hosea spoke exclusively of Israel's judgment or if he held out the possibility that Israel could avoid the projected punishment by returning to YHWH. The prophet's marriage to Gomer plays a major role in this issue in that the prophet's remarriage to Gomer in Hosea 3:1–5 portrays the willingness of YHWH to accept Israel's return, but the issue is clouded by many who maintain that the marriage represented in Hosea 3:1–5 is to a different woman or that the elements of restoration in Hosea's message are later redactional reworkings of the original Hosean text.

Despite these difficulties, the book of Hosea holds a great deal of potential for understanding the dynamics of prophetic interpretation during the late seventh-century reign of Josiah. Although the structure of the book is not well understood, the present form of the book of Hosea articulates a message of judgment against the northern kingdom of Israel and its kings. It calls for Israel and Judah to be ruled by one Davidic monarch, and concludes with an appeal for Israel to return to YHWH, all of which appear as important elements in Josiah's attempts to reestablish Davidic rule over the former northern kingdom and thereby to reunite the

2. See Wilhelm Rudolph, *Hosea*, KAT XIII/1 (Gütersloh: Gerd Mohn, 1966) 19–22. For a study of the text of Hosea, see H. S. Nyberg, *Studien zum Hoseabuch, zugleich ein Beitrag zur Klärung des Problems der alttestamentlichen Textkritik*, UUÅ 1935:6 (Uppsala: A.-B. Lundequistska Bokhandeln, 1935).

3. See esp. Davies, *Hosea*, for a summary of the discussion.

4. For studies of Hosea's marriage to Gomer in Hosea 1–3, see H. H. Rowley, "The Marriage of Hosea," *Men of G-d: Studies in Old Testament History and Prophecy* (London: Thomas Nelson, 1963) 66–97 and, more recently, Yvonne Sherwood, *The Prostitute and the Prophet: Hosea's Marriage in Literary-Theoretical Perspective*, GCT 2, JSOTSup 212 (Sheffield: Sheffield Academic Press, 1996); Davies, *Hosea* 79–92.

original twelve tribes of Israel around the Temple in Jerusalem. Within this general perspective, the main difficulties to be resolved are a specific accounting of the overall structure and political-theological outlook of Hosea and the extent to which this present literary form and message of the book are the product of the prophet Hosea or later tradents.[5]

For the most part, scholars hold that the overall structure of the book comprises three basic textual blocks: Hosea 1–3, which presents Hosea's marriage to Gomer as a paradigm for YHWH's relationship with Israel; Hosea 4–11, which articulates Hosea's message of judgment against Israel and concludes with YHWH's passionate outcry that denies the Deity's capacity to give up Israel or allow it to be destroyed; and Hosea 12–14, which reiterates the history of YHWH's relationship with Israel by employing elements of tradition that rehearse the grounds for Israel's punishment and call for Israel's return to YHWH.[6] Each of the three blocks begins with material concerning Israel's judgment and ends with material pertaining to restoration. This structure facilitates redaction-critical views that posit an original core of judgmental material from the prophet that has been softened or modified by the addition of material by later hands and which is designed to transform Hosea's message of judgment into one more favorably disposed to Israel.

Nevertheless, this view of the structure of Hosea is problematic in that it is not based entirely on an assessment of the literary features of the book in its present form that identify the speaker and addressee of a particular pericope, but on redaction-critical criteria that allow views concerning the book's compositional history to unduly influence scholarly assessments of its literary structure. This is evident in Hosea 1–3, for example, which is grouped together on the basis of the narrative literary form in chapters 1 and 3 and by the overall thematic concern with Hosea's marriage or marriages. But such a view tends to suppress important literary features, such as the narrative voice of the text. The narrative in Hosea 3 is autobiographical, whereas the narrative in Hosea 1 is written about Hosea in an objective form. Furthermore, the poetic material beginning in Hosea 2:4 is likewise styled as an address by the prophet directed to the people of Israel. Hosea 2:1–3, by contrast, is formulated in the objective style of chapter 1. This suggests that

5. For studies that are especially concerned with the literary structure and composition of the book of Hosea, see Edwin M. Good, "The Composition of Hosea," *SEÅ* 31 (1966) 21–63; Martin Buss, *The Prophetic Word of Hosea: A Morphological Study*, BZAW 111 (Berlin: A. Töpelmann, 1969); Yee, *Composition*. For studies that are especially concerned with the literary growth of the book through inner-biblical interpretation, see Ina Willi-Plein, *Vorformen der Schriftexegese innerhalb des Alten Testaments: Untersuchungen zum literarischen Werden der auf Amos, Hosea und Micha zurückgehenden Bücher im hebräischen Zwölfprophetenbuch*, BZAW 123 (Berlin and New York: Walter de Gruyter, 1971); Grace I. Emmerson, *Hosea: An Israelite Prophet in Judean Perspective*, JSOTSup 28 (Sheffield: JSOT Press, 1984); Thomas Naumann, *Hoseas Erben: Strukturen der Nachinterpretation im Buch Hosea*, BWANT 131 (Stuttgart: Kohlhammer, 1991); Martti Nissinen, *Prophetie, Redaktion und Fortschreibung im Hoseabuch: Studien zum Werdegang eines Prophetenbuches im Lichte von Hos 4 und 11*, AOAT 231 (Kevelaer: Butzon & Bercker; Neukirchen-Vluyn: Neukirchener, 1991).

6. See Hans Walter Wolff, *Hosea*, Hermeneia (Philadelphia: Fortress, 1974) xxix–xxxii; Yee, *Composition* 51–52; Davies, *Hosea* 102–107.

Hosea 1–3 do not comprise a single block, but perhaps two distinctly formulated textual blocks addressed by different parties to different audiences, viz., Hosea 1:1–2:3, which is addressed by the narrator of the book to the reader, and Hosea 2:4–3:5, which is addressed by the prophet alternatively to the people of Israel in Hosea 2:4–25 and to the reader in Hosea 3:1–5. Similar problems emerge in Hosea 4–11, which contain introductory address formulae, analogous to that of Hosea 2:4, that are directed to specific audiences among the people of Israel.-Such addressees include the people of Israel in Hosea 4:1; the priests, house of Israel, and kings in Hosea 5:1; unspecified audiences that are commanded to sound horns in Hosea 5:8 and 8:1; and Israel in Hosea 9:1. These addresses are intermixed with descriptive material about Israel, generally presented as the words of YHWH or the prophet to an unspecified audience, throughout these chapters. The same phenomenon appears in Hosea 12–14, in which Hosea 14:2 contains an address formula directed to Israel in the midst of material that is either descriptive of Israel or addressed specifically to the people. Finally, discussion of the form and contents of Hosea is complicated by numerous references to Judah, which suggest that the prophet's oracles may have been addressed to Judah as well as to Israel, or that they have been expanded by later redactors who attempted to relate Hosea to the concerns of the southern kingdom.[7]

This calls for a reassessment of the structure and generic character of the book of Hosea. Clearly, Hosea is not simply a three-part collection of the prophet's oracles to Israel. The book appears to have a much more complex structure, and it is formulated both to convey the prophet's oracles to Israel and to address an unspecified audience. In order to specify the book's structure, it is necessary to pay close attention to the formal literary features of the text that indicate its speakers and addressees and that convey its contents. By this means, the foundation will be laid for establishing the overall message and perspective of the book, together with the settings in which it was read.

To establish the structure of the book of Hosea, several initial observations concerning the form of the book are necessary. The book begins with a superscription in Hosea 1:1. As Tucker points out in his study of the superscriptions for prophetic books, the superscription must necessarily stand apart from the following material in that it serves as an introduction to the balance of the book that identifies its contents, author, and the historical setting in which the book is to be read.[8] In contrast to the contents of the book, which are attributed to Hosea as the word of YHWH to the prophet, the superscription cannot be attributed to Hosea, but to an anonymous narrator who presents the book to the reader. Interestingly, the work of an anonymous narrator appears again at two key points in the book. The first is the report of YHWH's speaking to Hosea in Hosea 1:2–2:3. The work of the anonymous narrator is evident in the initial statement of this pericope in Hosea 1:2a, "the beginning of YHWH's speaking with Hosea," and in the narra-

---

7. See esp. Emmerson, *Hosea*, for discussion of the references to Judah in the book of Hosea.

8. Gene M. Tucker, "Prophetic Superscriptions and the Growth of the Canon," in *Canon and Authority*, ed. G. W. Coats and B. O. Long (Philadelphia: Fortress, 1977) 56–70.

tive indicators of YHWH's speeches to the prophet and the prophet's subsequent actions throughout the balance of the pericope in Hosea 1:2bα[1], "and YHWH said to Hosea"; 1:3–4aα, "and he went and he took Gomer bat Diblaim and she conceived and she bore a son to him, and YHWH said to him"; Hosea 1:6aαβ, "and she conceived again and she bore a daughter, and he said to him"; and Hosea 1:8– 9aα, "and she weaned Lo Ruhamah and she conceived and she bore a son, and he said . . ." Hosea 2:1–3 is clearly included as a component of Hosea 1:2–9 in that the introductory formula of Hosea 2:1, *wĕhāyâ mispar bĕnê yiśrā'ēl kĕhôl hayyām*, "and the number of the children of Israel will be like the sand of the sea . . ." establishes syntactical continuity with the report of YHWH's speech to Hosea in Hosea 1:9aβ–b. Hosea 2:1–3 thereby constitutes a component of YHWH's speech to the prophet in Hosea 1:9aβ–2:3. A new pericope begins in Hosea 2:4, which clearly depicts the prophet's address to the children born in Hosea 1:2–2:3, rather than the narrative report of YHWH's address to the prophet. The balance of the book comprises the prophet's addresses to Israel or to an unspecified audience until Hosea 14:10, in which an anonymous narrator again addresses the reader, "Whoever is wise, let him understand these things, whoever is discerning, let him know them, for straight are the ways of YHWH, and the righteous shall walk in them but the rebellious shall stumble."

Overall, these observations indicate that the anonymous narrator plays a determinative role in constituting the structure of the book of Hosea. The book thereby comprises three primary structural elements, each of which is formulated by the anonymous narrator. The superscription in Hosea 1:1 constitutes the first major structural element of the book in that it identifies the contents of the book as "The word of YHWH which was to Hosea ben Beeri in the days of Uzziah, Jotham, Ahaz, Hezekiah, kings of Judah, and in the days of Jeroboam ben Joash, king of Israel." Hosea 1:2–14:9 then constitutes the main body of the book, which is formulated as the narrator's report of YHWH's speaking to Hosea in Hosea 1:2–2:3 and the report of Hosea's subsequent speeches based on that experience in Hosea 2:4–14:9. Finally, Hosea 14:10 constitutes the postscript of the book that calls upon the reader to understand the book properly and thereby to walk uprightly in the path of YHWH.[9]

This last point is particularly important in the overall interpretation of the book because it indicates that the book of Hosea is presented not simply as a transcript or report of the prophet's career and message, but that the book is presented for didactic or persuasive purposes—that is, the reader is intended to learn something from this book and to apply what is learned as a means to choose a preferred course of action over one that is considered to be undesirable. This observation indicates that the generic character of the book is didactic and parenetic as it is designed to persuade the reader to adopt a course of action based on the lessons learned from a proper understanding of the book. The major questions, of course, are to whom is the book of Hosea addressed, and what does it call upon the reader to do?

---

9. Cf. C. L. Seow, "Hosea 14:10 and the Foolish People Motif," *CBQ* 44 (1982) 212–224, who points out the interrelationship between Hosea 14:10 and various pericopes throughout the book in order to demonstrate that functions as the conclusion for the book of Hosea.

Consideration of the structure and generic character of the body of the book in Hosea 1:2–14:9 may be useful in answering these questions. Modern exegesis of Hosea has generally proceeded on the basis of the contention that the book of Hosea is addressed to the northern kingdom of Israel.[10] This is a natural conclusion to draw, given that Hosea is a northern prophet and that his message essentially focuses on the projected punishment of the northern kingdom. The calls for Israel's repentance likewise feed into this view. But the formal features of Hosea 1:2–14:9 call for a critical reevaluation of this contention. As already noted, the basic layout of this text includes two major components: the report by the anonymous narrator of YHWH's speaking to Hosea in Hosea 1:2–2:3 and the report of Hosea's speeches in Hosea 2:4–14:9.-The presence of the anonymous narrator is explicitly evident only in Hosea 1:2–2:3, and it conveys in the form of YHWH's words to Hosea some basic elements of the message of the book. The report of Hosea's compliance with YHWH's commands to take a wife of harlotry and to have children of harlotry certainly articulates an important element of judgment against Israel in the overall message of the book. It is clear from the report of YHWH's statements that this judgment is directed against the people in large measure because of the actions of the house of Jehu, which came to power through bloodshed in a coup against the previously ruling house of Omri. Nevertheless, the present form of the narrative does not focus exclusively on a message of judgment. The present form of Hosea 1:6–7, for example, indicates that YHWH will show no mercy to Israel, but that YHWH will pardon Israel and that YHWH will show mercy to and deliver the house of Judah, although not by military means. Furthermore, Hosea 2:1–3 articulates the patriarchal promise to Israel to become as numerous as the sands of the sea.[11] It thereby points to YHWH's intention not to destroy Israel entirely, and it makes this clear by its statements that the people will ultimately be considered "my people" and "pitied" in contrast to the names "not my people" and "not pitied" given to Israel previously in the first part of the narrative. Furthermore, this text indicates that as part of this process of restitution, the people of Israel and Judah will be reunited again under the rule of one king. At the end of the speech report, YHWH gives an instruction to speak this message of restoration to the people, "Say to your brothers, 'my people,' and to your sisters, 'pitied.'" Although this statement is part of YHWH's speech to the prophet, the imperative plural form of 'say' (*'imrû*) indicates that this instruction is not directed to the prophet alone, but to a larger group of people. This statement clearly does not address the people of Israel, for they are the objects, not the addressees of this instruction. Rather, it is addressed to the people of Judah, who are called on to accept the people of Israel as YHWH's people and as pitied at a time when Israel and Judah will be reunited under the rule of a single king. This statement suggests that the present form of the book as a whole is addressed not to the people of Israel, but to the people of Judah.[12]

---

10. See Seow, "Hosea, Book of," 293.

11. Cf. Genesis 22:17.

12. Rudolph, *Hosea* 58–59. Cf. Wolff, *Hosea* 28, who understands this verse as an address to the people of the northern kingdom, but it is precisely the people of the northern kingdom who are

This conclusion is supported by the formal features of the prophet's words that appear in Hosea 2:4–14:9. Although a great deal of this material is addressed explicitly to the people and leaders of the northern kingdom of Israel, as indicated by the introductory formulae in Hosea 2:4, 4:1, 5:1, and 14:2, as well as by other features of this material, there is a great deal of material that does not represent direct speech by the prophet or YHWH to northern Israel but that constitutes the prophet's or YHWH's speeches about Israel that are addressed to an anonymous audience. This is evident in Hosea 2:4–3:5, for example, in which Hosea 2:4–25 is addressed to the children or to the wife of 1:2–2:3, but Hosea 3:1–5 is addressed to an anonymous audience and speaks objectively about the people of Israel. It is likewise evident in Hosea 4:1–19, which includes material explicitly addressed to the people of Israel in vv. 1–6, 13b–16, but speaks objectively about Israel to an unspecified audience in vv. 7–13a and 17–19. Similar features appear through-out Hosea 5:1–14:9. Such an alternation of addressee could well be a rhetorical device employed by the prophet in a situation of oral address to an Israelite audi-ence, in which he alternatively addresses his audience directly and then turns for an aside that describes the people's wrongdoing to no one in particular. But in the context of a written book that is removed from the setting of oral speech, such addresses are directed to the reader. Insofar as the written form of the book is formulated to presuppose a Judean reading audience, that addressee becomes the Judean reader.

This has a bearing on the means by which Hosea 2:4–14:9 is read. Although these chapters contain a great deal of material that is directed explicitly to a northern Israelite audience, it is ultimately directed to a Judean reading audience and it is designed to lead that audience to a certain set of conclusions concerning YHWH's actions in relation to the northern kingdom of Israel as articulated by Hosea. Overall, the formulaic addresses to the people and leaders of northern Israel still provide the criteria for determining the basic structure of the text, but it is evident that those addresses are embedded in material that is directed to the anonymous audience of the book, identified above as a Judean audience. In this respect, the book employs the addresses to northern Israel as a means to articulate a series of contentions that are designed to enable the Judean reader to conclude that YHWH has brought about punishment against the people and leaders of northern Israel for acting in a manner that is considered to be abandonment of YHWH. The kings and priests of northern Israel take special blame for this situation, and the material of the book continually returns to the themes of Israel's unwarranted kingship, cultic apostasy, and alliance with Assyria as the basis for the charge of abandoning YHWH. The series holds out the possibility of Israel's return to

---

the objects, not the addressees, of this command. Others understand it as an address to the postexilic Judean community, for example, J. Jeremias, *Der Prophet Hosea*, ATD 24,1 (Göttingen: Vandenhoeck & Ruprecht, 1983) 36. For a survey of the options, see G. I. Davies, *Hosea*, NCeB (Grand Rapids, Mich.: William Eerdmans, 1992) 63–64, who identifies the addressee simply as "the community as a whole" (p. 63). F. I. Andersen and D. I. Freedman likewise attempt to escape the problem by iden-tifying Hosea's son Jezreel as the addressee, arguing unjustifiably that the oldest son should be addressed with a plural form (*Hosea*, AB 24 [Garden City, N.Y.: Doubleday, 1980] 212).

YHWH, however, and calls explicitly for this return in the concluding segment of Hosea 14:2–9.

The sequence of the structure and argumentation of the book may be represented as follows. The first major structural segment of Hosea 2:4–14:9 appears in Hosea 2:4–3:5. This text is demarcated initially by its shift in form from the report of YHWH's speech to the prophet in Hosea 1:2–2:3 to the prophet's speech throughout Hosea 2:4–3:5. It is initially directed to the children, who were reported to be born in the preceding section, and it calls on them to contend with their mother so that she might return to her husband.[13] Although the text is initially formulated as Hosea's appeal to his children, it shifts in 2:18–22 to a report of YHWH's address to Israel as his wife, calling upon her to return. It shifts again to a report of YHWH's statements concerning the people in Hosea 2:23–25 that articulates the projected restoration of the people who will be called "my people" instead of the initial "not my people" of Hosea 1:2–2:3. The prophet's autobiographical report in Hosea 3:1–5 of YHWH's command again to love an adulterous woman is tied syntactically to Hosea 2:4–25. It thereby returns the reader to the initial rhetorical situation of Hosea 2:4 in which the prophet is clearly speaking about the restoration of his marriage relationship.

Hosea 2:4–3:5 thereby constitutes the initial premise of the prophet's message following YHWH's instructions to him. It presupposes the prophet's marriage to Gomer and the birth of the children, and it builds these images into an allegorical portrayal of the relationship between YHWH and the people of Israel. It articulates both the disruption of the relationship, portrayed as Israel's "harlotry" in relation to other gods, and its restoration as YHWH takes back the estranged Israel just as Hosea will take back Gomer. The addressee of this particular pericope is anonymous, but the statements that Israel will lose its king and religious leadership and that Israel will ultimately seek YHWH as G-d and David as king suggest that the anonymous reading audience is Judean. Certainly, the portrayal of Israel's restoration corresponds to an ideal Judean view of the situation. This also has an impact on the reference to the Valley of Achor as a "Door of Hope" in Hosea 2:17. This reference is generally understood in relation to the tradition in Joshua 7 concerning Achan's attempted theft of holy war booty in connection with the campaign against Ai in the narrative concerning the Israelite conquest of Canaan.[14] The Valley of Achor functions as a symbol of judgment against Israel in which the people had to be cleansed of evil before they were able to take possession of the land. The same process is envisioned here, but with an added dimension. The Valley of Achor is a broad expanse of land on the northwest edge of the Dead Sea. It extends into the Wadi Kidron, which when followed

13. Cf. Wolff, *Hosea* 33, who identifies the children as the addressees of this passage, arguing that they represent the people of Israel to contend against the land of Israel. Rudolph, *Hosea* 64, likewise identifies the children as the addressees.

14. Cf. Wolff, *Hosea* 42–44, who is somewhat perplexed concerning Hosea's use of this motif, in part because he rejects Martin Noth's identification of Achor as the *buqê'ah*, which extends into the *wâdī en-Nár* or Wadi Kidron. For details of this discussion, see also C. Pressler, "Achor," *ABD* I, 56.

into the hills overlooking the Dead Sea leads one directly to Jerusalem. In this case, the appellation of Petah Tiqvah, "the door of hope," aids in defining Israel's restoration in relation to its reunification with Judah around Jerusalem.

The next major section of Hosea 2:4–14:9 appears in Hosea 4:1–19. This subunit is demarcated initially by the call to attention formula in Hosea 4:1, "Hear the word of YHWH, Sons of Israel," which introduces the prophet's proclamation of YHWH's lawsuit with the inhabitants of the land.[15] An analogous formula in Hosea 5:1 introduces the following unit. Overall, Hosea 4:1–19 develops the theme of harlotry from Hosea 1:2–2:3 by portraying Israel's lack of knowledge concerning G-d as the basis of its abandonment of YHWH. It is formulated as a prophetic judgment speech, although it alternatively addresses the people directly (vv. 1–6, 13b–16) and speaks objectively about the people to an unspecified audience (vv. 7–13a, 17–19). It builds on the earlier themes of the mother and the children by arguing that because the people have abandoned YHWH, YHWH will destroy the mother of the people (v. 5) and abandon their children (v. 6). Although the passage is addressed to the people at large, it focuses especially on the leaders of the people, including the priest and prophet who are responsible for seeing to the people's proper understanding of G-d. In this respect, it begins to focus more specifically on the metaphor of harlotry among the people introduced previously and the cause of that harlotry in the religious leadership of the northern kingdom. The passage thereby condemns the cultic establishment and leadership of the northern kingdom of Israel.

Following the presentation of Israel as a faithless wife called to return to her husband in Hosea 2:4–3:5 and the condemnation of Israel's religious leaders in Hosea 4:1–19, the core of the book then follows in Hosea 5:1–14:9. Whereas the previous two sections outline the general themes of the book, including Israel's abandonment of YHWH and YHWH's appeal for Israel's return, Hosea 5:1–14:9 engages in a detailed examination of the issues involved in YHWH's/Hosea's complaint against Israel, which of course aids in defining the conditions for Israel's repentance or return to YHWH. Fundamentally, this unit identifies an alliance between Israel and Assyria as the basic cause for Israel's abandonment of YHWH and the corruption of its royal and cultic establishment. It concludes with a call for Israel's return to YHWH. Again, these chapters constitute of mixture of materials directly addressed to Israel and those that speak about Israel but are addressed to an unnamed audience. The direct address forms in Hosea 5:1, 5:8, 8:1, 9:1, and 14:2 appear to be constitutive in defining the overall structure of the text in that the material conveyed directly to Israel serves as the basis for the prophet's comments to the reading/listening audience.[16]

The first major subunit of Hosea 5:1–14:9 is Hosea 5:1–7, which provides an introduction to the issues to be discussed throughout the balance of the unit. It

---

15. For discussion of "call to attention" and the "lawsuit" forms in this text, see esp. Wolff, *Hosea* 65, 67.

16. Cf. Wolff, *Hosea* xxx, who points to similar criteria in the identification of textual subunits.

begins with a three-part call to attention, which addresses the priests, the house of Israel, and the royal house, "Hear this, O Priests, and pay attention O House of Israel, and House of the King, give ear, for the judgment is for you . . ." This call thereby identifies all the principle parties involved in Hosea's indictment, the religious leadership, the nation Israel at large, and the monarchy. It identifies three localities associated with Israel's judgment—that is, Mizpah, Tabor, and Shittim, each of which expresses concern with the three parties identified in the call to attention. Mizpah is the place where Saul was first selected by the people as king over Israel (1 Sam 10:17–27). Mt. Tabor is the first place where Israel gathers as a settled people centered around the northern Israelite tribe of Ephraim to oppose an enemy, and thereby it sets the organizational pattern of the northern kingdom of Israel. Shittim is the place where the tribes of Israel apostatized against YHWH by devoting themselves to the worship of Baal Peor through cultic prostitution during the wilderness period (Num 25). The passage speaks generally of Ephraim's and Judah's guilt employing the metaphors of harlotry and the bearing of alien children, thereby rehearsing once again the initial themes of the book.

The initial imperative warning, "Blow the shophar in Gibeah, trumpets in Ramah, raise a cry at Beth Aven (Beth-El) after you O Benjamin," introduces a subunit in Hosea 5:8–7:16 that probes the causes or the issues behind Israel's abandonment of YHWH.[17] The unity of this section is widely disputed on the basis of formal criteria in that the text alternates between direct address to Israel (and Judah) and objective statements about Israel (and Judah). Both Ephraim and Judah are condemned in this passage, but the basic concern throughout appears to be an alliance concluded between Ephraim/Israel and Assyria and perhaps Egypt. This concern appears near the beginning of the unit in Hosea 5:13–14 and again near the end in Hosea 7:11–13, 16. Other themes throughout the passage likewise express this concern—that is, the fickleness of Israel's love for YHWH (Hos 6:4–6), the transgression of the covenant like Adam (Hos 6:7), Israel's harlotry (Hos 6:9), Ephraim's/Samaria's false dealings (Hos 7:1) and adultery (Hos 7:4), Ephraim's mixing with foreign peoples (Hos 7:8–10), and Israel's turning to Baal in the context of going to Assyria (Hos 7:14–16).

The command to sound the trumpet, "Unto your mouth (set) the shofar like an eagle/vulture over the House of YHWH, because they have transgressed my covenant and against my Torah they have rebelled," marks the beginning of a new subunit in Hosea 8:1–14.[18] A shift in the argumentation appears here in that the theme of Israel's alliance with Assyria still remains (Hos 8:7–10), but a new focus on Israel's kings and cultic establishment emerges.[19] Following the initial statements concerning Israel's rejection of YHWH's covenant and Torah, Hosea 8:4–5 points to Israel's appointment of kings in defiance of YHWH's will and the subsequent erection of the silver and gold idols and calves to serve as gods. Follow-

---

17. Cf. Wolff, *Hosea* 108–110, who likewise identifies Hosea 5:8–7:16 as a major textual block, whereas many other scholars end the unit earlier (cf. Jeremias, *Hosea* 79–80, on this point).

18. Cf. Wolff, *Hosea* 133–136; Rudolph, *Hosea* 161; Jeremias, *Hosea* 103–104.

19. For discussion of Hosea's views on Israel's kingship, see A. Caquot, "Osée et la Royauté," *RHPR* 41 (1961) 123–146; A. Gelston, "Kingship in the Book of Hosea," *OTS* 19 (1974) 71–85.

ing the above-noted reference to Israel's alliance with Assyria, Hosea 8:11–14 returns to this theme, asserting that Israel's cultic practice constitutes abandonment of YHWH and YHWH's Torah. By building palaces and fortified cities, the works of kings, Israel and Judah are charged with abandonment of their Maker.

The next address form in the series appears in Hosea 9:1, "Do not rejoice, O Israel, do not celebrate like the peoples, because you have played the harlot against your G-d." This address introduces a large unit that comprises Hosea 9:1–14:1 that focuses especially on agricultural metaphors and worship practices to express Israel's abandonment of YHWH.[20] In addition, this section employs a great deal of past tradition to express its message.[21] Hosea 9:1–9 employs these themes of improper fertility/agricultural worship as a basis for assertions that Israel will be exiled to Egypt and Assyria, thereby reiterating the earlier themes of alliance with Assyria and Egypt. The language then shifts beginning in Hosea 9:10 from address forms to largely descriptive language in the balance of the unit as the prophet employs natural and agricultural metaphors to express his views concerning YHWH's current relationship with Israel. Israel is portrayed as grapes or fruit found by YHWH in the wilderness, but they turned to Baal Peor (Hos 9:10–17). Israel is portrayed as a luxuriant vine that will be overgrown with weeds because of its idolatry (Hos 10:1–8). Israel is a trained heifer that has plowed iniquity and now must turn or be destroyed together with its king; although Israel was a beloved child found by YHWH in the wilderness, its turning from YHWH will result in a return to Egypt and Assyria until Israel returns once again to YHWH (Hos 10:9–11:11). Ephraim encompasses YHWH with lies in making an alliance with Assyria and Egypt, but like Jacob who was exiled from the land, Israel can return (Hos 12:1–14). Ephraim was once exalted to leadership status in Israel, but by turning to Baal and rejecting YHWH, Ephraim faces judgment and death (Hos 13:1–14:1).

The final address form of the series, "Return O Israel unto YHWH your G-d, because you have stumbled in your iniquity," introduces the concluding appeal for Israel's repentance in Hosea 14:2–9. It emphasizes the theme that YHWH is the true power who is capable of nourishing Israel and providing her with fruit. It thereby returns to the initial marriage theme of the book insofar as Hosea's estranged wife looked to other lovers to provide her with sustenance. It likewise rehearses the concern with Israel's alliance with Assyria and its idolatry, "Assyria will not deliver us, upon horses we shall not ride, and we shall not again say 'our G-d' to the work of our hands" (Hos 14:4a). Overall, this concluding appeal picks

---

20. Most scholars break this unit up into smaller components, but as the following discussion will demonstrate, the initial address to Israel introduces an extensive section, which reflects on Israel's actions in relation to traditional motifs from Israel's history.

21. On Hosea's use of past tradition, see esp. T. C. Vriezen, "La tradition de Jacob dans Osée XII," *OTS* 1 (1942) 64–78; P. R. Ackroyd, "Hosea and Jacob," *VT* 13 (1963) 245–259; J. Vollmer, *Geschichtliche Rückblicke und Motive in der Prophetie des Amos, Hosea, und Jesaja*, BZAW 119 (Berlin: Walter de Gruyter, 1971) 55–126; R. Vuilleumier, "Les traditions d'Israël et la liberté du prophète: Osée," *RHPR* 59 (1979) 491–498; Heinz-Dieter Neef, *Die Heilstraditionen Israels in der Verkündigung des Propheten Hoseas*, BZAW 169 (Berlin and New York: Walter de Gruyter, 1987); Else Kragelund Holt, *Prophesying the Past: The Use of Israel's History in the Book of Hosea*, JSOTSup 194 (Sheffield: Sheffield Academic Press, 1995).

up the concern with Israel's repentance and restoration of its relationship with YHWH that has been evident throughout the book.

The structure of the book of Hosea may therefore be portrayed as in table 15.1. This analysis of the structure and generic character of the book of Hosea provides the basis for several observations. First, the organization and presentation of the full form of the book indicates an interest to employ the Hosean material for didactic or parenetic purposes—that is, the book of Hosea is clearly intended to instruct its readers and to persuade them to undertake a course of action. This is evident from the concluding instruction to the reader in Hosea 14:10, who is to learn something from the material presented in Hosea and to apply that knowledge by acting in a manner that is consistent with the "straight paths of YHWH" in which the righteous walk. It is also evident in the retrospective introduction to the book, both in the superscription in Hosea 1:1, which places Hosea in historical context, and in the narrative report of YHWH's instructions to Hosea to marry Gomer and to name his children in Hosea 1:2–2:3. Both sections are clearly formulated to present the reader with background information on Hosea and his interaction with YHWH as a basis for understanding the words of Hosea that follow in Hosea 2:4–14:9. By this means, the narrator of the book of Hosea provides the basis by which the reader will study the book and draw the desired conclusions that the book calls for in Hosea 14:10.

Second, the contents of the body of the book in Hosea 1:2–14:9 are clearly organized to appeal for Israel's return to YHWH. This is clear from the introductory reports of Hosea's marriage to Gomer, which sets the basic paradigm for the portrayal of Israel as an adulterous wife whose husband seeks her return despite

TABLE 15.1   Structure of the Book of Hosea: Parenetic appeal for Israel's return to YHWH

Prophetic instruction	*Hosea 1–14*
I. Superscription	1:1
II. Parenetic appeal for Israel's return	1:2–14:19
A. Report of YHWH's speaking to Hosea: marriage and birth of children	1:2–2:3
B. Report of Hosea's speech concerning appeal for Israel's return	2:4–14:9
1. Report of Hosea's appeal to children for mother's return: restoration of united people under Davidic monarch	2:4–3:5
2. Report of YHWH's controversy against Israel	4:1–19
3. Detailed report of YHWH's call for Israel's return	5:1–14:9
a. Initial statement of issues: Israel's harlotry/alien children	5:1–7
b. Concerning Israel's alliance with Assyria/Egypt	5:8–7:16
c. Concerning Israel's kings and cultic apostasy	8:1–14
d. Concerning Israel's pagan cultic practice/rejection of YHWH	9:1–14:1
i. Announcement of punishment	9:1–9
ii. Israel as grapes found in wilderness/rebellion at Baal Peor	9:10–17
iii. Israel as luxuriant vine that will be grown over	10:1–8
iv. Israel as trained heifer that must repent/return	10:9–11:11
v. Ephraim's need for exile and return like Jacob	12:1–15
vi. Ephraim's exalted status turned to punishment and death	13:1–14:1
4. Appeal for Israel to return to YHWH/abandon alliance with Assyria	14:2–9
III. Postscript: Instruction for wise to understand (Hosea) and to act properly	14:10

her faithlessness. Following the initial presentation of this paradigm, the book provides an extended analysis of northern Israel's behavior that indicates its abandonment of YHWH together with repeated statements by YHWH and the prophet that Israel will be punished but that YHWH will also seek Israel's return. The concluding appeal for Israel's return in Hosea 14:2–9 is particularly important in that it points to the return of Israel as one of the primary goals of the work. But it also points to an interest in explaining and justifying the suffering of Israel as a punishment brought about by YHWH that will eventually result in Israel's return and the restoration of the relationship.

Third, the book of Hosea speaks generally of Israel's abandonment of YHWH based on the paradigm of Gomer's adultery in relation to Hosea as the basic problem in the relationship between Israel and YHWH. Religious apostasy therefore constitutes an important theme of the book as indicated by the addresses to the priests and prophets condemning them for their failure to instill proper "knowledge of G-d" in the people and by the frequent references to Israel's cultic sites—for example, Beth-Aven (Beth-El), Mizpah, Gilgal, Shechem, and so on—as places for illicit worship of pagan deities. But religious apostasy is not the only problem highlighted in the book. Hosea points especially to the kings of Israel as one of the fundamental causes for Israel's problems in that YHWH did not desire kingship for Israel in the first place and because the northern kings are so closely associated with the idolatry and violence that Hosea perceives throughout the land (see esp. Hos 8:1–6). One particular aspect of Israel's abandonment of YHWH appears again and again throughout the book: that is, Israel's alliance with Assyria and perhaps Egypt. This theme appears throughout the bulk of the book in the detailed discussion of Israel's "harlotry" in Hosea 5:13–14, 7:8–16, 8:7–14, and 12:2, together with references to Israel's exile to Assyria and Egypt in Hosea 9:1–3, 10:6, and 11:5, 10–11, and it appears in the final appeal for Israel to return to YHWH in Hosea 14:3, where Assyria is presented as unable to deliver the nation. Such an alliance would be undertaken by the kings of Israel, and it is portrayed as an action designed to protect the nation and facilitate its role in trade between Assyria and Egypt. In this respect, the king's alliance with Assyria is presented as the people's rejection of YHWH.

Obviously, this suggests that one means to repair the relationship between Israel and YHWH is to abandon the alliance with Assyria and to eliminate the various manifestations of pagan worship or contact that such an alliance might entail or encourage. In this regard, it is noteworthy that a great deal of the material in the book is directed to the northern kingdom of Israel in order to call for its return to YHWH. The analysis of the structure and generic character of the book indicates that, although much material constitutes the prophet's direct address to the northern kingdom, which articulates its punishment and calls for its return to YHWH, a great deal of the material is not directly addressed to Israel but speaks objectively about Israel to another party, viz., the anonymous audience of the book. Although the prophet may well have composed this material with a northern Israelite audience in mind, two features point to the identification of this anonymous audience as a Judean audience in the final form of the book.

First, there are numerous references to Judah's guilt and punishment alongside Israel, although it is always clear that Israel bears primary responsibility for wrongdoing and that it will suffer more in relation to Judah. These references have been investigated as potential redactional additions designed to adjust the message of the book for a Judean audience, but most seem to have been a part of the original composition rather than later additions to the text.[22] Nevertheless, they point to an interest in addressing Judah as well as Israel. Second, this interest in Judah appears to express the fact that Judah will be punished alongside Israel, but that Judah will find itself in a much better position than Israel in relation to YHWH. The narrative in Hosea 1:6–7 concerning the naming of Lo Ruhamah indicates that YHWH will ultimately forgive Israel, but that YHWH will have mercy on Judah and deliver Judah militarily, an option that is not open to Israel. Likewise, Hosea 12:1 indicates that Judah's relationship with YHWH is still secure.

This interest in Judah is particularly noteworthy in relation to the condemnation of the northern Israelite kings throughout the book. Hosea 10:15, for example, indicates that the northern Israelite king will be destroyed. Statements concerning the future political constitution of the people are enlightening in this regard in that they point to Judean interest. Hosea 2:1–3, for example, reiterates the patriarchal promise that the people of Israel will become as numerous as the sands of the sea, but it continues with a statement that the people of Israel and the people of Judah will be reunited and will appoint for themselves one king as a result of the day of Jezreel, which clearly condemns the northern dynasty of Jehu. Furthermore, Hosea 3:1–5 presents an autobiographical statement by the prophet concerning his (re)marriage, which concludes with statements that the people of Israel will dwell for many years without a king until the return to YHWH and David their king in the latter days. These last statements concerning a reunified people ruled by a Davidic monarch clearly speak to Judean interests.

These considerations establish the Judean identity of the anonymous reading audience of the book of Hosea. The objective descriptions of northern Israel's abandonment of YHWH throughout the book and the appeal to Israel to return to YHWH (and to David) clearly have Judean interests in mind. This indicates that the book of Hosea may be initially addressed to Israel, but it addresses Judah as well, and it does so in a manner that defines the return of Israel to YHWH as a return of Israel to Judah and the house of David. In such a context, the critique of Israel's cultic apostasy would have to be taken as a call for Israel's return to the Jerusalem Temple as well.

This analysis obviously raises questions concerning the setting of the book. Although many scholars see the final form of the book as the product of postexilic redaction, there appears to be little basis for the conclusion that any redaction of Hosea must be set in the postexilic period.[23] Nothing in the book speaks explicitly of the problems generated by the destruction of Jerusalem and the Temple, the Babylonian exile of Judah, or the potential return of the Babylonian exiles and the rebuilding of the Temple. The themes of the book focus entirely on the pun-

---

22. See Emmerson, *Hosea.*

23. Cf. Brevard Childs, *Introduction to the Old Testament as Scripture* (Philadelphia: Fortress, 1979) 377–380, who likewise warns against attempts to place the redaction of Hosea in the postexilic period.

ishment and exile of the northern kingdom of Israel during the Assyrian period. In cases where Judean suffering is addressed, it is only in the context of the Assyrian threat against Israel. Certainly, such themes could have been read in the context of the Babylonian exile as a model for understanding Judah's experience, but the composition of the book appears to have taken place prior to the Babylonian threat against Jerusalem and Judah.

The interest in calling for Israel's return to YHWH and in the reunification of Israel and Judah under a single Davidic monarchic is the key factor in establishing the setting for the composition of the book of Hosea. Given such an interest, it would appear that the period of Hosea's composition could extend any time from the lifetime of the prophet in the mid-eighth century B.C.E. through the reign of King Josiah in the late seventh century. Certainly, the reunification of Israel and Judah under a Davidic monarch is central to Josiah's concerns, but the evidence for a Josianic redaction of Hosea is somewhat ambiguous. The narrative material in Hosea 1:1 and 1:2–2:3 points to an author other than the prophet who formulates the initial material of the book and thereby provides the organization of the book and the premises upon which the balance of Hosea is read. But the concern to show mercy to Judah and the interest in reunited Israel and Judah under one king is hardly exclusive to the period of King Josiah. As indicated elsewhere in the studies of Amos and Isaiah, there is extensive interest in such issues during the time of King Hezekiah and perhaps before that time as well. Likewise, the explicit references to Israel's return to YHWH and David in Hosea 3:4–5 have frequently constituted the basis for conclusions of a Josianic (or later) redaction of Hosea.[24] Although Hosea frequently criticizes the northern kings and calls for their destruction or punishment, nowhere else does the prophet express such explicitly pro-Davidic sentiments. Nevertheless, the statement appears in the context of an autobiographical narrative, although it is not explicitly formulated as a first-person statement by the prophet and it is attached to vv. 1–3 by a causative *kî*.

Two major conclusions concerning the setting of Hosea's composition appear to be warranted. First, the narrative material in Hosea 1:1; 1:2–2:3 does not necessarily derive from the time of King Josiah; rather, it may well derive from the period of King Hezekiah or earlier during the late eighth century. The calls for Israel's return to YHWH and its reunification with Judah under one king certainly speak to Hezekiah's interests in undertaking a revolt against the Assyrian empire and in extending the power of Judah and the house of David. The narrative form of these passages is clearly the product of some author other than Hosea. Several features of this narrative and the book as a whole are therefore noteworthy.

---

24. See esp. Yee, *Composition* 57–64, for a full discussion of the redaction-critical issues involved in the interpretation of Hosea 3:1–5. Her contention that the entirety of Hosea 3:1–5 is redactional is based in part on faulty premises, viz., the *possibility* that first-person narrative form can be redactional and the lexical correspondences between Hosea 3:1–5 and prior texts that *must* demonstrate a later hand. Fundamentally, her conclusions are based on her view that Hosea comprises three basic structural elements in Hosea 1–3, 4–11, and 12–14, which she simply takes over from Wolff, and her view that each must end with redactional additions that speak to the restoration of Israel.

The superscription of the narrative places Hosea's activities in the reign of the northern monarch Jeroboam ben Joash and in the reigns of the Judean monarchs Uzziah, Jotham, Ahaz, and Hezekiah. This is remarkable in that, whereas Hosea is a northern prophet, the superscription completely omits reference to the kings of Israel who ruled after Jeroboam ben Joash, viz., Zechariah, Shallum, Menahem, Pekahiah, Pekah, and Hoshea, all of whom were contemporaries of the Judean kings listed herein. Second, Hosea 1:2–2:3 employs the symbolic name Jezreel for Hosea's first son as a basis for articulating its condemnation of Israel. This is a clear reference to the means by which the Jehu dynasty, of which Jeroboam ben Joash was the most prominent member, came to power, in that Jehu assumed kingship after assassinating the last elements of the house of Omri at Jezreel.

The references to Israel's alliances with Assyria also must be considered. Although many have seen these references in relation to Menahem's attempts to bring Israel into an alliance with Assyria, many scholars overlook Jeroboam's alliance with the Assyrians. Jeroboam is said to have ruled a powerful kingdom from Lebo Hamath to the Sea of the Arabah (2 Kgs 14:25), but he did so as an ally of the Assyrians. Shalmanezer III (858–824 B.C.E.) had forced Jehu to submit to Assyrian authority in the aftermath of his campaign against Syria in his eighteenth year (ca. 840 B.C.E., cf. ARAB I 590, 672). Joash likewise paid tribute to Adad Nirari III of Assyria.[25] During the reign of Jeroboam, Israel and Assyria were apparently able to divide Syria among themselves as Jeroboam controlled Syria as far north as Lebo Hamath and Assur Nirari V was able to impose a temporary alliance on Mati-ilu of Arpad in the north.[26] Such a situation would facilitate cooperation between Israel and Assyria in order to control Syria and to facilitate trade between Mesopotamia and Egypt in which both would profit.[27] This points to a situation in which Hosea was highly critical of Jeroboam ben Joash for maintaining an alliance with Assyria. Insofar as Judah was also an ally or vassal of Israel, it would be included in Hosea's criticism, although Israel was certainly the leading target of Hosea's critique. Given that Jeroboam's son Zechariah was assassinated by Shallum, and that Shallum was in turn assassinated by Menahem who immediately moved to submit to Assyria (cf. 2 Kgs 15:8–31), it is entirely possible that Hosea's criticism of Jeroboam and his alliance with Assyria was

---

25. See S. Page, "A Stela of Adad Nirari III and Nergal-ereš from Tell al Rimlah," *Iraq* 30 (1968) 139–153; cf. Hayes and Miller, eds., *Israelite and Judaean History* 414. See also Adad Nirari III's Calah inscription in which he claims to receive tribute from "the land of Omri," that is, Israel (*ANET* 281).

26. See the treaty with Mati'ilu of Arpad with Assur Nirari V, which dates to ca. 751 B.C.E. (Luckenbill, *ARAB I* 749–760), but internal problems caused Assyria to lose control of Arpad. Shortly thereafter, Mati'ilu was able to conclude another treaty with Bargayah, king of KTK (see *ANET* 659–661). The identification of KTK is disputed, but the treaty nevertheless points to Arpad's subjugation to Assyria at a time when the Assyrian empire needed allies. Jeroboam ben Joash would have been able to play a supporting role in Assyria's attempts to secure its western borders. Cf. Hallo and Simpson, *The Ancient Near East: A History* 131–132.

27. Note that later Assyrian expansion in the west was motivated especially by an interest in developing commercial contacts with Egypt and the eastern Mediterranean (cf. Moshe Elat, "The Economic Relations of the Neo-Assyrian Empire with Egypt," *JAOS* 98 [1978] 20–34).

somehow bound up with Shallum's coup against Zechariah and Menahem's countercoup against Shallum.[28] Under such circumstances, Hosea may well have found himself in a difficult situation when Menahem ascended the throne and concluded that his interests would best be served if he left Israel and settled in Judah.

This must remain speculative, of course, but it does explain why the superscription would name only Jeroboam in the north while naming a full array of kings in the south. It also would explain Hosea's interests in the destruction of the northern kings and in the reunification of Israel and Judah under one king. Such a perspective would likely be welcome in the court of King Hezekiah, although not in that of Ahaz, who turned to Assyria for support in the Syro-Ephraimitic crisis. Certainly, Hosea's message would be relevant in the time of Jotham and Ahaz, both of whom had to face the possibility of Israel's potential threat against Judah by considering alliance with Assyria. A critique of Israel's former alliance with Assyria would certainly provide an argument against such a move, even if it was ultimately ignored. In Hezekiah's time, such a critique would fuel efforts to revolt against Assyria and support an effort on the part of the monarch to restore Davidic rule over the north. In the aftermath of Assyria's destruction of the northern kingdom, Hosea's prophecies would be perceived as fulfilled and the time for Israel's return to YHWH would be ripe.

Again, such a scenario must remain hypothetical. It is entirely possible that the present form of Hosea 3:4–5 is the product of a Josianic hand that elaborated on earlier statements concerning the reunification of Israel and Judah under one monarch in Hosea 2:1–3. Nevertheless, these considerations point to the fact that the book of Hosea would have been read in the late seventh century B.C.E. as a prophetic justification for the reform program of King Josiah. In such a scenario, Hosea's critique of the northern kingdom, including its faithlessness, the failure of its religious leaders and kings, and its alliance with Assyria, would all be read as fulfilled prophecy in the time of Josiah. Only the last element of the prophet's message would need to be realized at such a time, viz., the reunification of the people of Israel with Judah and the return of Israel to YHWH and to the House of David.

---

28. The coup was likely motivated in part by fear of Assyria in the aftermath of Tiglath-Pileser's assumption of power. In such a situation, Shallum may well have struck in an attempt to sever Israel's ties with Assyria, whereas Menahem preserved them. For discussion of this period, see Hayes and Miller, eds., *Israelite and Judaean History* 415–434.

16

Amos

One would not normally think of Amos as a major source for the study of King Josiah's attempts at national restoration and religious reform in the latter part of the seventh century B.C.E. According to the superscription of the book in Amos 1:1, Amos spoke in the mid-eighth century B.C.E. during the reigns of King Jeroboam ben Joash of Israel (786–7466 B.C.E.) and King Uzziah (Azariah) ben Amaziah of Judah (782–742 B.C.E.) prior to the Assyrian invasions of the Syro-Israelite region in the late eighth century. For the most part, Amos is treated as the exemplar of the classical writing prophet, who eschews identification with the political, economic, and religious centers of national power to emphasize a message of social justice to a corrupt Israel, in which the rich upper class was systematically exploiting a poor lower class in order to enrich itself even more.[1] He boldly stands in the Temple at Beth-El, the royal sanctuary of the northern kingdom of Israel, and claims that King Jeroboam will die by the sword and that Israel will go into exile as a result of this wrongdoing. When questioned about his motivations for speaking such a message, Amos claims that he is neither a prophet nor the son of a prophet—that is, he is not a professional prophet, but a herdsman and dresser of sycamore trees whom YHWH sent to speak his prophetic message to the corrupt kingdom.

For the most part, scholars have begun to recognize that this portrait of Amos reflects the perspectives of modern liberal Protestant and Reform Jewish theology in the late nineteenth and early twentieth centuries more so than those of eighth-century Israel and Judah.[2] Furthermore, several methodological factors have

---

1. For a survey of research on the message and social views of Amos, see A. G. Auld, *Amos*, OTG (Sheffield: JSOT Press, 1986) 60–83; cf. Bruce Willoughby, "Amos, Book of," *ABD* I, 203–212.

2. For example, see the comments by Auld, *Amos* 80.

emerged in recent years concerning the study of prophetic literature that point to a need to reconsider the book of Amos in relation both to the eighth century B.C.E. and to the seventh-century reign of King Josiah.[3] These factors include a combination of literary and social perspectives in the study of prophetic literature that focus on both synchronic and diachronic readings of prophetic books in their present canonical forms and the function of prophetic writings in relation to the communities that formulated and read them.[4]

Throughout much of the twentieth century, modern scholarship has emphasized attempts to reconstruct the earliest forms of the prophetic literature in an effort to identify the actual words of the prophets and the historical events that they addressed and the settings in which they were spoken. In the case of Amos, the book was treated as a collection of short speech units that were spoken at various times and places throughout the prophet's career.[5] In such a paradigm, scholars argued that a great deal of later material intruded into the authentic words of the prophet's and represented the misunderstandings of Amos' words by later authors or attempts to modify the prophet's message with the concerns and ideas of later times.

During the years since World War II, however, developing interests in the literary character of texts per se rather than on the events they convey has prompted a shift in exegetical methodology from a focus on the short, self-contained generic unit as an indication of the prophet's original speech forms to longer, more developed literary texts that present a complex series of themes, motifs, and rhetorical features to convey a message to its audience of readers or hearers. As a result, increasing attention is paid to the book of Amos as a work of literature; this includes study of its overall structure and literary form, as well as the history of its literary formation, as scholars have attempted to reconstruct the process and stages by which the book evolved from the original sayings of the prophet to the present literary book. A number of such attempts, both to establish the literary structure of the book and the process of its formation, have been put forward, although none has gained general assent.[6] To the extent that they treat Amos as a book per se rather than as a disordered collection of oracles, they identify the three generic elements of the book as its constituent components: that is, the oracles against the nations in Amos 1:3–2:16, the oracles against Israel in Amos 3:1–6:14;

3. See esp. my article, "Formation and Form in Prophetic Literature," in *Old Testament Interpretation: Past, Present, and Future*, Fs. G. M. Tucker, ed. J. L. Mays, D. L. Petersen, and K. H. Richards (Nashville: Abingdon, 1995) 113–126, which treats methodological developments and their relation to the study of Amos.

4. See esp. John Barton, *Reading the Old Testament: Method in Biblical Study* (Lexington, KY: Westminster John Knox, revised edition, 1996) and Robert Morgan with John Barton, *Biblical Interpretation*, Oxford Bible Series (Oxford: Oxford University Press, 1988), for discussion of these issues.

5. See the commentaries on Amos by James L. Mays, *Amos: A Commentary*, OTL (Philadelphia: Westminster, 1969) and Hans W. Wolff, *Joel and Amos*, Hermeneia (Philadelphia: Fortress, 1977), for recent examples of this approach.

6. See the survey by Auld on literary issues in *Amos* 50–59 and Willoughby, "Amos, Book of," 207–210. In addition, see Shalom Paul, *Amos*, Hermeneia (Minneapolis: Fortress, 1991).

and the vision reports in Amos 7:1–9:15. Prominent later additions include, among others, elements of the oracles against the nations in Amos 1:3–2:16; the narrative concerning Amos' confrontation with Amaziah at Beth-El in Amos 7:10–17; and the oracle concerning the restoration of the "fallen booth of David" in Amos 9:11–15. Because the latter is generally seen as a postexilic expression of hope for the restoration of the destroyed monarchy,[7] the literary history of Amos is generally viewed to extend from the time of the prophet through the postexilic period.[8]

Despite the uncertainties pertaining to the literary structure and formation history of the book of Amos, two particular features of the present form of the book demand attention in relation to the concerns of the present study. The first is Amos' identity as a Judean from the village of Tekoa, some sixteen kilometers south of Jerusalem, who speaks in the northern kingdom of Israel. With regard to Amos' Judean identity, it must be recalled that, during the mid-eighth century B.C.E., the kingdom of Judah was allied as a vassal to the larger kingdom of Israel, which, according to 2 Kings 14:25, extended "from the entrance of Hamath as far as the Sea of the Arabah," that is, from Aram/Syria to the Gulf of Aqaba.[9] In such a situation, Judah would be obligated to pay a certain yearly tribute to Israel as part of its obligations as a vassal state. The requirements for such tribute would explain Amos' presence at the Beth-El altar, especially since he is self-described as a herdsman and dresser of sycamore trees, in that he came to bring a share of the Judean tribute due to Israel. This also would explain the extensive agricultural imagery throughout the book, such as the cart of sheaves that presses down due to the weight of its contents (that is, a reference to produce being carted from Judah to northern Israel, in Amos 2:1) or the reference to the "king's mowings" (that is, the share of the harvest due to the king, in Amos 7:1). This also provides some context for understanding Amos' diatribes against the rich and powerful who oppress the poor and needy; Amos was condemning the practices of the northern kingdom of Israel in taking a heavy tribute from Judean farmers such as himself.[10]

The second noteworthy feature of the book, the focus on the Beth-El altar, follows naturally from the first. Tribute paid by a vassal state to a suzerain is paid at the state sanctuary of the suzerain, in the case of Israel, at Beth-El. Overall, the present arrangement of the book of Amos seems to be designed to lead the reader from a general view of the punishment of Israel's enemies to the destruction of the Beth-El altar, the royal altar of the northern kingdom of Israel, as the ultimate focus or concern of the book. Not only does it provide the climax of the vision sequence in Amos 7–9, but also it forms the climax of the entire book. This is particularly important to consider for three reasons: (1) the initial oracles against the nations progressively list a series of nations in the Syro-Israelite region until

---

7. For example, Wolff, *Joel and Amos* 352–353.

8. See the discussion by Wolff, *Joel and Amos* 106–113.

9. See the notice in 2 Kings 14:8–14 concerning Amaziah's failed attempt to challenge the Israelite king Jehoash. Cf. Miller and Hayes, *A History of Ancient Israel and Judah* 307–313; Hayes and Miller, eds., *Israelite and Judaean History* 414.

10. Cf. Willoughby, "Amos, Book of," 203–204, who identifies Amos as a member of the well-to-do Judean landed class.

they culminate in the lengthy oracle against northern Israel as the climax of the section; (2) the oracles in Amos 3–6 focus especially on the social and economic wrongdoing of the northern kingdom of Israel; and (3) the oracle against Beth-El in Amos 9:1–10 is followed immediately by the oracle in Amos 9:11–15 that calls for the restoration of the "fallen booth of David"—that is, the restoration of the ruling house of David. Although most scholars have placed this concern in relation to the restoration of the house of David in the aftermath of its demise in the Babylonian conquest and destruction of Jerusalem, Paul recently has suggested that it might be a call for the restoration of Davidic rule over the northern kingdom.[11] Such a concern might well express the interests of the prophet in the eighth century B.C.E.; it certainly expresses the interests of King Josiah in the late seventh century, who demolished the altar at Beth-El and attempted to restore the former northern kingdom of Israel to Davidic rule.

Both of these factors demand a reconceptualization of the book of Amos. Such a reconceptualization must begin with an examination of the literary structure, generic character, and rhetorical perspective of the book in its present form.

Reconsideration of the structure of the book of Amos must begin with the superscription in Amos 1:1,[12] which identifies the contents of the book as "the words of Amos who was among the shepherds from Tekoa, which he saw concerning Israel in the days of Uzziah king of Judah and in the days of Jeroboam ben Joash king of Israel, two years before the earthquake." Several items thereby come to the reader's attention: (1) the generic identification of the material contained in the book as the "words" or "matters" of Amos, which refers to both speech and actions or events; (2) the identification of Amos as the "author" or subject of the following material; (3) the identification of Amos as a "shepherd" from the village of Tekoa in Judah; (4) the topic of his words on "Israel" (that is, the northern kingdom of Israel); and (5) the time period of his words during the reigns of Uzziah of Judah and Jeroboam ben Joash of Israel, two years before the earthquake. The order of the monarchs, with the Judean Uzziah listed first, may well reflect the Judean background of Amos or the composers of the book. The date of the earthquake is unknown.[13] Normally, a superscription stands apart from the material that it identifies, but the superscription of Amos is expanded by the "motto" in Amos 1:2, which is syntactically joined to the superscription by the *waw*-consecutive verbal form, *wayyō'mar*, "and he said."[14] This introduces a quotation by the prophet, "YHWH roars from Zion and from Jerusalem he gives voice, and the pasturelands of the shepherds wither and top of the Carmel dries up." Overall, this statement functions as an introduction or premise for Amos' message as presented in the balance of the book. It highlights YHWH's identifi-

---

11. Paul, *Amos* 288–295; cf. John H. Hayes, *Amos, the Eighth Century Prophet: His Times and His Preaching* (Nashville: Abingdon, 1988) 223–228.

12. For study of the form and function of superscriptions in prophetic books, see Tucker, "Prophetic Superscriptions and the Growth of the Canon."

13. Most scholars associate it with the earthquake that apparently struck Hazor ca. 760 B.C.E. See Paul, *Amos* 35.

14. Cf. Wolff, *Joel and Amos* 116–126.

cation with Zion/Jerusalem, and YHWH's mastery over the natural world, especially the Carmel, a term that refers generally to vineyard lands, a characteristic
land area of the northern kingdom, or specifically to the Carmel range of northern
Israel. In either case, the Judean political and religious stance over against northern Israel is clear. Together, the superscription in Amos 1:1 and the motto in
Amos 1:2 introduce the balance of the book in Amos 1:3–9:15.

The first major subunit of Amos 1:3–9:15 is the oracles against the nations in
Amos 1:3–2:16. This section is held together by its relatively consistent formulation of oracles against a sequence of nations. Each oracle begins with generic statements that indicate the prophet's quotation of a message by YHWH concerning
the punishment of the nation in question, "Thus says YHWH, 'for three transgressions of *PN* and for four, I will not revoke it' (i.e., the punishment)."[15] The oracle
then continues with a specific statement of the actions by the nation, which call
for punishment. Statements that outline the punishment to be visited by YHWH
upon the nation then follow, and, in most cases, a concluding oracular formula
closes the oracle. The sequence of nations includes the following: Damascus/Aram
(1:3–5), Gaza/Philistia (1:6–8), Tyre/Phoenicia (1:9–10), Edom (1:11–12), Ammon
(1:13–15), Moab (2:1–3), Judah (2:4–5), and Israel (2:6–16). The identity and
sequence of nations is essential to understanding the rhetorical impact of this section. Each of the nations listed prior to Israel is a vassal or ally of Israel during the
reign of Jeroboam ben Joash, and each of the crimes listed indicates some sort of
wrongdoing in the eyes of people from the northern kingdom—namely, Aram's
attempts to conquer the Trans-Jordan region in the ninth century, Philistine and
Tyrian cooperation against Israel and Judah for incursions into the Negev, Edomite
actions against Judah, Ammonite movements against the Gilead region, Moabite
attacks against Edom, and Judean rejection of YHWH's instruction.[16] Overall, the
listing of these nations and their crimes would suggest to an eighth-century northern
Israel audience that each of these nations was receiving its punishment as a result
of the resurgence of the northern kingdom at this time. But the culmination of the
oracle sequence with Israel would take a northern audience by surprise and drive
home the intended point, that YHWH's intentions were ultimately to punish northern Israel for abusing its position as an international power.[17] YHWH would punish Israel for taking unfair advantage of its subjects. The extended oracle against
Israel thereby emphasizes the overall concern with the northern kingdom and
prepares the reader for the next major section of the book.

The next major segment of Amos 1:3–9:15 appears in the oracles directed
against northern Israel in Amos 3:1–4:13. This section is characterized by its introductory calls to attention, directed first to "the sons of Israel" in Amos 3:1 and
second to the women of Israel or "the cows of Bashan" in Amos 4:1. Although it

---

15. For a discussion of the phrase, "I will not cause it to return," see Rolf Knierim, "'I Will
not Cause it to Return' in Amos 1 and 2," in *Canon and Authority*, ed. G. W. Coats and B. O. Long
(Philadelphia: Westminster, 1977) 163–175.

16. For discussion of the historical issues behind these oracles, see Paul, *Amos* 43–99; Wolff,
Joel and Amos 127–173.

17. Paul, *Amos* 76.

contains a wide variety of generic elements, the section is held together by an overall interest in laying out the wrongs committed by the people of the northern kingdom of Israel, in contrast to the following segment beginning in Amos 5:1 that calls for the people to turn from their ways. Amos 3:1–4:13 takes a special interest in condemning the people of the northern kingdom, especially in relation to well-established cultic sites, such as Beth-El and Gilgal (Am 3:14; 4:4–5), and the capital city of Samaria (Am 3:9, 12, 15; 4:1). Overall, the passage employs traditions characteristic of the northern kingdom to make its case. It begins in Amos 3:1–2 with reference to YHWH's redemption of Israel from Egypt; because of Israel's special relationship with YHWH, it will be punished. Amos 3:3–8 then employs a wisdom analogy to indicate that two related things do not happen in isolation; evil has befallen the city, the prophets are speaking, YHWH is acting to punish. Amos 3:9–4:3 call on the people to witness the various aspects of YHWH's punishments that are to be visited on the people of Israel for the wrongdoings with which they are charged. Amos 4:4–5 call on the people to continue their transgression with offerings at Beth-El and Gilgal. Amos 4:6–11 outlines YHWH's various actions that were designed to show divine power over the people, including acts of beneficence, but more commonly acts of punishment. Finally, Amos 4:12–13 provide the climactic statements that YHWH is preparing to punish the people.

Amos 5:1–6:14 then turns to the issue of Israel's potential repentance.[18] Like Amos 3:1–4:13, this section begins with an introductory call to attention in Amos 5:1 that is directed to the house of Israel and introduces the prophet's lamentation over the fall of Israel in Amos 5:2–3. The exhortational element of this section, and indeed of the entire book, then becomes clear in Amos 5:4–27 that the prophet calls on the people to seek YHWH and live rather than rely on the traditional northern Israelite cultic sites at Beth-El and Gilgal—that is, "For thus says YHWH of Hosts to the house of Israel, 'Seek me and live; but do not seek Beth-El and do not enter into Gilgal or cross over to Beer Sheba; for Gilgal shall surely go into exile and Beth-El shall come to nought.'" Amos 6:1–14 then employs woe oracles (cf. Am 6:1–3, 4–7) to warn the people, including those in Zion/Jerusalem as well as in Samaria, that YHWH is bringing punishment against the northern kingdom, described with typically northern traditional names such as Joseph (Am 6:7) and Jacob (Am 6:8). The passage ends with a description of the ruin to be visited against the people; verse 13 alludes to the sanctuary at Beth-El by labeling it "Lo-dabar," or, "not a word" or "not a thing," and by reference to the people taking Karnaim—that is, a reference to the "horns" (*qarnāyim*) of the altar as a sign of strength, for themselves. By alluding to the futility of relying on Beth-El in this manner, the passage prepares the reader for the final section of the book in Amos 7–9.

The final segment of Amos 1:3–9:15 appears in the vision reports of Amos 7:1–9:15. This section is identified by its generic character as a series of vision reports in which the prophet discusses a sequence of five visions from YHWH that culminate in the call for the destruction of the Beth-El sanctuary. The first

18. For discussion of the problems posed by Amos 5, see Auld, *Amos* 50–54.

two are formulated in a similar manner as autobiographical reports in which the prophet begins with the formulaic statement, "Thus YHWH G-d showed me," followed by a description of the specific vision and the prophet's protest that Jacob—that is, Israel—cannot stand against such a threat and the deity's promise to revoke the punishment in question. Amos 7:1–3 comprises the vision of the devouring locust, who strip the land of produce after the "king's mowings," leaving the people destitute and the vision of fire consuming the deep and the land in Amos 7:4–6, which again testifies to YHWH's role in the natural world of the farmer as a sign of action in the historical and political realm. Two further visions follow: the vision of the plumbline in Amos 7:7–17 and the vision of the basket of summer fruit in Amos 8:1–14, both introduced by the formula, "Thus YHWH G-d showed me," followed by a description of the vision and some elaboration of its meaning. The vision of the plumbline portrays YHWH measuring the people as a person might measure the straightness of a wall to determine the people's moral straightness. Upon finding them inadequate, YHWH announces that the high places and sanctuaries of the northern kingdom will be destroyed and the house of King Jeroboam will be put to the sword. The above-mentioned narrative in Amos 7:10–17 concerning Amos's confrontation with the priest Amaziah at Beth-El then illustrates this oracle. The vision of the summer fruit in Amos 8:1–3 employs a pun in which the basket of summer fruit (*qĕlûb qāyiṣ*) serves as a sign that the "end" (*qēṣ*) has come upon the people of Israel. The oracle in Amos 8:4–14 then highlights the reasons for that punishment with special reference to abuse of the poor and the cultic life of the people of Israel. The final vision of the sequence appears in Amos 9:1–15. It begins with the statement, "I saw YHWH standing upon the altar," as an introduction to YHWH's commands to destroy the sanctuary at Beth-El. Verses 1–10 describe inability of people to escape YHWH's punishment, and verses 11–15 describe the subsequent rise of the fallen booth of David in the aftermath of Beth-El's destruction together with the renewed fertility of the land. With this vision of restoration, the book concludes.

Overall, the present form of the book of Amos provides an extended critique of the northern kingdom of Israel that focuses on the rejection of YHWH in terms of abusive treatment of the poor and illegitimate worship at Beth-El and other traditional northern cultic sites. The book calls for proper treatment of the poor, the destruction of the Beth-El altar, and the restoration of the house of David as the means to "seek YHWH and live" (Amos 5:6). The book may therefore be characterized as an exhortation to return to YHWH directed to the people of the northern kingdom of Israel. The structure of the book may be portrayed as in table 16.1.

The preceding discussion demonstrates that the present form of the book of Amos is organized to articulate a critique against the northern kingdom of Israel, a call for its repentance, the destruction of the Beth-El altar, and the reestablishment of the house of David. All of these factors must be considered in establishing the setting of the present form of the book. As noted, scholars generally date the final form of Amos to the postexilic period, based primarily on the call for the reestablishment of the house of David in Amos 9:11–15.[19] But this position pre-

---

19. Cf. Wolff, *Joel and Amos* 106–107.

TABLE 16.1   Structure of the Book of Amos: Exhortation to return to YHWH

Directed to the Northern Kingdom of Israel	*Amos 1:1–9:15*
I. Introduction	1:1–2
A. Superscription	1:1
B. Motto	1:2
II. Exhortation proper	1:3–9:15
A. Oracles against the nations: indictment of northern Israel	1:3–2:16
1. Damascus/Aram	1:3–5
2. Gaza/Philistia	1:6–8
3. Tyre/Phoenicia	1:9–10
4. Edom	1:11–12
5. Ammon	1:13–15
6. Moab	2:1–3
7. Judah	2:4–5
8. Israel	2:6–16
B. Indictment of northern Israel	3:1–4:13
C. Call for repentance of northern Israel	5:1–6:14
D. Vision reports: call for destruction of Beth-El and rise of house of David	7:1–9:15
1. Vision of locusts	7:1–3
2. Vision of fire	7:4–6
3. Vision of plumbline	7:7–17
4. Vision of summer fruit	8:1–14
5. Vision of Beth-El's destruction and David's rise	9:1–15

supposes the complete destruction of the Davidic house in the postexilic period, whereas the placement of this oracle in the book of Amos simply indicates the reestablishment of Davidic rule over the north. Likewise, several scholars have postulated a Deuteronomic redaction based on references to Judah's rejection of YHWH's Torah (2:4–5), judgment against Tyre and Edom (1:19–12), an interest in prophecy (2:11–12), parenetic concerns (2:10–12), and chronological issues (1:1).[20] But such a piecemeal approach demonstrates no comprehensive interest in conceptualizing the book of Amos in relation to a general Dtr worldview; rather, it points to selected features of the text that might correspond to Dtr interests of the exilic period. This view is undergirded by the assumption that Deuteronomic thought is exilic, but the Dtr connection with Josiah's program is increasingly evident. Furthermore, the concerns listed here easily relate to preexilic concerns. The concern with Judah's rejection of Torah fits easily with Josianic concerns. The focus on Tyre and Edom need not be explained by an expanded exilic worldview, but by an attempt to outline the entire purview of the Assyrian presence in the Syro-Israelite region and Josianic concerns to consider those lands in relation to a Judean/Israelite restoration. Interest in prophecy is hardly an exclusive Dtr concern, and parenesis is characteristic of a prophetic interest in motivat-

20. Werner H. Schmidt, "Die deuteronomistische Redaktion des Amosbuches: Zu den theologischen Unterschieden zwischen dem Prophetenwort und seinem Sammler," *ZAW* 77 (1965) 168–193; Wolff, *Joel and Amos* 112–113.

ing change in its addressees. The chronological concern pervades prophetic books, whether or not they are Deuteronomically oriented.

These examples point to the need to develop alternative criteria for establishing the setting of the final form of the book. Several factors must be considered.

First is the overall indictment of Israel in relation to the concern with the destruction of the Beth-El altar and the reestablishment of the House of David. On the surface, such a concern would clearly relate to the interests of the Josianic period, and considerable effort has been expended to define a Josianic redaction in the book on just such a basis. But these efforts generally overlook the relevance of Amos' Judean identity and the suzerain-vassal relationship between Israel and Judah in establishing the message of the prophet. A call for the destruction of Beth-El and the reestablishment of Davidic rule would be characteristic of a prophet such as Amos, who appears in Beth-El to pay part of the tribute owed by Judah to Israel. Such a message would express the frustration of a Judean who had also suffered crop reversals, for example, the locusts and fires indicated in the first two visions. It is doubtful that the call for the reestablishment of Davidic rule would be realistic during the reign of Jeroboam ben Joash, but a Judean prophet would likely look upon the past period of Davidic rule over the north in more ideal terms.

Although a call for the reestablishment of Davidic rule over the north would certainly fit well with Amos' sociopolitical setting, it also would correspond well to several subsequent periods in Israel's and Judah's history. Jotham's refusal to join the Syro-Ephraimitic coalition against the Assyrian empire would provide one possible setting, in that Jotham may well have entertained thoughts of siding with the Assyrians as a means to bring northern Israel under his control. At times, the Assyrians were known to assign vassal territories to local chieftains or rulers who would administer the territory on Assyria's behalf.[21] This must remain speculative, however, as Jotham did not live long enough to call on the Assyrians for support. Ahaz's actions in calling for Assyrian support against the Syro-Ephraimitic coalition may well have been based on such a premise, however, and perhaps would reflect Jotham's thinking. Certainly, Ahaz and his advisors would consider the possibility of some reward from the Assyrians for such a demonstration of loyalty. Although fear of annihilation by the Arameans and Israelites is clearly a decisive factor, some form of control over the northern kingdom may well have motivated Ahaz. Whether or not Ahaz considered this possibility, there is no evidence that the Assyrians ever granted Judah a hand in administering a subdued or conquered Israel. At the conclusion of the Syro-Ephraimitic war, 2 Kings 16:10–18 indicates that Ahaz made modifications in the Temple and palace complex in

---

21. For a discussion of Assyrian administrative practices over both vassal territories and provinces, see Jana Pečírková, "The Administrative Methods of Assyrian Imperialism," *Archív Orientální* 55 (1987) 162–175. Normally, vassal states were ruled by native rulers, whereas provinces were ruled by Assyrian governors. The choice of a native ruler for a vassal territory could vary according to Assyrian needs, however. When Tiglath Pileser III invaded Israel in 734, he claims to have installed Hoshea, a usurper who assassinated Pekah, to the throne of Israel (*ANET* 284). Sennacherib likewise claims to have stripped territory away from Hezekiah in order to grant it to Mitinti of Ashdod, Padi of Ekron, and Sillibel of Gaza (*ANET* 288).

Jerusalem according to Tiglath Pileser's instructions, but it does not indicate that Ahaz was rewarded in any tangible way for his loyalty to the Assyrian empire other than to stay alive and retain his kingdom. The Israelite Hoshea controlled the kingdom of Israel in a reduced state following Tiglath-Pileser's invasions of 734–732, and Sargon II incorporated Israel as an Assyrian province following the fall of Samaria in 720.

Judah appears to have been completely cut out of the picture by the Assyrians in the late eighth century, and this may well have been a motivating factor in Hezekiah's later revolt against Sennacherib.[22] There is evidence that the prophet Isaiah supported the possible restoration of Davidic rule over the north in the aftermath of Israel's fall,[23] but Hezekiah's revolt would naturally put a halt to any consideration of Judah as a center for Assyrian administration of the Syro-Israelite region. Although Manasseh and Amon appear to have been cooperative Assyrian vassals, there is no evidence that they exercised any influence over the Assyrian province of Samarina. The motivation to restore Davidic rule over the north would only have reemerged during the reign of Josiah who viewed the fall of Assyria as an opportunity for Judean resurgence. The sanctuary at Beth-El would have been a major obstacle to such ambitions as the Assyrians were known to use local installations, such as cultic sites, to collect the tribute due to the governors of the empire.[24]

Nevertheless, none of these considerations justifies the identification of anti-Beth-El passages in the book of Amos as the products of Josianic redaction. These elements are too well ingrained in the overall structure of the book and its message; rather, they point to readings of Amos' message in later periods to justify the potential or actual actions of Judean kings such as Ahaz, Hezekiah, and Josiah. The anti-Beth-El perspective is easily the viewpoint of the Judean prophet and farmer Amos.

Second, the superscription in Amos 1:1 and the narrative in Amos 7:10–17 concerning Amos' confrontation with Amaziah, the priest at Beth-El, provide some basis for establishing the compositional history and date of the present form of the book. Both were clearly composed by someone other than the prophet, in that they relay information about the prophet rather than present themselves as the actual words of the prophet. The superscription represents a retrospective view of the prophet's activity in that it locates him historically in the reigns of Uzziah and Jeroboam ben Joash, two years before the earthquake. Unfortunately, we do not

22. Cf. Isaiah 10:5–34, in which the prophet Isaiah condemns the Assyrian monarch for threatening Jerusalem in the aftermath of the fall of Samaria in 720 B.C.E. (cf. M. A. Sweeney, "Sargon's Threat against Jerusalem in Isaiah 10, 27–32," *Bibl* 75 [1994] 457–470; Sweeney, *Isaiah 1–39* 205–209, for a discussion of the historical setting of this material). It would appear that Sargon missed a major opportunity to garner support in Jerusalem by treating Judah as a potential enemy at this time.

23. See my study, "A Philological and Form-Critical Reevaluation of Isaiah 8:16–9:6," *HAR* 14 (1994) 215–231, and *Isaiah 1–39* 175–198, for treatment of this theme in relation to Isaiah 8:16–9:6.

24. See Pečírková, "Administrative Methods," 169. For a detailed study of Assyrian taxation practice, see J. N. Postgate, *Taxation and Conscription in the Assyrian Empire*, Studia Pohl, Series Maior 3 (Rome: Biblical Institute Press, 1974).

know the date of the earthquake; perhaps it is the one that damaged Hazor in 760 B.C.E.,[25] but the reference to it demonstrates that someone looking back on the prophet's career, who viewed the earthquake as a significant event, wrote the superscription. A reference to such an earthquake, which is otherwise unmentioned in biblical literature, suggests some chronological proximity to the event. The failure to mention the destruction of Israel may suggest a date prior to 722–721, but this must remain uncertain. The reference to Uzziah prior to Jeroboam suggests that the writer is Judean.

The narrative concerning Amos' confrontation with Amaziah, by contrast, displays a very specific interest in Jeroboam's death and Israel's exile. It plays on the oracle in Amos 7:9 that calls for the destruction of Israel's sanctuaries and a violence against the house of Jeroboam. The statement in Amos 7:11, in which Amaziah reports Amos' claim that Jeroboam would die by the sword and Israel would be exiled, likely represent the prophet's words and views. Jeroboam was not killed by the sword; his son Zechariah was assassinated by Shallum ben Jabesh after six months on the throne. In turn, Shallum was assassinated by Menahem ben Gadi of Tirzah. The inaccuracy of the prediction of Jeroboam's death indicates that the oracle is, in fact, authentic to Amos. Likewise, the correlation of the theme of Israel's exile with other statements that Israel would go into exile in Amos 5:27 and 6:7 indicate this as a theme of Amos' speeches. Israel's exile is mentioned at the beginning of Amaziah's quotation of Amos' words in Amos 7:11, and it reappears in Amos' final words to Amaziah at the end of the passage in Amos 7:17. The emphasis on Israel's exile in the context of a secondary account of an episode in Amos' life is noteworthy in that it indicates a primary concern of the writer who formulated this narrative. Such a concern suggests that the writer was aware of Israel's exile and wrote this passage as a means to highlight this concern and to make clear that Amos prophesied Israel's exile before it actually took place. The most likely setting for such a concern would be in the aftermath the Assyrian defeat of Samaria and its exile of elements of the northern Israelite population in the years following 722–721 B.C.E. This would place the composition of Amos 7:10–17 in the late eighth century during the reign of Hezekiah. The correlation of this concern with elements of Isaiah's message concerning the exile of Israel and the potential reestablishment of Davidic authority over the former northern kingdom would support this hypothesis. The Assyrian destruction of Beth-El during this period would likewise lend fuel to an interest in reasserting Davidic authority over the north.[26]

Third, and finally, the oracles against the nations in Amos 1:3–2:16 deserve some attention as they frequently have provided a basis to argue for exilic or postexilic composition of Amos. The issues have centered around the oracles concerning Tyre (1:9–10), Edom (1:11–12), and Judah (2:4–5), all because they

25. Paul, *Amos* 35.

26. 26. See James Leon Kelso, "Bethel," in *The New Encyclopedia of Archaeological Excavations in the Holy Land*, ed. Ephraim Stern (Jerusalem: Carta and the Israel Exploration Society, 1993) 192–194.

deviate in some manner from the standard form of the other oracles and contain features that are difficult to relate to the time of Amos.[27]

In the case of Tyre, the oracle condemns Tyre by repeating the same charge that is levelled against Philistia, "because they delivered up a whole people to Edom and did not remember the covenant of brotherhood." Many have supposed that Aram and not Edom is intended here so that the oracle would reflect Phoenicia's turn against Israel at the beginning of the reign of Jehu dynasty.[28] But there is no textual evidence for this view, and it would be unlikely that Phoenicia would cooperate with Aram after having just lost its influence in Israel to the Arameans. The action does indicate some correlation with the Philistines, who would be a natural ally of the Phoenicians due to their location along the sea coast and to a common interest in containing an Israel during the ninth and eighth centuries. It also points to some cooperation with the Edomites.

Clearly, conflict between Israel and Edom is the key to understanding the oracles concerning Tyre and Philistia. In this regard, the history of conflict between Judah and Edom in the ninth and eighth centuries is noteworthy because Judah seems to have functioned as a vassal or ally to Israel during both the Omride and Jehu dynasties. Joram of Judah (849–842 B.C.E.) is said to have lost control of Edom (2 Kgs 8:20–22) in the mid-ninth century, and Amaziah (800–783 B.C.E.) is said to have smitten the Edomites in the Valley of Salt in the early eighth century. It was only under the reign of Jeroboam ben Joash of Israel, who controlled an empire "as far as the sea of the Arabah," that any hint of Israelite or Judean control of Edom appears, but the reference to the fact that Edom revolted until this day in 2 Kings 8:20–22 suggests that Edom was never fully under Israelite control. This points to a continuing situation of conflict between Edom and Israel/Judah through the ninth and eighth centuries that could easily stand behind the oracle against Edom in Amos 1:11–12. Such conflict would likely attract the Phoenicians and Philistines who would share an interest in opposing Israel and Judah during this period.

These circumstances point to Amos as the author of each of the oracles against Philistia, Phoenicia, and Edom. Further evidence comes from the arrangement of the oracles, which reflects a typical invasion strategy to be employed against the Syro-Israelite region by an invader coming from the north beyond Damascus. Such an invader would naturally pass through Damascus but bypass Israel, by traversing the Jezreel Valley and coastal plain in order to secure Philistia, thereby sealing off the region from Egyptian interference. The way would then be clear to pick off Phoenicia, followed by Edom, Ammon, Moab, and Judah, in order to isolate Israel in the central hill country. The basic invasion strategy of an early move against Philistia was employed by the Arameans after Jehu's revolt to secure control over the region and by the Assyrians in their various campaigns. The fact that the order presented here deviates from any known invasion—the Arameans and Tiglath Pileser did not move against Phoenicia and Sennacherib hit Phoenicia prior

27. See the discussion by Wolff, *Joel and Amos* 139–141.
28. See the discussion of this issue by Paul, *Amos* 59.

to Philistia—indicates that this is a projected invasion strategy, not a reflection of an actual event. Again, Amos can well be the source of the current order. The inclusion of all nations that come under purview of Jeroboam's empire likewise indicates that the present arrangement stems from Amos; he condemns nations that were forced to submit to or ally with Jeroboam as a prelude to drawing his audience in for the culminating condemnation of Israel.

The oracle concerning Judah is the only one that still presents problems. Its placement in the present order of oracles against the nations makes perfect sense in the eighth century as part of Amos' attempt to condemn the northern kingdom. Judah was allied as a vassal with Israel, and its presence here enhances Amos' rhetorical strategy. The problem stems from the contents of the oracle, which condemns Judah for rejecting YHWH's Torah. Certainly, such a statement corresponds well to the Deuteronomic language and interests of the Josianic period,[29] but the concern with Torah and keeping YHWH's statutes seems unusual for Amos. In this case, it is possible that an original oracle concerning Judah may well have been reworked in the Josianic period, but references to the Torah of YHWH appear in Isaiah 5:24 and 30:9 and to the Torah of our G-d in Isaiah 1:10 in contexts that date to a Judean setting in the late eighth century.[30]

Overall, these considerations indicate the likelihood that the entirety of the oracles against the nations in Amos 1:3–2:16, with the possible exception of Dtr language in the oracle concerning Judah in Amos 2:4–5, derive from the prophet Amos in the mid-eighth century. They express the prophet's attempt to employ calls for punishment against the various nations that stood under the authority of Jeroboam ben Joash's resurgent kingdom of Israel as a means to draw the audience into a mood that would support condemnation. The sequence also reproduces a likely invasion pattern to be employed by an invader from the north and further serves the prophet's interest in drawing the audience surreptitiously into his plan to spring a rhetorical trap. As the prophet approaches the climax of the sequence of nations to be condemned, it becomes apparent that the real target is Israel and that the sequence has deftly led an Israelite audience into condemnation of its own state and policies. But by the time the prophet reaches the oracle concerning Israel, it is too late to back away from the calls for condemnation that the prophet has created.

When this observation is considered, together with the observations related to other segments of the book discussed here, it appears that the present form of the book of Amos derives from the late eighth century B.C.E. Although the poetic oracles that constitute the bulk of the book appear to derive from Amos himself, the narrative material in Amos 1:1 and 7:10–17 appears to derive from the reign of Hezekiah, when concern with the exile of Israel would have been paramount. In this case, the book would have been read as a support for Hezekiah's policies of revolt against Assyria and the reestablishment of Davidic authority over the

---

29. See the discussion of terminology in this oracle and its relation to Deuteronomic literature in Wolff, *Joel and Amos* 163–164.

30. Paul, *Amos* 21–22.

northern kingdom of Israel. The book's arguments in support of the view that the northern kingdom and the altar at Beth-El must be destroyed as punishment for rejecting YHWH would underlie Hezekiah's attempts to reestablish Davidic authority in the north as a means to restore righteous rule and proper observance of YHWH's expectations. Likewise, the parenetic calls for return to YHWH would support the call for the reestablishment of Davidic authority at the end of the book.

This concern also would be relevant during the reign of Josiah in the late seventh century, as it would lend authoritative prophetic support to Josiah's destruction of the Beth-El altar and his attempts to reassert Davidic authority over the territory of the former northern kingdom of Israel. Such a concern is evident in the correlation of Josiah's actions against Beth-El in relation to the argument for Beth-El's destruction put forward in the book of Amos. It is also evident in the presentation in 1 Kings 13 of Jeroboam ben Nebat's condemnation by an unnamed man of G-d at the dedication of the Beth-El altar, which many scholars argue is modeled on Amos' confrontation with Amaziah at Beth-El in Amos 7:10–17.[31] Altogether, these considerations indicate that prophetic literature did not function merely as an archive but functioned within ancient Judah as a means to address contemporary situations and to affect change within Judean society.

31. For discussion of this issue, see Peter Ackroyd, "A Judgment Narrative between Kings and Chronicles? An Approach to Amos 7:9–17," in *Canon and Authority*, ed. G. W. Coats and B. O. Long (Philadelphia: Fortress, 1977) 71–87.

17

Micah

The book of Micah presents a potentially fruitful source for the study of the role of prophetic literature in relation to the reign of King Josiah. Although the superscription of the book in Micah 1:1 places the prophet's activities in the days of the eighth-century Judean kings Jotham, Ahaz, and Hezekiah, scholars generally agree that the present form of the book dates to the period following the Babylonian exile.[1] A variety of factors have entered into the debate, such as the interrelationship between judgment and salvation in the book, the liturgical form of Micah 7, the perceived exilic or postexilic setting of Micah 4–5, and the interrelationship between the book of Micah and the book of Isaiah, but the most telling piece of evidence is the reference to the exile of the people of Jerusalem to Babylon in Micah 4:10. Furthermore, the reference to the destruction of Jerusalem in Micah 3:9–12 is quoted in the narrative concerning Jeremiah's trial for sedition in Jeremiah 26 (v. 18) as a basis for defending the prophet as one who would intend to change royal policy and thereby to save the city. The date of Jeremiah 26 is disputed, but it does demonstrate that some form of the Micah tradition was read by those who composed the book of Jeremiah and perhaps by

---

1. For discussion of contemporary research on the book of Micah, see D. Hillers, "Micah, Book of," *ABD* IV 807–810 and esp. R. Mason, *Micah, Nahum, Obadiah*, OTG (Sheffield: JSOT Press, 1991) 11–53. Note esp. Mason's comments concerning the postexilic message of the text. Principle commentaries include Delbert Hillers, *Micah*, Hermeneia (Philadelphia: Fortress, 1984); James Luther Mays, *Micah: A Commentary*, OTL (Philadelphia: Westminster, 1976); B. Renaud, *Michée—Sophonie—Nahum*, SB (Paris: J. Gabalda, 1987) 11–173; H. W. Wolff, *Micah: A Commentary,* ContCom (Minneapolis: Augsburg, 1990). In addition, see David Gerald Hagstrom, *The Coherence of the Book of Micah: A Literary Analysis*, SBLDS 89 (Atlanta: Scholars Press, 1988); B. Renaud, *La Formation du livre de Michée*, EB (Paris: J. Gabalda, 1977); John T. Willis, "The Structure of the Book of Micah," *SEÅ* 34 (1969) 5–42.

Jeremiah's contemporaries.[2] In any case, the period of the composition of the book of Micah appears to straddle the period of King Josiah's reign, which suggests that it may well have been extant in some form at that time.

Nevertheless, scholars generally do not look to the period of King Josiah as a time for either the composition or the reading of the book of Micah. Surveys of scholarly discussion of the literary form and composition of Micah demonstrate that scholars disagree widely on the details of both of these issues, but they do seem to agree that the period of Micah and the period of the exile and beyond constitute the two major periods of the book's composition.[3] For the most part, scholars accept the oracles in Micah 1–3 as the product of the prophet, but the material in Micah 4–5 and 6–7 is believed by many to derive from the exilic period or later.[4] The grounds for such contentions combine both thematic and formal considerations. Micah 1–3 establishes an analogy between Samaria and Jerusalem in order to present a scenario of judgment against both the northern kingdom of Israel and the southern kingdom of Judah. Insofar as Micah lived during the period of the Assyrian invasions of Israel and Judah during the late eighth century B.C.E., the message of judgment in these chapters relates well to the situation faced by the prophet. Micah 4–5, by contrast, present a scenario of Jerusalem's salvation in the aftermath of its destruction and exile, in which the nations come to recognize YHWH's sovereignty on Zion. Likewise, Micah 6–7 contain liturgical material, especially in chapter 7, that anticipates the restoration of Jerusalem and the recognition of YHWH's power by the nations. In this regard, chapters 4–5 and 6–7 appear to fit well with the concerns of the exile and the early postexilic period, when the restoration of Jerusalem was of primary concern.

It is striking, however, that some rather stereotyped views concerning the respective historical settings of judgment and salvation themes in prophetic literature play such a large role in establishing this view of the composition of the book. Chief among them is Stade's position that judgment and salvation in Micah are irreconcilable polar opposites that could never have been written by the same hand; rather, judgment must pertain to the preexilic period and salvation to the period of the exile and beyond.[5] This axiom has been critically reconsidered in relation to other works of prophetic literature in the Hebrew Bible, most notably the books of Isaiah and Jeremiah, so that a more nuanced view of the historical interaction of these themes has emerged among scholars. With respect to Micah, it is noteworthy that the only clear reference to the Babylonian exile appears in

---

2. For treatments of Jeremiah 26 in relation to Micah 3:9–12, see Robert P. Carroll, *Jeremiah: A Commentary*, OTL (Philadelphia: Westminster, 1986) 510–522; William L. Holladay, *Jeremiah 2*, Hermeneia (Minneapolis: Augsburg Fortress, 1989) 107–108; Jun-Hee Cha, *Micha und Jeremia*, BBB 107 (Weinheim: Beltz Athenäum, 1996) 42–58.

3. See the discussion in Mason, *Micah, Nahum, Obadiah*, 27–42; Renaud, *La Formation* 383–420.

4. See B. Stade, "Bermerkungen über das Buch Micha," *ZAW* 1 (1881) 161–176; Stade, "Streiflichter auf die Entstehung der jetzigen Gestalt der alttestamentlichen Prophetenschriften," *ZAW* 23 (1903) 153–171, who is especially influential in establishing this view.

5. Stade, "Bermerkungen."

Micah 4:10, which portrays the exile and rescue of Zion; other references to the punishment, restoration, or exaltation of Jerusalem, Judah, and Israel give little indication of a setting in the exilic period. Furthermore, the portrayal of the nations in the book of Micah, a concern commonly identified with the exilic or postexilic period, is variegated; whereas Micah 4:1–5 presents a very tolerant view of the nations who will come peacefully to Zion to learn YHWH's teachings and who will worship their own gods, the balance of the book looks to their defeat and their submission to YHWH's power. This suggests that the compositional history of this material is much more complex than is indicated by a simple decision to assign it to the exilic or postexilic period. This issue is especially noteworthy in Micah 5:1–5, in which Assyria is explicitly identified as the nation that will face YHWH's judgment and in which a ruler of Israel from Bethlehem Ephrata is identified as the figure who will gather the people of Israel and play a role in overthrowing Assyria when it comes into the land of Israel. Many see this as a cryptic reference to a messianic period when foreign powers will be brought down,[6] but there is little reason to see Assyria rather than Babylon as a universal symbol of evil in the exilic or postexilic periods. As texts such as Isaiah 13–14 and Jeremiah 50–51 demonstrate, Babylon could be explicitly named in the prophetic literature of this period, even when Assyria served as the paradigm for defining Babylon's future. Such a scenario of Assyrian downfall in conjunction with the rise of a Davidic ruler does correspond well to themes that have been identified in relation to the restoration program of King Josiah, and it suggests the possibility that an edition of Micah may well have been composed, or at least read, in relation to the reign of Josiah.

These considerations point to the need to reconsider the compositional history of the book of Micah. Naturally, reconsideration of Micah's compositional history requires an assessment of the structure and literary character of the final form of the book. Such an assessment presents its own set of challenges: discussion of the literary structure and form of the book of Micah indicates that scholars vary widely in their interpretations of the book. This is due in large measure to the variety of positions articulated concerning the compositional history of Micah, as views of its present form frequently depend on views of its literary history. Nevertheless, the recent commentary by Mays and the dissertation by Hagstrom point to a promising basis for understanding the present form of the book.[7]

Contemporary discussion of the literary form of Micah has produced a variety of proposals for the structure of the book that emphasize four basic models: (1) Micah 1–3, 4–5, 6–7; (2) Micah 1–3, 4–5; 6:1–7:6(7); 7:7(8)-20; (3) Micah 1–5 and 6–7; and (4) Micah 1–2, 3–5, and 6–7.[8] These proposals are based primarily on a combination of thematic criteria, particularly the interrelationship between themes of judgment and salvation within the individual blocks, and views concerning the compositional history of the book. This is unfortunate; it indicates

6. See Wolff, *Micah* 128–149; Renaud, *Michée* 96–108.

7. Mays, *Micah*; Hagstrom, *The Coherence*.

8. For a survey of these positions, see Hagstrom, *Coherence* 11–22.

that the structure of the book is not considered in terms of its own particular linguistic features that normally define literary structure, but in relation to sets of criteria that derive from theological and literary-historical concerns. Such thematic/theological and literary-historical conclusions must be derived from an analysis of the literature itself; they must not be employed at the outset to define its character and concerns. Instead, the structure of the text must be defined in relation to its formal features and content—that is, its syntactical and semantic structure, its generic characteristics, and the interrelationship of the contents conveyed by its formal features.

The problem of defining the literary structure of the book of Micah is particularly evident in the nearly unanimous view that Micah 1–3 constitute the first major structural division of the book, because these chapters are widely believed to derive from the prophet Micah himself rather than from later writers. Several features of the text, however, suggest that other structural principles govern its presentation, such as the appearance of a superscription in Micah 1:1, the absence of a formal syntactical relationship between chapters 1 and 2 and between chapters 6 and 7, and the presence of formal syntactical connectives between chapters 3 and 4 and between chapters 4 and 5. Furthermore, thematic factors, such as the interaction of the themes of judgment and salvation within the book and the definition of the lame and dispersed who are brought to Jerusalem as the remnant of Israel (Mic 4:6–7; 5:6–7), must be considered. The current arrangement of the book suggests that salvation proceeds from the basis of earlier judgment and that Jerusalem constitutes the basis for the restoration of the remnant of Jacob or northern Israel.

At the outset, it is therefore necessary to observe that the first major structural component of the book of Micah is its superscription in Micah 1:1, which identifies the following material as "the word of YHWH which was unto Micah the Moreshite in the days of Jotham, Ahaz, Hezekiah, kings of Judah, which he saw concerning Samaria and Jerusalem." Superscriptions are generically and structurally distinct from the material that they identify and introduce.[9] Because there are no further superscriptions in Micah, the balance of the book in Micah 1:2–7:20 constitutes its second major structural component.

An analysis of the syntactical and semantic features of Micah 1:2–7:20 in relation to its contents demonstrates that this text comprises four major structural subunits, each of which begins with a syntactically independent formula that introduces a thematically and generically coherent textual unit.

The first major subunit is Micah 1:2–16, which constitutes a prophetic announcement of punishment directed against Samaria and Israel as a basis for pointing to the punishment of Jerusalem and Judah. The passage begins with the call to attention formula directed to the nations and the earth at large: "Hear, all of the peoples; Pay attention, all of the earth and its fullness, that the L-rd YHWH will be a witness to you, my L-rd from his holy Temple." Essentially, this formula

---

9. On the generic character of superscriptions and their role within the structure of a text, see Tucker, "Prophetic Superscriptions and the Growth of the Canon."

addresses the world at large concerning YHWH's intentions to punish the sins of Samaria, which, in turn, affects Jerusalem. Verses 2–7 employ trial genres and natural imagery in the prophet's announcement of YHWH's accusations against Samaria and thereby provide the basis for declaring judgment against the city. A major point of contention is that Samaria's sins have affected Judah and Jerusalem and brought them under threat. This is clear from the beginning of the prophet's lament in vv. 8–16, which provides his response to the accusations of vv. 2–7. Verses 8–9 state expressly that her (i.e., Samaria's) sins have come to Judah and the gate of Jerusalem, and vv. 10–16 trace an itinerary through many cities that appear to lie primarily in Judah. The itinerary in these verses apparently portrays the path of an enemy invasion through the Shephelah and constitutes an announcement that Judah is to suffer YHWH's punishment.

The next major subunit of the book appears in Micah 2:1–5:14, which presents the prophet's views in detail concerning the ultimate outcome of the judgment against Samaria or northern Israel and its consequences for Jerusalem—that is, destruction and exile to Babylon and its restoration as the remnant of Israel in conjunction with the submission of the nations to YHWH. Although Micah 2:1–5:14 combine a variety of generic subunits within the structure, the overarching genre of the passage must be identified as a prophetic announcement about the punishment and subsequent restoration of Jerusalem as the remnant of Jacob/Israel.

The unit begins in Micah 2:1–13 with the woe speech directed against those who are evil, identified in v. 7 as the house of Jacob (i.e., the northern kingdom of Israel), which culminates in vv. 12–13 with a portrayal of the gathered remnant of Jacob passing out of the breach in the walls of the city into captivity with the king at their head. This passage is generally construed as an oracle of salvation because of its similarities to the oracle of salvation in Micah 4:6 concerning YHWH's intentions to gather the lame and those driven away, as well as various analogous images in Deutero-Isaiah that pertain to the shepherd who guides the people back to Zion and safety.[10] Likewise, the use of the verbs *'ăsōp 'e'ĕōp*, "I will surely collect" or "I will surely take under protection," and *qabbēṣ 'ăqabbēṣ*, "I will surely gather," are frequently cited by scholars as terms that denote YHWH's actions to assemble and restore the people of Israel. When read in relation to the image of the king and YHWH at the head of the people as they pass through the breach in the wall, the image is often taken as one that represents YHWH's protective action on behalf of the exiled people of Israel. Overall, scholars understand this to be a portrayal of YHWH's protective action on behalf of the exiles of Jerusalem and Judah.

But this conclusion does not account for the threatening aspects of the imagery of sheep being led out of the security of their enclosure into the open. Key to this imagery is the use of the verb *prṣ*, "to break out, to make a breach," to portray

---

10. Wolff, *Micah* 67–88; Mays, *Micah* 73–76; Hillers, *Micah* 38–40; Hagstrom, *Coherence* 51–54; Renaud, *La Formation* 104–114. Cf. Ina Willi-Plein, *Vorformen der Schriftexegese innerhalb des alten Testaments*, 79–80, who argues that the passage is a later addition to Micah based upon syntactical criteria and the relationship of the text to later prophetic themes of salvation.

the departure of the sheep from the pens. Verse 13a states that "the scatterer/the one who makes a breach (*happōrēṣ*) has gone up before them" and that "they have broken out (*pārĕṣû*) and passed by the gate and gone out," which conveys images of one who breaches the security of the sheep pens and enables the sheep within to break out. Following upon the statement at the end of v. 12 that "you shall be in tumult because of human beings," this suggest that *happōrēṣ*, "the one who makes a breach," in v. 13 refers to some invader who compromises the security of the pens and allows the sheep to escape. The imagery here presents a metaphor for Israel's exile as the result of an attack; the portrayal of the king and YHWH at the head of the people reinforces this portrayal in that the king is exiled with the people and in that YHWH is held responsible for bringing about the exile in the first place.

In this regard, it is noteworthy that the language employed for the people— "Jacob" and "the remnant of Israel"—are designations for the northern kingdom of Israel, which indicates that Micah 2:11–12 refers to the exile of the northern kingdom in keeping with the language employed throughout the rest of Micah 2:1– 11 and the presuppositions of Samaria's and Israel's punishment in Micah 1:2–16. This points to the interrelationship between the portrayal of Israel's punishment and exile in Micah 2:1–13 and the portrayal of Jerusalem and Judah's punishment and restoration in Micah 3:1–5:14. Just as in Micah 1:2–16, the punishment of Israel sets the pattern for the punishment of Jerusalem and Judah, but the ambiguous nature of the statements that YHWH "will gather" Jacob and the remnant of Israel allows for a scenario of restoration as well. In the present case, Micah 2:1–13 presents a scenario of judgment and exile for the northern kingdom, but Micah 3:1– 5:14 then applies this image to Jerusalem and Judah in a manner that first establishes the analogy between Israel and Jerusalem in Micah 3:1–12 and then portrays YHWH's restoration of the exiled people of Jerusalem and Judah. The above-cited imagery of Micah 4:6, which portrays YHWH's gathering of the lame and the dispersed, facilitates this aim in that it reverses the portrayal of Israel's exile in Micah 2:12–13. Whereas YHWH brought about the scattering of the sheep in Micah 2:11–12, so YHWH will see to their rescue in Zion in Micah 4:6.

This understanding of Micah 2:11–12 appears to be confirmed by the structural and generic relationship established between Micah 3:1–5:14 and the preceding material in Micah 2:1–13. Overall, Micah 3:1–5:14 presents a scenario for Jerusalem's and Judah's restoration as "the remnant of Jacob" (Mic 5:6, 7; cf. Mic 4:2; 5:2) in the aftermath of Assyria's downfall (Mic 5:4–5) and the Babylonian exile (Mic 4:10). Micah 3:1–5:15 appears as the prophet's response to the image of YHWH's leading the people out of the sheep pens and into exile in Micah 2:12– 13, insofar as Micah 3:1–5:15 constitutes his projections concerning the eventual outcome of this exile. Micah 3:1–5:15 is introduced by the first-person speech formula in Micah 3:1aα[1], "and I said." This formula indicates that the prophet is the speaker, and the conjunctive *waw*-consecutive formulation ties this material to Micah 2:1–13, establishing its structural and syntactical dependence on the preceding material and thereby demonstrating its generic character as Micah's response to the announcement of Micah 2:1–13.

Following the first-person speech formula of Micah 3:1aα[1], Micah 3:1aα[2]– 5:15 constitutes the prophet's speech, which is formulated as a prophetic announce-

ment concerning YHWH's plan to exalt the remnant of Israel/Jerusalem following its judgment. The introductory call to attention formulae in Micah 3:1aα²–β,
"Hear now, O heads of Jacob and leaders of the House of Israel," and 3:9a, "Hear
now this O heads of the House of Jacob and leaders of the House of Israel," define the two basic components of the prophet's announcement. Micah 3:1aα²–8
announces that the prophets of Israel will fail to instruct the leaders of Israel in
their time of distress because of the evil that they have done in that they do not
know justice. The result is evil action on Israel's part that results in Israel's punishment as YHWH chooses to hide the divine face from the people.

Micah 3:9–5:15 then presents the scenario of Jerusalem's exaltation following
its destruction and the exile of its people. The passage begins with the announcement
of punishment in Micah 3:9–12 that Jerusalem/Zion will be destroyed as a result
of unjust action on the part of the heads of the house of Jacob. But the imagery
shifts in Micah 4:1–5:15 insofar as the formula "and it shall come to pass in later
days" provides a syntactical connection to Micah 3 and introduces a presentation
of Jerusalem's/Zion's future restoration in the aftermath of exile as the outcome
of the judgment articulated in the preceding material. Micah 4:1–5 presents an
image of the nations peacefully streaming to Zion in order to receive instruction
in YHWH's Torah and ways. This idyllic imagery is further defined in Micah 4:6–
5:15, introduced by the syntactically independent formula *bayyôm hahû'*, "in that
day," that presupposes the days portrayed by Micah 4:1–5. Micah 4:6–7 employs
shepherding imagery to present YHWH's gathering the lame and dispersed remnant of those cast in order to establish eternal rule from Zion. Micah 4:8–5:14
follows up with pointed questions, introduced by the statement, "and you," directed to Zion in Micah 4:8–14 and Bethlehem Ephrata in Micah 5:1–14 concerning their respective roles in YHWH's plans. Micah 4:8–14 announces that domin-
ion shall come to Zion despite its present situation in which the city cries out for
lack of a king (4:9–10), nations are assembled against it (4:11–13), and it is besieged and its ruler is struck on the cheek by a rod (4:14). Micah 5:1–14 is likewise addressed and informed that a ruler of Israel shall emerge from its midst who
shall act as a shepherd, standing and feeding the flock, and thereby take action to
restore the security of the people Israel (Mic 5:1–3). The results are defined in a
series of statements introduced by *wĕhāyâ*, "and it shall come to pass." Micah 5:4–
5 portrays Israel's future peace when Assyria is smitten by the shepherds of Israel. Micah 5:6 states that the remnant of Jacob shall dwell in the midst of many
people like dew from YHWH. Micah 5:7–8 states that the remnant of Jacob shall
dwell in the midst of nations like a lion among flocks of sheep, so that Israel's
enemies will be cut off. Micah 5:9–14 returns to the initial premises of the entire
passage (Mic 2:1–5:14) to state that Israel will lose its military might and its various forms of idolatry, but that the nations who did not obey will suffer YHWH's
vengeance in the process that leads to Israel's restoration in Zion.

The next major subunit of the book of Micah appears in Micah 6:1–16, which
constitutes a renewed appeal by the prophet to the people of Israel. The passage
begins with a syntactically independent call to attention formula, "Hear now that
which YHWH says," that marks its beginning as a new subunit distinct from
Micah 2–5. The call to attention formula, which appears to be directed to the

people, introduces an appeal for a response to YHWH's charges made during the course of YHWH's controversy or legal case against Israel (Mic 6:1–2). YHWH demands an answer and rehearses divine acts of beneficence on their behalf: exodus from Egypt, Moses et al., and Shittim and Gilgal (Mic 6:3–5). A final series of rhetorical questions establishes that the deity wants justice but has not received it (Mic 6:6–8). The second part of the unit (Micah 6:9–16) then proceeds with YHWH's statements that the punishment of Israel has begun because of the people's wrongdoing in acting after the pattern of Omri and Ahab. Overall, Micah 6 presents YHWH's expectation that the scenario laid out in Micah 2–5 concerning Israel's judgment and subsequent restoration will be fulfilled.

The final subunit of the book appears in Micah 7:1–20, which constitutes the prophet's psalm of confidence that YHWH will show faithfulness to Israel in the end. The introductory statement, *'alĕlay lî*, "woe is me," is syntactically independent from Micah 6 and establishes Micah 7 as a distinct subunit of the book. Furthermore, it establishes the prophet as the speaker, and it identifies the first part of the passage in Micah 7:1–6 as a lament by the prophet over the fate of the people. But Micah 7:7 expresses the prophet's confidence with the statement, "but I will look to YHWH, I will wait for the G-d of my deliverance, my G-d will hear me." The balance of Micah 7:7–20 then expresses the prophet's confidence that YHWH will show compassion, deliver the remnant of the people, and show faithfulness to the relationship with Israel established with the patriarchs Jacob and Abraham. In this manner, it functions analogously to Micah 6: it presents the prophet's expectation that the scenario of judgment and restoration laid out in Micah 2–5 will, in fact, be fulfilled.

The structure of the book of Micah may therefore be portrayed as in table 17.1. As the preceding analysis of the present form of the book of Micah indicates, it is clear that the book presents a scenario in which the prophet looks to the fulfillment of a process defined throughout the book, but especially in Micah 2–5, in which the punishment of Israel will lead to the restoration of the "remnant of Jacob" in Jerusalem. An important component of this scenario is the destruction of the city of Jerusalem and the exile of its inhabitants to the open country outside of the city, where YHWH will rescue and redeem them and prepare them for their return to Zion and restoration to YHWH's sovereignty. Although this scenario has obvious implications for reading the book in relation to the Babylonian exile, the only clear reference to the Babylonian exile appears in Micah 4:10, "Writhe and groan, O Daughter of Zion, like a woman giving birth, for now you shall go out from the city and you shall dwell in the open country and you shall come unto Babylon; there you shall be delivered, there YHWH shall redeem you from the hand of your enemies." Other passages are believed by some to derive from exilic settings, such as the portrayal of the nations flocking to Jerusalem in Micah 4:1–5; the scenario of Jerusalem's restoration in Micah 4:6–13; the claims for a restored Davidic monarch in Micah 5; the appeal for justice with its potential for restoration in Micah 6; and the cultic lament in Micah 7.

For the most part, the arguments for the exilic settings of these passages are based in the belief that the theme of restoration can only pertain to the exilic period and beyond; the experience of the preexilic period offered little hope for a sce-

TABLE 17.1   Structure of the Book of Micah

Prophetic anticipation of YHWH's plans for Zion's exaltation	*Micah 1:1–7:20*
I. Superscription	1:1
II. Body of book: Prophetic anticipation of YHWH's plans for Zion's exaltation	1:2–7:20
A. Prophetic announcement of punishment against Samaria/Israel as basis for punishment of Jerusalem/Judah	1:2–16
1. Accusations against Samaria/Israel	1:2–7
2. Prophet's response: lament for Jerusalem/Judah	1:8–16
B. Prophetic announcement concerning the punishment and restoration of Jerusalem and Judah	2:1–5:14
1. Woe speech against Israel culminating in Israel's exile	2:1–13
2. Prophet's response: announcement concerning YHWH's plan to exalt remnant of Israel/Jacob in Zion	3:1–5:14
a. Speech formula	3:1aα¹
b. Speech proper: prophetic announcement concerning YHWH's plan to exalt remnant of Israel/Jacob in Zion	3:1aα²–5:15
i. Concerning failure of Israel due to leaders	3:1aα²–8
ii. Concerning punishment and exaltation of Jerusalem/Judah	3:9–5:14
a) Concerning punishment of Zion	3:9–12
b) Concerning exaltation of Zion	4:1–5:14
1) Exaltation of Zion	4:1–5
2) Exaltation of Zion defined	4:6–5:14
A) Initial statement: YHWH/Shepherd will gather lame/dispersed for eternal rule on Zion	4:6–7
B) Addresses to Zion and Bethlehem Ephrata concerning YHWH's plans	4:8–5:14
I) To Zion: dominion will come after distress	4:8–14
II) To Bethlehem Ephrata: king will come to restore security of Israel	5:1–14
aa) Ruler/shepherd will emerge	5:1–3
bb) Future peace when Assyria is stricken	5:4–5
cc) Remnant of Jacob in midst of peoples like dew	5:6
dd) Remnant of Jacob in midst of peoples like lion so enemies are cut off	5:7–8
ee) Summation: Israel's punishment/cleansing leads to punishment of nations and Israel's restoration	5:9–14
C. Prophetic appeal to people to return to YHWH	6:1–16
1. Legal appeal for justice from Israel	6:1–8
2. Assertions of Israel's punishment for lack of justice	6:9–16
D. Prophetic psalm of confidence in YHWH's faithfulness to Israel	7:1–20
1. Lament over fate of people	7:1–6
2. Expression of confidence	7:7–20

nario of restoration. Yet the explicit references to the threats posed to Israel/Judah/ Jerusalem by the nations throughout these passages do not name Babylon as the source of punishment, except in the case of Micah 4:10, but point to Assyria as the major enemy instead. Micah 5:1–5 makes this especially clear when it portrays the downfall of the Assyrian empire during the course of its attempted invasion of the land of Israel. In this case, the Davidic monarch that will arise from Bethlehem bears primary responsibility for the defeat of the Assyrians when they attempt to tread on the land of Israel. As a result, the defeat of the Assyrians ushers in an era of peace for Israel under its Davidic monarch. Certainly such sentiments underlay Hezekiah's attempts to resist the Assyrian empire in the late eighth century B.C.E., as well as Josiah's efforts to reestablish an independent Davidic kingdom in Israel and Judah in the aftermath of the Assyrian collapse. Insofar as Micah 5 envisions a direct confrontation between a Davidic monarch and the Assyrian empire that will result in Assyrian defeat, it seems best to date this passage to the reign of Hezekiah. Although the sentiments would certainly serve Josiah's interests, a direct confrontation with Assyria in the land of Israel during the late seventh century seems remote; rather, the apparent collapse of Assyria at this time suggests that a Mican oracle from the time of Hezekiah concerning Assyria's defeat would be read and perceived as having been fulfilled during the reign of Josiah.

This has tremendous implications for dating other oracles in Micah that have been considered as postexilic. The reference to Babylonian exile in Micah 4:10, for example, is noteworthy in that it disrupts a relatively balanced passage in which two verbs concerning the exile of the people—"you shall go out (*tēṣ'î*) from the city and you shall dwell (*wĕšākant*) in the open country"—correspond to two verbs introduced by *šām*. "There" conveys YHWH's deliverance of the people, viz., "there you shall be delivered (*tinnāṣēlî*), there YHWH shall redeem you (*yigʾālēk*) from the hand of your enemies."[11] Not only does the appearance of the statement "and you shall come unto Babylon (*ûbāʾt ʿad-bābel*)" disrupt the present context, but also it conflicts directly with the following references to the downfall of Assyria in Micah 5. It appears to be an addition to this text or a gloss that serves as a means to contextualize Micah's words in relation to the later Babylonian exile, in which Micah's statements concerning the destruction of Jerusalem in Micah 3:9–12 actually were fulfilled.

This also has implications for Micah 4:1–5 and 5:9–14, the two passages that introduce and close the presentation of Zion's exaltation in Micah 4:1–5:14. Both passages appear to be exilic redactional pieces that employ material from Isaiah 2 to rework an earlier underlying textual base in Micah 4:6–5:8.

Two major problems emerge in the reading of Micah 4:1–5, which presents a scenario of peaceful acceptance of YHWH's instruction in Torah at Mt. Zion and expresses the notion that other nations should follow their respective gods while Israel will walk in the name of YHWH.[12] First, the statement in Micah 4:1–4 that the nations should walk in the ways of YHWH appears to contradict that of Micah 4:5, which accepts the principle that the nations will walk in the ways of their own gods. Second, the portrayal of the nations' peaceful acceptance of YHWH's instruction at Zion and the idyllic tolerance of the nations' observance of their respective gods appears to contradict the later assertions that YHWH or the Davidic king will defeat the nations that oppress Zion in Micah 4:6–5:14 and

11. See Wolff, *Micah* 139–140; Mays, *Micah* 105–106.

12. For discussion of Micah 4:1–5, see Renaud, *Formation* 150–181; cf. Sweeney, *Isaiah 1–39* 87–100.

thereby bring about an era of peace under YHWH's sovereignty. Although it is possible that the nations' flocking to Zion for YHWH's instruction could well be the result of their defeat, it is the reference in Micah 4:5 to their following their own gods that creates the bulk of the difficulties in this passage. Nevertheless, Micah 4:5 facilitates the transition to the following material and thereby constitutes a major literary thread that ties Micah 4:1–4 and 4:6–5:14 together.

Therefore, it is noteworthy that Micah 4:1–3 appears in a slightly different form in Isaiah 2:1–4. The interrelationship of these texts has been studied extensively, and, although scholars are not in full agreement on the issue, most conclude that the Mican and Isaian versions of the passage presuppose a liturgical text that derives from the period of the exile, perhaps in the late-sixth-century rule of Cyrus, when such a scenario of peace in relation to the nations was a real possibility.[13] During this period, Cyrus was portrayed as an agent of YHWH in Isaiah, and Cyrus' own policies in relation to subject nations stressed his efforts to identify himself as an agent of the respective deities of the lands that were under his control. Others argue that the Isaian version is original. In either case, Micah 4:1–5 emerges as the later passage.

The features of the Mican text in vv. 4 and 5 indicate that it is a reworked form of the passage. Micah 4:4 includes a statement that does not appear in the Isaiah version, "and each man shall dwell under his vine and under his fig tree, and none shall make him afraid, for the mouth of YHWH Sebaoth has spoken." The reference to YHWH's speech provides a fitting close to the passage that distinguishes it from the following statement in Micah 4:5 concerning the nations' walking after their own gods. Micah 4:4 thereby employs formulaic language that appears elsewhere in 1 Kings 8:5, 2 Kings 18:31/Isaiah 36:16, and Zechariah 3:10 as a means to describe a situation of peace. It is likely not original to the passage in that it would have appeared in the Isaiah version as well if the Isaian writer had borrowed the passage from an original Mican context. Instead, it appears to have been introduced here by the Mican writer as a means to emphasize the scenario of peace and to provide an appropriate transition to Micah 4:5, "for all the peoples shall walk each in the name of its own gods, but we shall walk in the name of YHWH our G-d for ever and ever."

Micah 4:5 likewise does not appear in the Isaian version, but the differentiation between Israel and the nations in Micah 4:5 introduces a scenario in which the restored remnant of Israel in Zion will strike out against the nations assembled against Zion. Subsequent Mican passages call upon the daughter of Zion to "Arise, thresh," to "beat in pieces many peoples," and to "devote their gain to YHWH, their wealth to the Lord of the whole earth" (Mic 4:12). In response to the threat of the nations, Micah 5:1–8 calls for the establishment of a new Davidic monarch who will defeat the Assyrians in the land and enable the remnant of Israel to be "among the nations . . . like a lion among the beasts of the forest, like a young

---

13. For discussion of Isaiah 2:2–4, see Sweeney, *Isaiah 1–39* 87–100; Sweeney, *Isaiah 1–4 and the Postexilic Understanding of the Isaianic Tradition*, BZAW 171 (Berlin and New York: Walter de Gruyter, 1988) 135–138, 164–174.

lion among the flocks of sheep, which, when it goes through, treads down and tears in pieces, and there is none to deliver" (Mic 5:6–7). Clearly the portrayal of Israel's defeat of the nations in Micah 4:6–5:8 and the scenario of peace articulated in Micah 4:1–4 stand in literary tension.

The reason for this tension becomes evident when one considers Micah 5:9–14.[14] Following the calls for Israel and the new Davidic monarch to punish Assyria and the nations, this passage conveys an oracle in which YHWH announces the overthrow of Israel's military power, cities, sorceries, idolatry, and so on, in a scenario that sees the punishment of the nations that did not obey YHWH together with the uprooting of all these presumably undesirable features within Israel. As in Micah 4:1–4, this passage appears to contradict the calls for Israel to strike against Assyria and the nations by maintaining that YHWH will strike against the capacity that Israel would use against the nations. When read in relation to the preceding material, it appears to provide some qualification to the calls for Israel's actions against the nations that accord well with the peaceful scenario of submission to YHWH at Zion in Micah 4:1–4. Although Israel may strike at the nations as part of the scenario outlined in Micah 4:6–5:8, Micah 4:1–4 and 5:9–14 point to YHWH as the one who will root out weapons, idolatry, and evil from both Israel and the nations and thereby bring about the peace portrayed in Micah 4:1–4.

This indicates that, like Micah 4:1–5, Micah 5:9–14 may be the result of redactional activity that was designed to modify an original Mican text in Micah 4:6–5:8 in order to address the issue of the destruction of Jerusalem and the Babylonian exile. In this regard, it is noteworthy that the vocabulary and themes of Micah 5:9–14 demonstrate that the passage is heavily dependent on Isaiah 2:6–21.[15] Both Micah 5:9–14 and Isaiah 2:6–21 envisage YHWH's cutting off horses and chariots (Mic 5:9; Isa 2:7), cities and strongholds (Mic 5:11; Isa 2:10, 15), sorceries and soothsayers (Mic 5:12; Isa 2:6), and various idols including "the work of your hands" (Mic 5:5:13–14a; Isa 2:8). It would appear that just as Micah 4:1–5 is derived from Isaiah 2:2–4, Micah 5:9–14 is derived from Isaiah 2:6–21, and that both were introduced redactionally into the Mican text to qualify the scenario of Israel's punishment against Assyria and the nations that is articulated in Micah 4:6–5:8.[16] Ultimately, it is not Israel who will overthrow the nations and establish peace,; it is YHWH who will bring about judgment against both Israel and the nations and establish peace in Zion with both the remnant of Israel and the nations. This provides a rationale for Israel's exile to Babylon in that Micah 4:1–5:14 follows immediately upon the reference to the destruction of Jerusalem in Micah 3:9–12 and thereby presents YHWH's actions in relation to the subjugation of the nations as well.

---

14. For a discussion of this passage, see esp. John T. Willis, "The Structure of Micah 3–5 and the Function of Micah 5 9–14 in the Book," *ZAW* 81 (1969) 191–214; Willis, "The Authenticity and Meaning of Micah 5 9–14," *ZAW* 81 (1969) 353–368, who views Micah 5:9–14 as an eighth-century composition of the prophet Micah. Contra Renaud, *Formation* 262–271, who sees the oracle as an exilic composition.

15. See Renaud, *Formation* 267.

16. Cf. Renaud, *Formation* 270–287, who points to Micah 4:1–5 and 5:9–14 as a redactional inclusion that defines Micah 4–5 as a coherent redactional text that dates to the fifth or fourth century B.C.E.

Overall, Micah 4:1–5 and 5:9–14 appear to constitute an exilic redaction of an earlier Mican text that is designed to bring it into some conformity with the scenario presented in Isaiah. The introduction of the reference to Israel's deliverance by YHWH in Babylonian exile (Mic 4:10) also appears to be a part of this exilic redaction. Insofar as the edited text envisions the restoration of Israel to Zion and the acknowledgment of the nations, it would appear that this redaction dates to the late sixth century, when Jews returned to Jerusalem to rebuild the Temple and the possibility of peaceful coexistence with the nations under Persian rule appeared to be the means by which the remnant of Jacob/Israel would continue into the future. The Mican presentation displays some differences and some similarities with the Isaian presentation. Micah presents a somewhat different scenario from that of Isaiah, in that Micah presupposes both the defeat of Israel by the nations and the subsequent defeat of the nations by Israel as the prelude to YHWH's intervention to defeat both Israel and the nations. The scenario of peace portrayed in Micah 4:1–4, however, constitutes the ultimate ideal outcome of the violent process portrayed in the Mican presentation. In contrast to Micah, Isaiah elsewhere presents Israel solely as the victim of the nations; it is only YHWH who takes successful action against the nations. As in Micah, the scenario of peace portrayed in Isaiah 2 in which Israel is invited to participate together with the nations in the learning of YHWH's Torah at Zion appears to be the ultimate goal of the Isaian presentation.

When Micah 4:1–5 and 5:9–14 are removed, together with the reference to Babylonian exile in 4:10, a very different scenario emerges, in which Micah 4:6–5:8 portrays the establishment of YHWH's sovereignty on Zion. It begins with a portrayal of YHWH's gathering the lame and dispersed to Zion, followed by a confrontation with the nations that ultimately sees the establishment of peace and Israel's domination of the nations that once afflicted it. Like the final form of Micah 4:1–5:14, the earlier text in Micah 4:6–5:8 is designed to follow upon the notice of the destruction of Jerusalem in Micah 3:9–12. It thereby presents a scenario in which a reconstituted remnant of Jacob/Israel based in Zion and a restored Davidic king defeats the Assyrians who invaded the land. Insofar as the earlier text in Micah 4:6–5:8 envisions Israel's and the Davidic king's reestablishment in the aftermath of Assyria's downfall, it appears to derive from the period of Hezekiah's revolt against Assyria in the late eighth century. The overall form of the book (and the argument presented therein) differs in minor respects from its final form. The book as a whole anticipates YHWH's plans for the reconstitution and exaltation of Jerusalem. Again, the prophet's announcement in Micah 1:2–16 concerning the punishment of Samaria and Israel provides the model for punishment against Jerusalem and Judah—that is, Jerusalem and Judah suffer because of northern Israel. The central section in Micah 2:1–5:8* likewise looks to Jerusalem's exaltation as the place for the restored remnant of Jacob. The oracle against Jerusalem in Micah 3:9–12 expresses the threat of destruction rather than its reality[17] and blames the rulers of the northern kingdom for Jerusalem's sorry

---

17. Cf. Wolff, *Micah* 108–109; Mays, *Micah* 86–92.

state. The restored remnant of Jacob in Micah 4:6–5:8 constitutes the restored remnant of the northern kingdom of Israel that finds its place in Jerusalem following its punishment, and ultimately succeeds in defeating Assyria when a new Davidic monarch arises to lead Israel against the nations. The concluding sections in Micah 6 and 7, respectively, call for justice on the part of the northern kingdom that follows the statutes of Omri and express the prophet's confidence that justice will be done. The book would thereby present prophetic legitimation to Hezekiah's attempts to revolt against the Assyrians who had subjugated Judah during this period.

This earlier form of Micah would be quite pertinent in the late seventh century, when Josiah attempted to restore the Davidic state in the aftermath of Assyria's collapse, and would likewise present prophetic legitimation to Josiah's restoration program as the anticipated outcome of YHWH's purposes in the aftermath of Assyria's collapse. Again, it presents a scenario in which the shortcomings of the northern kingdom of Israel are the cause for the humiliation and potential destruction of Jerusalem and Judah. It is only when the remnant of Jacob—that is, the northern kingdom of Israel—is reassembled and reconstituted in Zion/Jerusalem that it will be able to defeat the invading Assyrians under the guidance of a new Davidic monarch. The ramifications of such a message for Josiah's program are clear. Josiah is the anticipated monarch of the book of Micah, who enables the scenario of reunification and restoration in Jerusalem to take place. The concluding chapters of Micah, which call for justice on the part of Israel (Micah 6) and express the prophet's confidence that YHWH will act to restore Israel, thereby point to Josiah's reign as the time when the restoration will take place.

18

Habakkuk

The superscriptions for the book of Habakkuk in Habakkuk 1:1 and 3:1 provide no information concerning the historical setting for the prophet's activity, but scholars generally agree that the book presupposes the period immediately following the reign of King Josiah.[1] During this time, the Babylonian empire emerged as the dominant power in western Asia as a result of the Babylonian King Nebuchadrezzar's defeat of the Egyptians at Carchemesh on the Orontes River in 605 B.C.E. Following the victory at Carchemesh, Judah was obliged to shift its status as a vassal ally of Egypt to an alliance with Babylonia as the Egyptians were driven out of the Syro-Israelite corridor. This situation is reflected in Habakkuk 1:6, which speaks of the rise of the Chaldeans or Neo-Babylonians as a new menacing power and the various images in the book that speak of violence and oppression. Although the book dates to the period of Babylonia's ascendancy over Judah beginning in 605 B.C.E., it is nevertheless an important witness to the Josianic period in that it portrays the circumstances in Judah during the aftermath of Josiah's reign. In this regard, the book of Habakkuk provides an important perspective on the Josianic period as it highlights the sense of loss evident in Judah during this period and the contrast in outlook in light of the Babylonian posed against Judah versus that of Judean resurgence.

---

1. For surveys of research on Habakkuk, see Peter Jöcken, *Das Buch Habakuk: Darstellung der Geschichte seiner kritischen Erforschung mit einer eigenen Beurteilung*, BBB 48 (Cologne and Bern: Peter Hanstein, 1977); Rex Mason, *Zephaniah, Habakkuk, Joel*, OTG (Sheffield: JSOT Press, 1994) 60–96; Marvin A. Sweeney, "Habakkuk, Book of," ABD III, 1–6. In addition to the bibliography cited in these surveys, recent commentaries and studies include J. J. M. Roberts, *Nahum, Habakkuk, and Zephaniah*, OTL (Louisville, KY: Westminster John Knox, 1991); Klaus Seybold, *Nahum, Habakuk, Zephanja*, ZBK (Zurich: Theologischer Verlag, 1991); Marvin A. Sweeney, "Structure, Genre, and Intent in the Book of Habakkuk," *VT* 41 (1991) 63–83; Robert Haak, *Habakkuk*, VTSup 44 (Leiden: E. J. Brill, 1992).

The primary issues in the interpretation of Habakkuk have therefore never centered on the question of its historical date; rather, the primary issues in the interpretation of Habakkuk have centered around the interpretation of its contents in relation to events of 605 B.C.E. and following.[2] For the most part, scholars have assumed that the book of Habakkuk is designed to criticize wicked elements within Judah who have abandoned the covenant with YHWH and allowed wickedness and injustice to prevail (Hab 1:4). This is due in large measure to the general perception that prophets in the preexilic period functioned as critics of the monarchy and Judean/Israelite society and to the portrayal of Jeremiah's conflicts with King Jehoiakim who ruled Judah at this time. But this consensus leaves several questions unanswered. It does not satisfactorily address the issue of the identity of the "righteous" and the "wicked" that appear throughout the book in Habakkuk 1:4, 13 and 2:4 and the relationship of these figures to the rise of the Neo-Babylonians. The presupposition that the "wicked" in Habakkuk 1:2–4 must refer to wicked parties within Judah leads to the conclusion that YHWH brings the Neo-Babylonians in Habakkuk 1:5–11 to punish those wicked parties, but this is problematic in that the Babylonians then emerge as the subject of the prophet's condemnation in Habakkuk 1:12–17, as they become the "wicked" who swallow up those who are more righteous. A second question concerns the interpretation of Habakkuk 2:1–4. The passage is filled with grammatical problems, but the basic question comes back to the identification of the "righteous" versus the "wicked" of previous passages. Habakkuk 2:4 states that "the righteous shall live," but it is not clear who the "righteous" might be. Finally, the identity of the oppressor in the woe oracles of Habakkuk 2:5–20 presents problems in that scholars are divided as to whether the oppressor refers to an internal Judean group or to the Neo-Babylonians once again.

These problems are necessarily bound together with that of the book's literary form since literary form conveys content and therefore plays a major role in establishing the interpretation of the contents of Habakkuk. Therefore, it is not surprising to learn that the literary structure and genre of the book of Habakkuk also present problems. Most scholars maintain that the book falls into three major parts: a "dialogue" between the prophet and G-d in Habakkuk 1:1–2:4(5); a series of "woe" oracles directed against an unnamed oppressor in Habakkuk 2:(5)6–20; and a concluding psalm in Habakkuk 3:1–19, which many scholars view as independent.[3] But this view is problematic in that scholars have come to no clear understanding of the interrelationship between the three parts, including that between the psalm in Habakkuk 3 and the preceding material in Habakkuk 1–2, as well as that between the "dialogue" of Habakkuk 1:1–2:4(5) and the "woe" series in Habakkuk 2:(5)6–20. The problem is compounded by the fact that superscriptions of the book in Habakkuk 1:1; 3:1 point to two basic structural components, not to three. In addition, there is tremendous disagreement concerning the genre

---

2. For a detailed discussion of the following, see esp. Sweeney, "Structure, Genre, and Intent."
3. See Childs, *Introduction to the Old Testament as Scripture* 448.

of the work, which is described as a "liturgy,"[4] "prophetic imitation of liturgy,"[5] "report of visionary experience,"[6] and "wisdom" composition.[7]

A reassessment of the literary form of the book of Habakkuk is clearly necessary. It must begin with the observation that the literary features of the present form of Habakkuk indicate two basic structural components for the book, each of which is introduced by a superscription that identifies the content and genre of the following material. The superscription in Habakkuk 1:1, "the pronouncement which Habakkuk the prophet envisioned," introduces a block of material in Habakkuk 1:2–2:20 that may be identified as a prophetic "pronouncement" or *maśśā'*; the superscription in Habakkuk 3:1 introduces a block of material in Habakkuk 3:2–19, "the prayer pertaining to Habakkuk the prophet concerning lamentations."

The prophet pronouncement or *maśśā'* refers to a specific type of prophetic discourse that identifies how YHWH's intentions are manifested in human affairs.[8] It has no specific formal features other than the use of the Hebrew term *maśśā'*, "pronouncement" or "burden" as a technical term to identify the associated oracle. The *maśśā'ōt* are generally based on some sort of revelatory experience, and they may be formulated as visionary experiences, auditory experiences, or some combination of the two. In the case of Habakkuk 1:2–2:20, the text is formulated in a dialogue form, in which the text conveys an exchange of statements between the prophet and YHWH about the violence of the wicked that is now overtaking the land.[9]

Habakkuk 1:2–4 constitutes Habakkuk's first complaint to YHWH concerning the violence of the wicked and the oppression of the righteous. The text is demarcated by its first-person singular verbs and pronouns that identify the prophet as the speaker and its second-person singular verbs and pronouns that identify YHWH as the addressee. The subunit begins with the prophet's statement to YHWH: "How long, O YHWH, shall I cry out and you do not hear? I cry to you 'violence!' and you do not deliver?" The balance of the subunit continues the prophet's portrayal of violence and ends with a statement concerning the breakdown of order in the land: "Therefore, Torah declines, and justice does not continue to proceed, for the wicked encompass the righteous. Therefore, justice proceeds perverted."

4. For example, Jeremias, *Kultprophetie und Gerichtsverkündigung in der späten Königszeit Israels* 90–110.

5. G. Fohrer, "Das 'Gebet des Propheten Habakuk' (Hab 3,1–16)," in *Mélanges bibliques et orientaux en l'honneur de M. Mathias Delcor*, AOAT 215, ed. A. Caquot et al. (Kevelaer and Neukirchen: Neukirchener, 1985) 159–167.

6. For example, Wilhelm Rudolph, *Micha-Nahum-Habakuk-Zephanja*, KAT 13/3 (Gütersloh: Gütersloher Verlaghaus Gerd Mohn, 1975) 193–195.

7. Eckart Otto, "Die Theologie des Buches Habakuk," *VT* 35 (1985) 274–295.

8. For a discussion of the *maśśā'* genre, see Weis, "A Definition of the Genre *Maśśā'*."

9. Contra Michael Floyd, "Prophetic Complaints about the Fulfillment of Oracles in Habakkuk 1:2–17 and Jeremiah 15:10–18," *JBL* 110 (1991) 397–418, who argues that Habakkuk 1:2–17 is not a dialogue but a complaint. Floyd, however, misses the significance of the reporting form in Habakkuk 2:1–20 for defining the genre of Habakkuk 1:2–2:20 as a whole.

Habakkuk 1:5–11 constitutes YHWH's first response to Habakkuk in which the Deity takes responsibility for the violence overtaking the land. The text is demarcated by its second-person plural address forms, its first-person singular formulation in v. 6 that identifies YHWH as the speaker, and its third-person description of the Chaldeans. YHWH begins by calling on the audience, presumably Habakkuk and the people, to look at the work YHWH is doing among nations in the world. Verse 6 identifies the specific focus of this work in that YHWH takes responsibility for bringing the Chaldeans: "For behold, I am raising the Chaldeans, the bitter and swift nation, that goes to the ends of the earth to dominate habitations that are not its own." The balance of the passage focuses on descriptions of the terrible presence of the Chaldeans in the world and their potential for unhindered violence and domination of their victims. The statement in v. 7, "from it (i.e., Chaldea), its justice and its dominance go forth," contrasts with the prophet's earlier complaint in v. 4 concerning the perversion of justice that goes forth as a result of the domination of the righteous by the wicked. In the context of Habakkuk's complaint concerning the violence of the wicked in Habakkuk 1:2–4, YHWH's answer therefore indicates that YHWH is the one who brings the violence and oppression on the land. The situation about which Habakkuk complains is in fact a deliberate act of YHWH.

Habakkuk 1:12–17 constitutes Habakkuk's second complaint to YHWH concerning the evil nature of the Babylonians. This subunit is demarcated by its second-person singular address forms that are directed to YHWH, its first-person singular pronouns that identify Habakkuk as the speaker, and its third-person singular references to the Chaldeans. In addition, the passage is syntactically independent from both the preceding and the following material. The subunit begins with a set of rhetorical questions directed by the prophet to YHWH that ask why YHWH has brought such evil upon the land. The key question appears in vv. 12b–13: "O YHWH, you have appointed him (i.e., the evil one, Babylonia) for justice, and O Rock, you have established him for chastisement. . . . Why do you gaze upon the treacherous, (why) are you silent when the wicked swallows one more righteous than himself?" Verses 14–16 continue with the prophet's portrayal of humans like fish in the sea, which the wicked one/Babylonia traps in his net. The prophet's complaint ends with another rhetorical question in v. 17 that raises the issue as to why YHWH tolerates the oppression carried out by Babylon: "Will he therefore persist in emptying his net, to slay nations, he shows no pity?"

Habakkuk 2:1–20 constitutes the prophet's report of YHWH's second response to his complaints. The passage is demarcated by its third-person report forms in vv. 1–2aα, 5–6a, 18, and 20, which convey the various speeches contained therein, and by the first-person singular forms in vv. 1–2 that identify Habakkuk as the speaker or narrator. This section differs generically from the preceding sections in that it is explicitly formulated as a narrative report in contrast to the earlier segments that were formulated only as speeches by either Habakkuk or YHWH. Nevertheless, the contents of this section indicate that it responds to issues raised in the preceding material, and the narrative form indicates that the whole of Habakkuk 1:2–2:20 must be regarded as a report in which the dialogue between Habakkuk and YHWH is presented.

The basic structure of Habakkuk 2:1–20 is determined by the narrative reporting language in vv. 1 and 2aα so that v. 1 and vv. 2–20 stand as the two basic structural components of the passage. Verse 1 describes Habakkuk's situation as he stands at a watchtower, possibly reflecting the role of the Levitical watchmen in the Temple, while waiting for YHWH's response to his complaint. Verse 2aα is a simple speech report form that introduces YHWH's response to the prophet. YHWH's speech appears in vv. 2aβ-4. YHWH initially instructs Habakkuk in vv. 2aβ-3 to write the vision and wait for its realization. The content of the vision then appears in v. 4, "he (lit., "his life force within him") is arrogant, he (lit., "it") is not upright (lit., "straight"), but the righteous shall live by his steadfastness."[10] This statement refers to the Babylonians who were the subject of the prophet's complaint in the previous passages. The arrogance and instability of the Babylonians will ultimately result in their downfall, whereas the righteous in Judah must endure a period of oppression until, ultimately, they are delivered from the threat. Overall, YHWH's response calls for patience on the part of the prophet and the people until the Babylonian threat passes. Habakkuk then expounds on the meaning of YHWH's response in vv. 5–20, which round out the prophet's report of YHWH's response. In v. 5, Habakkuk builds on the theme of the collapse of the Babylonians by pointing to the outcome of gluttonous consumption of wine as an analogy for the behavior of the Babylonians who attempt to swallow everything in their path. Ultimately, just as a drunk collapses from too much wine, so the Babylonian empire will collapse as a result of its greedy subjugation of nations. In vv. 6–20, the prophet then presents a taunt song directed to the Babylonians, together with his summary or commentary on it. Verses 6–17 contain the taunt song proper, which is introduced in v. 6a and proceeds in vv. 6b-17 with a series of woes that condemn Babylon for plunder (vv. 6b-8), extortion (vv. 9–11), bloodshed (vv. 12–14), and rape (vv. 15–17). The prophet concludes with the summation or commentary in vv. 18–20 that contrasts Babylon's reliance on lifeless idols that profit no one with YHWH in the holy Temple before whom all the earth is silent.

The second major portion of the book of Habakkuk is the Prayer or Petition by Habakkuk to YHWH in Habakkuk 3:1–19.[11] The passage is demarcated initially by the introductory superscription in Habakkuk 3:1, which identifies the following material generically as Habakkuk's prayer concerning lamentations, presumably a reference to the problems raised in Habakkuk 1:1–2:20. The instructions to the choirmaster in Habakkuk 3:19b demarcate the end of the unit. The prayer proper appears in Habakkuk 3:2–19a in the form of a petition directed by the prophet to YHWH to defeat the enemies that threaten the land (vv. 2, 16). It begins with the introduction in v. 2, which states the basic petition to manifest divine power on behalf of the petitioner, "O YHWH, I have heard your reputation

---

10. For a discussion of the philological and formal problems of Habakkuk 2:4–5, see J. A. Emerton, "The Textual and Linguistic Problems of Habakkuk ii 4–5," *JTS* 28 (1977) 1–18; J. G. Janzen, "Habakkuk 2:2–4 in the Light of Recent Philological Advances," *HTR* 73 (1980) 53–78; Sweeney, "Structure, Genre, and Intent," 74–77.

11. For a recent study of Habakkuk 3, see Theodore Hiebert, *G-d of My Victory: The Ancient Hymn in Habakkuk 3*, HSM 38 (Atlanta: Scholars Press, 1986).

(lit. "your report"), I fear, O YHWH, your deed; in the midst of time (lit., "years"), make it happen (lit., "make it live"), in the midst of time (lit., "years"), make it known, in wrath remember mercy!" The body of the petition then follows in vv. 3–15 with a report of a theophany that describes the manifestation of YHWH's power against enemies that threaten the land. In keeping with the standard elements of the theophany report form,[12] vv. 3–7 describe the approach of YHWH from Teman and Paran in the east as the entire cosmos looks on and the tents of Cushan and Midian tremble at YHWH's approach. Verses 8–15 then describe YHWH's victory employing standard elements of the cosmogonic creation myths, such as combat against the rivers and the sea and the witness of the sun and moon. Overall, these verses portray the defeat of the enemies or nations who are trampled, whose heads are crushed, and who are pierced with YHWH's arrows. Finally, vv. 16–19a constitute the third major element of the petition by expressing the psalmist's confidence that YHWH will act: "I will wait quietly for the day of trouble to go up against the people that plunders us (v. 16b) . . . and I will rejoice in YHWH, I will exult in the G-d of my deliverance" (v. 18).

Many scholars have pointed to the literary independence of Habakkuk 3, especially because it contains no explicit references to Habakkuk 1–2 and because it does not appear in the Qumran Habakkuk pesher.[13] Although Habakkuk 3, in fact, may be an independent composition around which the present form of the book was built, the two major components of the book are intended to be read together.[14] Habakkuk 1–2 poses the problem of the book: Why has YHWH brought evil—that is, the Babylonian invaders—against the righteous land? In posing this problem, it also points to the eventual solution: YHWH will not tolerate this situation for long, and the Babylonians will eventually collapse. Habakkuk 3 takes up the elements of the previous section that promise YHWH's deliverance and expresses Habakkuk's confidence that YHWH will act. In essence, the book forms a sort of theodicy that points to YHWH as the cause of evil but argues that YHWH will act justly to resolve that evil. The book thereby affirms YHWH sovereignty and justice. The structure of the book may be portrayed as in table 18.1.[15] This analysis of the structure and generic character of the book of Habakkuk has major implications for establishing the historical context of the book and the concerns that it addresses. Clearly, the book presupposes that the Babylonians constitute a threat to Judah insofar as they are identified as the evil party that threatens the righteous throughout the book. Such a concern points to the year 605 B.C.E. as a focal point for the prophet's message: 605 was the year that Nebuchadrezzar defeated the Egyptians at Carchemesh and took control of Judah. It was at this point that the Babylonians emerged as a threat to Judah and Judah was relegated to vassal status. Babylonia continued to present a threat to Judah through the middle

---

12. For a discussion of theophany report form, see Jörg Jeremias, *Theophanie: Die Geschichte einer alttestamentliche Gattung*, WMANT 10 (Neukirchen-Vluyn: Neukirchener, 1965).

13. For example, B. Stade, "Habakuk," *ZAW* 4 (1884) 154–159; C. Taylor, "Habakkuk," in *The Interpreter's Bible*, vol. 6, ed. G. Buttrick (Nashville: Abingdon, 1956) 974.

14. Cf. Sweeney, *ABD* III, 4–5.

15. Cf. Sweeney, "Structure, Genre, and Intent," 81–83.

TABLE 18.1   Structure of the Book of Habakkuk

Prophetic affirmation of divine justice	*Hab 1:1–3:19*
I. Pronouncement of Habakkuk	1:1–2:20
A. Superscription: *maśśāʾ* pronouncement of Habakkuk	1:1
B. *Maśśāʾ* pronouncement proper: dialogue report form	1:2–2:20
1. Habakkuk's complaint to YHWH: concerning the oppression of the righteous by the wicked	1:2–4
2. YHWH's response to Habakkuk: YHWH has established the Chaldeans/Babylonians	1:5–11
3. Habakkuk's second complaint to YHWH: concerning evil nature of the Chaldeans/Babylonians	1:12–17
4. Habakkuk's report of YHWH's second response	2:1–20
a. Narrative situation: Habakkuk waits at watchtower for YHWH's response	2:1
b. Response report proper	2:2–20
i. Response report formula	2:2aα
ii. Response by YHWH	2:2aβ–4
a) Instruction: wait for vision	2:2aβ–3
b) Basic statement of vision: righteous shall live, wicked shall fail	2:4
iii. Explication of YHWH's response by Habakkuk	2:5–20
a) Concerning failure of oppressor: analogy to drunk full of wine	2:5
b) Report of taunt song against oppressor	2:6–20
I) Report of taunt song proper	2:6–17
A) Introduction	2:6a
B) Song proper	2:6b–17
i) 1st woe: plunder	2:6b–8
ii) 2nd woe: extortion	2:9–11
iii) 3rd woe: bloodshed	2:12–14
iv) 4th woe: rape	2:15–17
v) Prophet's summation/commentary	2:18–20
II. Prayer/petition of Habakkuk concerning laments	3:1–19
A. Superscription: *tĕpillâ* prayer of Habakkuk	3:1
B. Prayer/petition proper	3:2–19a
1. Introduction: petition to YHWH to manifest divine power against enemies	3:2
2. Theophany report	3:3–15
a. Concerning YHWH's approach	3:3–7
b. Concerning YHWH's victory over enemies	3:8–15
3. Conclusion: expression of confidence by psalmist	3:16–19a
C. Instruction of the choirmaster	3:19b

of the sixth century as Babylon invaded Judah in 598–597 to put down Jehoiakim's revolt, again in 588–587 to put down Zedekiah's revolt, and perhaps again in 582 in response to the assassination of Gedaliah. A variety of positions concerning the historical setting and concerns of the prophet have been put forward, but most scholars accept the view that Habakkuk's concern with evil must be understood as a critique of elements within Judean society, especially King Jehoiakim, who was so roundly criticized by Jeremiah.[16] Some date Habakkuk to the years 609–

16. In addition to the bibliographical surveys of Habakkuk cited above, see Roberts, *Habakkuk* 82–84.

605, arguing that Habakkuk sees the Babylonians as an impending threat against the Egyptian oriented rule of Jehoiakim. Others date Habakkuk to 605–597, arguing that the Babylonians are not a potential threat but a realized threat against the Judean kingdom. Others point to the years following 597 as the setting for the prophet and view the book as a retrospective meditation on the causes of the disaster that overtook Judah beginning in 597 B.C.E. In all cases, Jehoiakim thereby becomes a representative of the evil within Judah that is to be punished in the view of the prophet.

But this view must be questioned. As noted in the analysis of the structure and genre of the book presented above, the references to evil in the book of Habakkuk can only be understood in relation to the Babylonian empire. To interpret them as references to an inner Judean party leaves open a contradiction in which Habakkuk first argues that the Babylonians are brought by YHWH to punish an "evil" Judean group that threatens the "righteous," but then shifts his position to condemn the Babylonians as the evil party when they actually carry out the task for which YHWH establishes them. Such a conception requires a fragmented reading of the book of Habakkuk, in which its various elements must be read in relation to different historical periods without any indication from the text that this should the case. Furthermore, it presupposes a relatively unified stance among prophets that consistently criticizes the monarchy or the people of Judah. In this regard, the book of Jeremiah exercises undue influence in the interpretation of Habakkuk: Jeremiah consistently criticizes Jehoiakim and calls for submission to Babylon as an agent of YHWH's actions. But as the encounter between the prophets Jeremiah and Hananiah in Jeremiah 27–28 demonstrates, there is no consistent prophetic viewpoint on such matters. Hananiah's statement that Babylon would fall in two years is frequently held up as an example of false, nationalistic prophecy, but his message is completely consistent with that of Isaiah ben Amoz over a century before. Hananiah may have been wrong for his time, but that does not make him a cynical self-interested false prophet; he simply expresses a position contrary to that of Jeremiah, and in the course of the debate, proves to be wrong. Prophets can disagree among themselves over any given issue.

This insight must be applied to Habakkuk. As R. Coggins argues, Habakkuk represents an alternative prophetic tradition to that of Jeremiah.[17] Like Jeremiah, Habakkuk views the Babylonians as a threat to Judah brought about by YHWH, but he does not agree with Jeremiah concerning the need to punish Judah or the need to submit to Babylon. Whereas Jeremiah argues that Judah is guilty of abandoning YHWH and that the Babylonians constitute a fitting punishment for that abandonment, Habakkuk maintains that Judah is innocent. Whereas Jeremiah argues that Judah should submit to Babylon and ally itself to the Babylonians as an expression of YHWH's will for the future of the people, Habakkuk expresses outrage at the approach of the Babylonians and their actions in relation to Judah. In contrast, Habakkuk argues that Judah should simply wait and, ultimately,

---

17. R. Coggins, "An Alternative Prophetic Tradition?," in *Israel's Prophetic Tradition*, Fs. P. R. Ackroyd, ed. R. Coggins et al. (Cambridge, U.K.: Cambridge University Press, 1982) 77–94.

YHWH will eliminate the threat posed by the Babylonians. In this regard, his message is very much like that of Hananiah in Jeremiah 27–28, who argued that the people should be patient because YHWH will eventually bring down the Babylonians. Like Hananiah, Habakkuk holds an opposing viewpoint to Jeremiah. Unlike Hananiah, Habakkuk is no false prophet.

This has tremendous implications for understanding Habakkuk in relation to his historical context. Habakkuk must be placed in relation to the imposition of Babylonian hegemony over Judah in 605 B.C.E., but he does not oppose the Davidic monarchy.[18] Certainly the statement in Habakkuk 3:13a, "you went forth for the salvation of your people, to deliver your anointed," indicates that YHWH is portrayed as defending the monarchy, not attacking it. When this is taken together with his statements of outrage or astonishment at the approach and actions of the Babylonians against the righteous, the conclusion is inescapable that Habakkuk supports the Judean monarchy over against the threat posed to it by the Babylonians. Insofar as Jehoiakim is the sitting monarch at the time of the Babylonian takeover, Habakkuk must support Jehoiakim, or at least Habakkuk does not condemn Jehoiakim; his book certainly shows no evidence that he is opposed to Jehoiakim in particular or to the Davidic monarchy in general.

Habakkuk is clearly outraged by Babylon's subjugation of Judah in 605, but the reasons for his outrage also must be investigated. Certainly, one can point to the normal outrage that any person might feel on seeing his or her own country become subject to another. But Habakkuk's case is particularly interesting in that he does not raise the issue of Judah's subjugation to Egypt during the years 609–605. Judah did not lose its independence to Babylon in 605; Judah had already lost its independence to Egypt four years earlier when Necho killed Josiah at Megiddo. This was made especially clear when Necho exiled King Jehoahaz three months later in order to replace him with Jehoiakim, who apparently was more compliant with Egyptian hegemony. Indeed, Jehoiakim's revolt against Babylon in 598 indicates that Jehoiakim still acts as a loyal ally or vassal of the Egyptians who put him on the throne. Likewise, Jeremiah's opposition to him might be understood as a further indication of Jehoiakim's pro-Egyptian sympathies as Jeremiah consistently called for submission to and alliance with Babylon. Habakkuk does not condemn Egypt for its subjugation of Judah; he only speaks out against the Babylonians.

It is against this background that Habakkuk's outrage at Babylonia's subjugation of Judah must be understood. The reasons for Habakkuk's silence concerning the Egyptians may never be known, but he has ample reason to speak out against the Babylonians in 605. Babylon and Judah had been firm allies from the

---

18. For a discussion of the political context of Habakkuk, see Haak, *Habakkuk*. In contrast to the position taken here, Haak argues that Habakkuk supported Jehoahaz and opposed Jehoiakim, but his arguments are based upon a problematic reading of the text of Habakkuk and the presupposition that the "evil" mentioned throughout the book must be identified with elements within Judean society. Haak is heavily dependent on the discussion of Jay Wilcoxen, "The Political Background of Jeremiah's Temple Sermon," in *Scripture in History and Theology*, Fs. J. C. Rylaarsdam, ed. A. Merrill and T. Overholt (Pittsburgh: Pickwick, 1977) 151–166.

eighth century on when Hezekiah coordinated his revolt against Assyria with Merodach Baladan of Chaldea. The revolt failed, but Judah and Babylon had found common cause against the Assyrians, and that mutual interest continued throughout the rest of the seventh century. The exact nature of the relationship between Judah and Babylon cannot be fully known as there are no texts that testify to an alliance between the two countries. It is noteworthy, however, that Josiah's meeting with Necho took place at Megiddo at a time when the Egyptian army was advancing northward to support the remnants of the Assyrian at Haran against the Babylonians and their allies. Whether intended as such or not, Josiah's death at Megiddo and the resulting delay of the Egyptian march kept the Egyptians out of the final battle at Haran and helped secure the Babylonian victory over the Assyrians. Josiah's actions appear to be those of a Babylonian ally or sympathizer; in part as a result of Josiah's death, Babylon emerged as one of the major world powers in the aftermath of Assyria's demise. Furthermore, Josiah's son Jehoahaz was removed from the throne by Necho and exiled to Egypt at a time when Necho was preparing to face the Babylonians for control of western Asia. Because Judah had suffered greatly for its opposition to Assyria and Egypt, the primary enemies of Babylonia, it is not surprising that Habakkuk should be outraged at Babylon's treatment of Judah in 605. Judah had acted as a loyal ally of Babylon for approximately a century. To be treated as a subjugated vassal when the Babylonians finally emerged as the masters of western Asia must have been viewed by many in Judah, Habakkuk included, as outright treachery.

This analysis of Habakkuk points to an element of Josiah's reign that is not evident elsewhere, except perhaps in the book of Jeremiah. Whether intentionally or not, Josiah pursued a policy that supported Babylonian interests, and he died as a result of that policy. Jeremiah continued to support that policy throughout his prophetic career by arguing that Judah should submit to Babylon and thereby continue its "alliance." In this endeavor, he was supported by the house of Shaphan, one of the major advisors of Josiah during the monarch's reign.[19] Ahikam ben Shaphan delivered Jeremiah from the trial for sedition after he condemned the Temple (Jer 26); Gemariah ben Shaphan provided the chamber in which Jeremiah's scroll condemning Jehoiakim's policies was read (Jer 36); Elasah ben Shaphan delivered Jeremiah's letter to the exiles urging them to submit to Babylon (Jer 29); and Gedaliah ben Ahikam ben Shaphan was the Babylonian-appointed governor of Judah who was to protect Jeremiah in the aftermath of the Babylonian destruction of Jerusalem (Jer 40). But whereas Jeremiah accepted Babylonian hegemony as the inevitable will of YHWH, Habakkuk argued that YHWH would act to remove the Babylonian ingrates. In this regard, Habakkuk bears important witness to Judah's relationship with Babylon during Josiah's reign.

---

19. Cf. Wilcoxen, "The Political Background."

19

Conclusion to Part II

The preceding discussion demonstrates quite clearly that prophets and prophetic literature play a substantial role in relation to the reign of King Josiah and his reform. Prophets who were contemporary with Josiah actively addressed various aspects of his reform program and frequently point to aspects that are not evident in the DtrH account of his reign. Zephaniah, for example, calls for the purging of syncretistic elements within the Judean government and religious establishment, which is completely in keeping with the DtrH portrayal of Josiah's cultic measures, but he also sees in international events the signs that point to the future centrality and glorification of Jerusalem. Thus the defeat of Cush and the downfall of Assyria point to YHWH's actions in the international realm and provide a basis for Zephaniah's claims that Philistia, Moab, and Ammon must also submit to YHWH's and Jerusalem's power. Nahum, of course, presents a similar perspective, in that it views Nineveh's fall as an act of YHWH, who employed the Assyrians to punish Judah for transgression and then destroyed them for their arrogance after the task was completed. Nahum thereby argues that YHWH is the primary power of the universe who exercises substantial control of the course of human events and looks to the restoration of Jerusalem as the demonstration of YHWH's mastery. In his early period, Jeremiah called for the restoration of the former northern kingdom of Israel to the Davidic monarchy and the Jerusalem Temple; thereby, he saw in the Josianic program the opportunity to reunite the people of Israel. Like Zephaniah and Nahum, he looked to international affairs in relation to Josiah's reign, but he does not seem to emphasize Judean dominance over other countries.[1] Rather, his

---

1. It is possible that the oracles against the nations in Jeremiah 46–51 contain some early pronouncements against nations by the prophet that might have played some role in relation to Josiah's reform, but, in their present form, they appear to presuppose the threat of the Babylonian empire.

associations with the Shaphan family and his later statements indicate that he supported a policy of alliance with Babylonia, much like that pursued by Hezekiah a century earlier, which would align Judah clearly against the Assyrians and the Egyptians and thereby guarantee Judah's political independence. Habakkuk's protest against Babylonia's harsh subjugation of Judah in the aftermath of Egypt's defeat in 605 B.C.E. appears to presuppose cooperative relations between Judah and Babylon under the reigns of Hezekiah and Josiah. Clearly, Habakkuk feels that Judah has been betrayed by its former ally.

In addition to the perspective gained from the study of prophets who were contemporary to Josiah's reign, the works of several prophets who lived a century earlier during the period of the initial Assyrian invasions of Israel and Judah also seem to have played some role in relation to Josiah's policies; they appear to provide some sense of prophetic legitimation for various aspects of his reform. Although these prophets clearly spoke about the circumstances of their own period, they very clearly were read in relation to the late seventh century B.C.E. Thus, Isaiah points to the role of Assyria as an agent employed by YHWH to punish Israel and Judah and to demonstrate divine power, but Isaiah also points to the eventual downfall of Assyria when it oversteps its bounds and fails to acknowledge YHWH's mastery of the world. This presents the possibility that an ideal Davidic monarch would extend Judah's power over the northern kingdom and thereby reunite the people of Israel. In addition, the Davidic monarch would extend Judah's power over neighboring states that had once constituted a part of the Davidic realm, such as Philistia, Edom, Moab, Ammon, Phoenicia, and Aram. In Isaiah's time, such a scenario would be understood perhaps in relation to Hezekiah, but in the late seventh century, Isaiah's prophecies of an ideal monarch would point to Josiah. Hosea's diatribes against the religious practices of the northern kingdom of Israel and its alliances with Egypt and Assyria would certainly be relevant in the mid-to-late eighth century when he spoke, but they also were relevant to the time of Josiah as a means to validate YHWH's punishment and destruction of Israel and the call for Israel to return to YHWH. In Josiah's time, such a call would be understood as a call to return to the Jerusalem Temple and to Davidic rule. Amos's polemics against the northern kingdom, particularly against its sanctuary at Beth-El, would support not only an effort on the part of the house of David to reunite the people in the late eighth century but also a similar effort in the late seventh century. This would be particularly relevant to Josiah's destruction of the Beth-El altar in that the book of Amos would certainly provide prophetic legitimation for such an act. Finally, Micah establishes an analogy between the experience of punishment by the northern kingdom of Israel and that by the southern kingdom of Judah. Micah's statements would play a major role in justifying the long period of Judah's subjugation to Assyria as an act of YHWH's punishment prior to the restoration of the people.

Clearly, the prophets point to both the religious and the political character of Josiah's reform as a program that was designed to restore the unity of the people of Israel under Davidic rule, the centrality of the Temple and Jerusalem as their religious and political capital, and Davidic authority over various neighboring peoples that had once constituted the early Davidic kingdom. The results of this study are relevant to defining the role that prophecy played in relation to the reign of King Josiah and in illuminating various aspects of his reform program, but they also point to the means by which the tradition developed in the aftermath of his death and the failure of his program at religious reform and national restoration. Books such as Zephaniah, Nahum, and Habakkuk do not appear to have been modified substantially; rather, they appear to have been read eschatologically as projections of a more distant future when Jerusalem would be restored at the center of the nations and YHWH's enemies, symbolized by Nineveh or Babylon, would be destroyed. The Jeremiah tradition, by contrast, developed substantially in the aftermath of Josiah's death. Although the prophet still continued his anti-Egyptian and pro-Babylonian stance, many of his early statements concerning the punishment and potential restoration of the northern kingdom of Israel were applied to Judah as well. Like Israel, Judah would also go through a process of punishment and exile for its failure to adhere to YHWH's will as Jeremiah understood it—if it failed to recognize Babylon as YHWH's agent and thereby submit to Babylonian power. For Jeremiah, Josiah's death clearly demonstrated that even the Temple in Jerusalem could not guarantee Judah's security in the face of such a threat. Likewise, the Isaiah tradition continued to develop as the projections of punishment and restoration were applied to later situations. The portrayal of Assyria as YHWH's agent of punishment was projected onto Babylon, and Cyrus eventually emerged as the ideal royal figure who would see to the restoration of Zion in the second part of the book. Ultimately, the Persian empire would prove to be YHWH's agent in the book of Isaiah, and at the end of the book, YHWH emerges as the ideal king. Micah, too, was modified to account for the Babylonian exile; Judah would suffer as did Israel, but Babylon would be the agent of YHWH's punishment prior to the restoration of Jerusalem. Other books, such as Hosea and Amos, seem not to have been modified substantially, but they were certainly read in relation to the later circumstances of the Babylonian exile; again, Israel's experience would provide the model for that of Judah.

Obviously, the prophetic tradition continued to develop in the aftermath of Josiah's death as a means to reflect on and to define the significance of the Babylonian exile and the Persian period restoration. In the course of such development, the concern with Josiah appears to have faded as other more pressing concerns took their place in Judah's experience. Josiah once represented the promise of YHWH to the royal house of David that a united Israel would stand with its Temple in Jerusalem and with YHWH's glory and power recognized among the nations. Josiah's death and the failure to realize the goals of his reform clearly compromised his standing and significance, but the Josianic patterns and projections of restoration for the house of David, the Jerusalem Temple, and the united people of Israel appear to have provided the basis for later projections of restoration during the course of the Babylonian exile and beyond. In this sense, Josiah's legacy continued to live on in the prophetic tradition in that it provided Israel/Judah with the ideological strength necessary to face the challenges of national destruction and restoration. Without the prior model of Josiah, which informed the patterns of restoration evident in much of the preexilic prophetic tradition, restoration in the Persian period might well have been impossible.

Conclusion

Although Frost maintains that a "conspiracy of silence" surrounds the death of King Josiah in the Hebrew Bible,[1] the results of this study demonstrate a major concern with the reign and reform program of King Josiah of Judah in the early editions of the DtrH, Deuteronomy, and many of the prophetic books. Much of this literature was reworked following Josiah's death to address the issues of the Babylonian exile and the postexilic restoration, and it reveals important facets in the understanding of King Josiah and his program in the aftermath of his death. Josiah apparently saw himself as the king or messiah of a reunited and restored kingdom of Israel centered around Jerusalem and the Temple, but his unexpected death at Megiddo by the hand of Pharaoh Necho of Egypt resulted in the loss of that grandiose vision. Nevertheless, the memory of this great monarch appears to have influenced exilic and postexilic visions of restoration. There is little comment on Josiah's death per se, but his impact was clearly felt during his lifetime and beyond.

In its present form, the DtrH derives from the period of the exile and attempts to explain the exile by arguing that the sins of King Manasseh prompted YHWH to destroy Jerusalem and Judah. Indeed, Josiah is portrayed as the most righteous monarch of Israel, but his actions are useless in that even Josiah's righteousness cannot reverse YHWH's decision to destroy Jerusalem and the Temple on account of the sins of Manasseh and the people. An earlier form of the DtrH was written during the reign of King Josiah as a means to portray Josiah as the ideal king of the House of David who would reconstitute the covenant with YHWH based on observance of YHWH's Torah, reunite the people of Israel around the Jerusalem Temple, and fulfill the promise that a son of David would rule forever in Jerusa-

---

1. "The Death of Josiah: A Conspiracy of Silence."

lem. In turn, the Josianic DtrH appears to have been a revision of an even earlier form of the DtrH written during the reign of Hezekiah that was designed to portray the House of David as the righteous rulers of Israel and, perhaps prepare for the reinstitution of Davidic rule over the north. Overall, the Josianic DtrH presents the Ephraimite Joshua as an ideal ruler and model for Josiah, but argues that the continued presence of Canaanites in the land and Israel's interrelationship with them provided the impetus for Israel's problems that Josiah must eventually overcome. It argues that even in the period of the Judges, the northern tribes were Canaanized and incapable of ruling themselves properly. David was an exemplary but not ideal monarch, who allowed his lust to compromise his righteousness and prepare for Solomon's accession to the throne. Solomon came to the throne improperly as a result of David's lust; therefore, he caused a shift in the royal house as a new Jerusalem-based faction of the house of David came into power to replace the older Hebron-based branch. Solomon is presented as much like his father in that his own inability to control his lust for pagan women caused the division of the kingdom. The northern kingdom aptly demonstrated its Canaanite character and inability to rule itself and culminated in the exile of the northern tribes. Hezekiah demonstrated faith and adherence to YHWH like that of David, and thereby he provided a model for Josiah. Unlike Solomon, Josiah came to the throne properly by acclamation of the people and proceeded to correct the abuses of his predecessors in order to restore the unity of the people of Israel. In sum, the Josianic edition of the DtrH was designed to address the former northern kingdom of Israel in an effort to convince the Israelite people to reunite with Judah, to return to the Temple in Jerusalem, and to accept Josiah as their righteous monarch.

The book of Deuteronomy complements the historiographical and theological goals and outlook of the DtrH. It presents an extensive body of legal instruction that employs the Mosaic traditions of the northern tribes as a means to lend authority to its program for the centralization of cultic, economic, and political power by the Davidic king and the priesthood of the Jerusalem Temple. Deuteronomy employs the language of the Davidic tradition to assert the legitimacy of only one unnamed altar as the worship site for YHWH and the closure of all others. This ensures that the central sanctuary becomes the collection site for all the revenues of the land, which are brought by the people in the form of produce, animals, or cash, thereby concentrating the economic resources of the land at one site. When read in the context of the DtrH, this of course points to the Jerusalem Temple as the site of the one altar devoted to YHWH. Although Deuteronomy points to the Levitical figure Moses as the source of its authority, it undermines the position and authority of the Levitical priests by reducing their income, insofar as they must share it with the people, and by requiring them to come to the central sanctuary to receive their share of the offerings. Instead, it gives greater rights to the people of the land, who placed Josiah on the throne, to retain their land and income and to ensure the authority and stability of the family or clan as the basic social institution of the people. It provides the king with a great deal of authority: he can appeal to the authority of Mosaic Torah as the means to legitimize his actions. Overall, the book of Deuteronomy establishes an alliance between the people, the central sanctuary, and the monarch that bypasses the authority of the Levitical priesthood outside of Jerusalem, all the while portraying the Levite Moses as the authoritative source for such actions. In this respect, the Levite Moses in Deuteronomy provides the basis for the reunification of the people of Israel under Davidic rule.

Finally, this volume points to the role played by prophets and prophetic literature in support of Josiah's reform program. I argue that Jeremiah supported Josiah's program during his early years and that his oracles calling for the restoration of the former northern Israel to Davidic rule can be reconstructed in Jeremiah 2–4 and 30–31. I further argue that, in the aftermath of Josiah's death, Jeremiah continued to support the Josianic program of alliance with Babylon, as opposed to alliance with Egypt, and that he was supported by the Shaphan family, which had served among Josiah's advisors. Nevertheless, as an Elide priest steeped in Mosaic tradition, Jeremiah rejects Davidic ideology in principle. Neither the Temple nor the Davidic monarch indicates YHWH's protection of Jerusalem and the people; only adherence to YHWH's expectations based on the Mosaic tradition—for example, submission to Babylon and rejection of Egypt—can ensure the security of the people. As a result, Jeremiah is quite critical of the Davidic monarchs who followed Josiah; whereas Josiah's policies were based in Mosaic Torah, those of the later monarchs were not.

Other prophetic books likewise address Josiah's reign. The book of Zephaniah is a coherent exhortational text from the early years of Josiah's reign that calls on its audience to support and to identify with Josiah's reform program. Although later tradition reads Zephaniah as an eschatological scenario of worldwide punishment and restoration, it clearly points to the defeat of Josiah's enemies and the establishment of new Davidic state. Nahum must be read as a coherent composition that celebrates the downfall of the city of Nineveh as an act of YHWH and that demonstrates YHWH's control of historical events from the time of the initial Assyrian incursions. Nahum therefore dates to the last years of King Josiah's reign. Habakkuk dates to the period after the Babylonian subjugation of Judah in 605 B.C.E. and decries Babylon's actions against its erstwhile ally. Earlier prophetic books, such as Isaiah, Amos, Hosea, and Micah, were reworked or reread to support Josiah's program so that Josiah emerged as the promised righteous Davidic monarch who would preside over the reunited people of Israel and Judah. Isaiah presents Josiah as the righteous monarch who will preside over a unified Israel that will see the return of its exiles and subjugate nations once ruled by David. Hosea calls for the return of northern Israel to YHWH and Davidic rule. Amos calls for the destruction of the Beth-El Temple and the reestablishment of Davidic authority over the north. Micah argues that Judah will suffer like Israel, but that a righteous Davidic monarch will preside over the reunification of the people when the suffering is over.

This volume demonstrates that the ideology of Josiah's reform is present in a great deal of biblical literature and that, with the proper application of redaction-critical tools, it is possible to identify and reconstruct both the Josianic ideology and the literature in which it is expressed. Nevertheless, I recognize that Josiah's reform was an absolute failure. Both the nonbiblical evidence, including the results of archeological excavation of the land of Israel and contemporary ancient near-eastern literature, and the biblical evidence demonstrate that Josiah never

succeeded in realizing the goals of reunifying the people of Israel and reestablishing the old Davidic empire. Perhaps it was realized in part, but Josiah's death
at the hands of Necho in 609 B.C.E. certainly put an end to such plans.

These conclusions have implications for future work concerning the development of Judean religious and political ideology in the period following Josiah's
reign. Indeed, Deuteronomy, the Deuteronomistic History, and the prophetic books
examined in this study were programmatic works that were designed in part to
articulate visions for Israel's and Judah's life beyond the time of their respective
compositions. These works were meant to be read and their ideas and programs
were meant to be implemented as the exilic and postexilic Jewish communities
faced the questions of the meaning of the destruction of Jerusalem and the Babylonian
exile, as well as the potential for the restoration of the nation. Laato has already
addressed this issue in his study of Josiah as the "David Redivivius" figure in which
he argues that the image of Josiah is constitutive for the development of Judean
messianic expectations in the exilic period and beyond.[2] Based on his literary-
historical study of the DtrH, Jeremiah, Ezekiel, Haggai, Zechariah, Chronicles,
and Ezra-Nehemiah, he argues that the memory of the righteous Josiah influenced
messianic expectations during the last years of Judah, as well as during the exilic
and postexilic periods, because they fueled popular support for a reestablished
Davidic dynasty that would bring about Judean independence and the restoration
of the Temple in Jerusalem as the center of a reunited people returned from exile.
Much of this expectation, of course, appears to be centered around Zerubbabel,
who played a major role in rebuilding the Temple during the early Persian period.
Insofar as Zerubbabel was the grandson of Jehoiachin, he represented the potential restoration of the Davidic line in Jerusalem. With Zerubbabel's disappearance
or demise, messianic hopes tended to be eschatologized and the righteousness of
Josiah and the house of David were questioned. According to Laato, the DtrH
favors the monarchy and Josiah and during the exilic period thereby interprets
Josiah's death as a consequence of Manasseh's sins. At a much later time, the
Chronicler changed this position to charge that Josiah himself was responsible
for his own death.

Laato is certainly correct to point to the role that the image of Josiah plays in
shaping messianic expectations in the exilic and early postexilic periods, particularly as they pertain to Zerubbabel. But his exclusive focus on exilic and postexilic
text traditions forces him to miss some important dimensions of the perception of
Josiah during the late monarchy and beyond. Despite his righteousness, Josiah
was a failure, and the consequences of this failure were already having their effect prior to the time of Zerubbabel. In short, this volume points to the other side
of the debate concerning messianic expectations during these periods: essentially,
I show that many Judean thinkers were already beginning to abandon the concept
of a restored Davidic monarchy even before the time of Zerubbabel. Literature
such as the DtrH, Deuteronomy, and Isaiah point to the centrality of the Temple

---

2. Antti Laato, *Josiah and David Redivivius: The Historical Josiah and the Messianic Expectations of Exilic and Postexilic Times*, ConBibOT 33 (Stockholm: Almqvist and Wiksell, 1992).

and priesthood in their portrayal of YHWH and the future of the Jewish people, but the Davidic monarch already plays a relatively minor or subordinate role as early as the late monarchic and exilic periods.

The DtrH is a key case in point. The final form of the DtrH must be dated to the exilic period as indicated by its concluding notice of the release of King Jehoiachin from prison by the Babylonian monarch Evil-Merodach. It shows no awareness of the impending collapse of Babylonia, the rise of Persia, or the return of Jews to Jerusalem in the early Persian period, and therefore it cannot be securely dated to the postexilic period. Many scholars have seen a programmatic interest in restoration in the final form of the DtrH—namely, the release of Jehoiachin from prison reflects YHWH's promise to the Davidic house expressed in 2 Samuel 7 and elsewhere to ensure an eternal line of David.[3] But the DtrH expresses no programmatic interest in the return of the people from exile, and Jehoachin is presented as a relatively pathetic example of the Davidic line. He does not sit on the throne in Jerusalem; he dines at the table of the King of Babylon much as Mephibosheth, the son of Saul, dines at the table of David after the Saulide dynasty is deposed (2 Sam 9). The Davidic line continues to exist in the exilic DtrH, but if the exilic DtrH looks to the restoration of Davidic rule, it does so obliquely. Furthermore, it portrays Josiah, the ideal monarch of Israel, as a monarch who attempts to act in opposition to YHWH's will to destroy Jerusalem and exile the people for Manasseh's sins as expressed by the prophetess Huldah. In the exilic DtrH, Josiah is completely ineffective, despite his righteousness. Isaiah had already informed Hezekiah that his sons would be carried off to Babylon. Josiah is unable to reverse YHWH's decision to destroy Jerusalem and the Temple, and he only wins a reprieve from witnessing the destruction, much like Ahab did following his repentance. Because of this ineffectiveness, the continued monarchical role of the house of David is called into question.

Much the same perspective applies to the book of Deuteronomy, which is read prior to the DtrH. Although Deuteronomy 30:1–10 allows for the possibility that the people would repent and thereby be restored to the land of Israel from exile, the portrayal of proper leadership in the book likewise calls into question the role of the monarch. As noted in the discussion of Deuteronomy, the Torah of the King in Deuteronomy 17:14–20 portrays the monarch as one who must adhere to YHWH's Torah in order to rule and who is required to read YHWH's Torah daily under the supervision of the Levitical priests. Both of these factors may well derive from Josiah's interests—that is, the possibility of return from exile may originally have envisioned the return of northern exiles, and the portrayal of a Torah observant monarch apparently strengthened the hand of the Davidic king. Nevertheless, when Deuteronomy is read in an exilic context, a very different picture emerges. The potential for repentance and return is applied not only to northern Israel but also to the people as a whole who suffered the Babylonian exile. Furthermore, the portrayal of the righteous monarch clearly singles out Solomon as the antithesis of righteous monarchic rule because he violates every provision for royal behav-

---

3. For example, von Rad, *Studies in Deuteronomy* 74–91.

ior laid out in Deuteronomy 17:14–20. It is at this point that the supervision of
the Levitical priests becomes so important. From the perspective of Deuteronomy,
Moses the Levitical priest constitutes the ideal standard for rule of the people of
Israel. When read in relation to the DtrH, it becomes clear that the kings of Israel,
including both the northern kings and the house of David, failed to meet this standard. When read in relation to the period of the exile and beyond, when no Davidic
monarch sat on the throne but the Levitical priests served as leaders for the people,
the book of Deuteronomy and the DtrH put forward a different model of leadership for the people. No longer would the monarch rule; the Levitical priests would
guide the people instead. This perspective holds true not only in Deuteronomy
and the DtrH, but in the entire Pentateuchal tradition as well, in which Moses the
Levitical priest serves as leader of the people but no monarch appears. The portrayal of Moses as a Levitical figure may originally have served Josianic interests
to attract the people of northern Israel to Davidic rule by portraying Josiah as a
monarch modeled on a Levitical ideal, but in the aftermath of the collapse of the
house of David, the Mosaic or Levitical ideal would hold sway as a model for the
leadership of the people, and the Davidic ideal would not.[4]

This perspective is evident in the prophetical traditions as well. Laato points
especially to prophetical traditions that derive from the period following that of
Zerubbabel and that reflect qualification of Zerubbabel's perceived messianic role.
Haggai clearly points to Zerubbabel's messianic role as "the signet ring" of YHWH
(Hag 2:20–23) who will assume authority with the establishment of YHWH's
Temple in Jerusalem as the site to which the nations will come to acknowledge
YHWH's rule. The book of Zechariah, especially Zechariah 4 and 6, clearly pre-
suppose Zerubbabel's royal status, but the book has clearly been reworked to
present the priesthood as leadership figures, apparently in the aftermath of
Zerubbabel's disappearance or demise. The presentation in Ezekiel 34 and 40–
48 of the Davidic monarch as a subordinate "prince," who acts under the authority of the Temple priests rather than as an autonomous ruler, reflects the reworking of a positive view of the monarch to a much more qualified view following
Zerubbabel's attempt at reestablishing Davidic authority.[5] Finally, the portrayal

---

4. It is noteworthy that in Genesis 15, the covenant with Abraham is portrayed in royal Davidic
terms, insofar as it is an eternal covenant that assures Abraham of the continuity of his descendants,
much like the covenant portrayed for David in 2 Samuel 7, and that defines the land of Israel granted
to his descendants along the lines of the definition of the Davidic empire in 2 Samuel 8. Abraham's
covenant is portrayed as a royal covenant, but no king appears. For discussion, see R. E. Clements,
Abraham and David: Genesis XV and Its Meaning for Israelite Tradition, SBT 2/5 (London: SCM,
1967); M. Weinfeld, "Covenant, Davidic," *IDB*[S] 188–192. Note also that Chronicles ties the image
of the Davidic monarchs closely to Temple observance and the Levitical priesthood. As William
Schniedewind argues (*The Word of G-d in Transition: From Prophet to Exegete in the Second Temple
Period*, JSOTSup 197 [Sheffield: Sheffield Academic Press, 1995]), Chronicles presents a clear
messianic view that is designed to argue for the reestablishment of the Jerusalem Temple in the
postexilic period.

5. Laato sees the presentation of the pro-*nāśî'* ("prince") layer in Ezekiel 34 and 40–48 as
exilic, but argues that the conception of the prince was subjected to criticism by the Zadokite priests
in the postexilic period. See his discussion, *Josiah and David Redivivius* 179–185, 189–196.

of the Davidic monarch in Jeremiah 23:5–6 and 33:14–26 as "the righteous branch" of David clearly presupposes Zerubbabel, whose name in Akkadian means "branch of Babylon," and places YHWH's promise to David together with that to the Levitical priests. According to Laato, these traditions testify to the influence of Josiah's image on Zerubbabel but also reflect the reconceptualization of the Davidic monarch following Zerubbabel's failure.

Nevertheless, my study of Josiah's influence in the prophetic traditions points not to the period following Zerubbabel's failure, but to the late monarchic and the exilic periods as the time when a fundamental reconceptualization of the role of the Davidic monarchy begins. As noted in the chapter on the Jeremiah tradition, the prophet clearly questions Davidic authority and the Zion tradition in principle and only supports Davidic monarchs when they align themselves with the Mosaic tradition. At a much later period, statements are added about the establishment of a righteous Davidic "branch" (Jer 23:5–6; 33:14–26), apparently as a means to portray Zerubbabel as a monarch like Josiah, but even these references are qualified by their associations with promises to the Levites. As noted in the chapter on the Isaiah traditions, a Josianic edition of Isaiah clearly portrays Josiah as the ideal monarch or "branch" announced by the prophet. Isaiah the prophet and the Isaianic tradition are very clearly royalist or Davidic in orientation. Therefore, it is noteworthy that, already in the exilic period, the Isaiah tradition abandoned the notion of a Davidic monarch and posited that Cyrus, king of Persia, would serve as YHWH's messiah and Temple builder in place of a Davidic figure (Isa 44:28; 45:1).[6] In fact, no clear Davidic monarch appears in the Isaiah tradition from the exile on. The people of Israel at large are granted the "sure promises" of the house of David in Isaiah 55:3, and the Trito-Isaiah material presents YHWH as the true righteous monarch of Israel; no Davidic figure appears. Indeed, the oracle in Isaiah 11:1–16, which appears to have been written as part of the Josianic edition of Isaiah to announce Josiah as the righteous monarch envisioned by the prophet, has been reinterpreted in the Trito-Isaiah tradition to point to YHWH as the righteous monarch of Israel.[7] The entire book of Isaiah does not look to a Davidic monarch as the source of leadership; rather it looks to the Temple in Jerusalem and to YHWH as the manifestations of true sovereignty in Zion (cf. Isa 2:2–4; 24–27; 65–66). In such a scenario, the people of Israel serve as YHWH's priests.

The book of Micah follows a somewhat different pattern. In its exilic edition, it employs in Micah 4:1–5 a version of the same oracle that appears in Isaiah 2:2–4 to portray YHWH's Temple in Zion as the source for YHWH's sovereignty over the world. YHWH is portrayed as sovereign, but Micah 5:1–8 looks to the rule of a righteous Davidic figure who will preside over the ingathering of the exiled

---

6. Gressmann argues that perhaps the image of Josiah stands behind the image of the suffering servant, but this is disputed. For details of the discussion, see Herbert Haag, *Der G-ttesknecht bei Deuterojesaja*, ErFor 233 (Darmstadt: Wissenschaftliche Buchgesellschaft, 1993) 120–121.

7. See Marvin A. Sweeney, "The Reconceptualization of the Davidic Covenant in Isaiah," in *Studies in the Book of Isaiah*, BETL 132, Fs. W. A. M. Beuken, ed. M. Vervenne and J. T. A. G. M. van Ruiten (Leuven: Peeters, 1997) 41–61.

people. This oracle likely had its origins in a Josianic edition of Micah, but in the present form, it points to a debate with the Isaiah tradition over the nature of proper rule. Whereas the book of Isaiah posits Isaiah 2:2–4 as an oracle that leads ultimately to YHWH's rule following the period of Davidic rule, Micah employs Micah 4:1–5 as an oracle that points simultaneously to YHWH's and to Davidic rule. That Micah reacts to Isaiah 2 is clear from Micah 5:9–14, which employs language from Isaiah 2:6–21 to portray YHWH's destruction of war materials among the nations.[8] But it also indicates a debate within prophetic tradition as to whether a Davidic monarch would emerge in the exilic or postexilic period. Isaiah maintains that no such monarch would appear; Cyrus and YHWH serve that role. Micah, by contrast, maintains that a Davidic figure would preside over a period of peace and thereby represent YHWH's rule. Hosea and Amos, both of which call for the restoration of Davidic rule over Israel, would support such a position. Although the preceding analysis argues that their respective prophecies concerning the restoration of Davidic rule in Hosea 3:5 and Amos 9:11–15 were understood in relation to Josiah during the seventh century, both would have been read as prophetic texts that called for the restoration of the House of David in the exilic and postexilic periods. Perhaps these texts were instrumental in supporting the claims of Zerubbabel and in defining his role as YHWH's anointed. But these texts also must be read in relation to the Isaiah tradition, which apparently envisions no possible restoration of the Davidic monarch in articulating its vision of the future.

In sum, Josiah's reform and its failure to achieve its aims appears to have provoked considerable debate concerning the role of the monarchy in the period following Josiah's death from the late monarchic period, through the exilic period, and beyond. Clearly, the image of Josiah as the righteous Davidic monarch who would restore the unity of the people of Israel around the Jerusalem Temple greatly influenced messianic expectations, particularly in relation to Zerubbabel, in the early Persian period. Furthermore, the images that played such an important role in the articulation of Josiah's reign—the redemption of Israelite exiles and their return to Jerusalem, the establishment of the Jerusalem Temple as the center of the reunited people of Israel, and the establishment of sovereignty over nations from Zion—all are major elements of exilic and postexilic images of an ideal age. But many of the traditions raise questions about the role of a Davidic monarch and point instead to the Temple in Jerusalem as the focus for the future. Furthermore, exilic editions of the Deuteronomistic History, the book of Deuteronomy, and the book of Isaiah clearly call the expectations for the Davidic monarchy into question and posit instead the possibility of Levitical leadership and the central role of the Temple. By pointing already in the exilic period to the ideal leadership of the Levitical priesthood, the role of the Temple in Jerusalem, and, indeed, the royal leadership exercised by YHWH, these traditions undermine the claims of the House of David as rulers of the people of Israel. Josiah's rulership had failed, and the House of David never again regained the throne in Jerusalem. As a result

---

8. See also my commentary on Micah in *The Book of the Twelve Prophets* forthcoming.

of that failure, debate opened concerning the alternative models of leadership that were available to the people of Israel during the exilic and postexilic periods. These traditions portrayed the Levitical priesthood and the Temple in Jerusalem—not the monarchy—as the source of ideal leadership. Josiah's failure opened the way for the emergence of new patterns of leadership in the Second Temple period in the which the Levitical priests, centered in the Temple at Jerusalem, would provide authoritative guidance for the Jewish people during the periods of Persian and, later, Hellenistic and Roman rule. The death of Josiah was not met with silence, but with considerable discussion concerning new patterns of leadership as Judah entered the Second Temple period.

BIBLIOGRAPHY

Ackroyd, Peter R. "Hosea and Jacob." *VT* 13 (1963) 245–259.

———. "An Interpretation of the Babylonian Exile: A Study of II Kings 20 and Isaiah 38–39." *Scottish Journal of Theology* 27 (1974) 329–352. Reprinted in *Studies in the Religious Traditions of the Old Testament*, 152–171, 282–285. London: SCM, 1987.

———. "Isaiah 36–39: Structure and Function." In *Studies in the Religious Traditions of the Old Testament*, 105–120, 274–278. London: SCM, 1987. Originally published in *Von Kanaan bis Kerala*, ed. W. C. Delsman et al. Fs. J. P. M. van der Ploeg. AOAT 211. Neukirchen-Vluyn: Neukirchener, 1982.

———. "A Judgment Narrative between Kings and Chronicles? An Approach to Amos 7:9–17." In *Canon and Authority*, ed. G. W. Coats and B. O. Long, 71–87. Philadelphia: Fortress, 1977.

Ahlström, Gösta W. *The History of Ancient Palestine*. Minneapolis: Fortress, 1993.

Albertz, R. "Jer 2–6 und die Frühzeitverkündigung Jeremias." *ZAW* 94 (1982) 20–47.

Alt, Albrecht. "Die Heimat des Deuteronomiums." In *Kleine Schriften zur Geschichte des Volkes Israels*, vol. 2, 250–275. Munich: C. H. Beck, 1953.

———. "The Formation of the Israelite State in Palestine." In *Essays in Old Testament History and Religion*, 171–237. Oxford: Blackwell, 1966.

———. "The Monarchy in the Kingdoms of Israel and Judah." In *Essays on Old Testament History and Religion*, 311–335. Garden City, N.Y.: Doubleday, 1967.

Amit, Yairah. "Hidden Polemic in the Conquest of Dan: Judges xvii–xviii." *VT* 40 (1990) 4–20.

———. "Literature in the Service of Politics: Studies in Judges 19–21." In *Politics and Theopolitics in the Bible and Postbiblical Literature*, ed. H. Graf Reventlow and B. Uffenheimer, 28–40. JSOTSup 171. Sheffield: Sheffield Academic Press, 1994.

Anderson, Bernard W. "The L-rd has Created Something New." *CBQ* 40 (1978) 463–478.

Anderson, F. I., and D. N. Freedman. *Hosea*. AB 24. Garden City, N.Y.: Doubleday, 1980.

Anderson, G. W. "The Idea of the Remnant in the Book of Zephaniah." *ASTI* 11 (1977–78) 11–14.

————. "Some Observations on the Old Testament Doctrine of the Remnant." *Transactions of the Glasgow University Oriental Society* 23 (1969–1970) 1–10.

Anderson, Roger W., Jr. "Zephaniah ben Cushi and Cush of Benjamin: Traces of Cushite Presence in Syria-Palestine." In *The Pitcher is Broken: Memorial Essays for Gösta W. Ahlström*, ed. S. W. Holloway and L. K. Handy, 45–70. JSOTSup 190. Sheffield: JSOT Press, 1995.

Auld, A. G. *Amos*. Old Testament Guides. Sheffield: JSOT Press, 1986.

Bailey, L. R. "The Golden Calf." *HUCA* 42 (1971) 97–115.

Barrick, W. B. "On the 'Removal of the High Places' in 1–2 Kings." *Bibl* 55 (1974) 255–257.

Barth, Hermann. *Die Jesaja-Worte in der Josiazeit*. WMANT 48. Neukirchen-Vluyn: Neukirchener, 1977.

Barthelmus, Rüdiger. "Forschung am Richterbuch seit Martin Noth." *TRu* 56 (1991) 221–259.

Barton, John. *Isaiah 1–39*. OT Guides. Sheffield: JSOT Press, 1995.

————. *Reading the Old Testament: Method in Biblical Study*. Louisville, KY: Westminster John Knox, Revised edition, 1996.

Becking, Bob. "Divine Wrath and the Conceptual Coherence of the Book of Nahum." *SJOT* 9 (1995) 277–296.

————. "Is het boek Nahum een literaire eenheid?" *NTT* 32 (1978) 107–124.

————. "Passion, Power, and Protection: Interpreting the G-d of Nahum." In *On Reading Prophetic Texts: Gender-Specific and Related Studies in Memory of Fokkelien van Dijk-Hemmes*, ed. B. Becking and M. Dijkstra, 1–20. BibInt 18. Leiden: E. J. Brill, 1996.

Beit-Arieh, Itzhak, and Cresson, Bruce C. "Horvat ʿUza: A Fortified Outpost on the Eastern Negev Border," *BA* 54 (1991) 126–135.

Ben Zvi, Ehud. "The Account of the Reign of Manasseh in II Reg 21, 1–18 and the Redactional History of the Book of Kings." *ZAW* 103 (1991) 355–374.

————. *A Historical-Critical Study of the Book of Zephaniah*. BZAW 198. Berlin and New York: Walter de Gruyter, 1991.

————. "History and Prophetic Texts." In *History and Interpretation*, ed. M. P. Graham et al., 106–120. Fs. J. H. Hayes. JSOTSup 173. Sheffield: JSOT Press, 1993.

Berlin, Adele. *Zephaniah*. AB 25A. New York: Doubleday, 1994.

Beuken, W. A. M. "Jesaja 33 als Spiegeltext im Jesajabuch." *ETL* 67 (1991) 5–35.

Beyerlin, Walter. *Reflexe der Amosvisionene im Jeremiabuch*. OBO 93. Freiburg: Universitätsverlag; Göttingen: Vandenhoeck & Ruprecht, 1989.

Biddle, Mark. *A Redaction History of Jeremiah 2:1–4:2*. AThANT 77. Zürich: Theologischer Verlag, 1990.

Blenkinsopp, Joseph. *A History of Prophecy in Israel*. Revised Edition. Louisville, KY: Westminster John Knox, 1996.

Boecker, H.-J. *Law and the Administration of Justice in the Old Testament and Ancient East*. Trans. J. Moiser. Minneapolis: Augsburg, 1980.

Böhler, Dieter. "Geschlechterdifferenz und Landbesitz: Strukturuntersuchungen zu Jer 2,2–4,2." In *Jeremia und die "deuteronomistiche Bewegung"*, ed. W. Gross, 91–127. BBB 98. Weinheim: Belz Athenäum, 1995.

Böhmer, S. *Heimskehr und neuer Bund. Studien zur Jeremia 30–31*. Göttingen: Vandenhoeck & Ruprecht, 1976.

Boling, Robert G. and G. Ernest Wright. *Joshua*. AB 6. Garden City, N.Y.: Doubleday, 1982.

Boling, Robert G. *Judges*. AB 6A. Garden City, N.Y.: Doubleday, 1975.

Bozak, Barbara. *Life "Anew": A Literary-Theological Study of Jer. 30–31*. AnBib 122. Rome: Pontifical Biblical Institute, 1991.

Braulik, G. *Die deuteronomistischen Gesetze und der Dekalog: Studien zum Aufbau von Deuteronomium 12–26*. SBS 145. Stuttgart: Katholisches Bibelwerk, 1991.

Brettler, Marc. "The Book of Judges: Literature as Politics." *JBL* 108 (1989) 395–418.

———. "Text in a Tel: 2 Kings 17 as History." In *The Creation of History in Ancient Israel*, 112–134, 208–217. London and New York: Routledge, 1995.

Buccellati, G. *Cities and Nations of Ancient Syria: An Essay on Political Institutions with Special Reference in the Israelite Kingdoms*. Rome: University of Rome, 1967.

Buss, Martin. *The Prophetic Word of Hosea: A Morphological Study*. BZAW 111. Berlin: A. Töpelmann, 1969.

Buttrick, George, editor. *The Interpreter's Dictionary of the Bible*. 4 volumes. Nashville: Abingdon, 1962.

Campbell, Antony F. *Of Prophets and Kings: A Late Ninth-Century Document*. CBQMS 17. Washington, D.C.: Catholic Biblical Association, 1986.

Caquot, A. "Osée et la Royauté." *RHPR* 41 (1961) 123–146.

Cardellini, I. *Die biblischen "Sklaven"-Gesetze im Lichte des keilschriftlichen Sklavenrechts: Ein Beitrag zur Tradition, Überlieferugn und Redaktion der alttestamentlichen Rechtstexte*. BBB 55. Bonn: P. Hanstein, 1981.

Carmichael, C. *The Laws of Deuteronomy*. Ithaca and London: Cornell University Press, 1974.

Carroll, R. P. *Jeremiah*. OT Guides. Sheffield: JSOT Press, 1989.

———. *Jeremiah: A Commentary*. OTL. Philadelphia: Westminster, 1986.

———. "Prophecy and Society." In *The World of Ancient Israel: Sociological, Anthropological, and Political Perspectives*, ed. R. E. Clements, 203–225. Cambridge, U.K.: Cambridge University Press, 1989.

Cathcart, Kevin. *Nahum in the Light of Northwest Semitic*. BO 26. Rome: Biblical Institute Press, 1973.

Cazelles, Henri. "Sophonie, Jérémie, et les Scythes en Palestine." *RB* 74 (1967) 24–44.

Cha, Jun-Hee. *Micha und Jeremia*. BBB 107. Weinheim: Beltz Athenäum, 1996.

Childs, Brevard S. *Introduction to the Old Testament as Scripture*. Philadelphia: Fortress, 1979.

———. *Isaiah and the Assyrian Crisis*. SBT 2/3. London: SCM, 1967.

Chirichigno, G. C. *Debt-Slavery in Israel and the Ancient Near East*. JSOTSup 141. Sheffield: JSOT Press, 1993.

Christensen, D. L. "The Book of Nahum: The Question of Authorship and the Canonical Process." *JETS* 31 (1988) 51–58.

———. "The Book of Nahum as a Liturgical Composition." *JETS* 32 (1989) 159–169.

———. "Zephaniah 2:4–15: A Theological Basis for Josiah's Program of Political Expansion." *CBQ* 46 (1984) 669–682.

Claburn, W. Eugene. "The Fiscal Basis of Josiah's Reforms." *JBL* 92 (1973) 11–22.

Clements, R. E. *Abraham and David: Genesis XV and Its Meaning for Israelite Tradition*. SBT 2/5. London: SCM, 1967.

———. *Deuteronomy*. OTG. Sheffield: JSOT Press, 1989.

———. "Deuteronomy and the Jerusalem Cult Tradition." *VT* 15 (1965) 300–312.

———. *G-d's Chosen People: A Theological Interpretation of the Book of Deuteronomy*. Valley Forge: Judson, 1969.

———. *Isaiah 1–39*. NCeB. Grand Rapids: Eerdmans. London: Marshall, Morgan, and Scott, 1980.

———. *Isaiah and the Deliverance of Jerusalem: A Study of the Interpretation of Prophecy in the Old Testament*. JSOTSup 13. Sheffield: JSOT Press, 1980.

———. "The Isaiah Narrative of 2 Kings 20:12–19 and the Date of the Deuteronomic History." In *Isac Leo Seeligmann Volume*, ed. A. Rofé and Y. Zakovitch, 209–220. Jerusalem: E. Rubenstein, 1983.

Cogan, Mordechai, and Hayim Tadmor. *II Kings*. AB 11. New York: Doubleday, 1988.

———. "Israel in Exile—The View of a Josianic Historian." *JBL* 97 (1978) 40–44.

Coggins, R. "An Alternative Prophetic Tradition?" In *Israel's Prophetic Tradition*, ed. R. Coggins et al., 77–94. Fs. P. R. Ackroyd. Cambridge, U.K.: Cambridge University Press, 1982.

Coggins, R. J., and S. P. Re'emi. *Israel Among the Nations: Nahum, Obadiah, Esther*. International Theological Commentary. Grand Rapids, Mich.: Eerdmans, 1985.

Collins, Terence. *The Mantle of Elijah: The Redaction Criticism of the Prophetical Books*. BibSem 20. Sheffield: JSOT Press, 1993.

Conrad, Edgar. *Reading Isaiah*. OBT. Minneapolis: Fortress, 1991.

Cortese, Enzo. *Josua 13–21: Ein priesterschriftlicher Abschnitt im deuteronomistischen Geschichtswerk*. OBO 94. Freiburg: Universitätsverlag. Göttingen: Vandenhoeck & Ruprecht, 1990.

Crim, Keith, editor. *The Interpreter's Dictionary of the Bible: Supplementary Volume*. Nashville: Abingdon, 1976.

Cross, Frank M., Jr. "The Themes of the Books of Kings and the Structure of the Deuteronomistic History." In *Canaanite Myth and Hebrew Epic*, 274–289. Cambridge, Mass.: Harvard University, 1973.

Davies, G. I. *Hosea*. NCeB. Grand Rapids, Mich.: William Eerdmans, 1992.

———. *Hosea*. OTG. Sheffield: Sheffield Academic Press, 1993.

De Vries, Simon J. *1 Kings*. WBC 12. Waco, Tex.: Word, 1985.

———. *From Old Revelation to New: A Tradition-Historical and Redaction Critical Study of Temporal Transitions in Prophetic Prediction*. Grand Rapids, Mich.: William Eerdmans, 1995.

———. *Prophet against Prophet*. Grand Rapids, Mich.: Eerdmans, 1978.

Dearman, A., editor. *Studies in the Mesha Inscription and Moab*. ABS 2. Atlanta: Scholars Press, 1989.

Debus, Jörg. *Die Sünde Jerobeams: Studien zur Darstellung Jerobeams und der Geschichte des Nordreichs in der deuteronomistischen Geschichtsschreibung*. FRLANT 93. Göttingen: Vandenhoeck & Ruprecht, 1967.

de Pury, Albert, Römer, Thomas, and Macchi, Jean-Daniel, editors. *L'historiographie deutéronomiste à la lumière des recherches récentes*. Geneva: Labor et Fides, 1996.

Dietrich, Walter. "Josia und das Gesetzbuch (2 Reg. XXII)." *VT* 27 (1977) 13–35.

———. *Prophetie und Geschichte: Eine redaktionsgeschichtliche Untersuchung zum deuteronomistischen Geschichtswerk*. FRLANT 108. Göttingen: Vandenhoeck & Ruprecht, 1972.

Dietrich, Walter and Thomas Naumann. *Die Samuelbücher*. ErFor 287. Darmstadt: Wissenschaftliche Buchgesellschaft, 1995.

Dietrich, Walter and Milton Schwantes, editors. *Der Tag wird kommen: Ein interkontextuelles Gespräch über das Buch des Propheten Zefanja*. SBS 170. Stuttgart: Katholisches Bibelwerk, 1996.

Donner, Herbert. "The Syro-Ephraimitic War and the end of the Kingdom of Israel." In *Israelite and Judaean History*, ed. J. H. Hayes and J. M. Miller, 421–434. OTL. Philadelphia: Westminster, 1977.

Duhm, Bernard. *Das Buch Jesaia*. Göttingen: Vandenhoeck & Ruprecht, 1968.

Eissfeldt, Otto. "Lade und Stierbild." *ZAW* 58 (1940–41) 190–215.

———. *The Old Testament: An Introduction*. Trans. P. R. Ackroyd. Oxford: Blackwell. 1965.

Elat, Moshe. "The Economic Relations of the Neo-Assyrian Empire with Egypt." *JAOS* 98 (1978) 20–34.

Elliger, Karl, and Wilhelm Rudolph, editors. *Biblia Hebraica Stuttgartensia*. Stuttgart: Deutsche Bibelgesellschaft, 1977.

Emerton, J. A. "Sheol and the Sons of Belial." *VT* 37 (1987) 214–218.

———. "The Textual and Linguistic Problem of Habakkuk ii 4–5." *JTS* 28 (1977) 1–18.

Emmerson, Grace I. *Hosea: An Israelite Prophet in Judean Perspective*. JSOTSup 28. Sheffield: JSOT Press, 1984.

Epsztein, L. *Social Justice in the Ancient Near East and the People of the Bible*. Trans. J. Bowden. London: SCM, 1986.

Eynikel, Erik. *The Reform of King Josiah and the Composition of the Deuteronomistic History*. OTS 33. Leiden: E. J. Brill, 1996.

Fensham, F. C. "Widow, Orphan, and the Poor in Ancient Near Eastern Legal and Wisdom Literature." *JNES* 21 (1962) 129–139.

Finkelstein, Israel. "The Archaeology of the Days of Manasseh." In *Scripture and Other Artifacts: Essays on Bible and Archaeology in Honor of Philip J. King*, ed. Michael D. Coogan, J. Cheryl Exum, and Lawrence E. Stager, 169–187. Louisville, KY: Westminster John Knox, 1994.

Finkelstein, J. J. *The Ox That Gored*. TAPS 71/2. Philadelphia: The American Philosophical Society, 1981.

Fischer, Georg. *Das Trostbüchlein: Text, Komposition und Theologie von Jer 30–31*. SBB 26. Stuttgart: Katholisches Bibelwerk, 1993.

Floyd, Michael. "The Chimerical Acrostic of Nahum 1:2–10." *JBL* 113 (1994) 421–437.

———. "Prophetic Complaints about the Fulfillment of Oracles in Habakkuk 1:2–17 and Jeremiah 15:10–18." *JBL* 110 (1991) 397–418.

Fohrer, G. "Das 'Gebet des Propheten Habakuk' (Hab 3,1–16)." In *Mélanges bibliques et orientaux en l'honneur de M. Mathias Delcor*, ed. A. Caquot et al., 159–167. AOAT 215. Kevelaer and Neukirchen: Neukirchener, 1985.

Freedman, David Noel, et al., editors. *The Anchor Bible Dictionary*. 6 vols. New York: Doubleday, 1992.

Friedman, Richard E. *The Exile and Biblical Narrative: The Formation of the Deuteronomistic and Priestly Works*. HSM 22; Chico, Calif., Calif.: Scholars Press, 1981.

———. "From Egypt to Egypt: Dtr[1] and Dtr[2]." In *Traditions in Transformation: Turning Points in Biblical Faith*, ed. B. Halpern and J. Levenson, 167–192. Fs. F. M. Cross. Winona Lake, Ind.: Eisenbrauns, 1981.

Fritz, Volkmar. *Das Buch Josua*. HAT 1/7. Tübingen: J. C. B. Mohr (Paul Siebeck), 1994.

Frost, Stanley Brice. "The Death of Josiah: A Conspiracy of Silence." *JBL* 87 (1968) 369–382.

Galling, K. "Das Königsgesetz im Deuteronomium." *TLZ* 76 (1951) 133–138.

Gelston, A. "Kingship in the Book of Hosea." *OTS* 19 (1974) 71–85.

Gerbrandt, G. E. *Kingship According to the Deuteronomistic History*. SBLDS 87. Atlanta: Scholars Press, 1986.

Gertz, Jan Christian. *Die Gerichtsorganization Israels im deuteronomischen Gesetz*. FRLANT 165. Göttingen: Vandenhoeck & Ruprecht, 1994.

Gilmer, H. *The If-You Form in Israelite Law*. SBLDS 15. Missoula, Mont.: Scholars Press, 1975.

Ginsberg, H. Louis. *The Israelian Heritage of Judaism*. New York: Jewish Theological Seminary, 1982.

Gitin, Seymour. "Tel Miqne-Ekron: A Type Site for the Inner Coastal Plain in the Iron Age II Period." In *Recent Excavations in Israel: Studies in Iron Age Archaeology*, ed. S. Gitin and W. G. Dever, 23–58. AASOR 49. Winona Lake, Ind.: Eisenbrauns, 1989.

―――. "Seventh Century B.C.E. Cultic Elements at Ekron." In *Proceedings of the Second International Congress on Biblical Archaeology, June 1990*, 248–258. Jerusalem: Israel Exploration Society, 1993.

Glatt-Gilad, David. "The Deuteronomic Critique of Solomon: A Response to Marvin A. Sweeney." *JBL* 116 (1997) 700–703.

Gonçalves, F. *L'expédition de Sennachérib en Palestine dans la littérature hébraïque ancienne*. PIOL 34. Louvaine-la-neuve: Institut orientaliste, Université de Louvain, 1986.

Good, Edwin M. "The Composition of Hosea." *SEÅ* 31 (1966) 21–63.

Graffy, A. *A Prophet Confronts His People: The Disputation Speech in the Prophets*. AnBib 104. Rome: Biblical Institute Press, 1984.

Greenspahn, Frederick E. "The Theology of the Framework of Judges." *VT* 36 (1986) 385–396.

Grønbaek, Jakob H. *Die Geschichte vom Aufstieg Davids (1. Sam. 15–2. Sam. 5). Tradition und Composition*. Acta Theologica Danica X. Copenhagen: Munksgaard, 1971.

Gross, W. "Lying Prophet and Disobedient Man of G-d in 1 Kings 13: Role Analysis as an Instrument of Theological Interpretation of an Old Testament Narrative Text." *Semeia* 15 (1979) 97–135.

Gross, Walter, editor. *Jeremia und die "deuteronomistiche Bewegung."* BBB 98. Weinheim: Belz Athenäum, 1995.

Haag, Herbert. *Der G-ttesknecht bei Deuterojesaja*. Erträge der Forschung, 233. Darmstadt: Wissenschaftliche Buchgesellschaft, 1993.

Haak, Robert D. "'Cush' in Zephaniah." In *The Pitcher is Broken: Memorial Essays for GöstaW. Ahlström*, ed. S. W. Holloway and L. K. Landy, 238–251. JSOTSup 190. Sheffield: JSOT Press, 1995.

―――. *Habakkuk*. VTSup 44. Leiden: E. J. Brill, 1992.

Hagstrom, David Gerald. *The Coherence of the Book of Micah: A Literary Analysis*. SBLDS 89. Atlanta: Scholars Press, 1988.

Hallo, W. W., and W. K. Simpson. *The Ancient Near East: A History*. New York: Harcourt, Brace, Jovanovich, 1971.

Halpern, Baruch. *The Constitution of the Monarchy in Israel*. HSM 25. Chico, Calif.: Scholars Press, 1981.

Halpern, Baruch, and David Vanderhooft, "The Editions of Kings in the 7th–6th Centuries." *HUCA* 62 (1991) 179–244.

―――. "Jerusalem and the Lineages in the Seventh Century BCE: Kinship and the Rise of Individual Moral Liability." In *Law and Ideaology in Monarchic Israel*, ed. B. Halpern and D. W. Hobson, 1–107. JSOTSup 124. Sheffield: JSOT, 1991.

Hamilton, J. M. *Social Justice and Deuteronomy: The Case of Deuteronomy 15*. SBLDS 136. Atlanta: Scholars, 1992.

Hardmeier, Christof. "Die Redekomposition Jer 2–6. Eine ultimative Verwarnung Jerusalems im Kontext des Zidkijasufstandes." *Wort und Dienst* 21 (1991) 11–42.

―――. "Geschichte und Erfahrung in Jer 2–6: Zur theologischen Notwendigkeit einer geschichts- und erfahrungsbezogenen Exegese und ihrer methodischen Neurorientierung." *EvTh* 56 (1996) 3–29.

————. *Prophetie im Streit vor dem Untergang Judas: Erzählkommunkiative Studien zur Entstehungssituation der Jesaja- und Jeremiaerzählungen in II Reg 18–20 und Jer 37–40.* BZAW 187. Berlin and New York: Walter de Gruyter, 1990.

Hauser, A. J., and R. Gregory. *From Carmel to Horeb: Elijah in Crisis.* JSOT Sup 85. BLS 19. Sheffield: Almond, 1990.

Hayes, John H. *Amos, the Eighth Century Prophet: His Times and His Preaching.* Nashville: Abingdon, 1988.

————. *An Introduction to Old Testament Study.* Nashville: Abingdon, 1979.

Hayes, J. H., and J. M. Miller, editors. *Israelite and Judaean History.* OTL. Philadelphia: Westminster, 1977.

Hentschel, Georg. *Die Elijaerzählungen: Zum Verhältnis von historischem Geschehen und geschichtlicher Erfahrung.* Erfurter Theologische Studien 33. Leipzig: St. Benno, 1977.

Herrmann, Siegfried. *Jeremia.* BKAT XII/2. Neukirchen-Vluyn: Neukirchener, 1990.

————. *Jeremia: Der Prophet und das Buch.* ErFor 271. Darmstadt: Wissenschaftliche Buchgesellschaft, 1990.

Hess, Richard. "A Typology of West- Semitic Place Name Lists with Special Reference to Joshua 13–21." *BA* 59 (1996) 160–170.

Hiebert, Theodore. *G-d of My Victory: The Ancient Hymn in Habakkuk 3.* HSM 38. Atlanta: Scholars Press, 1986.

Hillers, Delbert. *Micah.* Hermeneia. Philadelphia: Fortress, 1984.

Hobbs, T. R. "Jeremiah 3, 1–5 and Deuteronomy 24, 1–4." *ZAW* 86 (1974) 23–29.

Hoffmann, Hans-Detleff. *Reform und Reformen: Untersuchungen zu einem Grundthema der deuteronomistischen Geschichtsschreibung.* AThANT 66. Zürich: Theologischer Verlag, 1980.

Holladay, William. *Jeremiah 1.* Hermeneia. Philadelphia: Fortress, 1986.

————. *Jeremiah 2.* Hermeneia. Minneapolis: Fortress, 1989.

Holt, Else Kragelund. *Prophesying the Past: The Use of Israel's History in the Book of Hosea.* JSOTSup 194. Sheffield: Sheffield Academic Press, 1995.

Hossfeld, F. L., and I. Meyer. *Prophet gegen Prophet. Eine Analyse der alttestamentlichen Texte zum Thema: Wahre und falsche Propheten.* BibB 9. Freiburg: Schweizerisches Katholisches Bibelwerk, 1973.

Irvine, Stuart A. *Isaiah, Ahaz and the Syro-Ephraimitic Crisis.* SBLDS 123. Atlanta: Scholars Press, 1990.

Ishida, Tomoo. "'The People of the Land' and the Political Crises in Judah." *AJBI* 1 (1975) 23–38.

Janzen, J. G. "Habakkuk 2:2–4 in the Light of Recent Philological Advances." *HTR* 73 (1980) 53–78.

Japhet, Sara. *I and II Chronicles: A Commentary.* OTL. Louisville, KY: Westminster John Knox, 1993.

Jeremias, Jörg. *Der Prophet Hosea.* ATD 24,1. Göttingen: Vandenhoeck & Ruprecht, 1983.

————. *Kultprophetie und Geschichtsverkündigung in der späten Königszeit Israels.* WMANT 35. Neukirchen-Vluyn: Neukirchener, 1970.

————. *Theophanie: Die Geschichte einer alttestamentliche Gattung.* WMANT 10. Neukirchen-Vluyn: Neukirchener, 1965.

Jöcken, Peter. *Das Buch Habakuk: Darstellung der Geschichte seiner kritischen Erforschung mit einer eigenen Beurteilung.* BBB 48. Cologne and Bern: Peter Hanstein, 1977.

Jones, Gwilym H. *The Nathan Narratives.* JSOTSup 80. Sheffield: JSOT Press, 1990.

Kaiser, Otto. *Introduction to the Old Testament: A Presentation of its Results and Problems.* Trans. J. Sturdy. Minneapolis: Augsburg, 1975.

———. *Isaiah 1–12: A Commentary*. OTL. Philadelphia: Westminster, 1983.

Kaufman, S. A. "The Structure of the Deuteronomic Law." *Maarav* 1–2 (1978–79) 105–158.

Keulen, Percy S. F. van. *Manasseh Through the Eyes of the Deuteronomists: The Manasseh Account (2 Kings 21:1–18) and the Final Chapters of the Deuteronomistic History*. OTS 38. Leiden: E. J. Brill, 1996.

Kilian, Rudolph. *Jesaja 1–39*. ErFor 200. Darmstadt: Wissenschaftliche Buchgesellschaft, 1983.

Kilpp, Nelson. *Niederreissen und aufbauen: Das Verhältnis von Heilsverheissung und Unheilsverheissung bei Jeremia und im Jeremiahbuch*. BTS 13. Neukirchen-Vluyn: Neukirchener, 1990.

Knierim, Rolf. "Criticism of Literary Features, Form, Tradition, and Redaction." In *The Hebrew Bible and Its Modern Interpreters*, ed. D. A. Knight and G. M. Tucker, 123–165. Chico, Calif.: Scholars Press, 1985.

———. "'I Will not Cause it to Return' in Amos 1 and 2." In *Canon and Authority*, ed. G. W. Coats and B. O. Long, 163–175. Philadelphia: Fortress, 1977.

Knight, Douglas A. and Gene M. Tucker, eds. *The Hebrew Bible and Its Modern Interpreters*. Chico, Calif.: Scholars Press, 1985.

Knoppers, Gary N. "The Deuteronomist and the Deuteronomic Law of the King: A Reexamination of a Relationship." *ZAW* 108 (1996) 329–346.

———. "Jehoshaphat's Judiciary and 'the Scroll of YHWH's Torah,'" *JBL* 113 (1994) 59–80.

———. "'There was None like Him': Incomparability in the Books of Kings." *CBQ* 54 (1992) 411–431.

———. *Two Nations Under G-d: The Deuteronomistic History of Solomon and the Dual Monarchies*. 2 vols. HSM 52–53. Atlanta: Scholars Press, 1993–1994.

Koenen, Klaus. *Heil den Gerechten—Unheil den Sündern: Ein Beitrag zur Theologie der Prophetenbücher*. BZAW 229. Berlin and New York: Walter de Gruyter, 1994.

Kraus, Hans-Joachim. *Geschichte der historisch-kritischen Erforschung des Alten Testaments*. 2nd ed. Neukirchen-Vluyn: Neukirchener, 1969.

Kuenen, Abraham. *Historisch-Kritische Einleitung in die Bücher des Alten Testaments*. Vol. 1. Leipzig: Otto Schulze, 1887.

Laato, Antti. *Josiah and David Redivivus: The Historical Josiah and the Messianic Expectations of Exilic and Postexilic Times*. ConBibOT 33. Stockholm, Almqvist and Wiksell, 1992.

Lasine, Stuart. "Manasseh as Villain and Scapegoat." In *The New Literary Criticism and the Hebrew Bible*, ed. J. C. Exum and David J. A. Clines, 163–183. JSOTSup 143. Sheffield: JSOT Press, 1993.

Lemke, Werner. "The Way of Obedience: 1 Kings 13 and the Structure of the Deuteronomistic History." In *Magnalia Dei/The Mighty Acts of G-d*, ed. F. M. Cross et al., 301–326. Fs. G. E. Wright. Garden City, N.Y.: Doubleday, 1976.

Levenson, Jon D. "Who Inserted the Book of the Torah?" *HTR* 68 (1975) 203–233.

Levinson, Bernard. "The Case for Revision and Interpolation in within the Biblical Legal Corpora." In *Theory and Method in Biblical and Cuneiform Law: Revision, Interpolation and Development*, ed. B. M. Levinson, 37–59. JSOTSup 181. Sheffield: Sheffield Academic Press, 1994.

———. *Deuteronomy and the Hermeneutics of Legal Innovation*. New York and Oxford: Oxford University Press, 1997.

L'Heureux, Conrad. "The Redactional History of Isaiah 5.1–10.4." In *In the Shelter of Elyon*, ed. W. B. Barrick and J. R. Spencer, 99–119. Fs. G. W. Ahlström. JSOT Sup 31. Sheffield: JSOT Press, 1984.

Liwak, R. *Der Prophet und die Geschichte: Eine literar-historische Untersuchung zum Jeremiabuch*. BWANT 121. Stuttgart: W. Kohlhammer, 1987.

Lloyd, S. *The Archaeology of Mesopotamia from the Old Stone Age to the Persian Conquest*. London: Thames and Hudson, 1984.

Lohfink, Norbert. "The Cult Reform of Josiah of Judah: 2 Kings 22–23 as a Source for the History of Israelite Religion." In *Ancient Israelite Religion*. Fs. F. M. Cross. Ed. P. D. Miller, Jr., P. D. Hanson, and S. D. McBride, 459–475. Philadelphia: Fortress, 1987.

―――. "Der junge Jeremia als Propagandist und Poet: Zum Grundstock von Jer 30–31." *Le livre de Jérémie: Le prophète et son milieu, les oracles et leur transmission*, ed. P. M. Bogaert, 351–368. BETL 54. Leuven: Peeters, 1981.

―――. "Kerygmata des Deuteronomistischen Geschichtswerks." In *Die Botschaft und die Boten*, ed. J. Jeremias and L. Perlitt, 87–100. Fs. H. W. Wolff. Neukirchen-Vluyn: Neukirchener, 1981.

―――. "Zur neuer Diskussion über 2 Kön 22–23." In *Das Deuteronomium: Entstehung, Gestalt und Botschaft*, ed. N. Lohfink, 24–48. BETL 58. Leuven: Peeters, 1985.

Long, Burke. *2 Kings*. FOTL X. Grand Rapids, Mich.: Eerdmans, 1991.

Lundbom, Jack. *The Early Career of the Prophet Jeremiah*. Lewiston: Mellen Biblical Press, 1993.

Lust, J. "A. Van Hoonacker and Deuteronomy." In *Das Deuteronomium: Entstehung, Gestalt und Botschaft*, ed. N. Lohfink, 13–23. BETL 68. Leuven: Peeters, 1985.

Malamat, Abraham. "The Kingdom of Judah Between Egypt and Babylon: A Small State Within a Great Power Confrontation." In *Text and Context*, ed. W. Classen, 117–129. Fs. F. C. Fensham. JSOTSup 48. Sheffield: JSOT Press, 1984.

Martin, James D. "The Forensic Background to Jeremiah III 1." *VT* 19 (1969) 82–92.

Mason, Rex A. *Micah, Nahum, Obadiah*. OTG. Sheffield: JSOT Press, 1991.

―――. *Preaching the Tradition: Homily and Hermeneutics After the Exile*. Cambridge, U.K.: Cambridge University Press, 1990.

―――. *Zephaniah, Habbakuk, Joel*. OTG: Sheffield: JSOT Press, 1994.

Mayes, A. D. H. *Deuteronomy*. NCeB. London: Marshall Morgan and Scott. Grand Rapids, Mich.: Eerdmans, 1979.

―――. *Judges*. OTG. Sheffield: JSOT Press, 1985.

―――. *The Story of Israel Between Settlement and Exile: A Redactional Study of the Deuteronomistic History*. London: SCM, 1983.

Mays, James L. *Amos: A Commentary*. OTL. Philadelphia: Westminster, 1969.

―――. *Micah: A Commentary*. OTL. Philadelphia: Westminster, 1976.

McBride, S. Dean, Jr. "Polity of the Covenant People: The Book of Deuteronomy." *Int* 41 (1987) 229–244.

McCarter, P. Kyle. *II Samuel*. AB 9. Garden City, N.Y.: Doubleday, 1984.

―――. "The Books of Samuel." In *The History of Israel's Traditions: The Heritage of Martin Noth*, ed. S. L. McKenzie and M. P. Graham, 260–280. JSOTSup 182. Sheffield: Sheffield Academic Press, 1994.

McCarthy, Dennis J. "II Samuel 7 and the Structure of Deuteronomic History." *JBL* 84 (1965) 131–138.

McConville, J. G. *Law and Theology in Deuteronomy*. JSOTSup 33. Sheffield: JSOT Press, 1984.

McKane, William. "The Composition of Jeremiah 30–31." In *Texts, Temples, and Traditions*, ed. M. V. Fox et al., 187–194. Fs. M. Haran.Winona Lake, Ind.: Eisenbrauns, 1996.

―――. *Jeremiah 1*. ICC. Edinburgh: T & T Clark, 1986.

―――. "Relations between Poetry and Prose in the Book of Jeremiah with Special Ref-

erence to Jeremiah III 6–11 and XII 14–17." In *Congress Volume: Vienna 1980*, ed.
J. A. Emerton, 220–237. VTSup 32. Leiden: E. J. Brill, 1981.

McKenzie, Steven L. *The Trouble with Kings: The Composition of the Books of Kings in
the Deuteronomistic History*. VTSup 42. Leiden: E. J. Brill, 1991.

McKenzie, Steven L. and M. Patrick Graham, editors. *The History of Israel's Traditions:
The Heritage of Martin Noth*. JSOTSup 182. Sheffield: JSOT Press, 1994.

Mettinger, T. N. D. *King and Messiah: The Civil and Sacral Legitimation of the Israelite
Kings*. ConBibOT 8. Lund: Gleerup, 1976.

Milgrom, J. *Numbers*. JPS Torah Commentary. Philadelphia and New York: Jewish Publication Society, 1990.

Miller, J. Maxwell and John H. Hayes. *A History of Ancient Israel and Judah*. Philadelphia: Westminster, 1986.

Miller, Patrick D., Jr. "The World and Message of the Prophets: Biblical Prophecy in its
Context." In *Old Testament Interpretation: Past, Present, and Future*, ed. J. L. Mays,
D. L. Petersen, and K. H. Richards, 97–112. Fs. G. M. Tucker. Nashville: Abingdon,
1995.

Montgomery, James A. and Henry Snyder Gehman. *The Books of Kings*. ICC. Edinburgh:
T & T Clark, 1951.

Moran, W. L. "The Ancient Near Eastern Background of the Love of G-d in Deuteronomy."
CBQ 25 (1963) 77–87.

Morgan, Robert and John Barton. *Biblical Interpretation*. Oxford: Oxford University Press,
1988.

Mowinckel, Sigmund. *Zur Komposition des Buches Jeremia*. Videnskapsselskapets skrifter 4,
Hist.-Filos. Klasse, 1913, No. 5. Oslo: Kristiana, 1914.

Murray, D. F. "The Rhetoric of Disputation: Re-examination of a Prophetic Genre." *JSOT*
38 (1987) 95–121.

Na'aman, Nadav. "Hezekiah's Fortified Cities and the LMLK Stamps," *BASOR* 261 (1986)
5–21.

———. "Sennacherib's Campaign to Judah and the Date of the *lmlk* Stamps," *VT* 29 (1979)
61–86.

———. "The Kingdom of Judah under Josiah." *Tel Aviv* 18 (1991) 3–71.

Naumann, Thomas. *Hoseas Erben: Strukturen der Nachinterpretation im Buch Hosea*.
BWANT 131. Stuttgart: Kohlhammer, 1991.

Neef, Heinz-Dieter. *Die Heilstraditionen Israels in der Verkündigung des Propheten
Hoseas*. BZAW 169. Berlin and New York: Walter de Gruyter, 1987.

Nelson, Richard. *The Double Redaction of the Deuteronomistic History*. JSOTSup 18.
Sheffield: JSOT Press, 1981.

———. "Josiah in the Book of Joshua." *JBL* 100 (1981) 531–540.

Nicholson, E. W. *Deuteronomy and Tradition: Literary and Historical Traditions in the
Book of Deuteronomy*. Philadelphia: Fortress, 1967.

———. "Deuteronomy's Vision of Israel." In *Storia e Tradizioni di Israele*, ed. D. Garrone
and F. Israel, 191–203. Fs. J. A. Soggin. Brescia: Paideia, 1991.

Nissinen, Martti. *Prophetie, Redaktion und Fortschreibung im Hoseabuch: Studien zum
Werdegang eines Prophetenbuches im Lichte von Hos 4 und 11*. AOAT 231. Kevelaer:
Butzon & Bercker. Neukirchen-Vluyn: Neukirchener, 1991.

Nogalski, James. *Redactional Processes in the Book of the Twelve*. BZAW 218. Berlin
and New York: Walter de Gruyter, 1993.

Noth, Martin. "The Background of Judges 17–18." In *Israel's Prophetic Heritage*,
ed. B. W. Anderson and W. Harrelson, 68–85. Fs. J. Muilenberg. London: SCM,
1962.

———. *Überlieferungsgeschichtliche Studien I*, 1–110. 2nd ed. Tübingen: Max Niemeyer, 1957. ET: *The Deuteronomistic History*. JSOT Sup15: Sheffield: JSOT Press, 1981.

Nyberg, H. S. *Studien zum Hoseabuch, zugleich ein Beitrag zur Klärung des Problems der alttestamentlichen Textkritik*. UUÅ 1935:6. Uppsala: A.-B. Lundequistska Bokhandeln, 1935.

O'Brien, M. A. "The Book of Deuteronomy." *CR:BS* 3 (1995) 95–128.

———. *The Deuteronomistic History Hypothesis: A Reassessment*. OBO 92. Freiburg: Universitätsverlag; Göttingen: Vandenhoeck & Ruprecht, 1989.

———. "Judges and the Deuteronomistic History." In *The History of Israel's Traditions: The Heritage of Martin Noth*, ed. S. L. McKenzie and M. P. Graham, 235–259. JSOTSup 182. Sheffield: Sheffield Academic Press, 1994.

O'Connell, Robert. *The Rhetoric of the Book of Judges*. VTSup 63. Leiden: E. J. Brill, 1996.

Oded, Bustenay. "Judah and the Exile." In *Israelite and Judaean History*, ed. John H. Hayes and J. Maxwell Miller, 435–488. OTL. Philadelphia: Westminster, 1977.

Oestreicher, Theodor. *Das deuteromistische Grundgesetz*. BFCT 27/4. Gütersloh: Bertelsmann, 1923.

Olson, D. T. *Deuteronomy and the Death of Moses: A Theological Reading*. OBT. Minneapolis: Fortress, 1994.

Orlinsky, Harry. "The Biblical Concept of the Land of Israel: Cornerstone of the Covenant Between G-d and Israel." In *The Land of Israel: Jewish Perspectives*, ed. L. A. Hoffman, 27–64. Notre Dame: University of Notre Dame, 1986.

Otto, Eckart. "Aspects of Legal Reforms and Reformulations in Ancient Cuneiform and Israelite Law." In *Theory and Method in Biblical and Cuneiform Law: Revision, Interpolation, and Development*, ed. B. M. Levinson, 160–196. JSOTSup 181. Sheffield: Sheffield Academic Press, 1994.

———. "Rechtsreformen in Deuteronomium xii–xxvi und im Mittelassyrischen Kodex der Tafel A (KAV 1)." In *Congress Volume. Paris 1992*, ed. J. A. Emerton, 239–273. VTSup 61. Leiden: E. J. Brill, 1995.

———. "Die Theologie des Buches Habakuk." *VT* 35 (1985) 274–295.

———. "Vom Bundesbuch zum Deuteronomium. Die deuteronomistische Redaktion in Dtn 12–26." In *Biblische Theologie und gesellschaftlicher Wandel*, ed. G. Braulik, W. Gross, and S. McEvenue, 260–278. Fs. N. Lohfink, S.J. Freiburg, Basel, Vienna: Herder, 1993.

Page, S. "A Stela of Adad Nirari III and Nergal-ereš from Tell el Rimlah." *Iraq* 30 (1968) 139–153.

Parpola, S. "Neo-Assyrian Treaties from the Royal Archives of Nineveh." *JCS* 39 (1987) 161–189.

Paul, M. J. "Hilkiah and the Law (2 Kings 22) in the 17th and 18th Centuries: Some Influences on W. M. L. de Wette." In *Das Deuteronomium: Entstehung, Gestalt und Botschaft*, ed., N. Lohfink, 9–12. BETL 68. Leuven: Peeters, 1985.

Paul, Shalom. *Amos*. Hermeneia. Minneapolis: Fortress, 1991.

Pečirková, Jana. "The Administrative Methods of Assyrian Imperialism." *Archív Orientální* 55 (1987) 162–175.

Peckham, Brian. *The Composition of the Deuteronomistic History*. HSM 35: Atlanta: Scholars, 1985.

———. "The Significance of the Book of Joshua in Noth's Theory of the Deuteronomistic History." In *The History of Israel's Traditions: The Heritage of Martin Noth*, ed. S. L. McKenzie and M. P. Graham, 213–234. JSOTSup 182. Sheffield:Sheffield Academic Press, 1984.

Perdue, Leo. "Jeremiah in Modern Research: Approaches and Issues." In *A Prophet to the Nations: Essays in Jeremiah Studies*, ed. L. G. Perdue and B. W. Kovacs, 1–32. Winona Lake, Ind.: Eisenbrauns, 1984.

Pohlmann, Karl-Friedrich. *Die Ferne G-ttes—Studien zum Jeremiabuch*. BZAW 179. Berlin and New York: Walter de Gruyter, 1989.

Postgate, J. N. *Taxation and Conscription in the Assyrian Empire*. Studia Pohl, Series Maior 3. Rome: Biblical Institute Press, 1974.

Pressler, C. *The View of Women Found in the Deuteronomic Family Laws*. BZAW 216. Berlin and New York: Walter de Gruyter, 1993.

Preuss, Horst Dietrich. *Deuteronomium*. ErFor 164. Darmstadt: Wissenschaftliche Buchgesellschaft, 1982.

———. "Zum deuteronomistischen Geschichtswerk," *Theologisches Rundschau* 58 (1993) 229–264, 341–395.

Pritchard, James, ed. *Ancient Near Eastern Texts Relating to the Old Testament*. 3rd edition. Princeton: Princeton University Press, 1969.

Provan, Iain W. *Hezekiah and the Books of Kings. A Contribution to the Debate about the Deuteronimistic History*. BZAW 172. Berlin and New York: Walter de Gruyter, 1988.

Rad, Gerhard von. *Deuteronomy: A Commentary*. OTL. Transl. D. Barton. London: SCM 1966.

———. *Old Testament Theology*. 2 vols. Trans. D. M. G. Stalker. New York: Harper & Row, 1962–65.

———. *Studies in Deuteronomy*. SBT 9. Translated by D. M. G. Stalker; London: SCM, 1953.

Redford, Donald. *Egypt, Canaan, and Israel in Ancient Times*. Princeton: Princeton University Press, 1992.

Renaud, Bernard. "La composition du livre de Nahum." *ZAW* 99 (1987) 198–219.

———. *La Formation du livre de Michée*. EB. Paris: J. Gabalda, 1977.

———. "Le livre de Sophone: Le jour de YHWH thème structurant de la synthèse rédactionelle." *RevScRel* 60 (1986) 1–33.

———. *Michée—Sophonie—Nahum*. Sources bibliques. Paris: J. Gabalda, 1987.

Rendtorff, Rolf. *The Old Testament: An Introduction*. Trans. J. Bowden. Philadelphia: Fortress, 1986.

Reuter, E. *Kultzentralization: Entstehung und Theologie von Dtn 12*. BBB 87. Frankfurt/Main: Anton Hain, 1993.

Richter, Wolfgang. *Die Bearbeitungen des "Retterbuches" in der Deuteronomischen Epoche*. BBB 21. Bonn: Peter Hanstein, 1964.

———. *Traditionsgeschichtliche Untersuchungen zum Richterbuch*. BBB 18. 2nd edition. Bonn: Peter Hanstein, 1966.

Roberts, J. J. M. *Nahum, Habakkuk, and Zephaniah: A Commentary*. OTL. Louisville, KY: Westminster/John Knox, 1991.

Römer, Thomas, and de Pury, Albert, "L'historiographie deutéronomiste (HD): Histoire de la recherche et enjeux du débat." In *Israël construit son histoire: L'historiographie-deutéronomiste à la lumière des recherches récentes*, ed. A. de Pury, T. Römer, and J.-D. Macchi, 9–120. Geneva: Labor et Fides, 1996.

Rosenberg, R. "The Concept of Biblical 'Belial'." In *Proceedings of the Eighth World Congress of Jewish Studies. Division A: The Period of the Bible*, 35–41. Jerusalem: World Union of Jewish Studies, 1982.

Rost, Leonhard. *Die Überlieferung von der Thronnachfolge Davids*. BWANT 42. Stuttgart: Kohlhammer, 1926. ET: *The Succession to the Throne of David*. Trans. M. D. Rutter and D. Gunn. HTIBS 1. Sheffield: Almond, 1982.

Rowlett, Lori L. *Joshua and the Rhetoric of Violence: A New Historicist Analysis*. JSOTSup 226. Sheffield: Sheffield Academic Press, 1996.

Rowley, H. H. "The Marriage of Hosea." In *Men of G-d: Studies in Old Testament History and Prophecy*, 66–97. London: Thomas Nelson, 1963.

Rudolph, Wilhelm. *Hosea*. KAT XIII/1. Gütersloh: Gerd Mohn, 1966.

———. *Micha-Nahum-Habakuk-Zephanja*. KAT XIII/3. Gütersloh: Gerd Mohn, 1975.

Schäfer-Lichtenberger, Christa. *Josua und Salomo: Eine Studie zu Autorität und Legitimität des Nachfolgers im Alten Testament*. VTSup 58. Leiden: Brill, 1995.

Schmidt, W. H. "Die deuteronomistische Redaktion des Amosbuches: Zu den Theologien Unterscheiden zwishen dem Prophetenwort und seinem Sammler." *ZAW* 77 (1965) 168–193.

Schmitt, Hans-Christoph. *Elisa: Traditionsgeschichtliche Untersuchungen zur vorklassischen nordisraelitischen Prophetie*. Gütersloh: Mohn, 1972.

Schneider, Tammi J. *Judges*. Berit Olam: Studies in Hebrew Narrative and Poetry. Collegeville, MN: Liturgical Michael Glazier, 2000.

Schniedewind, William M. "History and Interpretation: The Religion of Ahab and Manasseh in the Book of Kings." *CBQ* 55 (1993) 649–661.

———. *The Word of G-d in Transition: From Prophet to Exegete in the Second Temple Period*. JSOTSup 197. Sheffield: Sheffield Academic Press, 1995.

Schreiner, Josef. "Jeremiah und die joschianische Reform: Probleme—Fragen—Antworten." In *Jeremiah und die "deuteronomische Bewegung"*, ed. W. Gross, 11–31. BBB 98. Weinheim: Beltz Athenäum, 1995.

Schulz-Rauch, Martin. *Hosea und Jeremia: Zur wirkungsgeschichte des Hoseabuches*. CTM 16. Stuttgart: Calwer, 1996.

Seidl, Theodor. "Die Worterreignisformel in Jeremia." *BZ* 23 (1979) 20–47.

Seitz, Christopher R. *Theology in Conflict: Reactions to the Exile in the Book of Jeremiah*. BZAW 176. Berlin and New York: Walter de Gruyter, 1989.

———. "The Prophet Moses and the Canonical Shape of Jeremiah." *ZAW* 101 (1989) 3–27.

———. *Zion's Final Destiny: The Development of the Book of Isaiah. A Reassessment of Isaiah 36–39*. Minneapolis: Fortress, 1991.

Seow, C. L. "Hosea 14:10 and the Foolish People Motif." *CBQ* 44 (1982) 212–224.

———. "Joshua's Campaign of Canaan and Near Eastern Historiography." *SJOT* 4 (1990) 1–12.

Seybold, Klaus. *Der Prophet Jeremia: Leben und Werk*. Urban Taschenbücher 416. Stuttgart: W. Kohlhammer, 1993.

———. *Nahum, Habakuk, Zephanja*. ZBK. Zürich: Theologischer Verlag, 1991.

———. *Profane Prophetie: Studien zum Buch Nahum*. SBS 135. Stuttgart: Katholisches Bibelwerk, 1989.

Sheppard, Gerald T. "The Anti-Assyrian Redaction and the Canonical Context of Isaiah 1–39." *JBL* 104 (1985) 193–216.

Sherwood, Yvonne. *The Prostitute and the Prophet: Hosea's Marriage in Literary-Theoretical Perspective*. GCT 2. JSOTSup 212. Sheffield: Sheffield Academic Press, 1996.

Smelik, Klaas A. D. "Distortion of Old Testament Prophecy: The Purpose of Isaiah xxxvi and xxxvii." *OTS* 24 (1989) 70–93.

———. "King Hezekiah Advocates True Prophecy. Remarks on Isaiah xxxvi and xxxvii/ /II Kings xviii and xix." In *Converting the Past: Studies in Ancient Israelite and Moabite Historiography*, 93–128. OTS 28. Leiden: Brill, 1992.

———. "The Portrayal of King Manasseh: A Literary Analysis of II Kings xxi and

II Chronicles xxiii." In *Converting the Past: Studies in Ancient Israelite and Moabite Historiography*, 129–189. OTS 28. Leiden: E. J. Brill, 1992.

Smend, Rudolph. "Die Gesetz und Völker: Ein Beitrag zur deuteronomistischen Redaktionsgeschichte." In *Probleme biblischer Theologie*, ed. H. W. Wolff, 494–509. Fs. G. von Rad. Munich: Chr. Kaiser, 1971.

Smith, J. M. P., W. H. Ward, and J. A. Bewer. *A Critical and Exegetical Commentary on Micah, Zephaniah, Nahum, Habakkuk, Obadiah, and Joel*. ICC. Edinburgh: T & T Clark, 1985.

Soggin, J. A. *Introduction to the Old Testament*. OTL. 3rd Edition. Trans. J. Bowden. Louisville, KY: Westminster John Knox, 1989.

———. *Joshua: A Commentary*. OTL. Trans. R. A. Wilson. Philadelphia: Westminster, 1972.

———. *Judges: A Commentary*. OTL. Trans. J. Bowden. Philadelphia: Westminster, 1981.

Spronk, K. "Synchronic and Diachronic Approaches to the Book of Nahum." In *Synchronic or Diachronic? A Debate on Method in Old Testament Exegesis*, ed. J. C. De Moor, 159–186. OTS 24. Leiden: E. J. Brill, 1995.

Stade, B. "Anmerkungen zu 2 Kö 15–21." *ZAW* 6 (1886) 172–186.

———. "Bermerkungen über das Buch Micha." *ZAW* 1 (1881) 161–176.

———. "Habakuk." *ZAW* 4 (1884) 154–159.

———. "Streiflichter auf die Entstehung der jetzigen Gestalt der alttestamentlichen Prophetenschriften." *ZAW* 23 (1903) 153–171.

Steck, Odil Hannes. *Überlieferung und Zeitgeschichte in den Elia-Erzählungen*. WMANT 26. Neukirchen: Neukirchener Verlag, 1968.

Steinberg, Naomi. "The Deuteronomic Law Code and the Politics of State Centralization." In *The Bible and the Politics of Exegesis*, ed. D. Jobling, P. L. Day, G. T. Sheppard, 161–170, 336–339. Fs. N. Gottwald. Cleveland: Pilgrim, 1991.

Stern, Ephraim, et al., editors, *The New Encyclopedia of Archaelogical Excavations in the Holy Land*. 4 vols. Jerusalem: Carta; Israel Exploration Society, 1993.

Steymans, Hans Ulrich. *Deuteronomium 28 und die adê zur Thronfolgeregelung Asarhaddons: Segen und Fluch im Alten Orient und in Israel*. OBO 145. Fribourg: Éditions univeritaires. Göttingen: Vandenhoeck & Ruprecht, 1995.

Stone, Lawson G. "Ethical and Apologetic Tendencies in the Redaction of the Book of Joshua." *CBQ* 53 (1991) 25–36.

Suzuki, Y. "Deuteronomic Reformation in View of the Centralization of the Administration of Justice." *AJBI* 13 (1987) 22–58.

Sweeney, Marvin A."The Book of Isaiah in Recent Research." *CR:BS* 1 (1993) 141–162.

———. *The Book of the Twelve Prophets*. Berit Olam: Studies in Hebrew Narrative and Poetry. Collegeville, MN: Liturgical Michael Glazier, 2000.

———. "Concerning the Structure and Generic Character of the Book of Nahum." *ZAW* 104 (1992) 364–377.

———. "The Critique of Solomon in the Josianic Edition of the Deuteronomistic History." *JBL* 114 (1995) 607–622.

———. "Davidic Polemics in the Book of Judges." *VT* 47 (1997) 517–529.

———. "Form Criticism." In *To Each Its Own Meaning: Revised and Expanded Edition*, ed. S. L. McKenzie and S. R. Haynes. Louisville, KY: Westminster John Knox, 58–89.

———. "Formation and Form in Prophetic Literature." In *Old Testament Interpretation: Past, Present, Future*, ed. J. L. Mays, D. L. Petersen, K. H. Richards, 113–126. Fs. G. M. Tucker. Nashville: Abingdon, 1995.

———. "A Form-Critical Reassessment of the Book of Zephaniah." *CBQ* 51 (1991) 388–408.

———. "A Form-Critical Rereading of the Book of Hosea." *Journal of Hebrew Scriptures* 2 (1998) article 2.

———. *Isaiah 1–4 and the Post-exilic Understanding of the Isaianic Tradition.* BZAW 171. Berlin and New York: Walter de Gruyter, 1988.

———. "Isaiah 1–39 in Recent Critical Research." *CR:BS* 4 (1996) 79–113.

———. *Isaiah 1–39, with an Introduction to Prophetic Literature.* FOTL 16. Grand Rapids, Mich. and Cambridge, U.K.: William Eerdmans, 1996.

———. "Jeremiah 30–31 and King Josiah's Program of National Restoration and Religious Reform." *ZAW* 108 (1996) 569–583.

———. "Jesse's New Shoot in Isaiah 11: A Josianic Reading of the Prophet Isaiah." In *A Gift of G-d in Due Season,* ed. D. M. Carr and R. D. Weis, 103–118. Fs. J. A. Sanders. JSOTSup 225. Sheffield: Sheffield Academic Press, 1996.

———. "The Latter Prophets: Isaiah, Jeremiah, Ezekiel." In *The Hebrew Bible Today,* ed. S. L. McKenzie and M. P. Graham, 69–94. Louisville, KY: Westminster John Knox.

———. "A Philological and Form-Critical Reevaluation of Isaiah 8:16–9:6." *HAR* 14 (1994) 215–231.

———. "The Reconceptualization of the Davidic Covenant in Isaiah." In *Studies in the Book of Isaiah,* ed. M. Vervenne and J. T. A. G. M. van Ruiten, 41–61. Fs. W. A. M. Beuken. BETL 132. Leuven: Peeters, 1997.

———. "Reevaluating Isaiah 1–39 in Recent Critical Research." *CR:BS* 4 (1996) 79–113.

———. "Sargon's Threat against Jerusalem in Isaiah 10, 27–32." *Bibl* 75 (1994) 457–470.

———. "Structure and Redaction in Jeremiah 2–6." In *Troubling Jeremiah,* ed. A. R. Diamond, K. O'Connor, and L. Stuhlman. JSOTSup 260. Sheffield: Sheffield Academic Press, 1999) 200–218.

———. "Structure, Genre, and Intent in the Book of Habakkuk." *VT* 41 (1991) 63–83.

———. "Zephaniah: A Paradigm for the Study of the Prophetic Books." *CR:BS* 7 (1999) 119–145.

Tadmor, H. "'The People' and Kingship in Ancient Israel: The Role of Political Institutions in the Biblical Period." *Cahiers d'histoire mondiale* 11 (1968) 3–23.

Tagliacarne, Pierfelice. *"Keiner war wie er": Untersuchung zur Struktur von 2 Könige 22–23.* ATSAT 31. St. Ottilien: EOS, 1989.

Talmon, S. "The Judaean 'Am ha'Areṣ' in Historical Perspective." In *Fourth World Congress of Jewish Studies. Papers. Vol. I,* 71–76. Jerusalem: World Union of Jewish Studies, 1967.

Tatum, Lynn, "King Manasseh and the Royal Fortress at Horvat ʿUza," *BA* 54 (1991) 136–145.

Taylor, C. "Habakkuk." *The Interpreter's Bible,* vol. 6, ed. G. Buttrick, 973–1003. Nashville: Abingdon, 1956.

Thiel, Winfried. *Die deuteronomistische Redaktion von Jeremia 1–25.* WMANT 41. Neukirchen-Vluyn: Neukirchener, 1973.

Trible, Phyllis. *G-d and the Rhetoric of Sexuality.* OBT. Philadelphia: Fortress, 1978.

———. *Rhetorical Criticism: Context, Method, and the Book of Jonah.* GBS. Minneapolis: Fortress, 1994.

Tucker, Gene M. "Prophecy and Prophetic Literature." In *The Hebrew Bible and Its Modern Interpreters,* ed. D. A. Knight and G. M. Tucker, 325–368. Chico, Calif.: Scholars Press, 1985.

———. "Prophetic Superscriptions and the Growth of the Canon." In *Canon and Authority,* ed. G. W. Coats and B. O. Long, 56–70. Philadelphia: Fortress, 1977.

Tull, Patricia. "Rhetorical Criticism." In *To Each Its Own Meaning: Revised and Enlarged Edition*, ed. S. L. McKenzie and S. R. Haynes. Louisville, KY: Westminster John Knox, 1999) 156–180.

Ussishkin, David. "The Date of the Judaean Shrine at Arad," *IEJ* 38 (1988) 142–157.

Van Seters, John. "Cultic Laws in the Covenant Code (Exodus 20, 22–23, 33) and their Relationship to Deuteronomy and the Holiness Code." In *Studies in the Book of Exodus*, ed. M. Vervenne, 319–345. BETL 126. Leuven: Peeters, 1996.

————. "Joshua's Campaign of Canaan and Near Eastern Historiography," *SJOT* 4/2 (1990) 1–12.

————. *In Search of History: Historiography in the Ancient World and the Origins of Biblical History*. New Haven and London: Yale University Press, 1983.

Vaughn, Andrew G. "The Chronicler's Account of Hezekiah: The Relation of Historical Data to a Theological Interpretation of 2 Chronicles 29–32." Ph.D. dissertation. Princeton Theological Seminary, 1996.

Veijola, Timo. *Das Königtum in der Beurteilung der deuteronomistischen Historiographie: Eine redaktionsgeschichtliche Untersuchung*. Helsinki: Suomalainen Tiedeakatemia, 1977.

————. *Die Ewige Dynastie: David und die Entstehung seiner Dynastie nach der deuteronomistischen Darstellung*. Helsinki: Suomalainen Tiedeakatemia, 1975.

Vermeylen, J. *Du prophète d'Isaïe à l'apocalyptique*. 2 Vols. EB. Paris: Galbalda, 1977–78.

Viviano, P. A. "2 Kings 17: A Rhetorical and Form-Critical Analysis." *CBQ* 49 (1987) 548–559.

Vollmer, J. *Geschichtliche Rückblicke und Motive in der Prophetie des Amos, Hosea, und Jesaja*. BZAW 119. Berlin: Walter de Gruyter, 1971.

Volz, Paul. *Der Prophet Jeremia*. KAT X. Leipzig: A. Deichert, 1922.

————. *Der Prophet Jeremia*. KAT X. Leipzig: A. Deichert, 1928.

Vriezen, T. C. "La tradition de Jacob dans Osée XII." *OTS* 1 (1942) 64–78.

Vuilleumier, R. "Les traditions d'Israël et la liberté due prophète: Osée." *RHPR* 59 (1979) 491–498.

Weigl, Michael. *Zefanja und das "Israel der Armen": Eine Untersuchung zur Theologie des Buches Zefanja*. ÖBS 13. Klosterneuberg: Österreichisches Katholisches Bibelwerk, 1994.

Weinfeld, Moshe. *The Promise of the Land: The Inheritance of the Land of Canaan by the Israelites*. Berkeley: University of California, 1993.

————. *Deuteronomy 1–11*. AB 5. New York: Doubleday, 1991.

————. *Deuteronomy and the Deuteronomic School*. Oxford: Oxford University Press, 1972.

————. "Judge and Officer in Ancient Israel and in the Ancient Near East." *IOS* 7 (1977) 68–88.

————. "Judges 1.1–2.5: The Conquest under the Leadership of the House of Judah." In *Understanding Poets and Prophets*, ed. A. G. Auld, 388–400. Fs. G. W. Anderson. JSOTSup 152. Sheffield: JSOT Press, 1993.

Weippert, Helga. "Die 'deuteronomistischen' Beurteilungen der Könige von Israel und Juda und das Problem der Redaktion der Königsbücher." *Bibl* 53 (1972) 301–339.

Weis, Richard D. "A Definition of the Genre *Maśśā'* in the Hebrew Bible." Ph.D. Dissertation. Claremont, Calif.: Claremont Graduate School, 1986.

Welch, Adam C. *The Code of Deuteronomy: A New Theory of Its Origin*. London: James Clarke, [1924].

Wendel, Ute. *Jesaja und Jeremiah: Worte, Motive und Einsichten Jesajas in der Verkündigung Jeremias*. BTS 25. Neukirchen-Vluyn: Neukirchener, 1995.

Westbrook, R. "What is the Covenant Code?" In *Theory and Method in Biblical and Cuneiform Law: Revision, Interpolation, and Development*, ed. B. M. Levinson, 15–36. JSOTSup 181. Sheffield: Sheffield Academic Press, 1994.

Whedbee, J. W. *Isaiah and Wisdom*. Nashville: Abingdon, 1971.

Wilcoxen, Jay. "The Political Background of Jeremiah's Temple Sermon." In *Scripture in History and Theology*, eds. A. L. Merrill and T. W. Overholt, 151–166. Fs. J. C. Rylaarsdam. Pittsburgh: Pickwick, 1977.

Wildberger, Hans. *Jesaja 1–12*. BKAT X/1. Neukirchen-Vluyn: Neukirchener, 1972.

———. *Jesaja 13–27*. BKAT X/2. Neukirchen-Vluyn: Neukirchener, 1978.

———. *Jesaja 28–39*. BKAT X/3. Neukirchen-Vluyn: Neukirchener, 1982.

Willi-Plein, Ina. *Vorformen der Schriftexegese innerhalb des Alten Testaments: Untersuchungen zum literarischen Werden der auf Amos, Hosea und Micha zurückgehenden Bücher im hebräischen Zwölfprophetenbuch*. BZAW 123. Berlin and New York: Walter de Gruyter, 1971.

Willis, John T. "The Authenticity and Meaning of Micah 5:9–14." *ZAW* 81 (1969) 353–368.

———. "The Structure of Micah 3–5 and the Function of Micah 5:9–14 in the Book." *ZAW* 81 (1969) 191–214.

———. "The Structure of the Book of Micah." *SEÅ* 34 (1969) 5–42.

Wiseman, D. J. *The Vassal Treaties of Esarhaddon*. London: British School of Archaeology in Iraq, 1958. Republished from *Iraq* 20 (1958), Part I.

Wolff, Hans Walter. *Joel and Amos*. Hermeneia. Philadelphia: Fortress, 1977.

———. "Hoseas geistige Heimat." *TLZ* 81 (1956) 83–94.

———. *Hosea*. Hermeneia. Philadelphia: Fortress, 1974.

———. "The Kerygma of the Deuteronomic Historical Work." In *The Vitality of the Old Testament Traditions*, ed. W. Brueggemann and H. W. Wolff, 83–100. Atlanta: John Knox, 1975.

———. *Micah: A Commentary*. ContCom. Minneapolis: Augsburg, 1990.

Yee, Gale A. *Composition and Tradition in the Book of Hosea: A Redaction-Critical Investigation*. SBLDS 102. Atlanta: Scholars Press, 1987.

AUTHOR INDEX

343

SELECTED SCRIPTURE INDEX